THE CAMBRIDGE COMPANION
TO AUSTRALIAN POETRY

An invaluable resource for staff and students in literary studies and Australian studies, this volume is the first major critical survey of Australian poetry. It investigates poetry's central role in engagements with issues of colonialism, nationalism, war and crisis, diaspora, gender and sexuality, and the environment. Individual chapters examine First Nations writing and the archive, poetry and activism, print culture, and the practices of internationally renowned poets such as Lionel Fogarty, Gwen Harwood, John Kinsella, Les Murray, and Judith Wright. The *Companion* considers Australian leadership in digital poetries and hybrid forms like the verse novel, as well as Antipodean engagements with Romanticism and Modernism.

Ann Vickery is Professor of Writing and Literature at Deakin University. She is the author of *Leaving Lines of Gender: A Feminist Genealogy of Language Writing* (2000) and *Stressing the Modern: Cultural Politics in Australian Women's Poetry* (2007). She is the co-author of *The Intimate Archive: Journeys through Private Papers* (with Maryanne Dever and Sally Newman, 2009).

A complete list of books in the series is at the back of the book.

THE CAMBRIDGE COMPANION TO
AUSTRALIAN POETRY

EDITED BY
ANN VICKERY
Deakin University

Shaftesbury Road, Cambridge CB2 8EA, United Kingdom

One Liberty Plaza, 20th Floor, New York, NY 10006, USA

477 Williamstown Road, Port Melbourne, VIC 3207, Australia

314–321, 3rd Floor, Plot 3, Splendor Forum, Jasola District Centre, New Delhi – 110025, India

103 Penang Road, #05-06/07, Visioncrest Commercial, Singapore 238467

Cambridge University Press is part of Cambridge University Press & Assessment, a department of the University of Cambridge.

We share the University's mission to contribute to society through the pursuit of education, learning and research at the highest international levels of excellence.

www.cambridge.org
Information on this title: www.cambridge.org/9781009470230

DOI: 10.1017/9781009470186

© Cambridge University Press & Assessment 2024

This publication is in copyright. Subject to statutory exception and to the provisions of relevant collective licensing agreements, no reproduction of any part may take place without the written permission of Cambridge University Press & Assessment.

When citing this work, please include a reference to the DOI 10.1017/9781009470186

First published 2024

A catalogue record for this publication is available from the British Library.

Library of Congress Cataloging-in-Publication Data
NAMES: Vickery, Ann, editor.
TITLE: The Cambridge companion to Australian poetry / edited by Ann Vickery.
DESCRIPTION: Cambridge ; New York, NY : Cambridge University press, 2024. | Series: Cambridge companions to literature | Includes bibliographical references.
IDENTIFIERS: LCCN 2023058150 (print) | LCCN 2023058151 (ebook) | ISBN 9781009470230 (hardback) | ISBN 9781009470209 (paperback) | ISBN 9781009470186 (epub)
SUBJECTS: LCSH: Australian poetry–History and criticism.
CLASSIFICATION: LCC PR9610.2 .C36 2024 (print) | LCC PR9610.2 (ebook) | DDC 821.009/994–dc23/eng/20240226
LC record available at https://lccn.loc.gov/2023058150
LC ebook record available at https://lccn.loc.gov/2023058151

ISBN 978-1-009-47023-0 Hardback
ISBN 978-1-009-47020-9 Paperback

Cambridge University Press & Assessment has no responsibility for the persistence or accuracy of URLs for external or third-party internet websites referred to in this publication and does not guarantee that any content on such websites is, or will remain, accurate or appropriate.

CONTENTS

List of Figures	page ix
List of Contributors	xi
Acknowledgements	xv
Chronology	xvii

	Introduction ANN VICKERY	1

PART I   CHANGE AND RENEWAL

1	Models of Poet and Nation PHILIP MEAD	21
2	War, Crisis, and Identity in Australian Poetry DAN DISNEY	38
3	Cultivating Australian Poetry through Periodicals JOHN HAWKE	54

PART II   NETWORKS

4	Above and Below: Sublime and Gothic Relations in Nineteenth-Century Australian Poetry MICHAEL FARRELL	73
5	Romanticism, Sensibility, and Settler Women Poets KATIE HANSORD	89
6	Experiment and Adaptation: Modernist Poetry in Australia AIDAN COLEMAN	101

CONTENTS

7 The Post-war Golden Generation, 1945–1965   119
TOBY DAVIDSON

8 Generation of '68 and a Culture of Revolution   134
COREY WAKELING

PART III   AUTHORS

9 High Delicate Outline: The Poetry of Judith Wright   153
NICHOLAS BIRNS

10 Burning Sappho: Gwen Harwood's Incendiary Verse   167
ANN-MARIE PRIEST

11 Les Murray: Ancient and Modern   183
DAVID MCCOOEY

12 Lionel Fogarty's Poetics of Address and the Negative Lyric   197
DASHIELL MOORE

PART IV   EMBODIED POETICS

13 *The Strength of Us as Women*: A Poetics of Relationality and Reckoning   219
JEANINE LEANE AND NATALIE HARKIN

14 "Country Snarled / in Borders": Spatial Poetics in Asian Australian Poetry   236
KIM CHENG BOEY

15 Australian Poets in the Countries of Others   252
LOUIS KLEE

16 Writing the Body   274
ORCHID TIERNEY

17 Not the Poem Alone: *In Medias Res*   292
JOHN KINSELLA

PART V   EXPANDING FORM

18 Hybrid Forms: The Verse Novel, Prose Poetry, and Poetic Biography   315
PAUL HETHERINGTON AND CASSANDRA ATHERTON

19 Sound, Visual, Digital, and Conceptual Poetries in Australia 334
A. J. CARRUTHERS

Further Reading 351
Index 361

FIGURES

15.1 Oodgeroo Noonuccal, "Yussef"	*page* 265
15.2 Oodgeroo Noonuccal, "Yussef"	266
17.1 John Kinsella, "Graphology Botanical – Save Wheatbelt Habitat"	305
19.1 Alex Selenitsch, from *7 More Monotones* (1973 n.pag.)	340
19.2 Alex Selenitsch, from *7 More Monotones* (1973 n.pag.)	340
19.3 Chris Edwards, from *after Naptime* (2014 n.pag.)	342
19.4 Jas H. Duke, from *Destiny Wood* (1978 n.pag.)	343
19.5 Benjamin Laird, from *The Durham Poems* (2016)	347
19.6 Benjamin Laird, from *The Durham Poems* (2016)	347

CONTRIBUTORS

CASSANDRA ATHERTON is Professor of Writing and Literature at Deakin University. A leading expert on prose poetry, she has published numerous poetry collections and is the co-author of *Prose Poetry: An Introduction* (Princeton University Press, 2020) and co-editor of *The Anthology of Australian Prose Poetry* (Melbourne University Press, 2020). She also edited *Travelling without Gods: A Chris Wallace-Crabbe Companion* (Melbourne University Press, 2014) and *In So Many Words: Interviews with Writers, Scholars and Intellectuals* (Arcadia, 2013), and co-edited *Memory Book: Portraits of Older Australians in Poetry and Watercolours* (Hunter Publishing, 2021). She is also the author of *Flashing Eyes and Floating Hair: A Reading of Gwen Harwood's Pseudonymous Poetry* (Australian Scholarly Publishing, 2006).

NICHOLAS BIRNS teaches at New York University. He is the co-editor of *The Cambridge Companion to the Australian Novel* (Cambridge University Press, 2023) and *Teaching Australian and New Zealand Literature* (Modern Language Association, 2017). He is the author of *The Hyperlocal in Eighteenth- and Nineteenth-Century Literary Space* (Lexington, 2019) and *Contemporary Australian Literature: A World Not Yet Dead* (University of Sydney Press, 2015). He edited the US-based journal *Antipodes* from 2001 to 2018.

KIM CHENG BOEY was an Associate Professor at Nanyang Technological University before stepping down as Head of the English department in 2020. He has published six poetry collections, most recently *The Singer and Other Poems* (Cordite Books, 2022), as well as a travel memoir, *Between Stations* (Giramondo, 2009), and a novel, *Gull between Heaven and Earth* (Epigram Books, 2017). He edited *To Gather Your Leaving: Asian Diaspora Poetry from America, Australia, United Kingdom and Europe* (Ethos Press, 2019) and co-edited *Contemporary Asian Australian Poets* (Puncher & Wattmann, 2013).

A. J. CARRUTHERS is a critic and poet, and author of *Languages of Invention: Literary History and Avant-Garde Poetics in the Antipodes* (Edinburgh University Press, 2023) and *Stave Sightings: Notational Experiments in North American Long Poems* (Palgrave, 2017). *Languages of Invention* concerns the long-twentieth-century history of avant-garde poetry in Australia, from Symbolism and Dada to visual and sound poetry in the present day. Carruthers writes an ongoing long poem *Axis*, of which there is *Axis Book 1: 'Areal'* (Vagabond Press, 2014), *Axis Book 2* (Vagabond Press, 2019), and *Axis Z Book 3* (Cordite, 2023). Carruthers is Associate Professor at Nanjing University and was previously Lecturer at Shanghai University of International Business and Economics.

AIDAN COLEMAN is Senior Lecturer in English and Creative Writing at Southern Cross University. He is the author of three poetry collections, the most recent being *Mount Sumptuous* (Wakefield Press, 2020). He has also edited two anthologies and is completing a biography of John Forbes.

TOBY DAVIDSON teaches in the Department of English at Macquarie University. He is the author of *Good for the Soul: John Curtin's Life with Poetry* (UWA Publishing, 2021) and *Christian Mysticism and Australian Poetry* (Cambria Press, 2013). He edited Francis Webb's *Collected Poems* (UWA Publishing, 2011) and has published two poetry collections: *Four Oceans* (Puncher & Wattmann, 2020) and *Beast Language* (Five Islands Press, 2012).

DAN DISNEY teaches in the Department of English at Sogang University. He co-edited *New Directions in Contemporary Australian Poetry* (Palgrave Macmillan, 2021) and *Writing to the Wire* (UWA Publishing, 2016). He has published over ten poetry collections, including *accelerations & inertias* (Vagabond Press, 2021), *either, Orpheus* (UWA Publishing, 2016), and *Mannequin's Guide to Utopias* (Flying Islands Pocket Poets, 2013).

MICHAEL FARRELL is the author of ten poetry collections, including *Googlecholia* (Giramondo, 2022), *I Love Poetry* (Giramondo, 2017), and *Cocky's Joy* (Giramondo, 2015). He is also the author of *Writing Australian Unsettlement: Modes of Poetic Invention 1796–1945* (Palgrave Macmillan, 2015). He edited *Ashbery Mode* (Tinfish Press, 2019) and co-edited *Out of the Box: Contemporary Australian Gay and Lesbian Poets* (Puncher & Wattmann, 2011). He edits the little magazine *Flash Cove*.

KATIE HANSORD is the author of *Colonial Australian Women Poets: Political Voice and Feminist Traditions* (Anthem Press, 2021) and contributed to Anna Johnston and Elizabeth Webby's edited collection, *Eliza Dunlop: Writing from the Colonial Frontier* (Sydney University Press, 2021). She co-edited a special issue of *New Scholar* on "Cosmopolitanism and Its Critics" in 2014.

NATALIE HARKIN is a Narungga poet and scholar. She is a member of the Unbound Collective and is the author of *Archival-Poetics* (Vagabond Press, 2019) and *Dirty Words* (Cordite, 2015). She is Associate Professor in Indigenous Studies at Flinders University.

LIST OF CONTRIBUTORS

JOHN HAWKE is the author of *Australian Literature and the Symbolist Movement* (University of Wollongong Press, 2009) and co-editor of *Poetry and the Trace* (Puncher & Wattmann, 2013). He is also the author of two poetry collections: *Whirlwind Duststorm* (Grand Parade, 2021) and *Aurelia* (Cordite Books, 2015).

PAUL HETHERINGTON is Emeritus Professor of Writing at the University of Canberra. He has published over fifteen poetry collections, including *Ragged Disclosures* (Recent Work Press, 2022) and *Moonlight and Oleander* (UWA Publishing, 2018), and, with Cassandra Atherton, *Fugitive Letters* (Recent Work Press, 2020). He co-authored *Prose Poetry: An Introduction* (Princeton University Press, 2020) and is co-editor of *The Anthology of Australian Prose Poetry* (Melbourne University Press, 2020).

JOHN KINSELLA has published over forty volumes of poetry, most recently two of the three volumes of his *Collected Poems* with UWA Publishing, *Insomnia* (W.W. Norton, 2019), and, with Charmaine Papertalk Green, *False Claims of Colonial Thieves* (Magabala Books, 2018). He has also published fiction and life writing, including the recent novel *Pushing Back* (Transit Lounge, 2021) and the memoir *Displaced: A Rural Life* (Transit Lounge, 2020). His critical work includes *Legibility: An Antifascist Poetics* (Palgrave Macmillan, 2022) and *Activist Poetics: Anarchy in the Avon Valley* (Oxford University Press, 2010). He is Emeritus Professor in Literature and Environment at Curtin University and Fellow of Churchill College, University of Cambridge.

LOUIS KLEE is Junior Research Fellow at Clare College, University of Cambridge. He co-edited *The Cambridge Companion to the Australian Novel* (Cambridge University Press, 2023) and holds a Juncture Fellowship at the *Sydney Review of Books*. He has been awarded the Association for the Study of Australian Literature's A. D. Hope Prize and the *Australian Book Review*'s Peter Porter Prize.

JEANINE LEANE is a Wiradjuri writer, poet, and academic from south-west New South Wales. A new edition of her prize-winning first novel, *Purple Threads* (2011), was published in 2023 by University of Queensland Press in its First Nations Classic series. She has won the Oodgeroo Noonuccal Prize for Poetry twice and been the recipient of a Red Room Poetry Fellowship. She teaches Creative Writing and Aboriginal Literature at the University of Melbourne. She edited *Guwayu – For All Times: A Collection of First Nation Poems* (Magabala Books, 2020).

PHILIP MEAD is Emeritus Professor at the University of Western Australia and Honorary Professorial Fellow in the Melbourne Graduate School of Education, University of Melbourne. He co-authored *Literary Knowing and the Making of English Teachers: The Role of Literature in Shaping English Teachers' Professional Knowledges and Identities* (Routledge, 2022) and *Antipodal Shakespeare: Remembering and Forgetting in Britain, Australia and New Zealand* (Bloomsbury, 2018). He is the author of *Networking Language: Culture and*

History in Australian Poetry (Australian Scholarly Publishing, 2008) and the poetry collection, *Zanzibar Light* (Vagabond Press, 2018). He co-edited *The Penguin Book of Modern Australian Poetry* (Penguin, 1991) and edited *Kenneth Slessor: Critical Readings* (University of Queensland Press, 1997).

DAVID MCCOOEY is Professor of Writing and Literature at Deakin University. He is the author of four poetry collections, most recently *The Book of Falling* (Upswell, 2023). He is also the author of *Artful Histories: Modern Australian Autobiography* (Cambridge University Press, 1996) and co-editor of *The Limits of Life Writing* (Routledge, 2018). He was Deputy General Editor of *The Macquarie PEN Anthology of Australian Literature* (Allen & Unwin, 2009).

DASHIELL MOORE is an early career researcher at the University of Sydney. His research interests include world literature, postcolonial theory, and Indigenous studies, with a particular concentration on modern and contemporary Caribbean, Australian, and Pacific writing in English. He has published scholarly articles in several key journals, including *Textual Practice* and *The Journal of West Indian Literature*.

ANN-MARIE PRIEST is Senior Lecturer at Central Queensland University. She is the author of *My Tongue Is My Own: A Life of Gwen Harwood* (Black Inc, 2022), *A Free Flame: Australian Women Writers and Vocation in the Twentieth Century* (UWA Publishing, 2018), and *Great Writers, Great Loves: The Reinvention of Love in the Twentieth Century* (Black Inc, 2006).

ORCHID TIERNEY is Assistant Professor of English at Kenyon College. Articles and chapters have appeared in the *Journal of Modern Literature*, *SubStance*, *The Cambridge Companion to American Poetry and Politics since 1900* (Cambridge University Press, 2023), and the *Routledge Companion to Ecopoetics* (Routledge, 2023).

ANN VICKERY is Professor of Writing and Literature at Deakin University. She is the author of *Stressing the Modern: Cultural Politics in Australian Women's Poetry* (Salt Publishing, 2007) and *Leaving Lines of Gender: A Feminist Genealogy of Language Writing* (Wesleyan University Press, 2000). She is the co-author of *The Intimate Archive: Journeys through Private Papers* (National Library of Australia, 2007) and the co-editor of *Poetry and the Trace* (Puncher & Wattmann, 2013). She is the author of three poetry collections, most recently *Bees Do Bother: An Antagonist's Care Pack* (Vagabond Press, 2021).

COREY WAKELING is Associate Professor at Aoyama Gakuin University. He is the author of *Beckett's Laboratory: Experiments in the Theatre Enclosure* (Bloomsbury, 2021) and the co-editor of *Outcrop: Radical Australian Poetry of Land* (Black Rider Press, 2013). He is also the author of three poetry collections: *The Alarming Conservatory* (Giramondo, 2018), *Goad Omen* (Giramondo, 2013), and *Gargantuan Terrier, Buggy or Dinghy* (Vagabond Press, 2012).

ACKNOWLEDGEMENTS

I want first to deeply thank Ray Ryan at Cambridge University Press for his support of this book, and then to Edgar Mendez, Vinithan Sethumadhavan, and Tom Haynes at Cambridge University Press for their wonderful professionalism. I am very grateful for the contributors' persistence with their chapters during a period that saw considerable challenges around accessing materials as well as rapid changes in the way we teach. I acknowledge that this volume was edited on unceded land and pay respects to Aboriginal elders past and present. I particularly thank Aboriginal elder Professor Marion Kickett, who generously gave approval to one of the chapters. I want to thank Helen Johnson for permitting the reproduction of the remarkable *Leapyear Ladies Pop* (2022) for the cover, with photo credit to Andrew Curtis. As Johnson notes in an exhibition label at Monash University, this painting takes its name from a cartoon published in the *Police Gazette* (1876). Its interweaving imagery features a woman emerging out of the cartoon's hollowed centre and speaking versions of herself, "an attempt on the part of a subject to find purchase in the world." The exhibition was *Judy Watson and Helen Johnson: the red thread of history, loose ends* (10 September-12 November 2022). I want to further thank Philip Mead for ongoing discussions and feedback, Kyle Kohinga for their research assistance and discussions, Penny Harper for her wonderful copyediting, Jack Kirne for his research assistance, and Louis Klee for his generous insights from co-editing *The Cambridge Companion to the Australian Novel*. Lastly, a huge thank you to the Contemporary Histories Research Group at Deakin University for their support.

The authors want to thank the following for providing permission to quote material in this volume:

> Jessica Hepburn and Harriet Windsor for permission to reproduce excerpts from "Mare Bred by Pegasus" and "Divorce" by Anna Wickham.

ACKNOWLEDGEMENTS

Tom Thompson for permission to reproduce excerpts from "The Crane is My Neighbour" and "The Orange Tree" by John Shaw Neilson and "The Forest of Night" and "The Wanderer" by Christopher Brennan.

Samela Harris, Tom Thompson, and ETT Imprint to reproduce "Petit Testament" by Ern Malley.

John Harwood and Penguin Random House for permission to reproduce "The Sharpness of Death" by Gwen Harwood.

Lionel Fogarty. All works reproduced with permission from Lionel Fogarty.

Fryer Library for permission to reproduce Kath Walker (Oodgeroo Noonuccal), "Yussef," Oodgeroo Noonuccal Papers, UQFL84, Series A, Subseries 1, File 1, Fryer Library, University of Queensland. The two images have been reproduced with the permission of the copyright holder, courtesy of the Fryer Library.

John Forbes' Estate for permission to reproduce "Europe, endless."

Laurie Duggan for permission to reproduce excerpts from poems.

Ellen Van Neerven for permission to reproduce the excerpt from "Goan Fish Curry."

Charmaine Papertalk Green for permission to reproduce poems from *False Claims of Colonial Thieves*.

Jas H. Duke Estate for permission to reproduce the excerpt from *Destiny Wood*.

Chris Edwards for permission to reproduce the excerpt from *After Naptime*.

Alex Selenitsch for permission to reproduce poems from *7 More Monotones*.

Benjamin Laird for permission to reproduce poems from *The Durham Poems*.

~~CHRONOLOGY~~

A timeline or chronology is always incomplete and contestable. Accordingly, a strikethrough has been added to raise questions around the very constitution of histories. A strikethrough resists a privileging of Western understandings of temporality and poetry, and challenges how history in Australia is recorded and transmitted in light of ongoing settler colonialism. In compiling this chronology, I have been informed by the works cited in the volume's chapters. I would also like to acknowledge Joseph Steinberg for his careful chronology in *The Cambridge Companion to the Australian Novel*, which provided a generative parallel. While I hope that this timeline will foreground synchronicities between various poetries, I also hope it will indicate alternative, fragmented, and dispersed trajectories. I encourage scholars and students to read across and beyond the timeline in order to contextualise Australian poetries through their multiple connections and positionalities within the local, regional, and global.

65,000 BCE:	Archaeological evidence from Madjedbebe [Arnhem Land] in what is now known as the Northern Territory confirms the presence of Indigenous peoples on the Australian continent.
30,000 BCE:	Earliest dated Indigenous rock art.
1488:	Portuguese explorer Bartolomeu Dias starts European charting of the southern hemisphere and successfully navigates around the Cape of Good Hope, Africa. He becomes an advisor to Vasco da Gama, who establishes a sea route between Europe and India.
1605:	Spanish explorer Pedro Fernando de Quirós mistakes Vanuatu as part of the southern continent and names it Australia del Espírito Santo.
1606:	Dutch explorer Willem Janszoon looks for land and resources for the Dutch East India Company and is the first European to map the northern Australian coast. During the

CHRONOLOGY

	course of his travels, there would be a clash with the Indigenous Wik people, with a recording only of crew casualties.
1687:	William Dampier, *A New Voyage around the World* – the first Englishman to explore parts of the Australian coastline.
1700:	Trade at this time between the Aboriginal people of the Kimberleys and Arnhem Land and the Makassar people of Indonesia has been evidenced.
1703:	William Dampier, *A Voyage to New Holland in the Year 1699*.
1704:	Jonathan Swift, *A Tale of a Tub*.
1770:	James Cook claims land for the British Crown, renaming it New South Wales. The land was never ceded by the Indigenous peoples.
1786:	The British Government announces that a penal colony is to be established at Botany Bay.
1788:	Arthur Phillip, commander of the First Fleet, establishes a convict settlement at Sydney Cove, Port Jackson.
1789:	Erasmus Darwin writes "Visit of Hope to Sydney-Cove, Near Botany-Bay" to accompany a medallion made out of clay from the Colony of New South Wales and depicting a golden age.
1792:	Mary Wollstonecraft, *A Vindication of the Rights of Woman*.
1792–1802:	Pemulwuy, a Bidigal man of the Eora nation, leads resistance to European colonisation.
1794:	Robert Southey begins his *Botany Bay Eclogues*; first acknowledged massacre of Aboriginal people on Dharug land in New South Wales.
1798:	William Wordsworth, "The Convict" in *Lyrical Ballads*.
1801–3:	Matthew Flinders circumnavigates the continent of Australia. He maps it in *Voyage to Terra Australis* in 1814.
1803:	First European settlement near nipaluna (Hobart, Tasmania).
1804:	Castle Hill rebellion involving Irish convicts.
1815:	Governor Lachlan Macquarie establishes the inland settlement of Bathurst, resulting in a decade-long conflict with the Wiradjuri people, led by Windradyne.
1819:	Barron Field, *First Fruits of Australian Poetry*.
1823:	Australian-born William Charles Wentworth, *Australasia*.

1824: Thomas Kibble Hervey, *Australasia*, declaring that Australia is "destined to act a mighty part upon the theatre of the world."
1825: Letitia Elizabeth Landon (as L.E.L.), "The Female Convict" in *The Female Improvisatrice and Other Poems*.
1830: Lieutenant-Governor George Arthur instructs the making of the "Black Line," a chain of settlers to ensure capture of the remaining palawa people of lutruwita (Tasmania).
1833: Height of convict transportation, approximately 7,000 in a year.
1836: South Australia is established as a colony of free settlers.
1838: Eliza Hamilton Dunlop, "The Aboriginal Mother."
1839: Francis MacNamara (Frank the Poet), *A Convict's Tour to Hell*.
1842: Henry Parkes, *Stolen Moments: A Short Series of Poems*.
1846: Charles Harpur, "To the Lyre of Australia."
1847: First indentured labourers brought into Queensland from the South Pacific Islands.
1848: Wulatji publishes "Native Poetry" in *The Sydney Morning Herald*.
1851: The Colony of Victoria is established as independent to New South Wales. Gold is discovered in Victoria and New South Wales.
1854: Eureka Stockade of Ballarat miners swearing allegiance to the Southern Cross flag as independent from colonial administration; Caroline Leakey, *Lyra Australis: Or, Attempts to Sing in a Strange Land*.
1858: Mary Bailey, "The Sisters of Charity."
1867–72: Jong Ah Sing, "The Case."
1868: End of convict transportation to Australia.
1869: Charles Harpur, "The Kangaroo Hunt or a Morning in the Mountains"; Henry Kendall, *Leaves from Australian Forests*.
1870: Adam Lindsay Gordon, *Bush Ballads and Galloping Rhymes*.
1874: Catherine Martin, *The Explorers and Other Poems*.
1879: Bushranger Ned Kelly attempts to have his Jerilderie letter published. He is captured in 1880 and sentenced to death.
1887: Ada Cambridge publishes *Unspoken Thoughts* anonymously. It is quickly suppressed once Cambridge is identified as the author; Eliza Hamilton Dunlop, "The Aboriginal Mother"; Henry Lawson, "A Song of the Republic," inspired by riots protesting the Queen's Jubilee.

CHRONOLOGY

1888:	Louisa Lawson founds *The Dawn*; Grace Jennings Carmichael, "Tomboy Madge."
1889:	A. B. (Banjo) Paterson, "Clancy of the Overflow."
1892:	William Lane founds the New Australia movement. In 1893, he leads a group to Paraguay to found New Australia, a socialist utopia. The new colony divides in 1894, with Lane taking fifty-eight to Cosme, also in Paraguay. Mary Gilmore returns to Australia in 1902.
1893:	Charlie Flannigan, "Song Fellow," "Rodeo."
1894:	*Chinese Australian Herald* is founded.
1895:	A. B. (Banjo) Paterson, "Waltzing Matilda."South Australia grants voting rights to women, including Aboriginal women. Aboriginal men had been given the right to vote in Victoria, New South Wales, and South Australia in the 1850s whereas laws in Queensland (1885), Western Australia (1893), and the Northern Territory (1922) denied Aboriginal and Torres Strait Islander people the right to vote.
1897:	Christopher Brennan, *Musicopoematrographoscope* (published posthumously).
1898:	*Tung Wah News* (later *Tung Wah Times*) is founded.
1900:	Bernard O'Dowd, "Australia."
1901:	Establishment of the Commonwealth of Australia with the first federal election; beginning of the White Australia policy through the Australian Immigration Restriction Act which also required the writing of fifty words in a European language as dictated by the officer. This is reinforced by the Pacific Island Labourers Act; Henry Lawson, "The Shanty on the Rise."
1902:	The Commonwealth Franchise Act gives all men and women around Australia the right to vote in federal elections, excepting Aboriginal and Torres Strait Islander people unless they already had the right to vote before 1901; *Chinese Times* founded.
1905:	Louisa Lawson, *The Lonely Crossing*.
1908:	Dorothea Mackellar publishes "My Country" as "Core of My Heart" in *The Spectator* (UK).
1909–15:	C. J. Dennis, "The Songs of a Sentimental Bloke"; the Aborigines Protection Act is passed in New South Wales.
1914–18:	World War I.
1915:	Amendments to the Aborigines Protection Act enable the New South Wales Aborigines Protection Board to remove

Aboriginal children from their families; Yang Yuting, "My Experiences in Australia." The failed Gallipoli campaign in Turkey, followed by the Dardanelles campaign, resulted in 250,000 deaths on both sides. It is believed to have been integral to not only a burgeoning Australian and New Zealand national consciousness, but also for the independence movement in Turkey. The anniversary of the landings at Gallipoli on 25 April was later commemorated as Anzac Day.

1916: Zora Cross, *A Song of Mother Love and Other Verses*.

1918: Christopher Brennan, "Chant of Doom"; Lola Ridge, "The Ghetto."

1921: John Shaw Neilson, "The Orange Tree"; Zora Cross, *Elegy on an Australian Schoolboy*.

1922: Zora Cross, *An Introduction to the Study of Australian Literature*.

1923: *Vision* founded and runs for two years.

1924: Nettie Palmer, *Modern Australian Literature 1900–1923*.

1928–29: *The London Aphrodite* (magazine).

1931: Kenneth Slessor, "Five Visions of Captain Cook."

1938: *Conditional Culture*, by Rex Ingamells with Ian Tilbrook, heralds the Jindyworobak movement.

1939: Kenneth Slessor, *Five Bells*; A. D. Hope, "Australia"; *Southerly* founded.

1939–45: World War II. Robert Menzies becomes prime minister from 1939 to 1941.

1940: Clem Christesen founds *Meanjin Papers*, later shortened to *Meanjin*; Douglas Stewart takes over editing of *The Bulletin*'s "Red Page"; Max Harris, *A Gift of Blood*.

1941: The speech on 26 December in which Prime Minister John Curtin declares that "Australia looks to America, free of any pangs as to our traditional links or kinship with the United Kingdom" is prefaced by a stanza from Bernard O'Dowd's "Dawnward?" (1903); Beatrice Davis founds *Australian Poetry*; Flexmore Hudson founds *Poetry* (1941–47); Douglas Stewart, *Sonnets to the Unknown Soldier*, *Fire in the Snow*.

1942: Lionel Lindsay, *Addled Art*.

1943: James McAuley and Harold Stewart create the hoax poet Ern Malley and his work, *The Darkening Ecliptic*, is published in *Angry Penguins* in 1944.

CHRONOLOGY

1944:	The Realist Writers Group begins in Melbourne; Kenneth Slessor, "Beach Burial."
1945–65:	Around 2 million immigrants from Europe arrive in Australia.
1946:	Judith Wright, *The Moving Image*; H. M. Green, *Modern Australian Poetry*; Douglas Stewart, *Modern Australian Verse*; James McAuley, *Under Aldebaran*.
1948:	Francis Webb, *A Drum for Ben Boyd*; Rosemary Dobson, *The Ship of Ice*.
1949:	Robert Menzies becomes Prime Minister again, serving until 1966. This period also saw what was known as the Lavender Scare, where thousands of gay and lesbian workers were fired or lost their federal government jobs due to their sexuality.
1950–53:	Australia is one of the first countries to become involved in the Korean War.
1954:	Stephen Murray-Smith establishes *Overland*; Vincent Buckley, *The World's Flesh*.
1956:	James McAuley and Richard Krygier establish *Quadrant*; Robert Smith founds *Westerly*.
1957:	Vincent Buckley, *Essays in Poetry: Mainly Australian*.
1959:	Chris Wallace-Crabbe, *The Music of Division*.
1960:	James McAuley accepts a position at the University of Tasmania and quickly becomes chair of English.
1961:	Peter Porter, *Once Bitten, Twice Bitten*; Gwen Harwood publishes "In the Park" and two acrostic poems slyly savaging the *Bulletin* under the pseudonym of Walter Lehmann. Vincent Buckley had taken over editorship of the Red Page from Douglas Stewart; *Australian Book Review* begins.
1962:	Aboriginal people are given the option to enrol and vote in federal elections, but are not treated like other voters and required to vote until 1984. Aborigines were able to vote in state elections; Judith Wright is a founding member of the Wildlife Preservation Society of Queensland; Gwen Harwood, "Burning Sappho."
1962–73:	The Vietnam War begins in 1962, seeing Australian involvement until 1973.
1963:	Gwen Harwood, *Poems*; Angus & Robertson launch its Australian Poets series; *Australian Literary Studies* begins.
1964:	Oodgeroo Noonuccal (as Kath Walker), *We Are Going*; James McAuley, *Captain Quiros*; *The Realist* founded; Grace Perry founds *Poetry Australia*, which runs until 1992.

1965:	Judith Wright, *Preoccupations in Australian Poetry*.
1967:	A referendum results in 90.77 per cent voting yes to recognising Aboriginal and Torres Strait Islander people as part of the Australian population in the Constitution; Rodney Hall and Thomas Shapcott, *New Impulses in Australian Poetry*.
1968:	Bruce Dawe, "Homecoming"; Judith Wright, "Conservation as a Concept"; Rodney Hall and Thomas Shapcott, *New Impulses in Australian Poetry*; University of Queensland Press begins its poetry series.
1969:	Australian women workers granted equal pay for equal work.
1970:	First Earth Day; Thomas Shapcott, *Australian Poetry Now*; David Malouf, *Bicycle and Other Poems*.
1971:	Neville Bonner becomes the first Aboriginal member of the federal parliament; Martin Johnson, *shadowmass*.
1972:	Led by Gough Whitlam, Labor wins the federal election for the first time in twenty-three years; the Aboriginal Tent Embassy is established outside Parliament House; Alec Bolton begins Brindabella Press; Michael Dransfield, *The Inspector of Tides*; Alan Ginsberg visits Australia, leading to lectures on "Spontaneous Poetics" at Naropa (1976) that reflect his interest in Aboriginal understandings of breath, rhythm, and community participation.
1973:	With Australia withdrawing from the Vietnam' War, the White Australia policy of immigration restrictions to non-Europeans ends; Arabic language weekly *An-Nahar* is founded and runs until 2000; Kris Hemensley begins *Ear in a Wheatfield*; Vicki Viidikas, *Condition Red*.
1974:	Oodgeroo Noonuccal pens "Commonplace" and "Yussef" while aboard a British Airways flight that had been hijacked by terrorists campaigning for Palestinian liberation; Colin Talbot and Robert Kenny, *Applestealers*; Robert Gray, *Creekwater Journal*.
1975:	Governor-General dismisses the Whitlam government; International Women's Year; Kate Jennings, *Mother, I'm Rooted: An Anthology of Australian Women Poets*; Fremantle Arts Centre Press is established; James McAuley, *A Map of Australian Verse*; Alex Selenitsch, *Sonnets*; Rudi Krausman, *From Another Shore*; Dorothy Porter, *Little Hoodlum*; Geoff Page, *Smalltown Memorials*.

1977: Association for the Study of Australian Literature is formed; Les Murray, "The Buladelah-Taree Holiday Cycle."
1978: Sydney Gay and Lesbian Mardi Gras begins; *Australian Book Review* begins again; Jas H. Duke, *Destiny Wood*; Kevin Gilbert, *People Are Legends*; Bruce Beaver, *Death's Directives*; Lee Cataldi, *Invitation to a Marxist Lesbian Party*; the Sydney Women Writers Workshop (also known as No Regrets) begins; Jennifer Rankin, *Earth Hold*.
1979: *The Tasmanian Review*, later *Island*, is established; John Tranter, *The New Australian Poetry*; Billy Marshall Stoneking, *Ear Ink: Poems*.
1980: Lionel Fogarty, *Kargun*; Gig Ryan, *The Division of Anger: Poems*.
1981: Ania Walwicz, "Australia"; Peter Craven and Michael Heyward found *Scripsi*, which runs until 1994.
1982: The first case of AIDS is diagnosed, with a rapid increase occurring in the mid-1980s; Fay Zwicky, *Kaddish and Other Poems*.
1983: Margaret Bradstock, Gary Dunne, Davy Sargent, and Louise Wakeling, *Edge City on Two Different Plans*.
1984: Anna Couani, *Italy and the Train*.
1985: Komninos Zervos, *the komninos manifesto*.
1986: Pam Brown, *Selected Poems 1972–1978*; Robert Adamson, Juno Gemes, and Michael Wilding establish Paperbark Press; Gaetano Rando, *Italo-Australian Poetry in the 80s*; Alan Wearne, *The Nightmarkets*; John Scott, *St. Clair: Three Novels*; Lily Brett, *The Auschwitz Poems*; Mudrooroo, *The Song Circle of Jacky and Selected Poems*.
1987: Laurin McKinnon and Jill Jones found BlackWattle Press and *cargo* (1987–93); Ron Pretty establishes Five Islands Press; Dennis Gallagher, *Love and Death: An Anthology of Poetry and Prose*; Laurie Duggan, *The Ash Range*; Philip Salom, *Sky Poems*; Judith Beveridge, *The Domesticity of Giraffes*; Indigenous publisher Magabala Books is established; Ken Bolton begins *Otis Rush* (1987–96).
1988: Bicentennial celebrations; Survival/Invasion Day protests; Kevin Gilbert, *Inside Black Australia: An Anthology of Aboriginal Poetry*; Oodgeroo Noonuccal, *Kath Walker in China*; John Tranter, *Under Berlin: New Poems 1988*; John

	Forbes, *The Stunned Mullet and Other Poems*; Dimitris Tsaloumas, *Falcon Drinking*.
1989:	The opening of the Iron Curtain results in a peaceful end to the Cold War; Robert Adamson, *The Clean Dark*; Ken Bolton and John Jenkins, *The Ferrara Poems*.
1990–1:	Australia participates in the Gulf War.
1991:	Renate Klein and Susan Hawthorne found Spinifex Press.
1992:	Mabo decision: High Court rules that native title exists for all Indigenous people; Gillian Hanscombe, *Sybil: The Glide of Her Tongue*; Antigone Kefala, *Absence: New and Selected Poems*; Robert Harris, *Jane, Interlinear and Other Poems*; joanne burns, *on a clear day*.
1993:	Merlinda Bobis, *Cantata of the Warrior Woman Daragang Magayon: An Epic*; Sandy Jeffs, *Poems from the Madhouse*; John Kinsella, *Syzygy*.
1994:	Dorothy Porter, *The Monkey's Mask*; Ee Tiang Hong, *Nearing a Horizon*; Philip Hodgins, *Dispossessed*; Hazel Smith, *Poet without Language*. Louise Crisp, *pearl & sea fed*.
1995:	Ivor Indyk and Evelyn Juers establish Giramondo; Black Pepper Press begins; Lionel Fogarty, *New and Selected Poems: Munaldjali, Mutuerjaraera*; J. S. Harry, *The Life on the Water and the Life Beneath*; Ouyang Yu, *Moon over Melbourne: Poems*; John Anderson, *The Forest Set Out Like the Night*.
1996:	Lisa Bellear, *Dreaming in Urban Areas*; Kerry Reed-Gilbert, *Black Woman, Black Life*; PiO, *24 Hours*; Les Murray, *Subhuman Redneck Poems*; Ivor Indyk founds *Heat*.
1997:	The Bringing Them Home report is tabled in Parliament, detailing systemic removal of Aboriginal children from their families; John Tranter founds *Jacket*, which runs until 2010, and leads to the US-based *Jacket2*; Peter Minter and Adrian Wiggins found *Cordite Poetry Review*, with David Prater becoming managing editor from 2001 to 2012, followed by Kent MacCarter.
1998:	Jordie Albiston, *The Hanging of Jean Lee*; Merlinda Bobis, *Summer Was a Fast Train without Terminals*; Amanda Stewart, *I/T: Selected Poems 1980–1996*.
1999:	Les Murray drafts a preamble to the Australian Constitution with Prime Minister John Howard. This proposed change, as

	well as Australia becoming a republic, is rejected by referendum; Les Murray, *Fredy Neptune*; Alan Jacobs, *Enough Already: An Anthology of Australian Jewish Writing*; Michael Brennan founds Vagabond Press; John Kinsella, Clive Newman, and Chris Hamilton-Emery start Salt Publishing.
2000:	Sydney hosts the Olympic Games; Kerry Reed-Gilbert, *The Strength of Us as Women: Black Women Speak*; Jenni Kemarre Martiniello, *Writing Us Mob: New Indigenous Voices*; Raghid Nahhas founds and edits *Kalimat: An Australian-Arabic Literary Quarterly*; film adaptation of Dorothy Porter's *The Monkey's Mask*.
2001:	Four coordinated terrorist attacks involving commercial passenger airplanes are carried out on 11 September by the Islamic extremist group al-Qaeda against the United States; Bronwyn Lea, *Flight Animals*.
2002:	Kate Fagan, *The Long Moment*; Emma Lew, *Anything the Landlord Touches*; Ron Pretty begins *Blue Dog: Australian Poetry*.
2003–9:	Australia joins in the US-led invasion of Iraq in 2003 and is involved until 2009.
2003:	Johanna Featherstone founds Red Room Poetry; Louis Armand, *Strange Attractors*.
2004:	Lily Brett, *Auschwitz Poems*; Huang Ngoc-Tuan, *Cau Noi: The Bridge*; Martin Harrison, *Who Wants to Create Australia?*; Samuel Wagan Watson, *Smoke Encrypted Whispers*; Anthony Lynch begins Whitmore Press.
2005:	The annual Australian Poetry Slam begins; David Musgrave establishes Puncher & Wattmann; Cassie Lewis, *Bridges*; David McCooey, *Blister Pack*; Peter Minter, *blue grass*; Geoff Page, *Freehold*.
2006:	Robert Adamson, *The Goldfinches of Baghdad*; Claire Gaskin, *A Bud*; Peter Minter, *blue grass*.
2007:	Kim Cheng Boey and Michelle Cahill establish *Mascara Literary Review*; Angela Gardner, *Parts of Speech*.
2008:	Prime Minister Kevin Rudd makes a formal apology for the policies that led to Stolen Generations, the forcible removal of First Nations children from their families; Philip Mead, *Networked Language: Culture & History in Australian Poetry*.
2009:	Michael Farrell and Jill Jones, *Out of the Box: Contemporary Australian Gay and Lesbian Poets*; Adam Aitken, *Eighth Horizon*; Peter Boyle, *Apocrypha*.

2010: Australian Poetry Library established by John Tranter and Elizabeth Webby; Louis Armand begins *Vlak Magazine*; Pamela Brown, *Authentic Local*; Jill Jones, *Dark Bright Doors*; Jennifer Maiden, *Pirate Rain*; Jennifer Harrison, *Colombine: New and Selected Poems*; Mark Tredinnick, *Fire Diary*.

2011: The national organisation Australian Poetry (www.australianpoetry.org) is established out of a merger of former New South Wales and Victorian poetry organisations and begins *Australian Poetry Journal*; Jessica L. Wilkinson founds *Rabbit: A Journal for Nonfiction Poetry*; Ali Cobby Eckermann, *Ruby Moonlight*; Ali Alizadeh, *Ashes in the Air*.

2012: Prime Minister's Literary Awards extend to poetry after they were first begun in 2008; Linsay and John Knight begin Pitt Street Poetry; Ouyang Yu, *The Kingsbury Tales: A Complete Collection*; Jessica L. Wilkinson, *marionette: a life of miss marion davies*; Lisa Gorton, *Hotel Hyperion*; Toby Fitch, *Rawshock*; Mez Breeze, *Human Readable Messages_ [Mezangelle 2003–2011]*.

2013: Anne Elvey establishes *Plumwood Mountain: An Australian Journal of Ecopoetry and Ecopoetics*; Adam Aitken, Kim Cheng Boey, and Michelle Cahill, *Contemporary Asian Australian Poets*; Robert Gray and Geoffrey Lehmann, *Australian Poetry since 1788*; Justin Clemens, *The Mundiad*; Ivy Alvarez, *Disturbance*; Stephen Edgar, *Eldershaw*; Corey Wakeling and Jeremy Balius, *Outcrop: Radical Australian Poetry of Land*; Fiona Hile, *Novelties*; Kate Middleton, *Ephemeral Waters*.

2014: Omar Musa, *Here Come the Dogs*; Alex Skovron, *Towards the Equator: New and Selected Poems*; Bonny Cassidy, *Final Theory*; Nick Whittock, *hows its*; Petra White, *A Hunger*.

2015: Recent Work Press begins; Michael Farrell, *Cocky's Joy*; Natalie Harkin, *Dirty Words*; Chris Edwards, *After Naptime*; Cassandra Atherton, *Exhumed*; Tracy Ryan, *Hoard*; Lucy Dougan, *The Guardians*. Natasha Dennerstein, *Anatomize*.

2016: Bonny Cassidy and Jessica L. Wilkinson, *Contemporary Australian Feminist Poetry*; Martin Langford, Judith Beveridge, Judy Johnson, and David Musgrave, *Contemporary Australian Poetry*; Ellen Van Neerven, *Comfort Food*; Paul Hetherington, *Burnt Umber*; Dan Disney and Kit Kelen, *Writing to the Wire*; Tony Birch, *Broken Teeth*; Liam Ferney, *Content*.

2017:	Uluru Statement from the Heart calls for Voice, Treaty, and Truth for First Nations people to be enshrined in the Constitution. It is offered to the Australian Government but not accepted by Prime Minister Malcolm Turnbull; Ali Cobby Eckermann is the first Indigenous winner globally of the Windham-Campbell Prize; Andy Jackson, *Music Our Bodies Can't Hold*; Quinn Eades, *Rallying*; Amelia Dale, *Constitution*; Lachlan Brown, *Lunar Inheritance*; Eileen Chong, *Painting Red Orchids*; Heather Taylor Johnson, *Shaping the Fractured Self: Poems of Chronic Illness and Pain*.
2018:	Kate Lilley, *Tilt*; Candy Royalle, *A Trillion Tiny Awakenings*; Alison Whittaker, *blakwork*; Bella Li, *Argosy*; Charmaine Papertalk Green and John Kinsella, *False Claims of Colonial Thieves*; Benjamin Laird, *The Durham Poems*; Eunice Andrada, *Flood Damage*; Maryam Azam, *The Hijab Files*; Rae White, *Milk Teeth*.
2019:	Gay'wu Group of Women, *Song Spirals: Sharing Women's Wisdom of Country through Songlines*; David Stavanger and Anne-Marie Te Whiu, *Solid Air: Australian and New Zealand Spoken Word*; Omar Sakr, *The Lost Arabs*.
2019–20:	Black Summer results in 60 million acres or 94,000 square miles being burnt. The Gospers Mountain fire is the biggest forest fire in Australian history.
2020:	First case of COVID-19 in Australia is reported on 5 January, with community transmission being recorded in March. Australian borders to all non-residents are closed later that month. Australia had a zero-COVID suppression strategy until late 2021, with particular areas experiencing lengthy lockdown periods. A vaccination program began in February 2021. Alison Whittaker, *Fire Front: First Nations Poetry and Power Today*; Jeanine Leane, *Guwayu – For All Times*; Cassandra Atherton and Paul Hetherington, *The Anthology of Australian Prose Poetry*; Jill Jones, *A History of What I'll Become*; Melinda Bufton, *Moxie*; L.K. Holt, *Birth Plan*; Astrid Lorange, *Labour and Other Poems*.
2021:	Evelyn Araluen, *Dropbear*; Andy Jackson, *Human Looking*; Elfie Shiosaki, *Homecoming*; Saba Vasefi, Melinda Smith and Yvette Holt, *Borderless: A Transnational Anthology of Feminist Poetry*; Dan Disney, *accelerations & inertias*; Maria

	Takolander, *Trigger Warning*; Emily Stewart, *Running Time*.
2022:	Sarah Holland-Batt, *The Jaguar*; Gavin Yuan Gao, *At the Altar of Touch*; Rachel Potter, *Acanthus*.
2023:	The proposal to establish an Aboriginal and Torres Strait Voice to Parliament was rejected in a Referendum. The Gaza-Israel conflict begins, which is part of the longer Israeli-Palestinian conflict dating back to 1948. Alison Whittaker and Steven Lindsay Ross, *NANGAMAY dream MANA gather DJURALI grow: First Nations Australia LGBTQIA + Poetry*; Sara M. Saleh, *The Flirtation of Girls/Ghazal El-Banat*; Shastra Deo, *The Exclusion Zone*; A.J. Carruthers, *Axis Z Book 3*; Grace Yee, *Chinese Fish*.
2024:	David Brooks, *The Other Side of Daylight: New and Selected Poems*; Nam Le, *36 Ways of Writing a Vietnamese Poem*.

ANN VICKERY

Introduction

The new millennium has witnessed a resurgence in poetry as its condensed form, attention to feeling, and capacity to capture the zeitgeist attracts more readers than ever before. Australia has been at the forefront of experimenting with emergent and hybrid forms such as the verse novel, prose poetry, digital poetries, and poetic biography. Among the first to realise the potential of the Internet to create a vibrant cross-cultural dialogue around poetry and poetics, Australians initiated online journals that reached out globally like *Jacket* and *Cordite Poetry Review*. Australia's poets have increasingly garnered international recognition. Les Murray was dubbed "one of the superleague that includes Seamus Heaney, Derek Walcott and Joseph Brodsky" by the *Independent on Sunday* (quoted in Davie) while Dan Chiasson discerned in *The New Yorker* that Murray was "routinely mentioned among the three of four leading-English language poets." In 2017, Australian poet Ali Cobby Eckermann was the first Indigenous writer worldwide to be awarded Yale University's prestigious Windham Campbell Prize. Describing John Kinsella as "a prodigy of the imagination," Harold Bloom declared of Kinsella's mid-career *oeuvre*: "We are poised before the onset of what I prophesy will be a major art" (xxviii). It would be wrong, however, to view Australian poetry as marked principally by a few individuals. Australian poetry is a vast yet intricate network of energy and communities. As David Malouf remarks: "Poetry is, at the moment, the most flourishing of the literary arts in Australia."

Scholarship has tended to subsume much discussion of Australian poetry under the broader umbrella of 'Australian literature,' with the novel typically dominating in its narrativisation of nation. Yet, as Philip Mead discerns in his chapter, Australian poetry has currency in many ways, even quite literally, with poets appearing on banknotes along with other iconic representatives of Australian life. Chapters in this *Companion* consider the crucial role of poetry in shaping understandings of nation, yet also how it has provided a powerful means to unsettle the power dynamics of settler colonialism and nation, and imagined being otherwise. One of the first broadly framed critical collections on Australian poetry, this *Companion* is nevertheless highly aware of its own provisionality and limits. In accompanying the reader on a literary journey, *The Cambridge Companion to Australian Poetry* seeks to be less a gatekeeper than an enthusiast inviting wider conversations that can also be returned to over time. This is not to ignore that such discussions can become heated, to the point that John Forbes once famously characterised Australian poetry as being like a "knife fight in a phone booth" (Duggan). Poetry, whether written, visual, or heard, matters. It has ontological bearing, fathoming "how to be and how to relate," as much as it is epistemologically driven, "navigat[ing] terrains of what is known, what remains unknowable, and how we actively undertake knowing" (Vickery and Fagan 17).

Australian poetry offers a particular distinctiveness, demonstrating that "some of the world's oldest aesthetic and cultural stories are alive beside glimmers of forms and communities that are among the newest and most emergent" (Vickery and Fagan 17). Australia has one of the world's oldest continuing cultures, with the song cycles and orature of over 500 Indigenous groups occurring over 60,000 years in hundreds of languages. As A. J. Carruthers points out in his chapter, these are living songs that involve interworking between the bodily interior and the external land through sound.

In the European imaginary, Australia figured as the New World and was imagined as either holding utopic potential or, alternatively, disparaged as the 'arse end' of the world. Viewed primarily by the English as a tidy solution for its criminal population, the First Fleet arrived in 1788 and established a penal colony at Botany Bay. While free settlers began to arrive five years later, the establishment of further penal colonies at Van Diemen's Land and Norfolk Island led to Australia being indelibly shaped by a convict heritage. Unlike New Zealand, there was no recognition of the pre-existing Indigenous culture. With Australia deemed *terra nullius*, the history of Australian settler colonialism is simultaneously a history of Aboriginal genocide, resettlement, as well as the removal of Aboriginal children up to the 1970s.

Poetry has had a key role in the mechanics of settler colonialism while also being a major vehicle through which to both challenge it and navigate its ongoing impact. In his chapter, Philip Mead discerns that mythographic literature has played a constitutive role in the imagining of Australia. From Matthew Flinders' mapping of the continent in *Voyage to Terra Australis* in 1814, the narratives of geographic discovery and imperialism have been intertwined. In the nascent colonies, poetry functioned as a form of instruction, entertainment, and community formation, as much as a means to challenge structures of authority and governance. Henry Parkes, the longest serving premier of the colony of New South Wales, would rail against the "dung-hill aristocracy of Botany Bay" (Martin 15) as well as publish *Stolen Moments: A Short Series of Poems* (1842). Justin Clemens has argued that Barron Field's even earlier *First Fruits of Australian Poetry* (1819) reflects the judge's sense of being in a colony that was "both over-present and lacking" (23). He adds that Field's citation of Jonathan Swift's vision of a *Terra Australis incognita* in the satire *A Tale of the Tub* (1704) mediated Field's understanding of a real place while consolidating the legal fiction of *terra nullius* that Field was then urging in his taxation battle with Governor Macquarie (28–29). Irish convict-poet Francis McNamara, colloquially known as "Frank the Poet," would likewise cite Swift in "A Convict's Tour to Hell" (1839), including figures like Captain James Cook and past Governor Ralph Darling within its Dantean journey.

Field's infamous rhyming of "Australia" with "failure," for Michael Farrell, demonstrates anxiety over the colonial enterprise itself and he finds this echoed in subsequent settler poems. His chapter explores how settler poets reworked the sublime and the gothic through which to articulate their ambivalence over the circumstances of settlement. The sublime sits uncomfortably alongside the murderous or deathly, with Charles Harpur's "A Midsummer Noon in the Australian Forest" meditating on quietness as a point outside time or, alternatively the closeness in life to death. Banjo Paterson would mobilise the gothic convention of the live burial in his ballad "Waltzing Matilda." And in "The Shanty on the Rise" (1901), published in the same year as Australian Federation, Henry Lawson invokes and blurs high and low, presence and absence, present and past, and reality and dream. Farrell points out that Lawson conjoins the buried and unburied in "The Men Who Made Australia" to embody a mythic national spirit.

Precarity would also be felt by settler women poets, accentuated by gender constraints. Transportation from Britain was aimed at removing a convict's past identity, whether male or female, yet, as Katie Hansord discerns, there was little sense of individual identity and agency even for free female immigrants. She argues that white women poets created a sense of solidarity through a Romantic lens, and extended the bardic power of the poet to the poetess. While male poets also invoked sympathy, its association with female sensibility meant that settler women poets could publicly advocate for understanding those with no or fewer rights, whether these be white women, First Nations people, or prisoners. An example is Eliza Hamilton Dunlop's "The Aboriginal Mother" (1838), published after the Myall Creek

Massacre and subsequent court trial. Aileen Moreton-Robinson points out that such writings were still highly complicit with the structures of colonialism. There were also limits to more radical thought by settler women. Ada Cambridge, for instance, wrote of female sexuality and criticised the institution of marriage in the anonymous *Unspoken Thoughts* (1887), yet was forced to withdraw it once her authorship was identified. She then turned to the novel, its conventions around 'fiction' perhaps providing more of a buffer for her dissident ideas and dispelling the intensity of feeling that was so evident in her poems.

Farrell argues that one must look beyond conventional sources of the book and periodical to locate poetic texts by those on the colonies' margins. There is little record of early Chinese poetry in Australia, despite the Gold Rush of the 1850s seeing a wave of migration from China. Farrell cites Jong Ah Sing's diary, "The Case" (1867–72), written while in an asylum. He also foregrounds the drawing poems of Aboriginal stockrider Charlie Flannigan, produced while on death row. Huang Zhong and Wenche Ommundsen are in agreement with Farrell, arguing that researchers must look at the "large but largely hidden body of texts written in languages other than English" (1). We might therefore add the unpublished notebooks of anarchist Salvador Torrents, who was part of the wave of Spanish migrants who first arrived around 1907 to work on the sugar cane farms (Jacklin 178), and the notebooks of Aboriginal activist A. M. Fernando, who wrote protest "word poems" in London in the late 1920s (Paisley).

Just as anti-British sentiment increased in the second half of the nineteenth century, so too did racial anxiety among white Australians and a growing sense of geographic isolation. Individual colonies began to legislate restrictions on Chinese immigration. Henry Lawson's collective vision in "A Song of the Republic" (1887) did not extend to racial others like the Chinese and Aborigines, or those with mixed race. William Lane established the New Australia movement in 1892 along similar lines of eugenics-based purity, creating New Australia and Cosme colonies in Paraguay in 1893 and 1894. The Australian Immigration Restriction Act and the Pacific Island Labourers Act (known colloquially as the White Australia policy) would pass in the same year as Federation (1901), regulating national subjects. While white women would be recognised as citizens the following year, First Nations people were not.

The impact of the White Australia policy meant that the Chinese population reduced from 40,000 in the early 1860s to 30,000 in 1901, and then to 10,000 or less after World War II. Philip Mead points out in his chapter that nation has a narrow, short, and highly contested reality in Australia: "For white Australia it is a mythic and political collective with an unsettled origin and unreconciled present; for Aboriginal Australia it is an alien, domineering framework that ignores the history of their own unceded sovereignty." For Chinese Australians, it was a space of ambivalence. Chinese Australian newspapers started up around the same time as Federation. This included the *Chinese Australian Herald* (1894), the *Tung Wah News* (1898) (which became the *Tung Wah Times* in 1902), and the *Chinese Times* (1902). Zhong and Ommundsen's research into poetry published in the *Tung Wah Times* found frequent use of the Chinese word *ke* (guest) and expressions of alienation (7). Yang Yuting, an official with the Chinese Consulate-General in Australia, would openly write of the discriminatory laws of British colonisers towards Chinese arrivals in his poem "My Experiences in Australia" (1915) (Zhong and Ommundsen 6–7).

Carrying the banner of "Australia for the White Man," *The Bulletin* facilitated a 'bush school' of poetry that included Lawson and A. B. (Banjo) Paterson. It would also serialise C. J. Dennis's *The Songs of a Sentimental Bloke* (1909–15), immensely popular in its proud vernacular and comic portrait of Australian larrikinism. The *Bulletin*'s Red Page shaped literary opinion for many decades. John Hawke points out that when A. G. Stephens took over editorship of the Red Page in the 1890s, it acknowledged international developments in poetry by running a debate on French Symbolism. Stephens encouraged alternative poets like Christopher Brennan and John Shaw Neilson. Brennan's *Musicopoematographoscope* (1897) was penned in response to Mallarmé's *Un coup de dés*, while Toby Davidson's chapter analyses how Neilson's interchangeability of light and sound in "The Orange Tree" (1921) heightens the blurring of the mystic and ordinary.

Poetry functioned in World War I as a vehicle of national and imperial propaganda, as demonstrated in Christopher Brennan's "Chant of Doom" (1918). Yet it also began to question the cost of war, with poets like Zora Cross shifting from highly patriotic in *A Song of Mother Love and Other Verses* (1916) to the more critical *Elegy on an Australian Schoolboy* (1921). Dan Disney points out in his chapter that the ANZACs or 'diggers' were often portrayed as simultaneously ordinary and extraordinary, extending the larrikin mythos while also being heroicised. He analyses how a soldier-poet like Leon Gellert turns to the Shakespearean sonnet in "A Night Attack" (1917), while transposing a colonial lens to the battlefield. By World War II, poets were more openly ambivalent, Disney citing Kenneth Slessor's "Beach Burial" (1944) as emblematic in articulating a "growing weariness at war's futilities and death's finalities."

Poets like Gellert and Slessor were part of the artistic circle around Norman and Jack Lindsay. As John Hawke discusses in his chapter, the

Lindsay circle reacted against bush realism and a primitivist (and feminised) lens of modernism, advocating instead a Nietzschean-inspired vitalism that formed the base for the short-lived but highly distributed journal *Vision* (1923-24). Aidan Coleman also considers how Slessor was shaped by Vitalist principles, moving beyond the influence of T. S. Eliot to capture the energy, rather than ennui, of modern urban life. He adds that Slessor's nihilism would, however, turn the Lindsays' vision on its head, his elegy "Five Bells" demonstrating the impossibility of connection while still resonant with lyric intensity. Echoing the distilled symbolism of Shaw Neilson, Lesbia Harford transformed the Dionysian impetus of Vitalism into an impressionistic moment of transcendence:

> Pat wasn't Pat last night at all
> He was the rain,
> The Spring,
> Young Dionysus, white and warm,
> Lilac and everything. (115)

Although one of the first women to graduate with a law degree, Harford spent much of her life in menial jobs and became involved in union organising. Her brother would introduce her to modernist art and avant-garde movements like Vorticism. In his chapter, Coleman explores how Harford locates working-class agency in pockets of disruption to dull factory or commuter routines.

In their exploration of erotic transgression as embodied liberation, Harford's poems were shown only to a small, intimate circle. Most only became public when her close friend, Nettie Palmer, published them posthumously. In contrast, Zora Cross revised the sonnet form to proclaim female desire with an openness that made her a popular sensation. Although lecturing at the Sydney Teachers' College and one of the earliest to publish a volume of criticism on Australian literature, Cross was dismissed as lightweight by many contemporaries and subsequent scholars.[1] This included Nettie Palmer, an early promulgator of national literature with husband Vance Palmer. In *Modern Australian Literature 1900-1923*, Palmer wrote of Cross's work: "The sonnets are less original than the other poems, but the remarkable thing about them was their easy movement, as of some slender animal with strong, silken muscles" (51).

While Drusilla Modjeska argues that women writers increasingly turned to the novel in early twentieth-century Australia, it is more accurate to observe that those that did often attracted greater critical praise, particularly from later scholars, and especially feminist scholars. This period saw a prodigious number of (still overwhelmingly white) women publishing poetry, including in newly formed women's magazines that were critically dismissed for their middlebrow inclination. Many early-twentieth-century women writers would also travel, which either reinforced their sense of national identity (like Dorothea Mackellar in her 1908 poem, "My Country") or made them more reflective about cultural prescription. Raised in Australia before returning to England as an adult, Anna Wickham voiced a forthright, manners-be-damned feminism within British modernist circles. Another transnational modernist was Lola Ridge, who moved from New Zealand to Australia and onto the United States, where she celebrated the New York mixing pot in "The Ghetto" (1918) and critiqued forms of injustice.

Forums like the Red Page became less open to international influences and Jack Lindsay found England unreceptive to "anti-modernist Antipodean vitalism" in his short-lived magazine *The London Aphrodite* (1928–29). Alternatively, Max Harris successfully courted an international avant-garde and combined it with experimental local writing and art through his journal, *Angry Penguins*. The ambitions of Harris and his little magazine would incite soldier poets James McAuley and Harold Stewart to create the hoax poet Ern Malley as a way of debunking what they saw as nonsensical pretension. Purportedly whipped up in a few hours while at the Melbourne barracks, the resulting poems were created through chance operations and collaging from a wide range of sources that included army reports on mosquito control and Shakespeare. Harris took the bait, announcing Malley's surrealist genius in a special 1944 issue. Once unveiled, the hoax attracted nationwide notoriety (and an obscenity trial for Harris), while the poems themselves gained international admiration, including poets like John Ashbery.

With its self-conscious mocking of European inheritances, the incident signalled Australian bravura and independence. Toby Davidson argues that a growing need to distinguish national character after World War I and into World War II resulted in many poets turning to the lives of explorers or outlaws. Examples included Slessor's "Five Visions of Captain Cook" (1931), Douglas Stewart's verse plays *Fire in the Snow* (1941) and *Ned Kelly* (1942), Rosemary Dobson's *The Ship of Ice* (1948), Francis Webb's *A Drum for Ben Boyd* (1948) and *Leichhardt in Theatre* (1952), Rex Ingamells' *The Great South Land* (1951), and James McAuley's *Captain Quiros* (1964). Viewing such mythmaking as part of a larger cultural turn that included Patrick White's historical epics and the art of Sidney Nolan and Albert Tucker, Michael Griffith discerns that such works often reveal more about contemporary concerns than the past. It could also result in quite different angles being taken, Griffith citing Webb's interest in "stained and vulnerable" figures as an example (447–48).

In attempting to identify what was distinctive in Australian culture, the Jindyworobaks focused on the local, often in terms of place. The movement's name came from an Aboriginal word that Rex Ingamells translated as being "to annex, or to join" (4). *Conditional Culture* (1938), a manifesto penned by Ingamells with Ian Tilbrook, asserted that Australian poetry needed to free itself from "whatever alien influences trammel it" and that Aboriginal culture was key to authenticity. Ingamells' brother, John Ingamells, embraced a more inclusive approach in that "Australian literature must take *all* cultures into account – Chinese as well as English and American as well as Aboriginal or Pacific – yet still have marked individuality with regard to local themes" (7). Writers associated with the Jindyworobak movement (which was prolific in its fifteen anthologies, single-author collections, little magazines, and club) viewed their poetic practice through the lens of *joining* rather than cultural appropriation, and often still relied on Western lyric conventions. While Rex Ingamells viewed the Jindyworobak movement as an alternative to "pre-war nationalism" and "jingoism" (2), Ellen Smith argues that Victor Kennedy's subsequent manifesto, *Flaunted Banners* (1941), also positions the Jindyworobak movement as an alternative to the "destructive" energies of the European avant-garde (11). Subsequently condemned for how they used Aboriginal language and culture as source material, the Jindyworobaks were ridiculed by contemporaries like A. D. Hope, who likened them to the "Boy Scout School of Poetry ... playing at being primitive" (248).

Toby Davidson locates the emergence of a "golden generation" of Australian poetry as beginning when Douglas Stewart took over the editorship of the *Bulletin*'s Red Page in 1940 before assuming the reins of Angus & Robertson (along with Beatrice Davis) and turning it into a major post-war publisher of poetry. Stewart also served on the Commonwealth Literary Fund, which provided governmental funding for writers. While the Fellowship of Australian Writers began in 1928, World War II and the post-war era saw a rapid institutionalisation of the poetry field. A wave of new journals, such as *Southerly, Australian Poetry, Meanjin, Overland, Quadrant,* and *Australian Book Review*, provided forums for poetry and its critical reception. These were supplemented by new critical journals like *Australian Literary Studies*, and critical volumes, the latter spearheaded by H. M. Green's *Modern Australian Poetry* (1946) but also including Vincent Buckley's *Essays in Poetry, Mainly Australian* (1957), Judith Wright's *Preoccupations in Australian Poetry* (1965), and James McAuley's *A Map of Australian Verse* (1975).

The golden generation emerged out of a friendship circle that, like many literary coteries, was circumscribed by male homosociality. Women writers continued to impress themselves into the literary culture yet were, as Susan

Introduction

Sheridan has discerned, more isolated. This *Companion* includes chapters that concentrate on the work of four authors in depth. Two of them focus on Gwen Harwood and Judith Wright. Born five years apart, their careers demonstrate the limited trajectories then available to white women writers, one marking out marginality and the other exceptionalism. As a primary carer of four young children in the 1950s, Gwen Harwood did not publish her first collection until 1963. In her chapter, Ann-Marie Priest suggests that a series of rejections had made Harwood suspicious of the gendered judgement by editors and this was confirmed when she experienced more success using the names of Walter Lehmann and Francis Geyer. Published under the name of Lehmann, her poem, "In the Park" (1961), powerfully addresses the subsumption of self to maternal caregiving with its final line: "They have eaten me alive" (65). And it would be as Lehmann, in the same year, that she sent two acrostic poems to the *Bulletin* that spelled out "so long Bulletin" and "fuck all editors." Priest analyses how Harwood used personae as a means of play and to explore different perspectives around desire and creativity, sometimes controversially. Although diminished as a 'lady poet' or dismissed as a housewife in her younger years, Harwood later became a feted fixture of the literary circuit.

In contrast to Harwood's delayed recognition, Wright was a central figure of mid-century Australian poetry from the start and one of the first to have a select edition published by Angus & Robertson. As Nicholas Birns observes in his chapter, she engaged with "themes of landscape, frontier, and pioneering, themes that are more often associated with male poets," while also writing poems about intimacy and interiority. Her first collection, *The Moving Image* (1946), featured poems like "South of My Days" and "Bullocky," which reinforced the Georgic nexus between labour and land, while other poems like "Bora Ring" explored more ancient connections, albeit problematically, in its suggestion that "the song is gone." Birns points out that in the 1960s, Wright "moved beyond a rhetorical acknowledgement of Aboriginal presence in the land to a genuine engagement with Indigenous resilience and sovereignty." This included her friendship with poet Oodgeroo Noonuccal, which led in large part to addressing her own genealogy of settler colonialism and white privilege. Wright would also turn towards environmental advocacy, feeling a disjunct between the solitary act of writing and an activist urge to move beyond art and collaborate with others.

The third single-author chapter of this *Companion* focuses on Les Murray. Born in 1938, he shared the conservative outlook and some of the strategies of earlier mid-century poets. Describing himself as "the last of the Jindyworobaks," he sought to combine "all three main Australian cultures, Aboriginal, rural and urban" in poems during the 1970s. The best-known of these is "The Buladelah-Taree Holiday Cycle" (1977), which improvises from R. M. Berndt's translation of the Wonguri-Mandjikai Song Cycle of the Moon Bone in depicting white Australians on vacation. The poem's reception has shifted from praise to condemnation over its appropriative poetics. David McCooey points out that Murray's public interventions in Australian literary culture and broader politics also made him a controversial subject 'at home' in comparison to his highly esteemed international reputation. Although well educated, Murray cast himself as an outsider through his experience of childhood bullying, a rural rather than metropolitan outlook, anti-modernist stance, and neurodiversity. Yet, McCooey argues that Murray's poetry works more through an insider/outsider dialectic in relation to the land, the pastoral-Georgic becoming a space of emotional and material struggle, and, by extension, a stage for the pursuit of spiritual and national value. McCooey also considers Murray's comic flourishes and the startling defamiliarisation that occurs in his most virtuosic lyric. In his chapter, Philip Mead adds another insider/outsider framework in the consideration of Murray in Australia, relating how Prime Minister John Howard's invitation to collaborate with Murray on a Preamble to the Constitution only led to Murray's dismay as his "ageless language" or "wholespeak" became dismantled during the drafting process, and the Preamble was then soundly defeated by the 1999 Referendum.

The era of the Menzies government (1949–66) was marked by social conservatism and became a period where many mid-century poets consolidated their cultural capital. James McAuley, Vincent Buckley, and A. D. Hope all became professors of English, although Leigh Dale points out that there remained a belief that the discipline should focus on books of quality, which still meant books which had "made England great" (165). Having emigrated to England in 1951, Peter Porter became a significant part of its literary establishment as poetry editor of the *Times Literary Supplement*. As Louis Klee suggests in his chapter, who was recognised as an "expatriate poet" was still construed around an England–Australia nexus, later highlighted in Les Murray's argument of an Athenian and Boeotian divide of city and country. Toby Davidson reminds us that upon Queen Elizabeth II's visit to Australia in 1963, Prime Minister Robert Menzies quoted English poet Thomas Ford's "There is a Lady Sweet and Kind": "I did but see her passing by, / And yet I love her till I die." Such heteropatriarchal sentiment is aligned with the 'lavender scare' that occurred among federal government at the time and the introduction of anti-gay policies. In her chapter, Orchid Tierney cites the view of police superintendent Colin Delaney that homosexuality was "the greatest social threat" then facing Australia.

Introduction

Different voices needed to find alternative pathways. Oodgeroo Noonuccal, then known as Kath Walker, found support from the Brisbane Realist Writers Group, with both James Devanny and Mary Gilmore encouraging her before Judith Wright. Oodgeroo's *We Are Going* (1964) was the first poetry collection by an Aborigine. The title's focus on action was echoed in her second collection, *The Dawn Is at Hand* (1967). Oodgeroo's poetry found a wide audience. She also became an important figure in the Aboriginal rights movement and connected it with Black rights movements around the world. Occurring in the same year as the publication of *The Dawn Is At Hand*, the 1967 Referendum resulted in 90.77 per cent of the population voting that Aboriginal and Torres Strait Islander people be constitutionally recognised. It was one of a series of progressive steps in Australian culture. While Australia had pledged assistance (1962), then troops (1965) towards the Vietnam War, growing concern about the war culminated in moratorium marches in 1970 and 1971, followed by the gradual withdrawal of troops. Gig Ryan notes that when it came into power in 1972, Gough Whitlam's Labour Government would go on to legislate equal pay legislation, the single mother's pension, the lowering of the voting age to eighteen, and free university education.

In his chapter, Corey Wakeling discerns that the years between 1968 and 1975 saw a shift in both voices and candour. He points out that the generation of poets emerging in the 1970s and 1980s wrote through the emergence of sexual liberation, the women's movement, alternative lifestyles, and drug culture. Technological change meant little magazines could be easily produced by anyone, decentring the print culture from a few powerful publishers and encouraging counterculture expression. Wakeling argues that Australian poets were also preferring the "cultural reference, percept, register, and form exemplified in American contemporaries" over a deadening English tradition. Seeking to align the small press scene with the emergence of the New Left, John Tranter retrospectively applied the umbrella term of "generation of '68" in *The New Australian Poetry* (1979). Wakeling posits that, despite her absence from the anthology, Kate Jennings best embodied this nexus in her political agitation and encapsulation of grassroots community in *Mother, I'm Rooted* (1975). While the anthology stands out in creating popular and industry respect for women's poetry, Wakeling points out that many of the established poets – like Wright and Oodgeroo, but also Dorothy Hewett and David Malouf – often encouraged wider change in cultural attitudes than those publishing in small presses.

While the 1960s saw migration from South Africa during tensions around Apartheid, the end of the Vietnam War saw an influx of Vietnamese migrants from 1976 onwards. Mass migration from Southern Europe from the end of World War II to 1970 had transformed Melbourne into being the largest Greek city outside of Greece while there was also a strong Italian, Polish, and Croatian demographic. There would also be a wave of migration from Latin America and the Middle East in the 1970s, although there had been an earlier wave of migration from the latter region during the Gold Rush. Wenche Ommundsen points out that the Whitlam Government sought to support cultural diversity in Australian through the introduction of multicultural policy (74), resulting in a wide range of literary activities. This included clubs, such as the Spanish Club in Sydney and the Uruguayan Club in Melbourne. Journals emerged like *La Crónica* and *Versión*, and then later again, *Kalimat*. Anthologies, often beginning with the general umbrella term of 'multicultural writing' in the 1980s, branched out to particular ethnic or cultural groups, such as Gaetano Rando's *Italo-Australian Poetry in the 1980s* (1986), Alan Jacobs' *Enough Already: An Anthology of Australian Jewish Writing* (1999), and Huang Ngoc-Tuan's *Cau Noi: The Bridge* (2004). Yet a multicultural framework tended to distinguish writers from both the mainstream and 'Australian literature' as it was beginning to develop in the academy. Lebanese-Australian poet Wadih Sa'adeh would publish *Laysa Lil Massa' Ikhwah (Evening Has No Brothers)* in 1981 after circulating it in handwritten form during the 1970s. Greek-Australian poet ΠO (PiO) would self-publish *24 Hours* (1996), a 740-page epic which revelled in working-class, inner-suburban detail and vernacular. For Ania Walwicz who was born in Poland, Australia was both insular and misogynous. Philip Mead notes that her use of non-standard Australian English in "Australia" (1981) foregrounds the "role of grammar in the poetics of nation" while enacting difference with proud disdain. This is reinforced by her use of prose poetry that resists the lyric line and often proceeds through associative slippage.

Ouyang Yu, born in the People's Republic of China, similarly expresses anger and dislike for a country that reminds him of his otherness in poems like "Fuck You Australia." Yet in declaring, "I don't like china either" in "Fragments of an Evening Walk in Kingsbury," Ouyang articulates estrangement from any 'home' country. The lack of capitalisation refuses the propriety and containment of grammar in a strategy similar to Walwicz. Ouyang writes in Chinese as well as in English, exploring movement between both languages and cultures, and liminal moments where they meld. In his chapter, Kim Cheng Boey identifies a bifocal poetics in writers like Ouyang, Malaysian-born Ee Tian Hong, and Philippines-born Merlinda Bobis, and argues that it can manifest as an ambivalence towards place that can be either challenging or empowering. Suggesting that writers not be packed within a single formation like Asian Australian poetry, no matter how complex and evolving, Boey concludes that diasporic writers from Asia have resonances with other diasporic writers. Michael Jacklin's research into Hispanic-Australian writers, for instance, suggests some parallels in the careers of Ouyang Yu and poets like Victor Ramos, who published prolifically, wrote in both Spanish and English, edited a bilingual collection, and put together anthologies from the Spanish Club of Sydney over many years. Louis Klee also reminds us of the multilingualism of Australian poets who have engaged with the language of another, often adopted, country.

The final chapter to engage with a single author is Dashiell Moore on Yoogum and Mununjali writer Lionel Fogarty. Despite his centrality to the Aboriginal rights movement and the innovative techniques in which he explores interconnectedness, Fogarty has yet to receive extended attention in Australian literary surveys. This may be due, in part, to his publications occurring beyond dominant print culture but also because his reception in the twentieth century was not in the university but rather communities or other institutions like prisons, both in Australia and North America. Moore notes the significance of Philip Mead's chapter on Fogarty's resistant poetics in *Networked Language* (2008) being published in the same year as Prime Minister Kevin Rudd's apology for the removal of Aboriginal children from their families. As Moore points out, Fogarty's education at Cherbourg Aboriginal Reserve reinforced colonial English and delimited ancestral knowledge. Moore argues that a 1986 article by Mudrooroo, then Colin Johnson, centralised Fogarty's work within a tradition of Aboriginal self-determination that included Oodgeroo, Jack Davis, and Kevin Gilbert. Describing Fogarty as a "guerrilla poet," Mudrooroo argued that while Fogarty uses "the language of the invader," his experimentation with it generated a "new language free of restrictions" (49). In 1988, Gilbert published *Inside Black Australia: An Anthology of Aboriginal Poetry*, simultaneously a protest against the Bicentennial celebrations and a vehicle of Black solidarity. It is important to consider Fogarty's poetry as writing back to Oodgeroo and Gilbert as much as he distinguishes his approach from them. While Louis Klee suggests that Fogarty's writing also "interpolates the non-indigenous reader into the position of outsider" (930), Moore suggests that Fogarty decolonises through a negative lyric where the poetic 'I' "revisits, comments upon, and emerges out of a matrix of negative space."

While the Bicentennial protests energised Aboriginal poetry, the Mabo decision of 1992 recognising native title, further countered nationalist narratives of settlement. In 2000, Kerry Reed-Gilbert published *The Strength of Us as Women: Black Women Speak*. In their chapter of this *Companion*, Narungga poet Natalie Harkin and Wiradjuri poet Jeanine Leane foreground the importance of this anthology in enacting a poetics of relationality and Aboriginal women's solidarity. Rather than replicate the essay form that dominates Western scholarship, they undertake a conversation. Leane advocates a rhizomatic approach of docu-memory in resisting the violence of the colonial archive and foregrounds the body as archive. Harkin situates this alongside Chadwick Allen's concept of blood memory and proposes an embodied process of archival-poetics, giving the example of her own transformation of hand-written letters by women in her family (previously 'held' in the state archive) into a Ngarrindjeri basket. Another example, I would add, is Elfie Shiosaki's physical retracing of letters from the archive in *Homecoming* (2021). Her poem "Venus" redresses the elision of Aboriginal figures in modern urban life, retelling her grandmother's story of enjoying dances, live jazz, and silent films with white friends in the 1920s (33–34). Asserting that poetry is a sovereign act, Leane and Harkin foreground the significance of writing communities, particularly of Blak women and non-binary poets, in de-centring whiteness. Harkin cites Michi Saagiig Nishnaabeg poet-scholar Leanne Betasamosake Simpson's advocacy of strategic alliances with others who resist a heteropatriarchal colonialism.

John Kinsella's yarning and exchange of poetry with Charmaine Papertalk Green, a member of the Wajarri, Badimaya, and Nhanagardi Wilunyi people of the Yamaji Nation, in *False Claims of Colonial Thieves*, might be viewed as an example of strategic alliance. In his chapter, Kinsella discusses how a poem that seeks to be ecopoetic is limited in and of itself, and needs to be part of networked activities to effect material change. His chapter presents activism *in media res*, with poetry only one part of a collective effort aimed at preventing the construction of a mountain bike trail through Walwalinj, or Mount Bakewell, a mountain that is sacred to the Ballardong Noongar people. As he demonstrates, such collective resistance is led by the traditional owners and involves the poet alongside other actors, the non-literary as much as the literary.

Orchid Tierney's chapter considers how periodicals of the LGBT community provided forums for the intersection between aesthetics and activism. While homosexuality was slowly being decriminalised across Australia after 1975, individual poetry collections – such as those by David Malouf, Dorothy Porter, and Pam Brown – were being published and presses like BlackWattle, and its associated journal *cargo*, would also provide important forums for a gay and lesbian community. Some anthologies like *The Exploding Frangipani: Lesbian Writing from Australia and New Zealand* insisted on a separate lesbian community, emphasising and making visible female same-sex desire and subjectivity. Tierney points out that many of the anthologies of the 1990s and 2000s were mixed-genre publications, although *Out of the Box: Contemporary Australian Gay and Lesbian Poets* (2009) would focus solely on poetry while heralding a queer rejection of expected performances of identity. Tierney further discusses the strategic alliance between CALD (culturally and linguistically diverse) and First Nation LGBTQ+ poets in challenging white privilege and a heteropatriarchal colonialism. Lastly, she considers the emergence of embodied poetics in challenging the heteronormative body.

The final section of the *Companion* examines the diverse forms of Australian poetry. This includes the development and proliferation of the verse novel, which was particularly significant in Australia. Beginning with Dennis's *The Songs of a Sentimental Bloke* (1909–15), Cassandra Atherton and Paul Hetherington trace its momentum from the 1970s with the early work of Alan Wearne and Les Murray's *The Boys Who Stole the Funeral* (1979) and through the 1980s and 1990s. They consider how Dorothy Porter brought a broad audience to the subgenre with her exploration of female agency and sexuality, and cross-over with popular forms like crime fiction in *The Monkey's Mask*. Hetherington and Atherton point out that the flexibility of the form enables a wide diversity of themes in the twenty-first century, whether on missing persons in Anthony Lawrence's *The Welfare of My Enemy* (2011), the depiction of nineteenth-century colonisation in Ali Cobby Eckermann's *Ruby Moonlight* (2011), domestic violence in Ivy Alverez's *Disturbance* (2013), or disempowered youth culture in Omar Musa's *Here Come the Dogs* (2014). Moreover, the form has become hugely popular in the Young Adult market.

While Andy Jackson has argued that the verse biography has not received the same kind of attention as the verse novel, Hetherington and Atherton suggest that early exemplars like Webb's *A Drum for Ben Boyd* (1948) and McAuley's *Captain Quiros* (1964) were usually framed as long narrative poems. They argue that verse biography enables an extension of life writing that might enable collective biographies, creative encounters with the archive, and creative re-imaginings. Hetherington and Atherton also point to the proliferation of prose poetry in Australia, citing as Chris Wallace-Crabbe's prose suite, "Going to Cythera" (1971) and Rudi Krausman's *From Another Shore* (1975) as two early examples. They outline the enormous field that it has become, resulting in growing anthologisation such as the more recent *An Anthology of Australian Prose Poetry* and *The Indigo Book of Australian Prose Poems*, as well as the emergence of the additional, related subgenre of microliterature.

In their chapter, A. J. Carruthers discusses the significance of sound in Australian poetry, from Aboriginal songspirals to the performance ensembles of Amanda Stewart, Dada performances of Jas H. Duke, and "body talk" of New York-based Chris Mann. As Carruthers points out, any consideration of sound necessarily involves questions of reception and practices of listening. Carruthers also outlines the renaissance of visual experimentation in the 1970s, via the work of Alex Selenitsch and Duke's *Destiny Wood* (1978), before moving to the later experimentations such as Michael Farrell's comic strip poem *Break Me Ouch* (2006) Chris Edwards' collage techniques in *after Naptime: a poem profusely illustrated* (2014), the mixed media of Bella Li, Catherine Vidler's sonnets, and the cricket scorebook form of Nick Whittock's *hows its* (2014). Carruthers also draws attention to those who do not sit within the genealogies generally recognised within poetry, such as Vietnamese-Australian visualist Lê Văn Tăi, Chinese-Australian letter-and-character painter Zhao Baokang, and the Indigenous language art of Vernon Ah Kee. Lastly, Carruthers discusses the electronic poetries of writers like Mez Breeze, Hazel Smith, and Benjamin Laird, arguing that while they may overlap with conceptual poetry in their shared aim to experiment, electronic poetries do not want to undo the platform upon which they operate as conceptual poetry does.

Bronwyn Lea has declared: "The richness, strength, and vitality of Australian poetry is marked by a prodigious diversity that makes it as exhilarating to survey as it is challenging to encapsulate." Louis Klee also makes a point in his chapter that might seem obvious but can often be sidelined in collections pivoting around a concept of national literature: "Australians can be found just about everywhere, and the same goes for Australian poets." This can make it even harder to encapsulate in a single volume. Klee finds that many settler poets share a "bond of shame," citing Carlo Ginzburg's phrase, towards Australia in its continuing colonialism. The ties may not be positive; moreover, other ties may make for a shifting complexity. At the beginning of this introduction to the *Companion* I suggested that it might provide a sense of accompanying, or being alongside, the reader. While we often think of this in terms of proximity or closeness, I also want to recognise modalities of distance, whether cultural, geographic, spiritual, or affective. Anthony Giddens has pointed to the "intensification of worldwide social relations which link distant localities in such a way that local happenings are shaped by event occurring many miles away" (181). This volume demonstrates how poetry has been navigating what increasingly seem like overwhelming cultural, economic, and environmental forces. Yet, as the volume also demonstrates, poetry has the capacity to find form for movements that pull against such forces. I hope this *Companion* will encourage practices of reading that engage with poetry's cultural, aesthetic, and historic contexts, that may then lead to a greater understanding of poetry as a key (but not singular) mode of engagement and possibility.

Introduction

Works Cited

Bloom, Harold. "Introduction." *Peripheral Light: Selected and New Poems*, edited by John Kinsella. Fremantle Arts Centre Press, 2003, pp. xiii–xxviii.

Chiasson, Dan. "Fire Down Below: The Poetry of Les Murray." *The New Yorker*, 4 June 2007. www.newyorker.com/magazine/2007/06/11/fire-down-below.

Clemens, Justin. "*First Fruits* of a Barron Field." *Critical Quarterly* vol.61 no.1, 2019, pp. 18–36.

Dale, Leigh. "Australian Literature in the University." *The Routledge Companion to Australian Literature*, edited by Jessica Gildersleeve. Routledge, 2020, pp. 163–70.

Davie, Donald. "Boeotian Masters." *London Review of Books* vol.14 no.21, 5 November 1992. www.lrb.co.uk/the-paper/v14/n21/donald-davie/boeotian-masters.

Duggan, Laurie. "In Dialogue with Laurie Duggan," with David McCooey. *Double Dialogues* no.5, 2003. https://doubledialogues.com/article/in-dialogue-with-laurie-duggan/.

Giddens, Anthony. "The Consequence of Modernity." *Colonial Discourse and Postcolonial Theory: A Reader*, edited by Patrick William and Laurie Chrisman. Longman, 1994, pp. 181–89.

Griffith, Michael. "Francis Webb's Challenge to Mid-Century Mythmaking: The Case of Ludwig Leichardt in Australian Literature." *Australian Literary Studies* vol.10 no.4, 1982, pp. 448–58.

Harford, Lesbia. *Collected Poems: Lesbia Harford*, edited by Oliver Dennis. UWA Publishing, 2014.

Harwood, Gwen. *Poems*. Angus & Robertson, 1963.

Hope, A. D. "Culture Corroboree." *The Jindyworobaks*, edited by Brian Elliott. University of Queensland Press, 1979, pp. 248–52.

Ingamells, Rex with Ian Tilbrook. *Conditional Culture*. Preece, 1938.

Jacklin, Michael. "'Desde Australia para todo elm undo hispano': Australia's Spanish-Language Magazines and Latin American/Australian Writing." *Antipodes* vol.24 no.2, 2010, pp. 177–86.

Klee, Louis. "Reading Lionel Fogarty." *Textual Practice* vol.36 no.6, 2022, pp. 928–52.

Lea, Bronwyn. "Australian Poetry Now." *Poetry* vol.208 no.2, 2016, www.poetryfoundation.org/poetrymagazine/articles/89028/australian-poetry-now#:~:text=The%20richness%2C%20strength%2C%20and%20vitality,it%20is%20challenging%20to%20encapsulate.

Malouf, David. "States of Poetry." *Australian Book Review*. www.australianbookreview.com.au/poetry/states-of-poetry#:~:text=One%20measure%20of%20the%20positive,than%20the%20novel%20or%20any.

Martin, A. W. "Henry Parkes: Man and Politician." *Melbourne Studies in Education* vol.4 no.1, 1960, pp. 3–24.

Mead, Philip. *Networked Language: Culture and History in Australian Poetry*. Australian Scholarly Publishing, 2008.

Modjeska, Drusilla. *Exiles at Home: Australian Women Writers 1925–1945*. Sirius Books, 1981.

Moreton-Robinson, Aileen. *Talkin' Up to the White Woman: Indigenous Women and Feminism*. University of Queensland Press, 2000, reprinted 2020.
Mudrooroo. "Guerilla Poetry: Lionel Fogarty's Response to Language Genocide." *Westerly* vol.31 no.3, 1986, pp. 47–55.
Ommundsen, Wenche. "Multicultural Writing in Australia." *A Companion to Australian Literature since 1900*, edited by Nicholas Birns and Rebecca McNeer. Camden House, 2007, pp. 73–86.
Paisley, Fiona. *The Lone Protestor: A.M. Fernando in Australia and Europe*. Aboriginal Studies Press, 2012.
Palmer, Nettie. *Modern Australian Literature (1900–1923)*. Lothian, 1924.
Ryan, Gig. "*Fuori le mura*: Seven Vicki Viidikas Poems." *Cordite Poetry Review*, 1 May 2015. http://cordite.org.au/essays/seven-vicki-viidikas-poems/ .
Sheridan, Susan. *Nine Lives: Postwar Women Writers Making Their Mark*. University of Queensland Press, 2011.
Shiosaki, Elfie. *Homecoming*. Magabala Books, 2021.
Smith, Ellen. "Local Moderns: The Jindyworobak Movement and Australian Modernism." *Australian Literary Studies* vol.27 no.1, 2012, pp. 1–17. www.australianliterarystudies.com.au/articles/local-moderns-the-jindyworobak-movement-and-australian-modernism.
Vickery, Ann and Kate Fagan. "'The whole reflected world shuddering': Active Aesthetics and Contemporary Poetry." *Active Aesthetics: Contemporary Australian Poetry*, edited by Daniel Benjamin and Claire Marie Stancek. Tuumba Press, 2016, pp. 17–28.
Zhong, Huang and Wenche Ommundsen. "Toward a Multilingual National Literature: The *Tung Wah Times* and the Origins of Chinese Australian Writing." *JASAL* vol.15 no.3, 2015, pp. 1–11.

NOTES

1 Kenneth Slessor would ridicule Cross's sonnets in "Poetic License." *The Bulletin*, 24 July 2019, p. 24.

PART I

Change and Renewal

I

PHILIP MEAD

Models of Poet and Nation

The relations of poets and poetry to nations and national contexts is an ever-changing calculus of biography, history, geography, and language. Perhaps most significantly for poetic discourse, and for poets who live intensely within their language (or languages), there is no typical or stable alignment of language and nation. And for all their political, demographic, and territorial realities, nations are at the same time variable narrative and imaginary entities. C. P. Cavafy wrote in Greek, about Greek history, but never lived in Greece; Sorley MacLean lived in remote regions of the United Kingdom and wrote in English, Gaelic, and Scots; Louise Bennett wrote in Jamaican patois and creole as a Caribbean "nation language" (Brathwaite 259). Poets, sometimes celebrated ones, have also played a role in the fabrication of nations, deploying their writing in either patriotic endorsement of the state (Walt Whitman, Adam Mickiewicz) or in counterfeit stories of nation and national origins (Virgil, Petrarch, James Macpherson). Sadly, poets have also been the victims of state violence and abuse, for being poets (Mandelstam, Lorca, Neruda, Akhmatova). Nations are an order of human society that is often violently maintained, racially exploitative, and ecocidal. But if Ernest Renan is right, a nation can also be a people's "soul, a spiritual principle" (19). These deep dichotomies of nationhood and subjectivity are often felt most tensely in the lives of poets and the language of poetry, although an obvious consequence of this poetics is that the relation between poet and nation is never an innocent or simple one.

Australia is a present-day nation which happens to have a long literary prehistory. Mythographic literature played a constitutive role in the imagining of Australia long before it was constituted as a nation. Early narratives of The Great Southland, Terra Australis Incognita, Australia del Espíritu Santo, and a New Britannia all have an afterlife in the culture of continental Australia that Matthew Flinders defined cartographically in his *Voyage to Terra Australis* of 1814.[1] Much later, the 'Voyager' tradition of mid-twentieth-century Australian poetry looked back beyond white settlement and colonial origins to the putatively heroic age of pre-national (and imperialist) maritime narratives (Stewart). Another such exemplar was Major Thomas Mitchell, Surveyor General of New South Wales in the 1830s, who embodied a link between the earlier European poetry of discovery and colonial exploration. Mitchell published his journals of *Three Expeditions into the Interior of Eastern Australia: with descriptions of the recently explored region of Australia Felix, and of the present colony of New South Wales* in 1838 and his translation of the epic of da Gama's discovery of a sea route to India, the *Lusiad of Luis de Camoens*, in 1854, although he had written his translation much earlier. These poetic conjunctions of geographical enigma and imperial discovery circulated in a pre-federated Australia, only incipiently tethered to the genealogy of nations, and would be appropriated later, in various ways, for national and nationalist mythography.

In modern Australia the differentials of poet and nation are both distinctive and fundamentally divided, between the settler institutions of literature and poetry, and the Indigenous traditions, whatever their complex interactions. This calculus is part of the discursive genetics of the nation and its inter-nation history and prehistory in multiple ways, including its influence on shaping poets and poetry. In what is referred to as Australia, the history of more than 60,000 years of Indigenous cultural life, including the narrative universe of song cycles, or orature, predates both colonial settlement (or invasion) and, later, nationhood. The continent of Australia has been constituted as a 'nation' for only about 0.2 per cent of the period of its human habitation. And that constitution was initially deliberately exclusive, designed for British Australians only. Modern Australian settler literature, including poetry, was complicit in the politics of settlement, in its anxious pursuit of its own legitimacy and Anglo traditions. In recent decades it has become variously anxious about its role in the repression of, or ignorance about, this history. Its dawning awareness (and remembrance) of contested belonging is now reflected in various critiques of the historical and territorial nation as the horizon or limit of analysis and understanding, as the basis of an unquestioned sovereignty, and of the evils of nationalism.

While whole worlds of Indigenous orature, archives of knowledge, and language have been lost through the dispossessive violence of more than 200 years of settlement, there are also ongoing, valuable survivals throughout the colonising and contemporary eras. But these traditions belong to a different cultural universe, one where the relations between language, performance, knowledge, and song express the ancestral and spiritual life of people and country. For Aboriginal people living within their own languages and in their own country, the geopolitical entity Australia and its institutions, including sometimes the literary ones, are a mere overlay on country, and all that that means, or a colonising intrusion. Increasingly, though, there are also Indigenous writers who, in decolonising, dis-alienating projects, are exploring the forms and expressive potential of their versions of English and its literary heritage to represent their understanding of contemporary Indigenous realities. From this perspective the 'nation' is both a narrow, contested reality of short historical duration and an object of activist and imaginative remaking. For white Australia it is a mythic and political collective with an unsettled origin and an unreconciled present; for Aboriginal Australia it is an alien, domineering framework that ignores the history of the Aborigines' own unceded sovereignty.

There are many poets whose lives and work are emblematic of these histories and dichotomies of nation. Christopher Brennan, Francis Webb, Les Murray, Judith Wright, Peter Porter, Oodgeroo Noonuccal, and Lionel Fogarty are just a few Australian poets whose very different life courses and writings illustrate the vicissitudes and shades of national allegiance and oppositionality. Australia's role in World War I turned Christopher Brennan, a poet of the symbolist 'Absolute,' into a propagandist ("Chant of Doom" 1916); in Francis Webb we read the conjunction of the poetry of heroic Australian exploration and the space of an English psychiatric institution; Les Murray, a celebrator of poor, white rural lives, was engaged to write a preamble to the Australian constitution; Judith Wright's rewriting of her pioneering inheritance over decades ran parallel to realisations about settler history catalysed in the Mabo decision; Peter Porter chose expatriation and its themes but has been repatriated by critical readings of his life and work; Oodgeroo pioneered the poetry of Indigenous protest; Lionel Fogarty's political activism is embodied in a poetics of linguistic subversion.

A curious role for poets in the iconography of the nation is evident in a context of social exchange – one not usually subject to literary analysis – Australia's currency. There have been three poets depicted on Australian banknotes: Henry Lawson, Banjo Paterson, and Dame Mary Gilmore, four if we include Sir Henry Parkes. Parkes was on the old $5 note as the 'Father of Federation,' but he did publish a book of poems, *Stolen Moments: A Short Series of Poems* (1842) and was a lifelong friend of Charles Harpur. The figures on the banknotes have been iconic representatives of different fields of Australian life: inventors, scientists, architects, Antarctic explorers, social workers, pioneer businesswomen, military men, pastoralists, Indigenous leaders, and writers. But it is only poets who achieved such a high representation. There are no painters, for example, on any of the banknotes, and no prime ministers, and only one musician, Dame Nellie Melba. A design including Lawson's handwritten verse appears on the first issue of the $10 note, Paterson with lines from his high-country horse-opera "The

Man from Snowy River" and Gilmore with her anti-Japanese World War II poem "No Foe Shall Gather Our Harvest" on later issues of the $10 note. The design, production, and issuance of banknotes are elements of the financial system controlled entirely by the Reserve Bank of Australia, and the high profile of poets and poetry in this Australian capitalist semiotics is apparent when we look comparatively at the semiotics of other financial systems: the euro has no historical figures, only bridges, arches, and doorways; the US dollar bills have portraits of presidents; the UK banknotes have the reigning monarch on every note, and an iconic figure from British history on the reverse (Churchill, Nelson, Adam Smith, Alan Turing) – the only literary figure is Jane Austen on the reverse of the £10 note. This high profile of poets on the Australian currency is perhaps surprising, given the low valency of literary figures, like poets, in Australian culture generally, and the absence of any literary scholars on the Reserve Bank's Design Advisory Panel.[2] But the semiotic level of this monetary system of exchange seems to express a desire for poets to be equivalent to, if not more emblematic than, other (literally) notable figures from Australian history.

The biographies of poets signify much about the influences of nation and state on their writing. Sometimes such influences are a matter of life and death. The history of PEN, for example, since 1921, is the record of the international struggle against state repression of writers and of free speech. PEN's charter recognises that the problem is not just political, but specifically national: "PEN stands for the principle of unhampered transmission of thought within each nation and between all nations."[3] This perspective is especially fraught where the legitimacy of a nation itself, or sovereignty, is contested. Such questions are raised in the Australian context in the story of Les Murray's preamble to the constitution and in Evelyn Araluen's poem "Index Australis." As this chapter aims to illustrate, with reference to just a small number of poems across Australia's white history, it is in individual poems where the historically specific tensions of writerly lives, poetic expression, and the nation are most strikingly and concretely evident.

For colonial and early Federation poets, Australia was only imaginable as a nation in terms of the Global North and always in the context of colonisation that they found themselves in the midst of. For Charles Harpur (1813–68), for example, the futurity of Australia is a "national dream." "To the Lyre of Australia," a poem he wrote as a teenager, but published later in 1846, begins with an acknowledgement of Indigenous traditions, however generalised, as the precursors to a literate, patriotic poetry:

> Lyre of my country, remains it for me,
> From the charm-mutt'ring savages' rude-beating hand

Models of Poet and Nation

> To snatch thee; that so thy wild numbers may be
> No longer but writ on the winds of the land!
> And though he who thy chords would now master, may never
> Evince in his verse all thy rapture of tone,
> Yet – yet should Australia smile on the endeavour –
> The glory so won by the Bard were her own.   (722)

The verb "snatch" here has an uncomfortable suggestion of violence and dispossession, although at the same time Harpur recognises the "rapture of tone" of the Indigenous poets – "savages" nevertheless – that he may "never evince" in his own verse. Harpur's model here is the patriotic poet like Robert Burns, whom he mentions, and with whom he hopes to vie in "patriot fire." He is thinking of poems by Robert Burns like "The Patriot Bard." For colonial poets like him, their songs may be "unstudied" but are nevertheless "high" "[w]hen the glory of Future Australia's the theme" (723). This poem has a bitter footnote, though, about the ungratefulness of the poet's country towards his poetic efforts: "neither then nor since did my Country *deign* to award one smile of encouragement to the endeavours of her Poet. Her best and only gifts to him have been hunger and rags ... C.H." (723).

Burns' poetry of an independent Scotland was nationalist at every level, while Harpur's dream of a future Australia was a republican one, with an English provenance. As he wrote in a "Note to a Republican Lyric (From a Colonial Newspaper)" in 1855, "I am not only a democratic Republican in theory, but by every feeling of my nature" (Ackland 18). His motto, "Right Onward," was taken from Milton, "the great republican poet of England" (Ackland 19). This allegiance to a radical strand within English polity not only put him at odds with the monarchical imperialism of the mid-nineteenth-century colonial government he lived under, it also reflected a contradiction in the possibilities for independence, as he understood them, for colonial subjects. For instance, in a note to his poem of 1847, "The Tree of Liberty (As Song for the Future)," another expression of Harpur's "republican spirit," he argues that "it will be best for Australia to continue during the present century (at the very least) as part of the British monarchy" (Ackland 22). His reasoning is that

> even the state-botches of Downing Street are full fifty years in advance of our present half-educated wool-kings, and such forms of Government therefore, as they may from time to time fabricate for us, though upon the most threadbare models, will be altogether preferable to any things of the kind which the latter would or could tinker up in the event of a premature separation.   (Ackland 22–23)

This dissatisfaction with the present explains Harpur's emphasis on the future, and on the birth of a new generation of leaders and a "new birth of

Liberty" (Ackland 23). It is also an expression of the helplessness of the colonial republican poet.

For Henry Lawson, in his first published poem, "A Song of the Republic" (1887) the "ominous atmosphere" of the lead-up to Federation shares Harpur's sense of the colonial oppressor and the convict past:

> Sons of the South, awake! arise!
>   Sons of the South, and do.
> Banish from under your bonny skies
> Those old world errors and wrongs and lies.
> Making a hell in a Paradise
>   That belongs to your sons and you.   (5)

The sons of the South have the choice, in their fashioning of a nation, between "The Land of Morn and the Land of E'en / The Old Dead Tree and the young Tree Green." The time of the growing army of the sons of the South is near and Lawson's call is for them to "free" the coming republic from the "wrongs of the North and Past" (5). The exclusively gendered, military rhetoric of this poem is obvious, a young man's masculinist rallying cry as much as a "Song." But the driver of its idealism is demographic, the fact of the growing native-born population, a fact that Harpur could only dream about.

For Bernard O'Dowd (1866–1953), who published his poem "Australia" in the *Bulletin* on the eve of Federation (May 1900) the perspective is not so much sociopolitical as geographical, if not cosmographical. The first line of his poem describes the continent as a "sea-thing":

> Last sea-thing dredged by sailor Time from Space,
> Are you a drift Sargasso, where the West
> In halcyon calm rebuilds her fatal nest?
> Or Delos of a coming Sun-God's race?
> Are you for Light, and trimmed, with oil in place,
> Or but a Will o' Wisp on marshy quest?
> A new demesne for Mammon to infest?
> Or lurks millennial Eden 'neath your face?   (2)

This strange, poetic "Australia" stands in stark contrast to Edmund Barton's contemporaneous celebration of Australia as a new geopolitical unity – a continent for a nation, for the first time – and to Federation projects like *The Picturesque Atlas of Australasia* (1886–88) with its maps of wishfully connected infrastructure like railway and telegraph lines.[4] Both Barton's speech of 1897 and the *Atlas* are "isomorphic" (141) in Robert Dixon's description, expressing the wished-for alignment of literature, geography, and nation, or "landscape as the inscape of national identity" in Homi Bhabha's equivalent formulation (143). But O'Dowd's sonnet is more intuitive about the mirage of Australian nationhood. Through a series of five questions addressed to "you," about what exactly this belated, amorphous "sea-thing" is, or will be: "a drift Sargasso, where the West / In halcyon calm rebuilds her fatal nest?," he questions the island site of a coming race of gods (perhaps like Delos in the South Aegean, a demesne of Mammon, or a "millennial Eden"?). The poet is in more than one mind about both the nature and temporality of the nation, and his imagining is an illogical equation of mythic and symbolic traces:

> The cenotaphs of species dead elsewhere
> That in your limits leap and swim and fly,
> Or trail uncanny harp-strings from your trees,
> Mix omens with the auguries that dare
> To plant the Cross upon your forehead sky,
> A virgin helpmate Ocean at your knees. (2)

These "cenotaphs of species dead elsewhere" somehow have an antipodal life, as they "leap and swim and fly" within the limits of the pronominal "Australia." What the poet sees are only the "omens" and "auguries" these dead images of polity produce, one of which is the Southern Cross "upon your forehead sky" and another, a "virgin helpmate Ocean at your knees." These are only the bodily fragments of a continent and nation – forehead and knees – it is the stars and ocean that dominate the scene. Between the sky and the sea "Australia" appears as only a monstrous mess.

These complex, even confused dichotomies of national imagining persist into the immediate post-Federation decades of the twentieth century in the poetry of Dorothea Mackellar and A. D. Hope. Their poems "My Country" and "Australia" are two of the best-known poems of national sentiment, one a declaration of love for an anti-England and the other an acerbic critique of *Australia Felix*. These two poems are worth considering together, partly for historical reasons but also for their stark contrasts. Mackellar began writing "My Country" as a teenager on a tour of Europe with her wealthy parents, and the poem was first published in London in *The Spectator* in 1908 (as "Core of My Heart"). It begins with an address to an anonymous English person, a *Spectator* reader, who has

> The love of field and coppice
> Of green and shaded lanes,
> Of ordered woods and gardens
> ... running in your veins. (4)

Mackellar's speaker "knows" this English person's "love of grey-blue distance, / Brown streams and soft, dim skies" but she cannot share it, her "love is otherwise." Her prejudice against the English countryside is epitomised by the autologically Anglo word "coppice," a thicket of trees managed by annual cutting, in contrast to the "stark white ring-barked forests" of Australia at the beginning of the third stanza. After the first stanza the description of Australia – never named in the poem – is in terms of topography, extreme climate, weather, native flora: "sweeping plains," "ragged mountain ranges," "droughts and flooding rains," and "green tangle of the brushes." It is a landscape of "beauty and terror" in antipodal contrast to the "ordered woods and gardens" of the English countryside. The blue sky is "pitiless," the paddocks are "thirsty," the country is "wilful," if "lavish." This series of aerial shots reveal no human inhabitants nor any social conurbations of "my country," core of the poet's heart, only the deserted evidence of land clearing and pastoral settlement, the ring-barked forests, the paddocks, and the dying cattle. The sentimentality of Mackellar's poem lies in the figuring of the country as female: "her far horizons"; "her jewel-sea"; "she pays us back threefold" (4). As a nationally popular poem this quaint gendering of the unnamed Australia tends to annul the metaphorics of a pitiless, terror- and heartsick-inducing, and thirsty land.

A. D. Hope's "Australia" is a poem of 1939, and was written after Hope's return to Australia in 1931 after postgraduate study at Oxford. Unlike Mackellar's "My Country" the poem announces its national consciousness in both its title and its first line: "A nation of trees, drab green and desolate grey."[5] Hope's aerial shots also establish the antipodal topography of Australia, but the poet's perception of the southern land is coloured by the intuition of imminent European war, the Australian landscape appears "in the field uniform of modern wars." The effect is deeply contradictory – the northern landscape is not the "soft, dim skies" and coppices of Mackellar's poem – and foreshadows the rest of the poem's problematic reversals. At the beginning, Hope's Australian topography is not something he loves, it has no native attraction for him as it does for Mackellar. It has rather the appearance of an archaeological landscape of the Middle East: the hills like "endless outstretched paws / of sphinx demolished or stone lion worn away" (54). This landscape will reappear at the end of the poem, in biblical terms. Meanwhile Hope's poem also plays with the figuring of Australia as female, but not unselfconsciously as in Mackellar. Hope's objection is to the idea of Australia as a "young" country, a nation little more than three decades old when he is writing. His rhetorical move here mobilises the contradiction of the political and the geographical, but relying on the figuration of femaleness in a way designed to shock:

> They call her a young country, but they lie:
> She is the last of lands, the emptiest
> A woman beyond her change of life, a breast
> Still tender but within the womb is dry. (54)

Such post-menopausal metaphorics contradict the idea of Australia as reproductive, capable of bearing and nurturing new life, a disconcerting refiguring of national being. This country is past bearing any Sons of the South. The middle three stanzas of the poem are the most devastating in their negativity: Australia (she) "has no gods, no songs, no history," her actual rivers "drown among inland sands," but the "river of her stupidity" "floods her monotonous tribes from Cairns to Perth." Her inhabitants are not individuals but "ultimate types" whose boast is not "we live" but "we survive." Landscape has now receded, replaced by the "five teeming sores" of her cities, the built developments of "a vast robber state / Where second-hand Europeans pullulate / Timidly on the edge of alien shores" (54). (Hobart seems to have escaped this dire scenario.) White Australia is a population of timid, unoriginal types; for Hope there is no evidence of the independence and individuality of the native born. At this point there is a volta, signalled by the "Yet" at the beginning of the sixth stanza. For all its deficits and ugliness, the poet actually owns Australia as "home" and turns to it "gladly" "from the lush [northern] jungle of modern thought" (54). The startling dichotomy of the last two stanzas reflects that at the beginning of Mackellar's poem, although in human as well as landscape terms, where the "green hills" of "over there" are now the home of "cultured apes" and so-called civilisation. The syntax of these stanzas isn't straightforward though. They are all one sentence:

> Yet there are some like me turn gladly home
> From the lush jungle of modern thought, to find
> The Arabian desert of the human mind;
> Hoping – if still from deserts the prophets come –
>
> Such savage and scarlet as no green hills dare
> Springs in this waste, some spirit which escapes
> The learned doubt, the chatter of cultured apes
> Which is called civilization over there.

The syntactical complexity is a symptom of the unease at the heart of this nexus of nation and poetics. Having cleared the Australian desert of all myth and human presence, not recognising any kind of Indigenous civilisation, Hope has to transport the northern metaphorics of the Arabian desert and a biblical reference to prophets to convey his meaning. He hopes some "savage and scarlet" will spring from this wasteland, some prophetic spirit that will evade the mediocrity and the subhuman weakness of Anglo-European civilisation. But the "savage and scarlet" are deracinated signifiers, ambivalently nouns and adjectives: they will spring in the wasteland of Australia, which makes them sound like substantives, but what are they? They are descriptive, with nothing to modify. And the further grammatical ambiguity, if not confusion, is that the northern landscape would not "dare" them. The word "savage" in this context, a hot-button word in this poem, also has the inevitable suggestion that there is some residual link to Indigenous Australia – particularly the central desert – that Hope has otherwise so thoroughly elided in his vision of Australia as an archaeological site. Savagery in the Australian wasteland, if it springs up, will be strikingly coloured and spiritual, if not Indigenous, in contrast with the degenerate culture of Europe. Hope's imagining of nation here includes the dangerous counters of European evolutionary theory. The dichotomy of civilisation and savagery has a long and contentious history in Western thought, including the history of slavery and the science of racism. In the long conclusion to the poem – perplexing in syntax, sharp in imagery – Hope's planet-of-the-apes reversal is meant to privilege the southern savage, but it is not logically worked out, or organically imagined. He is presenting a structure of feeling: a sequence of striking images packed with latent political forces, some of them treacherous. Hope has strong feelings about the Australia he envisions but he is not exactly sure what it is, or will be.

Ania Walwicz's prose poem "Australia" (1981) is a kind of reprise of Hope's poem from the formally innovative and multicultural perspective. It is worth considering alongside Hope's poem for the way in which it also continues the foregrounding of grammar in the poetics of nation. The opening of Walwicz's poem is a more intensive critique of Australia than even Hope's: "You big ugly." And the litany of accusations is relentless: "You too empty. You desert with your nothing nothing nothing." Not even the illusion of archaeological ruins. And as with Hope and Mackellar there is the antipodal dichotomy, this time derogating the Australian side of the relation: "I came from crowded and many. I came from rich. You have nothing to offer. You're poor and spread thin. You big. So what. I'm small." The core scene of the poem seems to be the cruel rejection in the schoolyard: "Cold day at school playing around at lunchtime. Running around for nothing. You never accept me. For your own. You always ask me where I'm from. You always ask me. You tell me I look strange. Different. You don't adopt me. You laugh at the way I speak" (18). Whatever the linguistic culture of the playground, the poem displays its non-Standard Australian English way of speaking as an analogy for ethnic difference. Walwicz's ethnolect also stresses the speaker's experience of misogyny: "You don't like me and you don't like women. You put your arm around men in bars. You're rough. I can't speak to you. You burly burly" (18). The poem is in fact a subtle alternation of perfectly correct standard English sentences ("You don't have any interest in another country") and 'broken' English whose diction imbues the whole poem with its effects. The insistent repetition of the accusatory "you" has an othering countereffect to the othering that the speaker is suffering in her experience of a new country. Australia is not plural and diverse; via the obsessively repeated pronoun "you" it is reduced to a singular entity. Walwicz's speaker is unequivocal about what she thinks about 'Australia' and her equally forceful counter-othering goes to highlight the othering that her speaker has experienced.

The issue of Australia's becoming a republic was a matter of public interest and political manoeuvring in the early 1990s. As part of the Constitutional Convention in 1998 and 1999 it was the issue of a preamble to the Australian Constitution that emerged as a major focus of debate. No doubt the reason for this, as the historian Mark McKenna wrote, was that preambles

> by their very nature, articulate and give legitimacy to profound political change. They provide purpose and rationale, elucidate intention, and potentially serve as the declaration of belief for a political community. They are often the first words of 'the people,' their *raison d'etre* and their *cri de Coeur* (3).

And in the understanding of such high social ideals people reach for the genre of poetry as the appropriate expressive form:

> Unlike the flawed and grimy world of day-to-day partisan politics, many delegates hoped that a new preamble would be a means of lifting politics above cynicism and corruption. It should be something to revere – a tablet of stone to cherish. At times, it seemed as if the Convention was witnessing a profound change in the republic debate – a shift from pragmatism to poetry. (7)

As if the prime minister at the time, John Howard, understood such impulses he engaged Les Murray to co-write a new preamble with him.[6] The Howard–Murray draft preamble was an attempt at a prose poem of Australian national definition:

> With hope in God, the Commonwealth of Australia is constituted by the equal sovereignty of all its citizens.
>
> The Australian nation is woven together of people from many ancestries and arrivals.
>
> Our vast island continent has helped to shape the destiny of our Commonwealth and the spirit of its people.

> Since time immemorial our land has been inhabited by Aborigines and Tones Strait Islanders, who are honoured for their ancient and continuing cultures.
>
> In every generation immigrants have brought great enrichment to our nation's life.
>
> Australians are free to be proud of their country and heritage, free to realise themselves as individuals, and free to pursue their hopes and ideals.
>
> We value excellence as well as fairness, independence as dearly as mateship.
>
> Australia's democratic and federal system of government exists under law to preserve and protect all Australians in equal dignity which may never he infringed by prejudice or fashion or ideology nor invoked against achievement.
>
> In this spirit we, the Australian people, commit ourselves to this Constitution. (McKenna 12)

This was to be inserted into the Constitution proper and was intended to have no legal effect. At a press conference on 23 March [1999], John Howard described it as being collaborated on by "a great wordsmith ... and one or two other people" and would articulate, in an "ageless language," "a sense of who we are, a sense of what we believe in, and a sense of what we aspire to achieve in the future" (quoted in McKenna, Simpson, and Williams). McKenna, Amelia Simpson, and George Williams note that "Howard also announced that the Coalition Joint Party Room had endorsed a proposal to submit the draft to the people at the same time as the republic referendum." This draft preamble met with a hostile reception, from the opposition parties at the time, and from Indigenous groups. Women's groups, also, objected to the exclusively male term "mateship": "Judith Wright, observed, 'we are all men from Snowy River it seems. I hope women stamp on this'" (McKenna, Simpson, and Williams). The Tasmanian premier, Jim Bacon, objected to the reference to Australia as a "vast island continent," with its seeming omission of the island state. The preamble went through various further stages of redrafting, dictated by the political situation at the time, which included the Australian Democrats holding the balance of power in the Senate. The result of the referendum question on the preamble in November 1999 was a resounding NO vote in every State and Territory. The NO vote, nationally, was 60.7 per cent.

Les Murray was annoyed that his contribution to the original version of the preamble "was slowly taken apart and turned into mush in a process of political compromise" (McKenna, Simpson, and Williams). Nevertheless, David McCooey sees evidence of Murray's 'bardic' persona at work in the preamble, particularly in the last two clauses, which, while written in prose clearly illustrate[s] the trace of a 'poetic' language in its role as public speech. This was no doubt appropriate for a document that was wholly symbolic, with no legal instrumentality or standing. The use of anaphora and parallelism, and the serious tone, all suggest a rhetoric that is 'epideictic,' the ornate and figurative oratory of praise. (6)

The bardic mode, or "wholespeak" as Murray has referred to it (519), is designed to overpower the narrower modes of speech – like the law, politics, criticism – and represent a fuller human response. But in this instance the saturation boost of poetry seemed to have no power over the political realities of the language of national identity.

As it turns out, this set of literary and political conjunctions was far less influential, in terms of implications for national identity, than a single High Court instance of what Murray would have called "narrowspeak." This catalytic moment of collective self-understanding, and therefore in the dimensions of individual writers' understandings, is the degree zero of the High Court of Australia's 1992 judgment, commonly referred to as the Mabo decision. That case was about Indigenous land rights on a small island in the Torres Strait, but the judgment and its language went to the heart of the history of settlement and the foundations of the nation. The Mabo decision challenged the existing Australian legal and land tenure system from two perspectives: it overturned the assumption that the continent was *terra nullius* (no-one's land) at the time of European arrival and that Aboriginal and Torres Strait Islander people had no historical and cultural claim to their ancestral lands. The Uluru "Statement from the Heart" of 2017 – a recent claim by Aboriginal people themselves for constitutional recognition – extends the Mabo decision with its use of the word sovereign or sovereignty five times.[7] The Mabo case and its legal consequences (the Land Rights Tribunal, successful native title claims, etc.) brought to the fore and into the light of the everyday the social, historical, and political realities of what settlement meant – that the country was stolen, that it was founded on the violent and ongoing extirpation of the First Nation Australian people. While the decision didn't mention sovereignty it nevertheless brought the question of sovereignty, of political and national legitimacy, in other words, and the meaning of Indigeneity to the surface.

The ramifying effects of this shift in national understanding pervade every level of discourse about nation in Australia, especially literary discourse. In contemporary Indigenous poetics there is a recognition of the project of decolonisation that the Mabo decision helped to identify. Lionel Fogarty, Ellen Van Neerven, Alison Whittaker, Lorna Munro, Natalie Harkin, and Evelyn Araluen write in highly distinctive ways – sometimes in experimental lyric mode, sometimes within archival poetics, sometimes in hybrid language – about settler coloniality

> working in the long shadows of activists and organisers who have spent generations alerting us to injustice and oppression, who have written their refusal to be silenced and have fought for every inch of paper they're published on, trusting for no reason beyond necessity that their words will reach those most needing their imagining. (Araluen, "Story Is the Voice of History").

Where Les Murray and John Howard laboured on a prose poem of national definition, Evelyn Araluen's writing discerns the sectional, backward-looking and repressive assumptions underlying every sentence of that effort. Araluen is a descendant of the Bundjalong Nation and was born and raised in Dharug Country. In the note to her poem "Index Australis" from her collection *Dropbear* (2021) Araluen writes that the poem is in the form of "a dialogue and response to Soda Jerk's 2018 film *Terror Nullius*, and also features references to the songs of Nick Cave and the Bad Seeds, with some references to Nick Cave songs" (99). Soda Jerk's film, like Araluen's poetry, is a sequence of samples from multiple iconic films and songs of the media age – from *Skippy* to *Wake in Fright* to *The Piano*, to the *Mad Max* films, *Lantana*, and many more[8] – and the satirical mode is signalled by the first word of Araluen's poem: "Straya," the transcription of the broad Australian pronunciation of Australia. It also occurs within the frame of a book called *Dropbear*, the words for a hoax horror bush creature that could easily have appeared in *Terra Nullius*. That single word, "Straya" conveys the 'unwriting' or satirical rejection of national mythologies constituted by photographs of bodies at the beach or film narratives like *Priscilla, Queen of the Desert*, "Straya in sepia 35 mm with sweat rolling across a tan / With that thin shirt sticking to skin / Straya trailing tin foil through the red dirt / On its way to the pool party in the inland sea" (12).

The unwriting of popular myths of Australia is evident in the savage pillorying of these filmic representations and their disrespect for, or misunderstanding of, Aboriginal 'country' with the conjunction of samples of xenophobic political discourse, like John Howard's "We will decide" speech:[9]

> And well may we say, we will decide
> Who and how
> Well may we be not lectured and well
> May we do it slowly (12)

But Araluen is always alert to the complexity of these genres of political opposition, including her own poem. She is aware of how she is "both colonised by and [an] inheritor[s] of" these myths of nation ("Snugglepot and Cuddlepie"):

> But darl, this is a drama not a document
> Straya is a man's country
> And you're here to die lovely against the rock
> To fold linenly into horizon
> And sweat beautiful blonde on the beach   (13)

The feminist critique here, of both the film *Terror Nullius* and the poem "Index Australis" is around *Picnic at Hanging Rock* and its depiction of young womanhood and the spectacle of its mysterious, erotic death in the bush. The final lines are particularly savage, with their reminder of the human grief hidden behind these representations and their aestheticisation of death, in this case drowning: "Baby, don't you know this is a weeping song / And you'd be so beautiful in that brown creek" (13). The index of this poem, then, what it points to, are signs of contemporary Australian filmic representations and their complex, but popular constructions of myths of nation. Where earlier poets had centuries of the mythography of Australia, or the great Southland – the idea of Australia in the northern imagination – to draw on, Indigenous poets like Evelyn Araluen have a contemporary archive of narratives of nation that, in her case, are the subject of decolonising reading and creative response. The theoretical language of decolonisation provides a language to "express our movement against the settler-colonial interior" (Araluen, "Resisting the Institution").

These few samples of Australian poems from the colonial era to the present are distinctive instances of that complex calculus of the relations of poets, poetry, and nation. They are also very different in their formal aspects, but analogous in their recognition of the constitutive language of poetry. The story of poets, poetry, and nation is often not a happy one, too often tragic. In the case of Australia it is a story of unease, irresolution, and oppositionality. But it is also the story of how the poetic resources of language allow these writers to create memorable, resonant, and critical responses to a determinant of social and political life that is both resistant to change and capable of change.

Works Cited

Ackland, Michael. *That Shining Band: A Study of Australian Colonial Verse Tradition*. University of Queensland Press, 1994.

Araluen, Evelyn. "Resisting the Institution." *Overland* no.227, 2017. https://overland.org.au/previous-issues/issue-227/feature-evelyn-araluen/.

"Snugglepot and Cuddlepie in the Ghost Gum." *Sydney Review of Books*, 11 February 2019. https://sydneyreviewofbooks.com/essay/snugglepot-and-cuddlepie-in-the-ghost-gum-evelyn-araluen/.

Dropbear. University of Queensland Press, 2021.

"Story Is the Voice of History." 2 May 2021. https://womensagenda.com.au/life/evelyn-araluen-speech-sydney-writers-festival/.

Bhabha, Homi K. *The Location of Culture*. Routledge, 1994.

Brathwaite, Edward Kamau. *Roots*. University of Michigan Press, 1993.

Brennan, Christopher. "A Chant of Doom." *The Lone Hand* vol.19 no.112, 1 August 1916, pp. 145–46.

Dixon, Robert. "'A Nation for a Continent': Australian Literature and the Cartographic Imaginary of the Federation Era." *Antipodes* vol. 28 no.1, June 2014, pp. 141–54.

Harpur, Charles. *The Poetical Works of Charles Harpur*, edited by Elizabeth Perkins. Angus & Robertson, 1984.

Hope, A. D. "Australia." *Selected Poetry and Prose*. Halstead Press, 2000, p. 54.

Lambert, Helen. "A Draft Preamble: Les Murray and the Politics of Poetry." *Journal of Australian Studies* vol.27 no.80, 2003, pp. 5–14.

Lawson, Henry. "A Song of the Republic." *The Bulletin* vol.8 no.400, 1887, p. 5.

Mackellar, Dorothea. "Core of My Heart." *The Spectator*, 5 September 1908. Reprinted as "My Country," *Daily Telegraph* (Launceston, Tasmania), 9 January 1909, p. 4.

McCooey, David. "Poetry and Public Speech: Three Traces." *Journal of the Association for the Study of Australian Literature* no.9, 2009. https://openjournals.library.sydney.edu.au/index.php/JASAL/article/view/9757.

McKenna, Mark. *First Words: A Brief History of Public Debate on a New Preamble to the Australian Constitution 1991–99*. Research Paper 16 1999–2000. Politics and Public Administration Group, 4 April 2000. https://parlinfo.aph.gov.au/parlInfo/search/display/display.w3p;query=Id%3A%22library%2Fprspub%2FFV716%22.

McKenna, Mark, Amelia Simpson, and George Williams. "With Hope in God, the Prime Minister and the Poet: Lessons from the 1999 Referendum on the Preamble." *UNSW Law Journal* vol.29, 2001. http://classic.austlii.edu.au/au/journals/UNSWLawJl/2001/29.html.

Mitchell, Thomas Livingstone. *Three Expeditions into the Interior of Eastern Australia: with descriptions of the recently explored region of Australia Felix, and of the present colony of New South Wales*. T. & W. Boone, 1838.

Lusiad of Luis de Camoens: closely translated. T. & W. Boone, 1854.

Murray, Les. "Poemes and the Mystery of Embodiment." *Meanjin* vol.47 no.3, Spring 1988, pp. 519–33.

O'Dowd, Bernard. "Australia." *The Bulletin* vol.21 no.1056, 1900, p. 2.

Parkes, Henry. *Stolen Moments: A Short Series of Poems*. James Tegg, 1842.

Renan, Ernest. "What Is a Nation?" Translated and annotated by Martin Thom. *Nation and Narration*, edited by Homi K. Bhabha. Routledge, 1990, pp. 8–21.

Stewart, Douglas, ed. *Voyager Poems*. Jacaranda, 1960.

Walwicz, Ania. "Australia." *Made in Australia: An Anthology of Writing*, edited by Jim Kable, Oxford University Press, 1990, p. 18.

NOTES

1. The subtitle to Flinders' *Voyage to Terra Australis* was *Undertaken for the Purpose of Completing the Discovery of that Vast Country, and Prosecuted in the Years 1801, 1802, and 1803, in His Majesty's Ship the Investigator.*
2. See https://banknotes.rba.gov.au/production-and-distribution/design/design-advisory-panel/.
3. See https://pen-international.org/who-we-are/the-pen-charter.
4. See Robert Dixon.
5. The handwritten copy of this poem in Hope's papers at the National Library of Australia (MS55836) is dated at the end 1939.
6. Lambert observes:

    Murray was previously involved in writing for government in 1992, when he was asked to draft an updated Oath of Allegiance for migrants seeking Australian citizenship. This oath was never adopted in Murray's original draft form, due in part to the then Labor government's reaction to the implications of the last words: "And I expect Australia to be loyal to me."

7. See http://www.referendumcouncil.org.au/sites/default/files/201705/Uluru_StatementFrom_The_Heart_0.PDF.
8. The final credits to the film list the samples used in its making.
9. The reference is to John Howard's 28 October 2001 election speech: "But we will decide who comes to this country and the circumstances in which they come." https://electionspeeches.moadoph.gov.au/speeches/2001-john-howard.

2

DAN DISNEY

War, Crisis, and Identity in Australian Poetry

Little wonder soldiers fighting abroad loom so large, albeit problematically, in the discourse of Australian identity; at the end of the twentieth century, this country had sent its soldiers to be "involved in more major conflicts for more years than any other industrial nation" (Kent, "From the Sudan to Saigon" 155). The numbers quickly reveal the components (not to mention the calculi) of a mythography: newly elected to office in September 1914, Australian Prime Minister Andrew Fisher made good on his pre-election promise to "stand beside the mother country to help and defend her to our last man and our last shilling" (Curtis) and, in a recently federated nation numbering fewer than 5,000,000 citizens (Indigenous peoples deemed unworthy to be counted as "Australians" until 1967), 330,000 served in the Australian Imperial Force (AIF). The Australian War Memorial officially records the deaths of 61,604 personnel during World War I; when repatriated, a further 113,000 were deemed "unfit" (Tibbitts). A generation later, conservative Prime Minister Robert Menzies announced that "in consequence of the persistence of Germany in her invasion of Poland, Great Britain has declared war upon her ... as a result, Australia is also at war" ("Prime Minister Robert G. Menzies: Wartime Broadcast"). By 1939, the Australian population had swelled to 7,000,000; of these, "nearly 500,000 were engaged in munitions, or building roads or airfields, and over 1,000,000 joined the armed services" (Higgins), and these figures comprise both enlistees in a second iteration of the AIF alongside conscripted personnel participating in the 'Citizen Military Forces.' The Australian War Memorial records 39,655 deaths; when demobilised at the end of World War II, it goes without saying that a multitude of surviving armed services personnel returned in varying states of disfigurement and damage.

Though the number of Australian soldiers killed in the so-called 'Korean' and 'Vietnam' wars is significantly lower (340 and 521 respectively), and lower still in the North American-led invasions of the Middle East at the start of the twenty-first century, these figures in no way mitigate a resounding fact: very soon after federation, a newly fledged 'Australia' followed the British Empire into a series of ideological, global conflicts. By the middle of World War II, allegiances were switched from Britain to North America and, thereafter, there followed further national involvements in ideologically inflected wars. The result? For generations, old soldiers have walked among an Australian citizenry, enduring emblematically in tropes of sovereignty and statehood. Into the twenty-first century, codifications of the soldier-legend remain pervasive, performative, ritualised, and reifying. From the annual calendar in Australia (ANZAC Day, Remembrance Day) to the ubiquity of war memorials, honour boards in public buildings, RSL (Returned and Services League) clubs, and surplus equipment scattered across civic parks (canons, tanks, etc.), in this sovereign state that did not exist before 1901 the solider myth endures, a part of lore presented as if immemorial tradition.

Indeed, in this colonised, whitewashed country, symbols of war remain omnipresent. Some will argue there is an element of paralysis or compulsive repetition to the endless commemorations of our war dead as if, in the absence of other candidates, these figure spectrally as apostolic founders of a federated imaginarium. To a great many Australians, an AIF soldier remains a hagiographical amalgam of heroic traits, nationalised: to some, "tough and inventive, loyal to ... mates beyond the call of duty, a bit undisciplined ... chivalrous, gallant, sardonic" (Mandle, quoted in Kent, "The ANZAC Book" 376). To this, others would add notions of "the 'bushman,' the explorer, the adventurer, independent, egalitarian, a good shot and horseman, full of mateship, initiative, and courage [which] did not take a great deal of re-modelling to be transformed into an ideal soldier and in turn into a representative type of the nation" (Caesar 148). In "National Myths of Manhood: Anzacs and Others," Adrian Caesar evokes a Melbourne newspaper article proclaiming, in 1883, that "our men are splendid material for an army; very much above the average of the line in physique and intelligence" (147). In the same era, the *Bulletin* (operating from Sydney) can be seen as "a rallying point for Australian literary nationalism" (Stephensen); indeed, in his well-known essay from the interwar years, "The Foundations of Culture in Australia" (1936), P. R. Stephensen decries the impact of the *Bulletin* in the late nineteenth century as presenting "a larrikin view of Australian life. It has made the larrikin idea paramount, as in an earlier phase convictism was paramount."

At the onset of World War II, then, settler masculinities emerged from a backdrop of wilful positivism, a proto-Australian consciousness awaiting fulfilment while a standing reserve of subjects awaited service, bodies honed through formulating empire-issued performances towards colonially remodelled connections to land; these same repurposed as ready-made fighters who could, at any moment, be called upon to bolt headlong into theatres of war on behalf of the so-called motherland. In other words, these early constructions of a specifically Australian subjectivity had not arisen inside a vacuum: with an almost Oedipal collective blindness, colonial soldiers performed as if unable to see beyond inherited, ideologically subservient roles in which dénouement would require, from many, no less than the feat of their deaths. Thereafter, these martyrdoms would be rendered heroic, historicised as simultaneously extraordinary and mundane, these earliest AIF soldiers – 'ANZACs' and 'diggers' – finally presented as nonchalant, laconic, still larrikin-esque, and as if anaesthetically indifferent to the experience of fear or suffering.

The pantheon of Australian war poems boasts no "Channel Firing" or "Dulce et Decorum Est," and there exists no historical equivalent to Rupert Brooke's *1914 & Other Poems* (1915) or Siegfried Sassoon's *Counter-Attack, and Other Poems* (1918). Indeed, in "Literary Culture 1914–1939: Battlers All," Jennifer Strauss understands that "the entrenched image of Australia's national identity [is] baptised in the blood shed at Gallipoli and confirmed in the mud of French trenches," but remains surprised "how little of this mythology originated in memorable contemporary works of poetry and fiction" (107). This is not to assert that no literature exists; there is a preponderance of poetry pamphlets and collections manifesting more or less immediately in response to Australian participation in World War I (examples include Robert Nichols' *Invocation: War Poems and Others* (1915); Jessie Pope's *More War Poems* (1915); F. E. Westbrook's *Anzac and After: A Collection of Poems* (1916); L. E. Homfray's *Australians Awake and Other Poems* (1916); A. A. Johnson's *Soldier's Poems* (1918); and C. N. Hutchinson's *A Soldier's Poems* (1919)). But these works from amateur soldier-poets have more or less disappeared from view. If we are to locate an emblematic Ur-poem written by an Australian poet during World War I, then teacher-turned-soldier Leon Gellert's Shakespearean sonnet, "A Night Attack" (1915), demonstrates the formal contours of an attempt at representation:

> Be still. The bleeding night is in suspense
>   Of watchful agony and coloured thought,
> And every beating vein and trembling sense,
>   Long-tired with time, is pitched and overwrought.
> And for the eye, the darkness holds strange forms.
>   Soft movements in the leaves, and wicked glows
> That wait and peer. The whole black landscape swarms
>   With shapes of white and grey that no one knows;
> And for the ear, a sound, a pause, a breath.

> A distant hurried footstep moving fast.
> The hand has touched the slimy face of death.
> The mind is raking at the ragged past.
> ... A sound of rifles rattles from the south,
> and startled orders move from mouth to mouth. (30)

Gellert's adjectivally inflated iambics situate the war as peripherally close to a disembodied, synecdochic collective of whispers shifting in abstracted parts (the eye, the ear, footsteps, the hand, the mind) towards an impending fight. His poem places readers into heightened states of vigilance, and in so doing centralises anxiety as its motif. Duty seems a sole fortitude. Gellert was wounded at Gallipoli, where "A Night Attack" was written, but this poem forecloses on any view of explicit horrors, preferring instead to focalise towards the terror-stricken "beating vein and trembling sense" of impending doom. The second half of this sonnet's end-stopped lines are perhaps especially eerie, the poet setting a walking meter to newer uses, the narrative racing iambically – as soldiers charged, terminally – towards undefined enemy lines in darkness.

Simply put, Gellert's poem is the formal demonstration of a colonially imposed textual structure which, transported halfway around the world, more or less assumes "the guise of a reproduced, lesser version of British culture" (Rudy 4). But the poem is further imbricated with unwittingly colonial modes: suppose this sonnet were reframed, set a century earlier somewhere in the pre-federated British colonies. What then could be made of the "whole black landscape swarm[ing] / With shapes of white and grey"? What of the "coloured thought" and "strange forms"? Lyricising from within a colonially determined imaginarium, here is a poet seemingly accustomed to wrestling with nervous energies, exerting self-control while performing as part of a massed group of invaders awaiting orders (indeed, attempting to ideologically reorder already occupied, populated places). The poem is partisan in ways Gellert cannot have intended and, like any Shakespearean sonnet, it delineates a set of dialectical propositions: Gellert's argument asserts a self-aware and mission-bound obliging loyalty (at any cost) as central to Antipodean narratives. Nineteenth century: across unceded Indigenous domains wrongfully rendered non-historical and unpopulated, therein able to be colonised, we may cue all manner of atrocity against Indigenous others declared, at the point of British possession, to be mere outliers (those whom Agamben would term *Homo Sacer*, extra-sovereign non-subjects able to be "killed by anyone without committing homicide"(103)).

Twentieth century: the ANZACs and so-called diggers became Australia's first and foremost hero-emblems, voyaging abroad in order to be enshrined at home. If culture is *cultura*, a connectedness through tilling and cultivating lands, then what Strauss notices is just how thinly settler-descended citizens are culturally connected to the places of a recently made 'Australia.' In terms of the imperialist pogroms waged internally across pre-federated colonial places in the nineteenth century, there seems a total amnesia in mainstream accounts of a pre-nationalised identity; indeed, it took until 2008 for an Australian government to officially recognise the atrocities of dispossession, and formally apologise.

None will miss the irony of these prototypical soldier descendants of settler stock (those who had performed totalising displacements of Indigenous peoples) being shipped offshore in order to dig elsewhere, and by these means usher the phenomenological states of being-Australian into symbolic order. But a crisis endures across notions of an Australian identity, and this can be framed as a crisis of disingenuous inauthenticity. The ANZAC myth is first responder to the emergency of a national emergence. Our several urban centres, mostly on the eastern seaboard of the continent, have functioned as if pockets consolidating a colonial civilisation that shields settler-colonisers from Indigenous connections to land, holding out against a sublime territorialisation of space apprehended and repurposed, in Gellert's sonnet, as: "Soft movements in the leaves ... wicked glows / That wait and peer." Before the construction of the myth of the ANZAC digger soldier, the normative models of empire – infrastructures, language, rituals, roles, and personae – are imposed as if an inheritance working diametrically to simultaneously establish (one) and erase (other) cultures. The crisis of that inheritance is an ongoing crisis of identity enshrining a primary, central, and specifically Australian anxiety.

When theorising on trauma as a mode of becoming-Australian, Bruce Bennett and Jennifer Strauss enumerate examples: "the settlement, or invasion, of this country marked by the landing of Governor Phillip at Sydney Cove in 1788; the beginning of the First World War in 1914; the Second World War in 1939; and Australia's involvement in the Vietnam War from 1965" (4). Though the list is selective, and arguably places events in a descending order of impactfulness, versions of Australian history (and indeed that which gets to be landmarked constitutionally and made-historical) remain disfigured, our nationalising discourses haunted by ghosts either endlessly revivified (such as the ANZACs) or murderously exorcised, silenced, and made invisible (Indigenous peoples from historically situated cultural groupings). Of course, the term 'crisis' is located back in Hippocrates and Galen, and pinpoints a turn or change in symptoms preceding either recovery or death. The discourse of Australian identity, mediated through a survey of its war poems, indicates a country that remains in a symptomatically liminal state of neurotic non-recovery, in which artificial mythic structures are no more than a panacea, compulsively administered.

Recall that pre-federation, Barron Field chose to drop into his inaugurating collection a poem in which "Australia" is rhymed with "failure." The myth of Australian soldiering began a century later, and convulsed across the twentieth century as if a collective failure of imagination; and as World War II began, as if the next instalment in an episodic and intergenerational global cataclysm, a suite of poetic recapitulations of the Australian soldiering myth soon followed. Pamphlets and collections include Paul Buddee's *Stand To and Other War Poems* (1943); Maurice Clough's *The Fighting "Ninth" and Other Poems* (1943) and *We of the A.I.F. and Other Poems* (1943); Patrick Hore-Ruthven's *The Happy Warrior: Poems* (1943); Samuel Buckby's *They Shall Not Pass: And Other Poems* (1943); Maurice Biggs' *Poems of War and Peace* (1945); Colin Thiele's *Splinters and Shards: Poems* (1945); Pat Galligan's *To Those Who Survive: Poems* (1945); and H. D. Saunders' *Carnations in Tobruk and Other Poems* (1945). Were we to seek a poem performing exemplary myth-keeping labours, then from the first stanza, J. S. Manifold's "The Tomb of Lieut. John Learmonth, A.I.F." delineates a set of re-echoing imperatives:

> This is not sorrow, this is work:
> I build a cairn of words over a silent man,
> My friend John Learmonth whom the Germans killed.
> There was no word of hero in his plan;
> Verse should have been his love and peace his trade,
> But history turned him to a partisan. (197)

Through imagistically constructing a "cairn of words over a silent man," Manifold's text asserts a linguistic boundary within which, he perhaps hopes, will reverberate a worshipful, immanent silence. The respect of readers is anticipated, commanded even, and Manifold's language speaks univocally into a rhetorical space in which "old heroic virtues [can] still appear" (198). Later in the poem, Manifold directly addresses his imagined ideal readers: "Schoolboy[s]," who are to be enchanted by rhetoric presented as Australian tradition which, as Manifold would have it when ratcheting up the diction of his paean, combines "fierceness and resolve" (198). For those readers content to be lectured to, Manifold's didacticism will remain unproblematic, and we may share for his text's titular hero (who has demonstrated "courage chemically pure") similar feelings of "queer affection" (199). Manifold's upkeep of the soldiering mythos reaches an apex when asserting an unadulterated "panache / That sparkles" (199), nationalised, into perpetuity. This poem-as-monument both houses and promulgates a trove of carefully fabricated traits, promoted by Manifold as the coveted myths of Australian subjects needing to be schooled.

If 'crisis' derives from *krinein* (etymologically 'to separate, decide, judge'), then in the discourses of twentieth-century poetry, it is fair to say that simplistic gestures of reiterative myth-maintenance were not the only modes of responsiveness performed by Australian poets. Some poems written during World War II are openly ambivalent. Perhaps the most enduringly famous is Kenneth Slessor's "Beach Burial" (1944). Unlike Manifold's poem, there is no partisanship, rather, a different mythographic language elaborates a growing weariness at war's futilities and death's finalities: "Softly and humbly to the Gulf of Arabs / The convoys of dead sailors come; / At night they sway and wander in the waters far under, / But morning rolls them in the foam" (75). Slessor (whose father, at the outbreak of the previous world war, had changed the family surname from Schloesser; the poet's middle name was Adolph) knew from first-hand experience what he was writing against: acting as official war correspondent, Slessor followed the second AIF's campaigns across the Mediterranean and, later, into New Guinea. "Beach Burial" tracks the scenes of a hopelessly inadequate temporary consecration and, recording the tragedy, the poem acts as if eyewitness, member of a clergy, and judge: "Dead seamen, gone in search of the same landfall, / Whether as enemies they fought, / Or fought with us, or neither; the sand joins them together, / Enlisted on the other front" (13). This Australian poem-as-reportage openly ponders the dehumanisation of soldiers, and dares to speak beyond nationalising discourses. In surveying the ghoulish beaches at El Alamein in 1944, "Beach Burial" unemotionally explores death's encompassing common grounds. Here is a modernist poem that speaks beyond the preconditions of nation, towards a universal humanism.

This is not to say that Australian poets were shifting univocally towards tendentiously modern stylistic experimentations during World War II; indeed two Australian poets, (Corporal) Harold Stewart and (Lieutenant) James McAuley, more or less took care of impulses towards fervent linguistic innovation when, famously spending an afternoon at Melbourne's "Victoria Barracks" in October 1943, they attacked an emergent Australian avant-garde (championed by Max Harris's Adelaide-based journal, *Angry Penguins*) through creating the wholly fictitious "Ern Malley." For the most, it was English formalism that remained a more apt mode of expressing the complexities of elegiac sentiment, as seen in Douglas Stewart's *Sonnets to the Unknown Soldier* (1941). This sequence begins with an exhortation to: "Open the tomb, strip off the flags and the flowers / And let us look at him plainly," as if the components of the soldier myth required recalibration. For Stewart, these are heroes that still arrive reliably and on cue to "do[ ] the fighting," and it is incumbent on readers, these texts seem to imply, that we do the remembering. But while this suite may not explicitly celebrate war,

Stewart's loosely structured sonnets seem astonished and aggrieved at the explosion of a second global conflict: "We had built so much to hold back the onset of night, / ... / But the Flood is upon us, and down in the roaring waters, / Drowning with man, goes his work and the light of the world" (Sonnet 3 n.pag.). Geopolitical complexities are parsed here, the poem instead testifying to each soldier's heroism that is figured as: "The lonely flame of a life against the darkness" (Sonnet 3 n.pag.). Biblical references are central to Stewart's suite, as if in these desperately historical times, simpler figurations are required for readers in a place named by James McAuley (in the poem "Terra Australis") as a "land of similes" (228). In Stewart's jejune sensibility, Germans are demonic, Australians angelic. The partisanship is explicit, and these poems lionise England as a place that has twice "stood firm" against "the Germans ... like rock / Sure of the light in its heart" (Sonnet 5 n.pag.). Stewart then takes those who may not have been following on an openly propagandistic tour: "We who have heard / The animal howl of Hitler exulting in Poland / Invaded, Norway betrayed, Rotterdam bombed" (Sonnet 6 n.pag.). He adds, "The dark of the cave, the sea-floor, the bottomless pit / Where Lucifer fell and the creatures of chaos exult / Is the dark of the soul of Germany, and there its spokesman, / The snake at the roots of being, strikes at the light" (Sonnet 6 n.pag.).

These sonnets seek to wage rhetorical war and, at the time of publication, Stewart's reductive dichotomies may have been rousing. But as certainly as these poems model a chthonic struggle towards purity and illumination, in Bakhtinian terms Stewart's suite is a hermetically sealed mess. While purporting to "break up the monument, / Open the tomb" (Sonnet 1 n.pag.), these poems in fact re-encrypt national identity with an "authoritarian, dogmatic and conservative [language that is] sealing itself off from the influence of extraliterary social dialects" therein; similarly to Manifold's "cairn of words," Stewart's sonnets perform the labour of a "special 'poetic language,' a 'language of the gods,' a 'priestly language of poetry'" (Bakhtin 287) that assert their own monoglossic modes of totalitarianism. This is yet another recapitulation of those anxieties at large in twentieth-century Australian poetry, Stewart's sonnets shifting their Antipodean performers offshore in order to claim space in the "*Terra Nullius*": "When the Australians crashed singing on Tobruk / ... / Many times before the white dawn breaks on the world. / Look in the darkest past and the darkest future, / And a man goes down into hell to bring fire for mankind" (Sonnet 7 n.pag.). Imagine replacing the placeholder "Tobruk" with, say, "Van Diemen's Land." In Stewart's celebration of epically heroic dialectical death-drives, the evolution of a *bone fide* Australian is to be no less than a cosmological event of whiteness rising out of darkness *qua* civilisation settling structurally (indeed racially) into place. While Stewart's reasons for a "white dawn" cannot finally be known, it is impossible to read this sonnet as innocuously or innocently phrased. The text's newly Promethean day can be read less as an Antipodean version of *Sturm und Drang* but instead is arguably as racially odious as any ideological program that would consign the future to massed columns of *Übermensch*.

Of course, Australian poets with little or no experience of actively participating in war have also written at length about warfare, and these transmissions further entrench (and sometimes seek to problematise) the myth of Australian soldiering. A. D. Hope's epigrammatic "Inscriptions for a War" was published in his collection, *Antechinus* (1981); Hope did not enlist to fight in World War II and was too old for conscription during Australian involvement in the Vietnam War. His poem decries how: "We took their orders and are dead" (133), a line echoing the title of a 1971 anthology of Australian poems protesting the country's participation in the Vietnam conflict. Bruce Dawe's much quoted "Homecoming" (1968) also critiques that war. Dawe spent a career in the Air Force, and while opposition to Australian participation in North American-led infractions in Vietnam meant that a "Welcome Home Parade for the troops ... did not take place until October 1987" (Davis 34), Dawe remains an insider whose poem ironises those indiscriminate machineries which, if called upon, he too could operate: "All day, day after day, they're bringing them home ... in green plastic bags" (12). Dawe's anti-war panegyric frames dead soldier bodies as if a waste product; his poem locates a precursor text in Slessor's "Beach Burial." Like Dawe, Geoff Page has spent much of his career investigating the "domestic concerns of ... war and its effects on Australians" (McCooey 170), as witnessed in his collection *Smalltown Memorials* (1975). An abundance of poems written towards the end of the twentieth century reference both first and second iterations of the AIF; indeed, at the centenary of the ANZAC landing in Gallipoli, books such as Jordie Albiston's *Warlines* (which repurposes letters from 'diggers' at the front) and Robyn Rowland's more problematic *This Intimate War: Gallipoli / Çanakkale 1915* seem to do little beyond extend and vaguely re-stamp 'ANZAC' and 'digger' narratives as if brands inviting mythopoesis. Perhaps these books manifest a turn in Australian anxieties, materialising a misplaced sense of mnemophobia while wholly occluding the Frontier Wars that raged across Antipodean British colonies in the nineteenth century. A great many other poets have sought to dismantle the myth of Australian soldiering, from John Forbes' "Anzac Day," to Graham Rowlands' "The Queensland Cop," to Geoff Page's "Kokoda Corrective"; from Dorothy Hewett's excursive "Legend of the Green Country," to Katherine Gallagher's sanguine "The Meaning of War," to Lionel Fogarty's eviscerating and wide-ranging damnations in "Decorative Rasp, Weaved Roots."

But one particular poem stands out, albeit for the wrong reasons; Les Murray's "Visiting Anzac in the Year of Metrification" seems to do little more than re-empower the ANZAC myth with exciting syntax. David McCooey suggests Murray was "[a]mbitiously nationalistic, [attempting] to fuse rural, urban and Aboriginal strands of Australian culture" (172); one wonders how it is possible for a settler descendant to incorporate strands of Indigenous cultures into an aesthetic program without simply performing again (reinforcing, normalising) appropriation as key to keeping dispossessed peoples displaced. When recounting a visit in 1974 to Çanakkale, we understand Murray believes he is on those terrains Manning Clark famously terms a "sacred site" (461). In this poem that seems alert to the possibilities of misused names ("there's no place called *Gallipoli*," he fusses), Murray mentions how: "Our continent is uncrowded space, / a subtler thing than history" (121). The ironies seem to elude him – before the prisoners aboard conflict fleets and British troopers morphed into "squatters' and selectors' boys" (121), there was no place called 'Australia' – and in this poem Murray is simply programming a monoglossic language that would lumber redundancies, reasserting the coordinates of settler logic across offshore grounds. His weird diction makes for a complex aestheticisation:

> Those shelterless hardscrabble cols
> where even the *Heads* get *knocked*, were best
> assaulted in youth: we were handiest,
> the climbing was overt and in vogue
>
> and done with friends, in company.
> Pioneering there, building with planks,
> we showed the *battler* style to Death
> among hoarse screams and rosemary. (122)

Readers are never quite sure if these concluding stanzas depict the poet's visit or play out scenes of ANZAC soldiers arriving to fight, or both. While age may have wearied this poet, the landscape "best / assaulted in youth," Murray's venerations simultaneously locate the origins of the 'Aussie *battler*' as working-class or settler-colonial hero relocated to war zone, while also placing himself in their footsteps, hearing in their echoes a resonance with which the poem attempts harmony. History is made as if present, time's barriers as if collapsed, and the boundaries (physical, linguistic) shudder as if portals channelling sacred immanence. Murray's poem issues from a jingoistic mode of dark tourism, and invites readers to imagine themselves into ecstatic states of empathy: in sum, a concretisation of the Australian soldiering myth as veracious, a means of feeling connected (just so long as readers are descended from settler stock).

Murray's Australianisms are not only wilfully narrow but also proffer a false ontology. Anecdotally, this poet is said to have occasionally joked that he was "the last of the Jindyworobaks" (Elliot 283), that group of predominantly white male poets (including Rex Ingamells, Ian Mudie, and Roland Robinson) whose appropriative program proposed, at best naïvely, to enshrine colonial creative producers as those "Aryan Aborigines" (Tout 141) implied within P. R. Stephensen's "The Foundations of Culture in Australia: An Essay towards National Self-Respect" (1936). The Jindyworobak group was more than an early agglomeration of eco-poets, and indeed constitutes more than simply "a tin-eared manifestation of aggressive nationalism" (Strauss 118). They set out to articulate their difference from English settlers so as to legitimise claims to indigenising place by means of misrepresentation (indigenous stories as if their own), appropriation (indigenous terms brought into English syntactical structures), and annexation (simplistic hybridisations as a mode of cultural connection). Clearly, Murray's joke was a bad one (to say the least). When Ingamells asserts in *Conditional Culture* (1938) that: "Whether convicts or freemen, most of our early settlers were misfits here" (2), his logic for the Jindyworobak program lies in its attempts to fit, be suitable for, or relevant to, or consonant and congruent with lands that were invaded in the late eighteenth century, then forcibly and genocidally possessed. His proposed means of fitting in are nothing short of amnesiac: "'Jindyworobak' is an aboriginal word meaning 'to annex, to join,' and I propose to coin it for a particular use. The Jindyworobaks, I say, are those individuals who are endeavouring to free Australian art from whatever alien influences trammel it, that is, to bring it into proper contact with its material" (4–5).

With their own masquerades, the Jindyworobak group would overwrite possibilities of Indigenous speech acts being heard. Here was an aesthetic program that would not only select and steal Indigenous words and stories, but proposed to do so in order for colonisers to consolidate connections to land through assuming themselves to be ersatz Indigenes. In assuming a position from which to speak, the disingenuousness is breathtaking; this program that reasserts colonial blindness *qua* anxieties of unbelonging is neatly encapsulated in Murray's later assertion that *"we're country, and Western"* ("The Boeotian Strain" 64). This seems nothing less than an unapologetic war cry summarily expressing "a continuing desire in the white Australian imaginary ... for a species of cultural-racial syncretism" (Mead 560), while leaving in place all privileging, epistemological structures of colonial oppression.

Of course, not all commentators and contributors to twentieth-century discourses of Australian poetry were much taken with Ingamells' program: in James McAuley's first collection, *Under Aldebaran* (1946), we find the poem "Jindyworobaksheesh," while A. D. Hope labelled the group as a "Boy Scout School of Poetry" (Elliot 248). Beyond the Jindyworobaks, the 'interwar years' (a term used guardedly in the contexts of Australian history) gave rise to a number of nationally significant journals: *Southerly* (Sydney, 1939–current); *Meanjin Papers* (Brisbane, 1940–current, relocating to Melbourne in 1945 and shortening the name to *Meanjin*); *Angry Penguins* (Adelaide, 1940–46); *Barjai* (Brisbane, 1943–47). As geopolitical relationships developed and international allegiances complexified (shifting increasingly from Britain to North America), the lexicon of an 'Australia' as more than simply a set of amalgamated British colonies, 'Antipodean' as if by default, was to be contested inside these journals. It seems that the interwar years were as important in attempting to shape discourses of Australian identity as those formulated during wartime, but the very notion of 'interwar years' remains contingent on the angles from which one views 'Australia' as a place, assemblage, or set of ideas. What of the impacts of British colonisation in the nineteenth century, "ethnocidal and fatal for Aborigines" (Moses 92)? An unknown number of Indigenous peoples were killed in the Frontier Wars: some historians assert 20,000 people (Barta 237), others assert that the ratio of "black to white deaths could be 44 to one" (Daley). As such, shifting the parameters of the historiography of 'Australia' to include the Frontier Wars, it seems obvious that there is no such thing as either an ante- (or post-) bellum English-language Australian poetry.

Our writers still must wage discursive attacks on the logic of settlement that centralises its own mythic structures so as to assert its own epistemological regimen. In other words, the crisis of Australian identity continues, and may well continue into perpetuity until those Indigenous language-users generationally silenced since occupation in 1788 find their way, in and on their own terms, towards a mythographic discourse that radically displaces and decentralises narratives of Australian soldiering heroism. At the outset of the twenty-first century, in his essay "Contemporary Poetry: Across Party Lines" (2000), David McCooey asks readers to consider "what constitutes an *Australian* poetry" (158), before untangling a multitude of ideological and political visions in order to assert ours as "a worldly poetry, both celebratory of and anxious over the idea of an 'Australian inflection'" (180). Two decades later, McCooey's emphasis must be altered so as to ask, importantly, "what *constitutes* an Australian poetry," and by which means might these constraints be challenged and overwritten?

As the twenty-first century continues, it seems certain that answers will favour a gamut of forces unleashed by critically literate writers thus far overlooked in this chapter, which, in surveying those judderingly constitutional repetitions of the Australian soldiering myth, has engaged exclusively with white male voices. Of course, there is a polyphony of alternative inheritances able to be listened to, and the most enduringly valuable commentaries from the second half of the twentieth century in Australia may prove to comprise of contributions made by Indigenous and/or female poets and commentators. As the ecologically and equity-minded settler-descended Judith Wright found cause to assert in the early 1990s: "Our history isn't reassuring. We have been predators on this count. Few of us ever thought it necessary to learn from our mistakes and care for, maintain and restore raped landscapes; let alone learn from the Aborigines whose country it has been for untold millennia" (117). It beggars belief that the first collection of poetry written by an Indigenous poet was published in Australia as late as 1964, 145 years after the confection that was Barron Field's *First Fruits of Australian Poetry* (1819). Oodgeroo Noonuccal's *We Are Going* sold out within days, and collections by Indigenous poets Kevin Gilbert and Jack Davis soon followed. In her later collection, *My People* (1970), Oodgeroo asks: "Must we native Old Australians / In our land rank as aliens?" (37). Her provocation typifies an ethics that responds to the "conquest of the country by one people and the dispossession, with ruthless destructiveness, of another" (Barta 237), and catalyses a trope that had for too long been absent from conversations around Australian identity. Liminality, estrangement, non-connection, unbelonging: each is thematic to an occupier's positionality, but what of the spaces and experiences of Indigeneity (affective, cultural, linguistic, displaced and dispossessed, silenced)?

Increasingly, it seems that colonised spaces are opening to the presence of Indigenous counter-narratives speaking differently while languaging difference. This is a far cry from, say, the disgruntled ironies voiced in A. D. Hope's "Australia" in the mid-twentieth century: "Without songs, architecture, history: / The emotions and superstitions of younger lands, / Her rivers of water drown among inland sands, / The river of her immense stupidity" (119). On the face of things, Hope's is a mocking self-effacement of the colonial experience; it is also "devastatingly ignorant of anything other than a whitefella, civilizing view of settler-culture" (Harrison 25). One wonders on the affects able to be produced when Hope's evisceration of Australian dumbness is misread, purposefully, so as to take the colonial gaze in this text as surveying colonised others. The indefatigably militant Indigenous poet-activist Lionel Fogarty insists that there remains an inescapable "disease of stupidity in [colonisers'] language," and his guerrilla poetics exemplify a performative mode of using "English against the English" (ix). This is a far cry from the formalistic manifestations of the Australian soldiering myth, and a necessary move beyond the (perhaps well-intentioned) malfeasance of the Jindyworobaks. In a text dedicated to: "*ALL the brothers and sisters who have been fighting since the invasion of the white man, for our FREEDOM and INDEPENDENCE*," Fogarty's poetry unapologetically instructs: "Look pig / what you do to our people" (145–46). Closer examinations remain the work of future poetries.

In section one of "The Foundations of Culture in Australia" (1936), P. R. Stephensen asserts "we are Antipodeans; a gumtree is not a branch of an oak; our Australian culture will evolve distinctively" (n.pag.). In *My People* (1970), Oodgeroo responds: "The gum cannot be trained into an oak" and asserts: "We will go forward and learn. / Not swamped and lost, watered away, but keeping / Our own identity, our pride of race" (21). Just as Oodgeroo uses her text as a site to contest settler epistemologies, in the early twenty-first century we see a growing number of Indigenous voices using English in order to speak a mode of experiential truthfulness to colonial power. Indeed, a range of remarkable poets both emerged and emerging are fomenting a distinctive shift in the contours and coordinates of Australian poetry, including Samuel Wagan-Watson, Jeanine Leane, Alison Whittaker, Billy-Ray Belcourt, Romaine Moreton, Melanie Mununggurr-Williams, Elizabeth Jarrett, Kaitlen Wellington, Charmaine Papertalk Green, Natalie Harkin, Peter Minter, Lionel Fogarty, Evelyn Araulen, Ellen van Neerven, and Ali Cobby Eckermann. Their writing entails the possibility of radical resymbolisations energising notions of linguistic propriety, land management and the distribution of 'resources,' the telling of histories, communitarian/cultural connections, in short a *coming-to-terms* (orthographically, materially, postcolonially, politically, ideologically) to turn debates around Australian identity towards a more clear view of recent and ancient history. Before there can be such a thing as a post-bellum poetry in Australia, poets such as those listed immediately above must be allowed to speak, and must be closely (and widely) read, listened to, and heard.

Works Cited

Agamben, Giorgio. *Homo Sacer: Sovereign Power and Bare Life*, translated by Daniel Heller-Roazen. Stanford University Press, 1998.
Bakhtin, Mikhail M. *The Dialogic Imagination*, edited by Michael Holquist. Texas University Press, 1981.

Barta, Tony. "Relations of Genocide: Land and Lives in the Colonization of Australia." *Genocide and the Modern Age*, edited by Isidor Wallimann and Michael N. Dobkowski. Syracuse University Press, 2000, pp. 237–51.
Bennett, Bruce and Jennifer Strauss. "Making Literary History." *The Oxford Literary History of Australia*, edited by Bruce Bennett and Jennifer Strauss. Oxford University Press, 1998, pp. 1–5.
Caesar, Adrian. "National Myths of Manhood: Anzacs and Others." *The Oxford Literary History of Australia*, edited by Bruce Bennett and Jennifer Strauss. Oxford University Press, 1998, pp. 147–65.
Clark, Manning. *A History of Australia*. Chatto & Windus, 1994.
Curtis, Jonathan. "'To the Last Man' – Australia's Entry to the War in 1914." *Parliament of Australia*, 31 July 2014. www.aph.gov.au/About_Parliament/Parliamentary_Departments/Parliamentary_Library/pubs/rp/rp1415/AustToWar1914.
Daley, Paul. "Why the Number of Indigenous Deaths in the Frontier Wars Matters." *The Guardian*, 15 July 2014. www.theguardian.com/commentisfree/2014/jul/15/why-the-number-of-indigenous-deaths-in-the-frontier-wars-matters.
Davis, Geoffrey V. "'Wars Don't End When the Fighting Is Over': Adib Khan's *Homecoming* and the Australian Literature of the Vietnam War." *The Journal of the European Association for Studies of Australia* vol.8, no.2, 2017, pp. 32–45.
Dawe, Bruce. "Homecoming." *The Age*, 6 July 1968, p. 13.
Elliot, Brian. *The Jindyworobaks*. Queensland University Press, 1979.
Fogarty, Lionel. *Munaldjali, Mutuerjaraera: New and Selected Poems*. Hyland House, 1995.
Gellert, Leon. "A Night Attack." *Songs of a Campaign*. Hassell Press, 2017, p. 30.
Harrison, Martin. *Who Wants to Create Australia? Essays on Poetry and Ideas in Contemporary Australia*. Halstead Press, 2004.
Higgins, Matthew. "Australians at War." Australian Bureau of Statistics. www.abs.gov.au/AUSSTATS/abs@.nsf/featurearticlesbytitle/00753BC276CCB154CA2570FF000075A8?OpenDocument.
Hope, A. D. "Australia." *The Penguin Book of Modern Australian Verse*, edited by John Thompson, Kenneth Slessor, and R. G. Howarth. Penguin Books, 1958, pp. 119–20.
—. "Inscriptions for a War." *Two Centuries of Australian Poetry*, edited by Mark O'Connor. Oxford University Press, 1988, pp. 133–34.
Ingamells, Rex and Ian Tilbrook. *Conditional Culture*. F. W. Preece, 1938.
Kent, D. A. "The ANZAC Book and the ANZAC Legend: C.E.W. Bean as Editor and Image-Maker." *Historical Studies* vol.21 no.84, 1985, pp. 376–90.
—. "From the Sudan to Saigon: A Critical Review of Historical Works." *Australian Literary Studies* vol.12 no.2, 1985, pp. 155–65.
Manifold, J. S. "The Tomb of Lieut. John Learmonth, A.I.F." *The Penguin Book of Modern Australian Verse*, edited by John Thompson, Kenneth Slessor, and R. G. Howarth. Penguin Books, 1958, pp. 197–99.
McAuley, James. "Terra Australis." *The Penguin Book of Modern Australian Verse*, edited by John Thompson, Kenneth Slessor, and R. G. Howarth. Penguin Books, 1958, pp. 228.
McCooey, David. "Contemporary Poetry: Across Party Lines." *The Cambridge Companion to Australian Literature*, edited by Elizabeth Webby. Cambridge University Press, 2000, pp. 158–82.

Mead, Philip. "Nation, Literature, Location." *The Cambridge History of Australian Literature*, edited by Peter Pierce. Cambridge University Press, 2009, pp. 549–67.

Moses, A. Dirk. "An Antipodean Genocide? The Origins of the Genocidal Moment in the Colonization of Australia." *Journal of Genocide Research* vol.2 no.1, 2000, pp. 89–106.

Murray, Les. "The Boeotian Strain." *Kunapipi* vol.2 no.1, 1980, pp. 45–64.

"Visiting Anzac in the Year of Metrification." *Collected Poems*. Black Inc., 2002, pp. 119–22.

Noonuccal, Oodgeroo. *My People*. Jacaranda Press, 1970.

"Prime Minister Robert G. Menzies: Wartime Broadcast." *Australian War Memorial*. www.awm.gov.au/articles/encyclopedia/prime_ministers/menzies.

Rudy, Jason R. *Imagined Homelands: British Poetry in the Colonies*. Johns Hopkins University Press, 2017.

Slessor, Kenneth. "Beach Burial." *Southerly* vol.5 no.3, 1944, p. 13.

Stephensen, P. R. "The Foundations of Culture in Australia: An Essay towards National Self-Respect." W. J. Miles, 1936. www.australianculture.org/the-foundations-of-culture-in-australia-stephensen-1936/.

Stewart, Douglas. *Sonnets to the Unknown Soldier*. Angus & Robertson, 1941.

Strauss, Jennifer. "Literary Culture 1914–1939: Battlers All." *The Oxford Literary History of Australia*, edited by Bruce Bennett and Jennifer Strauss. Oxford University Press, 1998, pp. 107–29.

Tibbitts, Craig. "Casualties of War." *Australian War Memorial*. www.awm.gov.au/wartime/article2.

Tout, Dan. "Encountering Indigeneity: Xavier Herbert, 'Inky' Stephensen and the Problems of Settler Nationalism." *Cultural Studies Review* vol.23 no.2, 2017, pp. 141–61.

Wright, Judith. "It's Not the Planet That's the Problem. It's Us." *Going on Talking*. Butterfly Books, 1992, pp. 117–19.

3

JOHN HAWKE

Cultivating Australian Poetry through Periodicals

Verse in many forms, both sophisticated and primitive, was widely published in nineteenth-century Australian periodicals, including in even the most remote rural newspapers: John Shaw Neilson's earliest writings first appeared in the *Nhill Mail*. Louisa Lawson's *The Dawn* (1888–1905) provided a powerful platform for women writers, including international voices. But it was in the pages of the *Bulletin* that the first real attempt was made to foster an Australian literature that took poetry as its central focus. This was encouraged by the onset of 'ballad fever': A. B. Paterson published his first *Bulletin* poem in 1885, and his debut collection ran through multiple editions after selling out in a week in 1895; Henry Lawson's first volume followed a year later. The appointment of A. G. Stephens as literary editor of the "Red Page" in 1894 substantially broadened the scope of the *Bulletin*'s poetry offerings: a fervent internationalist, Stephens looked beyond the dominant Anglophone models of Kiplingesque balladry and Celtic revivalism, to currents in continental and especially French literature.

The two poets he particularly championed, both in the *Bulletin* and in his subsequent journal the *Bookfellow*, were John Shaw Neilson, who first appeared in the *Bulletin* in 1896, and Christopher Brennan. Both were poets who eschewed the representationalism of 'bush nationalism': Shaw Neilson created his own autonomous poetic landscape through pure lyricism; Brennan, knowledgeably influenced by his French Symbolist contemporaries, offered myth and techniques of suggestion and evocation in place of direct description. It is the pathway offered by these two poets that has most often been viewed as central to the evolution of modern Australian poetry through the twentieth century. While the accepted version of Australian culture takes the nationalism established in the *Bulletin* during the 1890s as its lodestone (and "Waltzing Matilda" remains our national song), this alternative current, receptive to the international avant-garde of the period, is equally apparent under Stephens' editorship. Brennan was even invited to lead a symposium discussion in the Red Page on the topic of "Was Mallarmé a Great Poet?" in November 1898: this was at a time when Stéphane Mallarmé was an obscure figure in the English-speaking world, apart from a few significant acolytes such as W. B. Yeats and Arthur Symons; and this discussion appeared on the leading page of the self-professed "Bushman's Bible".

This period of openness was not to persist. As A. A. Phillips notes in *The Australian Tradition* (1957), the confident optimism of the 1890s dissipated in the works of subsequent nationalist poets, such as Bernard O'Dowd and Frank Wilmot. By the 1920s, under the editorship of David McKee Wright, the *Bulletin* published verse that seems dated and stilted by the standards of comparable international poetry. Brennan re-emerged to contribute articles on nineteenth-century French poets in the mid-1920s, but there was little engagement with the more recent development of this approach within Anglo-American modernism. The Red Page was not to see a revival until the editorship of Douglas Stewart (1940–60), who initiated a new generation of poets, including Judith Wright, David Campbell, and Francis Webb, with an interest in representing national subjects in more sophisticated forms. Stewart was a follower of Norman Lindsay, and his influential exploration of archetypal Australian hero-figures, with Kenneth Slessor's "Five Visions of Captain Cook" (1931) as its model, bears distinctly Nietzschean overtones (most evident in his depiction of Ned Kelly). There is also the uncomfortable fact that the *Bulletin* published under the banner, "Australia for the White Man," for much of the twentieth century; this extended throughout Stewart's own era.

The sources for Stewart's approach can be identified in what is usually regarded as Australia's first 'little magazine,' the Lindsay-oriented journal *Vision* (1923–24). Mainly edited by a young Jack Lindsay (with assistance from Kenneth Slessor and Frank Johnson) as a mouthpiece for his father's ideas, *Vision* rejected both the "realism" of the nationalist school and the "primitivism" of modernism, which it viewed as a "devitalisation" symptomatic of a post-war malaise ("Foreword" May 1923, 2). It proposed instead a "vitalistic" Dionysism, derived loosely from Nietzsche, which would "see again the gods come to earth and living by the hearths of men: Apollo in the fields and Aphrodite on the lily-slopes" ("Foreword" August 1923, 4). This was chiefly evidenced in the Parnassian verse of Hugh McCrae, who provides a kind of poetic equivalent to Norman Lindsay's faun and nymph-replete artistic fantasias. It is especially apparent in the early poems of Slessor (collected in his 1923 volume *Thief of the Moon*), which address subjects such as the appearance of Greek deities in Norman Lindsay's garden. This activity led Jack Lindsay and Slessor to edit an anthology, *Poetry in Australia 1923*, which included McCrae, Shaw

Neilson, and Brennan alongside the work of emerging poets such as R. D. FitzGerald and Dulcie Deamer. In spite of its Lindsay-isms, this can be regarded as the first representative anthology of modern Australian poetry, although Slessor's contributions were regarded as improperly "fleshly" in a contemporary review in Adelaide's *Register* (4). *Vision* itself was short-lived, even though it claimed its four issues had sold several thousand copies; Jack Lindsay's subsequent attempt to bring this anti-modernist Antipodean vitalism to an international audience, in *The London Aphrodite* (1928–29), was predictably unsuccessful. Norman Lindsay nevertheless continued to exert an influence on a generation of Australian poets, including Slessor, Stewart, and Webb, and was a frequent contributor to the *Bulletin* in the 1940s.

The accepted view about the belated Australian response to literary modernism overlooks the existence of the Melbourne journal *Stream*, which published three issues in 1931. Edited by Cyril Pearl, with the assistance of Bertram Higgins – an expatriate poet who had returned to Australia in 1930 – *Stream* announced itself as "a medium of international art expression," promising that "the current European scene will be adequately interpreted by translations from the outstanding periodicals of France, Germany, Italy, Russia" (n.pag.). With an Art Deco cover featuring a nude figure with paintbrush in one hand and a copy of T. S. Eliot's "Poems" in the other, *Stream* presented articles on the international Modernist movement in art, music, theatre, film, and literature. The first issue (July 1931) took its "Credo" from Remy de Gourmont – the writer "should create his own aesthetics, and we should admit as many aesthetics as there are original minds." It featured an extended interview with Aldous Huxley by Frederic Lefevre, which discusses *Finnegans Wake* in relation to Surrealism; a story by the Dadaist Georges Ribemont-Dessaignes; an essay on film music by Arthur Honneger (Cocteau's collaborator); and a revealing discussion of the banned *Lady Chatterley's Lover*. As Cyril Pearl noted in his humorous wrap-up, "La Ligne Générale," the most advanced local literary taste of the era seems to have been demonstrated by the Federal Customs Department who had seized copies of *Dubliners* and *A Farewell to Arms*, along with other key modernist works (44).

Among the Australian contributions to *Stream* are examples of the proto-modernist poetry of Bertram Higgins, as well as 'free verse' by Alwyn Lee and others; further discussion of Higgins' work followed in later issues. Nettie Palmer reviewed Edmund Wilson's pioneering study of the Anglo-American modernists, *Axel's Castle*, which had just been published. Issue 2 (August 1931) extended the journal's cultural survey to include cinema, with a column quoting major statements by Eisenstein and Pudowkin, and featured an analysis of the theatre of Pirandello. It also included Fernand

Leger's essays "Modern Life and Art" and "The Cinema," making these key statements about modernity ("Speed is the law of the world") available to Australian readers for the first time. Evidence of the journal's contacts with leading international figures is provided in the note to this issue: "Ezra Pound, in a letter to the Editors, has granted *Stream* the Australian rights of publishing any of his new work. A selection of Mr Pound's recent writings will follow shortly" (n.pag.). While an extract from Pound's 1930 "Credo" concluded issue 3 (1945), the journal did not survive to fulfil this promise. However, this issue did feature Pound's English amanuensis, Basil Bunting, whose "Directory of Current English Authors" provided a bracingly modern survey that dismissed most English writers, championing instead authors such as Joyce, Wyndham Lewis, William Carlos Williams, and H. D., as well as the uncollected *Cantos*. A story by Robert McAlmon – another associate of Pound's – was also included in *Stream* 3, along with essays on Wagner, contemporary Soviet literature, and an interview with Thomas Mann (mostly concerning Nietzsche). There was also a translation of Russian Futurist Vladimir Mayakovsky's most celebrated poem, "A Cloud in Trousers," by Sacha Youssevich. This brief engagement with international modernism would not be pursued in Australia for another decade.

When it commenced in 1941, *Angry Penguins* was clearly an Adelaide student magazine – which is why its increasing profile attracted the envious attention of Sydney poets, such as James McAuley, associated with rival university journals *Hermes* and *Arna*. This led to McAuley's production with Harold Stewart of the "Ern Malley" hoax-poems, which are the journal's most significant contribution to Australian poetry. *Angry Penguins* was from the outset an organ for the dissemination of the apocalyptic poetry of its editor, Max Harris, though his lifelong associate, Geoffrey Dutton, was also an ongoing contributor. Harris' first book, *A Gift of Blood* (1940), was heavily promoted in the first issue, and his signature poem "The Pelvic Rose (to Salvador Dali)" provided a stylistic template for the journal's semi-surrealist poetics. These early issues claim that it is the only local magazine "contemporaneous in spirit and idiom" (*Angry Penguins* no.2, 7), evident in its championing of the experimentalism of *Finnegans Wake*, with the stated aim of providing an Australian equivalent to the US journal *New Directions*, with whom Harris established direct editorial contacts. This was particularly evident in its connections with the new wave of Antipodean modernist artists, such as Nolan, Boyd, and Tucker – but especially James Gleeson, whose poetry offers a genuine engagement with surrealist automatist practice (as do the "Malley" poems themselves).

The breakthrough in this regard occurred when Harris joined forces with John Reed, who brought not only the intellectual resources of the

Melbourne-based Contemporary Art Society, but also the material funding of the Baillieu fortune. The fourth issue signalled a notable advance: *Angry Penguins* was now "a literary and art journal proper" (1) – and the publication of Dylan Thomas' "Hunchback in the Park" (29) indicates the true model for Harris' poetry, an English neo-Romanticism, informed by the critical writings of Herbert Read, that displaces Auden's stylistic domination of the 1930s. This was supplemented by Sunday Reed's translations of Rimbaud, as the central precursor to modernist poetics (Rimbaud is also translated by Dutton in the fifth issue); contributions by Henry Treece, George Seferis, and Robert Penn Warren demonstrate the increasing internationalism of Harris' ambitions. The "Ern Malley" issue of 1944 (no. 6) was sumptuous and substantial, featuring a selection of US poets, headlined by Objectivist Harry Roskolenko, as well as translations of Rilke.

It is clear from the editorial that Harris felt that the evident qualities of the "Malley" poems, alongside the simultaneous publication of his own experimental novel, *The Vegetative Eye* (1943), would bring a new modernity to Australian literature (redressing the setback of the Dobell Archibald Prize scandal, and the recent publication of Lionel Lindsay's anti-modernist diatribe, *Addled Art* (1942)). But the admonitory quotation appended to the Malley poems, "do not speak of secret matters in a field full of little hills," reads like an epitaph to this minor attempt to engage with international modernism. And the hoaxers' satirical assertion that "[e]very poem should be an autarchy," with which Harris wholeheartedly concurred, underpinned their attempt to unmask the formalist claims of modernist poetics.

It would be a mistake, however, to think that the "Malley" hoax signalled the death knell to Harris' ambitions: the December 1944 issue, at nearly two hundred pages, continued the expansiveness of the previous volume, including translations of Rilke's "Letters to a Young Poet," as well as a selection of twelve poems by Lorca. The US section of issue 8, edited by Roskolenko, featured work by Kenneth Rexroth, a model for the emerging Beat generation. By 1946, Harris' focus had shifted to the more general cultural issues that would occupy his later career: the monthly *Angry Penguins Broadsheet* was not primarily a poetry journal, though it included work by W. S. Graham and Louis Aragon, as well as Dylan Thomas' "Fern Hill" (11), along with unflagging contributions from Harris himself. Its seventh issue gathered a symposium of international reviews heralding the publication of Thomas' *Deaths and Entrances*, seemingly to vindicate Harris' pro-Thomas stance in the teeth of his detractors.

Yet it would not be accurate to view *Angry Penguins* as an anomaly within mid-twentieth-century Australian culture: the commentators on the "Ern Malley" hoax in issue 7 of *Angry Penguins* include Nettie Palmer, who noted the precedence of Bertram Higgins' *Stream* (15). David Campbell, whose work was also informed by the image-centred surrealism of poets such as Lorca, suggested that the main problem with Harris' approach is simply lack of control: "the search for imagery," he wrote, "leads to inevitable obscurity and unrelatedness" (19). And the editorials of *Angry Penguins* were supportive of related attempts to foster a post-war renaissance in Australian literature, particularly *Meanjin*, although Harris remained dismissive of those (such as the Jindyworobaks) who retreated into pre-modernist nationalist concerns.[1] Most telling, perhaps, is the publication of an extract from James McAuley's apocalyptic "Incarnation of Sirius" in issue 8, under the title "In the Best Ern Malley Manner" (136), suggesting that the approaches and influences of hoaxers and hoaxed, while offering competing conceptions of poetic modernism, were never entirely opposed.

Harris was unsurprisingly dismissive of Flexmore Hudson's *Poetry* (1941–47), which favoured Jindyworobak writings and themes, with the fine early poetry of William Hart-Smith strongly represented. But it also included work by important emerging figures such as Judith Wright, Rosemary Dobson, A. D. Hope, Kenneth Mackenzie, and McAuley, as well as poems by a young Dorothy Hewett. And *Poetry* was notably receptive to international influences: most interestingly, it commissioned several poems from Langston Hughes, placing his Harlem Renaissance voice alongside the local interest in Indigenous experience. William Carlos Williams' "The Rock-Old Dogma" appeared in issue 20; and a letter by Williams is also featured in issue 25 discussing the case of Ezra Pound's incarceration. A selection of recent Indonesian poetry appeared in the same issue.

Southerly was viewed as an academic journal from its inception in 1939, and its initial number featured Harris' future antagonists, McAuley, Stewart, and Hope (Judith Wright first appeared in 1940). Indeed, the early issues of *Southerly* seem preoccupied with Harris' activities, including a review of the Adelaide student journal, *Phoenix* (the precursor to *Angry Penguins*), as well as negative notices of *The Gift of Blood*, and of each *Angry Penguins* as it appeared. *Southerly* included works by associates of *Angry Penguins* such as Elisabeth Lambert and Karl Shapiro, as well as by Harris himself. But this did not prevent them from including Beatrice Davis' scathing review of *The Vegetative Eye*, leading to Harris himself intervening to complain about the coverage. The direct influence of Kenneth Slessor emerged strongly in *Southerly* by the mid-1940s: his late poems "Beach Burial" (1944) and "Polarities" (1948) first appeared there, and the publication of his *One Hundred Poems: 1919–1939* in 1944 cemented his reputation as the central protagonist in Australian poetry. (Mary Gilmore's *Selected Poems*, published in 1948, had a similar impact, though she was by this time already a public figure.) Slessor's disapproval of Harris' version of modernism, which he described as "entirely misguided" in an essay on "Australian Literature" (1945), was perhaps the decisive opinion; Gilmore also contributed a sardonic poem titled "Angry Penguins" in 1948.

What emerges instead through the mid- to late 1940s is a generation of powerful poetic voices that would shape Australian poetry for decades: 1946 sees the publication of: Wright's *The Moving Image*; McAuley's *Under Aldebaran*, described by H. M. Green as "the best since FitzGerald and Slessor" ("Australian Literature, 1946," 212); Harold Stewart's *Phoenix Wings*; William Hart-Smith's *Christopher Columbus*; *A Drum for Ben Boyd* by the twenty-two-year-old Francis Webb; and collections by Rosemary Dobson, David Campbell, John Blight, and Kenneth Mackenzie. A. D. Hope would eventually join them with *The Wandering Islands* in 1955, while Douglas Stewart was seemingly omnipresent. In support of this groundswell of current activity, *Southerly* through the 1950s set about establishing a canon of poetic forebears, with Slessor as its central guide. Special issues were devoted to Brennan, Shaw Neilson, Norman Lindsay, and Hugh McCrae: nationalists such as Lawson were seldom to be seen (though his former companion, Gilmore, contributed some fine late poems to the journal during this period). Confidence in this poetry renaissance was reinforced through the annual *Australian Poetry* collections, and through the publication of anthologies that reflected the newly coalesced canon. Yet there were also signs of anxiety: Brian Elliot's 1956 article, "Australian Bards and American Reviewers" (182) highlighted a review by Kenneth Rexroth of Judith Wright's *Book of Australian Verse*, which stated that "Australian verse is still provincial." Rexroth bluntly summed up Wright and her collection: "[I]t isn't great poetry, and there isn't any great poetry in this book" (183). Evidently, in the rush to flee from the example of Ern Malley, something had perhaps gone missing.

The counterpoint to this tendency emerged with the establishment of *Overland* (incorporating "The Realist Writer") by Stephen Murray-Smith in 1954, which reasserted a ballad-driven nationalism. *Overland* opened with an article by John Manifold (at the time a forthright Stalinist) reclaiming A. B. Paterson, and the poetry of its early issues is mostly in ballad form, with Mary Gilmore also celebrated. Issue 5 (1955) featured A. A. Phillips' famous essay on "The Democratic Tradition," establishing a lineage that leads directly from the *Bulletin* to social realist contemporaries. Issue 8 (1956) placed Manifold and Gilmore alongside poems by Ho Chi Minh (a rare overseas contributor); its review of the Wright anthology by Laurence Collinson is predictably critical of her underrepresentation of poets from the nationalist tradition. The antagonist to *Overland* appeared with *Quadrant*, founded by James McAuley in 1956: McAuley's combative opening editorial was particularly scathing of "the ugly nineteenth-century vice of cultural nationalism" (3). As Murray-Smith commented in issue 9 of *Overland*, McAuley's position is "explicitly reactionary" in its rejection of "those values we have come almost to take for granted as the unifying thread, the spiritual core of Australian literature" (2). The accuracy of this opinion is confirmed by the publication of McAuley's conservative manifesto, *The End of Modernity* (1959), delicately reviewed by Chris Wallace-Crabbe in issue 16: McAuley's hardening political opinions and anti-modernist stance would shape *Quadrant*, which was never primarily a poetry journal.

By this time, however, a new counter to the nationalist tradition had emerged with the publication of Patrick White's major novels, especially the Miles Franklin Award-winning *Voss* (1957), which were widely viewed (by A. D. Hope and others) as attempts to transpose Symbolist poetry to the novel form. Ian Turner's verdict that *Voss* presents "a way of thinking that is foreign to most Australians" (37) – confirmed by White's own rejection of "dreary dun-coloured ... journalistic realism" ("The Prodigal Son") – was supported by Katharine Susannah Prichard, who found *Voss* "anaemic and completely out of tune with an Australian atmosphere and environment" (14). Slessor was also the subject of suspicion: his 1958 *Penguin Book of Australian Verse* (co-edited with John Thompson and Guy Howarth) was criticised for dispensing with all nineteenth-century poetry, especially that of Lawson. By the 1960s, though, *Overland* had become more mainstream in its poetry selection, broadening its coverage to include Wright as well as emerging poets such as David Malouf and Rodney Hall; even Max Harris, who was now pursuing folkloric themes similar to those of John Manifold, appears in its pages. And Patrick White himself was featured with the short story "Clay" in 1963.

A persistence of the nationalist tradition through the 1960s can be found in the pages of *Realist Writer* (later *The Realist*), which retained allegiances to the ballad form through poets such as Hewett and Manifold. *Realist* critics, including Ray Williams, Jack Beasley, and Judah Waten, asserted the centrality of the democratic-realist tradition, directly attacking the lineage of Brennan, Wright and White. *The Realist* also highlighted the importance of Mary Gilmore, especially in her sympathetic treatment of Aboriginal experience. The journal particularly celebrated the successful 1964 publication of *We Are Going*, not only the first book by Oodgeroo Noonuccal, then known as Kath Walker, but also the first book by an Indigenous author and sponsored by communist writers Len Fox and Jean Devanny (and famously supported by Judith Wright).

In his satire on the poetry scene of the 1940s, "The Denunciad," Alister Kershaw describes *Meanjin* (initially *Meanjin Papers*) as "*The Bulletin* in free verse" (8), and its early issues do reflect a nationalist interest, with Jindyworobaks such as Rex Ingamells and P. R. Stephensen featuring alongside younger Queensland poets including its editor, Clem Christesen. But by 1942, *Meanjin* had expanded to accommodate not only Harris and Kershaw himself, but also essays by critics such as A. R. Chisholm (a student of Brennan), which contested a narrowly local focus. *Meanjin*'s most important legacy to Australian poetry was its championing of the work of Judith Wright, who first appears in the eleventh issue in 1942 with "The Company of Lovers" (15). Wright's poems feature in nearly every issue of the journal through the 1940s and 1950s (she was listed as Christesen's "secretary"), often alongside the writings of her life partner, Jack McKinney, whose essays discuss the centrality of the poet's task in a time of crisis in Western thought. And while Wright's subjects are usually local and descriptive, an engagement with broader concerns emerges as her work evolves across her first three volumes.

The publication of A. D. Hope's "Australia" (1943) – "the river of her immense stupidity / floods her monotonous tribes from Perth to Cairns" (42) – provides a clinching statement on the nationalist argument. This was supported by Max Harris' anti-Jindyworobak essay, "Dance Little Wombat," in the following issue. McAuley also published some of his most important work in *Meanjin*: "The True Discovery of Australia" (1946) follows Hope in its own satire of Australian intellectual life, with a final dig at the Angry Penguins. By the late 1940s, however, *Meanjin* had become more selective in its publication of poetry, favouring more general cultural articles (and social realist fiction). A Melbourne influence emerged in the 1950s, in contrast to the accepted orthodoxies of *Southerly*: this is especially evident in Vincent Buckley's 1952 essay on the poetry of Kenneth Slessor, which reassesses his central role, criticising his "romantic grotesquery," and asserting: "there is in all his poetry a faint background of disgust with life" (30). As with *Southerly*, by the mid-1950s a confidence in the quality of the local canon was apparent: Hope, McAuley, and Buckley provide authoritative essays on issues of poetics, and the reputation of poets such as Wright is firmly established. It is quite a shock, then, to encounter Ezra Pound's "Canto 90" in the fourth issue of 1955, accompanied by an explanatory essay by eminent US critic, Guy Davenport. Pound's deployment of poetic collage and techniques of parataxis looks nothing like the accepted version of poetry advanced in Australian journals of this period. The sheer anomaly of its appearance is revelatory.

While each of these journals commenced with a specific focus on poetry, as they developed into more general literary magazines this emphasis receded, although at different times particular poetry editors would assert an important influence. This was the case with the appointment of Kris Hemensley as poetry editor of *Meanjin* in 1976, which gave the voice of the Melbourne poetic underground a position within the mainstream; Barrett Reid, a former Angry Penguin, brought a similar emphasis to *Overland* in the 1980s. These national journals were supplemented by regional literary magazines, with the establishment of *Westerly* (1956), *LINQ* (*Literature in North Queensland*) (1969), and *The Tasmanian Review* (later *Island*) (1979), which promoted poets distanced from the central networks of Sydney and Melbourne. However, by the mid-1960s, with the emergence of major new voices such as Les Murray and Bruce Dawe, the need for more dedicated poetry journals was apparent.

Poetry Magazine, the journal of the Sydney-based Poetry Society, published mostly minor poets through the early 1960s, though its contributors included Jindyworobak fellow-traveller, Roland Robinson, and the influential Bruce Beaver. Signs of transformation commenced under Robinson's editorship towards the end of the decade. By this time the poets of the 1940s, such as Hope, Stewart, and Webb, were consolidating their reputations through collected editions; an intermediate generation was represented in the Rodney Hall and Thomas Shapcott anthology, *New Impulses in Australian Poetry* (1967). A breakthrough is evident in 1968, with the debuts of Robert Gray and Vicki Viidikas (issue 4), swiftly followed by Robert Adamson and John Tranter (issue 5): both Adamson's "To Arthur Rimbaud" and Tranter's "Bardo Thodol" contain the word "acid." These young poets were distinctively different to anything that had previously appeared, and were also notable for their lack of respect for the 'establishment': Gray delivered a scathing review of the *New Impulses* survey, which he found "boring" (36). With the addition of Adamson to the editorial board, the magazine featured reviews of Mersey and Beat poets, as well as fresh voices such as J. S. Harry and Tim Thorne.

The real takeover occurred in 1969, with Adamson's editorial for issue 2 (titled "Young Poets' Issue Approximately") announcing "the circus is in town": the issue opened with two signature poems, Tranter's "Parallax" and Gray's "Kangaroo," and included a clear explanation of projective verse by critic and co-editor, Carl Harrison-Ford. Subsequent issues introduced future key figures in the new Australian poetry, including John Forbes, Martin Johnston, and Jennifer Maiden, as well as psychedelia such as Michael Dransfield's "Environmental Art," with its "fantastic beasts / jungled in hallucinogens" (34). By 1970, Robinson's name had vanished from the masthead, as Adamson and Harrison-Ford reached out to like-minded Melbourne poets from La Mama and Monash, including John Jenkins, Charles Buckmaster, Alan Wearne, and John A. Scott. The consolidation of this new generation was confirmed by the publication of debut collections by Tranter and Adamson, reviewed alongside one another by close friends Martin Johnston and Tim Thorne in August 1970. (Johnston's praise of Tranter's work for its "self-sufficiency" (41) would have been heartening to the young Max Harris.) Robert Gray's first book, and Bruce Beaver's *Letters to Live Poets*, were reviewed in the following issue. At this point *Poetry Magazine* turned into *New Poetry*, which would continue to advance the careers of this coterie of poets through the 1970s, culminating in the publication of Tranter's *New Australian Poetry* anthology in 1979.

The more mainstream rival to *New Poetry* during this period, *Poetry Australia* (1964–92), was also an offshoot of *Poetry Magazine*. Founded by Grace Perry, its typical contributors during the 1960s were *New Impulses* figures such as Beaver, Shapcott, and Hall, with Geoffrey Lehmann and Les Murray given increasing prominence. *Poetry Australia* also played an important role in highlighting regional poetries through special state-based issues over this period, foregrounding poets such as Randolph Stow and Gwen Harwood. Its "Young Poets' Issue" (issue 7, December 1965) included Dransfield and Thorne, as well as Tranter, whose work would appear frequently through the late 1960s. Critical discussion of US poets was featured in essays by James Tulip, which focused mainly on the Deep Image and Confessional poets collected in Donald Hall's *Contemporary American Poetry* anthology. International voices were also highlighted, through migrant poets such as Antigone Kefala, Margaret Diesendorf, and Sylvia Kantarizis, and European translations were common (issue 22/23 August 1968 was an "Italian Issue").

As with *Poetry Magazine*, the new generation became increasingly visible through the late 1960s: Viidikas and Harry were regularly featured, and the "Victorian Issue" (issue 27, April 1969) included John A. Scott and Walter Billeter alongside more established figures such as Wallace-Crabbe. The new poetry was acknowledged in issue 32 (February 1970): titled "Preface to the Seventies" and edited by Tranter, this special issue included younger poets who had previously appeared in the journal (Dransfield, Wearne, Viidikas), as well as Gray, Maiden, and Adamson. Thomas Shapcott, whose "Generation of 68" anthology, *Australian Poetry Now*, had just appeared, describes the scene as "a youthful romanticism as luxurious as anything in *Angry Penguins*" (47). And while this was followed by a more measured selection of New South Wales work, guest-edited by Leonie Kramer, the June 1970 issue was devoted to Tranter's debut collection, *Parallax*. (This was somewhat belated recognition of a movement that had burgeoned in short-lived 'little magazines' such as Richard Tipping's *Mok* and Hemensley's *Our Glass* for some years by this time.)

This initiated a climate of openness in the early 1970s when a diversity of major poems were featured in the journal: issue 42 (1972) includes Murray's "Walking to the Cattle Place" along with John Forbes' "T.V." and excerpts from Buckley's "Golden Builders"; Lehmann's "Ross's Poems" also first appeared during this period, as well as the work Robert Gray would gather for his breakthrough collection, *Creekwater Journal* (1973). However, with the appointment of Les Murray as associate editor in 1975, the magazine became increasingly partisan: a perceptive review of Murray's *Lunch and Counterlunch* by David Malouf in issue 57 (1975) identifies a "conservative mind" within Murray's poetry, and this is evident in his editorship (71). A canon was swiftly established that included Gray and Lehmann along with newer Canberra poets such as Geoff Page, Alan Gould, Kevin Hart, and Mark O'Connor; Jamie Grant savagely attacked the early volumes of John Forbes, Laurie Duggan, and Dorothy Porter in a review in issue 65 (1977) before being similarly dismissive of John Tranter in issue 67 (1978) and Ken Bolton in issue 69 (1979); while Robert Adamson was panned by Andrew Taylor in issue 58 (1976). With Murray's removal from the masthead in the 1980s, *Poetry Australia* returned to being a more open and inclusive journal under the managing editorship of the level-headed John Millett.

The trajectory of *New Poetry* over the same period was in some respects similar: energised by the Adamson 'takeover,' its early issues were packed with key poems and discussion of fresh conceptions of poetics. Its annual Poetry Award discovered major new works such as Duggan's "East" (1971) and Forbes' "Four Heads and How to Do Them" (1972); Martin Johnston's "The Blood Aquarium" appears in April 1971; and signature poems by Dransfield, Adamson, and Harry are regularly featured. Critical discussion of Charles Olson by Carl Harrison-Ford (1972), and of John Ashbery by Forbes (1972), elucidate the American influences essential to the new poetics; and the urbane approach of expatriate Peter Porter is rediscovered as a counter to traditional nationalist concerns. This internationalism broadened with the return to Australia of Melbourne underground luminary Kris Hemensley in 1973: Hemensley quickly established a new journal of his own, *Ear in a Wheatfield*, as "an international avant-garde journal," and the "Notes and Comments" he contributes to *New Poetry* during this period are unusually wide-ranging. This was also evident in related Melbourne 'little magazines' of this time, such as *Etymspheres*, edited by Billeter and Jenkins, which introduced important European voices, including Paul Celan. Other avant-garde elements were emerging through PiO's *Fitzrot*, in poems which emphasised the oral and visual components of the sign (as spoken performance and concrete poetry).

New Poetry itself altered focus in 1974, when Adamson assumed sole editorial control: the acute critical eye of Harrison-Ford is especially missed. An attempt to unify old and new is evident in volume 22, issue 2–3, which features poets of the 1940s (Hope, McAuley, Wright) alongside Forbes, Tranter, and Maiden. There was also an attempt to reach out to the *Poetry Australia* grouping in the first volume of 1975, which features Robert Gray and Vincent Buckley along with reviews of Murray (by Gray) and Gray (by Page). By the later 1970s, however, the journal mainly represents Adamson's own interests and influences – including its proclamation of a "New Romanticism" which did not apply to the majority of his peers – with the mid-1970s visits of US poets Robert Creeley and Robert Duncan particularly highlighted. With the shift to a more elaborate format in 1977, *New Poetry* continued to feature key works, including poems from Beaver's *Death's Directives* and Fay Zwicky's *Kaddish*, as editorial responsibilities were transferred to Adamson's wife, Cheryl, and a young Kate Lilley. Newer voices, such as Gig Ryan, Judith Beveridge, and Anthony Lawrence, were introduced at this time.

The role of *New Poetry* was overtaken by the leading Australian literary journal of the 1980s, *Scripsi* (1981–94), founded by Peter Craven and Michael Heyward. From its inception, *Scripsi* was a showcase for the work of Monash poets, Alan Wearne, John A. Scott, and Laurie Duggan, as well as their Sydney-based associates, including Ryan, Tranter, and Forbes (who would eventually assume the poetry editorship). Les Murray was given regular attention in the journal, but his *Poetry Australia* allies, such as Gray and Lehmann, were not generally featured (and many *New Poetry* regulars, such as Viidikas and Harry, also did not appear). Peter Porter was particularly celebrated, with his Audenesque approach finding a younger counterpart in the poetry of Peter Rose. With the journal's encouragement, each of their favoured authors produced award-winning work during this period: Wearne's *The Nightmarkets* (1986), Scott's *St Clair* (1986), and Duggan's *The Ash Range* (1987) were career-defining volumes, as was Tranter's major collection, *Under Berlin* (1988); Adamson joined them later in the decade with the poems included in *The Clean Dark* (1989). While younger voices, such as Kate Lilley, Adam Aitken, and Luke Davies, often appeared in *Scripsi*, established poets of an earlier generation were mainly emphasised.

Scripsi was notable for its genuine engagement with international currents within Anglo-American modernism. The English poet Christopher Logue's *War Music* was the focus of its second issue, which also included a poem by Gary Snyder. Its most important contribution in this regard was the attention given to the Objectivist generation of post-Poundian poets: this commences with an essay on Louis Zukofsky by Kris Hemensley, written in the informative epistolary style of his *Ear* journals. The following issue examined the poetry of Basil Bunting, and introduced the important writings of English literary critic Kenneth Cox through an essay on Hugh McDiarmid; Cox's articles on the related work of poets such as Gael Turnbull and Zukofsky were a significant scholarly contribution to the field. Alongside this, *Scripsi* drew attention to the contemporary San Francisco poet, August Kleinzahler, a student of Bunting and associate of Objectivist Carl Rakosi, whose work was also featured. More diverse figures in US postmodernism, Ronald Johnson, Robert Kelly, and Michael Palmer, appeared in 1985. There was also attention to New York School influences, with an essay on O'Hara by Forbes in 1985, and interviews in 1986 by Tranter with John Ashbery and Kenneth Koch, both of whom contributed poems. The confidence with which *Scripsi* presented its chosen Australian poets alongside highly regarded international figures is evident in the third issue of 1986, which celebrates the publication of Wearne's *The Nightmarkets* in direct parallel to that of Vikram Seth's rival verse-novel, *The Golden Gate*, giving equal emphasis to each.

Scripsi's selective approach to the field of local poetry narrowed further with the accession of John Forbes to the poetry editorship in the late 1980s. Poets from the 1970s 'little magazine' scene were never widely represented, although both Hemensley and Robert Kenny appeared in early issues, and during this period Hemensley continued his project through the roneoed journal *H/EAR*. Smaller contemporaneous journals offered connections with international currents overlooked by *Scripsi*. Ken Bolton's *Magic Sam* (edited with Anna Couani), and later *Otis Rush*, demonstrated the direct influence of New York School poets of the second wave. Pete Spence's *Post Neo* provided a forum for an avant-garde that extended to US poets associated with the emerging Language movement, as well as their local equivalents, including Chris Mann and Ania Walwicz. Other publications were more focused: PiO's *925* specialised in poems about the workplace, while Jeltje's *Migrant 7* offered a platform for multicultural writings; both continued their editors' formal interest in visual and oral poetics. Poetry with an explicitly feminist emphasis was represented in the long-running Melbourne journal, *Luna*. This wide range of smaller poetry magazines in the 1980s was fostered by generous Australia Council funding for literary journals available during this period, which would become more restricted over subsequent decades.

The 1990s brought increasing mainstream attention to multicultural and Indigenous writings, with *Meanjin* adopting a postcolonial focus, while Ivor Indyk's editorial contribution to *Southerly* highlighted publications such as

PiO's major poem of migrant experience, 24 *Hours* (1996). By the mid-1990s, however, the demise of both *Poetry Australia* and *Scripsi* had left a significant gap in the field. This was partially filled by John Kinsella's irregular magazine, *Salt*, which published key works by local figures such as Robert Harris and Adamson, as well as a range of international writing. But the major journal which emerged in response was Indyk's *Heat*, established in 1996 with the aim of providing a forum for established local writers, with a particular focus on poetry. *Heat* consolidated the reputations of leading poets – including Jennifer Maiden, Gig Ryan, and Judith Beveridge – through its publishing arm, Giramondo Press, while also introducing newer voices such as Emma Lew and Michael Farrell. However, a number of major poets, such as Murray, Tranter, and Kinsella, were never featured in its pages. And while *Heat* from its inception included examples of international work, its main focus was on a broad representation of the local scene, with former outsiders, such as Bolton, Couani, and Javant Biarujia, introduced to a more general audience for the first time.

A comprehensively international representation was instead provided by John Tranter's internet journal, *Jacket* (1997–2010), which swiftly gained recognition as one of the world's leading forums for poetics. Because of its online presence, *Jacket* was neither expressly Australian nor international – a resolution to the issues of provincialism and 'cultural cringe' which have beset poets and editors throughout our literary history. With its encyclopedic coverage, and the apparently limitless space it provided for critical discussion as well as poems of length, *Jacket* offered a model for digital publishing that has since been emulated but never equalled. Its main successor has been *Cordite Poetry Review*, which, especially under the active editorship of Kent MacCarter, has emerged as the major specialist poetry journal of the past decade. As this historical survey has indicated, poetry has always been integral to our literary magazine culture, and these journals have been essential to our national cultural life. Recent decisions to cut government funding for established literary magazines such as *Cordite*, and for the small press publishing ventures which support our poets, demonstrate an inadequate understanding of the vitally important role they have played for more than a century.

Works Cited

Adamson, Robert. *The Clean Dark*. Paper Bark Press, 1989.
Auchterlonie, Dorothy. "Rev. of *Voices, a Quarterly of Poetry* (USA), Australian Issue, September 1944." *Meanjin Papers* vol.4 no.2, 1945, pp. 146–47.

Beaver, Bruce. *Death's Directives*. Prism, 1978.
Buckley, Vincent. "The Poetry of Kenneth Slessor." *Meanjin* vol.11 no.1, 1952, pp. 23–30.
Campbell, David. (as A. Campbell). "Ego." *Angry Penguins* no.7, 1944, pp. 18–19.
Dransfield, Michael. "Environmental Art." *Drug Poems*. Sun Books, 1972, p. 34.
Duggan, Laurie. *The Ash Range*. Picador, 1987.
Elliot, Brian. "Australian Bards and American Reviews." *Southerly* vol.17 no.4, 1956, pp. 182–85.
Gilmore, Mary. "Angry Penguins." *Southerly* vol.9 no.2, 1948, p. 98.
Selected Poems. Angus & Robertson, 1948.
Grant, Jamie. "Children of the Revolution." *Poetry Australia* no.67, 1978, pp. 70–74.
"Such Rich Despair." *Poetry Australia* no.69, 1979, pp. 68–71.
Gray, Robert. "Untitled." *Poetry Magazine* no.6, 1968, pp. 34–37.
Creekwater Journal. University of Queensland Press, 1974.
Green, H. M. "Australian Literature, 1946." *Southerly* vol.8 no.4, 1947, pp. 212–27.
Hall, Rodney and Thomas Shapcott, eds. *New Impulses in Australian Poetry*. University of Queensland Press, 1970.
Harris, Max. *A Gift of Blood*. Jindyworobak Club, 1940.
"The Second 'Angry Penguins.'" *Angry Penguins* no. 2, 1941, pp. 7–8.
"Dance Little Wombat." *Meanjin* vol.2 no.2, 1943, pp. 33–37.
The Vegetative Eye. Reed & Harris, 1943.
Hart-Smith, William. *Christopher Columbus: A Sequence of Poems*. Caxton Press, 1943.
Hope, A. D. "Australia." *Meanjin* vol.2 no.1, 1943, p. 42.
The Wandering Islands. Edwards & Shaw, 1955.
Johnson, Frank C., Jack Lindsay, and Kenneth Slessor. "Foreword." *Vision: A Literary Quarterly* no.1, May 1923, pp. 2–3.
"Foreword." *Vision: A Literary Quarterly* no.2, August 1923, pp. 3–4.
Johnston, Martin. "Review." *Poetry Magazine* vol.18 no.4, 1970, pp. 41–43.
Kershaw, Alister. "The Denunciad." *Angry Penguins* no. 5, 1943, p. 8.
Leger, Fernand, "Two Opinions Modern Life and Art." *Stream* vol.1 no.2, 1931, p. 32.
Lindsay, Jack and Kenneth Slessor, eds. *Poetry in Australia 1923*. Vision Press, 1923.
Lindsay, Lionel. *Addled Art*. Angus & Robertson, 1942.
Malouf, David. "Subjects Found and Taken Up." *Poetry Australia* no.57, 1975, pp. 70–72.
Mayakovsky, Vladimir. "A Cloud in Trousers," translated by Sacha Youssevich. *Stream* vol.1 no.3, September 1931, pp. 35–37.
McAuley, James. "In the Best Ern. Malley Manner." *Angry Penguins* no.8, 1945, p. 136.
"The True Discovery of Australia." *Meanjin* vol.5 no.1, 1946, p. 27.
"By Way of Prologue." *Quadrant* vol.1 no.1, 1956, pp. 3–5.
The End of Modernity: Essays on Literature, Art and Culture. Angus & Robertson, 1959.
Murray-Smith, Stephen. "The Realist Writer." *Overland* no.1, 1954, p. 13.
Noonuccal, Oodgeroo. *We Are Going*. Jacaranda Press, 1964.
Palmer, Nettie. "All Who Run May Read." *Angry Penguins* no.7, 1944, pp. 14–15.

Pearl, C. Alston. "La Ligne Générale." *Stream* vol.1 no.1, July 1931, pp. 44–45.
Penn, J. "The Audacious Younger Poets." *The Register* (Adelaide), 5 January 1924, p. 4.
Phillips, A. A. *The Australian Tradition: Studies in Colonial Culture.* F. W. Cheshire, 1958.
PiO. *24 Hours.* Collective Effort Press, 1996.
Prichard, Katharine Susannah. "Review of Seedtime." *Overland* no.13, 1958, p. 14.
Rilke, Rainer Maria. "Letters to a Young Poet," translated by Horst Solomon. *Angry Penguins*, December 1944, pp. 34–37.
Scott, John. *St. Clair: Three Novels.* University of Queensland Press, 1986.
Seth, Vikram. *The Golden Gate.* Random House, 1986.
Shapcott, Thomas. "Hold Onto Your Crystal Balls, or: Cocksure in the 70s." *Poetry Australia* no.32, 1970, pp. 46–47.
Slessor, Kenneth. *Thief of the Moon.* Hand-press of J. T. Kirtley, 1923.
  One Hundred Poems: 1919–1939. Angus & Robertson, 1944.
  "Australian Literature." *Southerly* vol.6 no.1, 1945, pp. 31–36.
Stewart, Harold. *Phoenix Wings: Poems 1940–6.* Angus & Robertson, 1948.
Taylor, Andrew. "Smiles Singing B Sharp Together." *Poetry Australia* no.58, 1976, pp. 72–77.
Thomas, Dylan. "The Hunchback in the Park." *Angry Penguins* no.4, 1942, p. 29.
  Deaths and Entrances. J. M. Dent, 1946.
  "Fern Hill." *Angry Penguins Broadsheet* no.3, 28 February 1946, p. 11.
Tranter, John. "Bardo Thodol." *Poetry Australia* no.34, 1970, p. 22.
  "Parallax." *Poetry Australia* no.34, 1970, pp. 44–45.
  Parallax and Other Poems. South Head Press, 1970.
  Under Berlin. University of Queensland Press, 1988.
Turner, Ian. "The Parable of Voss." *Overland* no.12, 1958, pp. 36–37.
Wearne, Alan. *The Nightmarkets.* Penguin, 1986.
Webb, Francis. *A Drum for Ben Boyd.* Angus & Robertson, 1948.
White, Patrick. "The Prodigal Son." *Australian Letters* vol.1 no.3, 1958, pp. 37–40.
  "Clay." *Overland* no.26, 1963, pp. 4–13.
Williams, William Carlos. "The Rock-Old Dogma." *Poetry* no.20, 1946.
Wright, Judith. "The Company of Lovers." *Meanjin* vol.1 no.11, 1942, p. 15.
Zwicky, Fay. *Kaddish and Other Poems.* University of Queensland Press, 1982.

NOTES

1 Harris also provided commentary for an Australian issue of *Voices: A Quarterly of Poetry* (USA) in September 1944, that was edited by Roskolenko and Elisabeth Lambert. In her review for *Meanjin Papers*, Dorothy Auchterlonie found the editors' mapping of modern Australian poetry as a "surrealist drawing of abstract and unrelated elements" to be confusing and unrepresentative (146) but praised a translation of "The Song of Ankotarinja" as having "more than an anthropological interest" (147).

PART II
Networks

4

MICHAEL FARRELL

Above and Below

Sublime and Gothic Relations in Nineteenth-Century Australian Poetry

While the colonising landings of the English appear to be horizontal acts, the earth is not flat, and the structural logic of settler poetic texts in the nineteenth century is a vertical one, an antipodal one, concerned with the above and below. In Romantic, or European, terms, the 'above' can be associated with the sublime: the towering peak, the flight of a bird, a hyperbolic speech. The 'below' – especially below ground – indicates correspondences with the gothic: the trope of being buried alive, for example. This up/down relational structure, as found in colonial texts, is not primarily Christian, although there are exceptions: Barron Field's "The Kangaroo" (1819) which refers to God, Francis MacNamara's "A Convict's Tour To Hell," with its explicit Christian schema, and Mary Gilmore's later "Old Botany Bay" – although here the metaphor – of Australia as hell – is merely rhetorical. The north/south relation between England and Australia, while it may crucially inform this structure, is not, however, one that is usually made explicit. In what follows I attempt to resituate the sublime, and the gothic, within the Australian colonial rather than simply import them for analogous purposes, as if Australian poetics was simply an extension of English literature.

The defining relation of these nineteenth-century poems, or poetic texts, is, though ambivalent, between the speakers and the land itself. It is this particular ambivalence that concerns this chapter rather than "emotional ambivalence" – the family feeling, or, rather, family of feelings, which is the basis for the "emotive sublime" (Bloom 119). While this structure is not unique to Australian poetics, my reading of these texts is contextualised through the colonial circumstances of settlement. In referring to settling I do not mean to suggest a fait accompli but, rather, an attempt: because, due to whatever cultural or psychological forces, the settling of these poems' speakers' feet on the ground, between the above, and the below, ground, typically does not occur. There is, for example, the sublimely inflected brumby chase in A. B. 'Banjo' Paterson's "The Man from Snowy River" (220–25); alternatively, there is the gothic, ghostly, emanation of the drowned swagman in his "Waltzing Matilda." Both poems are concerned with the Australian land, and an inability to stand still on it, let alone sit. Nor does death bring rest: not in "Waltzing Matilda," whose protagonist's ghost continues to sing, and not in Adam Lindsay Gordon's "The Sick Stockrider," where the speaker listens to children stomping on his grave.

Barron Field (1786–1846) is generally considered to have written the first book of poetry in Australia, *First Fruits of Australian Poetry* (1819) (Currey). It includes "The Kangaroo": the Christian structure of which, of people on earth, being, necessarily, below that of God in heaven, is not the only above/below structure utilised in the poem. An epigraph by Virgil also signals above/below hierarchies through staging northern hemispherical precedence. The quote's substance: "mixtumque genus, prolesque biformis" (mixed race, two-formed offspring) is doubly double, and indicates Field's theory of the kangaroo as a divine cut-up of deer and squirrel. This is clearly a European perspective of an Australian creature. Further, the kangaroo, in its "bounding," can be read as being in ambivalent relation to the earth: neither at home within the land, like a wombat, snake, or even rabbit; nor finding its place above the land, like a bird, possum, or koala. This contrasts with at least one Aboriginal story collected by David Unaipon, where the kangaroo is a wise leader of other animals (25–41). As a land animal, Field displaces it (literally, as well as discursively) by an (eco-genocidal) economic imaginary of the earthbound cow and sheep. The historical precedence of "The Kangaroo," as well as its anxiety over Australia's rhyme with failure as an analogy to the colonial enterprise itself, makes it a benchmark poem for subsequent settler poems.

For my purposes, the colonial poetry corpus, as it participates in an above/below structure, is the 'mixed race, two-formed offspring' of the aesthetic concepts of the sublime and the gothic. Field's spotlighting of Virgil also evokes Dante's *Inferno*, and is a reminder that, although this reference comes from the Romanised pen of an Englishman, colonial Australian poetics receives poetic capital from Europe more broadly, not just from English poetics (even if via Europeanised England). As an apostrophised representative, "The Kangaroo" encapsulates above and below (and ambivalence), as "[t]hy fore half, it would appear, / Had belong'd to some 'small deer,' / Such as liveth in a tree" while the kangaroo's larger, lower, or hind half allows it to bound from ground predators – dogs and, implicitly, humans. The poem concludes:

> When sooty swans are once more rare,
> And duck-moles the museum's care,
> Be still the glory of this land,
> Happiest Work of finest Hand!

Is not, then, the kangaroo sublime? The animal is closely associated with God, and it is God's finest "Work." In the final lines we see Field pulling back from his irony, the excess of which, as Harold Bloom notes, destroys the sublime (119). The kangaroo is Art: but one that is sublimely free – unlike the duck-mole (platypus) – of the deadly, gothic care of the museum. In a footnote, Field returns to Rome to cite Juvenal's dubbing of the black swan ("cygnis niger") as rare ("rara avis"). This just after he refers readers up to heaven, and then back to earth again, as he imagines God's fashioning of the kangaroo. Australia seems to be the ultimate down under, as Field borrows the kangaroo's hind power to bound between conceptual spaces, inviting readers to "chace" him. This kind of poetic closure, of death and afterlife, will recur in numerous poetic examples: if none so literary, nor pretentious, nor so jolly, as Field.

Charles Harpur's major poem, "The Kangaroo Hunt; or, A Morning in the Mountains: A Descriptive Poem in Six Parts" (1860), is a verse narrative with preface and notes. This form was established, as George Rapall Noyes discerns, by Sir Walter Scott and Lord Byron (Mickiewicz 428). Its 1860 presentation (469–70) of verse and prose provides readers with a hierarchical structure, as if the poem is, in a sense, grounded in the prose, while the verse lines represent – the possibility at least – of scaling (or imaging) the sublime heights. Yet its later, posthumous presentation is as complicated as a trifle. It begins with an exaggeratedly more elaborate title, which is followed by a verse epigraph, before going on to the preface (where, at one point, Harpur considers the relative sublimity of mountains and hills(!) (455), poem, and notes. Its layering reminds us that above and below are not simple categories: that if we ride a horse the saddle and horse are between us and the ground; and if we lie on the ground, there may still be layers of plant and insect life between us and the earth.

Harpur (1813–68) is another first poet claimant, being, unlike Field, born in Australia. Harpur's parents were both convicts, so his achievements, while they may not have matched his aspirations, are high ones. In Harpur's best-known lyric, "A Midsummer Noon in the Australian Forest," the poem's speaker lies down in the shade (199–200). Here, Harpur follows a different Romantic example, that of John Keats' "Autumn," or perhaps something earlier, as "the noontime rest is a standard pastoral trope" (Schur 149). Poetic tension is produced by the contradiction of what the speaker is saying is happening, and what is not happening, and the concluding fact that the speaker is not in a position to do other than imagine where the poem's insects, for example, may be. If lying supine, the speaker might just be able to spot the "bedaubed" dragon-hornet, but not quite in the manner the poem suggests. In other words, there is a space constructed in the poem, through the literal position of the speaker, in relation to the speaker's imagination: the poem calls on the reader to join in the imagining of its various parts. The imagination is literally constructed as a higher realm – higher, that is, than the lower, grounded, speaker. The mobility of the imagination, its flight through the sky, its flow in the rill, relies, therefore, on its grounded source, that of the speaker lying on the earth, on the ritualised pastoral sublime, to combine Owen Schur's cited observation, and what Jaya Savige refers to as "the Australian sublime *qua* 'silence'" (174).

Gustave Flaubert has his mid-nineteenth-century character, Emma Bovary, opine that "life is *'quelque chose de sublime'* in Paris (or Madrid, or Moscow), and a desert everywhere else" (quoted in Moretti 52–53). That this seemingly sophisticated view is itself provincial, is affirmed by Flaubert in a letter, where he quotes a line of Moliere's, that "outside Paris there was no salvation for gentlefolk," adding: "That judgment seems to me provincial, that is, narrow" (Flaubert 161). Bovary's attitude, serves, in miniature, for the notion of sublime Europe, home in "The Kangaroo" to "sphynx and mermaid" versus the self-punning "barren wood" of Field's Australia. While this attitude serves as a (now rather tired) rhetorical approach, enabling the poem's production – and fuelling newspaper arguments between the city and the bush to this day – it also suggests a relation between this attitude, and the concept of *terra nullius*, that enabling term for colonialism, deployed by Field, who, as well as a poet, was a judge and an ingenious tax-evader (Clemens). This division of the metropolitan sublime and the empty Australian bush (a metaphor based on the cliché that a desert is empty) provides us with a starting point for a colonial sublime in relation to land. Sublime because empty of (European) thought, and memory.

The conceit of *terra nullius* enables settler destruction of Aboriginal life – disregarding a long history of Indigenous thought and culture – and produces a new, traumatic, history, for Australia's Indigenous inhabitants. In terms of literary discourse, it brings the sublime uncomfortably up against the murderous, the genocidal. It is not the desert – or the bush – or, necessarily, representations of these complementary spaces – that are sublime, but *terra nullius*, or, rather, its projection. Harpur sets up the idea of emptiness as both meditative subject and temporal moment. It is at noon that the bush is empty (of sound). How long does noon last? Noon is precisely noon for a minute, or a second, or infinitely less, depending on the perceiver's relative exactitude. And while Harpur's speaker is more general than exact, they also contradict noon's emptiness through reference to proximate insects. Harper presents emptiness as an idea that is contradicted through bodily experience. The poem concludes:

> O 'tis easeful here to lie
> Hidden from Noon's scorching eye,
> In this grassy cool recess
> Musing thus of Quietness. (200)

Harpur's speaker is, for the purposes of the poem, outside of time: in being hidden from "Noon's scorching eye" – presumably by tree branches, and through being in the state of imagination; and further, bringing the two together in the idea of the timelessness of the earth. Read in Theodor Adorno's terms, Harpur might seem foolish, his shady relaxation being like preparing himself for a bush grave; writing on Goethe, Adorno describes the relation of the moments before sleep and those before death as a "sublime irony": "Imperceptibly, soundlessly, irony tinges the poem's consolation: the seconds before the bliss of sleep are the same seconds that separate our brief life from death" (63). The very act of sleep, then, covered in the darkness of night – or shade, in Harpur's case – has a touch of the gothic.

The title of "Bell-birds" by Henry Kendall (1839–82) evokes bush sounds that resonate in the memory of the poem's speaker, now residing in the city. Here, the sublime is attached to the forest and this will become typical in the poetry of the late nineteenth century, and beyond. The pealing call of the bellbird consoles Kendall's speaker; the poem aligns the city's "alleys" with the "deep mountain valleys" of the bush, triangulating two low spaces with the high space of a forest canopy, from where the bird calls (10–11). The entry about bellbirds (also known as bell miners) on the *Birdlife Australia* website notes that they are "more often heard than seen." The entry adds: "The sound of Bell Miners calling in the bush is often greeted with a feeling of benign sentimentality, but this is not the case for the other species of birds trying to share the habitat with them. Bell Miners are territorial and pugnacious ..." This probably owes something to Kendall's poem, which, in its final stanza, explicitly places the memory of bellbirds in the speaker's childhood.

While sentimental means putting more emphasis on a feeling than its circumstances deserve, the *Birdlife* writer suggests that humans both lessen and sweeten the bell sound's signification, because it tolls not for them, but for other birds: if the sound is beautiful it may also be terrifying, that is, sublime. "Sublimation," Geoffrey Hartman argues, "always sacrifices to an origin stronger than itself. If it did not cherish or dread this origin – this 'hiding-place' of power – it would not shroud it from sight by displacement or falsification" (287). This, in a nutshell, brings together both the generalised human view of the hidden, yet powerful, bellbirds, and that of a humanised view of other bird species. As this chapter will demonstrate, it is the hidden aspect of the sublime that links it with the buried and the gothic.

Mary Gilmore (1865–1962) first began publishing in the twentieth century yet poems like "Old Botany Bay" (145) reflect a nineteenth-century orientation. For most of this short poem, the damned convict speaker occupies a position of lowness, being "the conscript / sent to hell" that is "the desert." Despite such conflation, the desert is shown to have the potential to be transformed by "living well" and "set[ting] us high." Australia itself becomes the sublime, through the sacrifices of its conscripted workers.

The theme of high and low conventionally, and conveniently, places Europe, or more precisely England, in the sublime position, and Australia in the gothic. For convicts in particular, the sentence of being sent to Australia could mean, metaphorically, being buried alive. In 1839, Irish convict Francis MacNamara (dubbed 'Frank the Poet') writes "A Convict's Tour To Hell" and opens through quoting fellow Irishman and satirist Jonathan Swift. While repeating Field's nod to antecedents, their epigraphs indicate national and class divisions between the English and Irish in the nineteenth century. Put simplistically, the English pronounced judgment on the Irish poor, sentencing them to hanging or transportation. Nevertheless, Virgil is not out of reach: MacNamara's poem is Dantean, in that his persona travels to hell. Many of the damned have been the poet's tormentors, but he also includes Captain James Cook, for he "discovered New South Wales," and Ralph Darling, the state's governor from 1824 to 1831. Like Dante's persona, MacNamara's ventures up to heaven where he is welcomed with a feast. While the final line has the speaker wake to discover "twas but a dream" (Murray 365–70), the poem demonstrates that the dream is another way that the soul may be (safely) enlarged through sublime experience (Axton).

Comparable to Harpur and Gilmore in output, Henry Lawson (1867–1922) is a poet whose work displays both sublime and gothic features. His poems are sometimes comic, sometimes tragic, and sometimes both. The fourteener ballad, "Faces in the Street" (1888) is a gloomy portrait of the poverty-stricken masses, and gothic in its "dreadful corner" and the line "[t]hey haunted me – the shadows of those faces in the street" (4–6). When the poor masses turn into an imagined Red Revolutionary army, the scene has the tinge of nightmare. It ends with the modern gothic line of: "In that pent track of living death – the city's cruel street." "Andy's Gone with Cattle," of the same year, is a lighter, more comic lyric, with its reference to Andy's "cheerful face." Its shorter lines make for a more optimistic rhythm, underscoring the hope of Andy's return. Both the sublime and the gothic can seem to be outside of Christianity, yet it is the Christian inflection that hints at the afterlife – the elsewhere – of heaven that gives the poem its hints of the sublime in the final stanza: "And may good angels send the rain / On desert stretches sandy; / And when the summer comes again / God grant 'twill bring us Andy" (7). Although Andy is "looking old and jaded" in the sequel "Andy's Return," he is "hearty yet." Nevertheless there is an ethereal tone of the eternal: "We'll be happy for ever / When he'll no longer roam, / But by some deep, cool river / Will make us all a home" (8).

A nostalgic long-lined (fifteen-syllable) ballad by Lawson, "The Shanty on the Rise" (57–58), about a beloved drinking hole, also verges on the morbid. Set upon the mountains in "the careless days that died," the "Shanty" is kept by a landlord referred to only as "Something-in-Disguise." Further ironies emerge with the second stanza as "[c]ity swells ... would have called the Shanty low." Having "vanished," settlement cannot really be thought, except as already post-: "And, upon the very centre of the greenest spot that lies / In my fondest recollection stands the Shanty on the Rise." The Shanty is a fiction that lies, like all romances, and is elevated, put on high, because it is in the speaker's mind, as if colonisation itself is a dream.

Banjo Paterson (1864–1941) is perhaps the most versatile of the nineteenth-century poets, producing the comedy of "Clancy of the Overflow," the thrills of the horse chase, "The Man from Snowy River," and the maudlin gothicism of "Waltzing Matilda" (67–69). Being (like Gordon), an able horse rider, meant Paterson had a certain, albeit mediated, agency with regard to the land. D. A. Russell translates Longinus, in a phrase that evokes Emily Dickinson, that *"whatever knocks the reader out* is sublime" (xiii). He adds that "[a]ny subject which can genuinely excite is capable of being handled in a 'sublime' way" (xiv), which is perhaps a more mundane version of Jean-Luc Nancy's claim that the "sublime is the destiny of art" (Ferguson 18). In such terms, Paterson excels in bringing exciting narrative together with topographical description. "The Man from Snowy River" is highly popular, still recited at bush festivals today, and depicted on the Australian ten-dollar note. The poem builds suspense as reader follows rider going up and down steep terrain. Its narrative dialectic, between the broken, ridden horses and those that are 'wild' and free, displaces consideration of Indigenous dispossession with a settler Romance. Yet this scene of the horse chase is not easily read as an imperial one; and Paterson's mention of the danger of wombat holes reminds us that we are nowhere else but Australia.

An implication of my argument (if we read Paterson in Russell's terms), of an apparent inability, or ultimate unwillingness, of this poem to settle on the land, is that if "The Man from Snowy River" is exciting enough, it is sublime, and therefore unsettled, but if it is not exciting, it is colonising and murderous. The poem is clearly about excitement: that of the riders who want to bring the station colt back from the wild herd, but also of their horses: "the stockhorse snuffs the battle with delight" (220). The second stanza contrasts up and down through Harrison, who rode best when his "blood was fairly up," and Clancy of the Overflow, who "came down to lend a hand" (221). These named characters provide both foil to and assessment of the "Man." Clancy defends the "Man," against Harrison, who advises the "Man" to stay behind, having made a poor estimation of the "Man['s]" horse (221). They follow the wild horses into "gorges deep and black," but the brumbies gallop "upward, ever upward" (222) towards the mountain's summit. Up hills and down towards gullies, the "Man" continues the chase while others stay and watch. The peak of the Snowy Mountains, Kosciusko, the highest mountain in Australia, is referred to in the final stanza, where, in a reversal of the Gospel of John, the fleshly "Man" is bathetically made a (household) word.

Paterson's internationally known "Waltzing Matilda," a ballad, tells the tale of a swagman, or hobo, who steals a sheep and drowns to avoid capture. Eve Kosofsky Sedgwick views "live burial" as a "gothic convention" (9) and this may extend to drowning, especially if the body is not recovered. That the swagman's voice ("voice" in the "original version" and "ghost" in the "popular version" 68; 69) "may [still] be heard" (68) enforces this gothic, dead but alive, aspect. This gothic trope appears in poems by Lawson, Gordon and Barcroft Boake (1826–92), and may assume reversal through the unburied dead. To lie on the land unburied is perhaps the most unsettling image conjured by Christian culture. Yet there is a squeamishly comic version of this scenario in Alexander Montgomery's ballad, "A Curious Reminiscence," which is introduced by his speaker as being: "Of all the awful bloomin' things, the awfullest I've knowed" (Stewart and Keesing 163–65): a couple of drunk men refuse to believe "Old Doolan" has just died and march him up to the bar, and try to make him drink.

While this chapter seeks to literalise, and ambiguously 'ground,' notions of unsettlement in its relations of land and colonisation, it is here, in the image of the settler dead – and of their bodies undead and unalive – that settler gothic fictions join most crucially to unsettlement in its affective aspect (Farrell 7). In Lawson's "The Men Who Made Australia," the buried and unburied dead unite, to embody a wakening national spirit. Andrew Smith discerns: "The dead ... occupy an unusual space in the Gothic because they repeatedly fail to function as sources of horror" (194). In Boake's "Where the Dead Men Lie" (Stewart and Keesing 93–95) the lamenting refrain ("That's where the dead mean lie") builds a cumulative feeling that is both threatening and perversely inviting. In "Waltzing Matilda," the (now patriotically celebrated) voice of the swagman – if not his body – remains alive, and, presumably, above water, asking us to revel in an ambiguous (because metaphorical but also because the original version ends with "[w]-ho'll come a-waltzing") dance of death: "You'll come a-waltzing Matilda with me" (Paterson 67–69).

The song itself is a siren, then. A more direct appropriation of a siren figure appears in "Lorelei," an 1874 translation by Catherine Martin (1848–1937) from Heinrich Heine's German original, "Die Lorelei." Heine's poem brings the sublime and gothic together in its figure by contrasting the Rhine (Rhein, in German), where the boatmen will drown, with the mountain where the siren Lorelei sings. In Martin's translation: "The mountain's height against heaven / Gleams in the late sunshine." This image might be considered sublime – if we have fear of heights, or God, or of the death which heaven implies. The sublime is further consolidated by the notes of Lorelei's song, which "are sweet and manifold, / As they rise loud and long" (245). Not only is the man's exact fate unsettled, in being unknown, it cannot be presumed even to culminate in any particular national riverbed, as the river flows through six European countries before entering the North Sea, from the Netherlands.

Similar themes appear in "A Fragment." Martin's speaker compares a forest in a storm to "waves wind-driven," while the leaves that lie on the ground are described as: "Borne by the wind from the nooks where they lay dead ... Finding no refuge, driven to and fro, / While their frail forms more meagre hourly grow." From here an explicitly human analogy is made to grief and memory. Waves return, in an altered metaphor: "Hav[ing] swept dear comrades to unnoted graves" (159). Finally, arrival in the Promised Land of the Old Testament is evoked, but as an empty promise, because of the memory of those who were lost on the journey. All this is an analogy to the grief that tinges the supposed happiness of a fulfilled life – yet is also readily available for those migrants of the mid-nineteenth century who found refuge in Australia (Martin herself arrived in South Australia from Scotland aged eight), but left loved ones behind, either in the land they came from – or in the sea. None of the poem's dead appear to be buried: they haunt the memory of the living; they roll in the "unnoted graves" of seabeds. The poem's theme of the importance of friendship is consistent with the conclusion – in German – of Martin's extended dedication to *The Explorers and Other Poems* (which includes both poems): "Who does not see the world in his friends does not deserve the world to know from him." Such a sentiment separates the idea of the world from that of the earth, and provides a clue to the images of the impossibility of settlement by Australian settler poets.

How might the sublime and/or the gothic be understood in less conventional, lesser known nineteenth-century texts that push how we understand the poetic? These include Christopher Brennan's belatedly published *Musicopoematographoscopes* (1981), Jong Ah Sing's diary "The Case," the prose poetics of Ann Williams and Sarah Davenport, and the drawing-poems of Aboriginal/Irish stockman, Charlie Flannigan. To consider the drawing-poems of Flannigan (d. 1893) within European poetics frameworks is to make a categorical shift but not an absolute one. Flannigan is not a settler, yet his Irish ancestry, the presence of the Roman alphabet and of English words, in the poems being composed (on imported paper – paper production in Australia did not commence until 1895) means that there is a relationality between Flannigan's poems and settler texts (Christopherson suggests that the lettering is imitated from the covers of *Punch* magazine (Tetlow and Byrne)), as well as with the long history of Indigenous art. That this relationality is forced is not immediately apparent in works like the "Song Fellow" and "Rodeo" poems (Tetlow and Byrne; Farrell 193–94), yet they would be created while Flannigan was in the Northern Territory's Fannie Bay gaol, in shackles and handcuffs, awaiting sentence for the murder of a 'master stockman' he worked – and argued – with, and for which he is finally hanged. What is not so easily apparent, at least to a settler reader, is the violence of such relationality itself, which, in his works, Flannigan solves as an artistic problem.

Both drawing-poems make use of high and low spaces: in one, the words "Song Fellow" float above the drawing of station buildings, as if the now-condemned Flannigan can float his word-self above the cares of his depicted everyday – and of his present circumstances. In the other, there is a division – possibly a rail – between the horse rider and audience; in the upper half of the drawing, capitalised letters and human figures cavort. The rider of the horse also appears above this line, while the horse appears below. The letters seem to form connected parts of a vine: humans swing on the vine, and possibly play wind instruments (or smoke exaggerated cigars). One human is a head only. The line also divides a tree: branches above and trunk below. The tree's leaves also serve as an emu's body. Capitalising on the dynamics of the visual, Flannigan makes a compelling image of life in flux, as never settled.

There is something sublimely narcissistic about looking into the past and seeing the contemporary – or even the future. Consider the now-canonical tones of Dickinson's terrifying scraps, or the beautifully cadenced threats of bushranger Ned Kelly: "I wish to acquaint you with some of the occurrences of the present past and future" (1). German art critic Jan Verwoert claims that: "This is why the moment you put a foot inside the sublime archive you know that the archive has already survived you. You are as good as dead" (Kékesi 65). Yet, using Derrida's idea of encryption, Frances Ferguson also discerns that the act of reading a work as art contains it: "I neutralize, or encrypt, its existence" (20).

Up until his death at Sunbury Asylum, Jong Ah Sing (c.1837–1900) and his unpublished diary, "The Case," were in gothic parallel. "The Case" was written between 1867 and 1872 during his incarceration in Yarra Bend Asylum, and deposited at the State Library of Victoria in 1880. His asylum sentence was an alternative to gaol, following a knife fight (over a hen) with other Chinese men in the Victorian goldfields. Written in English or, according to Shen, a hybrid of English language and Cantonese syntax (22), "The Case" is part of the history of English literature, where to be shut up in an asylum – or convent, room in a house, or castle – is a familiar gothic trope. Jong does not live on flat ground; he goes down to the creek for water; down a hole to smoke opium; and up the hill to diggings. "The Case" presents his life of mining and later imprisonment; the continuation of his story beyond it can only be speculated on. While appearing to be a journal immediately preceding the fracas, and Jong's subsequent imprisonment, "The Case" is referred to as a novel on its first page (and more generally as "CRANKEY NONSENSE"). As explicitly mentioned in its opening narrative, Jong is concerned with the ground – digging it up in the search for gold, unsettling it. He also refers to making a vegetable garden (4). As a Chinese settler, Jong is to some extent outside the English colonial world. While it is, I argue, a sublime text of major poetic importance, it does not appear to have the same unsettled aspect of the lyric poems considered thus far. The ground is the ground, or "MY=SITDOWN=BUSH" (11).

The handwritten facsimile, of the three-part "Musicopoematographoscope" (1897; the plurally titled book contains this, and a shorter "Pocket" version) by Christopher Brennan (1870–1932), has discernible sublime features: its first-page poster-style announcements, its large capital letters, its escalating numbers of exclamation marks, as well as the second page's call for "no audience," and in its difficulty: its multi-linearity; the syntactic abysses of its Mallarméan pastiche; and the concluding collage-parody of Brennan's critics. Having been retrieved from the archive and published by Brennan's biographer, Axel Clark, the buried alive aspect of *Musicopoematographoscopes* is, like that of all such retrieved texts, brought into gothic relief. The archival death, the death that kills death (Smith 14), is paradoxically implicated in the texts' posthumous life after death of being published. The work's visual appearance, deliberately echoing Stéphane Mallarmé's poem "Un Coup de Des," suggests a reading practice which self-consciously reads up and down the work's oversized page, in an up–down prosody that formally explodes conventional reading practice, and parodies the rise and fall of the narrative arc. Yet it is this marginalised experimentalism that condemns it to the archive, while the traditional work that it transcends continues to be recited and reprinted.

Adam Lindsay Gordon (1833–70) killed himself with a shotgun on Brighton beach in Melbourne. The narrator of his perfectly titled "The Sick Stockrider" (1870) also writes his own, gentler – yet gothic – ending. Getting off his horse, the Stockrider reminisces with his companion, Ned, about their heyday – and the changes (including the deaths of others) time has wrought. Reverie concluded, the Stockrider turns to the present and future, observing that as "[t]he deep blue skies wax dusky, and the tall green trees grow dim" he desires to "slumber in the hollow where the wattle blossoms wave / With never stone or rail to fence my bed." He concludes that: "Should the sturdy station children pull the bush flowers on my grave, / I may chance to hear them romping overhead" (7). Later editing the poem, Gordon gave it an extra eight lines. The first four of these provide further ambiguities about sleep, death, and the ground, heading towards generality, and away from the immediate circumstance:

> I don't suppose I shall, though, for I feel like sleeping sound,
> That sleep they say is doubtful. True; but yet
> At least it makes no difference to the dead man underground
> What the living men remember or forget.   (PoemHunter)

The authorised ending of Gordon's poem takes advantage of the sleep/death metaphor to suggest that the Stockrider might not be completely dead, and may still be able to hear in his "slumber." Life and light fail together (the failure of light also being a gothic trope, according to Francesco de Sanctis (41)). Sanctis's further contention that "[t]he ugly as well as the beautiful dies away in the sublime" (211) sounds like a theme for Gordon's poem. That the children may soon be desecrating, dancing on, even, the Stockrider's grave, is seen as liveliness rather than wickedness; yet without straining the image too far, they also seem to embody the mindlessness of colonialism. The children's pleasure-seeking – their high spirits – are not quite the image of settlement, but they are that of possession. A nation, Tzvetan Todorov asserts (citing French writers Renan and Barres), is "a cult of ancestors," an "ancient cemetery" (229). While we can see such a "cult" emerging, in its various versions, in the formation of the Australian national imaginary, an "ancient cemetery" cannot be produced through passing legislation, any more than through taking possession.

Lucy Frost, twentieth-century editor of Ann Williams and Sarah Davenport, describes the effusive style of certain educated writers of the nineteenth century as "'bad' ... contrived ... silly and obscure ... almost unreadable," while Williams' "spare directness and laconic tone," her "grammatical faults," are "familiar to a modern ear": the reader can "imagine quite precisely what her journey was like" (214). The journey referred to takes place in October 1882, and consists of three weeks travelling, within New South Wales, from Queanbeyan to Moruya, with husband, small child, bullock team, horses, and belongings. With Frost, we might imagine that a literary writer, with a conscious desire to afford the reader a taste of the sublime, would have approached the following quite differently:

> 2nd day Saturday morning Saw the commet this Morning and it is beautifull I never saw anything like it it rises about 4 oclock in the Morning (215)

It's arguable that Williams is unable to rise above unintentional bathos and could not get to grips with the sublime if she tried. Yet there is always something bathetic about representation, in that it is never the thing itself, never the sublime pitch of feeling absolutely alive. It could also be objected that if Williams participates in the sublime, then what writer doesn't? Perhaps none, perhaps Williams' short text is a limit of the greater text of the colonial sublime. However, it does touch on aspects of the sublime: the cosmic; the sublime of bushfire (she gets a fright when her campfire catches the bark of a nearby gum tree); the "big snake" she sees, and the sublime of colonial despair (217; 218).

The sublime is not an inevitable category; it does not exist outside of the idea of it. Williams' text is a reminder of the privilege of sublime experience, when her concern with the "Mountain" is not the mountain itself, nor her sensibility, but rather the difficulty of getting a bullock team around it (219–20). Her text, at moments, also represents a nineteenth-century version of the comic anti-sublime:

> I forgot to mention in my yesterdays travels that I saw the big sea but I would not have noticed it if Tom had not have told me that it was it it looked to me like a flat plain with distant mountains in the back and as I thought white houses but upon viewing it more closely I see that it was white foam on the rocks but I must go on with todays travels ... (225)

As satire it would be worthy of Beckett. Yet she is not a fictional ditherer, but a woman of action: she goes on to describe herself catching a runaway filly on horseback (226).

Sarah Davenport is similarly "a woman of ... pluck" (Frost 238). As she states in her "Sceth [Sketch] of an emigrants Life in austrailia from Leiving England in the year of our Lord 1841," Davenport, with her family, left Manchester for Liverpool on 4 October, and sailed for Australia three days later: "we was in all good hopes that we was coming to beeter [better] ourselves" (239). They only get as far as Hoylake, however, before their ship is wrecked, and they lose most of their belongings. When they set sail again later in the month, her baby is accidentally scalded by another passenger, and dies two days later. Davenport then goes into premature labour: "that babe was throne in the sea i was almost Dumb with grief" (242).

Here, concisely, are examples of settler trauma, yet a later scene shows Davenport's role in a more complex anecdote of racism, abuse, possession and dispossession, comedy and tragedy. A friend of Davenport's, also poor, is involved in a lawsuit for some property, but her young son has hidden a page of the document that proves her right to it. Davenport writes, "we knew he was affaraid of the blaks," so when he is "strip[p]ed" for his bath, she gets "some blaking and a brush" and threatens him: "i will black you all over ... and i will give you to the blaks." She begins to "blak his boddy" – the boy screams and gives up the parchment's hiding place (246). The entanglement of this scene in British dispossession of Aboriginal land, of the history of race relations between white settlers, including the Stolen Generations (when Indigenous children were taken from their parents into settlements, and given to white families), is too complicated to investigate here. The sublime and the gothic are entangled also. Sanctis writes, "the ugly is sublime when it offends our moral and our aesthetic sense and throws us into strong reaction" (211). With its racism, property dispute, and abuse of a child, Davenport's text is an ugly scene for contemporary readers. Davenport takes on sublime figuring in her own representation, yet while considering the struggle between darkness and light, the naked boy's being covered in blacking, and the crucial role of the hidden, it is also a gothic scene.

Does reading Davenport's (and Williams', and Jong's) texts as poetry "neutralise" and "encrypt" their "existence"? What then, would be the loss, or gain? This is not virtue, nor ethics. Rather, it is just that it is not the poet's job to bolster any human project (although Mead would suggest otherwise (400)), but rather to ironise it: to reimagine it. It may be, then, that the seeds of ethics, and of the task of reconciliation (between settlers and those whose sovereignty of the land has been severely disrupted by colonisation), lie in this very (nineteenth-century) irony, the seeds of which are alive in the archive.

Works Cited

Adorno, Theodor W. *Notes on Literature*, edited by Rolf Tiedemann and translated by Shierry Weber Nicholson. Columbia University Press, 2019.

Axton, Paul. "The Sublime Experience of God." *Forging Ploughshares: Cultivating the Peaceable Kingdom*, 5 November 2020. https://forgingploughshares.org/2020/11/05/the-sublime-experience-of-god/.

Birdlife Australia. "Bell Miner: Manorina melanophrys, Meliphagidae." www.birdlife.org.au/bird-profile/bell-miner.

Bloom, Harold. *Ruin the Sacred Truths: Poetry and Belief from the Bible to the Present*. Harvard University Press, 1991.

Brennan, Christopher. *Musicopoematographoscope & Pocket Musicopoematographoscope*, edited by Axel Clark. Hale & Ironmonger, 1981.

Clemens, Justin. "Barron Field and the Myth of Terra Nullius." *The Monthly*, October 2018. www.themonthly.com.au/magazine/october-2018.

Currey, C. H. "Barron Field (1786–1846)." *Australian Dictionary of Biography*. https://adb.anu.edu.au/biography/field-barron-2041.

Farrell, Michael. *Writing Australian Unsettlement: Modes of Poetic Invention 1796–1945*. Palgrave Macmillan, 2015.

Ferguson, Frances. *Solitude and the Sublime: Romanticism and the Aesthetics of Individuation*. Routledge, 1992.

Field, Barron. "The Kangaroo." *First Fruits of Australian Poetry*. George Howe, 1819. Reprinted in *Australian Poetry Library*. www.poetrylibrary.edu.au/poets/field-barron/poems/the-kangaroo-0017002.

Flaubert, Gustave. *The Letters of Gustave Flaubert 1830–1857*, edited and translated by Francis Steegmuller. Faber, 1981.

Frost, Lucy. *No Place for a Nervous Lady: Voices from the Australian Bush*. McPhee Gribble, 1985.

Gilmore, Mary. "Old Botany Bay." *Freedom on the Wallaby: Poems of the Australian People*, edited by Marjorie Pizer. Pinchgut Press, 1953, p. 145.

Gordon, Adam Lindsay. "The Sick Stockrider." *The Australasian*, 15 January 1870, p. 7.

"The Sick Stockrider." PoemHunter. www.poemhunter.com/poem/the-sick-stockrider/.

Harpur, Charles. "The Kangaroo Hunt; or, A Morning in the Mountains: A Descriptive Poem in Six Parts." *The Australian Home Companion and Band of Hope Journal*, 6 October 1860. https://trove.nla.gov.au/newspaper/article/72484897/6758409.

The Poetical Works of Charles Harpur, edited by Elizabeth Perkins. Angus & Robertson, 1984.

Hartman, Geoffrey. "Evening Star and Evening Land." *Post-structuralist Readings of English Poetry*, edited by Richard Machin and Christopher Norris. Cambridge University Press, 1987, pp. 264–93.

Kékesi, Zoltán. *Agents of Liberations: Holocaust Memory in Contemporary Art and Documentary Film*. Central University Press, 2015.

Kelly, Ned. *The Jerilderie Letter*, edited by Alex McDermott. Text Publishing, 2001.

Kendall, Henry. *Leaves from Australian Forests: Poetical Works of Henry Kendall*. 1869. Reprinted by Rigby, 1975.

Lawson, Henry. *Poems*. Angus & Robertson, 2000.

Longinus. *On the Sublime*, translated by D. A. Russell. Clarendon Press, 1965.

Martin, Catherine. *The Explorers and Other Poems*. George Robertson, 1874.

Mead, Philip. *Networked Language: Culture and History in Australian Poetry*. North Australian Scholarly, 2008.

Mickiewicz, Adam. *Poems*, edited by George Rapall Noyes. Herald Square Press, 1944.

Moretti, Franco. *Graphs, Maps, Trees: Abstract Models for a Literary History*. Verso, 2005.

Murray, Les. *A Working Forest.* Duffy & Snellgrove, 1997.
Paterson, A. B (Banjo). *The Penguin Banjo Paterson: Collected Verse.* Penguin, 1993.
Sanctis, Francesco de. *History of Italian Literature.* Vol. 1. Translated by Joan Redfern. Harcourt, Brace, 1931.
Savige, Jaya. "'Creation's Holiday': On Silence and Monsters in Australian Poetry." *Poetry* vol.208 no.2, May 2016, pp. 169–84.
Schur, Owen. *Victorian Pastoral: Tennyson, Hardy, and the Subversion of Forms.* Ohio State University Press, 1989.
Sedgwick, Eve Kosofksy. *The Coherence of Gothic Conventions.* Methuen, 1986.
Shen, Yuanfang. *Dragon Seed in the Antipodes.* Melbourne University Press, 2001.
Smith, Andrew. *Gothic Death 1740–1914: A Literary History.* Manchester University Press, 2016.
Stewart, Douglas and Nancy Keesing, eds. *Favourite Bush Ballads.* Angus & Robertson, 1977.
Tetlow, Miranda and Conor Byrne. "Charlie Flannigan's Death-Row Art Tells the Story of NT's First Hanged Man." *ABC Radio Darwin*, 10 March 2021. www.abc.net.au/news/2021-03-10/charlie-flannigan-fannie-bay-gaol-death-row-drawings-exhibition/13227854.
Todorov, Tzvetan. *On Human Diversity: Nationalism, Racism, and Exoticism in French Thought*, translated by Catherine Porter. Harvard University Press, 1993.
Unaipon, David. *Legendary Tales of the Australian Aborigines*, edited by Stephen Muecke and Adam Shoemaker. Miegunyah, 2006.

5

KATIE HANSORD

Romanticism, Sensibility, and Settler Women Poets

Settler women poets in nineteenth-century Australia have been overlooked in the masculinist projects of nation and empire building, and excluded or marginalised in the studies of Australian literature and Romantic poetry. These are not unrelated. Yet shifts in scholarship towards more global understandings of Romanticism have necessitated, as Carmen Casaliggi and Porscha Fermanis point out, "less teleological ways of thinking about periodicity and ... the inclusion of previously neglected and less easily accommodated writers" (viii). Rather than simply recuperate Australian women poets within a Romantic tradition, this chapter considers how they mobilised and extended both Romantic sensibility and the figure of the poetess to navigate the complex dynamic between liminality and voice. I argue that it is through the influence of and engagements with Romantic women's writing in Europe that the articulations of early settler women rights in Australian settler poetry can be better understood.

Challenges to ongoing gender-based exclusions from public intellectual and literary discourses, political rights, financial independence, and patriarchal domination typically involve shifting and interconnected relationships to sensibility and Romanticism.

The harnessing of both Romantic rights discourse and the particularly lively forums of colonial newspapers and periodicals meant that settler women poets were quite successful in entering public debates and offering new viewpoints on issues of justice and gender difference. This chapter examines how their adaptation of Romanticism differed from male counterparts, connecting with a female tradition that extended from Europe to North America and even to Japan. It considers how they reworked Romantic tropes around liminality and negativity to advocate freedom and social transformation for settler women living in precarity and how they also explored affective registers that extended beyond sympathy. Sampling writers like Mary Bailey, Eliza Dunlop, Caroline Leakey, and Ada Cambridge, this chapter demonstrates how their response to colonial and patriarchal structures may have been limited yet remains important for understanding the transnational flows and gendering of nineteenth-century Australian literary history.

Although subsequently absent in Australian and European literary canons, there were many settler women who wrote poetry in nineteenth-century Australia. Their work was well represented in newspapers and periodicals and some were even able to produce full poetry collections. Their poetry was often connected by themes and stylistic approaches signalling their engagements with developing rights discourses, especially through a Romantic proto-feminist poetics that extended across national boundaries and imperial networks. This poetics rallied around a political discourse on the 'domestic affections.' The positioning of women within marriage and the family was understood to be a model of political paternalism and spoke to gender-based exclusions from full political rights. Such patriarchal control was critiqued by Mary Wollstonecraft in *A Vindication of the Rights of Woman* (1792), and her ideas were crucial to the development of a female Romantic tradition. Wollstonecraft publicly advocated for a paradigm shift from the concept of the authority of the father to that of the welfare of the child as a locus for questions of social advancement (Mellor 38).

In focusing on 'domestic affections,' settler women poets like Eliza Hamilton Dunlop, Mary Bailey, and Caroline Leakey focused on themes of exile and transportation, but often linked them closely to the Romantic tropes of the 'fallen woman' or the death of the illegitimate baby. As Aileen Moreton-Robinson points out, Romantic proto-feminist poetics were "predicated on sex and gender differences" that resulted in the "creation of the universal woman" who was white, middle class, heterosexual, and whose life was primarily oppressed through patriarchy. In such a model, "white women's race privilege, conferred by association with white men, remains invisible" (33). Accordingly, early feminists like Wollstonecraft and Harriet Taylor "were not writing about the black or Indigenous women in Britain's colonies" (34).

It is important to recognise that even as they approached questions of gender, class, and precarity, the writing of settler women still presumed and was complicit with colonialism. Literary resistance by white women in nineteenth-century Australia manifested in gender-conscious challenges around the punitive and exclusionary aspects of settler society. Poetic responses drew upon discourses centred around so-called fallen womanhood, prisoner rights, and the financial dependency within heterosexual marriage. They also navigated questions of liminality and negativity, as a political program around the domestic affections widened in scope. Claire Knowles suggests that for these women "the performance of sensibility often offer[ed] women an important point of entry in the public literary sphere by bridging the gap between the material and the literary," and discerns that "an impassioned eighteenth-century language of sensibility metamorphose[d] into a domesticated nineteenth-century rhetoric of sentiment" (13).

Ann Vickery has pointed out that the trope of the female convict became a screen for British Romantic women writers to explore the parameters of their own authorial agency, citing L.E.L.'s "The Female Convict" in her popular collection, *The Improvisatrice and Other Poems* (1825). There was far less agency within convict literature itself. Vickery discusses an example of a letter that "measures a woman's cultural capital in the new world by the status of her virtue." She concludes: "Already there is a subtext of the female convict, particularly pregnant and abandoned, as unable to be recuperated as a civil subject." Women's sexuality outside of marriage tended to be "presented in much literature as a situation belonging to working-class women only, while middle-class women were widely associated with 'purity' and the domestic ideal" (73).

Yet fears around the consequences of female sexual desire meant that the 'fallen woman' became accentuated as a middle-class anxiety. Eliza Hamilton Dunlop's poetry reveals complex relationships to eighteenth- and nineteenth-century discourses around ideas of sensibility, class, women's rights, and the domestic ideal. Domestic affections and the domestic ideal in the nineteenth century increasingly equated the idealised middle-class woman with the home, love, and emotional sensitivity while conversely equating men with public life, commerce, and reason. This meant that critiques of gendered exclusions from citizenship and associated rights could be addressed through themes of precarity and sensibility as relating to collective experiences. An emotional liminality blurred boundaries between aspects of acceptable feminine sympathy, with expressions of sadness, fear, and hope being part of emotional ranges extending from the concept of domestic affections, love, and concepts of sympathy that could include expressions of anger and distress at injustices.

Dunlop experienced being a young single mother in Ireland, following the death of her first husband, James Sylvius Law. When her barrister father died in India in 1820, Dunlop's inheritance never eventuated (De Salis n. pag.). Increasingly negative attitudes towards women's sexuality due to a perceived link to 'sexual deviance' led to a focus on the trope of the female convict or exile in women's rights writing. Although she soon remarried, to David Dunlop, Dunlop's poem "The Dream" (published in 1838 as the first of her "Songs of an Exile" series in the *Australian*) draws on common themes of exile in relation to ideas of sin, exile, social exclusion, and atonement. The poem emphasises memory and feeling as connected to social punishment amid a financial fall, an experience clearly recalling 'fallen woman' narratives:

> Regret, and sorrow, past revealing.
> The dead, the dead! I heard her speak!
> I heard, the fond maternal blessing!
> And felt the tear, that wet her cheek!
> Her thoughtless, loving girl, caressing.
> Youth—fortune—friends—and love were mine,
> How could I dread of future danger?
> Or think, that at the world's cold shrine—
> I e'er should bow—a friendless stranger! (2)

Human feeling and emotion are contrasted, especially through ideas of maternal care and sorrow, with "the world's cold shrine." Dunlop subverts any redemptive responsibility from the "thoughtless, loving girl" to the unfeeling and cold public sphere.

The relationship between ideas of punishment, morality, sexuality, and capital were frequently signified by the figure of the poetess as colonial 'exile' and the metaphor of women's transportation. As Vickery discerns,

> Significantly, the British penal system, and transportation in particular, was designed to remove a subject's past identity and any agency attached to that identity – convict women were sent to Australia without their children and their previous marital status generally rendered irrelevant. Even free female emigrants had little claim to individualised identity and agency. (72)

For poets like Dunlop, this was understood as a collectively gendered experience. The figure of the poetess as an individual but interchangeable figure with other women was understood as a part of the broader Romantic movement that contested the patriarchal doctrine of separate spheres for men and women. Anne Mellor suggests that many women writers articulated a very different domestic ideology. Defining it as a feminine Romanticism, she adds:

> They proclaimed the value of rational love, an ethic of care, and gender equality as a challenge both to a domestic ideology that would confine women within the home and to a capitalist laissez-faire system that would set the rights of the individual, free will, or rational choice, and an ethic of justice above the needs of the community as a whole. (84)

Operating through the separate spheres in order to demonstrate the limits of its ideology, their 'feminine' poetics often invoked and centred around the concept of a wider circle of women. In this, they would extend Wordsworth's and Coleridge's concept of the poet's bardic power to the figure of the 'poetess,' whose expressive channelling generated sympathy and a call to action.

Such writing challenged individualist patriarchal authority, notably in relation to building arguments around enfranchisement and personhood through democratic ideals. Mellor further points out that within Romantic women's writing in England:

> Some reversed the political dynamic of the literature of sensibility. Rather than allowing the public realm to usurp the prerogatives and values of the private realm, they recolonized the public sphere under the governance of women and feminine virtue, celebrating the social and political domination of a domestic sphere located either in an idealised version of the feudal past or in a utopian future ... Others denied the moral and thus legal legitimacy of the public sphere altogether. (9–10)

Caroline Leakey describes her own poetry in the preface to her volume *Lyra Australis; Or, Attempts to Sing in a Strange Land* (1854) as being, in part, "wild and wilful." It's a phrase that allows for an affective range that encompasses anger, rage, madness, despair, and mourning. She states that her poetry is to better show "the spirit of trustfulness and resignation" (v) but in doing so throws into some doubt what is trusted and what resigned. Instead it centralises a feminist resistance to the social standing of the 'fallen woman,' and the social, financial, and literal legal punishments such women faced, with ideas of exile and transportation as its theme:

> They drive her back in vain to weep, —
> A twice made exile from the gate, —
> And doubly feel the sins which keep,
> Her wand'ring yet, and desolate   (175–79)

In framing the concept of sympathy through domestic Christian language, and as related to understanding, hope, connection, and generosity, Leakey positioned her writing against the sexual double standard while remaining mired in its constructs. Her articulations of emotional and psychological suffering connect to a Romantic women's poetics concerned with the injustice faced by women imprisoned or 'exiled' for sexual 'deviance,' and unwed mothers without support, who often died alone, or died by suicide, without access to any social or financial supports.

Mary Bailey married Reverend William Bailey in 1832, and in 1844, she and her son followed her husband to Tasmania when he was transported for life after a conviction for forgery of a promissory note in favour of his sister. Bailey's poetry can also be understood as part of a nineteenth-century imperial feminist approach that advocated institutional inclusion through the values of domestic affections and education. Besides writing on exile, she would also write on the classics, bluestocking identity, and later nineteenth-century feminists like Anna Jameson. Bailey's concerns with rights discourses included prisoner rights, often operating through a 'feminised morality.' In one poem, she articulates devotion to her husband, whose morality she felt could never be tainted by his transportation, as this was a reflection on the immorality of British authorities. Writing under her initials M.B. to the *Colonial Times* in 1847, she clarified details of "Roman Charity." She points to the story of Cimon and Pero, "that matron of Rome, who provided, in the yearnings of a daughter's love, from her own bosom, continuing sustenance for her *famishing* father, condemned by his judges to the awful death of starvation in a prison!" (16 February 1847, 3).

Bailey published poetry collections in England, including *The Months and Other Poems* (1822), *Palmyra* (1833), and *Musae Sacrae* (1835), as well as the prose *Reflections, Doctrinal, Practical and Devotional, Upon the Litany of the Church of England* (1833). Her writing appeared in London reviews and *Blackwood's Edinburgh Magazine* (1817–1980). Bailey's work is particularly associated with the *Colonial Times*, although her poetry appeared in other newspapers, including the *Hobart Town Courier* (1827–39), which became the *Courier* (1839–59), the *Geelong Advertiser and Squatters' Advocate* (1845–47), and the *Hobarton Guardian* (1847–54). Her later writings appeared in the Sydney *Freeman's Journal* (1850–1932), a Catholic newspaper. Bailey continued to publish poetry, particularly religious poetry, after her arrival in Sydney in 1858. From 1853 onwards she signed herself Mary Elizabeth Bailey rather than M.B. and began publishing poems under this name in the *Freeman's Journal* in the mid-1850s (the first seems to have been titled "Rome As It Was and Is," published in the *Freeman's Journal*). In 1853, Bailey wrote to the editor of the *Hobarton Guardian* during a period when it was edited by her husband:

> Sir, — I beg your insertion of the subjoined translation in your journal. I had hitherto adopted, invariably, the signature and address of "M.B., Sandy Bay" and I had thus, for several years, forwarded, to most portions of our colonial press, numerous miscellaneous contributions in prose and verse. (3)

Her attached poem, "Dies Irae translated from the original Latin in the Roman missal" was, for the first time, signed "Mary Elizabeth Bailey, Hobart Town, Macquarie Street." She adds that she had spent "almost the entire of my life a solitary invalid" (3). This description is the only mention she seems to make of personal experience of disability and no further details are given. Her decision to publish under her full name, although it was widely known that "M.B." was a woman, suggests her desire to be known as a woman writer. She appears to have moved from Hobart sometime between February and May of 1858, and from May her publications begin to be signed "Sydney" rather than "Hobart."

These later poems were published with her change of signature from "M.B." to "Mary Elizabeth Bailey." Following her conversion to Catholicism in 1855, Bailey published in the Sydney *Freeman's Journal*. Her poem "Sisters of Charity" (1858) can be read in relation to contemporary debates around women's work outside of the home and ideas of *Woman's Mission*, as well as Bailey's imperially inflected feminist approach to rights that related to financial hardship. Soon after its publication, William Bailey was reported on 10 March 1858 to be insolvent, a probable reason for their move from Hobart. As a convict transported for life, he was granted a pardon conditional on his remaining in the colonies. Bailey's earlier poetic practice was often concerned with translation, including hymns like "Hymn for Christmas Day," which appeared in the *Colonial Times*.

Bailey's "Verses: Written upon the author's recent reception into the Catholic Church at St Joseph's Hobart Town" (1855) marks the shift in her later poetry towards grappling with the separate spheres doctrine. Constance Buchanan has pointed to the tendency for religion to be associated wholly with the private sphere in reappraisals of nineteenth-century women's writing. However, the increased religiosity in much women's poetry during this period reflects a shift in women's poetry towards resolving problems associated with affective poetry. British Victorian women poets like Adelaide Procter and Alice Meynell also converted to Catholicism. The sales of Procter's "A Chaplet of Verses" (1862) raised money for the Sisters of Charity. Anna Jameson's lecture on the "Sisters of Charity" (1855) expresses similar concerns to Bailey's poem, and Jameson was also friends with Procter. As with Procter and Meynell, there is a move away from an earlier Romantic Hellenism, which focused much more overtly on questions of gender equality and white women's rights.

In "Sisters of Charity" (1858), and an attached note, Bailey discusses Florence Nightingale, and the Sisters of Charity to signal debates around women's professionalisation and public agency within women's movements:

> Sisters of heavenly Love! for others' woe
> Your tears of sympathetic suffering flow!
> Your bosoms pierced at sight of human grief;
> The friendly hand, stretched forth to bring relief—
> Unbought, unasked, in sorrow's darkest hour,
> *Then* most is seen your Faith's all-conquering power!
> 'Tis yours to stand around the dying bed
> With Christian love to stay the sinking head,
> To bear from Calvary's Mount the healing balm

Which can alone the troubled spirit calm!
The flaunting world, with all her votaries gay,
Will in oblivion soon have passed away.
The Beauty now who bows at Fashion's shrine
Soon will Mortality to Death consign:
All that was once delightful to the eye.
With worms, will then in deep corruption lie:
While those who in the Cross's holy school
Have learned their hearts, their thoughts, their lives to rule,
Vig'rous in Faith, with purest Hope serene,
The Love of Heaven in all their actions seen,
Will, o'er the wreck of worlds, triumphant rise,
Bright as the radiant stars which fill the spacious skies!

The poem focuses on the debate around the need to increase spaces for the professionalisation of middle-class women. This was a debate in which well-known figures like Florence Nightingale and Anna Jameson were integral and also included the concept of Woman's Mission (which Francis Nixon, the first Bishop of Tasmania had lectured on in 1856). Judith Lissauer Cromwell suggests that Nightingale, "a child of conventional, upper-class Victorian rearing ... identified an evil in the world: The waste of female talent. She yearned for something 'springing from a truer foundation than conventional life,' a profession, a 'necessary occupation,' something to satisfy and make full use of her faculties" (1).

Both poem and note suggest the importance that Bailey places on women's devalued labour. In the note attached to the poem, Bailey compared Nightingale explicitly and unfavourably with "the achievements of the Catholic nursing sisterhoods," writing:

> What a contrast does Miss Florence Nightingale, of Crimean celebrity, suggest to these crowds of holy women! She, for her brief period of benevolence, was honoured, feted, courted by monarchs and nobles, and states – her applauded name a very household word; the holy Sisters, during their whole life-time absorbed in their self-denying toils of love, their very names unknown to the world. How much greater their self-denial, how much less their worldly reward! (4)

Bailey's poem opens with the lines:

> Sisters of heavenly Love! for others' woe
> Your tears of sympathetic suffering flow!
> Your bosoms pierced at sight of human grief;
> The friendly hand, stretched forth to bring relief—
> Unbought, unasked, in sorrow's darkest hour,
> *Then* most is seen your Faith's all-conquering power!

Bailey would align herself with Anna Jameson's position in her lecture, "The Sisters of Charity," in advocating the elimination of the social concept of class:

> The Love of Heaven in all their actions seen,
> Will, o'er the wreck of worlds, triumphant rise,
> Bright as the radiant stars which fill the spacious skies!

In her accompanying note, Bailey cites the Countess of Blessington's comments on the "Sisters of Charity," suggesting that she may have been familiar with Jameson's lecture. Even if Bailey was not aware of Jameson's lecture, there is a clear similarity in their approaches. As scholars like Judith Johnston have pointed out, Jameson was also sensitive to the difficulties of working-class women with responsibilities in both earning and housekeeping. Jameson writes in "The Sisters of Charity":

> The great mistake seems to have been that in all our legislation it is taken for granted that the woman is always protected, always under tutelage, always within the precincts of a home; finding there her work, her interests, her duties, and her happiness: but is this true? We know that it is altogether false. There are thousands and thousands of women who have no protection, no guide, no help, no home; who are absolutely driven by necessity, if not by impulse and inclination, to carry out into the larger community the sympathies, the domestic instincts, the active administrative capabilities, with which God has endowed them ... (10)

In light of this, the conclusion of Bailey's poem takes on another meaning, one of women successfully overcoming these obstacles:

> Vig'rous in Faith, with purest Hope serene,
> The Love of Heaven in all their actions seen,
> Will, o'er the wreck of worlds, triumphant rise,
> Bright as the radiant stars which fill the spacious skies!

Appearing in a newspaper, Bailey's "Sisters of Charity" and its prose note can be read as a political commentary, contrary to assumptions about women's religious writing being relegated to the private sphere.

Ada Cambridge, also known as Ada Cross, contributed to international journals such as the *Atlantic Monthly* as well as the more local *Australian Ladies Annual*. She wrote for the *Australasian*, and ranged across the genres of fiction, non-fiction, and poetry. Her poetry was highly political and connected with British feminist traditions in outlook. Her collections included *Hymns on the Litany* (1865) and *Hymns on the Holy Communion* (1866) prior to arrival in Australia in 1870. She then published *The Manor House and Other Poems* (1875) and *Unspoken Thoughts* (1887), after her arrival although all were published in London. As Jill Roe notes, the poems in *Unspoken Thoughts* were regarded as "daring and even improper for a clergyman's wife" and were "hastily suppressed."

In its strong argument against the institution of marriage, "A Wife's Protest" exemplifies the volume's radical thinking. Discourses of "Purity" and "Law" are challenged as not only hypocritical, but also as soul-destroying and harmful for both so-called fallen women and married women alike. Cambridge describes a wife's emotional suffering as a kind of spiritual death. The poem's speaker lies in bed like a "prisoner on the rack" waiting for "creeping terrors" that "chill my blood / As each black night draws on!" While characterising herself as: "A guiltless prostitute in flesh, / A murderess in soul," she is able to maintain the "lustre" of "fair repute" because she obeys the law as a married woman. Alternatively, the ragged streetwalker is "[m]-arked for the world's disgrace," forced to "hide [ ] in shadows" compared to the speaker's visibility and presumed moral light. Yet Cambridge suggests a higher order than "church and law" and that in the "sight of God":

> She is more pure than I;
> The latchet of those broken shoes
> I am not fit to tie.
>
> That hungry baby at her breast –
> Sign of her fallen state –
> Nature who would but mock at mine,
> Has made legitimate.

These "unspoken thoughts" in being written, and published, are conscious of stigma and repression and deliberately shared, particularly among other women, actively amplifying collective gendered experiences around cultures of harm and shame. Cambridge emphasises commonality and shared experience with "[m]y ragged sister of the street" in challenging the false binary between the "fallen" and married woman.

For white settler women who wrote in the Romantic proto-feminist tradition after Wollstonecraft, underlying assumptions about the universal woman as white, middle class, and heterosexual were often not questioned. Dunlop, Bailey, Leakey, and Cambridge applied strategies of Romantic liminality, negativity, and sensibility and, with the latter, reversed the expected dynamics of sensibility. While they considered aspects of precarity through the themes of exile and transportation, they nonetheless often fail to acknowledge or question the structures of colonialism within which these paradigms and debates were occurring. They would use print culture to reinforce their presence and role within the colonies.

While settler women poets were unlikely to have been paid for their contributions to newspapers, Bailey certainly made money from her writing in the past, as well as from her role as an educator. It is likely that Bailey was familiar with Anna Jameson's "The Sisters of Charity" lecture, published three years before penning her own "Sisters of Charity" poem. Discussions of charitable work, class, and gender in Jameson's lecture suggested a broader proto-feminist conception of the symbolic significance of the "Sisters of Charity" to expectations around women's roles more generally and supported an argument for women's work outside of the home. Such precarity was engaged with by many of these poets through tropes of the 'fallen woman' as well as the so-called pure woman. Leakey's "Unuttered Thoughts" and her concerns are echoed in the title chosen by Ada Cambridge for her later volume, *Unspoken Thoughts*. All of these poets questioned how religion and emotional experience informed responses to cultures of regulation and punishment and their internalised ideas of value, purity, and redemption. However, the subsequent scandal arising from Cambridge's open poetic critique of purity discourse, the patriarchal institution of marriage, and of religious hypocrisy demonstrate the still substantial limits of imperialist approaches for women settler poets to advocate for women's empowerment and cultural transformation, even when mobilising a poetics of gender-conscious sensibility.

Works Cited

Bailey, Mary. *The Months and Other Poems*. C.J.G. and F. Rivington, 1822.
   Palmyra. 2nd ed. C.J.G. and F. Rivington, 1833.
   Reflections, Doctrinal, Practical and Devotional, Upon the Litany of the Church of England. 1833. Nabu Press, 2012.
   Musae Sacrae: A Collection of Hymns and Sacred Poetry. 1835. Nabu Press, 2011.
   "Hymn for Christmas Day." *Colonial Times*, 25 December 1846, p. 4.
   Letter. "Edward MacDowell, Esquire, and Filial Affection." *Colonial Times*, 16 February 1847, p. 3.
   "To the Editor of the Guardian." *Hobarton Guardian, or, True Friend of Tasmania*, 7 December 1853, p. 3.
   "Verses: Written upon the Author's Recent Reception into the Catholic Church at St Joseph's Hobart Town." *Freeman's Journal*, 14 April 1855, p. 4.
   "Sisters of Charity." *Freeman's Journal*, 20 February 1858, p. 4.
Buchanan, Constance. *Choosing to Lead: Women and the Crisis of American Values*, Beacon Press, 1997.
Cambridge, Ada. *Hymns on the Litany*. J. Henry and J. Parker, 1865.
   Hymns on the Holy Communion. Houlston and Wright, 1866.
   The Manor House and Other Poems. Daldy, Isbister, and Co., 1875.
   Unspoken Thoughts [1887]. 1997. https://adc.library.usyd.edu.au/data-2/v00026.pdf.

Casaliggi, Carmen and Porscha Fermanis. *Romanticism: A Literary and Cultural History*. Routledge, 2016.
De Salis, Margaret. *Two Early Colonials*. Margaret de Salis, 1967.
Dunlop, Eliza. "The Dream" ("Songs of an Exile Number 1"). *Australian*, 8 November 1838, p. 2.
Jameson, Anna. "The Sisters of Charity." *Lecture* (1855). Accessed online at Project Gutenberg.
Johnston, Judith. *Anna Jameson: Victorian, Feminist, Woman of Letters*. Scolar Press, 1997.
  "Anna Brownell Jameson and the *Monthly Chronicle*." *Victorian Journalism: Exotic and Domestic*, edited by Barbara Garlick and Margaret Harris. Queensland University Press, 1998, pp. 19–37.
Knowles, Claire. *Sensibility and Female Poetic Tradition*. Ashgate, 2009.
Landon, Letitia Elizabeth (L.E.L.). *The Improvisatrice and Other Poems*. Hurst, Robinson, 1825.
Leakey, Caroline. *Lyra Australis; Or, Attempts to Sing in a Strange Land*. Bickers and Bush, 1854.
Lissauer Cromwell, Judith. *Florence Nightingale, Feminist*. McFarland & Company, 2013.
Mellor, Anne K. *Romanticism and Gender*. Routledge, 2013.
Moreton-Robinson, Aileen. *Talkin' Up to the White Woman: Indigenous Women and Feminism* [2000]. University of Queensland Press, 2020.
Nixon, Francis. "Woman's Mission." *The Courier*. Hobart, 13 August 1856, p. 2.
Procter, Adelaide. *A Chaplet of Verses*. Longman, Green, 1862.
Roe, Jill. "Cambridge, Ada (1844–1926)." *Australian Dictionary of Biography*, https://adb.anu.edu.au/biography/cambridge-ada-3145.
Vickery, Ann. "Feminine Transports and Transformations: Textual Performances of Women Convicts and Emigrants to Australia from 1788 to 1850." *JASAL* vol.7, 2007, pp. 71–84.
Wollstonecraft, Mary. *A Vindication of the Rights of Woman*. Thomas and Andrews, 1792.

6

AIDAN COLEMAN

Experiment and Adaptation

Modernist Poetry in Australia

In the decades that followed Federation, Australian culture tended to be indifferent, even hostile, towards what it perceived as literary modernism. The absence of a robust local canon was detrimental to those poets who desired to make their work both contemporary and authentically Australian. The more original nineteenth-century versifiers, like Charles Harpur and Henry Kendall, had no descendants,[1] and local engagement with literary Romanticism, so crucial to developments in the United States, was limited at best. It was, in the words of critic and poet Paul Kane, "as if Australia, was some Rip Van Winkle, who fell asleep a neo-classicist and woke up as a Victorian" (10).[2] The nation's main shapers of taste preferred conservative forms to introspective or experimental poetry, and the dissemination of the major texts of American and European modernism was piecemeal and delayed.

Australian poets who wished to experiment had either to resign themselves to relative obscurity or seek a compromise between an imported modernism and those models the literary mainstream more readily accepted. Kenneth Slessor and John Shaw Neilson took the latter approach, while Christopher Brennan, Lesbia Harford, Anna Wickham, and the fictional Ern Malley took the lonelier path. The approaches of these six poets to modernism – which often coincided with a belated Romanticism – differed markedly, as did their politics, but, through a combination of experiment and the absorption of international influence, they would create a modern Australian poetry of enduring significance.

Christopher Brennan (1870–1932) effectively ushered in a new Australian poetry. Although he wrote little after the publication of *Poems 1913* (1914),[3] he produced the most experimental poetry in Australia to be written in the first half of the twentieth century. Brennan was deeply read in the Classics, the English tradition, and the German Romantics. His writings on French Symbolism demonstrate an understanding superior to that of his international contemporaries, and he corresponded with Stéphane

Mallarmé, who lavishly praised his poetry (Hawke 6–7).[4] A precocious intellect with a formidable Jesuit education, Brennan lost his Catholic faith at the University of Sydney, where he undertook a BA and later an MA in Philosophy. It was while in Berlin on a scholarship that he discovered Mallarmé's poetry, and also fell in love with his landlady's daughter, Anna Werth (Clark 66–70). He later married her in what was to prove an unhappy union. His bohemianism stymied his university career,[5] and he was dismissed early for misconduct (Clark 149–54).

Brennan's reputation rests, almost exclusively, on *Poems 1913*. In the spirit of Mallarmé, it is conceived as a sum greater than its parts, or a *livre composé*, and not a collection of individual pieces (Wilkes, *New Perspectives*). The book conveys a sense of intricate balance; there are subtitles within titles and numbered sections within each. The individual compositions dazzle with a variety of forms, from *terza rima* and the Petrarchan sonnet to odes and epigraphs. The lines vary, from languid alexandrines to punchy, staccato dimeters. Although he never ventured into free verse, Brennan's use of white space and expressive typography was decidedly modern.

Poems 1913 dramatises a gnostic quest for Eden and is divided into three major sections – "Towards the Source," "The Forest of Night," and "The Wanderer." The Law of Correspondences, which suggests not only a new model for the physical world but also relationships between that world and an ideal or spiritual realm, is fundamental to the work's symbolism. Brennan thought poetry and philosophy "the two means by which we come into connection with the higher and real-world. And of the two poetry is the most important" (*Prose* 110). In such a formulation, poetry is elevated to the status of a religion and the poet is priest, mediating between the two worlds.

"To the Source" opens with images of natural beauty, childhood, and Brennan's courtship, but these are contrasted with feelings of impotence and despair, which intensify in "The Forest of Night." The syntax becomes knotty, the tone heavier, and the allusions denser. The Talmudic figure of Lilith is of central importance to this section. Spurned by the first man, Adam, she torments her former lover with visions of paradise. Lilith is terrifying:

> She is the night: all horror is of her
> heap'd, shapeless, on the unclaim'd chaotic marsh
> or huddled on the looming sepulchre
> where the incult and scanty herb is harsh. (*Verse* 143)

But she also holds out the promise that sensual beauty can be reunited with the spiritual (Barnes 13)[6] – the possibility that self-knowledge can be gained if the speaker is prepared to journey deep into the subconscious recesses of his own night:

> All mystery, and all love, beyond our ken,
> she woos us, mournful till we find her fair:
> and gods and stars and songs and souls of men
> are the sparse jewels in her scatter'd hair. (*Verse* 144)

"The Forest of Night" ends in dissolution, with the paradisal instinct frustrated (McAuley, *C.J. Brennan* 20).

In "The Wanderer," the setting, while symbolic, also becomes tangible. In a poem that shares the heroic grandeur of the Anglo-Saxon original, the speaker is disabused of his illusions, and the language is appropriately chaste, purged of its rhymes and much of its poeticism. The failure to gain self-knowledge is excused as "a glory won in defeat." The syntax is smoother and the stress patterns of the long lines vary subtly, providing an easier music:

> I know I am
> the wanderer of the ways of all the worlds,
> to whom the sunshine and the rain are one
> and one to stay or hasten, because he knows
> no ending of the way, no home, no goal,
> and phantom night and the grey day alike
> withhold the heart where all my dreams and days
> might faint in soft fire and delicious death:
> and saying this to myself as a simple thing
> I feel a peace fall in the heart of the winds
> and a clear dusk settle, somewhere, far in me. (*Verse* 165)

The poem's resolution is a resignation, and it brings a hard-won peace. The failure of the quest is not an artistic failure, but it was an endpoint for Brennan. *Poems 1913*, which he had effectively completed by the age of thirty-two,[7] was the apogee of his ambition and achievement.

Brennan's two collections of war poetry, *The Burden of Tyre* (1903) and *A Chant of Doom, and Other Verses* (1918), have few redeeming features, and the poems he wrote for his lover, Violet Singer, while accomplished, are slight. However, *Musicopoematographoscope* (1897), written in response to Mallarmé's *Un coup de dés*, is unique in Australian letters and has attracted recent interest from avant-gardists.[8] Brennan's existential pessimism, and his interest in the subconscious and the flâneur, align him with some schools of twentieth-century modernism. While the influence of Victorian poetry diminished much of his work, Brennan's engagement with French Symbolism introduced radical new elements into Australian poetry, as he worked with scant encouragement to establish a credible high modernist tradition.

John Shaw Neilson (1872–1942) has been cast as the antithesis of Brennan, his sophisticated and erudite contemporary. Although he had little formal education, Shaw Neilson's letters show that he read widely. He was raised on the Bible, Scottish songs, and Robert Burns, who provided a model of innovation within the conventions of song and ballad (Hewson 28–34). His father was a published poet of considerable talent who encouraged his son's gifts. Afflicted by bouts of depression and poor health, Shaw Neilson subsisted on short-term labouring jobs for most of his life. It was not until his final years that his literary contacts managed to secure him an administrative position. From his early thirties, a congenital sight impairment limited his capacity to read, and he was forced to compose by dictating to various amanuenses.

Although he began writing seriously in the 1890s, Shaw Neilson's best poetry was written in the last three decades of his life. His symbolism sharply distinguishes his aesthetic from that of his nineteenth-century Australian predecessors. Like Brennan's, Shaw Neilson's symbols are highly personal, though in contrast to Brennan's systematic approach, his use of them is sometimes ad hoc (Douglas). Colours abound and their complex – and occasionally contradictory – meanings evolve throughout the course of his oeuvre. An unbidden synaesthesia also contributes to the sensuousness of his verse. His published letters show some familiarity with the French Symbolists, whom his mentor and literary agent, A. G. Stephens, also promoted through the *Bulletin* and the *Bookfellow* (Hewson 290).

Nature provided a suite of symbols for Shaw Neilson, but concrete reality was also important to his vision. In "The Poor, Poor Country [II]" the poet contrasts his family's penury with the "wealth" he found in nature, specifically in the splendour of water birds: blue cranes, swans, spoonbills, black and mountain ducks, plovers, and the "Pelican," which the boy-poet "crown [s] for a king" (356–57). These birds, and the sensual largesse of nature ("wild cherries and the slabs of honeycomb"), infuse the speaker's dreams and fuel a nascent poetic imagination. As in Wordsworth's childhood reminiscences, these early encounters with nature contribute to the poet's spiritual growth.

Shaw Neilson's mother raised him in a strict, life-denying Calvinism, with disproportionate emphasis on the separateness of God and the fallen nature of both humanity and the world. The poet wrestles with this divinity and establishes alternative conceptions. In "The Gentle Waterbird," he reflects on his childhood image of God, who "was terrible and thunder-blue" (334). In conventional Christian theology, Christ is both "gentle" and a "king," God's emissary and a mediator, but Shaw Neilson bestows these tropes on

Experiment and Adaptation: Modernist Poetry

the crane, through whom a more benevolent divinity is knowable. The theme is revisited in the best of Shaw Neilson's late poems, "The Crane Is My Neighbour." The title alludes to the parable of the Good Samaritan, which is Christ's answer to the question "[w]ho is my neighbour?" As the parable looks to extend kinship beyond tribal allegiances to the whole of humanity, Shaw Neilson's speaker extends it to all living things:

> The bird is my neighbour, a whimsical fellow and dim;
> There is in the lake a nobility falling on him.
>
> The bird is a noble, he turns to the sky for a theme,
> And the ripples are thoughts coming out to the edge of a dream.
>
> The bird is both ancient and excellent, sober and wise,
> But he never could spend all the love that is sent for his eyes.
>
> He bleats no instruction, he is not an arrogant drummer;
> His gown is simplicity – blue as the smoke of the summer.
>
> How patient he is as he puts out his wings for the blue!
> His eyes are as old as the twilight, and calm as the dew.
>
> The bird is my neighbour, he leaves not a claim for a sigh,
> He moves as the guest of the sunlight – he roams in the sky.
>
> The bird is a noble, he turns to the sky for a theme,
> And the ripples are thoughts coming out to the edge of a dream. (422)

The rigid God of Shaw Neilson's childhood, here represented by sermonising ("instruction") and brash displays of virtue ("arrogant drum[ming]"), is contrasted with the crane's expansive universe. The crane suggests a way of being. He is "a guest of sunlight" who lives each moment without regret ("he leaves not a claim for a sigh"). The bird, "both ancient and excellent, sober and wise," is an emissary of the divine, but surprisingly, and at great risk to the poem's elevated theme, he is also simultaneously "whimsical" and "dim." Nature, in the poem, contains paradoxes – sobriety and whimsicality, wisdom and dimness – anomalies which are to be celebrated. The bird does not strive for his nobility; it is something bestowed upon him, like grace, and the immediacy of this revelation is ignited by the poet's use of the present tense. The fourteen lines of the poem are longer than those of a conventional sonnet, and the rhyme scheme is simpler, each couplet self-contained. However, its surprising patterning shows Shaw Neilson is not afraid to risk variation in the poem's form, which supports a more generous vision than any his upbringing bestowed, as he aspires through "dream[s]" to the realm of the imagination.

Undoubtedly, Shaw Neilson's most anthologised poem is "The Orange Tree," in which a simple ballad meter belies the complexity of the argument. Light and sound are almost interchangeable in this lyric, suggesting the power of sensation and, by extension, intuition, over rationality. Hal Porter, who committed the poem to memory, compared it to reading smoke (Hewson 13–16), and critics are divided as to whether a flaw in its design caused its ultimate opacity.[9] The poem is a dialogue between a young girl, who represents innocence, and a verbose, nostalgic old man, who represents experience and sophistication. Ultimately, the dialogue favours the younger visionary, who cuts through the older man's complex utterances, to insist, in the mystical tradition, on a reality beyond words:

> Silence! the young girl said. Oh, why,
> Why will you talk to weary me?
> Plague me no longer now, for I
> Am listening like the Orange Tree. (355)

Shaw Neilson's lexicon is limited, and much of his work suffers from sentimentality as well as from the use of stock poeticisms. Yet despite these shortcomings, he crafted some remarkable poems, which in terms of their lyricism are, perhaps, unmatched in Australia.

The reputation of **Kenneth Slessor** (1901–71) rests on four collections of poetry, written between the two world wars. Born in Orange, New South Wales, of Scots and German-Jewish ancestry, Slessor became a journalist after leaving school, contributing comment, reviews, and light verse to tabloid newspapers. Later he worked as a war correspondent in New Guinea, Greece, and North Africa. Aside from this interlude, and a sojourn in Melbourne, Slessor lived most of his adult life around Kings Cross, a bohemian suburb of Sydney. A *bon vivant*, possessed of a superficially cheery disposition, he was married twice: first to Noela Senior, who died of cancer in 1945, and later to Pauline Wallace, with whom he had a son, Paul.

In his early twenties Slessor met the artists and writers associated with the short-lived Sydney magazine *Vision* (1924–25): Norman Lindsay and his son Jack, and the poets Robert FitzGerald and Hugh McCrae. Guided by Norman Lindsay's messianic devotion to the cult of Friedrich Nietzsche, *Vision* promoted "vitalism," which celebrated youth and beauty, with a masculine emphasis on sex. Although the tenor of *Vision* was anti-modernist, and his biographer Geoffrey Dutton thought it a baleful influence on the poet's development (59), Slessor credited Lindsay with teaching him the value of the concrete image (*Bread and Wine* 124). The magazine's peculiar brand of romantic Nietzscheanism made a lasting impression on

Slessor. The elevated and apolitical role he attributed to the artist, and his ambivalence towards women, derived from this period.

Slessor's third book, *Cuckooz Contrey* (1932), shows the influence of T. S. Eliot and other modernists, which imbued his work with a new precision and suggestiveness (Smith 260). Refinement in diction is balanced by a greater desire to deviate from traditional meter and rhythm, but the poems stop short of Eliot's experiments with disjunction and syntax, and they mostly eschew complex allusion. Comparisons with the older poet are instructive because both writers are guided by the image and by a remarkable sensitivity to phrasal music. Slessor's Prufrockian apprenticeship also betrays a measure of the Master's impersonality, and his disgust with aspects of modern existence. In the Australian poet, this sometimes borders on misanthropy. But unlike Eliot's, Slessor's poems – and his light verse in particular – are replete with the detritus of consumer culture: telephones, wirelesses, cars, aeroplanes, advertising, and the latest fashions (Caesar 67). The inhabitants of Slessor's Sydney are alienated from their environment, but where Eliot's cityscapes suggest spiritual languor, Slessor captures the excitement and the frenzied pace of modern life. "William Street" celebrates Kings Cross by deploying a surfeit of sensual detail: "The red globes of light, the liquorgreen, / The pulsing arrows and the running fire" and the "[s]mells rich and rasping," which "crimp the nose." "You find this ugly," the speaker asserts, "I find it lovely" (*Collected Poems* 132–33).[10] In an earlier poem, written in ballad meter, the protagonist is "living in the sky / and feeding on the view" ("Up in Mabel's Room," *Collected Poems* 120). The city lights may eclipse the moon and the stars, but the "fiery hedge" and "flagons of electric beer / and alphabets of light" exhibit a dynamic beauty. In contrast, Slessor's unpeopled landscapes are unrelentingly bleak. The bilious narrator of "South Country" – who notes "the monstrous continent of air," "rotting sunlight," and "[b]ruised flesh of thunderstorms" (*Collected Poems* 132) – betrays both colonial anxiety and existential terror at the land's immensity.

More has been written about the title poem of Slessor's final volume, *Five Bells* (1939), than any other work by an Australian poet. Ostensibly an elegy for Joe Lynch, a dissolute cartoonist who drowned in Sydney Harbour, the poem meditates on the grand themes of time, memory, and death. Everything Slessor had written in the two preceding decades served as material for this chef-d'oeuvre (McAuley, "Slessor's Poetry" 20). The poem dramatises with cinematic intensity[11] the speaker's desire both to communicate with his dead friend and draw some meaning from his demise. The elegy can be appreciated on two levels, as it draws a distinction between clock time, represented by the chiming of a ship's bell in the harbour, and what Henri Bergson once called "duration" – the sort of chronology that is produced only by memory. Slessor characterises this as "the flood that does not flow"(*Collected Poems* 120).

After the calm and philosophical tone of the italicised proem, the poem proper begins with some of Slessor's most profoundly beautiful lines:

> Deep and dissolving verticals of light
> Ferry the falls of moonshine down. Five bells
> Coldly rung out in a machine's voice. Night and water
> Pour to one rip of darkness, the Harbour floats
> In air, the Cross hangs upside-down in water   (*Collected Poems* 120)

In a gesture of emotional distancing, Joe is reduced simply to "dead man" as the narrator strains to evoke his "agonies of speech." There is a desperation to communicate and a simultaneous realisation that such dialogue is impossible – that no "mouth can fly the pygmy strait" between this world and the next. It is in this state of heightened awareness that he attempts to recall his old friend, but the circumstantial details he conjures up and the imagery of immersion seem only to prefigure the abyss. The echoes of Joe's splenetic vivacity seem only to underline time's crushing power. Throughout, the speaker is returned to the idea of mortality by the cold iteration of the ship's bell, which not only tolls for Joe, but proclaims the stern march of time to all.

In the penultimate stanza, the speaker's creative consciousness attempts to embrace Joe's as it participates vicariously in the moment of his death:

> I felt the wet push its black thumb-balls in,
> The night you died, I felt your eardrums crack,
> And the short agony, the longer dream,
> The Nothing that was neither long nor short;
> But I was bound, and could not go that way,
> But I was blind, and could not feel your hand.   (123)

Whereas in Eliot's *Four Quartets*, time intersects with the Transcendent, the dénouement of "Five Bells" sees time confront the timeless void of annihilation: a death stripped of all meaning in a godless universe. Judith Wright, who described Slessor as the most nihilistic of Australian writers, remarked that "the note of hollowness and hopelessness in Slessor's work is inescapable" (158). Neither the consolations of art nor the narrator's refusal to surrender to 'the void' or 'meaninglessness'[12] vitiate this judgement, as some have argued. The chilling auditory image of the tolling bell is final.

Although Slessor lived a further thirty-two years after the release of *Five Bells*, he only published three more poems. He edited *Southerly* and *The Penguin Book of Modern Australian Verse* (1961) with John Thompson. During these years he also adjudicated prizes, served on a number of government committees, and acted as a mentor to younger writers. Many of the male poets who began publishing at this time felt a deep loyalty to him, which extended to his oeuvre. He wrote much of the era's finest poetry, but was he, as Andrew Taylor asserts, "the only genuine Modernist poet that Australia has produced" (53)? Surely not if experimentation and modernism are synonymous. Slessor was rather, as James McAuley put it, "a careful semi-modernist" (*Map* 6). His reputation rose steadily during his lifetime, and unlike the more audacious modernists, he encountered little resistance. His standing has been remarkably buoyant ever since, though, like Brennan and Shaw Neilson, he is little known outside Australia.

While in the early years of the twentieth century women were visible among Australia's most eminent prose writers, no female poet of the period shares Shaw Neilson's or Slessor's reputation; nor do any rival the later achievements of Judith Wright or Gwen Harwood. It is difficult to know why this is the case. In her study of female novelists of the period, Drusilla Modjeska observes that late nineteenth- and early twentieth-century literary circles were largely a male preserve (6), and that such groups were more important to poets than to prose writers, who had better hope of market success.

Mary Gilmore, Zora Cross, and Dorothea Mackellar carved out a niche within the literary mainstream, but many of the qualities that recommended them to their contemporaries now tell against them. The editors of *The Penguin Book of Australian Women Poets* (1986) comment that Lesbia Harford (1891–1927) and Anna Wickham (1883–1947) are "probably the closest in mood and subject matter" to contemporary women poets (15). Both operated outside the mainstream of Australian literary culture; Wickham chose exile, and Harford, but for a handful of poems in fringe publications, wrote privately.

After attending convent schools, **Lesbia Harford** became one of the first women to study law at the University of Melbourne, where she became involved in radical politics. She joined the socialist organisation The Industrial Workers of the World (known as the Wobblies) in 1917, and was employed in factory work for a number of years, where she engaged in union activity. She was by all accounts an energetic and charismatic speaker who played a significant role in the anti-conscription campaign. In Sydney, she was briefly married to the working-class painter Pat Harford, who proved to be a violent alcoholic. Born with a congenital heart condition, she contended with ill health throughout her life and died aged thirty-six from complications related to tuberculosis.

Harford's lyrics are modernist in their political concerns and their frankness about sex. Her socialist convictions also guided her work; the diction is simple, purged of Victorian poeticism and sentimentality, and the address is disarmingly direct. Harford's verse also has an aphoristic power and a rough, unfinished quality, as if lifted straight from her notebook, which some of it is. The majority of her poems are short, but her range is wide. She writes of sexual desire, factory work, the quotidian, war, nature, and spirituality with equal conviction. Her three pieces titled "Periodicity" may be the earliest Australian poems to broach the topic of menstruation (Vickery 228): "Women, I say, / Are beautiful in change, / Remote, immortal, like the moon they range" (56).

Sappho is an influence not only on some of Harford's stanza forms, but also on the value she attributes to the fragment. Harford is a poet of both heterosexual and queer desire and, like many political radicals of the time, she affirms free love: "For no two lovers are a single person / And lovers' union means a soul's suppression" (92). Harford's desire for her philosophy tutor, Katie Lush, inspired some of her strongest lyrics: "I can't feel the sunshine / Or see the stars aright / For thinking of her beauty / And her kisses bright" (17).

This untitled poem ends in a wish to escape the stifling conformity of Melbourne for Sappho's Greece. The most strange and gnomic of her love lyrics is the five-line poem for her husband, who is transposed into the mythical and erotic: "Pat wasn't Pat last night at all. / He was the rain, / The Spring, / Young Dionysus, white and warm, / Lilac and everything (115).

Harford's activism led her to seek work in the textile industry, and her sketches of her female co-workers are both hard-headed and tender. The "sweet, little" girls going home after hours on the factory floor in "Day's End" are also "amazingly rude" (24), in contrast to the dullness of the middle-class commuters, while "Machinist Talking" (51–52) combines Harford's feminist and class concerns. Her other portraits are equally sympathetic, whether they be of Gertie who arrives at work less weary because she dreamt of her beloved homeland the night before (43), Emmie with "her insolent air" (44), or Maisie, who proudly shows off a love bite during the lunch break (82).

Harford brings a similar freshness to her treatment of the natural world. The poets Robert Gray and Geoffrey Lehmann consider "We Climbed That Hill" to be the first poem by a "non-Aboriginal" to depict "an Australian landscape in all its individuality, without an overlay of nineteenth century romanticism" (247–48):

> We climbed that hill
> The road flushed red in pride
> At being beauty's boundary. Either side
> Stretched beauty, beauty ever, beauty still.

> For on the left
> Rose sandhills bound together by the deft
> Long fingers of sea-grass
> Humped like the Punch and Judy of a farce,
> Comical, cleft
> With gaps for wind to pass
> Spotted
> With dark
> Clumped tea-tree, stark
> With rushes, fierce with burrs ... (76)

In the looser rhythms of free verse, the poem recounts a walk as experienced by an 'I' whom we might speculate is the poet, captivated by details, and a 'you' who is more concerned with the universal. The argument, which is still unresolved at the close of the poem, seems to pit the perspective of a poet against that of a philosopher. The poem's evocation of the scenery is stranger and more vivid than any by Harford's contemporaries, and seems to anticipate Slessor's striking depictions of Australian landscapes.

Literary London provided a place for Australian writers to remake themselves. Mary Fullerton wrote fiction and verse in Australia during the first two decades of the twentieth century, but moved to England for the last twenty-five years of her life, where she published some of her best poetry under the pen name "E." Her English-born contemporary Edith Alice Mary Harper, better known as **Anna Wickham**, returned to London at around the age of twenty after an Australian childhood. She took her *nom de plume* from a Brisbane street.

Wickham's neglect stems from her uneasy relationship with Anglo-Irish modernism and her ambiguous nationality (Vickery 27).[13] Her oeuvre includes both free verse and stricter forms: ballads, dramatic monologues, songs, and short epigrammatic lyrics. While her lesser poems lapse into doggerel (Rice 109),[14] her Australian contemporaries rarely matched the rhetorical force of her finest verse. "Mare Bred from Pegasus" begins:

> For God's sake, stand off from me:
> There's a brood mare here going to kick like hell
> With a mad up-rising energy;
> And where the wreck will end who'll tell?
> She'll splinter the stable door and eat a groom.
> For God's sake, give me room;
> Give my will room. (50)

This is a poetry of direct statement and accessible allegory, vivid with dark humour. In "Divorce," night is synonymous with the feminine and creative:

> A voice from the dark is calling me.
> In the close house I nurse a fire.
> Out of the dark cold winds rush free
> To the rock heights of my desire.
> I smother in the house in the valley below,
> Let me out to the night, let me go, let me go. (3)

Much of Wickham's work shows this deft handling of meter and fluent syntax. Her rhymes are usually simple, her diction plain, and her images elementary. Though she disregards Ezra Pound's anti-adjective prescriptions, her work is largely purged of Victorian ornament. The adjective "up-rising," in the first poem, surprises. In the second poem, the ambiguous verb "smother," untethered from an object, carries a sinister edge. In other work Wickham celebrates the domestic and depicts her sons with tenderness. Many of her poems are overt in their expression of lesbian desire; others have a queer subtext. She has been read as both a mystic and a metaphysical (Rice 122); the term "God" is ubiquitous in her work, and often shorthand for the good or an ultimate perfection. Her God is immanent, and perhaps closest to Blake's notion of deity.

No contemporary Australian poet was closer to the heart of international modernism than Wickham, and none were more widely published.[15] Katherine Mansfield, Laurence Durrell, George Bernard Shaw, D. H. Lawrence, and Dylan Thomas were among her circle of friends, and she was a regular visitor to Natalie Clifford Barney's French salon of women writers. Wickham's work, which suffered from decades of neglect, anticipates confessionalism. Its immediacy and its prescient sexual politics are likely to appeal to new generations of twenty-first-century readers.

The fictional poet **Ern Malley**, the greatest literary hoax of the twentieth century, was conceived by two aspiring poets then in their mid-twenties: James McAuley and Harold Stewart. Though they claimed in the press that Ern Malley's poems were "a serious literary experiment," free of personal malice (Brooks 58),[16] their main target and victim was the editor of *Angry Penguins*, Max Harris. Only twenty-two at the time, Harris had already published three books of poetry, and his work as a critic and editor had given him a national reputation. *Angry Penguins*, which he co-edited with John Reed, was an innovative journal of arts and culture, which aimed to connect Australia with international modernism. It ran from 1940 to 1947, publishing translations of Rimbaud, Rilke, Lorca, and George Seferis alongside work in English by Karl Shapiro, Robert Penn Warren, Kenneth Rexroth, and Dylan Thomas, and art by Australian painters such as Albert Tucker, Arthur Boyd, and Sydney Nolan. In contrast to Harris, the hoaxers were relatively unknown, and while Ern Malley's poems can be read as a critique of modernism, they are equally a manifestation of professional rivalry.[17]

To accompany Malley's slim offering of seventeen poems, McAuley and Stewart wrote a preface and tragic biography of a lonely outsider with little formal education, who died, like Keats, aged twenty-five years and four months. The poems and story were fed to Harris in instalments through the fictional cipher of Ern's sister Ethel, who, after nursing her brother through his final months of illness, had found the poems while clearing out his meagre possessions. With the exception of one fragment (Brooks 324), Harris published all the poems in *Angry Penguins*, together with a rhapsodic introduction. When the hoax was revealed as front-page news in a Sydney tabloid (Heyward 162–63),[18] McAuley and Stewart insisted the poems were "meaningless nonsense" which had been concocted spontaneously one idle afternoon, with the poets interrupting each other and making use of the *Collected Works of William Shakespeare*, a rhyming dictionary, and a report on mosquito breeding grounds.

To succeed, the poems had to be good enough to appeal to Harris and his clique but weak enough to unravel under close scrutiny. At their worst they are hyperbolic melodrama. Neologisms and obscure multisyllabic words often combine to create a jarringly awkward music. In other places like "Perspective Lovesong," the poem is simply banal: "Princess, you lived in Princess St." But bathos is their main strategy, as in "Petit Testament": "Reserving to myself a man's / Inalienable right to be sad / At his own funeral" (61). T. S. Eliot haunts Malley's work more than any other writer, but the poems can sound like a rough paraphrase or bad quarto of his most famous work. When the speaker declares in "Boult to Marina" that "I am not Pericles" (39), it lacks the resonance of Prufrock's "No! I am not Prince Hamlet nor was meant to be" (17). The hoaxers replace Eliot's cultural capitals (Jerusalem, Athens, Alexandria, London, Vienna) with Melbourne suburbs and street names. While this gesture is effective in terms of parody, it also suggests, via a kind of internalised cultural colonialism, an anxiety that local geography is unworthy of great art (Lloyd). Alongside such banalities exist sections of resonant poetry, as exemplified in this section from "Petit Testament":

> Dear we shall never be that bird
> Perched on the sole Arabian Tree
> Not having learnt in our green age to forget
> The sins that flow between the hands and feet
> (Here the Tree weeps gum tears

> Which are also real: I tell you
> These things are real) ... (61)

Ever since Harris first published *The Darkening Ecliptic*, the collection has ended powerfully – perhaps even prophetically – with the following lines:

> I
>
> Who have lived in the shadow that each act
> Casts on the next act now emerge
> As loyal as the thistle that in session
> Puffs its full seed upon the indicative air.
> I have split the infinite. Beyond is anything. (62)

In keeping with the chance procedures McAuley and Stewart purported to have used, the final line – which originally read "I have split the infinitive" – was improved by a typing error that has remained ever since.

Michael Heyward called Malley's poems "the most decisive piece of literary criticism ever produced in Australia" (238), and the work, as poetry, withstands analysis far more successfully than intended. The clues to authorship that the hoaxers provide, for example, function as one of many motifs that enrich the *livre composé*.[19] The hoaxers were accomplished poets, steeped in the forms of literary modernism that they were in the process of rejecting. The poems are written out of such knowledge, with all the contradictory conviction of recent apostates.[20] *The Darkening Ecliptic*'s opening poem was lifted from McAuley's own work, but other poems, too, show signs of careful construction (Brooks). The abandon with which many sections were composed,[21] together with the one-upmanship of the collaborative process, accounts for much of the work's idiosyncrasy and its daring brio. The poems draw on surrealism, the French Symbolists, and Pound–Eliot modernism, and the hoaxers' embraced Dadaist procedures, but Malley most resembles the New Apocalyptic poets so revered by the *Angry Penguins* circle. And yet, with the exception of Dylan Thomas, Malley proves more memorable than any writer of this school. Ultimately, the poems succeed too well as parodies, and become the real thing.

Ern Malley's influence on Australia's literary and artistic culture has been profound. In his novel *My Life as a Fake* (2003), Peter Carey revisits the hoax, creating the poet Bob McCorkle, a virile figure of Frankensteinian proportions, who returns to terrorise his mediocre creator. While Harold Stewart's reputation faded, Malley's grew, and since the 1990s he has been as generously represented in anthologies as McAuley himself. His recent inclusion in the sixth edition of *The Norton Anthology of Poetry* (2018) is another tribute to his canonical status. *The Darkening Ecliptic*'s explicit, and implicit, sexual content provided a bizarre epilogue to the hoax which saw Max Harris tried for obscenity. If poetry was not on trial – as Philip Mead has suggested (87) – avant-garde experimentalism was. In *The Penguin Book of Modern Australian Poetry* the editors characterise Malley as "a ghostly presence designed to self-destruct and take Modernism with him into the void" (xxviii), and it seems, to judge from the conservatism of the eminent poets of the following decades, to have succeeded.[22] It was largely left to the writers commonly known as the Generation of '68, who were in most cases born after the hoax, to take up formal experiment and redefine Australian literary modernism.

Works Cited

Barnes, Katherine. *The Higher Self in Christopher Brennan's Poems: Esotericism, Romanticism, Symbolism.* Brill, 2006.
Brennan, Christopher. *The Verse of Christopher Brennan*, edited by A. R. Chisholm and J. J. Quinn. Angus & Robertson, 1960.
   The Prose of Christopher Brennan, edited by A. R. Chisholm and J. J. Quinn. Angus & Robertson, 1962.
Brooks, David. *The Sons of Clovis: Ern Malley, Adoré Floupette and a Secret History of Australian Poetry.* University of Queensland Press, 2011.
Caesar, Adrian. *Kenneth Slessor.* Oxford University Press, 1995.
Carey, Peter. *My Life as a Fake.* Random House, 2003.
Carruthers, A. J. "The Lives of the Experimental Poets 1-3." *Jacket2*. https://jacket2.org/commentary/lives-experimental-poets-1to3.
Clark, Axel. *Christopher Brennan: A Critical Biography.* Melbourne University Press, 1980.
Douglas, Dennis. "The Imagination of John Shaw Neilson." *Australian Literary Studies* vol.5 no.1, 1971, pp. 18-23.
Dutton, Geoffrey. *Kenneth Slessor.* Viking, 1991.
Eliot, T. S. "The Love Song of J. Alfred Prufrock." *Collected Poems 1909-1962.* Faber & Faber, 1963, p. 17.
Farrell, Michael. *Writing Australian Unsettlement: Modes of Poetic Invention 1796-1945.* Palgrave MacMillan, 2015.
Hampton, Susan and Kate Llewellyn. "Introduction." *The Penguin Book of Australian Women Poets*, edited by Susan Hampton and Kate Llewellyn. Penguin, 1986, pp. 1-17.
Harford, Lesbia. *Collected Poems: Lesbia Harford*, edited by Oliver Dennis. UWA Publishing, 2014.
Hawke, John. *Australian Literature and the Symbolist Movement.* University of Wollongong Press, 2009.
Hewson, Helen. *John Shaw Nielson: A Life in Letters.* Miegunyah, 2002.
Heyward, Michael. *The Ern Malley Affair.* University of Queensland Press, 1994.
Kane, Paul. *Australian Poetry: Romanticism and Negativity.* Cambridge University Press, 1996.

Lehmann, Geoffrey and Robert Gray, eds. *Australian Poetry since 1788*. University of New South Wales Press, 2011.
Lloyd, Brian. "Ern Malley and His Rivals." *Australian Literary Studies* vol.20 no.1, 2001, pp. 20–32.
Malley, Ern [James McAuley and Harold Stewart]. *The Darkening Ecliptic*. ETT Imprint, 2017.
McAuley, James. *C.J. Brennan*. Oxford University Press, 1963.
— "Shaw Neilson's Poetry." *Australian Literary Studies* vol.2 no.4, 1966, pp. 235–53.
— *A Map of Australian Verse*. Oxford University Press, 1975.
— "Slessor's Poetry: A Survey with Some Commentary." *Considerations: New Essays on Kenneth Slessor, Judith Wright and Douglas Stewart*, edited by Brian Kiernan. Angus & Robertson, 1977, pp. 11–24.
Mead, Philip. *Networked Language: Culture and History in Australian Poetry*. Australian Scholarly Publishing, 2008.
Modjeska, Drusilla. *Exiles at Home: Australian Women Writers 1925–1945*. Sirius Books, 1981.
Oliver, H. J. *Shaw Neilson*. Oxford University Press, 1968.
Pender, Anne. "'Phrases between Us': The Poetry of Anna Wickham." *Australian Literary Studies* vol.22 no.2, 2005, pp. 229–44.
Rice, Nelljean. *A New Matrix for Modernism: A Study of the Lives and Poetry of Charlotte Mew and Anna Wickham*. Routledge, 2001.
Shaw Neilson, John. *Collected Verse of John Shaw Neilson*, edited by Margaret Roberts. UWA Publishing, 2012.
Slessor, Kenneth. *Bread and Wine*. Angus & Robertson, 1970.
— *Kenneth Slessor: Collected Poems*, edited by Dennis Haskell and Geoffrey Dutton. Angus & Robertson, 1994.
Smith, Vivian. "The Ambivalence of Kenneth Slessor." *Southerly* vol.31 no.4, 1971, pp. 256–66.
Stewart, Annette. "A New Light on 'The Orange Tree'?" *Australian Literary Studies* vol.5 no.1, 1971, pp. 24–30.
Taylor, Andrew. *Reading Australian Poetry*. University of Queensland Press, 1987.
Tranter, John and Philip Mead, eds. *The Penguin Book of Modern Australian Poetry*. Penguin, 1991.
Vickery, Ann. *Stressing the Modern: Cultural Politics in Australian Women's Poetry*. Salt Publishing, 2007.
Wickham, Anna. *New and Selected Poems*, edited by Nathaniel O'Reilly. UWA Publishing, 2017.
Wilkes, G. A. *New Perspectives on Brennan's Poetry*. Angus & Robertson, 1953.
— "The Art of Brennan's Towards the Source." *Southerly* vol. 21 no.2, 1961, pp. 28–41.
Wright, Judith. *Preoccupations in Australian Poetry*. Oxford University Press, 1965.

NOTES

1 See McAuley, *A Map of Australian Verse* 5.
2 On "romantic disinheritance," see Taylor 22–35 and Kane 8–23.

3 Simply *Poems* at publication, it is commonly referred to as *Poems 1913* to differentiate it from earlier volumes of the same title. The year of publication was actually 1914. The poems from the earlier, shorter volumes were collected in *Poems 1913*. See Clark 213.
4 In his letter, Mallarmé wrote of *"une parentée [sic] de songe"* between Brennan and himself (Barnes 3). While flattered, Brennan assumed the praise was politeness, but Mallarmé also defended Brennan at one of his Tuesday evening salons for artists, chiding a friend for a dismissive review (Clark 112–13).
5 Whether Brennan's continually being overlooked for a number of academic appointments he might have performed was due to his worsening intemperance, the perceived lewdness of his poetry, or his public opposition to the Boer War is a matter of debate.
6 Barnes at 13 sees Lilith as Brennan's central symbol, representing "the possibility that a higher self might be constituted by the union of the human mind with Nature."
7 All but a few of the poems were written between 1894 and 1902, but Brennan edited and rearranged the material until the time of the book's publication (Clark 111, 149). The chronology established by Wilkes (firstly in *New Perspectives on Brennan's Poetry* and then extended in "The Art of Brennan's Towards the Source" demonstrate that considerable restructuring took place between 1899 and 1906 (Barnes 5). Brennan's critical impulse was possibly too highly developed to allow his creative faculties free rein, and certainly he was harsh about his own work. Brennan told friends that "he lacked a gift with words" (Barnes 155).
8 See Farrell, which dedicates half a chapter to the work, and A. J. Carruthers' series on Australian avant-gardism in *Jacket* 2, which singles out *Musicopoematographoscope* as being of particular interest.
9 See McAuley, "Shaw Neilson's Poetry," 235–36, and Oliver 30, who see the poem as important but flawed. Annette Stewart (24–25) defends it against charges of vagueness and poor craft.
10 The word "lovely" carries particular poignancy as it is also deployed in the sonnet corona "Out of Time" (129) to describe the transcendent but fleeting "lovely moment."
11 Slessor worked as a film critic during the cinema's transition to sound, and Mead speculates on cinematography's effect on Slessor's poetry, analysing this poem in particular.
12 See Kane 97. Kane recasts Slessor's nihilism in Nietzschean terms as a strong visionary element that "bravely – and sometimes bitterly – confronts the classic disparity between vision and fulfilment: it enacts the incompatibility of mystery and demystification" (116).
13 Vickery argues that this neglect stems from the fact that Wickham is unaligned with any school of modernism. Also see Rice (109–12) who discusses Wickham's "alienation from the poetic movements of the early twentieth century" in postcolonial and feminist terms, positing that she is largely overlooked because of the "conjunction of feminism, form, and freedom" in her work and its "woman-centered subject matter."
14 Rice defends this doggerel, asserting that Wickham uses it "deliberately as a vehicle for her poetic politics" only when it suits her purpose.

15 See Rice, and Pender, for accounts of Wickham's publishing success in both anthologies and periodicals.
16 Quotation taken from the *Sunday Sun* supplement *Fact*, 25 June 1944.
17 See Lloyd. Neither McAuley nor Stewart had yet published a book, and the Sydney student magazines with which they were involved lacked the funding and reach of *Angry Penguins*.
18 The story was followed by coverage in international news outlets, including *Time*, *Newsweek*, *The New York Times*, and *The Spectator* (UK).
19 These references can equally be read as formulations of Eliot's theory of impersonality, as set down in "Tradition and the Individual Talent," or as romantic foreboding.
20 McAuley had recently completed an MA on the French Symbolists and Stewart had formerly admired these writers. See Brooks 95–135 in particular.
21 The London-based critic Herbert Read wrote in a telegram to Harris, "I TOO WOULD HAVE BEEN DECEIVED BY ERN MALLEY BUT HOAXER HOISTED BY OWN PETARD HAS TOUCHED OFF UNCONSCIOUS SOURCES INSPIRATION WORK TOO SOPHISTICATED BUT HAS ELEMENTS OF GENUINE POETRY": see Heyward 156.
22 Judith Wright, A. D. Hope, David Campbell, Gwen Harwood, and McAuley himself could be counted among this number. The most obvious exception is Francis Webb, a poet whose reputation has grown since his death in the 1970s.

7

TOBY DAVIDSON

The Post-war Golden Generation, 1945–1965

In 1964, Francis Webb wrote to Gwen Harwood expressing his admiration for her debut collection, *Poems*. He would speak excitedly of the post-war "efflorescence" in Australia that came from a generation of poets that included Robert D. FitzGerald, Douglas Stewart, David Campbell, James McAuley, A. D. Hope, Judith Wright, Vincent Buckley, Roland Robinson, and "this no-hoper who is actually a tiny little atom of it" (Griffith 273–74). For many poetry aficionados at the time and since, the post-war poets are nothing less than a golden generation who gave Australia a complex, cerebral tradition worthy of international attention. While lacking diversity by today's standards, they challenged the presumptions of colonialism, wowserism, insularity, and anti-intellectualism epitomised in the masthead of the influential *Bulletin* magazine until 1961: "Australia for the White Man." The post-war poets were products of, but also defied, a White Australia which often saw artists and writers as threats to public morality, racial "purity," and patriarchal orthodoxy. They were distinct from their predecessors in their enhanced access to modern and ancient international poets, including European and Asian poets in translation. This chapter focuses on seven major poets of the period from 1945 to 1965: Douglas Stewart, Rosemary Dobson, James McAuley, Francis Webb, David Campbell, Vincent Buckley, and A. D. Hope.

After an idyllic youth in New Zealand, **Douglas Stewart (1913–85)** migrated to Sydney in 1938. With one collection, *Green Lions* (1936), to his name and another, *The White Cry* (1939) on the way, he had also published widely in the *Bulletin*'s literary section, "The Red Page." In 1940, Stewart took over from Cecil Mann as editor of "The Red Page" and remained in this role for the next twenty years (Indyk). He expanded his influence still further by extensive work for the pre-eminent Australian publisher Angus & Robertson and by serving on the Commonwealth Literary Fund, the chief source of government assistance for writers. There were other literary presses such as Melbourne University Press or Edwards

& Shaw, and new journals such as *Southerly* or *Meanjin*, but none could match the combined reputation, scale, and distribution of "A & R" and "The *Bully*." These were the conditions under which a Kiwi became the most powerful gatekeeper in the history of Australian poetry.

Stewart married the painter Margaret Coen and moved to St Ives in northern Sydney, with nearby Ku-Ring-Gai Chase National Park inspiring his nature poems and fishing trips with poet friends like Kenneth Slessor and David Campbell. Like many mid-century Australian poets, Stewart found modernism's complexities at odds with his own poetic sensibilities. In a letter to Campbell in 1957, Stewart admitted he published Francis Webb's "Socrates" in the *Bulletin* for its "patches of force and lyricism," even if "it remains as a whole a blank to me" (*Letters Lifted* 122).

Stewart's verse plays for radio *Fire in the Snow* and *Ned Kelly* (broadcast 1941 and 1942 respectively) built upon prior Antipodean epics such as Slessor's "Five Visions of Captain Cook" to assert the lives of explorers and rogues as ciphers through which to test the character of a nation forced by war to reimagine itself. When Prime Minister John Curtin published his 'turn to America' declaration on 26 December 1941, it was prefaced by a stanza from Bernard O'Dowd's "Dawnward?" (1903). A few weeks prior, the same stanza had accompanied a Norman Lindsay cartoon in the *Bulletin* and Stewart, in "The Red Page," claimed the magazine deserved acknowledgement (Davidson, *Good for the Soul* 230–31). In addition to his own war poems in his third and fourth collections (*Elegy for an Airman*, 1940; *Sonnets to the Unknown Soldier*, 1941), Stewart clearly felt he had a hand in influencing the communications of a wartime leader renowned for quoting poetry.

Stewart's seventh collection *Sun Orchids* (1952) is widely considered his finest. In it, Stewart continued his evocation of the Antarctic epic he began with *Fire in the Snow* in "Worsley Enchanted." While *Fire in the Snow* follows the British explorer Robert Scott's ill-fated 1910–13 expedition, "Worsley Enchanted" accompanies New Zealand explorer Frank Worsley, captain of Ernest Shackleton's ship *Endurance*, on a later voyage where "[i]n an abstract beauty, a kind of flowering of light / The aurora flowed its colours across the mind? / We longed very much to stand on solid ground" (*Collected Poems* 176). A compelling counterpoint is the eponymous poem, "The Birdsville Track" (1955). Here, Stewart more than anywhere else moves beyond his stock-in-trade of explorer pieces, jovial missives, and gentle nature poems. "The Birdsville Track" was, he recalled, "written after I had visited the area in connection with the script of the Shell film *The Back of Beyond* (1954), on which I was working with John Heyer and Roland E. Robinson" – a rare collaboration between poets and film-makers (*The Birdsville Track* i).

Australians had flocked to the streets to catch a glimpse of Queen Elizabeth II during her visit in 1963, Prime Minister Robert Menzies fawningly quoted English poet Thomas Ford's "There Is a Lady Sweet and Kind": "I did but see her passing by, / And yet I love her till I die" (Maher). "The Birdsville Track" records another vision entirely. For a sequence written at the height of White Australia, in a nation still learning to look within, Stewart sympathetically depicts the presence, consciousness, and resilience of "blackfellows" and "Afghans." Stewart's curiosity extended to Indigenous Australian, Maori, and Pacific Islander themes in his final collection *Rutherford* (1962), albeit in less impressive works which border on what would be seen today as cultural appropriation. Shaping post-war Australian poetry more than any other figure, Stewart's conservatism was nonetheless indicative of his era.

An editorship at Angus and Robertson allowed **Rosemary Dobson** (1920–2012) to befriend other poets such as Douglas Stewart, Francis Webb, and Nan McDonald. There, she also met her husband and fellow editor Alec Bolton. They would move to London (1966–71), then return to Canberra, where Bolton established Brindabella Press and produced volumes by David Campbell, James McAuley, and A. D. Hope. Dobson once reflected, "I think it's the poet's task to illuminate everyday experience, not necessarily to teach or to point [to] a moral" and she maintained that she preferred to be judged as a poet, not a female poet (Dunlevy 10). Overt gender politics rarely feature in her work, yet she was closely influenced by resolute women such as the headmistress Winifred West, artist Thea Proctor, Angus & Robertson chief editor Beatrice Davis, and Dobson's sister, Ruth Dobson, Australia's first female ambassador.

A twenty-year-old Dobson confronted Douglas Stewart and dispelled his doubts that she might not have written the first poem she had submitted for the *Bulletin*, "shaking all over" (as she later recalled) with agitation and nervous energy (Dunlevy 10). The poem, "Australian Holiday, 1940," is remarkable for its painterly eye ("See, at the horizon / Pennons of smoke trail the unmindful steamer") but also its ingenuity as the blank verse of a childhood idyll is disrupted by taut quatrains projecting the horror of war (Dobson 17–20). The blank verse resumes in what becomes a triptych, with the holidaymakers transformed into "uncertain survivors" in an "infinity of sadness." When this piece reappeared in Dobson's first collection *In a Convex Mirror* (1944) beside the Vermeer-inspired title poem, it dominated the volume.

The Ship of Ice: With Other Poems (1948) established Dobson's reputation. The title poem, a dramatic blank-verse sequence, won the *Sydney Morning Herald*'s literary competition for poetry and reflects the influence of Douglas Stewart's Antarctic epics and radio plays. Fine art was a far greater influence, however, notably Dutch, Belgian, and Flemish painters such as Jan van Eyck ("Wonder"), Franz Hals, Adriaen Brouer ("The Devil and the Angel"), Pieter Brueghel the Elder ("Painter of Antwerp"), and Theodor de Bry ("Traveller's Tale"). Other poems offer meditations upon art's purpose ("Still Life," "Monumental Mason," "Every Man His Own Sculptor") and even the frozen English schooner *Jenny* in "The Ship of Ice" is "[f]ashioned of frost and ice... which almost it seems could be held in the hand... crew fixed like stars in appointed places" (*Collected Poems* 62). For Dobson, art itself operates as a challenge to presumed social truths by asserting its own higher truths.

Dobson's third collection *Child with a Cockatoo* (1955) privileges the artworks themselves. The ekphrastic title poem critiques European exoticism through a portrait of Anne, daughter of the Earl of Bedford, by Dutch painter Simon Verelst. Other galleries live on in the "well-dark" eye of the cockatoo as well as in the eye of Lady Anne in England, where the bird is reduced to a mere colonial souvenir instead of "an old adventurer" (*Collected Poems* 85). "Child with a Cockatoo" carries a profounder national relevance than the other ekphrastic poems in the collection ("Detail from an Annunciation by Crivelli," "The Martyrdom of Saint Sebastian," "The Mirror") due to the manner in which Dobson presents *both* girl and bird as silenced by forces who don't try to understand what their young and old eyes may (be)hold. To know that one does not know – that is there is a vast gap of historical knowledge – is a considerable achievement amid the insularity of the Menzies era, and a departure from Dobson's other ekphrastic works in which the subjects often speak.

Cock Crow (1965) expanded Dobson's field of interest to Greek mythology but also to Cold War fears, as in "Child of Our Time":

> I see the wounded moon, I fear
> The travelling star, the mushroom cloud,
> Beneath the perilous universe
> For you, for you, my head is bowed.   (*Collected Poems* 111)

In 1963, Angus & Robertson recognised Dobson and Judith Wright as leading poets of their era through selected editions. While both demanded to be considered on the same terms as their male counterparts, their achievement is even greater in light of the stifling male hegemony of the era and its explicit and implicit dismissals of female voices.

After undertaking a master's thesis on Symbolist poetry at the University of Sydney (Pierce), **James McAuley (1917–76)** worked briefly as a teacher at Newcastle Junior Boys' High School. As "[s]unset over the steelworks /

Bleeds a long rubric of war," his marriage to Norma Abernathy would be attended by Alec and Penelope Hope who "stood witness for an absent world" (*Collected Poems* 250, 252). From early 1944, McAuley worked for the Directorate of Research and Civil Affairs in Melbourne along with fellow poet and Fort Street alumnus Harold Stewart. With Stewart, he created the infamous Ern Malley hoax, discussed in prior chapters.

McAuley's first collection *Under Aldebaran* (1946) aspires to be much more than a wartime collection, but the war is inescapable as the factory turbines "[s]et up their hallowed roar" and "[m]en must awake betimes and work betimes / To furnish the supplies of war" (*Collected Poems* 11–12). In "The Blue Horses," the horror of not just war, but the sacralised modernity it ushered in, is countered by the creative power McAuley draws from German Expressionist painter Franz Marc's "The Tower of Blue Horses" (Ackland 64). Love, always the purest, ultimate state for McAuley, is expounded in multiple forms in *Under Aldebaran* as connubial love, lust, spiritual (Christian, Gnostic, and Classical) love and, in "Terra Australis," something evident in the land itself where "the angophora preaches on the hillsides with the wild gestures of Moses" (*Collected Poems* 21).

"Jesus" and "New Guinea Lament" are preludes to the central concerns of *A Vision of Ceremony* (1956) published a decade later. Primarily devotional, the collection has only one long poem, "A Letter to John Dryden," which castigates the undeserving from the Gnostics to the Communists. McAuley's profile as social crusader is more evident in his support for B. A. Santamaria and the Democratic Labor Party, his role as a founding editor of conservative literary journal *Quadrant* (with financial backing from the CIA), and his support for Australia's involvement in the Vietnam War (Pierce). Most of *A Vision of Ceremony* is spared this due to the New Guinea setting of "Memorial," "To a Dead Bird of Paradise," "To the Holy Spirit," "Palm," and "New Guinea," the last dedicated to French missionaries who inspired McAuley's 1952 conversion to Catholicism. Another reason is the sacralising of the poetic space itself in keeping with W. B. Yeats (in "Celebration of Divine Love"), John Dryden, Vincent Buckley ("An Art of Poetry"), and modern Austro-German poets he invokes in multiple works honouring, or translated from, Hugo von Hofmannsthal, Georg Trakl, and Friedrich Hölderlin.

In 1960, McAuley accepted a post at the University of Tasmania and rapidly became the chair of English, a position he held until his death in 1976. This put him in the orbit of Gwen Harwood, who playfully called him "The Devil," and away from the political and cultural squabbles on the mainland (Ackland 233). McAuley's first collection as a Tasmanian was *Captain Quiros* (1964), a book-length sequence which attempts a Catholic discovery of Australia through the Portuguese explorer Pedro Ferdinand de Quiros (1563–1614). While de Quiros died in Vanuatu, McAuley permits him a final prophetic vision of not just *Australia del Espíritu Santo* (The Australian Land of the Holy Spirit) but also its defilement:

> Then through a breach in timelessness I saw
> A colony begun – not as I planned –
> Under the shadow of harsh penal law;
> The natives shot and poisoned from their land;
> Christ's faith in rebel hearts condemned to be
> Disgraced, despised, flogged for infidelity;
> Blunder and greed disputing the command.   (*Collected Poems* 212)

There are echoes here of McAuley's snarl in "The Blue Horses" at men who "guard with malice, fraud and guile / The sacred enzymes of a world gone bad" and, as if to tease at this, an image of blue horses appears a few stanzas later. Yet dreadful, artless modernity is not the result this time, but rather a "fortunate and free" nation in which to sing "that canticle of praise / Which from all beings pours forth to the Spirit" (*Collected Poems* 214). *Captain Quiros* demonstrates some awareness of the initial horrors of colonisation (handily blaming the Protestant British) while ignoring its long-term horrors. Were it not for *A Vision of Ceremony*, McAuley's best work would be largely located in the final decade of his Tasmanian period, from *Surprises of the Sun* (1969) to his posthumous volume *A World of Its Own* (1977).

Francis Webb (1925–73) was raised by grandparents as a "strict, if not a 'puritanical' Catholic" (Webb, "Letter to the Editor" 47). When he was two, his mother, a singer, died from pneumonia and, six months later, his musician father was permanently institutionalised at Callan Park Mental Hospital for "acute melancholia" and then schizophrenia (Powell 4). Michael Griffith's 1991 biography *God's Fool: The Life and Poetry of Francis Webb* reveals that in order to explain these tragedies, their grandmother told Webb and his three sisters that their mother had become the brightest star in heaven and "Daddy had become very lost without her and couldn't play his music any more ... So he had gone searching for the brightest star and he himself was the wandering star" (12). Remarkably, Webb explicitly references this story in mature works such as "Hospital Night" and "St Therese and the Child." It is also there in his teenage works, such as "Cap and Bells" (c.1943), where Webb obliquely references his mother as "a careless singer" who is now part of the "grave great peace of the harbour" (*Collected Poems* 17).

Along with experiencing colossal symbols of Australian modernity like the Harbour Bridge, Webb also absorbed local modernist poets Christopher

Brennan and Kenneth Slessor and composed his own Antipodean responses to T. S. Eliot's "The Hollow Men" ("Images in Winter"), W. B. Yeats' "Cap and Bells," and Gerard Manley Hopkins' "The Wreck of the Deutschland" ("Disaster Bay"). After leaving school, Webb spent most of the war in Canada training with the Royal Australian Air Force, although he never saw active combat. Doomed, vanishing explorers were an early Webb obsession. In his debut collection *A Drum for Ben Boyd* (1948) it is left to John Webster, the last to see Scottish explorer Boyd alive in Guadalcanal, to wonder how "[h]is blurred shape grappled with the outskirts of the unknown … a shadow at the distant end / Of a tunnel of sunlight" (*Collected Poems* 71–72). Angus & Robertson published *A Drum for Ben Boyd* with illustrations by Norman Lindsay, and Douglas Stewart lauded it in the *Bulletin* as "[a]n Australian epic" and its composition by a mere twenty-two-year-old "an extraordinary achievement; without parallel, I imagine, considering its maturity and merits, in Australian literature" (*Collected Poems* 3).

Leichhardt in Theatre (1952) cemented Webb's reputation. In the title sequence, the Prussian explorer Ludwig Leichhardt vanishes along with the theatre in which his vanishing is performed. Other poems reflect Webb's time in Canada, including "For Ethel," addressed to his ex-fiancée. "The Gunner" and "Dawn Wind on the Islands" showcase Webb's abilities as a war poet, but there was also an internal war to contend with, one finally confirmed in "On First Hearing a Cuckoo," set in an English institution after Webb's first breakdown in 1949:

> Sad elongated faces, fine hands extended
> Downward, pouring the winds, shivering in the queasy
> Grey trickle of nightfall and mixing airs.
> Dissolving distances. Then the changeless words
> Unelectric among the going green and the advancing
> Colour of lights out and the nagging strands
> Of an anger. And cool before the cavernous
> Green of sleep which alone could lose them. (*Collected Poems* 101)

Webb was by no means the first canonical Australian poet to be institutionalised, but he was the first to openly discuss mental illness and treatment of the mentally ill. "Ward Two," the most extensive sequence, was written in Parramatta Psychiatric Hospital after Webb returned to Australia in 1960 after a second tumultuous period in England. Themes of innocence echo through "Ward Two" in figures "plucked from the world of common sense" such as the Down Syndrome patient Harry who writes letters "to the House of no known address" and the golden-haired woman in "Wild

Honey" who seems a refracted version of the love interest of John Shaw Neilson's "You and Yellow Air" (*Collected Poems* 318–19). The 1950s and 1960s were a period of great change in psychiatry and Webb's own diagnosis was a shifting one from 'persecution mania' to chronic schizophrenia (*Collected Poems* 124; Powell 3).

Webb was ahead of his time in his engagement with American Confessional poets such as Robert Lowell. During his time in America, he also reflected upon the aftermath of World War II: "Accounts of the concentration camps filled me with panic: race-hatred was the most unnatural hatred in man. Did it not happen in Aussie [Australia]?" (Griffith 89). Webb's third collection *Birthday* (1953) concludes with a verse play for radio about Hitler's final days. Yet two shorter poems are more radical in their attempt to re-imagine Sydney's colonial history, first in a surviving rock painting in "Ball's Head Again" and again in an attempt to reimagine Cook's landing at Botany Bay from the perspective of two Indigenous men in "End of the Picnic":

> When that humble-headed elder, the sea, gave his wide
> Strenuous arm to a blasphemy, hauling the girth
> And the sail and the black yard
> Of unknown *Endeavour* towards this holy beach,
> Heaven would be watching. And the two men. And the earth,
> Immaculate, illuminant, out of reach.   (*Collected Poems* 167)

Webb composed only one explorer sequence after this, 1961's "Eyre All Alone," in which the British explorer Edward John Eyre survives the Nullarbor Plain by renouncing his imperial quest and being alone with the desert, his thoughts and the gulf of understanding between himself and his Noongar guide Wylie. The sequence mirrors the Stations of the Cross, and as Roslynn D. Haynes has shown, if this interpretation is pursued to the end, it is Wylie, not Eyre, who is Christ (Haynes 237).

Webb's effect on the next generation can be seen in Gwen Harwood's response to "Eyre All Alone." In a 1962 letter to Vincent Buckley, Harwood called it "wonderful, profoundly moving; sometimes I'd like to tear up everything up I've done and start again" (157). Les Murray's 1974 obituary declared Webb "the gold standard by which complex poetic language has been judged" (15). For Webb himself, poetry was "a simple yet lovely sense of order which revitalizes all love of even the humblest things" in the manner of his namesake St Francis, celebrated in the dazzling 1953 sequence "The Canticle" (McLaren 158).

David Campbell (1915–79) impressed many as a talented sportsman, pilot, and grazier with matching movie-star looks. Yet on the page,

Campbell preferred the lyric to the heroic. His first collection, *Speak with the Sun* (1949) features war poems such as "Men in Green" and "Soldier's Song" beside the sacred bird of the title poem. "Speak with the Sun" echoes the verses of John Shaw Neilson, or even William Blake in its lines, "[w]ide on a tide of wind are set / Warp and woof of silvered air" (*Collected Poems* 20). Campbell swiftly became a *Bulletin* favourite. He would later reflect that as much as "[t]he surrealism of our landscape shimmers in the Australian mind ... I do not think of myself as a pastoral poet: a poet thinks with the images nearest to hand" ("Preface" i).

While Campbell loved Australian bush ballads and traditional British ballads and lyrics, his influences were also modern. His second collection *The Miracle of Mullion Hill* (1956) opens with an epigraph from T. S. Eliot's *Four Quartets* in "The End of Exploring" and a debt to W. B. Yeats' "The Hawk" ("Windy Gap"). Campbell also admired Russian poetry and attempted his own translations. "Beach Queen" serves as an example to Campbell's critique of modernity and urban excess, arguing against the "[b]lond multitudes upon the sand," "The city's elsewhere – Surely this is enough?" (*Collected Poems* 38–39). For Campbell, Sydney is inescapably the city of Kenneth Slessor, and it isn't hard to find the influence of Slessor's "Backless Betty from Bondi" here, or "William Street" in Campbell's own "In William St" where he converses with a "lady of the night": "neons flower against the dark; / And she yawned, 'Ah well, and so to work'" (*Collected Poems* 50). Unlike Slessor, Campbell was not a Sydney creature and he keenly felt a vital tension between the city's purported innocence and its lived experience.

Campbell's poems about women are often abstract or idealised, but this is transformed when bitter realities creep in. An example is "Mothers and Daughters" from *Poems* (1962), where the "cruel girls we loved" have had their beauty "stolen" by "subtle daughters" who now "mock" them "[w]ith their mothers' eyes" (*Collected Poems* 82). Here the bitterness is also the poet's own, transmuted into a form of intergenerational revenge. Unusually for a Campbell poem, no one comes out of this particularly well or having learnt much. "Droving," a sonnet from the same collection, is more optimistic, that "in spite of death and war / Time's not so desperate after all" (*Collected Poems* 83–84). The final line is a message to himself, the poet who brooded on time's finality from World War II through the Cold War. In later works before his death in 1979, Campbell expanded his attention to the Vietnam War ("My Lai") and Aboriginal rock art ("Ku-Ring-Gai Rock Carvings," "Letter to a Friend," "Devil's Rock and Other Carvings," "South Country," "Sydney Sandstone") as points of individual reflection quite apart from the Anti-Vietnam and Land Rights movements which shaped Australian poetry's next generation.

"Melbourne may at last have produced an important poet to break the Sydney monopoly," James McAuley teased in his *Sydney Morning Herald* review of Vincent Buckley's 1954 debut, *The World's Flesh* ("Out of the Mire" 11). As a teen, **Vincent Buckley (1925–88)** boarded in the city where he received a Jesuit education (Wallace-Crabbe). During the war, he was a clerk for the Commonwealth Department of Supply and Shipping and then enlisted in the RAAF, but was later discharged due to rheumatic fever from which he developed a permanent heart condition (McLaren 29). He would first study then teach at the University of Melbourne right up to 1987, a year before his death. A posthumous collection, *Last Poems*, appeared in 1991.

Buckley's autobiographical essays in *Cutting Green Hay: Friendships, Movements and Cultural Conflicts in Australia's Great Decades* (1983) outline his far-reaching literary connections. He took advantage of a 1952 trip to Sydney for a Newman Society conference to meet several poets, because "Melbourne was short of good poets ... I knew quite well that Sydney was where the strong poets were" (*Cutting Green Hay* 147). On that visit he lunched with Douglas Stewart and Robert D. FitzGerald and held a "prolonged, immensely friendly and insatiably boozy" meeting with James McAuley (*Cutting Green Hay* 150). Buckley had already befriended Francis Webb in Melbourne. A. D. Hope, a poet Buckley considered "visionary," proved even more vital. As Buckley recalls it,

> [I] began to know him as a friend only after I had become a tutor in the English department and he, as external lecturer and examiner, would come down regularly from the great new lucky dip of Canberra and consort with us ... I sent my poems swarming around him like blowflies, and he wrote of them at length, offering general commentary as well as "professional" suggestions ... My own bad book was out before his *The Wandering Islands* ... He wrote to me "You can learn nothing from me..." and suggested a study of *The Aeneid*. Too late. I was now a Published Poet. (*Cutting Green Hay* 151)

Buckley was a little sheepish that Hope's assistance had allowed him to beat Hope, nineteen years his senior, to the first-book milestone.

There has been a school of thought that Buckley's first two books *The World's Flesh* (1954) and *Masters in Israel* (1961) were lesser works, and in 1983 Buckley was happy to disparage the former. Only thirteen poems from both appear in *Collected Poems* (2009), and Buckley scholars, such as those featured in *JASAL*'s 2010 special issue, tend to favour his poetry after his third collection *Arcady and Other Poems* (1966). Another school of thought, one I have advanced in my own *Christian Mysticism and Australian Poetry* (2013), is that *The World's Flesh* and *Masters in Israel* are both extraordinary collections by a poet who – with a little help from

Hope – reeled off lines of glittering lyrical beauty and philosophical complexity right from the start.

The World's Flesh is a devotional collection which begins with "Poem – Of Ritual." Powerful family-centred poems appear in "A Prayer for Brigid" and the concluding sequence, "Land of No Fathers," is one of Australian poetry's most profound meditations on the psychology of the (Irish) migrant experience and its intergenerational echoes. By the time *Masters in Israel* was published in 1961, Buckley had also established himself as a poetry scholar. A Lockie Fellowship allowed Buckley to live in the United Kingdom and visit Ireland, where he composed a counterpoint to "Land of No Fathers" entitled "Walking in Ireland": "Everything here, strange in its very nearness, / Perplexes me like the shape of a foreign room ... How can I find my fathers in this darkness?" (*Masters in Israel* 32). "Sinn Fein: 1957" addresses the Troubles, while "Anzac Day" and "Wedge-Tailed Eagle" return to quintessentially Australian subjects. "Impromptu for Francis Webb" is the first dedicatory poem to Webb to appear in print: "Old friend, be careful: Words would become our home / And cosset us, till one dark day we find them / Dwindled to ash, or rigid as a tomb." He notes their task is "[t]o keep them swept and sure, / An open courtyard where the poor may find, / "Always, the walking love" (*Masters in Israel* 47). This was in contrast to the "fear and hatred" (47) of the Cold War, and both poets wrote in defiance of the 1949 Communist show trial and imprisonment of the Hungarian Cardinal József Mindszenty. "Before Pentecost," "Song for Resurrection Day," and "To the Blessed Virgin" continue in the Catholic devotional manner of *The World's Flesh*. Elsewhere in *Masters in Israel*, Buckley is far more whimsical. "Borrowing of Trees" shifts from personal allegory to the inner lives of "every limber / Landlord of wings" (*Masters in Israel* 20).

Buckley's *Arcady and Other Poems* (1966) was written during a time of personal turmoil. His father died in 1963 and this led to the seven-part elegy "Stroke." "Versions from Catullus" follows on from the "Catullus at Thirty" in *Masters in Israel* in its explorations of desire for his future wife Penelope Curtis from a safe Roman distance, and Penelope assisted with its composition (McLaren 222). *Arcady and Other Poems* marked a wider, permanent turn from the devotional to the social. Around this time, Buckley helped to foster a circle of poets and edited their anthology *Eight by Eight* (1963). Along with contributors such as Chris Wallace-Crabbe, R. A. Simpson, Alexander Craig, and David Martin, this group also expanded to include Bruce Dawe and Evan Jones, with Peter Steele in close proximity (McLaren 244). Efforts like these and Buckley's 1961 succession of Douglas Stewart as poetry editor at the *Bulletin*, ensured that no future Melburnian would have to travel to Sydney to engage with poets of influence and prowess. The era's other near-monopolies of gender, race, and sexuality would take far longer to dislodge.

Alec Derwent Hope (1907–2000) grew up between New South Wales and Tasmania as his Protestant minister father shifted parishes. He attended Fort Street High School in Sydney some years before James McAuley, but later met him at Sydney Teachers' College where Hope was lecturing (Ackland 63). Among Hope's activities at that time was a regular spot discussing poems and stories as "Anthony Inkwell" on ABC Radio's beloved children's program *The Argonauts*. In the adult world Hope was a far more brutal reviewer, as Max Harris, the Jindyworobaks, Patrick White, and others all discovered in short order. In 1950, Hope was appointed Professor of English at Canberra University College, which later became Australian National University. He taught until his retirement in 1968 and remained in Canberra until his death, maintaining friendships with Canberra-based poets such as Rosemary Dobson, David Campbell, and Judith Wright.

Hope was forty-eight when Sydney publisher Edwards & Shaw released *The Wandering Islands* (1955), drawn from a career dating back to the 1930s. Some have speculated that it may have been held back due to its erotic content which earnt the ire of reviewers – some for Hope's apparent obsession with sex, others for his almost puritanical unease towards it – for which Douglas Stewart and many others dubbed him "Phallic Alec" (Goldberg 61–62). The title poem "The Wandering Islands" proffers a masturbating shipwrecked sailor and his dreams of "big-hipped harlots," while "The Lingam and the Yoni," for all its daring ("The Lingam and the Yoni / Are walking hand in glove / O are you listening, honey? / I hear my honey-love") still reinforces the inescapability of the suburban gender roles it aims to subvert (*Collected Poems* 26).

"Imperial Adam," one of Hope's most (in)famous poems, confronts both the censors of its era and the twenty-first-century reader with a provocative version of Edenic reproduction. Hope was a wowser's worst nightmare, and readers today can appreciate his sex-positivity at a time of great sexual repression ("Chorale," "The Lingam and the Yoni"). Yet there is also the creepier Hope that Judith Wright objected to in *Pre-occupations in Australian Poetry* (1965). Wright felt the adolescent sexual liaisons and female grotesques in "Observation Car" revealed "the vulgarity of the man who has misjudged his listener ... the poem is a confidence-trick ... to emphasise his own anguish, to blackmail the reader as it were, into sympathy" (*The Double Looking-Glass* 83). She was relieved at the maturity and purpose on display in Hope's second collection, *Poems*.

Poems (1960) was published in London, a sign of increasing international attention. The collection features one of his best-known poems "Australia," which traverses the same artistic conundrum that Patrick White confronted in his 1958 essay "The Prodigal Son" – why return? Completed in 1939, "Australia" must have been influenced by Hope's 1931 return to Sydney from Oxford University, where he was taught by C. S. Lewis and J. R. R. Tolkien. Australia, Hope acerbically declares, is: "A Nation of trees, drab green and desolate grey," "The last of lands, the emptiest" and "A woman beyond her change of life ... Without songs, architecture, history: / The emotions and superstitions of younger lands"; her five cities amount to "teeming sores" of "a vast parasite robber-state / Where second-hand Europeans pullulate / Timidly on the edge of alien shores" (*Collected Poems* 13). The existence of any precolonial culture is denied at the same time as the colonial project of "a vast parasite robber-state" is acknowledged; no one's land has been stolen unless "robber-state" is read to refer to land theft rather than convict origins. In a review of Jindyworobak Roland Robinson's *The Feathered Serpent* (1956), Hope acknowledged traditional Aboriginal spirituality and culture, but imagined them so damaged that they "cannot be grafted onto our own civilisation ... [Robinson] reminds us of something we have lost beyond any possible recall" (*Native Companions* 86).

Poems features two long epistles, "An Epistle: Edward Sackville to Venetia Digby" and "An Epistle from Holofernes," the second to Judith of the Old Testament. An epistle to critic Dame Leonie Kramer followed in 1965's "A Letter from Rome." Hope's love of traditional forms and Classical/biblical subject matter (with some twentieth-century forays such as "Return from the Freudian Islands") lent his work a hardy, antique quality punctuated by wry humour which Anglo-American anthologists particularly admired. In 1965, Hope published *The Cave and the Spring*, a book of essays which clarified the English canonical figures he most respected and the moderns he despised:

> A whole generation of poets has followed T. S. Eliot into this waste land of prosody where verse, half-dead, trails its flabby rhythms and dispirited cadences across the page, on the plea that the old forms were dead and that this moribund prosody was a means of resurrecting the divine dance of language. [Yet] what Chaucer, Shakespeare, Donne, Dryden, Wordsworth, Tennyson and perhaps W.H. Auden have done in their time may be done again. The language itself provides continual new resources ...
>
> (*The Cave and the Spring* 49)

Dismissed by some as an elitist establishment figure, others applauded his brilliant mind as well as his refusal to conform to censorious post-war norms in Australian literature. Hope's finest poems do reach the heights they aspire to – perhaps the highest praise available to any poet – particularly so after he embraced a more sincere vulnerability towards the tragic questions of existence before which flouting the censors seems trivial.

The post-war generation are a golden generation, minus the scare quotes, in that their combined corpus of ambitious, future-facing works laid the foundation for an Australian poetry which was empathically Antipodean. For that they *are* golden, but they are "golden" too in that they are not above scepticism and were highly sceptical and questioned themselves. The standard they collectively set has, for some, never been bettered. For others, they are establishment figures from a time when the road to publication was a narrow one patrolled by old white men. What is indisputable is that the post-war generation fundamentally changed the way Australian poets saw themselves and what they could achieve. Before them, there were very few giants, few legendary talents who could sustain a national reputation, let alone one overseas. They utterly changed all that.

Works Cited

Ackland, Michael. *Damaged Men: The Precarious Lives of James McAuley and Harold Stewart*. Allen & Unwin, 2001.

Buckley, Vincent. *The World's Flesh*. Angus & Robertson, 1954.
Masters in Israel. Angus & Robertson, 1961.
ed. *Eight by Eight: Poems*. Jacaranda, 1963.
Arcady and Other Poems. Melbourne University Press, 1966.
Cutting Green Hay: Friendships, Movements and Cultural Conflicts in Australia's Great Decades. Penguin, 1983.
Collected Poems, edited by Chris Wallace-Crabbe. John Leonard Press, 2009.

Campbell, David. "Preface to the 1973 Edition." *Selected Poems*. Angus & Robertson, 1978, p. i.
Collected Poems, edited by Leonie Kramer. Angus & Robertson, 1989.

Campbell, David and Douglas Stewart. *Letters Lifted into Poetry: Selected Correspondence between David Campbell and Douglas Stewart 1946–1979*, edited by Jonathan Persse. National Library of Australia, 2006.

Davidson, Toby. *Christian Mysticism and Australian Poetry*. Cambria Press, 2013.
Good for the Soul: John Curtin's Life with Poetry. UWA Publishing, 2021.

Dobson, Rosemary. *Collected Poems*. University of Queensland Press, 2012.

Dunlevy, Maurice. "A Poet Divided in Purpose." *Canberra Times*, 4 March 1972.

Goldberg, S. L. "The Poet as Hero: A.D. Hope's *The Wandering Islands*." *The Double-Looking Glass: New and Classic Essays on the Poetry of A. D. Hope*, edited by David Brooks. University of Queensland Press, 2000, pp. 80–94.

Griffith, Michael. *God's Fool: The Life and Poetry of Francis Webb*. Angus & Robertson, 1991.

Harwood, Gwen. *A Steady Storm of Correspondence: Selected Letters of Gwen Harwood, 1943–1995*, edited by Gregory Kratzmann. University of Queensland Press, 2001.

Haynes, Roslynn D. *Seeking the Centre: The Australian Desert in Literature, Art and Film.* Cambridge University Press, 1998.
Hope, A. D. *The Cave and the Spring: Essays on Poetry.* Rigby, 1965.
Collected Poems 1930–1970. Angus & Robertson, 1972.
Native Companions: Essays and Comments on Australian Literature 1936–1966. Angus & Robertson, 1974.
Indyk, Ivor. "Stewart, Douglas Alexander (1913–1985)." *Australian Dictionary of Biography* vol.18, 2012. https://adb.anu.edu.au/biography/stewart-douglas-alexander-15726.
Maher, Louise. "Robert Menzies' Prized Possession: A Longfellow Verse Signed by WWII Allied Leaders Winston Churchill and Franklin Roosevelt." 15 September 2014. www.abc.net.au/news/2014-09-09/menzies-verse/5719800.
McAuley, James. "Out of the Mire." *Sydney Morning Herald*, 12 March 1955, p. 11.
Collected Poems, edited by Leonie Kramer. Angus & Robertson, 1994.
McLaren, John. *Journey without Arrival: The Life and Writing of Vincent Buckley.* Australian Scholarly Publishing, 2009.
Murray, Les. "The Death of a Poet." *Sydney Morning Herald*, 19 January 1974, p. 15.
Pierce, Peter. "McAuley, James (1917–1976)." *Australian Dictionary of Biography* vol.15, 2000. https://adb.anu.edu.au/biography/mcauley-james-phillip-10896.
Powell, Craig. *The Nameless Father in the Poetry and Life of Francis Webb.* Picaro Press, 2004.
Stewart, Douglas. *Green Lions: Poems.* Whitcombe and Tombs, 1936.
The White Cry: Poems. Dent, 1939.
The Birdsville Track and Other Poems. Angus & Robertson, 1955.
Collected Poems 1936–1967. Angus & Robertson, 1967.
Wallace-Crabbe, Chris. "Buckley, Vincent (1925–1988)." *Australian Dictionary of Biography* vol. 17, 2007. https://adb.anu.edu.au/biography/buckley-vincent-thomas-12261.
Webb, Francis. "Letter to the Editor." *Southerly* vol.21 no.2, 1961, pp. 47–49.
Collected Poems, edited by Toby Davidson. UWA Publishing, 2011.
Wright, Judith. "A. D. Hope." *The Double Looking Glass: New and Classic Essays on the Poetry of A. D. Hope*, edited by David Brooks. University of Queensland Press, 2000, pp. 80–94.

8

COREY WAKELING

Generation of '68 and a Culture of Revolution

The term 'Generation of '68' was assigned by poet and editor John Tranter to a group of writers which would then associate them with a larger culture of revolution that included anti-Vietnam War protest, May '68 anti-capitalist action, and second-wave feminism, as well as events particular to the Australian context, such as recognition of Aboriginal sovereignty mobilised through the 1967 Referendum. Tranter's influential anthology, *The New Australian Poetry* (1979), declared that a new direction, a kind of post-sixties modernism in Australian letters, had emerged out of this wider progression. Published in Sydney, it followed other timely anthologies *Applestealers* (1974), edited by Colin Talbot and Robert Kenny out of Melbourne, and *Australian Poetry Now* (1970), edited by Tom Shapcott out of Queensland.

All three anthologies signalled new strategies of free verse, new explorations of poetic persona, and a greater belief in the poet's role in advancing modernist and progressive agendas in the post-World War II culture of Australia. Moreover, this new trajectory included freedoms that had arguably not been given the chance to flourish under the then conservative state's conception of literary culture. A burgeoning youth counterculture, with its challenges for the existing order, powered a newly political and self-affirming revolution in expression.

This plurality of diverse, youth-led countercultural activity and civil disobedience in late 1960s and early 1970s Australia had perhaps only one shared orientation within its heterogeneity: an urgency to depart from the self-satisfaction of the post-war period with the White Australian mainstream, the same Australia that Donald Horne criticised in 1964 as "a lucky country run by second-rate people who share its luck" and that "lives on other people's ideas" (209). In the 1960s, intellectuals of many stripes agreed at least about this point. According to Meredith Burgmann and Nadia Wheatley:

Generation of '68 and a Culture of Revolution

> It is easy to point to the [Robert] Menzies government's support for policies such as White Australia and Assimilation, not to mention the military commitment in Vietnam, but just as bad was the cultural repression. Growing up behind the white picket fence of Menzies' Australia was *deadly boring*. (xiv)

Consequently, the years between 1968 and 1975 became a crucible for radical expression. We find concrete poems with anti-Vietnam War irony by Richard Tipping – "WE HAVE BEEN AUCTIONED OFF FOR TEN THOUSAND SQUARE SUBURBS OF DEAD CARS OR THREE FOR EVERY TWO CONSCRIPTS" (quoted by Dobrez 249–50); a new candour regarding gender relations and sex in poems by Vicki Viidikas – "They Always Come" (112–13), "Mad Hats of Desire" (102–3), and "O woman of the moon" (100); investigations into new frameworks of sense and perception – "the empty circus flutters / against my grey / face / and I submit to the pressures of the game" (Buckmaster, "Glen Ewart" 20); new diversities and internationalisms, say for example imagined in Martin Johnston's "Shadowmass" series – poem "Shadowmass iii": "Take the lightning's noontime, / the thunder's night into the caves of night; / the pine-trees' sorrow and the cedar's song / on mist wracked Lebanon" (n. pag.); unorthodox epigrams, such as in Jennifer Maiden's clipped, self-aware lyric in which the subject can "puff[] at / badly blended hash & sip[] / sour White, declaring that / the long finesse of kitsch is still / a question of consistency" (312); and deliberately unliterary escapades into revising the meaning of literature, such as Ken Bolton's dialogical poems: "'it's elegiac, / goodbye.' said the iron (interrupting) as it pressed the sheets / & went off, pressing in the distance, across the ocean bed, dreaming / its dream of 'a farewell / to poetry'" ("seven stupid poems" 53). Diverse in register, voice, subject, mode of address, positionality, linguistically diverse, even diverse in medium – a range of then unprecedented modes of poetries rapidly proliferated in Australia's small press culture from the mid-1960s onwards.

Crucially, such poetries have little of the unity represented in Shapcott and Tranter's anthologies. The Shapcott and Tranter projects of marking a generation both involved identifying and distilling a zeitgeist from a heterogeneous nebula, but that zeitgeist did not belong to poetry per se. As such, the problem of the name 'Generation of '68' as a movement is clear. Anthologists attempted to shoehorn Australia's radical poetics into what was a borrowed, narrower conception of innovation of North American modernism, most often associated with Donald Allen's anthology *The New American Poetry* (1960). Thus, as we shall see, a vexatious but also illuminating set of relationships exist between Tranter's manifesto, the constellation of poets whose careers started in the late 1960s, and the counterculture movement.

Two examples of works from Johnston's "Shadowmass" series were published alongside theories of transcendentalism, drug culture, and classifieds for people seeking others with interests in alternative lifestyles in the psychedelic magazine, *Chaos*, in 1968. Tipping's anti-Vietnam War concrete poem first appears in key radical culture magazine, *Mok: A Magazine of Contemporary Coffeebutts and Garlic*, edited by Tipping himself in Adelaide and featuring other pioneering concrete poems. Bolton's "seven stupid poems" appears in John Jenkins' Melbourne-based 'little magazine' *etymspheres*, beside experimental poems by other stalwarts of the generation such as J. S. Harry and Joanne Burns, along with international contributions by philosophical hyper-minimalist Robert Lax and print experimentalist Paul Buck. This heterogeneity arguably resembles heretofore unseen communities more than identifiable canons or generations. As Sophie Seita argues, "provisionality, periodicity, multiple authorship, heterogeneity of contents ... allow for a reflection on community formation that is historically more variegated and less reductive than an emphasis on individual works or authors" (11). Traditional definitions of authorship and poetic expression, and the literary-academic societies that once forged them, were being directly challenged by small press culture. A generation of young people growing up in the illusory calm of post-war, Menzies-governed Australia (1949–66) engaged with little small magazines to bypass the strict censorship regime and shirk the tastemakers of conventional verse. Small press in the 1960s offered a tentative, heterogenous commons, providing space and context to disaffection and alterity.

Censorship, then, was a constant obstacle to publishing on the subject of drugs, communism, anti-social activity, or sex. Psychedelic writing, protest and concrete poetry, insouciant deconstructions of sacred literary concepts and genres, and print experiments found somewhere to be fostered and networked across state and national boundaries. Such work's evanescence is critical to a historical account of that period's radicalism; much of the work does not retain the novel energy and influence today that it once did. Johnston, for example, would not republish the "Shadowmass" poems in future anthologies after *Chaos* and the eponymous collection *shadowmass* (1971). An anthology from 1979, such as *New Australian Poetry*, therefore already bears the judgemental, periodising eye of those looking back on a more anarchic time. The transient adventure of the little magazine for writers and readers itself, then, is critical to understanding post-1968 experimentalism, whether that print culture ultimately belongs to a generation, constellation, zeitgeist, or not.

Ear in the Wheatfield (edited and published by Kris and Retta Hemensley), *Free Poetry* (edited by Nigel Roberts in association with the Balmain readings Roberts organised in Sydney the 1960s and 1970s), *The Great Auk* (edited and printed by Charles Buckmaster in inner Melbourne), *Our Glass* (another Hemensley affair), and *Crosscurrents* (edited by Michael Dugan) were among many in this democratisation and experimentation with definitions and spaces for what could be deemed literature. Gig Ryan, a poet who developed among Generation of '68 affiliates from the late 1970s onwards, views the various radical activities concerning that generation as interrelated aspects of a larger progressive ecology of social change with consequences not only for activism but reading culture itself:

> Along with the intense political and social tumult of the 1960s and '70s, and the dynamically modernising upheavals wrought by the first Labor Government in 23 years (Australian troops withdrawn from Vietnam; Equal Pay legislation; Single Mother's Pension; voting age lowered from 21 to 18 years, free university education, etc.) the influence of recent anthologies, Donald Allen's *The New American Poetry: 1945–1960* (1960) and Donald Hall's *Contemporary American Poetry* (1963), had reinforced and revitalised this new generation of Australian poets. (n.pag.)

Debates around the so-called Generation of '68 often focus on the anthologies and the influence of American anthologies on them. But the assembly of poems beyond anthologies was itself undergoing revision. Tim Wright, for example, chronicles that the more adventurous media of the 1960s and 1970s involved poetry-centred magazines such as Melbourne-based Kris Hemensley's *Merri Creek-H/EAR*. More than merely a vehicle for presenting inventive language acts, they constituted a virtual meeting place for debate, knowledge construction, archiving, and speculation about topics that otherwise were not welcome in public at the time. Wright discerns that "it is not difficult to see in *Merri Creek-H/EAR*'s turn toward a more 'networked' approach a prefiguring of web-based forms such as the blog and the listserv" (9). Without immersion in the little magazines and social poetics, without the testimonies of the writers and editors themselves, histories of radical change will be limited to the minor biographical notes in the periodising anthologies. That Harry and Viidikas were viewed by peers as the "most achieved" of the poets participating in David Tulip's *Poetry Australia* – associated workshops in Sydney in 1969 would be overlooked, for example (Leves, "Constructing the Poetic Past" 156). The role of non-East Coast magazines, such as *Mok*, in enabling the work of now prominent figures such as Pam Brown, would be poorly known.[1]

The title of 'Generation of '68' deliberately draws an equivalence between cultural practices forwarded by a set of writers with the wider radical movement of 1960s liberation. We must ask then: does the work of writers circulating in the small press scene in Australia correspond to what Wheatley has called the "crucible year" (25) of 1968, the year of the Paris May '68 anti-capitalist student-led revolution central to the emergence of a New Left? Regarding the Generation of '68, the question inflects differently in relation to each of its poets. Those poets who most resemble the prominent activists of the period, who attended signal events in that history such as the 1970 Moratorium to end the war in Vietnam, tend to have marginal importance in terms of those anthologised in *New Australian Poetry*. For example, Kate Jennings, a key figure in radical literature of the post-sixties moment, is absent from *New Australian Poetry* entirely. Jennings' radical approach to (counter-)solidarity and women's liberation in "The Front Lawn Speech" testifies to the energy cogitating within the event of 1968 for Australian progressive culture, presenting the possibility of feminist correction of the Old Left in true New Left style through a focus on developing grassroots community and a newly confident mode of address:

> the women in the suburbs are no concern of yours? your mother is no concern of yours? so long as you think you're liberated, all's well. you and you sisters and the silent suburban women are all part of a capitalist PATRIARCHAL society which you cannot ignore. (8)

The Moratorium and the wider anti-Vietnam War movement in 1970, anti-abortion law reform, Gay Liberation group demonstrations in the early 1970s, the Aboriginal Tent Embassy established on 26 January (Invasion Day / Australia Day) 1972, pro-communist and anarchist culture, sexual liberation, anti-censorship exhibitions transgressing obscenity laws protecting the cultural preferences of polite society – the sheer number of landmark events demonstrate what an unprecedented amount of political and cultural change took place in a matter of a few years.

Despite its exclusion of Jennings, *New Australian Poetry* would position many poets within the Generation of '68 formation. Poets such as Laurie Duggan, Alan Wearne, Jenkins, Maiden, Tipping, Tim Thorne, Hemensley, and Bolton certainly carried the revolutionary urge accepted by the early 1970s into their encounter with literary culture. However, one major caveat must be attended to. Radical poetics understood through the framework of the Generation of '68 assumes that its associates have a closer relationship to New Left activism than established figures of the time in Australian letters. Such an assumption would be misguided. A number of popular establishment poets had a greater influence upon the public discourse about

Indigenous sovereignty, incipient LGBTQ+ ideas, or anti-censorship, for example, than those found in *New Australian Poetry* . Namely, Judith Wright, Oodgeroo Noonuccal (aka Kath Walker), Dorothy Hewett, and David Malouf had a great impact in transforming Menzies Australia and New Left causes. Such figures came to stand far more prominently for progressively minded literature too, each to a different extent, but at least with regards to literature participating in the radical transformation of Australia's mainstream society. Such contrast is inevitable, of course, since Wright, Noonuccal, Hewett, and Malouf all had prominence prior to the younger poets of the post-1968 poetry culture. As I will demonstrate, the revolution involving members of the Generation of '68 had less to do with speeches and picketing than with a revolution in language and literary capital. Understanding this nuance proves critical for demystifying what relation affiliates of this generation had to the spirit of May 1968.

Late 1975 saw the constitutional crisis that resulted in Gough Whitlam, Australia's first Labor Prime Minister in more than two decades, being deposed. Whitlam was a highly popular figure who, for many young Australians, symbolised the mainstreaming of progressive ideas. The Left had won some notable policy fights by this stage, such as resistance to attempts to reintroduce abortion prohibitions. The slow collapse of the Soviet Union's place in Leftist thought gave way to new mantras that embodied civil rights and decentralised, insurgent, coterie-led heterodox activism. This was a turn in part to the American Left. The concept that 'the personal is political' promoted by second-wave feminist figures like Carol Hanisch and compendiums like *Notes from the Second Year: Women's Liberation* (1970) reflect this turn. Anti-authoritarianism began to adopt greater multiplicity in terms of identity, social manner, and medium. Deliberately personified interpretations of sex and drugs as the chief pathway to expanded consciousness would be typified by Australian poets such as Michael Dransfield. Not all liberational pragmatics decentralising the principles of an old order led in the same direction. It is also worth keeping in mind the continuing and increasing influence of American globalisation upon both old Left and old conservative values. The overthrow of Whitlam would signal a wider influence of neoliberal forces that would begin steadily dismantling Australia's unions and welfare state as Australia's conservative party, the Liberal Party, became more free market-oriented.

Tranter's *New Australian Poetry* carries historical weight not merely due to its timely representation of new directions contemporary with 1960s–1970s activism, but for its chutzpah in articulating a zeitgeist with its own manifesto of literary consequence. Notably, Tranter's introduction is one of the few examples of endorsement of a set of poets and practices under the umbrella of the period's progressive youth 'generation.' As Martin Puchner writes, the manifesto constitutes a signal dimension of modernism as it tarries with history: "[avant-gardists] struggle with the specific temporality of modernity, a temporality of breaks and new beginnings ... appear[ing] nowhere as succinctly and strikingly as in the genre of manifesto" (7). That Tranter's 'Generation of '68' manifesto relied so heavily on a particular canon within a wider generation has been its historical undoing. Tranter was right to identify a new poetry, but a historian of that generation must visit other manifestos circulating in the little magazines to take stock of the emergence of a complex new poetics.

It is easy to forget the significantly international urge that underpinned the turn to America. The dominant literary order prior to 1968 was predominantly British, with its staid account of Victorian and Romantic literature, a conservative view of modernism as a short-lived experiment rather than a constellation of avant-gardes, and a linear Western genealogy ending, accordingly, with the modern neoclassicals, A. D. Hope and Vincent Buckley, who dismissed avant-gardism entirely. Tranter expressly opposed such a genealogy, deeply motivated as it was by a still-dominant view of colonial Australia as a sunburnt, Anglophile, faith-guided dominion. So, it was new American poetry and its amicability to both new world literary formations initiated in modernism and to decentred, cultural orientations which provided permission for a post-imperial internationalism. Australian poets were increasingly preferring the horizontal distribution of cultural reference, percept, register, and form exemplified in American contemporaries. Laurie Duggan, for example, is among the most formally multifarious of those attracted to innovations in American poetry. Duggan employs its many strands: its experimental social poetics of embodied writing practices in citation and temporality, the use of projective verse and the open field–approach to the page, and citational and bricolage techniques of unembellished found text intersecting with the visual arts. His osmotic textual approach to popular culture, medial stimuli, and documentary is demonstrated in his 1977 poem "A note":

>   to present/know that much of an area
>   as Alan Wearne, his poems,
>   their real history
> Windsor Rd
> & the legendary Forbes –
>   golf-links perve
>   nobody ever saw
>   Simon Stevens
>   – Sex Pistol before his time   (21)

That same year, Forbes would cite Duggan's work to distinguish New Australian Poetry from a Romanticism that Forbes deemed dishonest and wilfully ignorant:

> here hardly anyone has been able to relax and trust themselves to make their own formal decisions in the language so that what results is necessary & unique to a particular experience ... [Duggan] deals with it directly in a way that shows you that because the problem is basic and simple it's almost impossible to talk about it without falling off your chair in a rage that makes for the various "Romantic" solutions – from Norman Lindsay to the New Romanticism or Les Murray's willed Heartland – that just make things worse, putting the Heart on the sleeve and the Head in the sand. Duggan neither denies his intelligence nor makes a badge out of it and this gives him an energy & deftness in an area where almost everyone else looks silly. ("Wake Up Australia!" 73–74)

Duggan would become part of a generative but loose association that formed around Ken Bolton and Sal Brereton's squat in Coalcliff, south of Sydney. Bolton recalls: "[In 1980] [w]e saw a lot of Pam Brown and Laurie Duggan, Denis Gallagher, Kurt Brereton, Kate Richards. People moved down there, too. Rae Jones was already in the area and Alan Jefferies and Erica Callan arrived" ("Ken Bolton" n.pag.). At Coalcliff, the radical value of liberation from the usual academic or professional expectations then sustaining cultural production was affirmed via a new social poetics that was non-existent prior to 1968.

The central problem of a Generation of '68 orthodoxy about what amounted to new poetry can be highlighted by Michael Dransfield's reception. In his *New Australian Poetry* introduction, Tranter presents Dransfield as the closest representative of the "first serious attack on Neo-Classicism" practised by establishment figures such as Hope (xxiv). However, Dransfield's neo-romanticism, along with Buckmaster and Robert Adamson's, is a "clearly inadequate response to contemporary experience" (xxiv). Key to this shortcoming is a continuing faith in the poetic self, a problem only overcome when sufficiently experimental with the poetic subject or aware of its fictionality. By contrast, Patricia Dobrez and Livio Dobrez argue that neo-Romantic approaches to poetic persona are a valid alternative to the self-reflexive and impersonal approaches celebrated by Tranter. Dransfield's place in the Generation of '68 thus requires additional attention, given the partiality of Tranter's account.

Dransfield was ultimately more popular and more directly involved in the counterculture than, say, Forbes or Rae Desmond Jones. He, in some ways, should be viewed as a popular poet with a place more akin to Wright or Malouf's reception, and whose premature death gave rise to cult status.

Dransfield's vaunted surreal free-verse poems such as "Parnassus Mad Ward" and "Courland Penders: Going Home" explored consciousness-expansion and ontological peripeteia, building his reputation before his death in 1973 of drug-related ill health. Dransfield was not merely a representative of the type of artist opposed to Menzies Australia, but one shaped, as was his generation, by a profound discomfort with it:

> the election of a new Government [the Whitlam Labor Government of 1972] represented something extremely important: the end of Australia's participation in the Vietnam war. Since he was born the year before Menzies came into office, his life had been shaped by the Menzies years and successive conservative governments. (Dobrez, *Michael Dransfield's Lives* 489)

Tranter in *New Australian Poetry* evidently did not want 'Generation of '68' to designate a new Beat Generation. Herein lies another historiographic challenge. The case of Dransfield's interactions with the leading countercultural figures of the time, Beat poets Allen Ginsberg and Lawrence Ferlinghetti, is illuminating. Invited to launch his *The Inspector of Tides* (1972) at the Adelaide Festival, at which Ginsberg and Ferlinghetti would also be appearing, Dransfield elected to make a self-destructive Keatsian move:

> In the period leading up to the Adelaide Festival, during which he continued to live in Cobargo, Dransfield comforted himself with cocaine and black magic. Two black magicians visited Marchpane and stayed on. Dransfield bought a Kawasaki motorbike with some of the Marchpane profits, but had forebodings. He wrote to Geoffrey Dutton: "all poetry is a form of suicide. Motorbikes also." By the middle of February he had had three accidents. (*Michael Dransfield's Lives* 447)

Dransfield did make an appearance at the book launching on the Tuesday of Writers' Week, as Graham Rowlands, who was present, recalls: "I said to D that it was a pity he rejected the poets' panel [featuring Ginsberg and Ferlinghetti] because he could have accepted & blasted [A. D.] Hope. D said, his last words to me, 'It doesn't matter, Graham'" (*Michael Dransfield's Lives* 448).

Dransfield wasn't unfriendly towards America's Beat prophets. Patricia Dobrez confirms that Dransfield managed to spend time with them, even to the point of sharing a swim. Rather, deeply personal reasons – his father's recent death chief among them – underscored Dransfield's decision to drop out of an event that would entail an "upstag[ing]" by Ginsberg and Ferlinghetti; Livio Dobrez also suggests that Dransfield was less confident about his cultural capital than his prominence might otherwise suggest, and that Dransfield was doubtful about his ability to deal with in-person criticism levelled by those like Hope and Murray (338).

The Adelaide Festival affair illustrates how Dransfield was drawn to an introspective alternative when faced with the opportunity of representing Australian counterculture. There is little question that Dransfield opposed Hope's brand of neoclassicism and the values informing it. Yet his poetry was not an easily mobilised weapon equivalent to America's Beat poetry. Tranter was right to observe in the textual heterogeneity and permissiveness of more experimental poets of the period a more lasting critique of conservative English literature; this diversity has outlived the cultural capital once enjoyed by neoclassical poetry. At the same time, the countercultural turn to America for understanding the post-war self marks not just liberation, but also a broader continuing difficulty with aspects of Indigeneity, geopolitical autonomy, singularity, vernacular, and home in Australia.[2]

The neoliberal fascination with the United States was elegantly critiqued by Forbes in "To the Bobbydazzlers": "American poets! / you have saved / America from / its reputation ... & you saved me / too" (*Collected Poems* 69). Here, contemporary American poetry provides the inspiration for escaping an Australian theory of influence whereby acts of resistance merely end up affirming linear patrimony. Forbes' American poetry is poetry according to Ted Berrigan, not Robert Frost. Forbes does not celebrate America's nation state or culture either, in contrast with the country at large, which was ever looking to the USA for New World capitalist glamour. Americanisation too, the trend of greater globalisation according to US interests and its Cold War mentality, would be a trend that Forbes would parody elsewhere. No, American *poets* "save[]" Forbes, perhaps because these Americans would be the most informed of all about what to do about America, as it were. Ivor Indyk suggests that it was contemporary American poets that provided Forbes with the model for a "relaxed style" nonetheless full of "complication" (87). The "relaxed style" of Frank O'Hara or Berrigan gave permission to Australian poets exploring poetic registers hostile to neoclassical formalism, Romantic reverence, and the class-oriented literary register, providing an international ally in laconicism.

The intimate, subjective examination of what constituted individual opposition to conservatism, a mode Dransfield harnessed in his poetics, had its own allies in the period. Figures devoted to more denotative presentations of countercultural thought anthologised in *New Australian Poetry* include Nigel Roberts' casual chronicles of life experienced by young radicals and Viidikas's romantic nomadism. *New Australian Poetry* provides these two overtly countercultural voices less emphasis, in line with Tranter's critical view of the Romantic self, but a historian today can appreciate the attunement to the counterculture these examples from the anthology otherwise vexatiously evoke. Indeed, voicing the counterculture is the point for other thinkers who wish to use the term 'Generation of '68.' For Kerry Leves, for example, Viidikas could be called "the embodiment of the 'Generation of '68'" ("Foreword" 23). Jennings, though absent from *New Australian Poetry*, writes one of the major poems of the age, the 1975 poem "Couples," in which she utilises the hyper-subjective voice to remonstrate about one of the leading sixties causes, here second-wave feminism. Noting how "couples make me guilty of loneliness, insecurity, or / worse still, lack of ambition[,]" she adds,

> what do I do at the end of the day?
> lose him, weep him, think of catching a man,
> and eating him. (141)

Jennings would rail against the prevailing view of a radical poetry that overlooked hers when she complains that her influential anthology, *Mother I'm Rooted*, "has been downgraded ... shuffled off to the side, reduced to a curiosity" when in effect, and history testifies to this, "the effect [of the anthology] on the Australian poetry world was electrifying"; "[t]he boys were beside themselves. Their books sold 100 or 200 copies, maybe. Along came *Mother I'm Rooted* and sold 10,000" (15). So, the cardinal tensions existing within that generation are becoming clearer. The neo-Romantic mode, sometimes Beat-style, sometimes negative, typified by Dransfield and succeeded by Adamson and Viidikas, retained faith in the power of the poet-subject that Tranter wanted to demystify. That neo-Romantic mode, distinct from the modernist-postmodernist one, was nonetheless propelled by hyper-subjective criticality regarding the place of the poet in contemporary culture.

Like Duggan, the work of Pam Brown manages to bridge post-1968 countercultural change and postmodern criticality and exert a total shift in literary consciousness for the time. I mentioned earlier how Horne's critique of Lucky Country sensibilities were shared by both progressive and reactionary quarters in Australian literary culture, although in very distinct and differently motivated ways. One element of particular valency in the literary culture after 1968 is the transformation of satire into new critical modalities. Nicholas Birns rightly critiques the assumption that "rancour" be the sole domain of neoclassicals when radical women poets such as Maiden and Brown – and to that list the work of other similarly hypercritical voices of Ryan, Harry, Jennings, Anna Couani, and Burns – dominate the culture of socially critical wit in the post-1960s moment (115). Jennings' Front Lawn speech is a landmark example, typifying the multilayered nature of discontent underpinning the critical urge among women radicals. Not only did these women support the causes of New Left activism, they sought reform within the Left to advance civil rights for the marginalised and the subaltern within the culture itself, regardless of political orientation. Only with this intensity of deconstruction could mutually liberational futures become attainable for those historically excluded and obstructed from established institutions of radical discourse. Moreover, rancorous intensity could attend to the old biases of literary culture and open it up to cultural transformations playing out in the commons, both virtual and actual, the matters most actively concerning radical youth of that time. Affirmation of 1960s activist principles evidently itself was not enough to render cultural change, the disaffected poetics of Jennings, Brown, and others would retort.

Brown sought in the mid-1970s to keep the revolution of the personal alive, while rejecting the sentimentalities attached to particular modes of address that had by then lost, to quote Trotsky, the spark of permanent revolution. Brown's *Café Sport* (1979), for example, presents blackly comic poems about radical thought in "last ditch / after the revolution," drug culture in "Alternatives," squatting in "Queen of the Squats," while in the same instance presenting poems targeting conformity to the mainstream capitalist order in "Leaving" ("hello briefcase face. / hello screaming suitcase") and the pastoral imagination in deliberately laconic and peripatetic prose poems "stanthorpe 1953," "darling downs 1955," and "chinchilla 1958" that nonetheless, in their own profoundly intimate and subjective way, explore new modes of attention to the real and to memory (n.pag.). Devoted to the New Left concept of the personal as political, the true multiplicity of radicalism in the post-1960s moment undergoes reappraisal in the scathing critical voice and attentive eye of Brown. Brown's poetics in this period continues to affirm liberation from restrictive ideologies while pioneering new modes of textual-subjective record that empower diagnostic and even prophetic trajectories of negative feelings that emerge in late capitalism. Again, while certainly tending to the hypercritical end of the modernist-romantic divide, Brown continues the hyper-subjective tradition of forensic self-examination in poetry that Dransfield, Roberts, Viidikas, and so many others employed also.

Kevin Gilbert, another figure insufficiently represented by 'Generation of '68,' offers a different liberational perspective of the period. Affirming a 'personal is political approach' through his activism at the Tent Embassy, Gilbert's poetry also engages in more personal modes of political inquiry.[3] Gilbert's major collection, *People Are Legends* (1978), is perhaps the most hypercritical work of literature about settler Australia in twentieth-century writing. Gilbert's approach engages in detailed militant fantasies, blackly comic deconstructions of white society, and ironic diatribes about the mainstream white view of Indigeneity. Gilbert declaims the dissolution of revolutionary consciousness. "On Our Black 'Radicals' in Government & Semi-Government Jobs" resists the expectation of solidarity to affirm the essential role of justice instead (*People Are Legends* 28); opposition to white condescension appears in "The 'Better Blacks'" and "The Contemporary Aboriginal" (*People Are Legends* 26–27; 41); devastating and highly intimate use of second-person voice appears in "People Are Legends" and "Turn Back the Fold" (*People Are Legends* 54; 56–57); and throughout the collection the white coloniser is studied with a sharp critical eye. Gilbert was also a prescient thinker of the alliance of environmental activism and Indigenous thought. Matt Hall, for example, finds an anti-nuclear position critical to the radical ecological perspective deployed in Gilbert's later poems. He shows that the various echoes from 1960s causes, including anti-nuclear activism, reverberated continuously through the longer careers of figures who became active in the early 1970s. If we understand the Generation of '68 to be Australian poets radicalised by the 1960s and publishing anti-classical and hyper-subjective anti-Romantic countercultural poems in the 1970s, self-conscious about the failures of the 1960s project and stridently critical of the premises of the post-war Australian identity, then Gilbert presents an outstanding example of such a writer.

Looking back at this history of the so-called Generation of '68, one major figure whose long shadow was cast over the very field of play remains absent: Les Murray, Generation '68's most prominent opponent. While the appendage of 'so-called' has become all but necessary for the term by now, whatever substance lies within the constellation of poets either spoken about or spoken with the moniker of Generation '68, perhaps the name is most consistent when marking an opposition to Murray. Likely the sole Australian poet able to be named by those unfamiliar with Australian literature, Murray's book titles represent the essential characteristics of White Australia: the *Vernacular Republic* with its *"[s]ubhuman [r]edneck,"* Fredy Neptune, earthy, laconic, and carrying *"[ ] the [b]lack [d]og"* (i.e. depression), one who has a talent for *"[b]locks and [t]ackles"* and carries with *him* "[t]he [q]uality of [s]prawl." His poem "The Dream of Wearing Shorts Forever" even featured in the Australian Tourist Commission's advertising in 2004. Murray was also consistently hostile toward the Left and the counterculture.[4] The self-proclaimed last of the Jindyworobaks – that is, a nativist – Murray expressed an existential sympathy with Indigenous politics and its authenticity of habitus towards the land, so long as the settler was qualified to belong. Decolonial practices and material goals sought by anti-colonial contemporaries such as Gilbert, or indeed the politics of other established figures such as Judith Wright and her comrade, Oodgeroo, did not receive Murray's sympathies, however. Murray perversely utilised Indigeneity to affirm settler vernacular dominion. Consider, by contrast, how Forbes confronts the same principles of vernacular Australia with suspicion and doubt, a contrast formative to Indyk's view of Forbes.[5] When Murray would spell out the principles of his cultural politics, "Romantic" and "avant-garde" continued to be the expressed adversaries; Australia was, in essence, a natural haven of the Boeotian in an Athens–Boeotia binary of city versus country, intellect versus the passions: "Athenians do not really belong in Australia and might as well follow [Peter] Porter's own example of self-exile [in London]" ("The Boeotian Strain" 57), he once declared. No wonder Murray was for affiliates of the 'Generation of '68' the central opponent, at least prior to becoming established poets. Murray's perspective recapitulates the colonial notion of Australian culture more emphatically than any other figure of the time, and literature beyond the Commonwealth has little to no status in such a canon.

This chapter has questioned the relation between the poetry of Australia's Generation of '68 and the broader political and theoretical significance of radical counterculture, signalled by May 1968. Moreover, this chapter reviews such poetries' radicalism, in light of grassroots activism for sexual liberation, consciousness expansion, and anti-censorship. I maintain that Tranter's manifesto for *The New Australian Poetry* carried enormous power for incorporating the spirit of revolution into Australian literature. Socially and culturally, the term 'Generation of '68' is best thought of as a phantasmatic affiliation, but one with shifting historical value. The actual revolution was never anthologised. Those excluded from *New Australian Poetry* do not offer some alternative that might guide the reassembly of a truer generation either. My reassessment has attempted to restage many of the stakeholders concerned with the dissemination and promotion of poetics of the time in light of a more heterodox view of radical thought and action associated with the heady 1960s. The same roots have been discovered: the critical role of civil rights activism, the pursuit of a liberational commons, the emergence of a newly political subject, and an evolution in how new print cultures could transgress the existing order. Poetry by those anthologised in *New Australian Poetry*, and some of those who were not, generated new possibilities for literature to ally with grassroots activities of the age.

Works Cited

Allen, Donald. *The New American Poetry 1945–1960*. Grove Press, 1960.
Birns, Nicholas. *Contemporary Australian Literature: A World Not Yet Dead*. Sydney University Press, 2015.
Bolton, Ken. "seven stupid poems." *Etymspheres* vol.2 no.2 ("Cheeries and Quartermasters"), 1975, pp. 46–53.
"Ken Bolton: In Conversation with Peter Minter." *Jacket* 27, April 2005, http://jacketmagazine.com/27/bolton-mint.html, n.pag.
Brown, Pam. *Café Sport*. SeaCruise Books, 1979.
"Pam Brown's Sydney Poetry in the 70s: In Conversation with Corey Wakeling." *Cordite Poetry Review*, 1 May 2012. http://cordite.org.au/interviews/wakeling-brown/.
Buckmaster, Charles. "Glen Ewart." *Drunken Tram: Six Young Melbourne Poets*, edited by Michael Dugan. Stockland Press, 1972, pp. 20–21.
Burgmann, Meredith and Nadia Wheatley, "Introduction." *Radicals: Remembering the Sixties*, edited by Meredith Burgmann and Nadia Wheatley. NewSouth, 2021, pp. xi–xix.
Dobrez, Livio. *Parnassus Mad Ward: Michael Dransfield and the New Australian Poetry*. University of Queensland Press, 1990.
Dobrez, Patricia. *Michael Dransfield's Lives: A Sixties Biography*. Miegunyah Press, 1999.
Dransfield, Michael. *The Inspector of Tides*. University of Queensland Press, 1972.
Duggan, Laurie. *Selected Poems: 1971–2017*. Shearsman, 2018.
Firestone, Shulasmith and Anne Koedt. *Notes from the Second Year: Women's Liberation*. Radical Feminism, 1970.
Foley, Gary. "A Reflection on the First Thirty Days of the Embassy." *The Aboriginal Tent Embassy: Sovereignty, Black Power, Land Rights and the State*, edited by Gary Foley, Andrew Schaap, and Edwina Howell. Routledge, 2014, pp. 22–41.
Forbes, John. "Wake Up Australia!" *New Poetry* vol.25 no.2, June 1977, pp. 73–79.
Collected Poems. Brandl & Schlesinger, 2010.
Gilbert, Kevin. *People Are Legends*. University of Queensland Press, 1978.
"Speech at the Aboriginal Tent Embassy, Canberra." *Anthology of Australian Aboriginal Literature*, edited by Anita Heiss and Peter Minter. McGill-Queen's University Press, 2008, pp. 85–86.
Grant, Jamie. "The Generation of '68 – and me!" *Southerly* vol.59 no.3–4, 1999, pp. 213–16.
Hall, Matthew. "Reading Kevin Gilbert: Nuclear Weaponry, Media Ecologies and a Community of Memory." *Journal of the Association for the Study of Australian Literature* vol.18 no.2, 2018, pp. 1–10.
Hanisch, Carol. *The Personal Is Political*, [1970] 2006. www.carolhanisch.org/CHwritings/PersonalIsPol.pdf.
Horne, Donald. *The Lucky Country*. Penguin, 1964.
Hose, Duncan. "Instruction for an Ideal Australian: John Forbes's Poetry of Metaphysical Etiquette." *Journal of the Association for the Study of Australian Literature*, 2010, pp. 1–12.

Indyk, Ivor. "The Awkward Grace of John Forbes." *Homage to John Forbes*, edited by Ken Bolton. Brandl & Schlesinger, 2002, pp. 87–101.
Jennings, Kate. *Trouble: Evolution of a Radical: Selected Writings 1970–2010*. Black Inc., 2010.
Johnston, Martin. "Shadowmass iii." *Chaos* vol.1 no.1, 1968.
  shadowmass. University of Sydney Arts Society, 1971.
Leves, Kerry. "Constructing the Poetic Past: A Response to Jamie Grant." *Southerly* vol.61, 2000, pp. 151–60.
  "Foreword." *Vicki Viidikas: New and Rediscovered*, edited by Barry Scott. Transit Lounge, 2010, pp. 13–23.
Maiden, Jennifer. "Kitsch." *Meanjin* vol.34 no.3, September 1974, pp. 312–13.
Morris, Meaghan. *Ecstasy and Economics: American Essays for John Forbes*. emPress, 1992.
Murray, Les. "The Boeotian Strain." *Kunapipi* vol.2 no.1, 1980, pp. 45–64.
  Vernacular Republic: Poems 1961–1981. Angus & Robertson, 1982.
  "The Dream of Wearing Shorts Forever." *Selected Poems*. Carcanet, 1986, pp. 128–30.
  Subhuman Redneck Poems. Duffy & Snellgrove, 1986.
  Blocks and Tackles: Articles and Essays 1982 to 1990. Angus & Robertson, 1990.
  Killing the Black Dog. Black Inc., 1997.
  Fredy Neptune. Duffy & Snellgrove, 1998.
  The Quality of Sprawl: Thoughts about Australia. Duffy & Snellgrove, 1999.
Puchner, Martin. *Poetry of the Revolution: Marx, Manifestos, and the Avant-Gardes*. Princeton University Press, 2006.
Ryan, Gig. "Fuori le mura: Seven Vicki Viidikas Poems." *Cordite Poetry Review*, 1 May 2015. http://cordite.org.au/essays/seven-vicki-viidikas-poems/.
Seita, Sophie. *Provisional Avant-Gardes: Little Magazine Communities from Dada to Digital*. Stanford University Press, 2019.
Shapcott, Thomas, ed. *Australian Poetry Now*. Sun Books, 1970.
Talbot, Colin and Robert Kenny, eds. *Applestealers*. Outback Press, 1974.
Tipping, Richard. "MOK MAGAZINE 40th ANNIVERSARY CELEBRATION!" *poetry & ideas*, 11 November 2009. http://collectedworkspoetryideas.blogspot.com/2009/11/mok-magazine-40th-anniversary.html.
Tranter, John, ed. *The New Australian Poetry*. Makar Press, 1979.
Viidikas, Vicki. *Vicki Viidikas: New and Rediscovered*, edited by Barry Scott. Transit Lounge, 2010.
Wakeling, Corey. "John Forbes's 'Miraculous Fluidity.'" *Cordite Poetry Review*, 11 April 2016. http://cordite.org.au/essays/miraculous-fluidity/.
Wheatley, Nadia. "The Girl Who Threw the Tomato." *Radicals: Remembering the Sixties*, edited by Meredith Burgmann and Nadia Wheatley. NewSouth, 2021, pp. 16–32.
Wright, Tim. "Migrating Ears: Kris Hemensley's *The Merri Creek, Or, Nero* and *H/EAR*, with some brief comments on the earlier publications *Our Glass*, *Earth Ship*, and *The Ear in a Wheatfield*." *among the Neighbours* vol.7, 2019. https://library.buffalo.edu/pl/pdf/7-migrating-ears-kris-hemensleys-the-merri-creek.pdf.

NOTES

1 See Pam Brown, "Pam Brown's Sydney Poetry in the 70s" and Richard Tipping, "MOK MAGAZINE 40th ANNIVERSARY CELEBRATION!"
2 See Meaghan Morris's study of John Forbes' critique of the neoliberalisation of Australian socialist values, exposing parallels between the failure of the modernist poet in Australia and the neoliberalisation of the Labor Party in the figure of Paul Keating. Morris's prescient study *Ecstasy and Economics: American Essays for John Forbes* (1992) links the cultural stakes of Forbes' American imagination with how the Australian subject must deal with America when shedding the colonial yoke.
3 See Gary Foley, "A Reflection on the First Thirty Days of the Embassy." See also Gilbert's "Speech at the Aboriginal Tent Embassy, Canberra."
4 See, for example, commentary on this in *Michael Dransfield's Lives*, p. 337; Birns, p. 25; and Jamie Grant, "The Generation of '68 – and me!" pp. 213–16.
5 Indyk, "The Awkward Grace of John Forbes," pp. 91, 94. For how the poetic subject and Australian myth are untangled in Forbes' work, see Duncan Hose. For the political dimension of Forbes' style, see Corey Wakeling, "John Forbes's 'Miraculous Fluidity.'"

PART III
Authors

9

NICHOLAS BIRNS

High Delicate Outline

The Poetry of Judith Wright

Judith Wright (1915–2000) is one of Australia's greatest lyric poets, and the Australian poet who most expresses the ironies, deceptions, and pathos of white settlement. Living through the twentieth century and writing in response to three very different Australian landscapes (New England in northern New South Wales, Queensland around Brisbane, and Canberra and the relatively near rural landscape of Braidwood where she had her last home), she approached themes of landscape, frontier, and pioneering, often more associated with male poets, alongside explorations of marriage, motherhood, and, at times, madness. Even before the words gained currency, Wright was an environmental and ecological poet who explored connections between settler colonialism and the Anthropocene. Through her friendship and collaboration with the Indigenous poet Oodgeroo Noonuccal, Wright moved beyond a rhetorical acknowledgement of Aboriginal presence in the land to a genuine engagement with Indigenous resilience and sovereignty. By describing her own white ancestors and herself as "conquerors and self-poisoners" (*A Human Pattern* 152),[1] Wright sensitively and honestly confronted the settler colonialism of which she was still a part. While her male contemporaries wrote poems eulogising explorers and sought to define Australian identity simply in terms of national pride and independence from Britain, Wright questioned the very basis of the white presence in Australia. Though generally writing in rhyme and meter and using established formal devices, J. J. Healy aptly describes Wright's poetry as leading to "a heightened consciousness of Australia, in Australia" (181). Yet Wright's work also has far broader implications in its groundbreaking social and environmental message. Despite impingements on the global reception of Australian poetry in the mid-twentieth century, it reached an international audience during her lifetime and has since reached many more readers interested in environmental justice.

Wright was descended not just from European settlers but from European settlers who constituted the closest thing to an Australian rural upper class or even gentry. The 'squattocracy' held large estates and, as Georgina Arnott notes, families such as Wright's "sat at the top of a feudal-like society" (53). In Wright's case, this was the New England region of northern New South Wales near Armidale. Patrick White, who emerged as the leading Australian prose writer at the height of Wright's poetic production, came from a similar squatter/grazier background. Wright's father, Philip Arundell Wright, was a grazier who owned a property named Wallamumbi near what came to be the university town of Armidale. The Wright line was descended from the Wyndham family, whose Australian founder was George Wyndham (1801–70). Wyndham was a Harrow and Cambridge-educated Englishman. He migrated to the Hunter Valley of central New South Wales and then pioneered north-westward through the mountains to the New England region. Wright's mother was Ethel Bigg, also a descendant of the New England squattocracy. Her family named their Armidale-area estate Swallowfield after their original home in Sussex, England. Wright's ancestry thus incarnated a distinctly Australian identity based with close familiarity with a landscape they farmed. It also possessed adamant ties to an English past and possession of wealth and of class privilege far greater than most white Australians. While Wright's pastoralist ancestry once seemed politically non-ideological, if undeniably privileged, Georgina Arnott has more recently unearthed the involvement of Wright's paternal grandparents in rural conservative politics and the Country Party (Arnott 53).

Early Career

Wright studied at the University of Sydney in the mid-1930s but by the mid-1940s had moved to Brisbane where she worked at the University of Queensland. Her first collection, *The Moving Image*, was published in 1946. Two poems in this collection, "South of My Days" and "Bullocky," stand out as exemplifying the strengths of Wright's early work. The title, "South of My Days," refers to her own mobility, yet it is a poem less of individual than of generational memory in looking back to the frontiersmen whose toil helped to establish the region in its modern form. "South of My Days," as a title, also points to internal difference within Australia. It suggests a regional consciousness arising out of a multiplicity of places in Australia and thus prevents the poem from simply being a patriotic paean.

The poem begins by at once setting a scene, prompting a memory, and making an argument:

> South of my days' circle, part of my blood's country,
> rises that tableland, high delicate outline

of bony slopes wincing under the winter,
low trees, blue-leaved and olive, outcropping granite —
clean, lean, hungry country. (11)

New England is an interstitial region in Australia, neither city nor outback, not on the coast nor deep into the interior. That there is some vegetation, and that the landscape is "delicate," tells the reader that the landscape shares the dramatic quality of the Australian bush but is also temperate – or why else would it wince under the winter – and agricultural. The "high delicate outline" is a shape at once topographical, aesthetic, and attitudinal. The landscape is the object of personal memory for Wright. But the memory is as much about separation from as identity with the land. This presages a deeper feeling of incompleteness in Wright's topographical gaze. The argument is one not just for the distinctiveness but the importance of this country. Furthermore, the poem is not given over to her privileged, pastoralist ancestors, but to working-class men of the past. These were not her ancestors. They were the men who worked for her ancestors.

The second stanza marks a transition from Wright's voice to the memories of an old drover of times gone by. The invocation "O cold the black frost night," takes the reader back to a state of reverie, in a winter so cold that yarn-spinning is the only plausible activity. Notably, the poem does not pose as including a story told by "old Dan," the drover per se, but puts the entire narrative into the conditional state as a yarn he "can spin." The story is one conjectured as something Dan might tell, but not simply inscribed to the poem as a deposited oral history.

The third stanza is in the drover's voice: "During that year / Charleville to the Hunter / nineteen-one it was, and the drought beginning." The slightly archaic way of saying 1901 puts the action generations back, before Wright was born, and in the year of Australian federation, although the lack of any overt national credo is conspicuous. "Charleville to the Hunter" is going south-easterly, from the tablelands down into the fertile Hunter Valley. It is a journey whose compass points only someone deeply acquainted with Australia would understand. Most Australians can probably locate the Hunter Valley yet not know where Charleville is. Charleville, in south central Queensland, is a small town today. But it was once prominent as a stagecoach and, later, railway terminus. Thus the very referent "Charleville" asks the reader to go back to a different time with different spatial coordinates. Charleville to the Hunter is over seven hundred miles, a long journey for droving live cattle, and indeed "sixty head" are lost along the way. We are meant to admire the sheer physical perseverance of the drover's journey. As John Ferry said of the colonial Armidale of Wright's ancestors, status went to the "young, the strong, the killed, and the intimidating" (134). The poem privileges a certain sort of masculine stamina of the white pioneer (although the "yellow boy" who dies "in the sulky" could possibly be Asian). Due to Wright's class elevation, there is a sense, without necessarily condescension, of the poet taking care to acknowledge the effort provided by the drover and his comrades, and to let the story unfold in his own voice. If, taking Arnott's point into account, the stance is more politically neutral than Wright's true family history warrants, the neutrality also raises the memory to the status of legend.

The fourth stanza narrates other journeys: escaping a blizzard in the Bogongs by bringing cattle down early, and evading the attentions of law enforcement near Tamworth. There is a sense of Australian masculinity as rebellious, humorous, but also loyal and steadfast. While a highly recognisable feature in Australian national mythologies it is nonetheless personalised by Wright's voice. The poem is powerfully evocative of landscape and memory, but falls just short of being tendentious in its argument that a modern, urbanising, post-World War II Australia should remember the valour and effort of these men in these places.

The poem ends, nonetheless, on a melancholy note: "the yarns are over / No one is listening." There is a sense of aftermath, of futility, a forlorn quality. The poem recapitulates and goes back to where it started: "South of my days; circle." A circle is a very different form than the linear, if jagged, journey from Charleville to the Hunter: one with no origin or destination. The "old stories" keep walking in the poet's sleep, permanently in dream space, but now, in living time, only in that space. The poet can still project confidence in her ability to distill these stories, that, as she says in "For New England," in her poetry "orchards fruit in me and need no season" (13).

"Bullocky" is also a poem of the white Australian frontiersman, but one who goes mad and cannot glimpse the fruits of his labour in the future:

> Beside his heavy-shouldered team
> Thirsty with drought and chilled with rain
> He weathered all the striding years
> Till they ran widdershins in his brain.   (9)

The archaic word "widdershins," a Scots-flavoured word meaning counter-clockwise or, inferentially, every which way, is key here; the poet is positing it not as a word the bullocky (oxen-driver) literally used but as a word he might have used. Again, the woman poet's speaking persona merges within the man of the past. Describing his disturbed mental state, she gives him a word old-fashioned and colloquial enough that he might use but poetic enough that she might use it. Unlike the drover in "South of My Days" who faces drought and storm yet endures to tell the tale, years of hard work in hard country have undone the bullock until he loses his wits. The bullocky's madness has a Blakean, vatic quality about it: "he filled the steepled cone at night / with shouted prayers and prophecies."

Wright here uses a frontier-Biblical register reminiscent of the nineteenth-century poet Charles Harpur, who she later praised in her poem "Extinct Birds." The bullocky sees himself as "old Moses" and his team as the slaves Moses led out of Egypt. The bullocky's death is not explicitly chronicled. Instead, it is signalled by a sonic effect that is also strangely temporal: Wright sees the bullocky as mourned by "centuries of cattle-bells." Centuries here means hundreds. But the word also suggests that the cattle-bells have accelerated time and made the scant generations that have passed since his death seem primordial eons. The word "centuries" is both spatial and temporal. Only as a dead body fertilising the soil can it be true that "Moses feeds the grape / and fruitful is the Promised Land." Unlike the drover in "South of My Days," the bullocky will be forever anonymous, immured in the natural cycle. These poems affirm Australian identity as something new and different from England and Europe. Yet, as Wright realised and wrote about in her later work, this new identity did not justify the usurpation of Indigenous land.

Even in *The Moving Image* (1946), Wright included "Bora Ring," a poem which explores another vanished past far more ancient than that of the bullocky. "The song is gone; the dance / is secret with the dancers in the earth" (2). All that is left is the guilty consciousness of the white settler for usurping lands, "the fear as old as Cain" (3). Though Veronica Brady has argued for a preoccupation with spirituality in Wright's poetry, it is neither an orthodox creed nor one applied in a mechanistic way to Australian circumstances. As in the bullocky/Moses analogy, the comparison of white guilt to Cain's guilt plays off both the applicability and inapplicability of the Biblical figures to a very different situation, landscape, and, in terms of the Indigenous people, culture. This idea of inapplicability comes later in Wright's "The Harp and The King," a retelling of the story of the young David playing the harp to King Saul, although the characters are never named in Wright's poem. The poem outlines an allegory wherein the king stands for Australian settler egotism and the harp for poetic atonement for that egotism. Wright sees settler identity as laden with both the arrogance and the potential madness of Saul (a point also made by the nineteenth-century Canadian poet Charles Heavysege) but the solution is not just for David to replace Saul but for the sound of the harp to fashion a new music not contingent on past archetypes, "some new tremendous symbol for the soul" (Brady 97).

"Bora Ring" still has significant problems. By saying "the song is gone" Wright seems to place Indigenous life on the same archival level as the bullocky and the "Remittance Man" to the second sons of British gentry who became Australian settlers, also written about in her poem of that name. With regard to Indigenous Australians, a more apt way of putting it is by Wright's friend and fellow activist Kath Walker, later Oodgeroo of the Noonuccal people, who agrees that the old ways are gone, but that "[w]e are going." Going, but not gone entirely: not yet dead.

The collection's title poem, "The Moving Image," turns from these nostalgic and introspective meditations to launch a poem ambitious and (somewhat in the manner of British poetry of the 1940s) overly romantic in syntax. Sounding clock-time, modernity, and warfare, but resembling the other poems in canvassing madness ("Tom of bedlam / naked under the sun") and nostalgia ("the green world of a child"), it is rife with fear of the destructiveness human reason can wreak upon itself.

Mid-Career

Wright's next volume, *Woman to Man* (1949), was written in the early years of her relationship with Jack McKinney, an environmental thinker and philosopher twenty-four years her senior. Wright gave birth to the couple's only child, Meredith, in 1950. *Woman to Man* features several superb short lyrics. "Night after Bushfire" and "Camphor Laurel" depict a startling, Gothic landscape, a place of "charcoal and moonlight" (28) and "tideless night" (26). "The Cycads" is an extraordinary poem. Cycads are seed plants that were once, in earlier geological ages, more dominant, and which bear witness to the biological inheritance of the Australian continent. The cycads are so old they "watch the shrunken moon, but never die" (29) and "seem a generation carved in stone." Australian human time has multiple iterations – the bora ring, the bullocky, the moving image. So does Australian natural life have different temporalities, as the cycads, later-generated plants, and introduced species all coexist. The poem augurs a deep time that is almost beyond human conception. Yet the volume revolves around Wright's experience of partnership and pregnancy. Wright's poem, "Woman to Man," is one of her most famous. As Arnott indicates, Wright was told when a teenager that she could never have children (242), and her subsequent attitude towards motherhood and to family life in general may have been sharpened because it was an area of life experience that could have been denied to her. "Woman to Man" speaks of the foetus in the womb as an "eyeless labourer in the night" and "the blind head butting at the dark," a nascent new life made by the love of a woman and a man. This point is strengthened in "Woman to

Child" which concludes, "I am the stem that fed the fruit / the link that joins you to the night" (22). "Woman to Man" ends with the female speaker saying to her male partner, "[o]h hold me, for I am afraid" (20). This might seem deferential and vulnerable in a gender-stereotyped way. The polymathic British critic Martin Seymour-Smith accused her of being "puritanically bourgeois" and of favouring "[o]ld-fashioned values" (190). But Shirley Walker has read it as meaning that the poet realises "the cost of this commitment" (5). In a later poem, "To Another Housewife," Wright sees everyday domesticity as a riposte to violence and potential nuclear destruction.

It might also be a mistake to see "hold me" as simply a statement of submission or one renouncing autonomy. Wright clearly valued vulnerability and contingency in the human subject in general, and indeed her lack of a strong rhetorical ego enables her to make statements like that in the later "Two Fires," "I am born of the conquerors." This is an 'I,' the vulnerable 'I,' even in poems like "The Blind Man" where the 'I' is uttered by a male persona. Often this is manifested in the way the syllable 'I' is distended in the poem or put in an isolated or visually salient position, as in "Old Women's Song" where "This Branch I hold" and "So I carry home" (113) puts the 'I' not as central and oracular but as grammatically contingent and mid-line. One of the levels of her interest in marriage is the way that companionship makes a new "field of power" out of the meeting of "the I and the you" (91). 'I' is not the egotistical sublime nor even a typically autonomous agent in Wright.

Wright was fascinated by male individualist poets such as the Englishman Thomas Traherne and the Australian Christopher Brennan, to both of whom she dedicated poems. But these men needed to hold onto their personal idiosyncrasies to relate to the universe. Wright's poetic selfhood is more supple and manoeuvrable. Lines such as "hold me, for I am afraid," or "move in me, my darling" (21) are less a deference to patriarchal power than as an affirmation of the contingent self. A decentring makes Wright more able to step away from her racial and class privileges than if she had advocated a more insistent subjectivity. Like other Australian women writers of mid-century – Christina Stead and Eleanor Dark – Wright linked herself more to her male partner's intellectual identity than would the next generation of women writers, even writing a poem called "In Praise of Marriages." But, as with Stead and Dark, Wright's lack of an overtly feminist position did not preclude her from being socially radical on other issues, in her case, race and the environment.

The Gateway (1953) is the least discussed of Wright's first four volumes. It reflects on Wright and McKinney's move to the rainforest of Mount

Tamborine in Yugambeh country, located in south-eastern Queensland. In "The Flame Tree," the poet asks, "[h]ow to live, I said, as the flame-tree lives?" (57). This might seem a misplaced or earnest desire to merge with nature. Human beings by definition cannot live like flame trees. But it soon becomes clear that this is not a poem of the Romantic order of Keats' speaker momentarily wishing to be as the nightingale. Instead, the patience of the flame tree, its ability "to wait / in quietness" is likened to the tolerance needed for a human partnership to succeed. It is a question of qualities, not of identification. Wright recognises nature, and deplores human depredations or neglect of it, but this does not mean she, as a poet, thinks she can be at one with nature, or that this state is desirable.

The collection's title poem narrates a journey into death. Yet, logically, this cannot be in the first person in the direct sense, so in the second line we receive a parenthetical "(the traveller is speaking)" (66). This is just a foreshadowing of what the traveller finds out, that to arrive into the state of death they will have to lose not just their life but their self:

> Self, my justification,
> Sole lover, sole companion,
> Slipped from my side. (66)

Because of this stripping of the self, intensified by the anaphoric syllable 's' extending over three lines, even the articulation of the poem is something of a challenge. The traveller admits they cannot "recall that time. That country" (67). There is a language of negativity and of drastic paradox. This is far more abstract than Wright's usual strewing of botanical and geographical specificities would indicate. Indeed, "The Gateway" underscores the extremities of absence and erasure that always lie underneath Wright's seemingly more bucolic or descriptive landscapes:

> In the depths of nothing,
> I found my home.
>
> All ended there,
> Yet all began. (67)

It is because "The Gateway" is an atypically stark poem for Wright that it is significant in revealing the full spectrum of her talents.

The Two Fires (1955) was one of Wright's more heralded volumes. The title poem is spectacular in its deployment of the opposition of the primordial fire of earth and the novel "man-created fire" (70) of the Anthropocene. When Wright ends the poem by saying "the world's denied" (71) she was writing, in Brigid Rooney's words, with a "nuclear-age consciousness" (15).

Different urgencies have now arisen. But the imagery of fire as having two different aspects, a nurturing/destructive force ingrained in deep time and a purely destructive force attendant on modernity, remains plangent and catalysing. As in the later "Two Dreamtimes" and the poems of address, "Woman to Man" and "Woman to Child," there is an emphasis on duality in Wright's work. This duality is distinct from the trope of the double or binary opposition. The duality has the effect of forestalling any rhetoric of unity in what is otherwise Wright's affectively close relation to the landscape. It also lends her formal structures a more self-conscious effect, for she both inhabits them but also casts them off in the process of their enunciation. The point of "Sanctuary" is that there is no sanctuary, larger than "the word the board holds up" (93). Yet the presence of a pair of doves on a high-voltage wire offers a perilous sign of ambiguous hope. "At Cooloolah" decisively merges the concerns, articulated in "Bora Ring" and "Bullocky," of the Indigenous and the white settler: "The blue crane fishing in Cooloolah's twilight / Has fished there longer than our centuries" (83). As in "The Cycads," not just different orders of natural phenomena, but different orders of time, are juxtaposed here. Whereas nineteenth-century Australian poets would defend the crane as being as beautiful as any English bird, Wright recognises the exteriority of her tradition's representation of it. She cannot share the claim of the crane – again, more on the order of the tolerance-emulation of "The Flame Tree" than a wholesale identification with nature – as she is "come of a conquering people." Whereas in "Bullocky" and "South of My Days" Wright wrote about working-class men from whom she could distance herself by descent as well as temporality, here she mentions that her "grandfather was beckoned by a ghost- / a black accoutred warrior." At the end, the poet recognises that neither poetic awareness, the modern century, nor a more developed sense of white guilt makes her different from her grandfather, both with "a heart accused by its own fear." Wright never uses the frequent dualities in her poetry to erect hierarchies. Indeed, the emphasis on duality makes the forms she uses less confining and more open, something seen in her remarkable late experiments in the ghazal form.

The Two Fires emerged into an Australia where Patrick White's *The Tree of Man*, published in the same year, had, similarly, asked that readers take seriously the fires and floods, rich and poor farmers, of rural Australia. Whereas White, though, had spent extensive time in Europe and the United States, and brought to his work an aesthetic agenda clearly informed by literary modernism, Wright did not travel nearly as much and wrote in an idiom more Georgian or even Edwardian. But Wright in one way went deeper, as she wrote even less as to advance a specifically national idea of Australia. Wright wrote about specific places, about her own state of feeling, or about humanity as such, and she wrote about what it was to know her people did not have legitimate possession of the land. But she did not write about Australia in either a rousing or diagnostic way. She names Australia most declaratively at the end of her career, in her sequence of four poems set in New Zealand. Stating New Zealand is "Not My Country" (219), the speaker picks up a stone on the beach and says "choose it for you, for another country / loving you, loving another country." While "another country" is obviously Australia, she does not say it is her country. This was not because of lack of identification – Wright's was as indelibly Australian as any writer the country has produced. It was out of her desire to broadcast deep identification with the land while divesting herself of any claim to possessing it.

Late Career

In the last part of her career, Wright diversified as a writer. She composed histories of her family and works of environmental advocacy which render in prose form many of the major concerns of her poetry. Wright also wrote literary criticism. *Preoccupations of Australian Poetry* (1965) can stand with James McAuley's *A Map of Australian Verse* (1975) and R. D. Fitzgerald's *The Elements of Poetry* (1963) as a personal overview of Australian poetry thus far. Some of Wright's comments on other poets are also revealing of her own work. For instance, when she speaks of the treatment of love in the poetry of John Shaw Neilson (a poet whose works Wright also edited) as surpassing merely interpersonal relation (*Preoccupations* 118–19), this parallels the way ecological love interacts in Wright's work with erotic and parental love.

In 1963, Wright began a friendship with the poet Oodgeroo of the Noonuccal people. As the third stanza of "Two Dreamtimes," her poem about the friendship, says: "So it was late I met you, / late I came to know, / they hadn't told me the land I loved / Was taken out of your hands." Referring to it being later in her own life and late in the time of settlers in Australia Wright, upon meeting Oodgeroo and reading her poetry, embraced her as "my sister with the torn heart." This denotes both affective kinship and a fundamental dichotomy of experience. Oodgeroo and Wright shared what Peter Minter calls a close, complex friendship of "mutual entanglement and dutiful negotiation" (63) which led to a shared "decolonised transcultural ecopoetics" (61). But there are pitfalls to a utopian reading of the friendship. Stuart Cooke has said that Wright in "Two Dreamtimes" posits Oodgeroo as a denatured, binary listener, neglecting a dialogue that could take into account the topographical specificity of Indigenous custodianship (62–63). Wright also at times seems to enforce a mandatory blackness on Oodgeroo: "With a knifeblade flash in your black eyes / that always longed to be blacker." Without trying to identify with Oodgeroo, Wright seeks common ground in their love of the land and their marginalisation in the public sphere as poets. Poetry's social marginality as well as its, occasionally askance, relationship to truth-telling looms large for Wright in this poem. The addressee is warned: "Trust none – not even poets." By this Wright basically means that any white words about Indigenous experience will be incomplete.

A poetic dialogue between a white woman and a black woman where the white woman has to enable the black woman to signify is no true dialogue. Wright takes care to avoid what would later be called white saviour syndrome in her relation to Oodgeroo. Yet the protocol she has to adopt to avoid this default option is stringent. More generally, no matter how close the friendship between Wright and Oodgeroo and how much the white woman recognised the literary gift and cultural heritage of the Indigenous woman, a friendship between two people cannot resolve centuries of oppression. Nor can it be posited as a role model for Australians more generally, especially given Wright's considerable and unrepresentative socio-economic privilege. Personal affect can contribute to a social solution, and perhaps more to a strictly aesthetic one. But in neither case it is all-determinative. Wright, at one point, comes too close to an alignment between speaker and addressee. The poem states that both speaker and addressee have lost their dreamtimes. For whites "what's stolen once is stolen again," inferentially by capitalism and the exploitative depredation of the land. Yet there is a distinct difference between environmentalist and Indigenous rights agendas, even though they may have many of the same opponents. Wright perhaps elides the way in which environmental damage and settler occupation are analogous but not really parallel in a way that underplays her own complicity. It is hard to put any issue of, to quote Oodgeroo's "The Past," "the accidental present" on the same level as how the Indigenous presence in Australia reveals that "[n]ow is so small a part of time" (*The Dawn Is At Hand* 130). Wright says in the opening of "Two Dreamtimes": "You were one of the dark children / I wasn't allowed to play with / riverbank campers, the wrong color, / (I couldn't turn you white)." Wright addresses her own privilege in one sense, but their own individual powerlessness in another. Wright says all she has "to give" Oodgeroo for her "sad eyes" is "a poem." "Two Dreamtimes" is probably saved as an ethical document by the own awareness of the different ways poetry can, and cannot, be substantive.

McKinney died in 1966. A few years later Wright moved to Braidwood, in the countryside but only an hour's drive from Australia's capital, Canberra. This move coincided with her more activist turn, and augured a new phase in her poetry. In "Moving South" she goes even more south of her Queensland days, to a clime "closer to the pole" (211). "Brief Notes on Canberra" gives an ambivalent but not entirely negative, portrait of the city:

> The tawny basin in the ring of hills
> Held noting but the sunlight's glaze..
> A blue blank opaline mirage,
> Sharp crabbing flies, the magpies' warble,
> Burley Griffin brimmed it with his gaze (193)

Wright does not exactly extol Walter Burley Griffin, the American architect who designed Canberra. But she does not attack him for violating primeval nature either. "Brimmed," a superbly ambiguous verb, does distributed and variegated work here. She recognises the creativity and design necessarily to render a new capital. Indeed, Wright may well have been more able to write about the planned city of Canberra more sympathetically than the more organic urban spaces of Sydney and Melbourne, not deliberately built as dwellings for both peoples and ideals.

Fourth Quarter (1976) which contains Wright's Canberra poems and *Phantom Dwelling* (1985), Wright's valedictory collection, contain some fine poems and often experiment in stance, setting, and form. Yet, as Anne Collett has argued, these poems have tended to encounter neglect on the part of literary scholars. As Sarah Day has pointed out, Wright's late poems are aware of their linguistic circumstances and the paradoxes of their public and private address, and do not just subside into a poetic substrate. Wright published no poetry after 1990. She responded to the many requests by editors for new poems by stating she was now dedicated solely to environmental activism.

As Tim Bonyhady suggests, Wright at once felt an urge to suspend her poetry in favour of activism but also partially resented the impingement her political activities made on her craft. Even without that, and the onset of old age and deafness, there may have been other factors driving Wright to silence. The younger poets who wrote in formal meter were doing so as conscious formalists, sometimes with an avowed conservative or neo-traditionalist bent, whereas most who had similar imperatives or adherences as Wright wrote in a consciously avant-garde, experimental, and often non-referential style. Wright herself said, in her 1988 Perth lectures, that politically committed art was not truly part of literature. But, as Bridget Vincent argues, Wright achieved a mode of expression at once "artistic and non-artistic" (163). Cooke comments that Wright's environmentalist critique did not mean that her poetic forms became correspondingly innovative (40). This remained embedded in the forms of nineteenth-century Romanticism, although Oodgeroo's combination of traditional form and decolonial content offers an example of form being deployed in an anti-racist way.

John Kinsella has suggested that Wright's late interest in non-Western "patterns" such as ghazals and haikus, as well as writing in slightly freer metrical forms, betoken a drift away from strict formalism (337). But Wright consistently maintained more of a high wall between poetry and other modes of linguistically self-conscious expression than did her Australian poetic successors. As she told Fiona Capp, writing was "a solitary job" (5) whereas activism was not. Wright's independence from Marxism or any form of socialism or even leftism, decried by Cooke (47), is one of the aspects that makes her thought original. Wright was a European-descended woman unravelling European privilege from within her own assumptions. There is more of a mourning and a warning than a hectoring or sense of propaganda in Wright's poetry. This renders it effective as it comes out of deep personal feeling and not simply an ideological impulse that fits like a puzzle piece into related ideologies.

Wright did most of her conservationist work before the full awareness of anthropogenic climate change, before terms like 'The Anthropocene' and 'ecofeminism' became mainstream. Her poem "For the Quaternary Age" uses the term of that geological era in much the same way as 'Anthropocene' would be later used. When there seemed a rather large gap between environmental activism and aesthetic craftsmanship, Wright intertwined them. As Arnott notes, despite Wright's dramatic swerve away from the pastoralist outlook of her ancestors, there is an element in her overt politics of the priorities of the Country Party simply turned round and adapted to the defense of nature as such rather than to the rights of landowners (53). In the subsequent generations, this was not tenable. Poets like John Kinsella – who wrote the introduction to Wright's *A Human Pattern: Selected Poems* (2010) – Anne Elvey, Louise Crisp, the Yamaji poet Charmaine Papertalk Green, and the Wiradjuri and Gamilaroi poet Lorna Munro manifest experimental poetics with and as environmental activism, fusing their art and the quest to save the planet. These poets took Wright's critique further than she could herself. Judith Wright's advocacy of Indigenous rights, which continued until nearly before her death, and her fostering of active awareness of Indigenous identities and rights in the Australian public sphere, is a great part of not just her ethical but her imaginative legacy. The "high delicate outline" she glimpsed in the Australian landscape continues to trace a challenge to entrenched assumptions of settlement, conquest, and exploitation.

Works Cited

Arnott, Georgina. *The Unknown Judith Wright*. UWA Publishing, 2016.
Bonyhady, Tim. "Torn between Art and Activism." *Eureka Street*, May 2005. www.eurekastreet.com.au/article/torn-between-art-and-activism.
Brady, Veronica. *South of My Days: A Biography of Judith Wright*. Angus & Robertson, 1998.
Capp, Fiona. *My Blood's Country: In the Footsteps of Judith Wright*. Allen & Unwin, 2010.
Collett, Anne. "*Phantom Dwelling*: A Discussion of Judith Wright's Late Style." *Journal of Australian Studies* vol.37 no.2, 2015, pp. 243–59.
Cooke, Stuart. *Speaking the Earth's Languages: A Theory for Australian-Chilean Postcolonial Poetics*. Rodopi, 2013.
Day, Sarah. "Reading Judith Wright during the Tasmanian Forest Wars: The Intersection of Public and Private in Poetry." Paper delivered at the ASAL (Association for the Study of Australian Literature) conference, July 2020.
Ferry, John. *Colonial Armidale*. University of Queensland Press, 1998.
Fitzgerald, Robert D. *The Elements of Poetry*. University of Queensland Press, 1963.
Healy, J. J. *Literature and the Aborigine in Australia, 1770–1975*. University of Queensland Press, 1978.
Kinsella, John. *Spatial Relations: Vol: 1, Essays, Reviews, Comments, and Chorography*, edited by Gordon Collier. Rodopi, 2016.
McAuley, James. *A Map of Australian Verse: The Twentieth Century*. Oxford University Press, 1975.
Minter, Peter. "Kath Walker (Oodgeroo Noonuccal), Judith Wright and Decolonised Transcultural Ecopoetics in Frank Heimans' 'Shadow Sister.'" *Sydney Studies in English* no.41, 2015, pp. 61–74.
Noonuccal, Oodgeroo. *We Are Going*, as Kath Walker. Jacaranda Press, 1964.
  The Dawn Is At Hand: Collected Poems. Marion Boyars, 1992.
Rooney, Brigid. *Literary Activists: Writer-Intellectuals and Australian Public Life*. University of Queensland Press, 2009.
Seymour-Smith, Martin. *Macmillan Guide to Modern World Literature*. Macmillan, 1985.
Vincent, Bridget. "'Sorry, Above All, That I Can Make Nothing Right': Public Apology in Judith Wright." *Australian Humanities Review* no.61, May 2017, pp. 160–72.
Walker, Shirley. *Flame and Shadow: A Study of Judith Wright's Poetry*. University of Queensland Press, 1991.
Wright, Judith. *The Moving Image*. Meanjin Press, 1946.
  Woman to Man: Poems. Angus & Robertson, 1949.
  The Gateway. Angus & Robertson, 1953.
  The Two Fires. Angus & Robertson, 1955.
  Preoccupations of Australian Poetry. Oxford University Press, 1965.
  Fourth Quarter. Angus & Robertson, 1976.
  Phantom Dwelling. Angus & Robertson, 1985.
  A Human Pattern: Selected Poems, edited by John Kinsella. Carcanet, 2010.

NOTES

1 All cited poems by Judith Wright are from *A Human Pattern: Selected Poems*.

10

ANN-MARIE PRIEST

Burning Sappho

Gwen Harwood's Incendiary Verse

In the mid-twentieth century, Gwen Harwood was Australian poetry's pre-eminent trickster figure. "Not since the golden age of the Ern Malley hoax have we had such an entertaining personality in the literary world here," Wilson Blackman enthused in a radio review of her first book, *Poems*, in 1964. He was referring to Harwood's use of pseudonyms, by means of which "the poetess" – as Blackman calls her – had hoaxed a series of literary editors. Most spectacular was the so-called *Bulletin* hoax of 1961, in which, under the name Walter Lehmann, Harwood smuggled two acrostic poems into the literary pages of Australia's iconic magazine. Ostensibly high-minded sonnets about medieval lovers Abelard and Eloise, the poems spelled out "so long Bulletin" and "fuck all editors." In the resulting media furore, the revelation that the author of these 'obscene' works was a woman – and a respectable mother and housewife, at that – was the juiciest element.

Her use of 'unseemly' language was only one of the ways in which, as a poet, Harwood challenged the cultural conventions of womanliness. She refused to write in the genteel style expected of a "lady poet" (8) (as Donald Horne dubbed her in the aftermath of the hoax) – or, indeed, in the traditional mode of Australian lyric poets: "a poem about a bird, a flower or animal, from which they draw some generalisation about life" (Dunlevy 14). Instead, she wrote about contemporary urban life in ways that were unsentimental, dramatic (as opposed to lyrical), and careless of taboos. She adopted multiple poetic personae and points of view, trying out different voices and styles, and working, as Diane Dodwell noted, "on many different levels of seriousness and lightness" (74). In her early work, she often adopted a male perspective, the default point of view, then, for poetry. But in the 1960s, she began to work her way towards a poetic persona that was clearly, unashamedly, and sometimes agonisedly a woman, one who accepted the traditional female roles thrust upon her but who nevertheless suffered from a desire that – as she put it in her poem "Boundary Conditions" – flared beyond her "fate" (55).[1] In this persona, she wrote startlingly original poems that challenged the ideology of "Holy Motherhood"; she created a dazzling series of love poems with female desire at their heart; and she reworked the Romantic ideal of the Byronic poet, the isolated, detached, demon-haunted man, to create a poet-persona who is lovingly engaged with the world, a woman who "chooses," as in "Littoral," to be "woven in other lives" (187), and whose creative angst arises from the tension between her need for connection and her needs for self-expression, transcendence, and solitude.[2]

Harwood herself struggled to find time for her own writing in the 1950s, as a full-time housewife and mother of four young children. She was in her forties when her first book, *Poems*, appeared in 1963,[3] and very aware of the gap between her poetic personae and her private ones. She could imagine the whispers: "What is that forty-four-year-old mother-of-four doing with a book of burning poems?" Her answer was simple: "I may look like an aging choirboy ... but I don't think like one" (Edgar 74). Despite her age, she was quickly linked with the emerging poets of that era – the likes of Thomas Shapcott, Rodney Hall, Roger McDonald, David Malouf, and Chris Wallace-Crabbe, some fifteen years younger than she was. Indeed, Hall and Shapcott included her among the poets who were "breaking fresh ground" (1) in their 1968 anthology *New Impulses in Australian Poetry* – for which her poem "New Music" provided the epigraph. She also featured, in the guise of a young male poet, Timothy Kline, in the 1970 anthology *Australian Poetry Now*, which focused specifically on "young poets" who were "rejecting and rediscovering, making loud claims for themselves and their ideas" (Shapcott, *Australian Poetry Now* ix). Outing her as Kline's progenitor, one reviewer noted that Harwood was "sending up the whole youthquake with typical expertise" (Sylvia Lawson 23). But though there was an element of satire in her impersonation of an 'angry young man,' Harwood was perfectly at home in this company. As Dodwell noted in her 1977 review of Harwood's first *Selected Poems* (1975), Harwood's poetry was "intransigently anti-establishment," with "a quality of wildness such as to startle and challenge the reader" (78). After Harwood's death, Peter Porter would similarly observe that "[t]here is scarcely any conventional morality in her work but always a lively endorsement of youthful sexuality and daring" (7).

At the same time, Harwood took great care to distance her life from her poetry. Very aware of the social opprobrium that was heaped upon women who violated social norms, she worked hard to ensure that readers could draw no inferences about her private life from her poems. Her use of pseudonyms was one way she shielded herself; another was her deployment of what Trigg calls a "range of distancing effects" in the poems themselves, including the use of male or carefully non-gendered speakers (81). In her public life, she cultivated a persona of irreproachable respectability. She rejected critics' attempts to connect her so-called suburban poems of the early sixties with the later women's liberation movement, and stared down any suggestion that her erotic poems might have sprung from extramarital experience. Unlike her contemporary, Dorothy Hewett, she avoided any hint of scandal in her private life, and in her seventies presided over the mainstream literary circuit of festivals, prize ceremonies, and readings with sweet benignity, a twinkling-eyed "grandmotherly figure" (Trigg 75). In her home state of Tasmania, she willingly stepped into the role of unofficial poet laureate, writing accessible poems on demand to celebrate civic occasions, and becoming, in Porter's words, "undoubtedly Australia's most loved poet" (7). This carefully cultivated persona, however, has worked to obscure the subversive nature of Harwood's contribution to Australian poetry. This chapter focuses on the many challenges in her work to gendered conceptions of motherhood and sexuality, arguing that she led the way in bringing female experiences of the domestic realm into poetry and in creating works of explicitly female eroticism.

*

Harwood's early work includes a sequence of poems featuring a fictional character named Professor Eisenbart, a misanthropic scientist who may or may not be engaged in the development of weapons of mass destruction.[4] Written in the 1950s, in the shadow of Hiroshima, these poems were unusual in Australian poetry, as Strauss points out, for their "extended creation of character" (*Boundary Conditions* 65). They were unusual, too, in their attack on the valuing of science and reason, and in their overt sexual immorality. Eisenbart is a powerful man, successful in his field, celebrated in the community, yet he is full of rage, anguish, and self-doubt. He likes to see himself as the panther of the poem "Panther and Peacock," brooding and deadly, but cannot rid himself of the fear that he is really the vain and vapid peacock, helpless like everyone else before the "dark beast" of time and death (54).[5]

The ageing Eisenbart has a "young mistress," revealed in one poem, "Prize-Giving," to be a schoolgirl; several of the Eisenbart poems feature him either in bed with her or planning to be. But though the poems are dramatic in form, with scenes and dialogue, their style is far from naturalistic. They are tightly constructed in terms of both rhythm and rhyme, their language dense and ornate; the characters' utterances, in particular, tend to read like an exchange of formal set pieces in a verse play. This formality works as a kind of counterweight to their radical subject matter. In "Professor Eisenbart's Evening," for instance, the poem hinges on Eisenbart's mistress refusing him sex because she has her period (surely one of very few references to menstruation in mid-century Australian poetry), but the interaction is all but concealed by elegant abstraction. Eisenbart says only "[c]ome, now," and she replies: "The moon forestalls you, dear" (51). Her refusal sparks a furious – but elegantly elaborated – rant from her lover, directed ostensibly at the moon itself, in which he declares that he will destroy anything that thwarts his desire. His mistress is unimpressed, teasing him in rolling iambic tetrameter before going calmly off to sleep. Eisenbart continues to brood in exalted Romantic language, elaborating a dark fantasy of a poisonous cloud seeping through the town, "[i]nvulnerable, and swift to kill," before he, too, falls asleep.

Harwood's use of traditional metrical forms often seemed at odds with her subject matter, and more than one critic has seen this as deliberate. As early as 1976, Rodney Hall wrote that Harwood used her "carefully modulated and tuned" forms as a "guarantee of poetic respectability" (quoted in Strauss, *Boundary Conditions* 131). No matter how wild a poem's content, its form was tightly controlled – and thus the poet could not be dismissed as "insane or irresponsible." Harwood herself once said that the more deeply felt a poem was, the tighter its form should be.[6] Over her career, however, she would develop an increasingly conversational tone and diction. In the mid-sixties, she told a friend that she was "slowly growing away from the old encrusted ornate adjective-hung style,"[7] and in the 1990s, Elizabeth Lawson would observe that Harwood's use of formal structures had loosened "through time, both within set forms ... and in freer use of longer lines in later poems" (20).

The Eisenbart poems belonged to the earlier period, however, in which radical content was contained by traditional form. In addition to Eisenbart's sexual relationship with a schoolgirl, he also attempts, in "Ganymede," to bed a young boy, seemingly a child prostitute. Tired of his mistress's "sweetness" (56), the poem tells us, Eisenbart turns his lustful attention to "a boy whose wealth / of beauty" had "seduced" him (57) (a dangerous inversion of the truth of Eisenbart's "unwelcome longing" (56)), and leaves his hotel room in search of him. The poem invokes the ancient myth of Ganymede, a beautiful boy seized upon by Zeus in the guise of an eagle and whisked up to Mount Olympus to serve the god's pleasure. But Eisenbart is no Zeus, dropping upon the child "as a hawk swoops to serve its nature" (57). Instead, like Von Aschenbach in Thomas Mann's *Death in Venice* (another of Harwood's influences), he is unable to consummate his lust. Despite the sheltering umbrella of Greek mythology, the poem remains genuinely shocking, not only in its depiction of an adult male's desire for a child but also in the child's willing participation in his own "corruption" (57). Eisenbart is mocked by the child and, seemingly, by the poet for his failure to consummate his lust. "Ganymede" ends with the restless scientist drowning his "longing" (56) in work, foolishly seeking in "symbols" the "divine affirmative" only life itself can give (58).

"Ganymede" was published in *Meanjin* in 1958, which also published "Daybreak" (1956) and "Prize-Giving" (1959). Harwood struggled, however, to get her other Eisenbart poems into print. She suspected they were too confronting; editors sought poems that were "sexless and pretty," neither of which criterion "Ganymede" met (*A Steady Storm* 95). "I must get to work on my pink & blue epic, The Parish Church," she told a friend; "it will tell, in unrhymed eccentric pentameter, how the choir made paper chains out of their hymn books."[8] Certainly, the appearance under a woman's name of this angry, destructive, sexually ambiguous character must have been startling, to say the least. The male-dominated literary world still had fixed conceptions of the style and subject matter of "lady poets" (Horne 8), and a strong, if largely unexpressed, sense of what constituted 'proper' subject matter for women.[9] Editors were wary of Eisenbart, as Harwood's letters show. The series consisted of eight substantive poems, all of which were complete by the end of 1958;[10] by the end of 1959, only four were in print; two would only appear in her first collection. Her growing frustration at the many rejections of her poems (including those that did not feature Professor Eisenbart), along with her increasingly critical view of editorial judgement, led her to write the first of her hoax poems, and begin publishing under pseudonyms.[11]

She soon found that her poems were more acceptable to editors under the names of Walter Lehmann and Francis Geyer than her own. Douglas Stewart at the *Bulletin* and James McAuley at *Quadrant*, in particular, showed themselves much more amenable to publishing both Lehmann and Geyer than they had ever been to publishing Harwood. Indeed, Stewart told Geyer he would "rather like to know" who he was and asked him to "call in" at the *Bulletin* offices "any day about 12.30" (*A Steady Storm* 111). Such invitations had never been extended to Gwen Harwood. "I rankle at [Geyer's] easy success," Harwood wrote to a friend. "[W]hat's he got that I haven't except his name?" (*A Steady Storm* 116). She found the pseudonyms liberating, however. They enabled her to write more freely, without the fear that what she wrote would be held against the real-life Mrs Harwood.

One of the things she wrote about under the shelter of Lehmann's name was the toll that 1950s-style domestic life took on women who found themselves immured in it. "In the Park," which would become one of her most celebrated works, was first published as a Lehmann poem. In this tightly constructed sonnet, a young mother takes her three children to the park, where she runs into an old lover. Through his eyes, she sees herself as she has become: dowdy, careworn, defeated. Making polite conversation, she mouths the pleasant platitudes of motherhood, but when her old friend has gone, she sinks into despair. Holding her youngest child, she says to the wind: "They have eaten me alive" (65).

The sentiment was profoundly challenging for its time. The idea that a woman's children could consume her very being was entirely antithetical to the dominant discourse of motherhood, in which a woman was supposed to find her only true fulfilment in bearing and raising children. Even worse was the suggestion that a mother might resent this unthinking consumption of herself by her offspring. One of the key tenets of "Holy Motherhood" was that any woman worthy of the name would willingly give her life for her children; no burden was too heavy, no sacrifice too great. For a woman to challenge these cultural norms was to risk being labelled 'monstrous.' As Sheridan shows, in the post-war period, "[w]omen were supposed to be grateful for their modern suburban homes and proud of their enhanced domestic roles, but not to ask for anything more" (144). To push back against these cultural norms was to challenge the foundations of post-war society.

"In the Park" was somewhat more acceptable as the work of a man than a woman. Men could be expected to have 'tough' views even on domestic matters, whereas women were expected – as Harwood herself expressed it – to be "softer and sweeter." She was gratified to hear a reader opine that "a woman couldn't have written 'In the Park' because she would be too self-pitying ... takes a man to look at it like that!"[12] As Lehmann, Harwood could cast off the trappings of femininity and adopt the supposedly masculine qualities of objectivity and detachment. Indeed, her friend and fellow poet Vincent Buckley, who was in on the secret of Lehmann's identity, praised Lehmann precisely for these qualities. Buckley was, he told Harwood, "particularly attracted by the firmness and crispness with which [Lehmann's poems] objectify the personal emotions in their themes."[13] He found these works "neat, self-contained, and dramatic" in a way her other poems – those published under her own name – supposedly were not. To him, "In the Park" was "almost terrifying" in its "precision and fierceness of feeling." The terror, presumably, sprang from his awareness that the hand that held Lehmann's pen was a woman's.

"In the Park" was Lehmann's only poem of "feminist complaint" (Sheridan 159). His "A Kitchen Poem: The Farmer to His Wife" does acknowledge a trapped woman's yearnings for "a scintillating life" in a world "where brats and all their fierce demands / don't happen" – but it ensures her rebellion is contained within a broader narrative extolling the "rich" world of "[c]hildren and work and daily bread" (68). Harwood continued what Sheridan calls her "bold experiment" (151) in writing of the feminine world of suburbia under a different pseudonym: Miriam Stone. Following Lehmann's unmasking after the *Bulletin* hoax, her new pseudonym – "a lovely lady poet, married (of course, how else would she have any grasp of the world's sorrows?) with child" – was intended to put suspicious editors off the scent: "Nobody will be expecting me to be a lady poet" (*Idle Talk* 95). Both Sheridan and Trigg have argued that Stone's so-called suburban poems were transgressive for their time – and startlingly original. "It may be hard to credit how *dis*favoured such subjects were in the 50s and 60s, when high modernism disdained the popular and the domestic," writes Sheridan (151). Yet Harwood insisted that the domestic experience of women was a subject worthy of art. Trigg points out that poems such as "Suburban Sonnet" and "Suburban Sonnet: Boxing Day" work "by opposing the dominant discourse of maternal joy with the lived realism of endless chaos and repetitive chores" (37–38). The cliches of domestic bliss fall dismally flat for Harwood's exhausted housewives. The situation is exacerbated, as Sheridan points out, by the "violent contrast" between the protagonists' current situation and their previous "aspirations and hopes for love and creativity" (145). Harwood's housewives are former or aspiring artists – one is a musician, at least two are writers. In "Lip Service" and "Burning Sappho," poems that are in some ways mirror images of one another, the first-person narrator, immured in domesticity, is a poet. The chaos and exhaustion of her domestic life is exacerbated by her longing for time and solitude to do her own creative work. Her heart beats, as the protagonist of "Lip Service" puts it, like a "winged stone" – desperate for flight but incapable of leaving the ground (128).

"Lip Service" doubles down on the controversial image in "In the Park" of a woman being eaten alive by her children. Torn apart by the conflicting demands of her household and her art, the protagonist determines to put an end to her torment by jettisoning the part of her that longs to write. "No more I'll walk at a late hour / Restless about the house," she vows. "I'll not / Wrestle with words, nor show one sour / Look in my neat domestic plot." She will achieve this by the simple stratagem of cutting out her own core, wherein lies the longing that destroys her peace and that of her household. She will remove the "seeds" of her own discontent just as she would core an apple, in order to serve up the "the mild / Fruit of myself to fill the needs / Of husband and importuning child." It will be a kind of liberation: freed from her writing ambitions, her winged heart will no longer "beat in vain." Yet her self-mutilation leaves her unrecognisable to herself: "A sad face with an idiot grin."

Harwood sent this poem with two others to the *Bulletin* in early 1962 as Miriam Stone. It was rejected by the then poetry editor Vincent Buckley, who had not yet realised that Stone was really Harwood. He recognised Stone's work as "highly individual, with a powerful jet of feeling and a willingness to probe the life-centre in a way that would frighten most contemporary poets under their beds in pork-pie hats." Nevertheless, he felt that "Lip Service" worked only in "bits," "not as a whole."[14] "Burning Sappho," a companion piece to "Lip Service," he accepted. Where the speaker of "Lip Service" turns her anger inwards, in the form of self-loathing and despair, the speaker in "Burning Sappho" directs it outwards, in the form of murderous rage. It tells the story of a woman seeking a few moments in the busyness of her day to work on a poem, and being mercilessly thwarted by the endless demands of those around her – her whining child, a visiting friend, the rector, her amorous husband. In each stanza, she plots a remorseless revenge on those who stand between her and her work: sticking pins in a voodoo doll of her daughter, pouring prussic acid into her visitor's tea, chopping her husband to bits. With "devils burning in [her] brain," her fantasies are venomous (158). Yet she takes no violent action at all. Instead, she quietly goes about meeting the needs of everyone around her, and rises before dawn the next morning to try once more to "find / my truth, my poem, and grasp it yet."

Though the protagonist of "Burning Sappho" attacks no-one, her simmering rage is shocking in itself – particularly when directed at her child (in the original published version, "[s]omething like hatred forks between" mother and child, but in later versions Harwood changed "hatred" to the less confronting "anger"). Harwood felt uneasy about the poem once it was in print. When it was selected for the 1962 volume of *Australian Poetry*, she withdrew it, telling a friend she "hated" Miriam Stone "for writing Burning Sappho."[15] She was anxious to ensure her husband did not see it – it was "too nasty," as she confessed to another friend (Priest, "Baby and Demon" 72). Though she included it in her second volume, she left it out of all her subsequent collections. Yet this poem, like "In the Park," was one of those that spoke most strongly to her readers. As fellow poet and novelist Nancy Cato wrote to Harwood in 1969, the Stone poems expressed "what every woman stifled by suburbia & being a housewife and mother has felt; particularly that savage hatred of one's 'nearest & dearest' for getting in the way of creative work: 'you have eaten me alive.' 'Burning Sappho,' indeed!"[16]

It is not surprising that, once her pseudonyms had been stripped away, Harwood sought to distance herself from these poems. If readers of "In the Park" suspected her of not loving her children (as she would discover when she read the poem publicly), what inferences might they draw from "Burning Sappho"? Yet these were groundbreaking works whose power and relevance became ever-clearer with the emergence of second-wave feminism in the late 1960s and early 1970s. Indeed, Trigg argues that these poems inaugurated a new genre in Australian poetry in which "women writers give voice to the constraints of domesticity that are normally presented by the popular media and traditional ideologies as fulfilling and satisfying" (37–38), seeing parallels with the contemporaneous work of US poets such as Sylvia Plath and Adrienne Rich. Sheridan goes further, arguing that the "suburban" poems were not only ground-breaking in their time, but continue to challenge new generations of readers by drawing attention to "the persistent tensions inherent in the concepts of suburbia and domestic modernity" (151).

Jennifer Strauss points out, however, that it is not possible to draw any simple conclusions about Harwood's own view of motherhood and domesticity from her poems. As with so many other subjects, her work is ambiguous on these topics, speaking in many voices and inhabiting often conflicting points of view. An early poem entitled "To My Children" glorifies the traditional view of motherhood, while the later "Poet to Peasant," a work of Timothy Kline, speaks contemptuously of women's supposed desire for the banality of "suburban sweetness": "A nice house, and a soft foam bed, / Respectable love, not too intense" (205). Still later poems such as "Mother Who Gave Me Life" and "An Impromptu for Ann Jennings" can be read as "wonderfully convincing celebrations of motherhood" (Strauss, "Gwen Harwood" 68). Yet even in such celebratory works, the anguished cry of the immured woman is often heard. For the women mired in domesticity in "An Impromptu," "spirit beat at flesh as in a grave // from which it could not rise" (231). "I am I: give me my element or let me die," cries the wife-protagonist in "Iris" (251). Even the speaker in "The Old Wife's Tale" is restless in her domesticity, craving "some combat worthy of my sword" (17).

By giving voice to women's restlessness in the domestic sphere, and revealing the painful leaching away of female potentiality within the patriarchal household, Harwood's poems give vivid life to the sense of compression and deformation many women experience in their attempts to fulfil traditional gender roles. At the same time, however, they explore and acknowledge the joy that can come from familial connectedness, mothering, and friendship. The problem for Harwood was not motherhood or domesticity in themselves but the irresolvable conflict women experienced within a patriarchal society when they sought both motherhood and a life of their own. "I dream of a world in which there is no insoluble choice for women," she once wrote to Ann Jennings. "[N]ot in our lifetime, I fear, but it will come if enough of us refuse ... the male interpretation" (*A Steady Storm* 116).

*

In the early 1970s, some ten years after she wrote the last of her Miriam Stone poems, Harwood began a series of love poems that were as groundbreaking in their way as her earlier 'suburban' poems had been. Like those earlier works, these poems have a woman's experience at their heart. Trigg points out that in the 1970s, this in itself was revolutionary. Works such as "Carnal Knowledge I & II" and "Meditation on Wyatt I & II," among others from Harwood's "middle period," overturn the traditional love poem by writing "from a woman-centred sexuality" (Trigg 89). In these poems, the woman is "always the subject of love, never the object" (90) – a reversal of centuries of poetic tradition. In addition, Harwood's female protagonists speak "with a passion and desire that are often spiritual and emotional, and often simply carnal" (75).

Far from turning love into something bodiless and ethereal, as women were conventionally reputed to do, the women in Harwood's poems boldly claim their own lust. Though she was raised within the Christian tradition and was intensely religious for a brief period in her early twenties, Harwood's erotic poetry is entirely free of the language of sin. Sexual love in her poems is never morally wrong in itself, and is often allied with a sublime spirituality. In this, she may have taken her lead from the poet-priest John Donne, whose love poetry was an important early influence (Priest, *My Tongue Is My Own* 76). Certainly, his assertion that sex is the "right, true end of love" ("Elegy XVIII: Love's Progress") resonates through Harwood's oeuvre. An early poem, "Tom the Rhymer," applies Donne's phrase to an adulterous affair, the illicit lovers finding "love's right / true end in bodies" (87); it appears again, among many echoes of Donne, in a much later poem, "A Valediction," in which a woman finds solace after her beloved's departure in the knowledge that: "My lover / Will come again to me, my body / to its true end will give him joy" (335).

Not only was sex never sinful for Harwood, it was also a way to nourish, even liberate, the soul; the physical and the spiritual were not antithetical, as in the Christian tradition, but interdependent. In a number of her early poems, sex is depicted as having transformative power. Through sex, the body assumes "godheads of light and fire," making the human divine ("In Zurich by the Tideless Lake" 39); the "spirit" or "soul" is set free to walk "a floor of light" ("Tom the Rhymer" 87). "Triste, Triste" speaks of a lover drifting into a delicious post-coital lethargy – the "space between love and sleep" – and finding his spirit freed from the body to wander the earth in luminous joy: "away from the tomb of bone, / away from the guardian tents / of eyesight, walking alone / to unbearable light" (60).

The poem compares this sexual liberation of the soul to Christ's resurrection, a sublime, miraculous transcendence of the physical limits of the self.

But the lover's ecstatic fulfilment is fleeting. At the end of the poem, "spirit" sinks back into the body, sacrificing its incandescence in a gesture of loving compassion toward "heart," abandoned and alone in the "prison" of the body.

"The Wine Is Drunk" begins from this place of mourning: once "the woman" has been "known," the ecstatic plenitude of sexual rapture is lost, and the lover finds himself alone in "gross darkness," hopelessly yearning for "what's not found / in flesh, or anywhere" (6). The poem adopts a male point of view, but Harwood assured a friend that "of course it is my own voice on my own themes; it sounds odd in the feminine voice" (*A Steady Storm* 160). The idea in "The Wine Is Drunk" that a woman might prefer sexual bliss to "love's waking face" (6) – the prosaic dailiness of love – may well have seemed 'odd' at a time when women were seen as the objects, rather than the subjects, of sexual passion. But for Harwood, the experience explored in this poem was not gendered: both women and men could fall prey to the spirit's eternal hunger once the joy of a sexual encounter had faded. The lover in this poem is grappling with the same painful truth that haunts Professor Eisenbart: that "[f]lesh must perish" (6). But while Eisenbart seeks to bring human mortality under his own control through violence, the lover in "The Wine Is Drunk" strives to accept and embrace the limitations of mortality.

The idea that our human subjection to death is relieved, even subverted, by rapturous moments in which we apprehend our true immortality appears throughout Harwood's work. Such moments are not solely associated with sex: they also come through art (particularly music), friendship, and nature. In these moments, we wake "alive from the sleep of time," she writes in "The Double Image," and are "caught in the pulse of *now*" (105). Time ceases to exist: in the "tenseless/ *now* that embraces present, past, / and future" ("Retirement into Life" 550), we are immortal, safe from death and darkness in an ecstatic realm of light. Sex is the apotheosis of this experience, lifting us out of ourselves, freeing us from our subjection to time.

The early poems are cautious in their assertions, relying on dense and sometimes obscure allusions to the Bible or Greek mythology to make their case, and employing Trigg's "distancing strategies" to frustrate any identification of the poems' protagonists with their author. The later love poems, however, speak with ease and directness from a lyric 'I' who is confidently female. In these works, the physicality of sex is celebrated as the source and end of the spiritual, and our best riposte to mortality. The brief fourth poem in "The Sharpness of Death" is exemplary. Here, the speaker addresses a personified Death directly, exulting in the sexual rapture she has known and taunting him with the power it gives her over him:

> Death, I will tell you now:
> my love and I stood still
> in the roofless chapel. My
> body was full of him, my
> tongue sang with his juices, I
> grew ripe in his blond light.
> If I fall from that time,
> then set your teeth in me. (296)

The physicality of the imagery, the depiction of a woman revelling in sex, is typical of Harwood's love poems of this era. But the poem also has a powerful metaphorical dimension. In situating her love-making in a sacred space – a chapel, but one that has no roof, that is open to earth and sky – she makes sexual love a rival religion, the sexual woman a new Christ. In the utter plenitude of the carnal, the speaker is invulnerable: death itself cannot touch her. It is a recalibration of the Biblical declaration in the Song of Songs that love is stronger than death.

Other love poems are similarly explicit. Trigg notes, for example, that the speaker of "Carnal Knowledge I" situates herself as both the initiator of sex and the creator of the world: she "builds a world 'from what's to hand,' the penis she caresses" (87). She adds: "It is a most confident rewriting of traditional scenarios, and evinces a commanding sexual politics" (87). Harwood's characteristic playfulness with language reaches new heights in these poems, with joyous puns and double entendres abounding (in "Carnal Knowledge II," for example, the speaker lies "cockeyed with love / in the most literal sense" (264)). In the love poems of the early sixties, the dominant theme is the impossibility of staying in that rapturous moment outside of time, but in these later poems, there is little sense that death is waiting to pounce. The flare of love's light promises to drive away the darkness for good.

*

Harwood's late poems – beginning in *The Lion's Bride* (1981) and encompassing *Bone Scan* (1998) and her final collection, *The Present Tense* (1995) – are less rapturous. The lyric confidence of the female 'I,' perfected in the 1970s poems, does not falter; she would never return to the veiled, ornate style of her earliest work. But there is little in the late poems of the earlier joyous certainty that the transcendent moment – whether accomplished through sex, love, or art – can vanquish death. As Harwood moved into her sixties, she seemed always to be in mourning. "Many I loved are gone," says the speaker of "Sparrows," while "Three Poems for Margaret Diesendorf" declares, "Death has them in his net" (316). The speaker in this poem can no longer reason or rationalise, or invoke the eternal now, only cry out against God: "Why does he let them fall / if he loves the world at all?" But if the poems of *The Lion's Bride* are, as Elizabeth Lawson notes, "preoccupied with death (and dying), enough to risk seeming to form repetitive variations on a theme" (67), they also move increasingly towards the simple, untransfigured present. The poet sings "this ordinary day," which is "increasingly particularised, valued and celebratory" (67).

Though the poems of Harwood's sixties and early seventies lack the exuberance of those of her fifties, they are, for many readers, her most powerful. As Geoff Page argues: "The earlier work was just as observant but rarely as moving in such a directly personal way" (114). The late poems are grimmer; as depicted in "Night Thoughts," the poet wrestles until dawn with Jacob's angel, but wrings no new knowledge from her adversary, no transfiguring revelation. Instead, she must confront the bitter truth where, as she puts it in one of her fishing poems, "Mid-Channel": "A day will come, / matter-of-fact as knife and plate, / with death's hook in my jaw, and language / unspeakable, the line full out" (414). Her great poems of death (among them, poems such as "Herongate" and "Resurrection") evoke both its matter-of-fact quality – death is something with which we are all familiar, and in which, in fishing from a dinghy as much as in sitting at the dinner table, we all participate – and its immitigable horror. Indeed, for Strauss, "one of the major human values of Harwood's art is that it enables us to imagine death without either debilitating self-pity or false heroics" ("Gwen Harwood" 68).

At the same time, as a public figure, Harwood was writing an increasing number of occasional poems – poems that were solicited by dignitaries or friends for specific occasions. Her extraordinary range of tones and styles became even more pronounced in her final decade. She wrote comic and satirical poems, topical essays and lectures in verse, pastorals and commemorative works alongside agonised elegies and deeply felt poems of childhood. Her standing within Australia was unchallenged: she was widely acknowledged as, in Peter Porter's words, a "true master" and "the most accomplished poet the country produced in the twentieth century" (7). Younger poets sought her out, seeing her as "an inspirational figure ..., a yardstick of technical accomplishment and emotional involvement against which they aspire to measure themselves" (Page 115). Her fame was slowly growing overseas, too, despite her long-standing inability to travel due to her husband's ill-health. Her first *Collected Poems* was published in London in 1991, and in 1994, the UK Society of Authors selected Harwood, alongside Ruth Fainlight, Elizabeth Jennings, and John Mole, as one of the winners of the Cholmondeley Award, a prize of £2,000 given to four 'distinguished poets' each year. In the year of her death, 1995, she was invited to go to the USA to read and lecture at Johns Hopkins University and Holyoke College, among other places. By this time, however, she had been diagnosed with terminal cancer. The definitive *Collected Poems* was published in 2003, and two collections of her letters have been published since her death. With the publication of the first biography in 2022, it may be possible to look beyond her late persona as a benign old woman and recover the bold and subversive poet she was. As a woman writing of women's lives in the second half of the twentieth century, her work was path-breaking, giving poetic form to aspects of experience not previously found in Australian poetry and overturning moribund conceptions of women as poets.

Works Cited

Blackman, Wilson. "Four Poets in One: Gwen Harwood." The Creative Arts [audio recording], Radio Australia, 5–7 April 1964.

Dodwell, Diane. "Worlds Beyond Words: Gwen Harwood's Selected Poems." *Westerly* no.2, June 1977, pp. 73–79.

Douglas, Dennis. "A Prodigious Dilemma: Gwen Harwood's Professor Eisenbart and the Vices of the Intellect." *Australian Literary Studies* vol.6 no.1, 1973, pp. 77–82.

Dunlevy, Maurice. "Poet of Man's Regrets." *Canberra Times*, 29 June 1968, p. 14.

Edgar, Stephen. "An Interview with Gwen Harwood." *Island Magazine* no. 25–26, 1986, pp. 74–76.

Hall, Rodney and Thomas W. Shapcott, eds. "Introduction." *New Impulses in Australian Poetry*, edited by Rodney Hall and Thomas W. Shapcott. University of Queensland Press, 1970, pp. 1–13.

Harwood, Gwen. *Poems*. Angus & Robertson, 1963.

A Steady Storm of Correspondence: Selected Letters of Gwen Harwood: 1943–1995, edited by Gregory Kratzmann. University of Queensland Press, 2001.

Collected Poems: 1943–1995, edited by Alison Hoddinott and Gregory Kratzmann. University of Queensland Press, 2003.

Idle Talk: Letters 1960–1964, edited by Alison Hoddinott. Brandl & Schlesinger, 2015.

Horne, Donald. "The Hoax That Misfired." *The Bulletin* vol.82 no.4253, 19 August 1961.

Hudson, Flexmore. "Slim Volumes." *Australian Book Review* vol.3 no.7, 1964, p. 132.

Lawson, Elizabeth. *The Poetry of Gwen Harwood*. Sydney University Press, 1991.

Lawson, Sylvia. "Review of *Australian Poetry Now*." *The Australian*, 19 December 1970, p. 23.

Page, Geoff. *A Reader's Guide to Contemporary Australian Poetry*. University of Queensland Press, 1995.

Porter, Peter. "Satires in C Major." *Times Literary Supplement*, 9 May 2003, p. 7.
Priest, Ann-Marie. "Baby and Demon: Woman and the Artist in the Poetry of Gwen Harwood." *Hecate* vol.40 no.2, 2015, pp. 67–83.
—"'The Hoax That Misfired': Gwen Harwood's Cultural Dissent." *Southerly* vol.77 no.1, 2017, pp. 115–36.
—*A Free Flame: Australian Women Writers and Vocation in the Twentieth Century.* UWA Publishing, 2018, pp. 7–31.
—*My Tongue Is My Own: A Life of Gwen Harwood.* LaTrobe University Press/ Black Inc., 2022.
Shapcott, Thomas W. "Correspondence." *Australian Book Review* vol.3 no.9, 1964.
—ed. *Australian Poetry Now.* Sun Books, 1970.
Sheridan, Susan. "Suburban Sonnets: 'Mrs Harwood,' Miriam Stone and Domestic Modernity." *Australian Literary Studies* vol.23 no.2, 2007, pp. 140–52.
Strauss, Jennifer. *Boundary Conditions: The Poetry of Gwen Harwood.* University of Queensland Press, 1992.
—"Gwen Harwood: 1920–1995." *Quadrant*, April 1996, pp. 67–68.
Trigg, Stephanie. *Gwen Harwood.* Oxford University Press, 1994.

NOTES

1. All cited poems by Gwen Harwood are from *Collected Poems: 1943–1995*.
2. For Harwood's challenge to "Holy Motherhood" see Sheridan, pp. 140–52 and Trigg, pp. 37–38; for Harwood's radical eroticism, see Trigg, pp. 75–94; for Harwood's reworking of the figure of the creative artist see Priest, *A Free Flame*, pp. 7–31.
3. The book is dated 1963 even though it did not appear until February 1964.
4. Cf. Unpublished letter from Gwen Harwood to Vivian Smith, 12 April 1959, National Library of Australia, MS4853/2/41-43: "Is Eisenbart really a nuclear physicist, or is he mad … . Who knows?" Harwood was here anticipating a debate on this very topic between critics A. D. Hope and Dennis Douglas in *Australian Literary Studies* in the early 1970s.
5. See Douglas, and Strauss, *Boundary Conditions*, p. 68.
6. Unpublished letter from Gwen Harwood to Tony Riddell, 27 August 1963, Fryer Library, University of Queensland, UQFL45 Box 7, Folders 4–18: "I think the more passionate the feelings are, the stricter the form should be if the thing is not to sprawl."
7. Unpublished letter from Gwen Harwood to Tony Riddell, 22 March 1964, Fryer Library, University of Queensland, UQFL45 Box 7, Folders 4–18.
8. Unpublished letter from Gwen Harwood to Edwin Tanner, 5 December 1958, Fryer Library, University of Queensland, UQFL45 Box 6, Folder 21.
9. Reviewing Harwood's *Poems* (1963), Flexmore Hudson praises her for writing with "a sinewy toughness and a power that are rare in a woman's poetry" and asserts that it is only when she is writing as Walter Lehmann (i.e. as a man) that she "tells the truth of her [womanly] tenderness and compassion" (p. 132). In the same issue of *Australian Book Review*, Thomas Shapcott refers to Rosemary Dobson's "womanly sensitivity" (p. 132).

10 This total does not include Harwood's self-parody "Fuse Lightning" and the much later "The Death of Eisenbart."
11 For a full account of Harwood's hoaxes and pseudonyms, see Priest, "The Hoax That Misfired."
12 Gwen Harwood, Interview with Alison Hoddinott (audio transcript). National Library of Australia, 1988, p. 68.
13 Unpublished letter from Vincent Buckley to Gwen Harwood, 26 August 1961, Fryer Library, University of Queensland, UQFL45 Box 1, Folder 6.
14 Unpublished letter from Vincent Buckley to Mrs Stone, 28 March 1962, Fryer Library, University of Queensland, UQFL45 Box 1, Folder 6.
15 Unpublished letter from Gwen Harwood to Vivian Smith, undated [16 August 1962], National Library of Australia, MS 4853, Series 2, Folders 41–43.
16 Unpublished letter from Nancy Cato to Gwen Harwood, 5 April 1969 (Fryer Library, University of Queensland, UQFL45 Box 1, Folder 8).

11

DAVID MCCOOEY

Les Murray

Ancient and Modern

Les Murray, National Poet

During the last decades of his life, Les Murray (1938–2019) routinely figured in the media as 'Australia's national poet,' a potential poet laureate in a country with no such position. He was also recognised as Australia's best-known poet internationally, routinely namechecked in the 1990s and 2000s alongside the Nobel laureates Derek Walcott, Seamus Heaney, and Joseph Brodsky. That Murray's status as a national poet went hand in hand with a poetic style that was highly idiolectic, even to the point of obscurity, is striking. His style – usually expansive and highly allusive – was comprised of a mix of ordinary language, specialist vocabulary, and eccentric syntax. In terms of subject matter, Murray was certainly interested in national history and national issues, and (as I will discuss) his poems were habitually pastoral and georgic in nature, concerned with those most putatively 'Australian' loci, the bush and the farm. But Murray's version of rural Australia was not merely celebratory or sentimental, his concerns were often transnational in scope, and his attitude to Australian history was clear-eyed about the violence of colonialism.

A number of poems in Murray's third collection, *Poems against Economics* (1972), such as "The Conquest" and "The Ballad of Jimmy Governor," show an emerging postcolonial interest in cross-cultural encounters between First Nations and settler-colonial peoples. Perhaps as an extension of this interest in Australian colonial history, one of Murray's projects in the 1970s, as discussed in his essay "The Human-Hair Thread" (1977), was the fusing of "all three main Australian cultures, Aboriginal, rural and urban" (*The Paperbark Tree* 92). This may be evidence of a postcolonial attraction to hybridity and creole culture, and illustrate a strong concern with social cohesion rather than division. Yet the poem that embodied this project, "The Buladelah-Taree Holiday Cycle" (from *Ethnic Radio*, 1977), once one of Murray's most celebrated poems, is now usually seen as a work of cultural appropriation. It is based on R. M. Berndt's 1948 translation of the Wonguri-Mandjikai Song Cycle of the Moon Bone, which Murray describes in "The Human-Hair Thread" as being possibly "the greatest poem ever composed in Australia" (90). Murray's use of this song cycle can be seen in the poem's associative imagery (the Pacific Highway, for instance, is implicitly compared to the Rainbow Serpent), and in its use of long, accumulative lines, active verbs, and repetition as analogues for Berndt's rendering of the song cycle's oral style. Murray's poem represents (white) Australians on holiday – seen as the semi-ritualistic return to spirit places, as shown in the stylised catalogue of place names.

> Fresh sheets have been spread and tucked tight, childhood rooms have been seen to,
>
> for this is the season when children return with their children
> to the place of Bingham's Ghost, of the Old Timber Wharf, of the Big Flood That Time,
> the country of the rationalized farms, of the day-and-night farms, and of the Pitt Street farms,
> of the Shire Engineer and many other rumours, of the tractor crankcase furred with chaff,
> the places of sitting down near ferns, the snake-fear places, the cattle-crossing-long-ago places. (137–38)[1]

These place names echo Berndt's rendering of place names, such as "the place of the Dugong, of the Tree-Limbs-Rubbing-Together" (29). "Borrowing is an act of respect" (71), Murray writes in "The Human-Hair Thread," but notwithstanding this, "The Buladelah-Taree Holiday Cycle" is characterised as nothing less than "uncomplicatedly evil" by Jonathan Dunk in the obituary he wrote shortly after Murray's death (n.pag.). Dunk's indictment is on the grounds that the poem is an "extremely sophisticated version" of the "containment and erasure of Aboriginal people" (n.pag.). This moral condemnation is the apotheosis of a growing sense of disquiet about the poem since the late 1980s,[2] with critics drawing attention to the poem's appropriative poetics. However, all commentators on the poem, including Dunk, note the cycle's poetic skill, while "The Human-Hair Thread" makes it clear that Murray wrote out of genuine respect for the source work.

As Murray also points out in "The Human-Hair Thread," all arts are synthetic, and the poet was not advocating (or at least expecting) a 'fusion' of cultures outside art, but it remains the case that Murray's project has, at the least, dated badly. Interestingly, in 1992 (and later reprinted in 2001), Christopher Pollnitz argues that, in its simple celebration of white Australians on vacation, "the poem's social agenda is something worse than appropriation: it is an argument for self-congratulatory complacency" (55). Whatever its faults, it is clear that "The Buladelah-Taree Holiday Cycle" is generally considered problematic today. However, this poem (with its precipitate, though not universal, fall in critical estimation) also illustrates a feature that appears (usually) in more benign ways in Murray's poetry: the fusion of ancient and modern frameworks, forms, and subject matter. In particular, as I will argue, Murray's poetry is notable for its engagement with the ancient tradition of the pastoral and georgic modes within a poetic idiolect that could be characterised as late- or neo-modernist. The first of these is everywhere apparent in Murray's poetry; the second is less obvious and might even seem inconsistent with the first. Both these 'ancient and modern' features, with their shared emphasis on place, are consistent with Murray's concern with Australian themes, whether that concern is seen as being nationalist or postcolonial in spirit.

Dunk's characterisation of "The Buladelah-Taree Holiday Cycle" is the most pointed illustration of how Murray's status at home is more ambiguous – if not contested – than it is internationally. While Murray's poetry has been widely praised in his home country, his interventions in local literary culture, his forays into public life, and his association with figures on the right of politics (as well as his position as the poetry editor of the ring-wing journal *Quadrant*) often made him a source of controversy and disquiet. Critics have often focused on the apparent tension between Murray's self-evident linguistic skill and his disputatiousness. The poet Gig Ryan, writing in the wake of Murray's most contentious collection, *Subhuman Redneck Poems* (1996), sums this up when she claims that "Murray's books nearly always contain his signature bipolar mix of syntactical largesse and vivacity on the one hand, and pinched unadorned belligerence and dogma on the other" (199).

Such a summation suggests that each feature is apparent in equal parts, but attention to the poetry itself (rather than Murray's extra-poetic pronouncements) shows that the former outweighs the latter. Largesse and vivacity are evident in Murray's pronounced linguistic inventiveness and love of comedy. This is often best expressed in Murray's ebullient use of surprising imagery, such as his description of "a risen / loaf of cat on a cool night verandah" in "A Retrospect of Humidity" (*The People's Otherworld* 204), or his passing reference to the crocodile's "pineapple abdomen" in "Flood Plains on the Coast Facing Asia" (*The Daylight Moon* 223). Murray's poems are also filled with quips, puns, and comic imagery: "No stench is infra-dog" ("The Nostril Songs," *The Biplane Houses* 571); bikies are "Santas from Hell" in "The Harleys" (*Conscious and Verbal* 456); "[p]uns pique us with the glare / of worlds too coherent to bare / by any groan person" ("Black Belt in Martial Arts," *The Biplane Houses* 566).

Playfulness also appears in the more discursive, even argumentative, of Murray's poems. "Second Essay on Interest: The Emu" (from *The People's Otherworld*), as the title suggests, is essayistic, but it begins with a comic description of the eponymous bird:

> Weathered blond as a grass tree, a huge Beatles haircut
> raises an alert periscope and stares out
> over scrub. Her large olivine eggs click
> oilily together; her lips of noble plastic
> clamped in their expression, her head-fluff a stripe
> worn mohawk style ... (201)

This defamiliarising comedy gives way to the related discussion of the poem's other subject: 'interest.' This specialised meaning of the word presents interest as a European (and therefore implicitly colonial) mode of regard that both overwrites Indigenous culture ("men started renaming the creatures" 202) and is in thrall to fashionable thought ("Now only life survives, if it's made remarkable" 202). In "Poems and Poesies" (1986), an essay on the "poetic experience," Murray characterises poetry as the "fusion of dream and reason" (*A Working Forest* 377), a process that is not only cerebral, but also embodied, involving "breath and bodily movement." A somatic intensity ("the laws of the dance") occurs in fully achieved poems, but where it is absent (in works that Murray labels "poesies") it is "replaced at best by its humanistic substitute, interest." Interest as an activity of mind is, as Murray writes in his essay, essentially aristocratic in origin and dates back to the eighteenth century. It is "full of judgment and scorn" and a mode of fashion, something derided by Murray, since it can "switch away from any object the moment it threatens to become passé" (383).[3] "Second Essay on Interest: The Emu" ends by contrasting the "brigand sovereignty" of "the lords of interest" (terms that suggest colonial perceptions of Australian fauna) with "God's common immortality / whose image is daylight detail, aggregate, in process yet plumb / to the everywhere focus of one devoid of boredom" (203).

The appeal to the divine relates to the connection that Murray – who formally converted to Catholicism in 1964 – habitually makes between poetic and divine attention. As "Poetry and Religion" (from *The Daylight Moon*) illustrates, Murray figures poetry and religion in a circular relationship where one is the analogue of the other: "Religions are poems. They concert / our daylight and dreaming mind, our / emotions, instinct, breath and native gesture // into the only whole thinking: poetry" (265).

The valorisation of authentic poetry over interest and "poesies" is indicative of a suspicion of modernity, with its emphasis on rationality and prose discourse. In "Poems and Poesies," Murray labels poems (and the truly poetic) "wholespeak," while poesies and prose are "narrowspeak." Murray's propensity to think in terms of such dyads can have negative effects on his stated aim to overcome social division. This can be seen, too, in his poetry. For instance, while Murray's elegy for his father, "The Last Hellos" (from *Subhuman Redneck Poems*), enumerates numerous examples of the integrated relationships that Murray's father had with his family and community, the poem ends (in an apostrophe to the poet's late father) with the observation that "[s]nobs mind us off religion / nowadays, if they can. / Fuck thém. I wish you God" (432). The emphasis on the third-person pronoun in the final line ("thém") could suggest a degree of facetiousness (in the way it perhaps mimics vernacular speech), but in context this line adds an anti-elegiac breaking of decorum, unequivocally sounding a note of discord. This suggests that his hopes for reconciliation (between urban and rural, Indigenous and non-Indigenous) can easily flip to its opposite: division and tribalism.[4]

As this example suggests, despite Murray's commitment to the integration of difference, his self-image was that of an outsider. J. M. Coetzee is not alone in exhibiting a degree of impatience with this self-image, dismissing it as "not an accurate picture" (2011). Murray was, after all, university-educated, and subsequently feted by academia. He benefited significantly from state-based financial support for his writing, and he won many major awards, both locally and internationally. Notwithstanding these facts, Murray's sense of himself as an outsider was clearly authentic, stemming in large part from his foundational experiences, especially of being a poor, "word mad" child from the country, who was bullied at school. It may also stem from his putative neurodiversity. (Murray often spoke, long before it became common, of being on the autistic spectrum, though this is a biographical feature that has only been given serious consideration in recent years.[5]) Murray's self-image as an outsider is related to the anti-metropolitan, anti-modernist positions that are hinted at in "First Essay on Interest: The Emu," and that he habitually assumed, especially in his essays. In concert with these positions, Murray figured his outsider status as an argument with ideology itself, articulated especially through pronouncements against 'elites' of all kinds (prefiguring the weaponising of that word by the political right in the 1990s), of which those in the media and academia were prime targets.

Les Murray, the Pastoral-Georgic Tradition, and (Neo-) Modernism

Murray's putative outsider status also stemmed from a primary source of his status as national poet: his investment in the pastoral, both as subject and mode. Murray's poems routinely figure pastoral settings as sources of renewal and social cohesion. But these settings are also often embattled, declining, and the provenance of a half-vanished vernacular that, as I will show, Murray pits against metropolitan discourse. As evident in Murray's first collections, *The Ilex Tree* (1965) and *The Weatherboard Cathedral* (1969), his evocation of pastoral contexts was always sophisticated in articulation. For instance, "Tableau in January," a portrait of the main street of a country town, evokes the confounding heat and light of an Antipodean summer through striking, sometimes surreal, imagery: "In the cool of doorways, shirts drink lemonade. // January, noon. The unreal, idle street. / There is more light than world" (2). (It is hard not to see the "idle" / 'idyll' pun as intentional.)

Murray grew up on his father's dairy farm, and returned there in later life. His concern for the history and material practices of farming in his poetry shows that his pastoral interests are more specifically related to the georgic tradition. This tradition, which stems from Virgil's *Georgics* (29 BCE), is concerned with practical agricultural matters. However, Virgil's poem, and the tradition it inaugurated, was self-consciously concerned with poetic as much as farming work. As *The Princeton Encyclopedia of Poetry and Poetics* puts it, Virgil's "poem offers a complex meditation on the affinities and differences between the tending of words and the culture of the ground. It is no accident ... that the *Georgics* are the most carefully wrought and densely allusive of Virgil's works" (Greene and Cushman 556). Murray's own "carefully wrought and densely allusive" poems are not just generally concerned with pastoral settings, but with the specifics of farming (the word 'farm' and its cognates appear over a hundred times in the *Collected Poems*), especially with regard to cattle farming. Cattle appear numerous times as subjects, most notably in "Walking to the Cattle Place: A Meditation" (from *Poems against Economics*). The observation by Sue Edney and Tess Somervell that georgic is "a genre distinctively strange in its combination of high literary learnedness and empirical groundedness" (6) is particularly pertinent with regard to Murray's ambitious sequence. Formally diverse, "Walking to the Cattle Place" brings together an extraordinary array of references regarding bovine culture, myth, and history, including that of India, Africa, Ireland, Ancient Greece, and Aboriginal Australia, as well as Murray's own local settler culture. Cattle are also the source of much evocative imagery in Murray's shorter poems, such as the reference in "SMLE" to "[r]aw saplings [that] stand like cattle / in the distance of farms" (49).

The distinction between Murray's pastoral poems and his more specifically georgic ones is more than just semantics. Recognising the georgic element of Murray's poetics more accurately represents Murray's incipient eco-critical inclinations, whereby his interest in 'nature' is explicitly concerned with the interplay between human and environmental agents. As David Fairer argues, with regard to the eighteenth-century georgic tradition, the georgic, as opposed to the pastoral (with its emphasis on idealisation), addresses the "practical realities and negative pressures [that] have to be negotiated in any truly committed ecology" (215). Georgics such as "The Mitchells," "Laconics: The Forty Acres" (both from *Ethnic Radio*), and "The Idyll Wheel" sequence (from *The Daylight Moon*) figure the land as overwritten with the values and work of prior generations. "Forty Acre Ethno" (from "The Idyll Wheel") illustrates this through the speech of the poet's father:

> Dad speaks of memories, and calls his fire homely:
> when did you last hear that word without scorn
> for something unglossy, or some poor woman?
> Here, where thin is *poor*, and fat is *condition*,
> "homely" is praise and warmth, spoken gratefully.
> Its opposite lurks outside in dark blowing rain. (290)

As these lines suggest, the attraction to pastoral-georgic subjects and values is bound up in Murray's complex playing out of an insider/outsider dialectic, here literalised with regard to homeliness and "dark blowing rain," but also recognisable in the tension between pastoral and metropolitan values found in the different lexical valences. The use of an insider/outsider dialectic, then, is inherently ideological in nature. Indeed, in "Forty Acre Ethno," the poet refers to how, before returning to the rural home (a version of the traditional pastoral 'retreat'), society had for him "vanished into ideology" (290).

This is consistent with Robert Dixon's observation that Murray's project resonates with "pastoral's reputation for social conservatism, anti-modernism, and opposition to the fashionable and materialistic values of the metropolis" (286). Dixon's characterisation of the pastoral leans heavily towards a twentieth-century suspicion of the mode, in which the stylised rendering of the pastoral scene mystifies the material and ideological realities that can be found there (such as the exploitation of labour, animals, and land). As with Murray's work as a whole, however, this is too simple a diagnosis of Murray's representation of bucolic scenes, especially if we recognise Murray's engagement with georgic as well as pastoral matters. While conventional, if not sentimental, representations of bucolic settings can be found in Murray's poems, his poetry does not generally idealise the pastoral-georgic setting. This is in keeping with the mobility of pastoral and georgic themselves. As Terry Gifford writes, "the pastoral can be a mode of political critique of present society, or it can be a dramatic form of unresolved dialogue about the tensions in that society, or it can be a retreat from politics into an apparently aesthetic landscape that is devoid of conflict and tension" (11). Murray engages with all these pastoral frameworks, though the last appears most faintly. Perhaps more pointedly, Murray's representation of farming folk, as well as his self-image as an outsider with both erudite and practical knowledge, is remarkably consistent with Laura Sayre's observation that "the ecopoetics of the georgic suggest a connection to the land that is independent of academia. The farmer is a good emblem for the autodidact, the outsider intellectual, the poet-naturalist, in possession of knowledge that is in danger of being lost, disregarded by the university or the ivory tower" (195). Such figures and such knowledge are endemic in Murray's poetry, and not confined to the poet's father. "It has its roots in meadows deeper than Gaelic, / my uncle's knowledge" (40), Murray writes in "Towards the Imminent Days" (from *Poems against Economics*), which also makes explicit, and unironic, reference to "[t]he Georgic furrow [that] lengthens // in ever more intimate country" (39).

"Towards the Imminent Days" is an epithalamium (or nuptial poem), and therefore inherently invested in social cohesion. As such, and not surprisingly, the poem represents the georgic scene in its most benign form. The poem ends in apostrophic address to the nuptial couple: "For your wedding, I wish you the frequent image of farms" (43). But Murray's engagement with the pastoral-georgic tradition is often explicitly anti-sentimental, as seen in his many poems that figure farms and the bush as places of emotional and material struggle. The representation of emotional struggle is most often seen in autobiographical poems, especially those that deal with the death of Murray's mother, Miriam, when Murray was twelve years old. Miriam had died after a delay in sending an ambulance to her after she miscarried a child and began haemorrhaging. "Burning Want" (from *Subhuman Redneck Poems*) begins with Murray relating the emotional consequences of this event:

> From just on puberty, I lived in funeral:
> mother dead of miscarriage, father trying to be dead,
> we'd boil sweat-brown cloth; cows repossessed the garden.
> Lovemaking brought death, was the unuttered principle. (429)

This inverted idyll is a place of death, rather than life. Work – which, in the pastoral and georgic traditions, is conventionally a disguised form of leisure or a source of dignity – links the father and son both in their abjection (boiling "sweat-brown cloth" (429)) and dereliction (the cows repossessing the garden). Meanwhile, "the unuttered principle" shows that Arcadia is not the source of eros, but rather the site that begins the process of what Murray terms later in the poem "erocide" (429), a process that is fully enacted at the school where he was bullied.

Material struggle features throughout Murray's pastoral-georgic poems. "The Tin Wash Dish" (from *Dog Fox Field*) is a poem about rural poverty and the shame associated with it, but it is also notable for its deep attention to sound and rhyme. This intense investment in stylisation is, as noted, consistent with the georgic tradition. We see this also in "Rainwater Tank" (from *Ethnic Radio*), which employs intense stylisation to figure the pastoral-georgic scene as a place of material struggle. The rainwater tank, along with the windmill, is an iconic metonym for Australian farming life. But Murray does not idealise the pastoral-georgic setting, or present it as a place where one can retreat from economic (and therefore political) realities. Referring to the thread of a spider on the tankstand as "spittle" (153) suggests, in a negative way, the dryness around. Murray's comparison between the rainwater tank and the banker's roll of shillings shows that the poetic image can have profoundly mundane, as well as extra-mundane, implications. (In this case, the simile makes the point that, on a farm, a lack of water leads to a lack of money.) At the same time, the periphrastic description of the tank as "roof-water drinker" (153), with its suggestion of Old Norse 'kenning' or Homeric epithet, highlights the long poetic heritage that Murray is working with. This epithet starts a complex chain of personification, in which the downpipe – in a synaesthesia-like confusion of the senses – "stares drought" into the tank (153), the kitchen tap turns on without apparent human agency, and the tank onomatopoeically passes on its bad news. All of this occurs within the stylisation of a limited sonic palette that emphasises voiced and unvoiced fricatives (such as 't,' 'd,' 'b,' and 'k').

It is not inconsistent, then, that Murray pursues his pastoral-georgic project, even as he, in Dixon's words, lays "strategic claim to metropolitan sophistication" (289). This "metropolitan sophistication" is pronounced, and is as much the source of Murray's literary reputation as his engagement with rural Australia as the locus of (half-lost) national values. It would be inaccurate to say that Murray's pastoral-georgic interests were merely cover for his metropolitan sophistication, since that sophistication was always self-evident. Nevertheless, and as already noted, Murray's use of the pastoral-georgic tradition seems consistent with his oft-stated antipathy to modernism. In "Memories of the Height-Weight Ratio" (from *Subhuman Redneck Poems*), he writes that "[m]odernism is not modern: it's police and despair" (409), presumably in reference to the cultural movement's alleged stylistic obligations (or what he elsewhere terms "academic obedience" (*A Working Forest* 358) and pessimism. Elsewhere, Murray's complaints against modernism are largely conventional: it is "rootless" (*A Working Forest* 264), elitist, and out of touch with the vernacular forms of ordinary readers.

Murray's poetry undoubtedly engages with the vernacular, but it is not simply vernacular in style. This can be seen most conspicuously in "Presence: Translations from the Natural World" (from *Translations from the Natural World*), the long 1992 sequence of poems that gives idiosyncratic voice to a host of (usually Australian and sometimes agricultural) animals. Each poem is notable for its highly stylised linguistic rendering of something beyond language: non-human presence. This stylisation is seen in the poems' use of disordered syntax, technical or outré language, and neologism, as seen, for instance, in "Echidna": "I feast life on and sleep it, / deep loveself in calm. / I awake to spikes of food-sheathing, of mulling fertile egg" (364). The linguistic artistry of the sequence is most evident in "Bats' Ultrasound," which ends with a virtuosic rendering of the flying mammals' ultrasonic voices for "[a] rare ear": "*ah, eyrie-ire, aero hour, eh? / O'er our ur-area (our era aye / ere your raw row) we air our array, / err, yaw, row wry – aura our orrery, /our eerie ü our ray, our arrow*" (355).

According to Peter F. Alexander, Murray's biographer, the inspiration for these lines was two Welsh englynion consisting of only vowels and the consonant 'r.' While Alexander avers that the lines illustrate a "sheer technical innovation of a power none of his 'experimental' contemporaries could equal" (244), one could argue that such a display shows as much a family resemblance to the sound poetry of the modernist artist Kurt Schwitters as to Celtic mouth music.

We have moved a long way from the pastoral-georgic vision of "Forty Acres" and "The Mitchells." Nevertheless, the zoological focus of "Presence: Translations from the Natural World" retains, if in an attenuated way, a link to the pastoral's impulse to retreat from urban culture, and the georgic's attention to an ecology that encompasses human and non-human agents. What is notable about the intense stylisation of this sequence is the degree to which it brings together apparently opposing stylistic elements: the supposedly conventional impulses of the pastoral-georgic traditions and the innovative impulses of modernism (negatively hinted at by Murray's biographer).

As mentioned, Murray's poetic style is notable for its intensely idiolectic nature, a kind of 'vernacular of one' that places Murray, however paradoxically, in the modernist tradition. For all Murray's stated antipathy to modernism, his poetry can, as others have noted, be difficult.[6] Murray has a modernist's concern with producing poetry that engages intensely with its medium, even to the point of opacity. Counter-intuitive though it may seem, one can recognise Murray's engagement with the pastoral-georgic tradition as part of a wider neo-modernist project. I use the term 'neo-modernist' in this context as it is used by Neal Alexander in *Late Modernism and the Poetics of Place* (2022): to designate a transnational group of poets born in the 1920s and 1930s who sought "to renew, reconfigure, or recycle the techniques and ethos of earlier generations of modernist writers in a period characterised both by anti-modernist reaction and the ascendancy of postmodernist paradigms" (201). Such poets' work is primarily concerned with the 'geographical imagination' and is prefigured by late-modernist poets such as Basil Bunting, Lorine Niedecker, and Charles Olson.

Alexander identifies three key features of late (and neo-modernist) poetry, all of which resonate strongly with Murray's poetry. Firstly, Alexander associates late modernist poetry with a concern with longer forms, "sequences, serial poems, mid-length and long poems" (10). Secondly, he identifies late modernist poetry with a concern with the poetics of place, which reveals "a conception of place as open and in process, subject to the changes wrought by time and constituted by their relations with other places at a range of spatial scales from the local to the transnational" (11). Lastly, he argues that late modernist poetry has a "tendency to foreground the cultural significance of peripheral and non-metropolitan places" (12).

These features are all strongly apparent in Murray's writings. "Sequences, serial poems, mid-length and long poems" (10) are everywhere in Murray's *Collected Poems*, and often stand as lynchpins of their respective collections. This attraction to sequences and serial poems is related to Murray's concern with place (pastoral and georgic inherently being poetries of place), which is poetically understood as something existing across axes of time and space. The historical and the contemporary, the local and transnational, are always in dialogue in Murray's poems. Lastly, Murray's ecological conception of space (identified, for instance, by Leer, 17) is both consistent with his engagement of the pastoral-georgic traditions and his (anti-colonial) foregrounding of peripheral and non-metropolitan places. Such places are the loci of both pastoral and georgic, but they are also indices of Australia's status as being culturally, as well as geographically, 'peripheral.'

These characteristics take us back to "The Buladelah-Taree Holiday Cycle," that long, highly stylised sequence of poems that imagines non-metropolitan places in trans-temporal ways. But they can be seen less tendentiously elsewhere in Murray's oeuvre, especially in major works such as "The Idyll Wheel" and "Walking to the Cattle Place." Even his later, usually shorter, poems illustrate a neo-modernist poetics of place. This is perhaps seen most radically in "A Dialect History of Australia" (from the 2006 collection, *The Biplane Houses*), a catalogue poem made entirely of proper nouns. The poem's extreme use of parataxis (a key feature of modernist aesthetics) and catalogue (the most ancient of poetic forms) powerfully illustrates the way in which Murray's poetry is a dialogue between the ancient and the modern. This can be poignantly seen in the poem's opening lines: "Bralgu. Kata Tjuta. Lutana. // Cape Leeuwin Abrolhos Groote Eylandt" (562). These two lines, set off from the main body of the poem, starkly represent Indigenous and colonial times and places, and they are followed by a long, lyrical list of historically and geographically resonant names from "Botany Bay" to "Timor." These names, intensely evocative of the geographical imagination, also act on a purely sonic level, redolent again of a modernist aesthetic.

Anti-colonial (if not conventionally postcolonial), anti-hierarchical, and transnational in spirit, as well as difficult – even awkward – in style, Murray, is not, then, an anti-modernist poet, but rather a neo-modernist working with the pastoral-georgic traditions. No doubt this conjunction, along with Murray's populist and anti-modernist pronouncements, led to a misapprehension by some regarding Murray's poetics. Through its startling imagery, unorthodox syntax, and idiosyncratic lexis, Murray's poetry clearly works with a (neo-modernist) defamiliarising mode of attention, but from within the apparently conventional scenes of the pastoral and georgic. Murray, then, is an outsider-national poet, oxymoronically working with ancient and modern traditions.

At his most post-Romantic, Murray believes the poetic image itself can collapse all such contradictions. In "The Trade in Images" (1988), he writes that:

> Images are at their least disruptive in art, where they are at their most mysterious and many sided and inexhaustible, food for contemplation rather than precipitate action. In art, imagery and conflict alike are raised beyond embodiment in action to a more perpetual embodiment where their life needs nothing further from the world to feed itself. Art is thus, in Christian terms, effectual but vicarious. It has arrived, without having to find its way there through tyrannies, at the true ambiguity of things, and can let all things, even opposites, be true at once. (*A Working Forest* 349–50)

This is, of course, only true to a point, and that point is poetic. While some may find things in poetry that are problematic (or even "uncomplicatedly evil"), Murray's appeal to the benignity of images, utopian though it no doubt is, draws attention to an impulse in poetry that is both ancient and modern: to render language as a dynamic encounter with being. As Murray writes in "From Where We Live on Presence," "[a] human is a comet in language far down time; no other / living is like it" (378).

Works Cited

Alexander, Neal. *Late Modernism and the Poetics of Place*. Edinburgh University Press, 2022.
Alexander, Peter F. *Les Murray: A Life in Progress*. Oxford University Press, 2000.

Berndt, Ronald M. "A 'Wonguri-Mandjikai Song Cycle of the Moon-Bone.'" *Oceania* vol.19 no.1, 1948, pp. 16–50.
Coetzee, J. M. "The Angry Genius of Les Murray." *The New York Review of Books*, 29 September 2011. www.nybooks.com/articles/2011/09/29/angry-genius-les-murray/.
Dixon, Robert. "Two Versions of Australian Pastoral: Les Murray and William Robinson." *Imagining Australia: Literature and Culture in the New World*, edited by Judith Ryan and Chris Wallace-Crabbe. Harvard University Committee on Australian Studies, 2004, pp. 286–304.
Dunk, Jonathan. "The Stump: Looking Back on the Republic of Murray." *Overland*, 7 June 2019. https://overland.org.au/2019/06/the-stump-looking-back-on-the-republic-of-murray/.
Edney, Sue and Tess Somervell. "Introduction." *Georgic Literature and the Environment: Working Land, Reworking Genre*, edited by Sue Edney and Tess Somervell, Routledge, 2022, pp. 1–9.
Fairer, David. "'Where Fuming Trees Refresh the Thirsty Air': The World of Eco-Georgic." *Studies in Eighteenth Century Culture* no.40, 2011, pp. 201–18.
Gifford, Terry. *Pastoral*. Routledge, 1999.
Greene, Roland and Stephen Cushman, eds. *The Princeton Encyclopedia of Poetry and Poetics*, 4th ed., Princeton University Press, 2012.
Leer, Martin. "'This Country Is My Mind': Les Murray's Poetics of Place." *The Poetry of Les Murray: Critical Essays*, edited by Laurie Hergenhan and Bruce Clunies Ross. University of Queensland Press, 2001, pp. 15–42.
Malouf, David. "Some Volumes of Selected Poems of the 1970s, II." *Australian Literary Studies* vol.10 no.3, 1982, pp. 300–10.
Murray, Les. "The Art of Poetry No. 89." *Paris Review* no. 173, 2005, pp. 38–79.
———. *Collected Poems*. Black Inc., 2018.
Perrett, Bill. "Les A Murray and the 'Aboriginal Way.'" *Meridian* vol.7 no.1, 1988, pp. 73–79.
Pollnitz, Christopher. "*Folie*, Topography and Family in Murray's Middle-Distance Poems." *The Poetry of Les Murray: Critical Essays*, edited by Laurie Hergenhan and Bruce Clunies Ross. University of Queensland Press, 2001, pp. 43–63.
Rowe, Noel. "Justice, Sacrifice and the Mother's Poem." *The Poetry of Les Murray: Critical Essays*, edited by Laurie Hergenhan and Bruce Clunies Ross. University of Queensland Press, 2001, pp. 142–56.
Ryan, Gig. "And the foetid air and gritty..." *Heat* no.5, 1997, pp. 196–203.
Sayre, Laura. "'How/*to* Make Fields Fertile': Ecocritical Lessons from the History of Virgil's *Georgics* in Translation." *Ecocriticism, Ecology, and the Cultures of Antiquity*, edited by Christopher Schliephake. Lexington Books, 2016, pp. 175–95.
Tink, Amanda. "Les Murray Said His Autism Shaped His Poetry." *The Conversation*, 23 August 2022. https://theconversation.com/les-murray-said-his-autism-shaped-his-poetry-his-late-poems-offer-insights-into-his-creative-process-188212.

NOTES

1 All cited poems by Murray are from *Collected Poems* (2018).
2 See Perrett.

3 On the other hand, interest, according to Murray, is not wholly negative in connotation, since it is "nothing if not entertaining" and it "protects itself from premature commitment, and may help to protect us all from power-seeking myths" (383).
4 A more nuanced and generous explanation is posited by Noel Rowe, who (in a reading primarily about "The Steel," concerning Murray's late mother) sees the provocative and/or defensive ending as protecting the parent "from explanations that would leave [him] only dead and ensure that justice is forever denied [him]" (150).
5 See, for instance, Tink. Murray's *Paris Review* interview is one of a number of times that Murray refers to himself as "mildly autistic" (242).
6 This observation can be traced back at least to the early 1980s (see Malouf 309).

12

DASHIELL MOORE

Lionel Fogarty's Poetics of Address and the Negative Lyric

Conscious of the implications of discussing Yoogum and Mununjali poet Lionel Fogarty within a resource that will guide scholars and students in their critical engagement with Australian poetry, this chapter examines the constitutive tension between poetics and politics that animates Fogarty's poetry. His writing, I argue, unifies the promise of an exacting literary form with political action. Yet it also resists this estimation by claiming a distinctive poetic mode opposed to imposition, appropriation, and representative form. In this chapter, I discuss how Fogarty anticipates the politics of reception for more than forty years, focusing particularly on his capacity to recuperate the 'negative' of the lyric self and his development of what Louis Klee describes as "complex rhetorical and poetic games of address" to local and international interlocutors (928). Through his poetry, Fogarty undermines and destabilises various stereotypical depictions of Aboriginal peoples in order to reconstitute the negative space that defines the concept of Aboriginality. Like Waanyi novelist Alexis Wright, Fogarty reworks the meaning of that which is deemed to be discarded as a defining identifier of his poetic self, a strategy that I describe as a negative lyric. Put simply, Fogarty's poetic 'I' emerges from a mediated, recycled matrix of negative space.

By using the terms of negative discursive production, Fogarty develops a decolonial mode of resistance to the various institutional and political forces defining his work. This strategy enables the poet to shape his own reception at a time where his work is defined by paradox, allowing his poems take on a spectral afterlife in future readings. Fogarty may have this in mind when he states in an interview with Timmah Ball that the dictionary, a mode of stripping language to universally understood (if contested) meanings, represents an extension of '*terra nullius*' by assuming or prescribing a particular set of definitions and associations ("An Interview" 133). Or, as he states in his introduction to *New and Selected Poems* (1995), "the white man will always criticise written pieces of paper" (x). John Kinsella suggests that Fogarty recycles the written when he describes Fogarty's page as "a representation of a field of myth-thought, of song-dream continuity, a place that refuses closure" (200).

Fogarty's development of negative lyricism also underscores his commitment to various forms of encounter. Klee also makes this point by arguing that Fogarty's poetry at once "interpolates the non-Indigenous reader into the position of outsider ..., whilst also yearning for intimacy with the comrade-reader with whom it shares the vision and promise of internationalist solidarity" (930). From this perspective, Fogarty's poetry is defined by a pursuit of understanding and closeness, albeit on his own terms. These connections reflect an idiosyncratic world view shaped by the linguistic and cultural environment of Cherbourg Aboriginal reserve, pan-Aboriginal political sensibilities, as well as a strident belief in an internationalist politics of solidarity. Fogarty uses poetry to communicate in both local and transnational contexts as a vehicle of cross-cultural understanding and transformative change. In this sense, Fogarty's material reality and his poetic meaning-making underpin and intercede upon one another. With this in mind, this chapter encourages new readings that explore the intersection of experimental poetics and political action both within and outside of 'Australian literature.' While I do not suggest that Fogarty's poetry solely operates in the service of its reader, his works explicitly engage interlocutors, readers, fellow poets, and family members without surrendering to transparency. Through his capacity to invert or recycle the 'negative' of the lyric self, Fogarty's commitment to interlocution reflects a complex and uncompromising ideas of poetic and artistic expression that cannot be reduced to either abstraction or political address. As he says in an interview with Michael Brennan, it is poetry that "changes the bloody law," "boosts love of intelligence" in others, "gives ... people courage ... to overcome ... emotional slaughters," and lets "communities of the world see ... that we can live" ("Interview with Lionel Fogarty" n.pag). In this sense, Fogarty's poetry evokes the insider-outsider construction of Aboriginality, not simply that his Aboriginal identity determines or limits his poetry, but because it is an intersubjective field of meaning defined by encounters and representation, to paraphrase Marcia Langton's definition. So too is his poetry shaped and determined by the voices that enter into and out of it, the conversations it emulates and the exchanges that emerge.

A Critical Overview, "Like Pieces of Paper to a Fire"

Fogarty developed his distinctive poetic and political approach in the cultural and linguistic milieu of Barambah Mission (renamed Cherbourg Aboriginal Reserve) in South Queensland. Established following the

Queensland Aboriginals Protection and Restriction of the Sale of Opium Act of 1897, Cherbourg housed Aboriginal peoples removed from their homelands across Australia's Eastern coastline. Fogarty has kinship connections to the Yoogum Yoogum people from the Beaudesert area via his grandfather, Roy Fogarty, and to the Kudjela and Wakka Wakka peoples across Queensland. In Cherbourg, Fogarty has stated that he received a "detribalised" education in Cherbourg ("Australian Poet Lionel Fogarty" n.pag.). Fogarty refers to the fact that he had no access to ancestral knowledge through kinship or familial transmission. Managed "like an apartheid system" ("Australian poet Lionel Fogarty" n.pag.), Cherbourg imposed a colonial English education and system of governance that Fogarty challenged through his early writing. In "Puzzled," Fogarty describes the perplexity of negotiating contested relations between language groups in the reserve:

> Blacks so confused
> Now we are forced into dumps
> where nation upon nation
> turn to face each other
> Puzzled
> but struggle will bring life
> there will be no puzzle. (*Lionel Fogarty* 32)

Fogarty's upbringing in Cherbourg stimulated his desire to seek out and understand language and cultural knowledge across and between other language groups. He shared with Philip Mead that his earliest sense of poetry came from moving beyond Cherbourg "to the township of Mergon and in the park areas there or in the outskirts of Mergon, or even in Cherbourg, just sitting down with young folks as well as old folks and just listening to their gossip, rumours, yarns, storytelling – that was poetry to me" ("Australian Poet Lionel Fogarty" n.pag.). "Remember Something Like This" (n.pag.) records one such event, where the poem's speaker recalls hearing storytellers around the campfire begin speaking with the phrase, "I remember something like this." Fittingly, the poem opens with a child figure represented as a receptacle of story: "Long ago a brown alighted story was told / As a boy, looked up on the hall walls / water flowed to his eyes." The boy receives the story of a "wild blackfella / from up north" who escaped the British soldiers "headed for the caves / just near Milky Way," whose memory is tied to the taboo of entering secret and sacred areas, "that's why you don't swim too late / at this creek created." The story ebbs and flows, intercut with intermissions in its telling, "come boys get more wood, we'll stay / here all night," only for the story to proceed forward, "just near the bunya tree you can see / this middle age woman, long black hair."

Finally, we are left with the rise of a morning light: "A light story past thru windows / on to you all / never forget / remember more ..."

In his reading of this poem, Morrissey discerns that "words become embodied, images resonate, chains of narrative form surprising connections," leaving the reader with a chain of associations that represent "the creative process for the man who writes this poem" (23). Fogarty's associative capacity in "Remember Something Like This" (n.pag.) establishes sinuous and rhythmic connections between linguistic elements stripped of conventional meaning, as in "hall walls" and a later description of soldiers "bent to dip, sip" at a waterhole. Importantly, these mnemonic connections develop a form of relation in despite of external governance, "saw / saw ... nuh ... you didn't saw him." Reading through association is central to these poems and remains a central strategy of reading Fogarty. In this example, the associations form the puzzle pieces of Murri cosmology, presented behind a poetic veil of "a light story past thru windows" ("Remember Something Like This" n.pag.).

Leaving school at fifteen, Fogarty moved to Brisbane and became an active Aboriginal militant at the height of an authoritarian Bjelke-Petersen state government in Queensland. Fogarty was an early member of the Australian Black Panther Party (established in 1971 by Denis Walker and Sam Watson) and helped establish community programs such as free Aboriginal medical, legal, and housing services, as well as a National Black Theatre. In 1974, the Bjelke-Petersen government delivered trumped-up charges of conspiracy against Walker, John Garcia, and a teenage Fogarty, all of whom faced fourteen-year maximum jail sentences. The 'Brisbane Three,' as they were called, were accused of visiting the president of the University of Queensland Union to raise funds for the Aboriginal community in Palm Island, an action that challenged the state's capacity to control the movements of Aboriginal peoples. Sixteen at the time the charges were brought forward, Fogarty was sent to appear in the children's court, where the charges were dismissed.

Upon turning seventeen, Fogarty was promptly recalled before the adult court, where the 'Brisbane Three' were acquitted of all charges after a lengthy trial. Fogarty records his response to the event in the poem, "Related Charged": "Charges have been set. / Arrested in lies. / Welcome here, you son of a cunt, /   This pig said to me" (*Selected Poems* 42). "Related Charged" has an "arrested" momentum punctuated by repetitive full stops, an unusual stoppage given the duplicative force of Fogarty's poetry, often "driven on by the poet's faith in ... the 'magical potency' of his words" (Morrissey 20). This sense of delay fixes the reader in place of the lie that frames the poem, "arrested in lies."

Following his acquittal, Fogarty joined his then partner and eventual publisher Cheryl Buchanan on several visits to Aboriginal communities fighting for land rights. After attending the 1976 International Indigenous Treaty Council, Buchanan and Fogarty returned to Brisbane, where Fogarty assisted Buchanan in establishing the Black Resource Centre Collective and the Black News Service. The poem "Jephson Street Brothers Who Had None" honours the Black Resource Centre community: "Brothers come in all levels so low / Brothers go upon anger so low" (*Lionel Fogarty* 38). Through the Black Resource Centre, Fogarty engaged early Black Studies courses, familiarised himself with the work of Malcolm X, Franz Fanon, African American music, and, interestingly, Marxist economic theory. In a rare editorial penned under his last name at birth, Lionel Lacey, and appearing in *Honi Soit* alongside Buchanan, Fogarty writes: "I am ... going to study a number of books such as Mandels, Introduction to Marxist Economic Theory, Wages Price and Profit ... because I want to understand how capitalist society is structured and how it operates" (4). Fogarty's critique of capitalism allows him to recognise that Black Studies must work collectively to challenge a society "that works on keeping us divided." Buchanan would go on to self-publish three of Fogarty's poetry collections, *Kargun* (1980), *Ngutji* (1984), and *Jagera* (1990).

Through his forty-plus years of poetic production, Fogarty has been positioned by critics in several cultural, political, and literary milieus, most notably the political turn to assimilation from self-determination in the 1990s. Morrissey argues persuasively that Fogarty's work is "overdetermined by the interpretative frames of resistance, activism, anger and protest" (19). Goorie/Koori scholar Evelyn Araluen also points out that Fogarty "is rarely interrogated beyond its more didactic political demands; his linguistic defiance is usually explored from positions which ultimately privilege English as a poetic standard" (9). This is especially the case in the early reviews of Fogarty's poetry. From the 1980s to the 1990s, Fogarty's poetry was primarily read as an authentic expression of Aboriginality. In a 1983 review of Fogarty's poetry collection *Yoogum Yoogum* (1982) in *Social Alternatives*, Coralie Kingston likens the experience of reading Fogarty to eavesdropping on a sacred ceremony: "I am eavesdropping on the sacred history of an unbeaten and proud people. Lionel Fogarty's poems are like a door that opens into the life experience of Blacks in Australia today .... Reading these poems is walking on sacred ground" (78). While Kingston's essentialism clearly diminishes Fogarty's highly experimental and complex use of language, her review reflects Fogarty's ability to position his readers through different hermeneutic pathways. In this, and in many subsequent reviews, he appears to withhold an interior from those assuming the position of critic, who often liken the experience to being on the precipice of understanding.

At the close of the 1980s, Mudrooroo, then known by his first name, Colin Johnson, and Adam Shoemaker made compelling claims for Fogarty's creative use of language. Mudrooroo was a particularly pivotal supporter in preserving Fogarty's early writings by advocating for the landmark publication of *New and Selected Poems: Munaldjali, Mutuerjaraera* in 1995. In 1986, Mudrooroo gave arguably the most influential reading of Fogarty's poetry to date: "It is impossible to read Lionel without realising that he is Black; it is impossible to read him and not realise the crimes committed against the Aboriginal people, and it is impossible to read him and not realise that here is a poet using the English language in a unique and new way" ("Guerilla Poetry" 49). Drawing on Fanonian rhetoric, Mudrooroo memorably described Fogarty as a guerrilla poet "using the language of the invader in an effort to smash open its shell and spill it open for poetic expression" (Mudrooroo 49). When he introduces Fogarty in this way, Mudrooroo creates a rare precedent in the published history of Aboriginal literature by establishing a politics of Aboriginal canonisation. Mudrooroo described Fogarty as the central figure of self-determination following what he saw as the assimilationist forms of Oodgeroo Noonuccal, Jack Davis, and Kevin Gilbert. While Davis and Gilbert write in ways that are "open in meaning and sentiment to all," Fogarty's later work represents a significant departure that creates "a new language freed of restrictions and erupting a multi-meaning of ambiguity" (49). Mudrooroo's critique of poetic assimilation centred Fogarty as the idealisation of an "undiluted" Aboriginal reality" defined by its refusal of discourse with white Australian readers in an application of political power (50). By emphasising Fogarty in so singular a fashion, Mudrooroo created a terminology and criticism for reading Aboriginal literature that has led a number of critics to ascribe Fogarty's creative experimentalism to a particular cultural and political slant. Despite this, Mudrooroo continues to provoke new readings of the cultural politics of Aboriginal literary production. He anticipates readings of Fogarty's linguistic creolisation, which he rejects as "Kriol and Pidgin ... criticised on their use of English and Aboriginal remnant words" (*Indigenous Literature* 1).

In an era of reconciliation, Fogarty's reviews exemplify a pronounced appreciation of his capacity for poetic experimentation. Following Mudrooroo's example, Barry Hill suggests that readers come to terms with the field represented by Fogarty's poetry by taking non-standardised reading approaches, such as by reading "backwards, starting with the selections from Fogarty's early works" (21). In 2002, Sabina Hopfer also drew on Mudroooroo's conceptualisation of Fogarty's poetry as a "larger whole, or field" (55). Hopfer's explicit recognition of Fogarty's poetic authority dovetailed with a growing awareness of his work overseas through Europe and

North America, a decade following Fogarty's international reading tour of Europe in 1993. While critics have been quick to criticise Hopfer's likening Fogarty's poetry to the endurance of falling hailstones in "complete exhaustion and despair" (47), she productively argued for taking multiple hermeneutic modes together in 'rereading' Fogarty, "to enter even a single poem from as many angles as possible" through a "multiple, or retroactive, reading procedure" (47). One could trace this reading through contemporary criticism on the multiple registers, applications, and intentions behind Fogarty's poetry, including anger, pleasure, love, friendship, and solidarity.

In the post-reconciliation criticism that follows Hopfer, we find a Fogarty defined by his capacity to unsettle regional and national literatures from a position of marginality. In 2008, the Australian prime minister Kevin Rudd delivered his famous speech apologising to the Stolen Generations on behalf of the Australian government in recognition of the governmentally sanctioned practice of separating Aboriginal children from their families. The same year, Philip Mead foregrounded the significance of Fogarty's resistant poetics within Australian literature in *Networked Language* (2008). Pointing to Fogarty's absence from anthologies (notably from Robert Gray and Geoffrey Lehman's anthology, *Australian Poetry in the Twentieth Century* (1991)), Mead argues that an Australian readership may be incapable of listening to Fogarty's poetry, but that Fogarty's "poetic language" exemplifies the best kind of "(critical) talking cure for the linguistic disorders that the Australian settlement suffers from" (454). The first example of Fogarty's inclusion in a 'national' essay collection on Australian literature comes a year after Mead in Penny van Toorn's chapter on "Aboriginal Poetry Now" in *Reading Down Under: Australian Literary Studies Reader* (2009).

Fogarty's relative absence in anthologies and criticism of Australian literature continues to the present day. With a few exceptions, this book is one of the first 'national' critical volume of essays to designate a chapter to Fogarty despite his continuing, prolific poetic production over forty years. The belatedness of Fogarty's recognition reflects the lack of attention paid to a great many other Aboriginal writers until relatively recently. What are the implications of incorporating Fogarty into the field of Australian literature at this stage of his literary career? Fogarty's poetry exhibits a vehement opposition to compromise, appropriation, and representative politics. If there is any singular location that encompasses Fogarty's poetry, it can be found in a growing body of scholarship on Aboriginal literature by Aboriginal Australian critics, writers, and scholars, as well as the poet's own reflections on poetry. His work exists outside of standardised literary publications, having been taught in prisons in Australia and North America,

203

as well as in schools for language teaching, as exemplified by his children's book, *Booyooburra: A Story of the Wakka Murri* (1993). Throughout his career, Fogarty has advocated for literature as an instrument of meaningful political change, whether for the empowerment of Aboriginal voices, language revitalisation, or the creation of an Aboriginal university. In each of these contexts, Fogarty's poetry demands higher moral standards of Australia's poetry community, while refusing the formalisation of poetry and morality in performative and empty gestures. Still, Fogarty's poetry will not resolve Australian literature's 'linguistic disorders' if it is not met by a reader eager to listen, to paraphrase Mead. To recognise Fogarty's contribution to Australian literature is to always work towards an unsettled future, where the act of recognition is never formalised or settled. At the same time, this may obscure the poet's intentions for his own legacy, as signalled in the poem, "Mr Professor": "Thanks, Mr Professor / for those kind gestures / but I'm doing my thing . . ." (*New and Selected* 37).

Recycling the Negative 'I' of Reception into Poetry: "No More My Damned Name"

With all of this said, how do we read Fogarty's poetry? While Fogarty deliberately disassembles conventional interpretative frameworks, he does not leave his readers without directives or cues. At times, these are hidden behind a layer of poetic language like the end of a rainbow in the poem, "Would Ever Remember . . .": "If hidden life is hid then a / rainbow must colour / any lonely place. I'll be there" (*Lionel Fogarty* 218). In a recent poem, "Like Pieces of Paper to a Fire" (284), Fogarty describes his work as a manifestation of a larger bonfire encompassing 40,000 years of Aboriginal creative production, "40 thousand fire." In the same poem, he characterises his work by the creative force of "protest," "liveable images arting my / writing justices combines," a product that leaves the "world's readers" with the task of "corporat[ing] my central" reading "in translation," for there's "a lot off page." When Fogarty describes a poetry that lives "off page," he insinuates that his work unifies a lived reality with textual practice, a line of thought clarified by recent critiques of poststructuralist concepts by Aboriginal scholars, most notably Roland Barthes' "Death of the Author." While Barthes revised this later in life, he initially posited that the literary text is an "oblique into which every subject escapes, the trap where all identity is lost, beginning with the very identity of the body that writes" (142). Barthes suggests that meaning is distilled from a text by and through the reader, according to the internal meanings of the text itself. Bundjalung novelist Melissa Lucashenko describes this critical concept as a continuation of the 'dying race' tropes foisted on Aboriginal people, adding that "the Aboriginal author is not dead" despite "the long-lived colonial attempt at shunning and destroying Aboriginal voices and stories" (1). In "No Longer Malleable Stuff" (2020), Wiradjuri poet and scholar Jeanine Leane follows Lucashenko by repositioning Barthes in a "long trajectory of European appropriation, blind to its own cultural standpoint, western literary colonialism, and the consumption of minority cultures by invading, colonising powers" (11). In his poetry, Fogarty repeatedly satirises the idea of the 'dead author.' For instance, in his poem "You Sound Like Your Flirting" he humourously plays on the trope of the 'Dead Poets Society': "Let no poet writers jump no dead desks" (*Lionel Fogarty* 214). Fogarty's aversion to the disavowal of authorial intention stems from a long-standing desire to inform his own reading. As a result, his poetry indexes a distinct composite of literary form and linguistic connections that exceed the "narrowed range of official Austlit as it is represented and institutionalised in modes of research, publishing and teaching" (Mead, *Networked Language* 454).

One example of Fogarty's literary resistance is exemplified in his use of the lyric 'I' to illuminate the negative space created by settler colonialism, what Mudrooroo describes as an "anti-poetry" that reflects "an anti-language of experience" ("Guerilla Poetry" 49). Whether defined as a poem of "short, intense and exquisite redactions of impassioned speech" (Greene 216) or one that uses musical language to convey "one moment's state of feeling" (Booth 73), the lyric is conventionally defined by a speaker reflecting on their relation to various entities (a mountain, a woman, a distant land). By contrast, Fogarty's use of the 'I' erases the distinction of subject and object to evoke a myriad of voices and forces negated by the lyric. Hence, as Mead discerns, Fogarty "unsettles all concepts of self-formation and national identity" (*Networked Language* 422). In so doing, Fogarty illuminates colonialism's capacity to force dispossessed peoples to place themselves within an individualist schema of identity defined by various degrees of difference from a universal norm. In *Aboriginal People, Colonialism, and International Law* (2015), Irene Watson makes exactly this point by describing Fogarty's capacity to "centre his Aboriginal self" against "his colonised being" (67). Watson cites Fogarty's avid reading of Fanon's *The Wretched of the Earth* during his early activism: "Because it is a systematic negation of the other person and a furious determination to deny the other person all attributes of humanity, colonialism forces the people it dominates to ask themselves the question constantly: 'In reality, who am I'?" (Fanon 203). While Fogarty has publicly qualified the influences of Fanon and Malcolm X, Fanon's quote cogently illustrates the decolonial logic of Fogarty's 'I.' To Fanon, the singular 'I' reiterates the negation of colonised subjectivities by centring unequal terms of individual and collective comparison. In his poetic play with this problem, Fogarty appears to recycle the negative of the lyric tradition as a rich and emergent space of meaning. By animating objects held to have a negative value, Fogarty creates a radically new discursive and epistemological system of association from the lyric mode negated by colonialism.

Fogarty's resistance to the representative 'I' takes a powerful shape in his poem "First Off His Tribe Castrated", which illustrates his distinctive political position through repeated rejections of negative tropes:

> We ant's your modem Aborigines
> We ant's your code to heaven
> We ant's your talking without a face
> We ant's your sterilized irrefutably chords.
> I the man who not wrote but action the words
> [...]
> We ant's your herald Aborigines no feral
> We ant's your half stumble benches back for spears can't broken, for hearing.
> We ant's your bread recognized ray to race
> I am sundown up-sun every night you all don't want me desolate
> We ant's your oration invaders,
> Generation will spilt blood yet not our blood rocks. (*Lionel Fogarty* 206)

In this swirl of repetition, Fogarty rejects the poles by which Aboriginality is measured: the voiceless ("sterilized irrefutably chords"), the apologist ("we ant's your code to heaven"), the Enlightenment 'noble savage', the "herald Aborigines," and the "feral." Repetition defines the negative space surrounding the poem's speaker, who defines what they are by what it "ant." In so doing, Fogarty creates a field of opacity inhibiting our perception of the subject speaking the poem. Fogarty illuminates a speaking position through this veil, which distorts images and events as if to appear inverted. There is the slippage between "modem" and 'modern,' "up-sun" instead of 'sun-up,' the elision of 'c' from "ant" forcing the reader to make the connection to 'can't' (or another word starting with c), and the union of past ("yet") and future tense ("will") in "will spilt blood yet," an internal tension that promises an unrealised, unfulfilled revenge. The sun rises at night in "up-sun every night" to convey an inverted sensation of time and space caused by the imposition of a foreign culture. By doing so, Fogarty inverts the "desolate" to appear productive within an assertion of Aboriginal sovereignty, "you all don't want me desolate." In "Tired of Meaning," Fogarty explains the shift when defines poetry by "putting something / from nothing, that's my practice" (*New and Selected Poems* 109).

Fogarty throws a social and environmental ecology into disarray through a pattern of images and sequences that destabilise and recycle particular associative and linguistic codes. Mudrooroo eloquently describes this in a poem for *The Indigenous Literature of Australia: Milli Milli Wangka*: "Lionel takes our lives into his mouth, / Spits them out, crying with our needs, / Our desires, our wants and triumphs (12). Fogarty's negative lyric animates an entire ecology negated by the lyric tradition. Peter Minter also makes this point when he posits that the lyric separation of subject and object "extracts aesthetic value, otherwise known as beauty, from nature" (3). Fogarty's poetry opens subject–object distinctions to encompass different modes of habitus in a given environment, as noted by Stuart Cooke: "[T]he 'I' becomes all manner of things, from the frill-necked lizard and the king brown taipan, to digging sticks, seeds, and a woomera .... His 'I' is highly flexible; it can be of his local community, of his ecosystem, or even of Aboriginal people across the whole continent" (239–41). Warraimaay scholar Victoria L. Grieves usefully accounts for the indistinguishability of Fogarty's 'I' when defining Aboriginal spirituality as a "wholistic notion of the interconnectedness of the elements of the earth and the universe, animate and inanimate, whereby people, the plants and animals, landforms and celestial bodies are interrelated" (7).

Fogarty's 'I' represents a recycled expression of ecological relations and social connections denied to him in a 'detribalised' education. He animates these links using the lyric 'I' in "Imarbara I Am – Generation of Existence":

> I am a living entity, you belong to me. I AM.
> I am of earth and space
> I am a son of the world
> I am the religious law
> I am the kin to all creatures
> I am kin to this creation   (*Lionel Fogarty* 148)

Here, Fogarty pluralises the 'I' to stage ecological connections between human and non-human forms: "I am kin to all creatures." Deborah Bird Rose defines Aboriginal spiritual concepts of plurality through defining Country in *Nourishing Terrains* (1996) as a "place that gives and receives life. Not just imagined or represented, it is lived in and lived with" (7). Fogarty's duplications are never mono-logical or distinguished by separation. As "kin to this creation," Fogarty is responsible for the entities who emerge with the act of naming, as those who share the 'I' with him, and therefore, are responsible for creation itself: "I am the birds dat die / I am the snakes dat die."

Fogarty delivers arguably the most developed expression of negative lyricism in "Abstract Salt Pans." Like the titular salt pans, the poem appears to shimmer in defence of itself as the eye attempts to pull it into various shapes and patterns. The deflective poem critiques a reader's expectation of an 'I' that can be isolated and extracted into individual parts within a whole:

> I am we to the river in sky before the rain fell from the ground
> I am softly in wild nest in the city decent as veins land cut over devils dust
> My gum mouthed washing cling all mountainsides   (*Lionel Fogarty* 220)

The "I" evokes a timescape of rainfall wet with incoming rain that slides upwards into the open sky, a place where "rivers" flow into waiting streams in the sky. The poem proceeds by removing the word described as "softly," in "softly in wild nest in the city decent," to conceal the speaker's continuity between different forms of habitus in the "city" and the "wild." The two oppositions spill out towards the end of the line to air what may lie beneath "as veins land cut," a gesture that implicitly challenges the desire to metaphorically 'cut' the land/poem open to extract an internal value. The last line asserts the discursive potential of intuiting, rather than extracting, the negative lyric: "My gum mouthed washing cling all mountainsides." Rather than see into the poet's "gum[s]" from an external perspective, we emerge from the poet's mouth, what lies beneath the poem, flung into speech and meaning-making power. The following two words, "washing cling," string linguistic particles together in the guise of a washing line, so that the results appear 'gum mouthed' or inside out (inverted by the spin cycle of the poet's linguistic machinery), to be clipped to "all mountainsides" to dry. Fogarty continues:

> I am those Australians snow hugged in the hot aerial elaborate systems
> I am wombat ready and the fight plains were road kill them everyday
> [...]
> Now artist concentric the motif ... I am the Pop art
> reassembled   (*Lionel Fogarty* 220)

Fogarty uses the 'I' to encompass the settler negated by their own imposition of foreign ideas abroad, "those Australians snow hugged" by heat. One is reminded of Paul Carter's observation that explorer Charles Sturt named Mount Misery after "the absence of ... desirable" features (51). Fogarty unifies colonising metaphors within an ecology of recycling that gains in repetition and inversion: the 'I' is "wombat ready" to be killed, still living. He likens the 'I' to a "reassembled" art like pop art, which also recuperates imagery from sources deemed peripheral to artistic production. However, where pop art duplicates and fragments the origin of the image to blur the boundaries between 'high' and 'low' art, Fogarty reassembles the 'I' to articulate new forms of subjectivity and expression. He organises these patterns into a new whole: the decolonised 'I.'

A Poetics of Address: "The Beauty in Seekers Is Who Was Found Fast Last"

Fogarty's recuperation of the 'I' undergirds the poetics of address he uses to reach his readers on his own terms. As Klee recognises, Fogarty frequently addresses his poems to family, lovers, and friends who are largely concealed from the reader's field of vision (939). This layer of opacity develops a lineage in despite of settler-colonial governance, a strategy alluded to in his prose poem, "The Mununjali Exemption Man To My Great Grandfather Fred Fogarty," in which he writes, "my great grandfather was an aboriginal man dat is divide from me cos the history has changed camps. But I have moved too, yet ... I will find you waiting in Mununjali Dreaming realities" (*New and Selected Poems* 8). Through interviews and accompanying notes to poems in *Lionel Fogarty Selected Poems 1980–2017*, Fogarty has divulged many of these connections in ways that will distinguish emerging historicist approaches to his work, as well as Fogarty's contribution to future historical studies of Australian colonialism. In the notes, Fogarty explicitly addresses "Wobnah," to "an old Wakka Wakka man in Cherbourg, who knew all the languages and used to talk to Lionel's father" (298), "Nyarki's Place" to "Hugh Williams, a boxer Lionel used to watch on TV Ringside" (295), and "And It Rained This Night," to Jimmy Chi's musical, *Bran Nu Dae* (1990) (297).

Fogarty's more specifically understood poetics of address underscore a collectivism that may stem from his early membership in the Black Panthers and the Black Resource Centre, as well as his friendships with already-established Aboriginal writers like Jack Davis, Oodgeroo Noonuccal (formerly Kath Walker) and Kevin Gilbert. Oodgeroo, in particular, was an early champion of Fogarty. Describing Fogarty's first volume of collected poems, she states, "I would rather see Aborigines write a book called *Kargun* than pick up a shotgun" (quoted in Shoemaker 179). Fogarty references Oodgeroo's influence in a number of poems, including "Kath Walker" (*New and Selected* 81), "N.A.I.D.O.C. 1982" (*Yoogum* 61), and "You Sound Like Your Flirting" (*Lionel Fogarty* 214). Fittingly, Fogarty emulates the balladic composition of Oodgeroo's famous poem, "We Are Going" in the first line of "Kath Walker": "We are coming, even going / I was born in 1957 / the year after I became a realist" (*New and Selected* 57). Fogarty reverses the trope of the dying race in "we are going" to "we are coming," while adding his own distinctive agrammatical slip to Australian slang in an "even going." By playing with the concepts of arrival and departure, Fogarty unsettles the pre-established history of an Aboriginal people born into colonialism, which he associates with his own birth. Oodgeroo's writings gift Fogarty a rebirth into an alternative future, where "we are the conquerors to take over / not Christ."

Fogarty addresses Gilbert, Oodgeroo, and Davis to establish a self-defined exchange in the poem "Disguised, Not Attitude" (*New and Selected* 89–90), which concludes with the following lines:

> Now all books speak, land ecology never have holiday
> when nuclear murderers
> but ash writers test peered interests
> not over us' fella
> for again published musts are
> 'Long live Davis, Walker, and Gilberts
> writers
> We yours.'   (*New and Selected* 90)

The poem appears to challenge the use of praise to resolve the problem of literary recognition, a limited end that may be inimical to the kind of work necessary to defend "land ecology ... when nuclear murderers." Praise falls like "ash" across a writer's brow, who appears to exert their "interests" over their peers, "not over us' fella," in order to answer the demand of Australia's publishing industry, rather than commit to service, "never have holiday." However, the poem generates a multi-perspectival view of the scene that obscures this image: we are asked to peer over "peers," while "not over us' fella," a line that simultaneously suggests high-low perspectives. Through these multiple connotations, Fogarty conceals his praise for Davis, Oodgeroo, and Gilbert from the "boast tongue" or the "venom academics" who assume "felicity in scenery." Fogarty reinforces this effect by placing the final lines in speech marks to qualify the statement or relay its repetition from another voice separate from that of the poet himself. Through this 'disguised' form of address, Fogarty destabilises the representational politics of literary canonisation in order to activate a lived idea of the poet, whereby a figure like Oodgeroo "walks her texture of eternity / pedestals are matched cries in the winds" (*New and Selected* 89).

Fogarty's poetics of address heighten with his grief for the murder of his eighteen-year-old brother, Daniel, at the hands of the police in 1993. Daniel's murder triggered a series of political marches across Queensland and Australia in which Fogarty was a key member. In the wake of these events, Fogarty delivers a series of poems addressing his brother, such as "Murra Murra Gulandanilli – Waterhen":

> Dayock is a-calling contempt
> To evil policie
> Dayock is a-singing to the souls

> Aborigine revolution coming
> [...]
> You're on the other side, the light you see
> The light you see is where you're from
> Is where you're going to be the from of feeling that was within you
> Can't you forget
> Can't you remember
> As long as I am a-grieving
> You'll see justice will be done
> Baba Yubbu
> I will love you always   (*New and Selected* 6)

Fogarty provides echoes of his poetic encounter with his late brother across various times and spaces, as signalled by the resonances created by the alliteration of "calling contempt" and "singing to the souls," the mirroring of "a-calling" and "a-singing," and anaphoric repetition of "can't you forget / can't you remember." Fogarty's use of resonance across the poem reflects the paradox that emerges at its close, "the light you see is where you're coming from," which is then rewritten in a future-perfect lens: "is where you're going to be the from of feeling." Moving from one line to the other, the reader is positioned towards a fading light already dying, before thrown back into its original source. Hopfer suggests that the poem activates "a circular pattern of time and reality informed by the interlinkage of past, present and future" (49). While her criticism occurs after the Royal Commission into Aboriginal Deaths in Custody concluded in 1991, Aboriginal deaths in police custody remain topical in Australian society and reinforces the poem's tragic resonance for contemporary readers. In a report timed to release with the Black Lives Matter protests in the USA and Australia in 2020, *The Guardian* revealed that there had been 437 deaths since the Royal Commission. Of these, inquiries show that judicial and health agencies (police stations and hospitals) did not follow their own procedures in 41 per cent of those events (Allam et al.). At the time of writing this chapter, there have been seven deaths in custody in the last two months. For this, and through Fogarty's poetics of address, the poem provides a poetics of an endlessly echoing call: "as long as I am a-grieving / you'll see justice done."

While always working in concert with local connection to literary figures such as Buchanan, and more recently, Yankunytjatjara poet Ali Cobby Eckermann, Fogarty's poetic writings on solidarity give him a distinctive view of the world. Recently, a range of scholars have attempted to trace Fogarty's arc across the world: Ameer Chasib Furaih suggests that Fogarty's radical poetry is "part of a larger, international revolutionary 'Black' literary movement" (10), Stuart Cooke identifies lines of connection between hyper-local frames in Australia and South America (2013), and I have drawn attention to Fogarty's writings on inter-Indigenous encounters across the Pacific (2019). Currently situated in his own Country at Undullah, Fogarty travels to poetry festivals across Australia regularly, and is well known in the international literary circuit, having visited "the United States, United Kingdom, Latin America, Thailand, Indonesia, China, India, Holland, Germany, Italy, and Spain" (Morrissey 291). Fogarty's belief in collectivist resistance against individualist representation, colonial oppression, and extractive industries shapes his internationalist writings. In "Bhinneka Tunggal IKa – Ha Mon Kee in Diversity Diver City," a poem written at a literary festival in Indonesia, Fogarty clamours to "bring an end to inhaling poisonous gas / Used by the B.H.P. C.S.I.R.O or any cemetery" (*Lionel Fogarty* 177). His environmentalist critique is shaped by an overarching resistance to governance, as signalled by the corporate bodies that emerge in these lines. Fogarty challenges the capitalist governance structures allowing for extraction of resources in the last section of the poem: "Your candidate joins no public serves / The beauty in seekers is who was found fast last" (180). To Fogarty, any appointed "candidate" is divorced from the public they seek to represent. His play between "fast" and "last" appears to signify that a "beauty" can be "found" among those who do not seek leadership, but the duplicative rhyming logic of "fast last" unsettles this conclusion as if to suggest that no one can be found fast last, and, by implication, there is no "beauty" to be found at all in seeking a "candidate."

Fogarty's radical, idiosyncratic political voice has imagined connections to a wide range of political groups across the world. Consider, for example, his poetic address to Iraqi politician Saddam Hussein, published in 2004 a year after the United States' (and Australia's) invasion of Iraq, "Sad Saddam I Support." In a note accompanying a 2017 version of the poem, Phillip Morrissey and Tyne Daile Sumner suggest the poem was inspired by a "meeting with a man from Kuwait who was writing a thesis on the Black Panther movement" (300):

> Old boys running cunning
> complexities by a entering
> politics challenge
> [...]
> War is being condemned yet all
> must die for all beliefs 'let dem pray'
>
> The moral may be experimented
> by old boys wars

> Require liaison when war
> came, some acquisition
> native Arab home land
>
> Old boys I have a political
> statement here in 1991 I take
> side, with the holy war cos
> they on a mission from God Allah (*Lionel Fogarty* 165)

In a "political / statement" propelled by duplications ("old boys") and internal rhyme ("running cunning"), Fogarty draws attention to a shared commitment to defend one's homeland ("native Arab home land") from "acquisition" by Western forces. Here, Fogarty unifies the figure of the poet as prosecutor and the dictator, mutually tasked to decide whether "all / must die for all beliefs." His idiosyncratic comparison of the two figures illustrates the distinctiveness of his poetic and political outlook. Not bound to political conformity or national allegiance (Australia was fighting in Iraq alongside the United States at the time of the poem's publication in 2004), Fogarty emphasises international solidarity to all peoples suffering oppression, unbound by representative or ideological commitments. In the process, he creates his own poetic arc of production and reception defined by that which is negated by individualist and extractive logics.

Fogarty works within a decolonial tradition of breaking open linguistic, historical, and cultural models through unconventional syntax, spelling, and grammar to reterritorialise discursive space. I say 'reterritorialise,' as Fogarty often appears to return language to a central locus of enunciation. Hence, in the poem, "Murra Murra Gulandanilli – Waterhen," he writes: "Is where you're going to be the from of feeling that was within you[?]" (5). Fogarty describes a commitment to his own sense of orientation, to "where you're going," a steadfastness that is its own value, where progress is measured by a return to the "from of feeling." While inescapably limited to a given field of vision, Fogarty's literary experimentation exemplifies an idiosyncratic outlook that disrupts the accepted notions of literary expression, political thought, identity and culture, and history itself. Fogarty's endless process of meaning-making refutes solely negative or political readings of his poetry, while encouraging an acute awareness of the regenerative and adaptive nature of his poetic style. Fogarty's poetry intercedes to make a nonsense of his own measurement: a singular poetic self-defined by negation. Out of this negative matrix, Fogarty's poems spiral outward in their many duplications to form an alternative means of poetic self-definition in keeping with Indigenous epistemologies and ontologies.

Works Cited

Allam, Lorena, et al. "Aboriginal Deaths in Custody: Black Lives Matter Protests Referred to Our Count of 432 Deaths. It's Now 437." *The Guardian*, 9 June 2020. www.theguardian.com/australia-news/2020/jun/09/black-lives-matter-pro testers-referred-to-our-count-of-432-aboriginal-deaths-in-custody-its-now-437.
Araluen, Evelyn. "Resisting the Institution." *Overland* no. 227, 2017, pp. 3–10.
Barthes, Roland. "The Death of the Author." *Image, Music, Text*, translated by Stephen Heath. Hill and Wang, 1977, pp. 142–48.
Booth, Mark. *The Experience of Songs*. Yale University Press, 1981.
Buchanan, Cheryl and Lionel Fogarty. "You or Me – You and Me." *Honi Soit* vol.20 no.1, 1997, pp. 3–4.
Carter, Paul. *The Road to Botany Bay: An Exploration of Landscape and History*. University of Minnesota Press, 2010.
Cooke, Stuart. *Speaking the Earth's Languages: A Theory for Australian-Chilean Postcolonial Poetics*. Rodopi, 2013.
Fogarty, Lionel. *Kargun*. Cheryl Buchanan, 1980.
  Yoogum Yoogum. Penguin, 1982.
  Booyooburra: A Story of the Wakka Murri. Hyland House, 1993.
  New and Selected Poems: Munaldjali, Mutuerjaraera. Hyland House, 1995.
  "Australian Poet Lionel Fogarty in conversation with Philip Mead." *Jacket* no.1, October 1997. http://jacketmagazine.com/01/fogartyiv.html.
  "Remember Something Like This." *Jacket* no.1, October 1997. http://jacketmagazine.com/01/fogpoems.html.
  "Interview with Lionel Fogarty," by Michael Brennan. *Poetry International*, 3 July 2011. www.poetryinternational.com/en/poets-poems/article/104-20646_ Interview-with-Lionel-Fogarty/.
  "Interview: Lionel Fogarty," by Timmah Ball. *Etchings Indigenous: Treaty*, edited by Timmah Ball and Scott Halligan. Illura Press, 2011, pp. 129–35.
  Lionel Fogarty Selected Poems 1980–2017, edited by Philip Morrissey and Tyne Daile Sumner. Re.press, 2017.
Furaih, A. "'For Their Fights Affect Our Fights': The Impact of African American Poetics and Politics on the Poetry of Lionel Fogarty." *Journal of the Association for the Study of Australian Literature: JASAL* vol.17 no.1, 2017, pp. 1–12.
Gray, Robert and Geoffrey Lehmann, eds. *Australian Poetry in the Twentieth Century*. Heinemann, 1991.
Greene, Roland. "The Lyric." *The Cambridge History of Literary Criticism*, edited by Glyn Norton. Cambridge University Press, 1999, pp. 216–28.
Grieves, Victoria L. *Aboriginal Spirituality: Aboriginal Philosophy, the Basis of Aboriginal Social and Emotional Wellbeing*. Cooperative Research Centre for Aboriginal Health, 2009.
Hill, Barry. "Working the Country." *Australian Book Review* vol.176 no.21, 1995, pp. 21–22.
Hopfer, Sabina. "Reading Lionel Fogarty: An Attempt to Feel into Texts Speaking of Decolonisation." *Southerly* vol.62 no.2, 2002, pp. 45–64.
Kingston, Coralie. "'Yoogum Yoogum' Huggiby Lionel George Fogarty." *Social Alternatives* vol.3 no.3, 1983, p. 78.

Kinsella, John. *Spatial Relations, Vol. 1: Essays, Reviews, Commentaries, and Chorography*. Rodopi, 2013.
Klee, Louis. "Reading Lionel Fogarty." *Textual Practice* vol.36 no.6, 2022, pp. 928–52.
Leane, Jeanine. "No Longer Malleable Stuff." *Overland* no.241, 2020, pp. 11–18.
Lucashenko, Melissa. "I Pity the Poor Immigrant." *Journal of the Association for the Study of Australian Literature* vol.17 no.1, 2017, pp. 1–10.
Mead, Philip. *Networked Language: Culture & History in Australian Poetry*. Australian Scholarly Publishing, 2008.
Minter, Peter. "Writing Country: Composition, Law and Indigenous Ecopoetics." *Journal of the Association for the Study of Australian Literature* vol.12 no.1, 2012, pp. 1–10.
Moore, Dashiell. "The Inter-Indigenous Encounter." *Journal of Commonwealth Literature* vol.57 no.2, 2019, pp. 354–70.
Morrissey, Philip. "Introduction." *Lionel Fogarty Selected Poems 1980–2017*, edited by Philip Morrissey and Tyne Daile Sumner. re.press, 2017, pp. 15–28.
Mudrooroo. "Guerilla Poetry: Lionel Fogarty's Response to Language Genocide." *Westerly* vol.31 no.3, 1986, pp. 47–55.
The Indigenous Literature of Australia = Milli Milli Wangka. Hyland House, 1997.
Rose, Deborah Bird. *Nourishing Terrains: Australian Aboriginal Views of Landscape and Wilderness*. Australian Heritage Commission, 1996.
Shoemaker, Adam. *Black Words, White Page: Aboriginal Literature 1929–1988*. University of Queensland Press, 1989.
Van Toorn, Penny. "Aboriginal Poetry Now: From Dramatic Monologue to Hip Hop and Rap!" *Reading Down Under: Australian Literary Studies Reader*, edited by Amit Sarwal and Reema Sarwal. SSS Publications, 2009, pp. 182–92.
Watson, Irene. *Aboriginal People, Colonialism, and International Law: Raw Law*. Routledge, 2015.

PART IV
Embodied Poetics

13

JEANINE LEANE AND NATALIE HARKIN

The Strength of Us as Women
A Poetics of Relationality and Reckoning

Introduction

>Australia is an archive of secrets
>cloaked in daggered deceit
>dressed in borrowed robes
>no Pandora's Box can contain
>what this nation will not speak
>and all it has unspoken
>Australia is a violent translation.
>
>(Leane)

This chapter reflects on a series of conversations between two Aboriginal women poets and scholars from unique Wiradjuri and Narungga standpoints on the transformative power of Indigenous poetry, and its significant contributions to the literature of the world. Through our own methods of Gathering and Archival-Poetic praxis, we seek to better understand those entangled past-present-future contexts and theoretical strengths from which texts emerge and consider the counter-narrative potential of poetry to collective memory, shaping national consciousness and identity.

In 2000, the late Wiradjuri elder, poet, and activist Aunty Kerry Reed-Gilbert edited a landmark anthology, *The Strength of Us as Women: Black Women Speak*. This collection of poetry and short prose has become an enduring and relational touchstone for us, and we honour those critical voices that inform and bolster our thinking still today.

> If you want to know the reality of inside Black Australia, this book is for you. The women who speak within these pages allow you, the reader, to look into their hearts, minds, bodies and souls. Share with them their journey, the journey of life. (Reed-Gilbert 9)

We recognise these journeys as our own; as embodied and lived, but also 'officially' traced via the official state colonial archive. This chapter considers what the archive means to us, framed by a politic of relationality, refusal, and reckoning. We consider what happens when the archive box is opened, and when records speak and are heard for the first time. We share insights on the potential and possibility of poetry as an affective tool and literary intervention, and of our individual praxis as a means to actively transform out from the archive box and rupture the ongoing violence of the colonial state. Through literary ekphrasis, we consider the influence of other poets on our own work, including Aunty Kerry. This is our poetics of relationality and love, as active honouring.

Natalie: Standpoint/Relationality and Responsibility

As a Narungga woman living on Kaurna Country, I am a product of layered histories and disruptions, intergenerational and collective memories, and (re) connections to country. My writing is driven by lived experience underpinned with a deep sense of acknowledgement, accountability, and responsibility that extends beyond the present. My sense of belonging through relationship to place is necessarily woven into the fabric of the land on which I live and work, and knowing its colonial legacies. Cherokee writer/ scholar Daniel Heath Justice also refers to the responsibility of 'not knowing' to honour those mysteries that both connect and distinguish us; to respect the silences and recognise when and where to tread lightly, if to tread at all ("Global Native Literary Studies"). This is a resonant theme for so many Indigenous writers, theorised by the late Standing Rock Sioux writer, historian, and activist Vine Deloria Jr as the concept of 'relativity,' where the earth and universe are alive, related, and connected. Such critical relationality centres Indigenous ways of knowing, being, and doing to observe the natural world and make meaning as relational, related, and real. It is learnt through "reciprocity, obligation, shared experiences, coexistence, cooperation and social memory" (Moreton-Robinson, "Relationality" 71) and is grounded in holistic interconnectedness between and among all living things.

Many Indigenous writers position voice, freedom, and responsibility as central to the art of writing, and for the continuation of our stories, including those displaced from traditions through colonial disruption.[1] Muscogee poet Joy Harjo refers to the "responsibility of remembering"; the need "to continue the stories, to write and tell what we know, whether they are stories of growing up on country with community, or stories of displacement, loss and survival" (quoted in Perrault at 200).

Aunty Kerry Reed-Gilbert's book *The Strength of Us as Women* is a clarion call for responsibility through such critical relationality. She drives a direct challenge to non-Indigenous readers to understand multiple ways of belonging, and to act and engage in the political struggle with Indigenous Australians: "Responsibility is learning this country, sharing the stories. Sharing the pain, the hurt. Sharing the untruths. Who's responsible? You are. If you call this country home, you are" (13).

My own research initially set out to follow ghosts and paper trails in search of answers to some missing links in my family story. My desire to go back to the origin of the archive manifested as a restless gathering and a feverish hoarding of records that provide a chilling and intimate snapshot of lives lived under extraordinary surveillance and control. The files were predominantly located in State Aboriginal Records, Children's Welfare Records, the South Australian Museum, and the National Archives of Australia. Collectively, they expose a culture of biopolitics underpinning the science-based social policy experimentation that all Indigenous families were subjected to across Australia during this time. An insurmountable collation of data has been gathered, dovetailing between the Aborigines Protection Board and the Children's Welfare Board, and their associated departments. These records also revealed the government's focus on Aboriginal girls for targeted removal from their families and placed into domestic service labour as part of the great assimilation experiment.

This colonial archive is not an easy place to navigate. As Narungga and Wiradjuri researchers we approach the colonial archive tentatively, sometimes feverishly, and always with caution. We enter with our senses heightened; each experiencing these potent documents and sites in particular ways. We know these official records are not the source of an objective truth, but are, as Trawlwoolway artist and writer Julie Gough states, "ledgers leaking attitudes" ("Transforming Histories" 64) that bring particular meaning to our work. When you enter the archive, you have to really prepare yourself for the coloniser's madness. Despite the trepidation on this archival journey, access to certain material has actually heightened my sense of belonging and has become central to reckoning with my personal histories, and in turn, the collective histories of community, state, and nation.

Our praxis contributes to a growing body of Indigenous-led research engaging with the violence of the colonial archive concerning issues of access and transparency, the state's archivisation processes, and questions of surveillance, representation, agency, and truth-telling. As poets and educators, I feel like we're in a unique position to flip the gaze so these "ledgers" become our ultimate cabinets of curiosity; ripe for decolonising and critique so that beyond blood-memory recognition, our ancestors can exhale with ease towards a just future. We want to place the spotlight back on the state, where it firmly belongs.

Jeanine: Standpoint and Positionality

I am Wiradjuri. I was born in the middle of the freshwater cradle of southeastern Australia. I grew up on Country as one of three generations of Aboriginal women – my nanna was born in 1887, the eldest of the two aunties in 1909, the other in 1923, and my mother in 1937.

My body (like all bodies) is an archive where memories are etched, stored, and anchored. This is the living archive that I inherit, and my mind and body become a repository of my family's Aboriginal history – even before it was told to me and even now as some of it remains untold or is still missing. My work is the politics of memory. It is to remember a dismembered but still living past as it haunts, pervades, and *lives in* the present.

Memory politics is transgenerational – beyond the span of a lifetime; it is the greater body politic of Aboriginal memory. We had ways of gathering and storing, communicating, and transmitting our histories long before the invasion and intervention of state and its wide and wavering nets – its infrastructure – the archives, the 'History' with a capital 'H.' National history and the archiving of all things Aboriginal has been just one among many interventions – invasions into the lives of Aboriginal people. The original invasion of 1788 was followed by a series of smaller but no less significant or pernicious interventions into and invasions of Aboriginal lands and bodies and *attempts* to invade our mind. For this reason, I see my work as a poet and researcher more as *memory work* than archival work.

I've always found the image of an 'archive box' as it is presented and represented in Western literary history fraught. And confronting. And confusing. And deeply troubling. There's something about the shape – the angular hard sidedness, the sharp corners, and the lid that seals shut imprisoning all within that jars me. And then there's the airlessness. Anything inside would be starved of breath and light.

The box – its shape, its form, what it represents, what it contains, and what it doesn't – has a lot to answer for in this post-invasion nation. I become the stalker of what once stalked me – the bits and pieces of my family's lives captured in an archive – the violent translations of moments taken out of their control. Moments written of in English that uses smooth words to mask violent things – pillow-soft words that smother the truth. Like *interference* for *rape* and *assault*. Like *disturbance* for *domestic violence*. Like *insubordinate* and *aggressive* for *self-defence*.

I was taught not to be afraid of ghosts. I was taught to respect them. This means to listen. Even if you don't want to sometimes. And that's what draws me to the box – the giant archive box of the nation – Australia and all the little boxes that prop it up like a tower of blocks that is not so formidable or solid as it first appears.

Natalie and I have spoken and written before of how the records of those whose memories we embody – whose experiences are encrypted within us – call out to us and we hear them. Just as they are not objective, records are not inanimate or passive either. They are alive – making their presences felt, harbouring their resistance. And waiting to speak.

Natalie: Responsibility and Writing for Transformation

We may be intimate knowers of our own histories, but we have not been in control of the dominant narrative of our lives. Writing allows us to cultivate sovereignty of the mind and regain the plotline of our lives.[2] As a sovereign act, poetry is a means to rise up and transcend containment, boundaries, and essentialist labelling; a therapeutic means to "name our oppressions and our oppressors" (Bellear 70) and dangerous to hegemonic power.[3] I think about this often; the power and the importance of staying safe with others who also yearn to live in a more just and 'beloved community'; a bell hooks-inspired community that is formed "not by the eradication of difference but by its affirmation, by each of us claiming the identities and cultural legacies that shape who we are and how we live in the world. To form beloved community, we do not surrender ties to precious origins" (265).

Our poetry engages the language of "love and war alike" (Justice, *Why Indigenous Literature Matters* 60) imbued with the autobiographical voice: life-writing, personal narrative, memory-work, auto-ethnography, and story work; rooted in body-politics, deep and real; flesh, mind, and spirit; past, present, and future. When whiteness is the dominant invisible norm, and racist-, gender-, and homophobic-fuelled violence is a daily reality for so many, poetry can become the will to survive and stay safe with words; to "face the reality of dealing with pain" (Bellear 70); to trust one's own voice, that it may give voice to others, and to live passionately, imaginatively, and creatively, beyond embodied and genealogical pain. Our writing communities are indeed generative spaces that decentre whiteness and make meaning on our terms through a sense of collective community resurgence.

As Alexis Wright describes, we have been locked in this storytelling war from the point of first contact; a war that still fosters and maintains negative, racialised, stereotyped narratives about who we are, and invades every sense of our sovereignty and resistance ("What Happens"). As contemporary agents of memory, there are multiple ways to share the weight of these stories; to collectively move through a decolonising project of poetic refusal, resistance, and memory-making, through and beyond the colonial archive.

Indigenous writers and creative practitioners have become increasingly concerned with the politics of representation and question of sovereignty, authenticity, and voice; a continuum response to being defined, categorised, and written about by cultural institutions of power that historically rendered us voiceless.[4]

I'm not surprised that many of my first-year university students admit to ways of 'knowing' Aboriginal people that are steeped in resounding colonial myths and stereotypes. For migrant and international students, such racialised thinking is often perpetuated within their own communities. The semester's road towards transformation is long, and Indigenous-led curriculum and resources are crucial. Tony Birch's "The Invisible Fire: Indigenous Sovereignty, History and Responsibility" is particularly resonant. In it he refers to the important work of Joseph Pugliese, who advised migrant communities to "do their homework" in order to actively disrupt the colonial relations of the past; to not be "complicit agents in the reproduction of contemporary colonialism" (116). Birch calls for an "active stance of anti-colonialism"; for Indigenous and migrant communities to recognise commonalities, forge alliances, and refuse the status of marginalisation in order to become "a genuinely post-colonial nation" (116). Bundjalung poet/researcher Evelyn Araluen also echoes this sentiment, reminding non-Indigenous decolonial poets and literary scholars to carefully consider what is returned to communities, and to meaningfully engage with the Indigenous struggle beyond the sandstone walls of the academy. As Michi Saagiig Nishnaabeg poet/artist/scholar Leanne Betasamosake Simpson describes:

> We need to be creating a present that will inspire a radically different future than the one settler colonialism sets out for us. This means taking on heteropatriarchy, white supremacy, capitalism, and anti-blackness, and actualizing Indigenous alternatives on the ground, not in the future, but in the present. ("Indigenous Resurgence" 32)

Our sistergirl, Bundjalung author/poet/scholar Melissa Lucashenko, reminds us to choose our own reference points from where our stories are told; to interrogate colonial fantasies and be "vigilant about what we allow into our consciousness and what we recognize as the very Big Lie of colonialism" (n.pag.). Simpson also urges us to think big: to forge strategic alliances with others who refuse Western patriarchal structures of colonialism; build movements with intellectual-warriors in Black communities and radical communities of colour; and seek inspiration from those creative, compassionate visionaries who are interested in building new worlds that affirm and reinsert our Indigenous presence. These kinds of conversations, framed by Black, queer, postcolonial, and Indigenous feminisms, have been critical

A Poetics of Relationality and Reckoning

to my own thinking on poetry as decolonial praxis.[5] They have helped me better understand those intersecting dynamics of power and oppression, and think through alternative systems of accountability for race-, class-, and gender-based violence; grounded in a resistance-poetics vision of refusal to be silent or silenced.

As warrior woman activist/poet/scholar Audre Lorde notably states, "poetry is not a luxury" (36). The very act of writing is vital to existence and provides a way to transform dreams and hopes into action "toward survival and change"; imagining and enacting hopeful futures here and now, as well as on "the farthest horizons" (37). Simpson identifies something similar; writing as an obligation to the responsibility of "freedoms to come" (Simpson and Brand n.pag.); a means to build alternatives in the present, because today's actions give birth to the future, so our children will know "what freedom feels like ... so they know what to fight for" (Simpson, "Indigenous Resurgence" 33).

Jeanine: Memory Work – Defying the Records

History is not what happens. Nor is it the past – or not all of it anyway. History is a Western method of recording and cultural transmission. History as we currently inherit it – or perhaps more aptly have it thrust upon us and about us – is originally a Greek term beginning with Herodotus who authored an early work in anti-middle eastern propaganda called *The Histories* in the fifth century BC (before Christ and Cook). This text, later interpreted by modern Anglo-European scholars to mean 'facts of history,' has become the white-print for how to author colonial history ever after. Greco-Roman historical method is inherited by the British Empire and becomes the stuff of the colonial archive continuing.

Collective memory is the *only thing* that can hold the history of this nation to account. Memory can defy an archive of violent translations.

My aunties defied colonialism in everything they did. Colonialism is not just one big amphora structure descending from above. It is everywhere and in the everyday. In the way women were made to work; the way they were expected to dress; to speak. Colonialism is a series of macro and micro aggressions. Resistance comes first from the locale – where you are. An old saying rings true that the best place to hide something is under someone's nose. The best way to nurture and grow resistance under the nose of colonialism is behind the veneer of conformism.

My grandfather, descendant of English protestants from Devonshire, died in 1967 on his ninetieth birthday – the same year I turned six and the year before I faced the Western classroom. I grew up at the end of the reign of my grandfather, who like many other white men conducted their own personal eugenics/assimilation practices in the colonies.[6] He was descended from the Puritans who believed, among other things, that female subordination in earthly matters was God's will and that manifestations of sin were always gendered. Being born woman meant an automatic disposition to sin. Being born a Blak woman meant the word was made flesh and dwelt on earth to either tempt or be tamed and controlled by white men. He was on a mission, believing his own pathway to assimilation would be the individual and personal role he played (or at least sought to) in the colonial eugenics project.

He forbade, among other things, bright colours in clothing or decor, music other than hymns, dancing, and all other idle pleasures, like art, ornaments, jewellery, and flowers. Yet right under his nose the women began to grow a garden. The story goes that Nanna, and my eldest aunt, began to plant bulbs, cuttings, and seeds that my aunty gathered during her domestic work in the homes of the white women of the town between rows in the vegetable garden that the women were tasked with tending.

By the time I was born in 1961 there were beds and beds of all sorts of flowers and shrubs – both native and introduced – alongside herbs and vegetables. My sister and I played jungle games in the garden while Aunty worked. She liked to feel the dirt, she said. She often worked barefoot and loved nothing better than the heat of high summer in the western Riverina, working in the sun. I didn't know it then, like many things that were told to me bit by bit, and I didn't get the full picture until I was older, but the garden wasn't just pretty, it was, like many other things the women in my life did that seemed so benign at first glance, an act of rebellion, and a space for women to talk. I think of many small acts of radicalism. Covert radicalism – stealth, camouflage, ulterior radicalism, sub rosa.

My garden is an archive and a memorial and an investment. I think this because it is cultivated from seeds, roots, cuttings, bulbs, tubers, and rhizomes from many women I know and have known. Many women past and present. Memories of them still grow in my garden. I think most of my eldest Aunty who planted a garden, with her mother, my grandmother, as an act of defiance and a space for the women away from the house, and work, and the demands of white men. She insisted I make a garden to get out and work with the soil I live on, to feel the place through my hands and to bring things from home to a new place. And, because she always said, like Nanna said, flowers and stories will go forever if you take care of them.

I look out thirty years later at my garden for all seasons and know the women were right. These were the women as I knew them outside of anyone else's archive. There's more truth and story in my garden than any state agency about the lives of the Wiradjuri matriarchs of my family. My eyes always fall last on a stand of deep-purple bearded iris, one of the first things Aunty gave me. Tough and hardy, perennial and beautiful she told me as she handed me a single rhizome of bearded iris. "A bit like us!" she grinned through now 80-year-old toothless gums.

Their rhizomes have spread through my garden to form irregular clumps and drifts ever since. Memory is like a rhizome. It spreads like the surface of a body of water, spreading towards available spaces or trickling downwards towards new spaces through fissures and gaps, pushing through whatever is in its way. Rhizomes have no start or finish; they are always in the middle, like in-between things, always inhabiting the interface of many directions always at the intersection, at the junction of offshoots that grow and take on their own life.

Thinking about a rhizome as a metaphor for research means I can work in all different directions and with the non-linear narratives that have been busted up by the Western archival system of record-keeping. It means I can gather the memories, the objects, the letters, the pictures that live outside an archive to speak back to the violence within. These intergenerational and body memory practices and behaviours have shaped me and informed my method – like gathering, and growing things for the future. Intergenerational memory is the *only thing* that can hold a colonial archive to account.

Natalie: Archival-Poetics as Method and Praxis

As a method, Archival-Poetics emerged as a slow, situated unfolding; an embodied reckoning with Australia's state colonial archive and those traumatic, contested, and buried episodes of history that inevitably return to haunt. It developed as a means to disrupt and reimagine contemporary legacies of colonialism, including the inconceivable volume of Indigenous records, objects, artefacts, and human remains held in state collections all over the world; material, cultural, and intellectual property that was stolen, recorded, categorised, and contained in the name of empire and conquest. These archives hold histories of preservation painstakingly maintained, a fixed consignment process of hierarchy and order where provenance, objectivity, and security are assured. As institutions of future memory, they also signify sites and histories of immense loss for all that was discarded and deemed irrelevant for the record.

I unwittingly replicated the very thing I was attempting to disrupt, *the Archive Box*; locked in and vacuum sealed with my ancestors, navigating a violent entanglement of myth and truths, buoyed and sustained by imperial fantasies to shape official realities. The only way for me to reckon with it all was to examine the origins of the archive itself, consider new offerings for the future record, write poetry, and weave my way out.[7] This culminated in a body of poetry and text-based/mixed-media work featuring family archives with intention to reveal their agency and attest to their strength, courage, and proactive engagement with the state, and to shine a light on their legacy of intelligence, refusal, and activism.[8]

A selection of handwritten letters by my nanna and great-grandmother from the state's archive revealed critical minor histories where the gendered and racialised conditions of empire play out in the mundane intimacies of the everyday.[9] They were replete with references to home, to family, and a domestic-trained life controlled by the state and provided insight to stories and legacies otherwise smoothed over, hidden, or forgotten. As a labour of love, weaving became central to my poetic praxis culminating in the physical and metaphorical transformation of their letters into a Ngarrindjeri basket; a new archival-poetic site of resistance, a shared-history location, and a means to honour a very different story to what was officially recorded about them.[10]

Jeanine: Gathering/Docu-poetry and the Politics of Memory

I was the first generation of my family to confront an archive in its narrowest sense of the word – the building where the paper gods are enshrined. I was the first generation to be given the words – and the access to the words through the labour and unwavering activism of generations of Blak women preceding me. The women whose bodies I am descended from; and the Blak women who wrote – poems, stories, testimonials, and essays. Women who turned the word from a tool of incarceration to one of potential emancipation.

I think of Oodgeroo, who was the only Blak poet I read at school; writers like Margaret Tucker, Ida West, Shirley Smith, Glenyse Ward, and Sally Morgan, whose life-writing throughout the 1970s and 1980s challenged the national narrative of peaceful settlement, prosperity, and masculinity. I think about Aunty Jenni Kemarre Martiniello, poet, author, essayist, teacher, academic, and artist whose writing, glass-weaving, and essays, alongside generous mentoring and teaching, have inspired and launched the writing/artistic careers of a generation. I think about Aunty Kerry Reed-Gilbert – late Wiradjuri word-warrior, poet, artist, mentor, teacher, and friend whose words of strength to us as Blak women Natalie chose to open this sovereign women's conversation. I look to the strength of these women's words, and those of women and non-binary poets writing now like Aunty Alexis Wright, Aunty Jackie Huggins, Yvette Holt, Aunty Barbara Nicholson, Charmaine

A Poetics of Relationality and Reckoning

Papertalk Green, Natalie Harkin, Ellen van Neerven, Evelyn Araluen, and Melissa Lucashenko.

The politics of Aboriginal memory when applied to the state archive of surveillance that has officially defined Aboriginality can examine ways in which the past still haunts us and maintains its influence on the present, particularly how the layers of meaning in events or texts, previously consigned to history's shadows, can be exposed through creative expression. The archive has come into the spotlight and under the microscope of writers, and more importantly, it has been brought into conversation with writers – particularly but not exclusively those who seek to *remember* a past *dismembered* by the colonial archive. So, the archive is both exposed and brought into the public sphere by Aboriginal writing – that is the spotlight image – but it is also scrutinised, dissected, and examined under the microscope of Aboriginal readers who bring our intergenerational stories and secrets and read for the silences and the cultural metaphors that recast us in a largely deficit discourse. And what this does is challenge and, in this context, reverse to *some extent*, at least, the existing power dynamic of the colonial paradigm by putting the white history of Aboriginal Australians on the cutting board, where previously our people have spent too much time and experienced many personal and emotional invasions.

My creative intervention with archival material and records, such as newspapers and government-issued identification papers, is docu-memory. Docu-memory writing is a meeting place – as meeting places are central cultural metaphors for Aboriginal peoples – where memory meets documents or, the other way around, documents and memory collide to break down the force field of history as it has contained us thus far. The records – the written records – are the epicentre of the confinement. In this reverse invasion – intergenerational memory – body memory invades the archive or the record defying the paper god that is the heart of Western empires. It is like stepping back through the object – the paper – and coming out the other side to rewrite it.

My poetry is a gathering of not only archival interrogation. It is a critique of textual violence and national symbols and historical discourses. It is an intervention to disrupt calcified national narratives that have ensnared us in webs of deceit and misrepresentation like the colonial spider that Alexis Wright referred to.

My method is to smuggle things – like the information I find but cannot take back – out of the archive and bring them into the creative realm where they can breathe and speak. Trawlwoolway artist and scholar Julie Gough speaks of "detective work" ("The Artist" 835) as part of her method to understand and speak back to the gaps and violence the archives hold for many Aboriginal families. I think of my creative responses and interventions with the archives and history as informed imagination. My imagination, when I come to the records of the women I knew and loved and respected, is not unanchored, nor is it a tabula rasa that might just 'build characters' or 'create voices.' My imagination is grounded in body memory, and it is responding to the hauntings of my family. I can write the characters and voices of my Blak aunties and my nanna to defy the archive. The records, documents, and reports come face to face with the rest of the person – the Blak body outside the box embodied and empowered by intergenerational memory written of and to by archival, documentary, textual, and epistolic poets like Natalie, and Charmaine Papertalk Green, Elfie Shiosaki, and Evelyn Araluen, for example.

So, the physical record may remain with the institution of the state. But the state does not have the last word as the writings of First Nations poets speak back.

Natalie: Blood Memory, Haunting, and Ekphrasis

As a signature literary trope 'blood memory'[11] became central to *Archival-Poetics* as a reclamation response to personal and collective loss; it is an active remembering, recollection, recuperation, and refining relationships to knowledge to strengthen a sense of self, identity, and place with "blood trails that we follow back toward a sense of where we come from and who we are" (Owens 150). This obligation to remember relates to writing one's family, community, and ancestors through the landscape and the body, as an interrelated site of struggle; a sifting of one's Indigenous roots through generational movement and storytelling.[12] It is our corporeal connectedness and belonging through genealogy-narrative across time and place.

As a narrative tactic, blood memory is a means to write back to the state's colonial discourses and fixed imaginings on blood, constructions of race and identity, and the construction of personal story.[13] It is also a means to reimagine history and contribute to communal memory through the inter-generational transmission of knowledge pumping through individual and collective bodies and societies. Our blood memory is vital and unending, and given our histories of intense dislocation and removal from lands, families, and communities, it does not always flow easily.

As a literary tool, blood memory explored through an epistemology of haunting makes sense to me; a means to understand and theorise that which is silent, hidden, or absent, but is nevertheless acutely present and felt. Reckoning with history's ghosts through a framework of *recognition, transformation,* and *action* enables profound honouring; a form of restorative justice for local stories to rupture and inform larger narratives of history.[14] Theorising haunting from our local Indigenous standpoints can also challenge and counter problematic representations of the Indigenous *ghost* in literature; interrogate how spectres of colonialism still haunt our Indigenous subjectivities today; and dismantle colonial systems, processes, and fixed imaginings via reckoning with spectres of, and in, the colonial archive. Offering up new narratives of history and storytelling has the potential to shift local and national consciousness towards some kind of justice, through either a reckoning with ghosts, an aesthetics of action, or a politics of vision.[15] There are spectres everywhere, calling and willing us to investigate. In the wake of Australia's active forgetting as a form of cultural amnesia and erasure, writing is a kind of therapy through the work of mourning where the possibility of a just future lies in the ability to live in remembrance of history's injustices.[16]

Through ekphrastic markers of relationality and respect, I am drawn to particular Indigenous poets, writers, and artists who also engage archive and memory through decolonial praxis, including Evelyn Araluen, Lisa Bellear, Tony Birch, Ali Cobby Eckermann, Jim Everett, Lionel Fogarty, Charmaine Papertalk Green, Anita Heiss, Yvette Holt, Jeanine Leane, Romaine Moreton, Kerry Reed-Gilbert, Elfie Shiosaki, Ellen van Neerven, Sam Wagan Watson, Allison Whittaker, and Herb Wharton (to name but a few). They write invisible, silenced, and forgotten worlds, from nothing into existence, to expose what Tony Birch calls Australia's "national secrecy about colonialism," unveil what Kim Scott calls "Australia's continuing neurosis" (Scott, "Continuing") and keep the wounds open, as Alexis Wright states, to reverse the prescribed forgetting with a "steadfast telling of the truth" ("Politics"). Our most acclaimed literary-warriors bear witness and reckon with colonial histories of exclusion, as a proactive poetics of haunting and an embodied means to weave stories into a framework of common knowledge and pride.[17]

Their work captures me in unexpected-uncanny moments and at potent places, and they tell me something new and profoundly nostalgic about my own story. In these moments of embodied recognition, invisible spaces opened up to write and create into. Such literary ekphrasis can trigger critical interventions beyond the self, towards resounding and collective reckoning; an archival-poetic response where the potency of place, colonial histories, and blood memory collide.

Jeanine: Body Memory

> The body is the first sign of sovereignty.
> (Moreton in Brewster 61)

As discussed, blood memory is a powerful literary trope that has also been influential in my own work. But it also doesn't always encompass the way

I remember and write. My life and therefore my work takes inspiration from and is shaped by the physical, intellectual, and cultural labour of women. It is shaped by and through the bodies of women. The body holds all that is material of us – blood, bone, flesh, organs, and skin. Skin is the first point of contact between peoples.

> The body is the first archive
> yet the archive disembodies
> I'm seeking to re-embody.

Memory lives under the skin. Skin covers the body and hides all that is inside. People can't shed their skin like snakes. Even if they could, we'd still be the same person underneath. The experiences, body memories of the women before me are embroidered under my skin – stitched into my body.

Conclusion

This is a sovereign-woman conversation, devoid of any colonial filter that might read us in ways we do not intend; a contemplation on history, poetry, and our relationship with the state's gendered and racialised colonial archive. As Aboriginal women poets and educators, we recognise the shape of each other's stories and memories. This is an intimate recognition that is grounded in shared histories and our unique Narungga and Wiradjuri woman standpoints, despite our cultural, spatial, and temporal differences. We also find solace with constellations of poets, writers, and artists who navigate old terrain, imagine and labour through words and archives, and who ache with perpetual mourning because we refuse to leave the trauma of the past alone.

Our grandmothers, from forever away and not so long ago, invited themselves once again to join us, urging us to write and rewrite these narratives of belonging, and reinscribe voice and agency to our loved ones and Country. These conversations shape our becoming as a proud and diverse community of literary activists, anchored by a rich legacy of voices that keep us afloat, vigilant, and accountable. We have a responsibility to remain alive on the page; to rise up and keep fighting and staying strong with our words. We are compelled to counter the deficit gendered and racialised narratives, and demonstrate our survival, intelligence, beauty, and pride.

Aunty Kerry Reed-Gilbert encouraged us to find our voice, write with open hearts, minds, bodies, and soul; to know that we are connected to Country and that our ancestors are always with us:

> Our Dreaming continues for time eternal, there is no ending.
> Yours in unity and sovereignty. (Reed-Gilbert 9)

Works Cited

Allen, Chadwick. *Blood Narrative: Indigenous Identity in American Indian and Maori Literary and Activist Texts.* Duke University Press, 2002.
Anzaldúa, Gloria and AnaLouise Keating, eds. *This Bridge We Call Home: Radical Visions for Transformation.* Routledge, 2002.
Araluen, Evelyn. "Resisting the Institution." *Overland* no.227, 2017. https://overland.org.au/previous-issues/issue-227/feature-evelyn-araluen/.
Bellear, Lisa. "Healing through Poetry." *The Strength of Us as Women*, edited by Kerry Reed-Gilbert. Ginninderra Press, 2000, pp. 70–71.
Birch, Tony. "Promise Not to Tell: Interrogating Colonialism's Worst (or Best) Kept Secrets." First Person: International Digital Storytelling Conference, ACMI, 4 February 2006. www.acmi.net.au/global/media/first_person_birch.pdf.
Brewster, Anne. *Giving This Country a Memory: Contemporary Aboriginal Voices of Australia.* Cambria Press, 2015.
Bunda, Tracey. "The Sovereign Aboriginal Woman." *Sovereign Subjects: Indigenous Sovereignty Matters*, edited by Aileen Moreton-Robinson. Routledge, 2020, pp. 75–85.
Cameron, Emilie. "Indigenous Spectrality and the Politics of Postcolonial Ghost Stories." *Cultural Geographies* vol.15 no.3, 2008, pp. 383–93.
Cariou, Warren. "Haunted Prairie: Aboriginal 'Ghosts' and the Spectres of Settlement." *University of Toronto Quarterly* vol.75 no.2, 2006, pp. 727–34.
Deloria Jr, Vine. "Relativity, Relatedness, and Reality." *Spirit and Reason: The Vine Deloria, Jr. Reader*, edited by Barbara Deloria, Kristen Foehner, and Sam Scinta. Fulcrum Publishing, 1999, pp. 32–39.
DeShazer, Mary. *A Poetics of Resistance: Women Writing in El Salvador, South Africa, and the United States.* University of Michigan Press, 1994.
Eckermann, Ali Cobby and Lionel Fogarty, eds. "A Handful of Sand: Words to the Frontline." *Southerly* vol.71 no.2, 2011, pp. 8–11.
Galeano, Eduardo. "In Defense of the Word." *Days and Nights of Love and War.* Trans. B. Ortiz. Pluto Press, 1983, pp. 169–78.
Gordon, Avery. *Ghostly Matters: Haunting and Sociological Imagination.* 2nd ed. University of Minnesota Press, 2008.
Gough, Julie. "Transforming Histories: The Visual Disclosure of Contentious Pasts." Diss., University of Tasmania, 2001. http://eprints.utas.edu.au/2644/.
"The Artist as Detective in the Museum Archive: A Creative Response to Repatriation and Its Historic Context." *The Routledge Companion to Indigenous Repatriation: Return, Reconcile, Renew*, edited by Cressida Fforde, C. Timothy McKeown, and Honor Keeler. Routledge, 2020, pp. 835–53.
Green, Joyce. *Making Space for Indigenous Feminism.* Fernwood Publishing, 2007.
Harkin, Natalie. "The Poetics of (Re)Mapping Archives: Memory in the Blood." *Journal of the Association for the Study of Australian Literature* vol.14 no.3, 2014. https://openjournals.library.sydney.edu.au/index.php/JASAL/article/view/9909/9798.2014.
Archival-Poetics. Vagabond Press, 2019.

"Weaving the Colonial Archive: A Basket to Lighten the Load." *Journal of Australian Studies* vol.44 no.2, 2020, pp. 154–66.

Heiss, Anita. *Dhuuluu-Yala To Talk Straight: Publishing Indigenous Literature.* Aboriginal Studies Press, 2003.

"Black Poetics." *Meanjin* vol.65 no.1, 2006, pp. 180–91.

hooks, bell. *Killing Rage: Ending Racism.* Henry Holt & Co., 1995.

Justice, Daniel Heath. "Global Native Literary Studies Panelist Daniel Justice Presents Words in the World: Literatures, Oratures, and New Meeting Grounds Symposium." University of Hawaii, 19 July 2013. https://scholarspace.manoa.hawaii.edu/handle/10125/29708.

Why Indigenous Literature Matters. Wilfrid Laurier University Press, 2018.

Kilpatrick, Jacquelyn. *Louis Owens: Literary Reflections on His Life and Work.* University of Oklahoma Press, 2004.

Leane, Jeanine. *Gawimarra: Gathering.* University of Queensland Press, 2024.

Lorde, Audre. *Sister Outsider: Essays and Speeches.* Crossing Press, 2007.

Lucashenko, Melissa. "Writing as a Sovereign Act." *Meanjin Quarterly* (Summer 2018). http://meanjin.com.au/essays/writing-as-a-sovereign-act/.

Momaday, Scott. *House Made of Dawn.* Harper & Row, 1968.

Moraga, Cherrie and Gloria E. Anzaldúa, eds. *This Bridge Called My Back: Writings by Radical Women of Colour.* 4th ed. State University of New York, 2015.

Moreton-Robinson, Aileen. *Talkin' Up to the White Woman.* University of Queensland Press, 2000, p. 16.

"Relationality: A Key Presupposition of an Indigenous Social Research Paradigm." *Sources and Methods in Indigenous Studies*, edited by J. M. O'Brien and C. Andersen. Routledge, 2017, pp. 69–77.

Owens, Louis. *Mixedblood Messages, Literature, Film, Family, Place.* University of Oklahoma Press, 1998.

Perreault, Jeanne. "Memory Alive: An Inquiry into the Uses of Memory by Marilyn Dumont, Jeanette Armstrong, Louise Halfe and Joy Harjo." *Indigenous Women and Feminism: Politics, Activism, Culture*, edited by Cheryl Suzack, Shari M. Huhndorf, Jeanne Perreault, and Jean Barman. UBC, 2010, pp. 199–217.

Reed-Gilbert, Kerry. *The Strength of Us as Women: Black Women Speak.* Ginninderra, 2000.

Scott, Kim. *Benang: From the Heart.* Fremantle Press, 1999.

"Australia's Continuing Neurosis: Identity, Race and History." The Alfred Deakin Lectures, 14 May 2001. https://archive.is/CzH2t.

Sharpe, Christina. *In the Wake: On Blackness and Being.* Duke University Press, 2016.

Simpson, Leanne Betasamosake. "Indigenous Resurgence and Co-resistance." *Critical Ethnic Studies* vol.2 no.2, 2016, pp. 19–34.

As We Have Always Done: Indigenous Freedom through Radical Resistance. University of Minnesota, 2017.

Simpson, Leanne Betasamosake and Dionne Brand. "Temporary Spaces of Joy and Freedom." *Literary Review of Canada*, 2018. https://reviewcanada.ca/magazine/2018/06/temporary-spaces-of-joy-and-freedom/.

Stoler, Ann. "Tense and Tender Ties: The Politics of Comparison in North American History and (Post) Colonial Studies." *Haunted by Empire: Geographies of*

Intimacy in North American History, edited by Ann Stoler. Duke University Press, 2006, pp. 23–67.

Suzack, Cheryl, Shari Huhndorf, Jeanne Perreault, and Jean Barman, eds. *Indigenous Women and Feminism: Politic, Activism, Culture*. University of British Columbia, 2010.

Van Wagenen, Aimee. "An Epistemology of Haunting: A Review Essay." *Critical Sociology* vol.30 no.2, 2004, pp. 287–98.

Wright, Alexis. "Politics of Writing." *Southerly* vol.62 no.2, 2002, pp. 19–20.

——. "What Happens When You Tell Somebody Else's Story?" *Meanjin* vol.75 no.4, 2016, pp. 58–76.

NOTES

1 See Justice, *Why Indigenous Literature Matters*; Owens.
2 See Lucashenko; Wright, "Politics of Writing."
3 See Bunda; Moreton-Robinson, "Talkin' Up"; DeShazer; Heiss, "Black Poetics"; and Lucashenko.
4 See Heiss, "Black Poetics"; Wright, "What Happens."
5 See Anzaldúa and Keating; Green; Moraga and Anzaldúa; Simpson, *As We Have Always Done*; and Suzack, Huhndorf, Perreault, and Barman.
6 Noongar novelist Kim Scott's 1999 novel *Benang: From the Heart*, set in Western Australia in the aftermath of A. O. Neville's "breed out" eugenics, depicts an extreme example of this among settler men and Aboriginal women and its legacy of intergenerational trauma for future generations.
7 See Harkin, *Archival-Poetics*.
8 Harkin, "(Re)Mapping Archives" and "Weaving."
9 See also Stoler.
10 See Harkin, "Weaving."
11 See Allen; Momaday; and Owens.
12 Allen; Kilpatrick; Momaday; and Perreault.
13 See Allen.
14 See Gordon; Van Wagenen.
15 See Cameron; Cariou.
16 See DeShazer; Galeano; and Sharpe.
17 See Eckermann and Fogarty.

14

KIM CHENG BOEY

"Country Snarled / in Borders"

Spatial Poetics in Asian Australian Poetry

In a 1967 lecture, Michel Foucault diagnosed the postmodern condition thus: "The present epoch will perhaps be above all the epoch of space. We are in the epoch of simultaneity: we are in the epoch of juxtaposition, the epoch of the near and far, of the side-by-side, of the dispersed" (23). This spatial turn has intensified since then, with work on space and spatiality done by Henri Lefebvre, Yi-Fu Tuan, Edward Soja, and Fredric Jameson, with the latter calling for "an aesthetic of cognitive mapping" which "seeks to endow the individual subject with some new heightened sense of its place in the global system" (54). This "spatial turn," wrought by factors like time-space compression of contemporary living, technology, migration, and the global flows of ideas and people, is evident across the arts and humanities, but is especially pronounced in diaspora writing. Migration, voluntary or involuntary, is an act of displacement from the original homeland and relocation to a new home, enforcing a questioning and reviewing of the place left behind and the adopted home, and of where and how migrant subjects locate themselves.

Among Asian Australian poets, there is a discernible spatial poetics, an urgent need to locate the self vis-à-vis the adopted home and place of origin, to discover a poetics of location to counter the dislocations of diaspora. It entails what Adrienne Rich calls "the location of the self" (181), a self-mapping that is ambivalent and tentative, markedly different from the stable sense of place anchoring the poetry of mainstream Australian poets like Les Murray and Robert Adamson, which is grounded in country places, Bunyah and the Hawkesbury respectively. Asian Australian poets' sense of place is more uncertain, untethered to any fixed nationalist idea of country and place; it is haunted by places and memories of the ancestral homeland. Their poems are underwritten by what James Clifford calls "the empowering paradox of diaspora," which is "that dwelling *here* assumes solidarity and connection *there*" (296). They ride the tension between countries, cultures, and languages, their poetics navigating the liminal spaces in the migrant's map, exploring the fluid, shifting spaces between the new country and the old world. A salient feature of their spatial poetics is the bifocal and in some cases multi-locale way of mapping and reading space and place, the diasporic subject revealing "ways of living at home abroad or abroad at home – ways of inhabiting multiple places at once at once, of being different beings simultaneously, of seeing the larger picture stereoscopically with the smaller" (Pollock 14).

The oft-hyphenated label 'Asian Australian' suggests dual if not multiple attachments and affiliations, a complex, layered, and often conflicted sense of home and place. Like the term 'Asian American,' the compound label is more a convenient than accurate term, as it fails to capture the heterogeneity and diversity of the Asian diaspora. In "Asian Australian Diasporic Poets," Adam Aitken asks: "What is Asia anyway but a convenient blanket term for a diversity of regions?" He adds: "It is reductive to conjoin Asian Australian poets with that ambiguous hyphen, which runs the risk of packaging ethnicities for an Australian-centric readership" ("Asian Australian"). Compared to their Asian American counterparts, Asian Australian poets are situated closer to Asia; the shadows of ancestral homeland may thus dominate the Asian Australian imaginary more. Their attachments and affiliations, diasporic roots and routes are arguably more foregrounded; the liminal spaces to be negotiated by poets are accentuated and compounded by Australia's ex-centric position geographically and politically in relation to Asia. These intersections of geographical, political, and cultural spaces generate internationalist perspectives, and a transnational, cross-cultural poetics among Asian Australian writers which rejects the ideology of white Australia and any monolithic national formation or homogenising Australianness. As Aitken observes, this complex spatial poetics is subversive of any absolutes of place and identity: "Diasporic poetics raise more questions than they answer and are just as much about dis-placement as about place, just as much about a 'poetics of uncertainty' as about certainties of style/nation/identity" ("Asian Australian").

Aitken's "poetics of uncertainty" is akin to what Asian American poet Meena Alexander calls the "poetics of dislocation" (26), diasporic poetry that speaks from a profound loss of home, from a neither-here-nor-there space. If, as Iain Chambers explains, migration "involves a movement in which neither the points of departure nor those of arrival are immutable or certain," then what ensues is "always transit, the promise of homecoming . . . becoming an impossibility" (5). But the poetics of dislocation is only part of the spatial poetics in Asian diasporic poetry. Its counterpoint is the poetics of return, the trope and theme of the journey back, imaginary or real, to the original homeland. This is a particularly dominant reflex among first-generation Asian Australian poets, who have carried a heavy freight of personal and familial narratives from the old to the new country. Unlike second or third generations, their memories of the ancestral homeland are lived and strong, creating binaries of old homeland/host country, past/present. Their poems carry "a lived tension, the experiences of separation and entanglement, of living here and remembering/desiring another place" (Clifford 255). This tension is most palpable in the poetry of Ee Tiang Hong, who migrated to Australia in 1975 after the Whitlam Government had officially removed the White Australia Policy and installed multiculturalism as a national policy. Ee's new citizenship thus coincided with a watershed moment in Australian political and cultural history, and his post-migration work makes a pioneering Asian Australian voice that would begin to alter Australian literary demographics and landscape.

As an adult migrant who had spent a good part of his life in Malaysia, Ee's efforts at establishing a new home were constantly shadowed by the past and his place of birth. What results is an ambivalent sense of place, a bifocal, comparative topopoetics that reads one place in terms of another, often yielding a spatial montage rather than a fixed orientation to space and place. In the poem "Perth," there is no stable point of reference: "The city has no centre, focal landmark, / no Place de la Concorde, Padang Merdeka, Tien An Men, / no particular square, terrace, public park" (40). The rollcall of place names, including Ee's birthplace, reveals the placelessness of the déraciné poet who has lost the vital centre of his life. In Ee's diasporic work, a dual perspective conjugates two places together, eliding their boundaries. Perth slips into Malacca, his place of birth, an abiding presence in his work, an absence that haunts his life as an Australian. In "The Burden," a snatch of music in Perth brings Malacca back to him and his father "is alive, in a laterite grave / in Bukit Piatu, in his family grove / of green and brown tembusu" (20). The vision erases the boundaries between past and present, Perth and Malacca, and the landscape becomes destabilised, the positioning of the migrant subject ambiguous: "And I am here, and there, and back again. / wallowing in mud, cool slush, this waterhole / my home, in the freedom of another wilderness" (20).

The proximity of Perth to Malaysia allows Ee to make regular visits 'home.' In "Melaka," Ee is "Returning / empty-handed, incognito/ to visit old haunts" (18). It is a failed homecoming, as there is "no ceremonial / welcome" and "[f]aces I meet in the street / betray no recognition." The voice is weary, that of the native-turned-alien, while the metonymy conveys an uncertain and ambiguous relationship to place; he encounters only "remnants of empire, / monumental ruins" (18). There is no nostalgic recall, nothing to suggest a sense of attachment or belonging.

The return trajectory is countered by efforts to make a home in the present, in the ground of his adopted home. The poems in his posthumous collection *Nearing a Horizon* reveal Ee's divided spatial poetics, but he appears to be on the brink of achieving a poetics of home before his death in 1990. In "Resolution," he avows: "Here, halfway up the Swan, I chose / to build my home, for the last time / having to come to terms with my new home" (41). In the concluding lines of "Perth" Ee plants his pastoral idyll on the banks of the Swan River: "no looking back to brood, and not too far ahead, / just the opposite foreshore, Bassendean. // And the Swan, quiet, deathly pale at evening" (40). The poem musters determination to make a home from home, and establishes his passage to naturalisation. In an elegy to a fellow émigré "For Wong Lin Ken" Ee arrives at an accommodation with his new place, "[o]ur cases being different, / yours in Singapore, / mine Australian now, / I have to choose the Swan." While his "house and lawn /overlook the river" and is "where my wife children, mother are— ," the poem concludes "may it also rain sometimes / from here to Malaysia, / and Singapore" (4). Ee's last poems seem liberated from binaries like exile and homeland, Malacca and Perth, arriving at a multi-locale poetics, shuttling between geographical and cultural spaces of Malaysia, Singapore, and Australia; the sense of place and home has become fluid, blurring the local, regional, and global. Home has ceased to be tied to a single location but is assembled through a transnational lens.

Sharing Ee's poetics of place and displacement is the Hangzhou-born Ouyang Yu. Ouyang's poems can sound angry, outraged, confronting the bigotry of white Australia, excoriating the shallowness and tokenism of Australian multiculturalism, mostly clearly exemplified in the "Howl"-like poem "Fuck You, Australia" (*Moon over Melbourne* 79). Beneath these ironic outbursts is a profound sense of dislocation and pain of the migrant reckoning with the consequences of migration. By abandoning the place of birth, he has forfeited the certitudes of home and belonging; at the same time he feels an alien in his adopted country, acutely conscious of his difference, his conspicuous Chineseness attracting questioning glances. In the suburb of Kingsbury, Melbourne, where he has settled with his family, Ouyang practises an ambulatory poetics that negotiates the difficult, mundane terrain he has to call home. "Fragments of an Evening Walk in Kingsbury" tracks a migrant family's stroll through the Melbourne suburb, a quotidian activity that shows up the dis-ease and alienation of the migrants. The suburban landscape is described without affection: "the grass / half dead" and "the eucalyptus standing tall and dark-green / against a darkness / that was gathering behind the darkened / mute houses" (182). The migrants' presence seems to trigger avoidance, even rejection, in the "averted eyes" of two women walking their dog. The second-person pronoun exacerbates the alienation and self-division:

> suddenly the silent streets seemed startled
> when they heard you say:
> i don't like Australia
> i don't like china, either (183)

The sense of not-belonging to either the adopted home or the place of birth prevails at the end of the poem, with the persona returning to a "rented home," the feeling of displacement unassuaged. While Ouyang enjoys bicultural and bilingual mobility, he is prone to feelings of *dépaysement*, of belonging to neither China nor Australia, a migrant condition which Salman Rushdie describes thus: "Sometimes we feel we straddle two cultures; at other times, that we fall between two stools" (18).

With a bifocal lens Ouyang sees Australia through China and China through Australia. His migrant condition is a doubleness, a split, schizoid state of ambivalence and ambiguity. In "An Identity CV" Ouyang describes himself as "a cross-cultural fucker" who is an "australian for the last couple of year; / chinese for the first 43; / unashamed of / either; having a bit of problem / with both" (*New and Selected Poems* 3). Ouyang's poems are riven by this sense of division, revealing a need to locate the self in spaces that have opened up between his new and past lives. Whether in China or Australia, a neither-here-nor-there feeling persists, so that he can no longer be at home. In *The Kingsbury Tales* Ouyang evinces an acceptance of his in-between condition. In "New Accents," he observes how deeply immigration has altered the demographics of his adoptive suburb, Kingsbury: "P from Wuxi spoke of / Once travelling down a street in Melbourne / I'd never heard of that's called Neechosen Street" (*The Kingsbury Tales* 46). The poem demonstrates a spatial poetics that is alert to social transformations, reflected by the new nuances of street names inflected with new accents. Ouyang finds himself speaking a new language that is more "Anguish" than "English" (46). In "Place Names, A Tale of Chinese Invasion," Ouyang aims a dig at right-wing politicians bent on stopping Asian immigration by revealing "how Chinese have sinicised Australia": "xueli (Snow Pear) is their name for Sydney / moerben (Ink That Book) is theirs for Sydney ..." (*The Kingsbury Tales* 59). An inexorable process of cultural and demographic translation unfolds as Chinese words seep into Australian place names.

But the process of translation, of being changed irrevocably, applies not just to his adopted home but also to Ouyang's natal country. In Wuhan, Ouyang experiences a liminal moment when two places meet:

> In an ancient country one gets ancient quick
> One's thoughts slowed down by the futility of even thinking
> If there is anything colourful it is the bed linens
> That they hang out to sun on the open tops of those high rises
> There is an Australian quietness here
> Broken only by someone announcing his collecting 2nd hand
> televisions.   (*The Kingsbury Tales* 45)

Then Ouyang quotes a Chinese poet to underscore his hybrid sense of place: "Is the moon walking in the water or is the boat moving between the lake and the hills / Not knowing where I am, I feel like turning into a deity beyond the dust" (45). In the acts of migration and return, Ouyang's perceptions of place and self have undergone a sea change and home has become something ineffable. Shuttling between Australia and China, he holds what Aihwa Ong dubs "flexible citizenship," which allows one to "convert political constraints in one field into economic opportunities in another, to turn displacement into advantageous placement in different sites …" (134). Such transnational mobility breeds an ambivalent sense of place and self, which can be both empowering and creative on the one hand, and debilitating and confusing on the other.

The bifocal, bilingual approach to space and place in Ouyang Yu's work is also discernible in Filipina-Australian Merlinda Bobis, whose works also commute between two countries and cultures, weaving them together in a hybridised, transnational space. Bobis often splices two or more spatial perspectives in her spatial practice. In "driving to katoomba," there is a complex imaginative cartography unfolding as the poet and her partner drive into the Blue Mountains: "today, you span the far mountains / with an arm and say, / 'this I offer you – / all this blue sweat / of eucalypt'" (*Summer Was a Fast Train* 3). Even as the local flora and fauna appear, they are supplanted by a foreign ecology, the sense of place sliding into a more fluid perspective, first with the introduction of Tagalog words, then a complete change in climate and landscape:

> I, too, can love you
> In my dialect, you know,
> Punctuated with cicadas
> And their eternal afternoons:
> "*mahal kita, mahal kita.*"   (*Summer Was a Fast Train* 3)

The mapping is spatial and temporal, the drive triggering a journey into the past. But the poem transcends the binary of old and new country, the Philippines and Australia, as the composite pastoral idyll gives way to unsettling glimpses of conflict elsewhere – Bosnia, Tibet, East Timor, and

Sri Lanka – the transnational gaze disrupting the present, blurring political and temporal boundaries. Bobis' spatial poetics destabilises any fixed notion of Asia or indeed of Asian Australia.

The border as trope and theme recurs in Bobis' poetry. Borders and borderlands are spatial and metaphorical representations of diasporic liminality, of the states of in-betweenness migrants negotiate. It is an embodiment of Homi Bhaba's "third space," which "opens up the possibility of a cultural hybridity that entertains difference without an assumed or imposed hierarchy" (4). In "Double-Crossed," two women living in displaced conditions are both separated and united by "a wall / so high / between us, / we are both / invisible" (334). Instead of rejecting the border as alienating and isolating, Bobis' diasporic feminist poetics sees it as a site of possibility and redemption: "At the border, / we almost met / and caught / each other's eye / and saw in there / how safe we are, / how free" (335).

Bobis locates her work in liminal spaces that can be empowering, creating new ways of seeing and being through juxtapositions of past and present, memory and imagination, and interactions of different cultures and languages. In "Border Lover," Bobis makes a real or imaginary return to the Philippines, seeking sustenance in her roots as embodied by her grandmother, whose culinary skills yield a paradigm for how to handle dualities (*Summer Was a Fast Train* 12). Grandmothers are dominant figures in Asian diasporic poetry, a sustaining influence and custodian of Asian cultural and familial wisdom, appearing frequently in Asian American poems and in poems by Australian poets like Bobis and Eileen Chong. In "Grandmother and the Border," Bobis returns to Estancia in the Philippines, where her grandmother is a mediator, one who shows how it is possible to live in harmony even with a border separating two families fighting for land and ownership of a jackfruit tree. Against the sons' quarrel over their "land's border" (336), the grandmother's decisive gesture of fruit-sharing offers a reconciliatory way of reading space and place.

Bobis' younger compatriot Eunice Andrada also grapples with borders in her poetry. In "recognitions" from her debut collection *Flood Damages*, Andrada asserts: "I will only find my mouth / its own country snarled / in borders," as her grandmother's "language turns heads" on a Sydney train and Andrada expects "someone to tell us / to go back to where we came from" (83–84). The poem reveals the vulnerability of Asian migrants to racist discrimination and attacks, but it also reveals the liminality of the migrant's position and an ambivalent spatial poetics. Almost imperceptibly the present moment is displaced by a fleeting visitation of the past, a Tagalog line surfacing as her grandmother's hybrid voice speaks, and they are transported to her grandmother's "living room in Parañaque" (83). By grafting

Tagalog onto English, Andrada, like Bobis, asserts her difference and what Lisa Lowe calls "the heterogeneity, multiplicity, hybridity" (24) of Asian diaspora. It is also an act of resistance to the pressures of assimilation into the monolithic, dominant host culture and language. The poem ends in a liminal moment, with the immigrants suspended between worlds, straddling borders.

Like Bobis, Andrada mobilises the journey trope to convey the state of transit and liminality. Images of the sea, littoral tropes, motifs of sea-crossing fill her work, the poems tapping on the liminality latent in them. Andrada opens "(because I am a daughter) of the diaspora" with an evocation of "the open sea," affirming her natal connection to the Philippines archipelago with the voice of her mother "a selfish tide, / claiming words that are not meant / for her" and the acknowledgement "[i]n the end / our brown skin / married to seabed" (9). It is a return poem, but the homecoming is tinged with unease and the knowledge that the émigré can no longer enjoy the pre-migration sense of being-at-home and belonging:

> When I return to the storm
> of my islands
> with a belly full of the first world,
> I wrangle the language I grew up with
> yet still have to rehearse. (9)

Beyond physical uprooting, migration is a transformative and translational act, involving changes at the deepest levels of being, culture, and language. Choosing to write in the language of the adoptive country, the migrant betrays her mother tongue; this linguistic dilemma is an issue that many first-generation diasporic writers face, and is compounded if they come from a country with a history of colonial occupation. Andrada's displacement from her native tongue is palpable in the moment, when the poem moves to a street in Manila, and a homeless man asks the poet in "practised English": "*Where are you going?*" This is a threshold moment, the poet wakening to her presumed status, "the words a recognition / of the mongrel flag / I call my face":

> I want to say to him, *We are the same.*
> *Pareho lang po tayo.*
> My bleached accent,
> the dollars in my wallet
> sing another anthem.
> *How long have you been here?* (10)

Andrada concludes, "I am above water, holding / onto a country that drowns / without or without me." Migration has altered her irreversibly, the tokens of her foreignness marking her as alien to her native place, even if outwardly she is "the same." She describes herself as "mongrel," a word coined by Rushdie for postcolonial and migrant identities (394). Tellingly the poem ends with a watery image of her unstable state.

"second coming" also tracks a return, plumbing the fraught state of the emigrant visiting her "grandmother's old Parañaque apartment" (28). Once more the water element is vital, as the poet hires a boat and swims in "the prismatic" water. Again, she experiences the liminal moment and knowledge: "There is the unrelenting deep and the uncertainty of return." Upon return to the mainland, the boatman asks Andrada where her mother is from and she replies "*Iloilo*," the place name triggering a liminal moment with which the poem closes:

> How it never failed to sound like a river, no matter how broken her voice had become. How the name for the people she had come from translates to where the water flows down. The boatman says he can tell from the way I speak. I look to my feet. They are lost underwater. (29)

There is no sense of homecoming or arrival; the paradoxical state of fluidity and immobility at the end hints at the undertow of unease that comes with being between worlds. The hybrid form of the prose poem, hovering between lyric and narrative, mirrors this state of transit and flux. There is no narrative closure, neither the assurance of homecoming nor the finality of departure.

For first-generation migrant writers, the tug of the memory and the past, the pull of the place of birth and ancestral homeland are palpable forces conflicting with the resolve to forge a new life in the adopted country. The poets explored earlier resist the pitfalls of nostalgia and practise a spatial poetics that seeks some accommodation between lives, between culture and languages, negotiating and mapping liminal spaces that migration has opened up. Eileen Chong's poetry also rides the tension between return to her original home, Singapore, and locating herself in a new environment and engaging in the process of homemaking. The return visits are marked by a sense of disconnection and alienation, as though by emigration the native has turned foreigner and forfeited the right to belong. In "Boat Quay, Singapore," an emptiness hangs over the historical hub of the city, with its "empty stretches" reminding the poet "how tranquil this city can be / in the hours before it rouses." But the peace is marred by the failed homecoming:

> in my old country there is no one
> left to call. A man stands on the roof
> of a bumboat: he mops every square inch fastidiously.
> I wave, but he won't look at me: I simply do not exist.
> (*Painting Red Orchids* 39)

The emigrant elicits no recognition or acceptance from her natal place. The sparse imagery and the detached, lonely voice betray the irrevocable rupture and distance between the diasporic subject and the place of origin.

Deborah Madsen states that "the migrant can never 'return'; blood cannot bridge the chasm of time that separates departure from any return." She adds: "The failure to belong completely to a new home, or to return to the home left behind, is powerfully characterised by the diasporic motif of 'neither here nor there'" (120). This insight elucidates failed homecomings among migrant poets like Chong. The exclusion that she experiences in Singapore compounds the marginalisation she feels in Australia. In "Country," Chong recounts how on a visit to the outback she is shouted at: "*Go back to your own country*" (*Rainforest* 39). At a supermarket in Sydney, a woman hurls "*Chinese cunt!*" at the poet. This prompts an examination of instability of racial constructs, and the inadequacy of categories like Chinese and Asian; the poet is mistaken for being Japanese, Korean, Taiwanese, and Chinese. The poet concludes: "In Singapore, I am a quitter, a leaver. / In Australia, a new arrival" (*Rainforest* 40). In another poem, "My Hakka Grandmother," Chong tracks her diasporic liminality to her ethnic roots; she is Hakka or "guest people," an ethnic minority from the south of China, one of dialect groups that make up the Chinese community in Singapore: "We are guest people / without land or name, moving south and south, / wild birds seeking a place to call home" (*Burning Rice* 8). Chong's diasporic narrative is complicated by these tangled web of routes and roots, and overturns any essentialist notions of Chinese identity. Her Hakka heritage is doubly transplanted and translated, an evolving story which demonstrates the diversity and heterogeneity of the Chinese diaspora.

In her efforts at homemaking, Chong resorts to what Shirley Lim calls "ethnopoetics." Lim notes that among Asian American writers, exclusion and marginalisation, and the fear of "loss of identity" (52) that comes with assimilation, engender an ethnopoetics (the deployment of ethnic themes and motifs) that can subvert monolithic nationalism and embody the complex aspects of Asian American identities. In Chong's poems, the tropes of grandmother and food yield complex insights into memory and heritage, and how they are renewed and transformed in the diasporic consciousness and matrix, rather than transposed wholesale to the adopted country and culture. Poems like "Burning Rice," "Grandmother's Dish," and "Rice-dumplings" do not merely assuage the nostalgia and longing for the lost home (*Burning Rice* 3, 10; *Peony* 19). They are performative in that, according to Judith Butler, "bodily gestures, movements and enactments of various kinds constitute the illusion of an abiding gendered self" (270). The culinary actions, the remembering and re-enactment of recipes, as well as the gustatory and alimentary acts, are constitutive of a gendered diasporic space and body. "Rice-dumplings" sees the poet "[r]eviving the art / of rice dumplings in an inn-city apartment in Sydney / five minutes' walk from Chinatown" (*Peony* 19).

Food and the shared meal become the locus for creating a cross-cultural diasporic space where the braided themes of home, heritage, and identity could be negotiated. Restaurant meals recur in Chong's work, among them "Winter Meeting," where Chong and an Asian poet meet in a Chinatown restaurant, a diasporic space par excellence. Diasporic affiliations and attachments are evoked in a familiar cultural setting, where, "surrounded by smells of home" (*Burning Rice* 46), the alimentary act of a shared meal triggers a moment of human connection through a common heritage and history. In "Family," Chong is invited to the home of fellow poet Lachlan Brown, whose hybrid make-up is described in another poem thus: "His Chineseness is blurred at the edges" and he "sits comfortably in his Australianness" (*Painting Red Orchids* 46). "Family" embeds snapshots of a family and its diasporic history within its domestic space:

> Lachlan's house smells like home.
> His mother has been cooking. I step
> into the kitchen – steamed chicken on a platter,
> clear soup on the boil, ginger scenting the air. (48)

The culinary imagery conjures up a diasporic space of connection and homecoming, as the poet crosses the threshold from displacement into a moment of cultural bond and identification. She participates in the cooking and eating, the actions performative of a gendered migrant persona being liberated into a new diasporic space where new affiliations are discovered: "We sit and eat – / for a few hours, I am family" (49).

The dedicatee of Chong's poem is one of the products of migration, hybrid and translated "people who have been obliged to define themselves – because they are so defined by others – by their otherness; people in whose deepest selves strange fusions occur …" (124–25). In a review of Lachlan Brown's *Lunar Inheritance*, Chong observes: "Brown's mixed ethnic heritage leads him to the realisation that Asian-ness and Australian-ness are identities to be invented, performed, and resisted against, by himself or by others" ("Time's Mobius Strip"). Second or successive generation diasporic poets are hybrids with composite and hyphenated identities inhabiting a neither-here-nor-there space where questions of home, identity, and belonging require unceasing negotiation. Brown sees himself reflected in the eyes of Australian whites as a "mashed-potato-fried-rice-vigour-half-caste" (55). In a "Hurstville BBQ restaurant," his family gets "weird glances" because his father is "the only white guy in the place, his joyous fork / dividing joints and marrow, tendons and tripe" (6). Unlike Chong's "Winter Meeting," Brown's Chinese restaurant is not a stable place where ethnic identity could be recuperated but a site that reveals an intersectional spatial poetics of shifting borders of inclusivity, diversity, and belonging.

Returns to the ancestral homeland are also key themes among Australian-born Asian poets like Brown. *Lunar Inheritance* plots his quest in the land of his Chinese ancestors "whose double- / helixed existence necessitates this setting out and return" (34), a return that ends in the knowledge that "[w]hat you inherit is no ancestral village," that there is no possibility of real "homecoming" (25). In "grandmothercountry," he discovers that modernising globalisation has erased much of his grandmother's country: "First night in Kaiping centre and China repeats itself. / The same HK chain stores sit over Bruce Lee's Kung-fu eatery, which is roundhouse kicking a KFC where ..." (18). Another poem, "life-hyphen," enacts what Amy Ling calls "a double consciousness" or the "feeling of being between worlds, totally at home nowhere" (105):

> The way you don't know (what) you are in Austral
> ia until someone yells out 'Fucken gook' from the
> bus window is the way you don't notice the Guang-
> zhou rain falling until you look up and it has slick-
> ed over everything. (19)

Brown straddles two cultures and inhabits two places at one time, revealing the bifocal vision of the diasporic subject. The travels and places in China trigger comparative views with Australia that suggests a permeability of borders: arrival in Guangzhou recalls his poet's grandfather meeting "the clan / back on Dixon Street, Sydney" (3); the Sun Yat-sen monument "framed by Guangzhou skyscrapers" reminds him of his grandmother's "Sun Yat-sen medallion" (9); a Shanghai real estate agency prompts images of "the Sydney market" and "Randwick apartment blocks or sandstone freestanders" (52). These are moments of border-crossing, when borders become porous and the diasporic subject moves fluidly between past and present, between places and between cultures, his spatial mobility allowing time to become spatialised. They yield glimpses of the traveller's doubleness or his "selfied face in reverse" (19).

In the global age, the new generation of Asian Australian poets, attuned to multicultural cosmopolitanism and transnational flows of ideas and people, adopt transcultural strategies of negotiating diasporic border zones. Maryam Azam's spatial poetics evokes playfully the transformations of her Pakistani heritage in the context of Sydney's multicultural milieu. In "A Brief

Guide to Hijab Fashion," the hijab can be worn as a laff scarf, or "in the khaleeji aka Dubai style, or the Turkish or "the turban style," depending on the circumstance (14). This debunks the idea of Muslim identity as orthodox or fixed, its fluid, evolving nature reinforced by another poem "That Hijabi from Strathfield Girls," where the poet's friend is spotted wearing "a typical Pakistani hijab" one day, then hijab-free on another occasion, with her "thick wavy hair / in a ponytail," and finally with the hijab back on in the final stanza (19). Adopting a similar defamiliarisation strategy in "Places I've Prayed," Azam takes Islam out of the mosque and performs her prayers in a ladies room in Opera House, in "a Westfield parking lot" and in a cineplex "on George Street" (20).

Azam's spatial practice is translational and transformative, mapping Sydney's changing demographics and urban-scapes, celebrating the diasporic diversity of Western Sydney . Extending the boundaries of Asianness, one can include Arab Australian Omar Sakr, whose work is also plugged into the dynamic multiculturalism of working-class Western Sydney. In an interview Sakr says: "Depending on who you ask, I am not gay enough, not Arab enough, not Turkish enough, not man enough, not Muslim enough, and definitely not Australian enough" ("Political Reckoning"). His poetics is intersectional, mapping new spaces of "unbelonging" and "non-ownership" where he can achieve his "most complex and open self, far from false certainties" ("Political Reckoning"). In "Moratorium on Cartography," Sakr envisions a place freed from geopolitical claims and identity politics that is grounded in ideas of an authentic racial or cultural formation: "My country resists language. / It does not want to know you. / It has its own knowledge, and no/ holes for flags" and "[n]ow what it means to be free is in pieces and there" (*The Lost Arabs* 63). But Sakr's country is not an abstract or deterritorialised space cleansed of constricting nationalist and cultural definitions. It is anchored in the realities of the working-class spaces of Western Sydney, of Coles where boys stuff "pockets with stolen answers," of "Sydney Road, a replica of home, / all the Leb bread, smoke & men," a place of "[m]igrants labouring ... all of with a country / Waiting" (*The Lost Arabs* 10, 8, 31). If the idea of home is possible at all, its map has to also include Lebanon and Turkey, where Sakr's diasporic routes and roots lead. In his essay on diasporic Caribbean poetry, Demetrio Yocum calls the diasporic poem "the text-map" which "expands its own borders by moving and opening up the territory of a possible "encounter," a *road* which invites us to rethink our stable positions, to cross our own boundaries, and to take a journey towards diversity" (226–27). This is an apt description of Sakr's poetics, and the spatial practice of many Asian Australian poets, which resolutely resists any fixity of position or perspective in favour of fluidity and openness. Just as it is impossible to reduce the rich diversity and heterogeneity of the Asian diaspora and simplify the fraught disruptor 'Asian Australian,' Asian diaspora poetry in Australia cannot be packed into a single formation and label. It is growing and evolving in this global, transnational era, fed by a complex weave of roots and routes, of divergent and convergent narratives of displacement, movement and settlement, and histories of entanglements and negotiations, of places, cultures, and languages. There are new voices and styles, new spatial poetics to map the shifting and changing spaces that diaspora has created.

Poets like Adam Aitken and Bella Li eschew the predictability of identity politics and place-bound poetics. They shun familiar tropes and themes of Asian diaspora writing, choosing a more elliptical and experimental spatial poetics. Aitken's cosmopolitan irony and wit, language play, associative train of thought and imagery, and narrative disruption, create spaces that are uncertain, hybrid, and fluid, as in "The Anti-travel Travel Poem," where places slip into one another, borders are crossed and blurred: "the anti-travel poem does not / ask for directions on a road no-one's taken (*Eighth Habitation* 27). Bella Li's cross-disciplinary mix of poetry, photography, painting, and travel narrative in *Argosy* (2017) stitches together a sequence of prose poems and visual collages that creates an aesthetic, speculative space held together by allegorical narratives and dream-like imagery; its travel themes and motifs cover a wide spectrum of geography in an imaginative border-crossing cartography that rejects the certainties of identity politics and familiar diasporic tropes. The new generation of poets do not suffer the anguish or anxiety about place, identity, and belonging as much as first-generation poets. Though the theme of return also informs their work, they do not have the weight of lived memories in the ancestral or parental homeland that exerts an inexorable pull on the Asian-born poets. Noticeably absent in their work is the tension that derives from binary oppositions between past and present, country of origin and adopted country, Asia and Australia. Instead, these younger poets practise a transnational spatial poetics, moving freely between places, cultures, and languages, and provide new, complex mappings that build on the work done by the first-generation migrant poets. But across the generations, there is a preoccupation with space and place, and a shared diasporic poetics that brings two or more places, "the near and far" and "the dispersed" together in a moment of "simultaneity" and "juxtaposition" (Foucault 23). They bring Australia and Asia together in startling, refreshing configurations and mappings, offering compelling readings of what it means to be Australian and Asian in this era of the spatial turn.

Works Cited

Aitken, Adam. *Eighth Habitation*. Giramondo, 2009.
"Asian Australian Diasporic Poets: A Commentary." *Cordite Poetry Review*, 1 August 2012. http://cordite.org.au/essays/asian-australian-diasporic-poets/.
Alexander, Meena. "Is There an Asian American Aesthetic?" *SAMAR* vol.1, 1992, pp. 26–27.
Andrada, Eunice. *Flood Damages*. Giramondo, 2018.
Azam, Maryam. *The Hijab Files*. Giramondo, 2018.
Bhabha, Homi. *The Location of Culture*. Routledge, 1994.
Bobis, Merlinda. *Summer Was a Fast Train without Terminals*. Spinifex Press, 1998.
"Double-Crossed." *To Gather Your Leaving: Asian Diaspora Poetry from America, Australia, UK and Europe*, edited by Kim Cheng Boey, Arin Fong, and Justin Chia. Ethos, 2019, pp. 334–35.
"Grandmother and the Border." *To Gather Your Leaving: Asian Diaspora Poetry from America, Australia, UK and Europe*, edited by Kim Cheng Boey, Arin Fong, and Justin Chia. Ethos, 2019, p. 336.
Brown, Lachlan. *Lunar Inheritance*. Giramondo, 2017.
Butler, Judith. "Performative Acts and Gender Constitution: An Essay in Phenomenology and Feminist Theory." *Performing Feminisms: Feminist Critical Theory and Theatre*, edited by Sue-Ellen Case. Johns Hopkins University Press, 1990, pp. 270–82.
Chambers, Iain. *Migrancy, Culture, Identity*. Routledge, 1994.
Chong, Eileen. *Burning Rice*. Pitt Street Poetry, 2012.
Peony. Pitt Street Poetry, 2014.
Painting Red Orchids. Pitt Street Poetry, 2017.
"Time's Mobius Strip: Eileen Chong on Lachlan Brown." *Sydney Review of Books*, November 2017. https://sydneyreviewofbooks.com/review/lunar-inheritance-lachlan-brown/.
Rainforest. Pitt Street Poetry, 2018.
Clifford, James. *Routes: Travel and Translation in the Late Twentieth Century*. Harvard University Press, 1997.
Ee, Tiang Hong. *Nearing a Horizon*. UniPress, 1994.
Foucault, Michel. "Of Other Spaces." *Diacritics* vol.16 no.1, 1986, pp. 22–27.
Jameson, Fredric. *The Geopolitical Aesthetic: Cinema and Space in the World System*. Indiana University Press, 1992.
Li, Bella. *Argosy*. Vagabond, 2017.
Lim, Shirley. "Reconstructing Asian-American Poetry: A Case for Ethnopoetics." *MELUS* vol.14 no.2, 1987, pp. 51–63.
Ling, Amy. *Between Worlds: Women Writers of Chinese Ancestry*. Pergamon Press, 1990.
Lowe, Lisa. "Heterogeneity, Multiplicity, Hybridity: Marking Asian American Differences." *Diaspora* vol.1 no.1, 1991, pp. 24–44.
Madsen, Deborah L. "'No Place Like Home': The Ambivalent Rhetoric of Hospitality in the Work of Simone Lazaroo, Arlene Chai, and Hsu-Ming Teo." *Locating Asian Australian Cultures*, edited by Tseen Khoo. Routledge, 2008, pp. 117–32.

Ong, Aihwa. *Flexible Citizenship: The Cultural Logics of Transnationality*. Duke University Press, 1999.
Ouyang, Yu. *Moon over Melbourne: Poems*. Papyrus Publishing, 1995.
New and Selected Poems. Salt Publishing, 2004.
The Kingsbury Tales: A Novel. Brandl & Schlesinger, 2008.
"Fragments of an Evening Walk in Kingsbury." *Contemporary Asian Australian Poets*, edited by Adam Aitken et al. Puncher & Wattmann, 2012, pp. 182–83.
Pollock, Sheldon et al. "Cosmopolitanisms." *Cosmopolitanism*, edited by Carol A. Breckenridge et al. Duke University Press, 2002, pp. 1–14.
Rich, Adrienne. *Blood, Bread and Poetry: Selected Prose*. Norton, 1986.
Rushdie, Salman. *Imaginary Homelands: Essays and Criticism 1981-1991*. Granta, 1991.
Sakr, Omar. *The Lost Arabs*. University of Queensland Press, 2019.
"Political Reckoning and Personal History Unite in *The Lost Arabs*." Western Sydney University, 9 May 2019. www.westernsydney.edu.au/newscentre/news_centre/story_archive/2019/political_reckoning_and_personal_history_unite_in_the_lost_arabs.
Yocum, Demetrio. "Some Troubled Homecomings." *The Post-Colonial Question: Common Skies, Divided Horizons*, edited by Iain Chambers and Lidia Curti. Routledge, 1996., pp. 221–27.

15

LOUIS KLEE

Australian Poets in the Countries of Others

Kerosene in Honey Tins

In 1978, Les Murray delivered a lecture in the Danish city of Aarhus on the "Boeotian" strain in Australian culture (Rutherford 188). At first it is far from obvious what Boeotia, a pastoral region in ancient Greece, has to do with Australia. Murray begins with its connection to Hesiod's *Theogony*. Pasturing his flock on the Boeotian slope of Helicon, Hesiod claims to have been visited by the Muses, who "breathed a 'godly voice' into him, and commanded him to make poems" (Murray "Boeotian" 48). For Murray, Hesiod stands "on one side of a rift that runs through the whole of Western culture": the "war between Athens and Boeotia" (49). This is a war of cultural and aesthetic principles – one succinctly conveyed in "The Boeotian Count" section of Murray's poetic sequence "Walking to the Cattle Place" (1972). Rather than catalogue cattle numerically, as a rational Athenian might, the poem's speaker refers to each cow by name,

---

The title of this essay is borrowed from Slimani's 2020 novel *Le pays des autres* [*The Country of Others*] and McGuiness's *Other People's Countries* (2014). In the context of First Nations sovereignty, the title could refer to both Australian poets overseas and many Australian poets in Australia itself. I would like to express my enormous gratitude to all the poets who corresponded with me about their time overseas and to those who agreed to be interviewed for this chapter: Adam Aitken, Lily Brett, a.j. carruthers, Dan Disney, Will Druce, Laurie Duggan, Marty Hiatt, Marc Jones, Nicholas Jose, Cassie Lewis, Nicholas Powell, David Prater, Jaya Savige, Joel Scott, Ellen van Neerven, and Corey Wakeling. Unattributed quotations in this chapter are from unpublished interviews and correspondence with them. I would also like thank Michael Farrell, Jeanine Leane, and Brendan Casey. A very big thank you to the Fryer Library for their invaluable help with aspects of this research, especially to Lindo Justo for securing copyright permission for the reproduction of the Oodgeroo archival images, and to Jeff Rickertt for excellent assistance and advice.

"a typically Boeotian device," arraying their names on the page as if mapping their place on the pasture:

>   Maudie
>   Maisie
>   Shit-in-the bail
>   Quince
>   Blossom   Daisy
>   shy Abigail
> Primavera
>   Strawberry   Doris   (*Collected Poems* 65)

Urban Athenians might sneer at this rustic idiosyncrasy, but Murray reminds us that it is the Boeotians, not the Athenians, who the Muses have blessed: "poetry, of all but the dramatic sort, is ultimately a Boeotian art" ("Boeotian" 51). The conceit of Murray's lecture is that Australian culture is "still in its Boeotian phase" ("Boeotian" 55).

Murray prefaced his talk in Aarhus by reading Peter Porter's poem, "On First Looking into Chapman's Hesiod" (1975). In fact, the aim of Murray's essay, which was originally titled "On Sitting Back and Thinking about *Porter's* Boeotia," was to offer a reply to Porter, who was himself sitting in the audience at Aarhus.[1] In the words of Porter's poem, "yes, Australians are Boeotians," but the "blunt patriotism" of these "Taree smallholders splitting logs / And philosophising on ... dangling billies" sounds a lot like "long-winded, emphatic, kelpie yapping" (*Collected Poems* 210). Porter's poem ironises the self-styled Boeotian, the Australian poet who pursues authenticity in the trappings of rural life:

>   One day on the campus,
>   The next in wide hats at a branding or
>   Sheep drenching, not actually performing
>   But looking the part and getting instances
>   For odes that bruise the blood.   (211)

Nevertheless, the final stanza of Porter's poem turns introspective. Relevant here is the fact that Porter lived as an Australian immigrant in London for most of his life. "On First Looking into Chapman's Hesiod" valorises a sensibility that Murray would consider quintessentially Athenian. It offers a defence of homelessness, or at least a kind of "homelooseness" (Wood 284):

>   Sparrows acclimatise but I still seek
>   The permanently upright city where
>   Speech is nature and plants conceive in pots,
>   Where one escapes from what one is and who

> One was, where home is just a postmark
> And country wisdom clings to calendars,
> The opposite of a sunburned truth-teller's
> World, haunted by precepts and the Pleiades. (211)

In their poetic exchange, Murray and Porter not only set up a dichotomy but invite us to categorise them by its terms – as Boeotian and Athenian respectively. In the process, they confound two of the enduring oppositions in Australian literary history, mapping the distinction between the 'city' and the 'bush' onto the division between the Australian literary 'expatriates' and the 'stay-at-homes' (Kershaw 144). The resulting dichotomy has the air of an ultimatum: either remain in Australia and seek, in the words of Porter's poem, to "fuse with the land," or else flee to a foreign metropolis (211). Even if "home-grown Athenians" exist, they do not, as Murray puts it, "really belong in Australia and might as well follow Porter's own example of self-exile" ("Boeotian" 57).

Porter is often considered "Australia's greatest expatriate poet" (Bennett and Pender 144). His "On First Looking into Chapman's Hesiod" is the most celebrated reflection on the emigrant poet who seeks to make a home in writing itself (see Porter, "Country Poetry" 48). But not all Australian poets overseas are Athenians, let alone 'expatriates' or 'exiles,' just as Murray's "Boeotia" is a manifesto for Australian poetry so peculiar it hardly comprehends the development of his own work. The contention of this chapter is that Australia's emigrant and travelling poets constitute a far more complex phenomenon than our existing critical vocabularies suggest.[2] For our purposes, the most revealing moment in Murray's essay is when he quibbles with Porter's reference to "kerosene in honey tins." "[U]p Home," he says, "it was mostly honey in kerosene tins" ("Boeotian" 56). Porter responds that the muddle was deliberate: he was sacrificing authenticity for "a felicity of scansion. I simply thought that the line sounded better if I reversed the order of the words" ("Country Poetry" 43). Honey in kerosene tins, kerosene in honey tins: Boeotian, Athenian: the starkest oppositions may seem, from another perspective, to be the narcissism of small differences.[3] After all, Murray's quarrel with Porter was partially about how, in a specific historical moment, Australian poets might present themselves to the world (not, he thought, by adopting a "metropolitan tone," but by presenting an Australia's distinctiveness to the world: "Colonially obedient in so many ways, we yet fail to heed the metropolis when it tells us to be ourselves") ("Boeotian" 55). And in many respects Murray was as mobile and international as Porter, something memorably satirised by Laurie Duggan, who says of "Our Les":

Australian Poets in the Countries of Others

> To all things a season
> to harvest, to plant,
> to jet Midwest
> on a Guggenheim grant,
>
> to shun international
> modernist glam
> in Merthyr Tydfil
> and Amsterdam. (224)

As illuminating as Murray's exchange with Porter may be, Aarhus 1978 is not the only time Australians have reckoned with what it means to be a poet in the countries of others. The aim of this brief survey is to sketch some of the remarkable, varied, and sometimes neglected histories of Australian poets overseas. To offer this chapter's itinerary, first I give an historical overview, examining the terms that poets and critics have applied to the condition of being overseas. Then, I turn to two examples: Lola Ridge and Oodgeroo Noonuccal. To approach their work from the perspective of 'Australian poetry overseas' is at once awkward and revealing. It reveals, above all, the limitations of past conceptual framings, and points to new ways of thinking about that unavoidable theme in Australian literature: poetry and place.

A Lexicon for Living Away

When Australians travel overseas, they cross – in the words of an economist – "into statistical anonymity" (Nixon). The figures are speculative, but for more than two decades demographers have estimated that, "[o]n any given day, there are approximately one million Australians outside Australia" (Fullilove and Flutte 1).[4] Though mostly concentrated in the cities of Europe, Asia, and the Americas, Australia's diaspora is "widely dispersed across every continent" (Fullilove and Flutte 15). Australians can be found just about everywhere, and the same goes for Australia's poets. To count them in a Boeotian way, there is Dorothy Hewett, who came to the Soviet Union "in the year of Stalin ... / And saw flowers growing out of the blinkers on my eyes" (5) and Evelyn Araluen standing "[o]n Invasion Day ... in the stone walls of Cambridge University [as] the sharp call of Murrawarri mulga rings through the quadrangle" (*Dropbear* 80); there are Fay Zwicky's "China Poems 1988," David Prater's "Nagasaki Crows," and the Kolkata poems inspired by Colin Johnson's (later Mudrooroo) time as a Buddhist monk in the 1960s; there is Anna Wickham, queer modernist in interwar London, "writing a kind of 'confessional' poetry some decades before the term was invented" (Pender 231); there is Cassie Lewis thinking of

Melbourne's "chain smoking sky" (33) from San Francisco, "foggiest city in the world" (44), and John Forbes talking with a fair-haired woman while driving on a freezing highway in "Europe, endless" (1994):[5]

>   'it's true' she said
>   'our rock music's shit
>   but we invented sexual attraction
>   didn't you know? In the 12th Century–
>   I mean they had it before
>   but not
>   as a central, defining principle
>   in the Subject's relation to the Other'
>   I looked across at her–
>   her fine boned face
>   & deep, serious eyes–
>   Thanks, I said
>   Thanks a lot. (178)

But we must be a little Athenian too: for all this easy and potentially endless miscellany, there have been important social and economic trends that have sent Australian poets overseas. These are evident if we turn to the existing scholarship. Overwhelmingly, the focus has been on Australian writers who moved to Britain, especially London.[6] In *Lusting for London* (2011), Peter Morton argues that the emigration of Australian writers to London is "one of the most identifiable and enduring themes in the socio-economics of Australian letters" (2). It is not only significant in terms of numbers – Morton identifies roughly 150 Australian authors living and working in London in the period from 1870 to 1950 – but how much it has shaped Australian literature itself (9).[7]

Henry Lawson is one of Morton's most prominent examples. When Lawson set sail for London on 20 April 1900, he was in his thirties, a lauded author of bush ballads and stories (Morton 15ff.). London seemed the place to test his literary ambitions (and perhaps also the place to quit drinking) (Morton 17).[8] His poems from the period, like "The Rush to London," depict the emigrant's heady aspirations but later unpublished verses are more plaintive and rueful: "We were but married children and but lately put to sea / We sailed for Eldorado in the *Golden Vanity*" (quoted in Morton 15, 18). Lawson also elegised Grace Jennings Carmichael, an emigrant poet who died in poverty at thirty-six: "A lonely woman, fought alone / The bitter fight in London town" (quoted in Morton 108).

For all this, the significance of the 'expatriate' in Australian literary history has very little to do with the experiences of poets like Lawson or

Jennings Carmichael. It stems, rather, from a series of influential polemics *against* emigrant writers. Eager to establish a distinctly Australian literary canon, radical nationalists like Miles Franklin and P. R. Stephensen wrote influential invectives against what they called the "exodists" and "shirkers," meaning, in Stephensen's words, that "colony of young Australian writers … in Chelsea or Bloomsbury, aspiring to set the Thames on fire, because the Yarra and the Parramatta seemed too damp" (Quoted in Morton 42, 196). Murray and Porter's exchange fits into a longer history: the emigrant has been long derided for cutting themselves off from the Australian source of their poetic inspiration, squandering their talent, and thus abetting the wider impoverishment of Australia's literary culture. Though written in a more personal register, the most famous instantiation of this narrative is arguably Patrick White's reply to Alister Kershaw's essay "The Last Expatriate" (1958). White suggests that he would never have written his greatest literary works – the colour would not have rushed back into his palette – if he had decided to stay in Europe "talking brilliantly to Alister Kershaw over a Pernod on the Left Bank" ("The Prodigal Son" 127).

One consequence of these polemics is that the terminology for Australian literary emigrants feels loaded and inapt. The term 'exile' – though evoked from time to time, most probably for its gravitas and association with literary modernism – is self-evidently inappropriate in the context of Australian literature, where the vast majority of writers *voluntarily* lived and sojourned in foreign countries (Bones 14–15). Though emigrants may "share in the solitude and estrangement of exile," as Edward W. Said puts it, "they do not suffer under its rigid proscriptions" (181). In fact, 'exile' is more likely to refer to the fact of being *in Australia* than being away from it: narratives of 'exile', 'expulsion', and 'exodus' have been fundamental to the "Australian historical mythology" of settlement, as Ann Curthoys argues (3). This means that some subjects of the British Empire, even those born in Australia, experienced expatriation to the European metropole as a kind of homecoming (Denoon and Mein-Smith, with Wyndam 445; Morton 20–22). Interestingly, the theme of Australia-as-exile persists in contemporary migrant writing. Ouyang Yu's "Song for an Exile in Australia" (1994), for instance, describes being "doubly alienated" in a poem where each phrase is trailed by the weary epistrophe "in Australia" (50).

By far the most common and long-standing label applied to poets in the Australian diaspora is 'expatriate' or 'expat.' The *Macquarie Dictionary* defines "expat" as "someone living or working in a country of which they are not a citizen," but it is far from a neutral term. Even the plosives of the word can seem charged, as Morton suggests, with negative connotations: "fear, envy, contempt, and bullying. If you didn't go, it was because you suspect you were no good; if you did go, you were a traitor; if you went and came back, you were a failure" (Morton 42). Much like the 'cultural cringe,' critics and writers continue to wishfully insist that 'expatriation' is now an anachronism. "[P]eople who talk about expatriates are still living in the nineteenth century," claims David Malouf, while Clive James – in a gleefully unhinged squib against a book on Australian expatriates – contends that "[a]n artist is the incarnation of his country, wherever he might happen to hang his hat" (quoted in Morton 213; 6). In recent decades, critics have habitually claimed that "satellite communications and the jumbo jet" have spelt an end to "[a]ny reality associated with the term [expatriate]" (Packer 1–2). Because these claims are rarely accompanied by compelling evidence, they can feel like breezy attitudinising, "globaloney" (Huggan 51–52). But today the term 'expatriate' is more likely to be dismissed for other reasons, especially for its racial undertones. In a 2015 essay, Mawuna Remarque Koutonin observes that "expat is a term reserved exclusively for western white people going to work abroad. Africans are immigrants. Arabs are immigrants. Asians are immigrants." Koutonin's argument has already had an impact on Australian literary scholarship. In an essay on Silvia Cuevas-Morales (a Chilean-born Australian poet who writes in Spanish and lives in Madrid), Michael Jacklin questions the "unvoiced assumption" that Australia's emigrant poets write in English: "Given Australia's richly diverse, multigenerational multicultural and multilingual heritage, could there be Australian writers living abroad who write and publish in other languages? And, if so, should they be identified as expatriate, or something else?" (3).

"[S]omething else," most poets would answer. And being poets, they have their own coinages ready. Will Druce, who has lived in Chile and Spain, playfully describes being "not underseas"; Javant Biarujia suggests emigration is a state of "outlandishness" (a calque from the German *ausländisch*, meaning 'foreign'); in an essay on the Prague-based poet Louis Armand, Ali Alizadeh outlines a poetics of "unplacement"; Marc Jones, in Paris, borrows Alan Loney's idea of "writing beyond one's place of birth," while Marty Hiatt, who lives in Berlin, talks quite simply of "living away." Already in this miniature lexicon we witness how divergently poets transmute a seemingly shared experience. Even poets who appear, on the surface, to have followed fairly conventional patterns of literary emigration (moving from Australia to London or New York), can register it poetically in entirely different ways. Lily Brett, for instance, was born in a displaced person's camp in Germany in 1946, the daughter of "two people who had each survived years of imprisonment in Nazi ghettos, labour camps and death camps" ("'Inevitably Catastrophic'"). She grew up in Melbourne and moved to New York in 1989. It could be said that her poetry deals with displacement, but it is not so much geographical as historical – the displacement of intergenerational trauma. "I have no sense of geography," she says, "but I retain what people say to me" ("'Inevitably Catastrophic'"). In "Even the Sea," a poem in her first collection *The Auschwitz Poems* (1986), the Polish city Łódź, where "you were red-haired then" is not one that the poet could visit, but a place of reported speech: "the beauty of the town / they said / and clever so clever" (176). Brett's poetry responds to the moment, in her words, when it became impossible "to separate my mother's experience from my own experience." The need to speak on behalf of her voiceless parents has, she says, "shaped everything I've written."

It is also worth emphasising that Cuevas-Morales is not an outlier for writing in a language other than English. While for some this means writing in their non-English mother tongue, for others it means learning the language of an adopted country. Adam Aitken, for example, thinks of his engagement "with French and France as a method of deliberate *ostranenie* or making the familiar strange," while Nicholas Powell describes how he has developed a more "skittish" style in response to the "solemnity and intense interiority of Finnish modes". For Corey Wakeling, who has lived in Japan since 2015, this has meant the conscious effort to become a "second-language Japanese writer":

> Beckett sought in French ... a self-othering experience that would force transformation .... I too thought I would have an experience like Beckett's, having my maximalism inherently confronted with critique, have a radical break from literary inheritance made painfully obvious, and so on and so forth. But no one tells you that writing in a second language is deeply embarrassing. Was Beckett's French just so fine that the obvious common experience of writing sentences considered awkward in the language ... wasn't his experience? ... Because writing in a second-language does not instantly make you Raymond Queneau, realising instantly compelling tangents to common style and convention. No, in the most simple terms, you feel that you are simply a less accomplished writer .... I have entered a second childhood.

Wakeling's more recent English poetry bares the imprint of this experience: his poem "Traveller" (2021), for instance, plays on "two formerly inconsecutive lines" of Nishiwaki Junzaburō: 詩のないところに詩がある ["Poetry is where poetry is not"] and うつつは淋しい ["Reality is lonesome"].

There is one recent trend among poets in the Australia diaspora that is yet to be fully explored in the critical literature. Morton claims that no Australian writer, "as far as is known, went to live abroad *expressly* because they were frightened or disgusted by the xenophobia, popularism, puritanism, or racism of their homeland" (244). Yet for a growing number of settler Australian poets, feelings of shame, anger, and guilt have become a significant aspect of how they understand their motivations for leaving Australia.[9] Today many emigrant poets feel tied to Australia by what Carlo Ginzburg calls a "bond of shame"; for them, "the country one belongs to is not, as the usual rhetoric goes, the one you love but the one you are ashamed of" (35).[10] And what they are ashamed of is Australia's violent colonial history, especially the dispossession of First Nations people. Will Druce states candidly that he harbours "a deep resentment and hatred" of his status as a white settler-colonial subject, and initially felt that "I may be able to deglove myself of my Aussieness by ... having my sense of self somehow absorbed by other places, languages and people – to have my Australianness somehow diluted and therefore more bearable." It is easy to read this into the restlessness and dislocation of his poem "great artesian nowhere" (2019), which declaims: "we live on liquified pastures ... in silent stupefaction / of being here at all." In a similar vein, Marty Hiatt speaks of his emigration as "a kind of 'running away' or desertion" from the "permanent repressed tension of colonial violence": "Living away was ... a way out of the Australian hellscape of mortgaging your life to pay for a mass-produced miniature fortress on stolen land." Again, Dan Disney, who has lived in Seoul since 2010, notes how painfully aware he was, growing up in Gippsland, of the "land materialis[ing] traumas of colonisation." Leaving Australia, he says, was the direct consequence of his "shame" and his refusal "to be complicit in a nation-sized lie." Finally, in a somewhat different vein, Jaya Savige, who has lived mostly in London since 2009, speaks of "the tension that comes with being a postcolonial satellite-creature transplanted to the European imperial mothership." As "a half-Indonesian kid" without family ties to Britain, he knew he would never "slot [into the country] in the way, say, Peter Porter or Clive James did," and yet he still registered an "unsettling" feeling when studying at the University of Cambridge: "a sense that the stunning architectural wonders of the colleges were bound up ... with the spoils of empire ...: at times I almost visualised the blood seeping out of the stupendously imposing old buildings." Though I would avoid any easy periodisation, forceful and lucid articulations of settler positionality mark a significant shift in how some writers understand what it means to be an Australian poet overseas.

Flotsam of Five Oceans

An emigrant is also an immigrant, but sometimes only one of these categories influences a poet. For Lola Ridge, it was being an immigrant in a city of immigrants that mattered most. Ridge is today remembered as a "largely forgotten modernist and feminist poet" (Tobin, "Introduction" 11), which is to say her critical neglect is taken as the point of departure. She is often presented as a heroic, even "saintly" figure – one journalist, reporting on a vigil for the anarchists Sacco and Vanzetti, witnessed her alone and unflinching before a column of police horses (Tobin, "Modernism" 66). Ridge was associated with prominent anarchists, held editorial roles in the little magazines *Others* and *Broom*, and threw parties where, her biographer, Terese Svoboda, imagines, "William Carlos Williams and Robert McAlmon hatched plans for their magazine *Contact*, twenty-year-old Hart Crane flirted with everyone in sight, Marianne Moore read early drafts of her own work, and Vladimir Mayakovsky stomped on her coffee table." *The Ghetto and Other Poems* (1918), her first and best-known collection, depicts the poverty and dynamism of New York City, a place where "world-voices" sound "[m]ajestic discordances / Greater than harmonies," where the loafing homeless by a fountain at night appear as "[f]lotsam of the five oceans / Here on this raft of the world" (Ridge 59, 71).

Reviewing *The Ghetto*, one of her contemporaries notes: "It seems strange ... that it has remained for one reared far from our chaotic centres to appraise most poignantly the life that runs through our crowded streets. ... [H]er early life in Australia has doubtless enabled her to draw the American city with such an unusual sense of perspective" (Louis Untermeyer, quoted by Berke 30). Though Ridge was described in her first US publication as "a young Australian poet ... not without fame in her own land," she was conceivably an emigrant of several countries by the time she settled in New York (Giles 335). Perhaps 'Australian' was an suggestive and efficient way of saying 'foreign,' as Gail Jones says (133). Ridge was born an Irish Catholic in Dublin in 1873. While she was young, she moved with her widowed mother to Sydney. They lived briefly in Redfern, and then settled in New Zealand, where Ridge was raised in the West Coast settlement Hokitika in "a three-room shack, among immigrants, [Māori], and Chinese workers" (Tobin, "Introduction" 13). In 1903, she left an unhappy marriage to a gold mine manager and returned to Sydney. She studied painting with Julian Ashton in The Rocks and presented a poetry manuscript, *Verses*, to A. G. Stephens, a major literary figure and the editor of the *Bulletin*'s "Red Page." Stephens ran more than twenty of her poems in the *Bulletin* (Leggott).

Ridge's early work fits well alongside the *Bulletin*'s iconic bush poetry. "Under Song," for example, exalts the understated music of the Australia bush:

> The mystical, the strong
>   Deep throated Bush
> Is humming in the hush:
>   Low bars of song:
> Far singing in the trees
>   In tongues unknown –
> A reminiscent tone
>   On minor keys   (Ridge 305).

The speaker's uncanny feeling that she hears the bush repeat a familiar song in a minor key conveys the 'weird melancholy' of the Australian landscape in a way roughly as conventional as half-rhyming "bush" and "hush" (a half-rhyme that also appears, for instance, in Banjo Paterson's "Song of the Future").[11] From time to time, critics suggest that Ridge's bush poetry exerts a subtle influence on her later modernist verse. Perhaps most inventively, Paul Giles argues that Ridge's "Australasian provenance" shaped her "appulsive imagination," by which he means "a poetics of turning things around the other way," of bringing political revolution into alignment with the "diurnal revolutions of the earth." To demonstrate this, Giles marshalls planetary imagery from across Ridge's work, from the "emerging sun" that appears "up-turned" in a vision of Sydney through to America "with her great flanks on the globe" and "the skies whirling above" (Giles 335–38; Ridge 199, 92).

But I think there is another continuity between "Under Song" and *The Ghetto*. In "Under Song," it is the landscape that sings, while the poet is an impersonal figure, the "One" who, "peering through the husk / Of darkness thrown / May hear it in the dusk / That ancient tone." Though ballads are typically impersonal, "Under Song" explicitly thematises the poet's search for a surrogate voice – poetry emerges from overhearing the "voices of the Bush." Perhaps Ridge published an edited version of "Under Song" in *The Ghetto* because she felt that it shared her enduring concern with the vicariousness of lyric. In *The Ghetto*, Ridge's characteristic address is "To the Others," to "you, refulgent ones":

> Burning so steadily
> Like big white arc lights...
> There are so many of you.
> I like to watch you weaving –
> Altogether and with precision
> Each his ray –
> Your tracery of light,
> Making a shining way about America. (108)

But at the same time as she admires the weave of others' luminescence, the poet has vanished: "you do not yet see me / Who am a torch blown along the wind" (108).

This self-effacing "I" is crucial to the title poem, "The Ghetto" – a nine-part sequence in which a non-Jewish speaker observes the intricacies of Jewish life.[12] Though addressed "*To the American People*," and filled with passages where bodies dissolve into "a hot tide of flesh" and egos into the anonymous force of "Life – / Pent, overflowing," "The Ghetto" builds to these crescendos of poetic afflatus from an almost anthropological attentiveness to the lives of Eastern European Jewish immigrants in the crowded tenements and garment factories of the Lower East Side (40, 42, 65). Ridge's speaker "rooms at Sodos," in a boarding house on Hester Street where even the parrot speaks in Yiddish (43, 54). Around the time Ridge wrote "The Ghetto," "31 percent of the population of New York City was Jewish, and Yiddish was the dominant language spoken in a 20-square block area" around the open-air market of Hester Street (Miller 458). Despite being an outsider without knowledge of Yiddish[13], Ridge's speaker carefully observes the tensions between different generations of Jewish migrants. Young women converge on "the forums and meeting halls" with their "heads uncovered to the stars," while the old, with their wigs "of smooth black hair," beat rugs on fire escapes and light candles for Shabbat. Sadie, one of the young women, "wears her own hair," "dances madly" at festivals, has non-Jewish lovers, attends protests, and attempts to organise the garment workers: "Slow down – / You'll have him cutting us again!" (42–45, 54–55). It is easy to lose sight of the observer in this congested scene. We glimpse her offering an orange to a little girl who "stammers in Yiddish," but then the girl darts away "through the crowd / Like a little white panic" (48). Life, too, is always escaping Ridge's speaker: it "baffles me when I try to examine it, / Or hurls me back without apology. / Leaving my ego ruffled and preening itself" (63). To the extent that we glimpse the speaker of "The Ghetto," it is through the intensity of her concentration on the lives of other immigrants. This is not simply a portrait of one kind of immigrant reflected in another, but something else: 'migration' of an almost metaphysical, vitalist kind: as *migrāre*, a change of form, as the endless "flux of life" (65).

Never Mind Place

A few years before Murray and Porter convened in Aarhus, Oodgeroo Noonuccal (then Kath Walker) was on a flight back to Australia. She had been in Nigeria to serve on the steering committee of the Second World Black and African Festival of Arts and Culture (FESTAC 77). It was an historic occasion – the first time "Australia had been represented at an international event by an all Black delegation" (Cochrane 110). During a brief layover in Dubai, some of the delegates disembarked to stretch their legs, while Oodgeroo stayed on board, hoping to catch up on sleep (Walker, "Hi-Jacker" 8). She woke later to a strange sound. When she looked at up, she saw "a very tall, handsome black man" pointing a revolver at her. "I stand up," as she recalls, "ignore the revolver and ask, 'Is this a hi-jack?'" She soon established that the group of hijackers, who were "cradl[ing] their repeating rifles over their arms, like a waiter cradles a rare bottle of wine," were Palestinians, demanding the release of militants imprisoned in Cairo and the Netherlands. The hijackers first divided their hostages by nationality. Eventually, those with "Indian and Pakistani passports were allowed to leave the plane." Here Oodgeroo posed a problem: the hijackers wanted to know if she was "Pakistani or Indian." The chief steward turned to her at one point and said: "Say you are an Indian love." Instead, Oodgeroo told them: "I am Aboriginal Australian and proud of it," and submitted the hijackers to an impassioned lecture. While as an Aboriginal she felt solidarity with Palestinian struggle, she told them "I think [your] actions are stupid and not in the best interest of [your] cause." The internationalism of poetry and the arts, the kind of global gathering she was helping to organise in Nigeria, would better serve their aspirations than violence. She delivered this speech through a translator who, as it turned out, was a hostage too. "Whether he told the commandos what I said, I shall never know" (Walker, "Hi-Jacker" 8).

Over the forty-six-hours of her captivity, Oodgeroo wrote several poems on "unlikely stationary" – a pencil and a British Airways sick bag (Cochrane 110). One of these poems, "Yussef (Hi-Jacker)" (Figure 15.1; Figure 15.2) takes the form of an intimate address to the hijackers' leader, who had left his career as a pediatrician to become a militant. It begins: "Yussef, my son / What do you do here / With your dreamy eyes / That tell of moonlight / And sun" (Walker, "Yussef (Hi-Jacker)" 8). The poet imagines something that her addressee, Yussef, does not say. "The soft lines around your mouth," she says, "Tell of endearments / You dare not speak." Her "vision" is what she reads from his "[s]unburned" body. This is even more striking given that the poem was written while the writer was hostage in the stationary plane: "The hot sun of the desert," as Oodgeroo recalls, "penetrated the plane. I actually felt my skin getting sunburned through." Though the hijacker holds a "repeating rifle," the only repetition in the poem is of "a girl's embrace" (this is reinforced by the sickbag draft, which shows Oodgeroo replacing "machine gun" with "repeating rifle" and adding in the second "girl's embrace" with pen). Positing herself as Yussef's mother, the poem's speaker deciphers this embrace from his "dreamy eyes" and the "soft lines around your mouth," as though an absent female body has left a legible

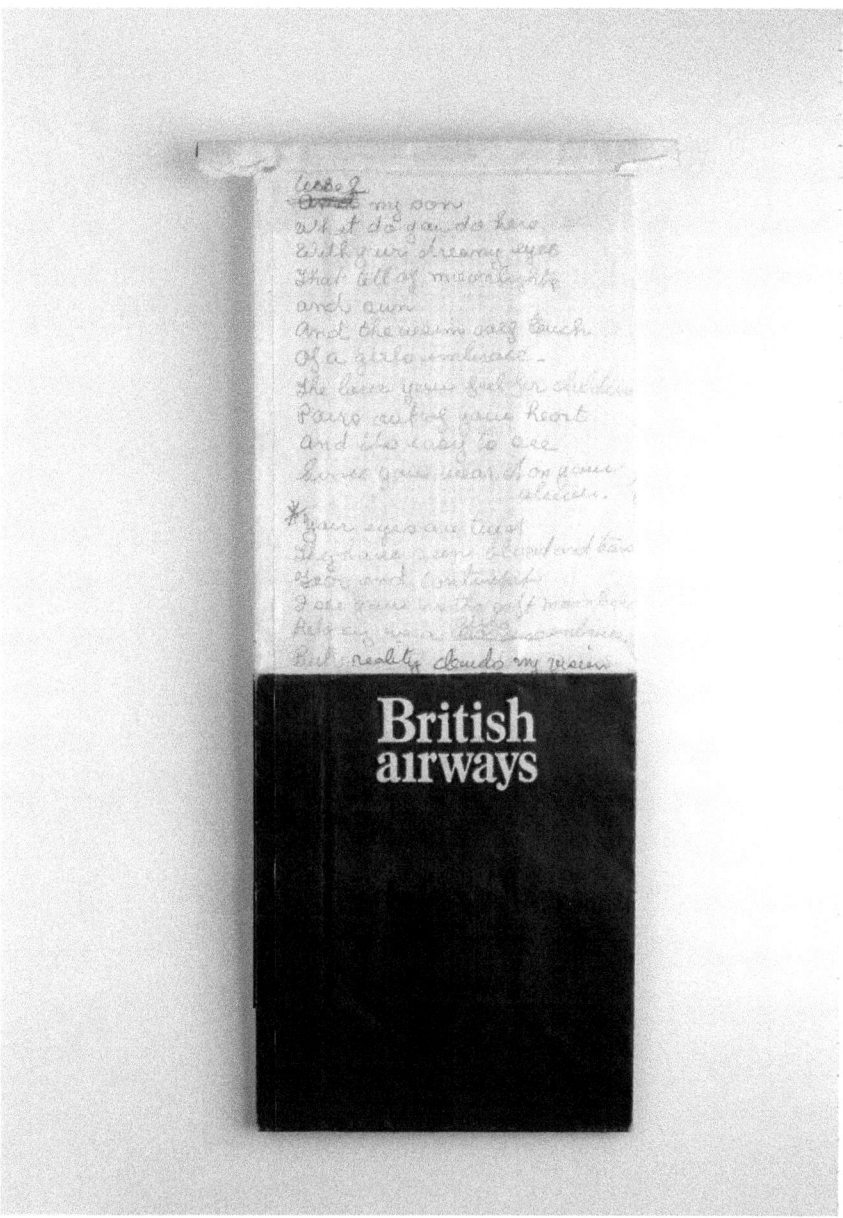

Figure 15.1 Oodgeroo Noonuccal, "Yussef"

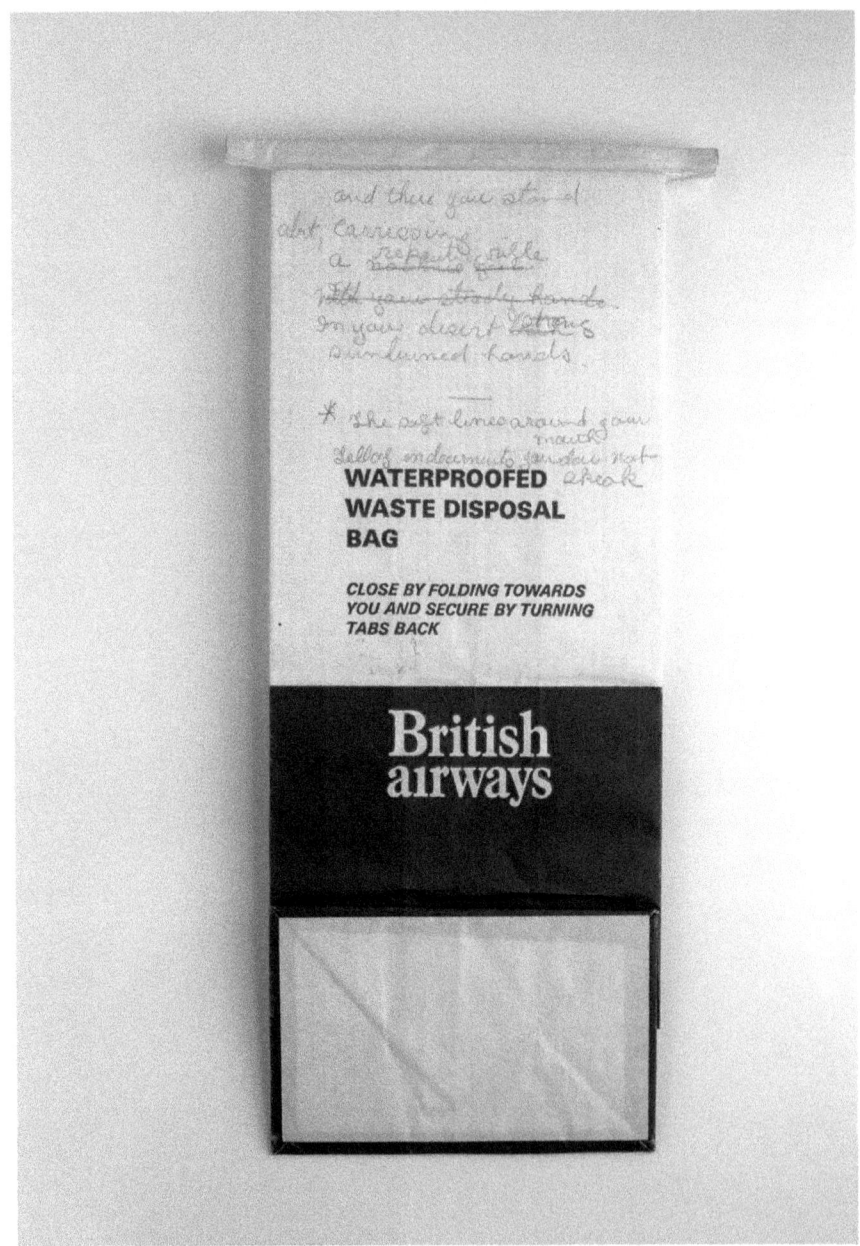

Figure 15.2 Oodgeroo Noonuccal, "Yussef"

imprint on Yussef's body (Walker, "Hi-Jacker" 8). By the end of the poem, the speaker's imaginary efforts falter with a deliberate ambiguity that recalls Keats: "Was it a vision, or a waking dream? / Fled is that music:—Do I wake or sleep?" (288). But though "reality clouds" her vision, the hijacker's body remains. "Reality" is just as corporeal, only his body is now unreadable: "For there you stand / Erect, / Alert" (Walker, "Hi-Jacker" 8).

Oodgeroo travelled widely in her lifetime, in places as far flung as the Soviet Union, Fiji, Papua New Guinea, India, and the United States (Cochrane 105ff.; Swan 73ff.). As she once wrote in her poem 'All One Race': "I'm international, never mind place" (1). Away from Australia, she was sometimes at her most prolific. The weeks she spent in China in 1984 were particularly momentous: she wrote a series of sixteen poems, later published in English and Mandarin as *Kath Walker in China* (1988). Nicholas Jose describes these poems as an "open, fluid, wry and insightful response to China," noting that their "free, spare, elliptical immediacy" is "less public, less oratorical than her more familiar work" (48). They offer glancing reflections on the meaning of travel: "[p]erhaps I have strayed too long / In this beautiful country," the "spirit of my Aboriginal Mook-Mook / Taps me lightly on the shoulder" (*Kath Walker in China* 53, 40). In another poem, Oodgeroo and the historian Manning Clark sing "Waltzing Matilda" to a group of "young pioneers":

> I think they liked it,
> Or, maybe, they were
> Showing us,
> How polite they can be.   (*Kath Walker in China* 24)

As they are leaving, Oodgeroo and Clark "cupped out hands, and called for them / Our / Australian coo-ee" (*Kath Walker in China* 24). These poems – arguably "the first Aboriginal writing published in China" – have served as an inspiration to other First Nations poets since. Wiradjuri writer Jeanine Leane's "Sunrise-Sunset in Yangshou" stands, in the words of Ellen van Neerven, "both as a tribute to Oodgeroo and a connector between two generation of Indigenous poets travelling to China" (Ellen van Neerven on Oodgeroo Noonuccal" n.pag.).

Gamatj leader Garralwy Yunupingu once remarked on the irony that (as Ann Curthoys paraphrases it):

> Aboriginal people who stay on their own land as far as they are permitted, to protect it, become in white Australian mythology the wanderers, the nomads, on "walkabout" ..., while those inveterate wanderers the European immigrants who have crossed oceans and strayed far from their homelands ... are named the settlers, those who stay at home.   (14)

Further ramifying this irony is the fact that settler colonial ideology took First Nations 'wandering' as evidence for the legal fiction of *terra nullius* at the same time as conceiving of Indigenous people as bounded to the land and only European settlers as truly mobile (Standfield 2–3). In recent years, historians have sought to unseat the legacies of these assumptions and begun to investigate the complex histories of First Nations transnationalism and mobility.[14] But there has been no comparable attention given to First Nations mobility among literary scholars. Striking instances like Oodgeroo Noonuccal's travels have inspired stand-alone essays, but there has been no sustained effort to reflect on what First Nations mobility means for the critical literature on Australian poets overseas. Even a term like 'overseas' may be suspect here. "Aboriginal poetics have always existed," as Evelyn Araluen puts it, and Indigenous poets have journeyed across the borders of the continent's First Nations and lived in diaspora for tens of thousands of years before the invasion of Australia ("Too Little"). This brief chapter cannot offer the corrective that Australian literary criticism needs, but I hope it might serve as an invitation for scholars to ask new questions.

For one thing, Oodgeroo was not the first Aboriginal writer and activist in London. When, in the 1960s, she sat down in London to write "White Racism and White Violence," she had been preceded by several decades by the "solitary Aboriginal activist," A. M. Fernando (who was himself preceded by one of the most famous First Nations visitors to Britain, Bennelong) (Paisley xiii).[15] Fernando (b. 1864) lived in interwar London, where he picketed Australia House in a coat sewn with "tiny toy skeletons around his shoulders to symbolise ... the culture of death and exploitation in Australia" and gave lengthy speeches in Hyde Park on what he called "the slaughter house of Australia" (Paisley xix, 125). Though he was self-educated, the experience of surviving Australian colonialism was, in his words, itself a "bitter education" (Paisley 125). In *The Lone Protester* (2012), Fiona Paisley portrays him as having "courageously translated these experiences of dislocation and life-long exile into a vibrant source of political expression on behalf of Aboriginal people" (xiii). Paisley also comments on the "complex poetics" of Fernando's protest monologues (something evident even in a stray phrase like the "law of England has outlawed us") and examines what she calls a "word poem ... reminiscent of modernist expressionism" in one of the surviving notebooks in which he detailed his daily life in London (142, 125, 154). Paisley scans a version of this "word poem" from 1929 as follows:

> Filth is adoration
> Lice is prostitution
> White man's adulation

> Murder and plunder in exploration
> Blasting the good name of who
> Trustful victim. (154)[16]

In the decades since Fernando's "word poem," there have been other First Nations visitors and further "'[p]ostcolonial' musings" in Europe – or "Urup," as Ellen van Neerven mischievously transliterates the name of the continent. While van Neerven was living and teaching in Bremen in 2019, they became intrigued by the disparity between Germany's reckoning with its collective responsibility for the Shoah (its *Vergangenheitsbewältigung*, or "coming to terms with the past"), and the lack of recognition of the country's history as a colonial power. Poems van Neerven wrote during this period draw attention to sites in Germany that "show evidence of colonisation: the trees that were chopped down, the wealth of the buildings, the way that the rivers have been shaped, and all the stuff that was stolen" (*Throat* 36–37). In an essay on "the figure of the tree in poems by Aboriginal poets," Peter Minter notes how the "dead trees at the core of sailing ships and the centers of wheels were spectral portents of the looming impact of colonisation and the razing of forests" (57, 61). There is a particularly startling example of what Minter calls "the coloniality of tree felling" in van Neerven's Bremen poems: van Neerven writes of a "ship-shaped hole in the forest" from the elms and pines cut to make vessels that sailed to Australia (63; *Throat* 35).

Van Neerven sometimes says that it was travel and living away that provided the impetus for their shift from prose to poetry. They think of *Comfort Food* (2016), their first poetry collection, as a kind of "travelogue" written in the creative lull after *Heat and Light* (2014). *Comfort Food*'s poems are like sensuous souvenirs: "Coffee in Toronto," "fourteen hours in Hong Kong," "[f]inally, a tamale in Texas" (27, 33). By reflecting on examples like these – from van Neerven and Oodgeroo to Lola Ridge – the limitations of past framings of Australian poetry overseas become obvious. But more than simply pointing to these limitations, I hope that this chapter's argument by way of example offers up new ways of imagining Australian literature as such. Van Neerven's observation in "Goan Fish Curry" resonates with many of the poets in this chapter:

> poetry travelled with me
> like rivers
> I didn't ever eat alone   (*Comfort Food* 32)

Works Cited

Alizadeh, Ali. "The Poetics of Unplacement." *Poetry International Archives*, 6 July 2012. www.poetryinternational.org/pi/cou_article/22434/The-poetics-of-unplacement.

Alomes, Stephen. *When London Calls: The Expatriation of Australian Creative Artists to Britain*. Cambridge University Press, 1999.
Araluen, Evelyn. "Shame and Contemporary Australian Poetics." *Rabbit*, no. 21, 2017, pp. 117–127.
―. "Too Little, Too Much." *Meanjin*, 6 July 2020. https://meanjin.com.au/blog/too-little-too-much/.
―. *Dropbear*. University of Queensland Press, 2021.
Arnold, John. "Australian Books, Publishers, and Writers in England, 1900–1940." *Australians in Britain: The Twentieth-Century Experience*, edited by Carl Bridge, Robert Crawford, and David Dunstan. Monash University Press, 2009, pp. 101–9.
Bennelong, "Letter to Mr Phillips, Lord Sydney's Steward." *Macquarie PEN Anthology of Australian Aboriginal Literature*, edited by Anita Heiss and Peter Minter. Allen & Unwin, 2008, p. 9.
Bennett, Bruce and Anne Pender. *From a Distant Shore: Australian Writers in Britain 1820–2012*. Monash University Publishing, 2013.
Berke, Nancy. "'Electric Currents of Life': Lola Ridge's Immigrant Flaneuserie.' *American Studies* vol.51 no.1–2, 2010, pp. 27–47.
Biarujia, Javant. "X Marks the Parataxis: Louis Armand, John Kinsella and Jessica L. Wilkinson." *Cordite Poetry Review*, 1 May 2014. http://cordite.org.au/essays/x-marks-the-parataxis/.
Bones, Helen. *The Expatriate Myth: New Zealand Writers and the Colonial World*. Otago University Press, 2018.
Brett, Lily. *Auschwitz Poems*. Suhrkamp, 2004.
―. "'Inevitably Catastrophic': Author Lily Brett on the Politics of Hatred." *Sydney Morning Herald*, 16 June 2018. www.smh.com.au/national/inevitably-catastrophic-author-lily-brett-on-the-politics-of-hatred-20180611-p4zksb.html.
Clarke, Marcus. *Marcus Clarke*, edited by Michael Wilding. University of Queensland Press, 1976.
Cochrane, Kathie. *Oodgeroo*. University of Queensland Press, 1994.
Curthoys, Ann. "Expulsion, Exodus and Exile in White Australian Historical Mythology." *Journal of Australian Studies* vol.23 no.61, 1999, pp. 1–19.
De Bolla, Peter. *Art Matters*. Harvard University Press, 2001.
Denoon, Donald and Philippa Mein-Smith, with Marivic Wyndham. *A History of Australia, New Zealand and the Pacific*. Blackwell Publishers, 2000.
Druce, Will. "great artesian nowhere." *Cordite Poetry Review*, 25 November 2019. http://cordite.org.au/chapbooks-features/apewf2019/great-artesian-nowhere/.
Duggan, Laurie. "The Great Tradition." *Southerly* vol.40 no.2, 1980, pp. 222–25.
Farrell, Michael. *Writing Australian Unsettlement: Modes of Poetic Invention, 1796–1945*. Palgrave Macmillan, 2015.
Forbes, John. *Collected Poems, 1969–1999*. Brandl & Schlesinger, 2010.
Freud, Sigmund. *Civilization, Society and Religion*, edited by Albert Dickson, translated by James Strachey. Penguin, 1985.
Fullilove, Michael and Chlöe Flutte. *Diaspora: The World Wide Web of Australians*. Lowy Institute for International Policy, 2004.
Giles, Paul. *Antipodean America: Australasia and the Constitution of US Literature*. Oxford University Press, 2013.
Ginzburg, Carlo. "The Bond of Shame." *New Left Review* no.120, 2019, pp. 35–44.

Grogan, Kristin. "'Thorns Served on Honey': Lyric Difference in Lola Ridge's 'The Ghetto.'" *American Literary History* vol.35 no.4, 2023, pp. 1617–37.
Hewett, Dorothy. "The Hidden Journey." *Overland* no.36, 1967, pp. 5–8.
Huggan, Graham. "Globaloney and the Australian Writer." *Journal of the European Association for Studies on Australia* vol.1 no.1, 2009, pp. 45–63.
Jacklin, Michael. "Silvia Cuevas-Morales: A Chilean-Australian Expatriate Writer?" *JASAL: Journal of the Association for the Study of Australian Literature* vol.19 no.1, 2019, pp. 1–12.
James, Clive. "When London Calls: The Expatriation of Australian Creative Artists to Britain." *Times Literary Supplement* no.5052, 2000, pp. 6–7.
Jones, Gail. "'Growing Small Wings': Walter Benjamin, Lola Ridge, and the Political Affect of Modernism." *Affirmations: of the modern* vol.1 no.2, 2014, pp. 120–42.
Jose, Nicholas. "Oodgeroo in China." *Australian Literary Studies* vol.16 no.4, 1994, pp. 42–54.
Keats, John. "Ode to a Nightingale." *Major Works*, edited by Elizabeth Cook. Oxford University Press, 2008, pp. 285–88.
Kershaw, Alister. "The Last Expatriate." *The Oxford Book of Australian Essays*, edited by Imre Salusinszky. Oxford University Press, 1997, pp. 144–46.
Konishi, Shino. "Crossing Boundaries: Tracing Indigenous Mobility and Territory in the Exploration of South-Eastern Australia." *Indigenous Mobilities: Across and Beyond the Antipodes*, edited by Rachel Standfield. ANU Press, 2018, pp. 35–55.
Koutonin, Mawuna Remarque. "Why Are White People Expats When the Rest of Us Are Immigrants?" *The Guardian*, 13 March 2015. www.theguardian.com/global-development-professionals-network/2015/mar/13/white-people-expats-immigrants-migration.
Leane, Jeanine. "Sunrise-Sunset in Yangshou." *Peril* no.8, December 2015. https://peril.com.au/back-editions/edition22/sunrise-sunset-in-yangshou/.
Leggott, Michele. "Lola Ridge Journal Publication 1892–1920." *ka mate ka ora: a New Zealand Journal of Poetry and Poetics* no.12, 2013, pp. 119–28.
Lewis, Cassie. *Bridges*. Walleah Press, 2005.
Macquarie Dictionary. Macmillan, 2023. www.macquariedictionary.com.au/.
McGuinness, Patrick. *Other People's Countries: A Journey into Memory*. Vintage, 2014.
Metzenrath, Rita. "Bennelong's Letter." *AIATSIS*, 21 August 2017. https://aiatsis.gov.au/blog/bennelongs-letter.
Miller, Cristanne. "Tongues 'Loosened in the Melting Pot': The Poets of *Others* and the Lower East Side." *Modernism/Modernity* vol.14 no.3, 2007, pp. 455–76.
Minter, Peter. "All the Trees." *New Directions in Contemporary Australian Poetry*, edited by Dan Disney and Matthew Hall. Palgrave Macmillan, 2021, pp. 55–69.
Morton, Peter. *Lusting for London: Australian Expatriate Writers at the Hub of Empire, 1870–1950*. Palgrave Macmillan, 2011.
Mudrooroo. *The Song Circle of Jacky and Selected Poems*. Hyland House, 1986.
Murray, Les. "On Sitting Back and Thinking about Porter's Boeotia." *The Peasant Mandarin: Prose Pieces*. University of Queensland Press, 1978, pp. 172–84.
——. "The Boeotian Strain." *Kunapipi* vol.2 no.1, 1980, pp. 45–64.
——. *New Collected Poems*. Carcanet, 2003.
Nixon, Stewart. "Australian Needs A Diaspora Census – Analysis." *East Asia Forum*, 14 September 2021. www.eurasiareview.com/21092021-australia-needs-a-diaspora-census-analysis/.

Noonuccal, Oodgeroo. "Yussef (Hi-Jack)." University of Queensland Fryer Library Manuscripts, Oodgeroo Noonuccal Papers, UQFL84-Series A-Subseries 1.
— *My People*. Wiley, 2021.
Ouyang, Yu. "Song for an Exile in Australia." *Kunapipi* vol.16 no.2, 1994, pp. 49–50.
Packer, Clyde. *No Return Ticket*. Angus & Robertson, 1984.
Paisley, Fiona. *The Lone Protester: A.M. Fernando in Australia and Europe*. Aboriginal Studies Press, 2012.
Paterson, A. B. "Song of the Future." *The Penguin Banjo Paterson*, edited by Clement Semmler. Penguin, 1993, pp. 132–36.
Pender, Anne. "'Phrases between Us': The Poetry of Anna Wickham." *Australian Literary Studies* vol.2 no.2, 2005, pp. 229–44.
Porter, Peter. "Country Poetry and Town Poetry: A Debate." *Australian Literary Studies* vol.9 no.1, 1979, pp. 39–48.
— *Collected Poems*. Oxford University Press, 1984.
— "John Forbes in Europe." *Homage to John Forbes*, edited by Ken Bolton. Brandl & Schlesinger, 2002, pp. 21–33.
Prater, David. "Nagasaki Crows." *Morgenland*. Vagabond Press, 2007, n.pag.
Ridge, Lola. *To the Many: Collected Early Works*, edited by Daniel Tobin. Little Island Press, 2018.
Rutherford, Anna. "Conferences." *Kunapipi* vol.1 no.2, 1979, pp. 182–98.
Said, Edward W. "Reflections on Exile." *Reflections on Exile and Other Essays*. Harvard University Press, 2003, pp. 173–86.
Savige, Jaya. "'Chops and Surrender': Nam Le Interviews Jaya Savige." *Cordite Poetry Review*, 1 October 2020. http://cordite.org.au/interviews/le-savige/.
Slimani, Leila. *Le Pays des Autres*. Gallimard, 2020.
Standfield, Rachel. "Moving across, Looking Beyond." *Indigenous Mobilities: Across and Beyond the Antipodes*, edited by Rachel Standfield. ANU Press, 2018, pp. 1–33.
Svoboda, Terese. "Lola Ridge: The Radical Modernist We Won't Forget Twice." *Boston Review*, 18 February 2016. https://bostonreview.net/articles/terese-svoboda-lola-ridge/.
Swan, Quito. *Pasifika Black: Oceania, Anti-Colonialism and the African World*. NYU Press, 2022.
Tan, George, Andrew Taylor, and Kelly McDougall. "COVID Has Made One Thing Clear – We Do Not Know Enough about Australians Overseas." *The Conversation*, 6 May 2021. https://theconversation.com/covid-has-made-one-thing-very-clear-we-do-not-know-enough-about-australians-overseas-159995.
Tasker, Meg and Lucy Sussex. "'That Wild Run to London': Henry and Bertha Lawson in England." *Australian Literary Studies* vol.23 no.2, 2007, pp. 168–86.
Tobin, Daniel. "Modernism, Leftism, and the Spirit: The Poetry of Lola Ridge." *New Hibernia Review* vol.8 no.3, 2004, pp. 65–85.
— "Introduction." *To the Many: Collected Early Works*, edited by Daniel Tobin. Little Island Press, 2020, pp. 11–34.
Van Neerven, Ellen. *Comfort Food*. University of Queensland Press, 2016.
— "Ellen van Neerven on Oodgeroo Noonuccal: Poetry and Place." *Melbourne Writers Festival*, 22 October 2018. https://mwf.com.au/blog/ellen-van-neerven-oodgeroo-noonuccal-poems/> [link no longer active].
— *Throat*. University of Queensland Press, 2020.

Wakeling, Corey. "Traveller." *Overland* no.245, 2021. https://overland.org.au/previous-issues/issue-245/poetry-traveller/.
Walker, Kath [Oodgeroo Noonuccal]. "Yussef (Hi-Jacker)." *Semper Floreat* vol.45 no.2, 1975, pp. 8–9.
   Kath Walker in China, translated by Gu Zixin. Jacaranda Press and the International Culture Publishing Corporation, 1988.
White, Patrick. "The Prodigal Son." *The Oxford Book of Australian Essays*, edited by Imre Salusinszky. Oxford University Press, 1997, pp. 125–28.
Wood, James. "On Not Going Home." *Serious Noticing: Selected Essays*. Vintage, 2019, pp. 270–93.
Zwicky, Fay. "China Poems 1988." *Collected Poems*, edited by Lucy Dougan and Tim Dolin. UWA Publishing, 2017, pp. 141–48.

NOTES

1 My emphasis. See Murray, 'On Sitting Back."
2 For an argument by "force of example," see de Bolla, p. 5.
3 On the "narcissism of small differences" [*der Narzißmus der kleinen Differenzen*], see Freud, p. 305.
4 Cf. Tan, Taylor, and McDougall.
5 On Forbes' time in Europe, see Porter, "John Forbes in Europe."
6 See Alomes, Morton, and Bennett and Pender. Cf. Bones' revisionary argument vis-à-vis New Zealand literature in *The Expatriate Myth*.
7 See also Arnold.
8 On Lawson's emigration, see Tasker and Sussex.
9 See in particular Evelyn Araluen's essay, "Shame and Contemporary Australian Poetics." *Rabbit*, no. 21, 2017, pp. 117–127.
10 Thank you to Laurie Duggan for suggesting this essay.
11 On 'weird melancholy,' see Marcus Clarke, *Marcus Clarke*, edited by Michael Wilding. University of Queensland Press, 1976, p.33.
12 For a more extensive reading, see Kristin Grogan's "'Thorns Served on Honey: Lyric Difference in Lola Ridge's 'The Ghetto,'" *American Literary History*." vol.35 no.4, 2023, pp.1617–37.
13 See Grogan 1627ff.
14 See, for instance, Konishi.
15 In 1792, Bennelong visited England. His "Letter" (1796), considered "the first known use of written English by an Aboriginal Australian," says of his three-year visit: "Not me go to England no more. I am home now" (Metzenrath). Farrell has argued that the "Letter" could be read as a "short poem" and speculated on how Bennelong's style responds to his time in England. Farrell describes his approach as one that "attends to the textual decisions effected by Bennelong, one that is partisan for Bennelong as an Aboriginal *writer*" (28–32).
16 See also the digitised "A.M Fernando Notebooks," *AIATSIS*, https://aiatsis.gov.au/collection/featured-collections/am-fernando-notebooks.

16

ORCHID TIERNEY

Writing the Body

Gay Liberation and Emergent Communities

In the mid-twentieth century, gay and lesbian poetry occupied a peripheral place in the mainstream Australian literary ecology, but international developments, coupled with significant shifts in social attitudes, encouraged the emergence of novel voices that foregrounded multifaceted identity and community formations. Dennis Altman noted in his foreword to the groundbreaking 1983 gay and lesbian anthology *Edge City on Two Different Plans* that LGBT literature had emerged from "a community of lesbians and/or gay men, which has only come into being in our lifetimes" (13). When compared to progressivism of the LGBT community in the United States, Australian gay and lesbian poets had few national models despite a flourishing gay commercial scene in Sydney and Melbourne in the late 1970s. To some extent, gay and lesbian poets were forced to become their own mentors and make their own manifestos. While it is possible to trace the presence of gay and lesbian writing after the 1788 invasion of Australia,[1] Altman's observation here stands for it gestures towards the steady consolidation of activist and literary infrastructures during the 1970s, which unravelled the stability of heteronormative literary traditions and categories of national identity.

Australian poets who emerged at the onset of gay liberation in the 1970s did so in a turbulent period of hostility and social reform. Following World War II, the so-called lavender scare had spread throughout the Australian federal government. Policies were enacted to weed out gay men in its ranks, who were seen as vulnerable to communist propaganda. Indeed, Colin Delaney, the one-time superintendent of police in New South Wales, called homosexuality "the greatest social threat" confronting Australia (Wotherspoon 113). As David K. Johnson notes, Australian security agencies, like their British and Canadian counterparts, employed American anti-gay practices in order to maintain favourable connections with officials in the United States (133). Anti-gay policies later entailed the aggressive policing of gay men, who frequented local beats (Willett 10). Moreover, successive governments actively censored books, magazines, films, and plays that hinted at homosexual content until the late 1960s and reportedly well into the 1970s (Willett 13). In other words, being 'out' for gay and lesbian writers meant navigating legal barriers that overshadowed attempts to build coalitions between social reform and literary groups.

The push for legal reform did not exist in a political vacuum but was part of a wider decentralised movement of social reckoning that was reflected throughout Australian literary culture. The liberalisation of attitudes towards the emergent LGBT community coincided with national and international developments. These included the slow decriminalisation of homosexuality in Australia starting from 1975; second-wave feminism; anti-racist, environmental, and anti-Vietnam demonstrations; and the publication of Dennis Altman's *Homosexual Oppression and Liberation* (1971), which offered a vocabulary for gay and lesbian coming-out narratives (Calder 6). The Stonewall Riots in Greenwich Village, New York, on 28 June 1969, also galvanised the gay liberation movement in Australia as it did the United States. While it is difficult to trace openly gay and lesbian writers prior to 1970, this date also proves to be a major turning point in the history of a visible LGBT literary community. The Sydney-based group Campaign Against Moral Persecution, or CAMP, formed in 1970 and was one of the first LGBT groups in the country to actively pursue the reform of anti-gay laws. The group also produced *CAMP Ink*, an irregularly printed newsletter from 1970 to 1977. *CAMP Ink* typically published polemical essays on reform but the magazine also included poetry from 1972 under editor Stefanie Bennett (Fisher 2). The poems were often erotic or sapphic in content and were clearly secondary to the newsletter's political agenda, but they also underscored an attempt to appeal to a wider literary readership.

Although marginal in the literary marketplace, a small number of gay and lesbian poets were beginning to publish openly in independent presses and little magazines in Australia and abroad against this backdrop of social reform. David Malouf's *Bicycle and Other Poems* (1970) and *Neighbours in a Thicket: Poems* (1974) set him up to become a major figure of the quotidian and homosocial aesthetics. Dorothy Porter's *Little Hoodlum* (1975) explored open lesbian desires that intersected with illicit, Christian, and pagan undertones, while playwright Laurence Collinson published homoerotic poems in *Hovering Narcissus* (1977). Pam Brown's *Selected Poems 1972–1978* indexed the countercultural desires of the period that underscored a refusal of social conformity: "all the time," she writes, "i was wearing / the kind of shoes / that being alive / makes so dirty" (17). Brown's rebellious poetry is typical for it documented the period's permissive drug and sex culture that sexual liberation and the growth of mass media nurtured: "we sat / collating pornographic magazines / me stoned on snow /and wanting Andy Warhol" (29).

Early poets such as Porter, Brown, and Lee Cataldi, who published *Invitation to a Marxist Lesbian Party* in 1978, signalled an open commitment to a socially inflected poetics that broke away from notions of heteronormative respectability to favour erotic pleasures and private feelings. The personal, in other words, was political, although this focus on private sensuality did not preclude grappling with a broader scope of subjects relating to Australian national identity, as well as mobilising the pastoral and avant-garde experimentalism to critique gay discrimination or explore the quotidian. Emerging poets, such as Javant Birujia, Denis Gallagher, Paul Knobel, and joanne burns, did not summarise a singular vision of what it meant to be gay or lesbian in Australia during this moment, but their poems did evince a colloquial and defiant voice in lyrical, confessional, and experimental modes that competed with the masculine heteronormative poetry in the Australian literary tradition.

Michael Hurley notes that "[w]hile much of the early community-based discussion of Australian gay and lesbian writing and publishing configured it as separate from, if not excluded by, mainstream publishing, this discussion was largely concerned with the publication of fiction and anthologies, particularly coming-out narratives" (50). Indeed, gay and lesbian writing that entered public forums generally took the form of fiction, although poetry and writings on gay and lesbian poetics did circulate in print venues during what Bill Calder calls the "golden era" for LGBT media after 1970, and these – often short-lived – little magazines need to be considered alongside the emergence of gay and lesbian poetry (xi). *Gay Changes* (1977–79), *Gay Community News* (1979–82), and *Gay Information* (later rebranded as *Journal of Gay Studies*) (1980–87) were notable examples where the literary and activist circles intersected. For example, Dave Sargent, who edited *Gay Community News*, was a fiction writer as well as a poet. On at least two occasions, *Gay Information* printed articles on American and British gay, lesbian, and feminist poetry that uncovered a hidden history of LGBT writers, who were otherwise excluded from heteronormative national canons.

Small presses and little magazines proved to be important early networks for writers like Sargent who entwined literary activism with infrastructure building. Despite modest beginnings, by the 1980s gay and lesbian poetry was experiencing a minor – but growing – circulation due to these foundational efforts. In 1980 the Sydney Gay Writers Collective published a pamphlet collection of poetry and fiction, *InVersions*, followed by

InVersions 2 in 1981 under the organising efforts of Margaret Bradstock, Gary Dunne, Louise Katherine Wakeling, and Dave Sargent. At the outset, *InVersions* foregrounded a gay and lesbian culture that was defined by a spectrum of human activities. As the editors noted in the first issue: "Living in a capitalist society organised in ways that directly oppress us has strengthened our resolve to express our versions of the way things are, and by so doing set homosexuality firmly into the context of human behaviour" (n.pag.). Highlighting an LGBT culture privileged a nuanced engagement with private erotic life, intimate sensuality, and popular culture over explicit sexual connections. By the time the Sydney Gay Writers Collective published *Edge City on Two Different Plans*, Gary Simes identified a subtler tone of a nonsexual gay experience in LGBT poetry after "the remorseless detailing of sexual encounters" (33).

The late twentieth and twenty-first century witnessed a clearly visible presence of LGBT literature as gay and lesbian poets entered mainstream publishing. In 1987 Laurin McKinnon and Jill Jones founded BlackWattle Press, which promoted established and emerging gay and lesbian voices. Jones and McKinnon simultaneously published *cargo*, a journal that alternated between gay and lesbian writing, from December 1987 to January 1993. BlackWattle Press published a varied catalogue of poetry along with fiction, including Ian MacNeill's *TV Tricks and Other Poems* (1989), Denis Gallagher's *These Tattoos: A Personal Miscellany, 1975–1990* (1990), Margaret Bradstock's *Flight of Koalas* (1993), and Chris Jones' erotic verse novel *The Times of Zenia Gold: A Verse Novel* (1992). The press closed in 2006 with McKinnon and Gary Dunne moving the catalogue and infrastructure online under the banner of gay-ebooks.com and later lesbian-ebooks.com. Here, they distributed the lesbian and queer magazines *Flaunt* and *Perverse Verse*, the latter of which was associated with the now regular Mardi Gras festival and the Sydney Feminist Bookshop's queer reading series. These digital magazines published poetry by a variety of new writers, such as Kate O'Brian, Ray Tyndale, Michael West, Bronwyn Winter, and Uma Kali Shakti. Neither magazine had a consistent editorial voice, and poetry typically varied in form and topics although love, romantic relationships, break-ups, or critiques of heterosexism often fell under the lens. More importantly, a rapidly pluralising LGBTQ+ community was migrating into digital spaces and identifying new audiences beyond their immediate sociogeographic literary scenes.

The 1990s and 2000s saw more deliberate anthologising of a now diversely networked community of LGBTQ+ poets with mixed genre publications such as *The Exploding Frangipani: Lesbian Writing from Australia and New Zealand* (1990), *Pink Ink: An Anthology of Australian Lesbian and Gay Writers* (1991), *Sappho's Dreams and Delights: The Australian Anthology of Lesbian Poetry* (2001), and *The Penguin Book of Gay Australian Writing* (2002). Robert Dessaix's editorial agenda in the 1993 Oxford edition of *Australian Gay and Lesbian Writing: An Anthology* included work containing gay themes by non-gay contributors, which suggested that LGBT identity was predominately performative. Underlying this approach was the question 'what is a gay text?'

Later anthologies pushed back on including work by non-gay poets and instead broadened the spectrum of LGBTQ+ poetry to recognise the intersections of situated experiences with regards to other markers of identity such as class, race, ethnicity, and location. *Out of the Box: Contemporary Australian Gay and Lesbian Poets* (2009), edited by Michael Farrell and Jill Jones, for example, underscored the queer expansion of gay and lesbian poetry with the inclusion of work from early figures such as Pam Brown, Kerry Leves, Paul Knobel, Denis Gallagher, and Margaret Bradstock to newer figures in the community such as Michael Farrell, Peter Rose, Susan Hawthorne, Martin Harrison, Kate Lilley, Chris Edwards, Wendy Jenkins, Keri Glastonbury, and Jenni Nixon, who began their careers in the late 1980s, 1990s, and early 2000s. The *Out of the Box* anthology was notable for a historically informed editorial approach that illustrated the influence of queer theory on an expanding acronym of LGBTQ+ identity. Poems in the collection, for example, speculated on variegated formations of gender and embodiments while anticipating that the queer experience meant reworking public life with the view that sexuality did not necessarily define queer identity. The anthology predicted a dramatic shift of the queer horizon whereby the unstable subject – the incoherent 'I' – defied expected performances of identity for its own sake. As Kate Lilley later wrote in the 2018 LGBTQIA+ special issue of the nonfiction poetry journal *Rabbit*: "I never really came out / just started turning up with lesbians" (124). If gay and lesbian poetry had now entered mainstream publishing as marketable commodities, *Out of the Box*, and subsequent collections by LGBTQ+ poets, speculated upon what these changes might mean for inclusive queer identities within a receptive literary market.

Concurrent Developments

Even before the emergence of queer theory, however, a defiance towards gender essentialism had long been integral to the development of gay and lesbian voices since the 1970s. The formation of an open lesbian identity saw the articulation of both butch and femme expression that challenged ideas of rigid positionalities in the poetry community. Specifically, the 1984 dual author anthology, *Small Rebellions*, by Louise Katherine Wakeling and Margaret Bradstock, exemplified this rejection of stable gender binaries. Wakeling and Bradstock attended to polymorphous embodiments through their exploration of hermaphroditism, androgyny, and feminine-embodied masculinity in cross-dressing icons such as Isabella Eberhardt and Pope Joan:

> the spoors
> of female saints led me
> to monasteries where women lived as monks (anticipating Origen
> who said that on the last
> flamboyant day we women
> would be changed to men) (31)

Lesbian poets pushed against the perceptions of gender reductionism and biological determinism while gesturing towards the representational interests they shared with straight feminist writers, who sought to recover a lost history of female poets. Still, frustrations towards the explicit erasure of lesbian voices underlay the representational politics in anthologies such as *The Exploding Frangipani* and *Sappho's Dreams and Delights*, which engaged with women's quotidian experiences at the crossroads of race, class, and nation-state. These anthologies overtly resisted the invisibility of same-sex desire and female subjecthood that contrasted sharply with the experiences of gay male poets. As Cathy Dunsford and Susan Hawthorne wrote in their introduction to *The Exploding Frangipani*, lesbian poets "resist the temptations of passing as heterosexual or of accepting the rules of the dominant culture" (9), a point reiterated in Linda Weste's poem in the collection: "who / will / represent us except us" (55).

The 1980s and 1990s saw a flush of new work in lyrical, autobiographical, confessional, and narrative registers from poets such as Susan Hampton, Carolyn Garrish, Susan Hawthorne, Jenni Nixon, Lynne Jennings, Kate James, Sandy Jeffs, Maralyn Rush, Beatriz Copello, Jill Jones, and Tricia Dearborn who, with Debra Hely, was a founding member of Sydney's OutWriters (1995–2000). Dorothy Porter's verse novels, *Akhenaten* (1992), *The Monkey's Mask* (1994), and *What a Piece of Work* (1999) undertook a long form view of what might constitute a lesbian narrative voice. *The Monkey's Mask*, an erotic crime thriller, centred on a lesbian private investigator solving the murder of a university co-ed, brought Porter considerable national and international success. In the same narrative vein, Gillian Hanscombe's 1992 collection *Sybil: The Glide of Her Tongue* and Susan Hawthorne's *Cow* (2011) and *Lupa and Lamb* (2014) explored the conditions of lesbian representation by empowering a herstory of women's literary traditions and mythologies through lyric modes and archival practices. As Hanscombe's *Sybil* laid bare: "Only dykes are proud of other dykes. People say live and let live but why should we?" (7). Long poems and poem sequences invoked not only a lesbian intellectual history by exploring mythologies, iconographies, and archives, but they also tested the limits of lyrical poetry, revealing that lesbian poets were just as invested in experimental aesthetics as their male counterparts.

It is clear that by the late twentieth century gay and lesbian poetry was yoking upon variegated literary traditions and participating in broader conversations about language, discourse, and embodiment. Two notable examples are Tricia Dearborn's *Frankenstein's Bathtub* (2001) and *Autobiochemistry* (2019), which offered an intervention into the masculine voice of Australian poetic identity. For example, "The Pouch of Douglas" in *Frankenstein's Bathtub* interrogates masculine physiological discourses that imposed the medical gendering upon reproductive organs. The science-informed nature of the collection undertakes a clinical inspection of physical and mental constitutions: "My memory still retains the whir and clink of magnetic stirrer, the acrid-sweet smell of oven-dried mould" (13). Other poets such as Stuart Barnes, Peter Rose, Michael Farrell, Martin Harrison, and Jill Jones brought to the fore an observational lens to their work that expressed complex portraits of the self in society and drew on the poets' provisional relationships to their situated realities. Jones' later works *A History of What I'll Become* (2020) and *Wild Curious Air* (2020), for example, represent the heterogeneous contours of LGBT voices that engage authoritatively with alienating assemblages of human experience: "Even when the mind / is homeless / the world is there real and difficult" (*A History* 77). Here, Jones reveals an interest in the ordinary that renders legible the overly familiar aspects of the everyday, often foregrounding the way that natural surroundings mirror an inner emotional world: "I hold my thoughts / close to my disquiet, I hold my tightness like / a resistance, I'm not trespassing in the world, this / path is my own breath" (*A History* 24). If, by the early decade of the twenty-first century, gay and lesbian poetry had abandoned the private voice of sincerity, which had emerged as a result of early gay activism, these later experiments reflected mature engagements with everyday life as spaces for multiple contestations between the self and the world at large.

Queer Poetics

The emergence of queer theory and queer studies in universities in the 1990s reworked ideas about politics and private life as public, inclusive, disruptive, and general. The open field of queerness, as Eve Kosofsky Sedgwick then proposed, "is the open mesh of possibilities, gaps, overlaps, dissonances and resonances, lapses and excesses of meaning" (8). From the 1980s and 1990s, work by theorists such as Judith Butler, Michel Foucault, Gayle Rubin, José Esteban Muñoz, Leo Bersani, and Laurent Berlant encouraged a turn to queer life that re-examined gender performativity and stable categories of sexual identity. They also looked towards the gaps and disruptions in society where social justice might unfold. In more general terms, queer theory unpacked and recycled cultural encoding, sometimes to the point where it could be used to empower minority positionalities or short-circuit dominant identifications. Importantly, the emphasis on queer, bisexual, and transgender subjecthood encouraged deeper intersectional engagements across group interests with respect to markers of state power, economics, race, exile, and Indigeneity.

By and large immigrant, Asian, and First Nation LGBTQ+ poets – such as Andy Quan, Dîpti Saravanamuttu, Omar Sakr, Ellen van Neerven, Gemma Mahadeo, Gabriele Journey Jones, Janet Jiahui Wu, and Eva Johnson – have underscored hyphenated and/or plural positionalities to illustrate the cuts of national conflict, racial injustice, and displacement in the colonised or migrant subject. In the process, these poets have challenged the cohesiveness of national belonging and the construction of White subjecthood that has excluded marginalised LGBTQ+ poets of colour who live under political threats of state violence or exclusions from national canons. A notable example is Gomeroi poet Alison Whittaker, whose *Lemons in the Chicken Wire* (2016) and *Blakwork* (2018) highlight how queer bodies are politically produced as sites of colonisation and resistance. The poem "Whatcha," for example, describes normative body functions like menstruation that are socially performed as female with painstaking honesty:

> Whatcha bleedin' in the bath for, girl?
> Don't kid me, I can see it
> See, there, a clot near the drain 'ole
> And your cunt pashed the rim while you were shavin'   (*Lemons* n.pag.)

"Whatcha" dissects the excess of affect and gender codes through a simple refusal of exoticisation. Rather the colloquial, idiomatic, and vernacular voice engages with the ordinary messiness of the menstruating body that is further extended intimately and sensually in poems "-ING; -LY" and "The First Coolest Thing." At first blush, Whittaker's work demonstrates a familial undercurrent, one that can be viewed as both a departure from, and an extension of, the autobiographical impulses of earlier LGBTQ+ poets, who perused the content of their lives for socio-political commentary. *Lemons in* the Chicken Wire and Blakwork, however, centre inventive hybrid or mixed forms to invoke a discursive tone that challenges conventional lyrical modes.

Additionally, this queer experimentalism is vital for examining the urgent situated experiences of working class and/or First Nation communities. Whittaker's oeuvre envisions the queer body not as a self-contained entity but one entangled with other marks of positionality including labour, colonialism, and the environment. In "The Abattoir," for example, Whittaker connects the more-than-human body with human labour and embodied rituals:

> My Pop's on the offal floor, sends the lamb up to my father as a gift – dozens a day like so many traditions would do to acknowledge his entry into the family. This family, all wholesome harvesters of flesh crops. From oesophagus to anus – the body is scoured of any engine that would suggests a lived life, and passed on. (Blakwork 35)

Blakwork reveals that sociopolitical contexts cannot be disengaged from one's lived reality. Indeed, other poems in the collection, such as "Exhibit Tab" and "The Skeleton of the Common Law," address the outcomes of systemic racism, revealing that the personal isn't just political but a means for critiquing the mechanisms of empire and colonisation. In 2023, Whittaker and Steven Lindsay Ross published *NANGAMAY dream MANA gather DJURALI grow: First Nations LGBTQIA+ Poetry*. Demonstrating the diversity of voices in this first poetry anthology of the rainbow mob, Whittaker and Ross declare: "We dream of another possibility. We gather, build community and family with one another. And we grow until our voices echo all over the continent" (17).

Other LGBTQ+ poets have similarly used poetry as a medium for critique of the nation-state and community expression, including Omar Sakr with *These Wild Houses* (2017) and *The Lost Arabs* (2019), and Candy Royalle with *A Trillion Tiny Awakenings* (2018). Royalle (1981–2018), who was a spoken word performer and activist, brought a sharp sense of transgressive orality into her poems to throw social injustice into sharp light: "How can I / write about the sensation // of you and me in the night / hands clasped bodies tight / when colonists are experiencing // what the colonised have been living" (67). Similarly, in the poem "Do Not Rush," Sakr limns the dehumanisation of Arabic peoples who are reduced to their body counts and statistics in American bombing campaigns: "you can savage a body at speed" (*Lost* 252). For such poets, the poetic text is reconfigured as a medium for cultural inquiry into a fraught racist reality. The overall effects of such a manoeuvre are varied, but for Whittaker, Royalle, and Sakr, this poetics refuses not only nostalgic ideas about the contemporary Australian nation-state but also usefully critiques the idea of a coherent Australianness.

Embodied Poetries

Of the poets who have emerged at the turn of the twenty-first century are those for whom the text reveals intersections between theory, lexicality, and/or the performing body. Rather than foreclosing difference, contemporary collections by queer, transgender, and genderqueer poets illustrate deep investments with theorising embodiment within philosophical, feminist, cultural, and literary frameworks. Poets such as Rae White, Em König, and Quinn Eades represent in varying degrees this thematic concern that attends to the spaces where bodies and texts are both constructed. König's *Breathing Plural* (2020), for example, challenges normative reading practices as the textual arrangement of poems mean that pages literally have to be flipped upside down. Their poetry demonstrates a desire to dismantle gender and textual codes that enforce rigid norms, including conventions relating to acts of reading and writing. Yet of special note here is the nonbinary poet Rae White, who begins *Milk Teeth* (2018) with an epigraph from another queer poet, Alex Gallagher: "I'm tired of being broken by language / when it is the only safe place I've ever known" (n.pag.). Like Gallagher and König, White recognises the lexical sign as inherently transgressive, and their poetry playfully resists gender binaries and social algorithms often through the use of digital metaphors and references:

```
<!DOCTYPE cis-centric>
<optionvalue= "biological"> MALE </option>
<option= "TRUE">            female </option>
<option= "other">           404      404</not-an-option>
>>Gender not found<< (26)
```

The collection challenges how gender is "flagged" and "suspended," often requiring constant performances for validation (27). These performances strive against misgendering and misnaming, sometimes to the point of exhaustion:

> in truth, i'm just fucking tired
> of the marching, the crawling (see also : indulging) : see also :
>   exhausted / pooped / snoozed out
>   of the cis-tem & sick-to-choking
>   on yr systemic lasagne-layered revulsion
> let me try again :   (31)

White's style articulates the structural violence in a society where transgender rights are not yet guaranteed in all aspects of legal and social life. The role of social media in *Milk Teeth* requires special mentioning for White's idiosyncratic language and punctuation reflects how Twitter/X and Instant Messaging disperse one's identity throughout online and offline spaces. This coalescence of digital and vernacular language forensically comments on the ways that social media have transmitted and authorised microaggressions towards transqueer and nonbinary bodies. Of course, LGBTQ+ poets are not universally participating in such resistant poetics that only refute transphobic discourses. But it is clear that White eschews ordinary stable arrangements of language through linguistic experiments to deconstruct reductive notions of gender and subjecthood in a very contemporary context.

Also observable in twenty-first century LGBTQ+ poetry is a turn to autotheory, whereby the body is construed as a map for intertextual and theoretical intervention. Indeed, *Cordite*'s 2018 Transqueer issue, edited by Stuart Barnes and Quinn Eades, frames transqueer poems as "poem-bodies" to order to attend to the abundant ways the textual body informs the body of the poet and vice versa. Taken seriously, "poem-bodies" suggests that acts of writing and reading produce one's sensations of embodiment and by extension positionality. This idea is legible in Eades' work, which richly highlights the academic interest in autotheory, which has shaped recent hybrid collections. As an illustration, Eades' *Rallying* (2017) was written alongside his hybrid autobiography *all the beginnings: a queer autobiography of the body* (2015). The poems are, on the one hand, self-reflective. *Rallying* accumulates – or, as the title suggests, gathers – the poet's former names and experiences of girlhood, sex work, addiction, love, birth, parenthood, and children that build up a repository of tactile sensory embodiments, including skin-to-skin contact, bruising, pain, trauma, and joy: "she learns how to bruise bleed her knuckles by slamming her left fist into fences and walls" (15). On the other hand, Eades' projects treat the body as multiple theoretical and intertextual encounters. Naturally, feminist Lacanians like Hélène Cixous are vital to his approach towards analysing embodiment, which is eventualised through the acts of writing:

> When I speak about the writing body, I am not only speaking about the hand that holds my pen, or the fingers that tap down on these keys. When I speak about the writing body, I am saying that text, that written thing, the signifier and the signified, comes out of me and I situate myself, not in the grey mass that resist in the cup of my skull, but somewhere lower down. (*Beginnings* 67)

In other words, writing, for Eades, produces the body through text, a point that Eades frequently reiterates throughout his current oeuvre: "She imagines what it would be like, to write. To make text. She picks up her pen. She writes that she is trying to write" (*Rallying* 17).

One way to understand Eades' work then is to apprehend the ways in which his writing refuses to segregate embodiment and composition. This means his work is remarkably frank with regards to his expressions of pain, trauma, and illness. Wounds and gaps are concurrent themes. "When bodies write (and particularly when wounded bodies write)," as he proposes, "they will use the language of the body to touch on sense. They will protest against the 'unspeakable,' the 'limit,' and the 'impossible' by speaking" ("Queer Wounds" 192). Eades' poetics refutes reductionist narratives of embodiment, but rather evidences examples of pain or interruptions for which there is no easy language:

> You bloom, necrotic, spotted, carrioned.
> Dead egg carrier you torse, you double, you
> shout at the tear that is my
> groin back ribs leg knee
> throat back back back back back.
>
> He can't find you. They talk
> about us in third person not knowing
> we are fourth person poetic split by pain.
> They want to send us home.   (*Rallying* 109)

Poetry, or writing more broadly, is not a recuperative or healing act. Rather Eades' poems demonstrate the role that violence, pain, and trauma – as well as joy and pleasure – play in fragmenting a subject's cohesiveness. The overall effect of this politics is a retooling of poetry to render legible unstable and discursive forms of embodiment to articulate trans autonomy and identity. Contemporary trans and genderqueer poetics might be described as one that combines aesthetics and politics in projects exploring difficult, painful, *and* joyful embodiments, not as a form of testimony but rather as a means to articulate what has been left unsaid.

Eades' poetics also gestures to the representation of the body as multiple encounters, whereby queerness, disability, and illness strain against what Robert McRuer calls "compulsory able-bodiedness" (2). In his poem "ash and breath," Eades describes bushfire smoke accumulating in his asthmatic lungs: "I try not to think about particles, / my inflamed lungs" (*Rallying* 105). Given the history of pathologising both, any discussion of the intersections between queer and crip embodiment comes easily. Whereas the medical model of disability views disabled bodies as defective, which necessitates cure, a social model of disability makes a clear distinction between physical or cognitive impairments and the social dissonances that prevent community participation, accommodations, or access. In this light, it is possible to see that both queer and crip theory challenge discourses of normativity and foreground the conditions of social and political life that are acted out on the body.[2]

The role of poetry then in articulating a social model of disability is a significant one. American disabled poets have long applied a crip or disabled poetics to critique of ableism in public and private life. Such a trend might seem obvious, but it is also a relatively recent one. In 2007 Jim Ferris was among the first to propose that crip poetry "demonstrates an awareness of sensitivity to the body which may not be unique to poetry with a disability aesthetic but is certainly present" ("Crip Poetry"). Scholars such as David Mitchell, Eli Clare, Michael Davidson, and Rosemarie Garland-Thomson have laid out frameworks for engaging not only the aesthetics of disability but also the extent that the 'body-mind,' to use Eli Clare's term, is an entanglement of values, mobilities, and desires that migrate across other identifications (*Brilliant Imperfection* xvi).[3] Accordingly, health and access have multiple valances and lived realities, which poets have sought to represent.

Yet in Australian literature, disabled poets have been poorly represented within any canon. Of course, not every disabled poet has engaged with identifications of the body. A case in point is Lex Banning (1921–65), who wrote playful, witty, and romantic poetry that rarely touched his experiences with cerebral palsy. To some extent, the early history of disabled poetry is harder to trace, largely due to the instability of disability and illness as categories of identity. People naturally acquire disability and illness with varying proximities over their lifetime. Still when treated broadly, poetry engaging with, or responding to, disability or chronic illness has assumed a small presence in the literary field, although this work is generally hard to categorise. While recognising that illness, disease, and disability do not necessarily overlap, notable early examples include Denis Gallagher's 1987 anthology *Love and Death: An Anthology of Poetry and Prose*, which responded to the impact of the AIDS pandemic on the gay community. Additionally, Sandy Jeffs' collections *Poems from the Madhouse* (1993), *Chiaroscuro* (2015), and *The Mad Poet's Tea Party* (2015) engage the poet's lived experiences with schizophrenia. Other important anthologising efforts include the 2016 special issue Writing Disability in *Southerly* and the 2019 DIS issue of *The Australian Poetry Journal*. Guest-edited by Jennifer Harrison and Andy Jackson, DIS included poets writing across the spectrum of disability and illness, such as Quinn Eades, Rae White, Claire Gaskin, Sandy Jeffs, Fiona Murphy, and Kerri Shying. Finally, the 2017 anthology

Shaping the Fractured Self: Poetry of Chronic Illness and Pain, edited by Heather Taylor Johnson, is one of the first literary publications dedicated to chronic illness with poems by Susan Hawthorne, Stuart Barnes, Rachael Mead, Peter Boyle, and Kevin Gillam.

Emma Rees suggests that "[w]riting the body always necessitates an approximation due to the insufficiency and contingency of the raw linguistic materials" (5). And this is true in poetry, where metaphor, metre, sight, sound, and performance place physicality and able-bodiedness at the centre of meaning making.[4] Consequently it is worth considering the manoeuvres by which a disability poetics in Australia has challenged notions of body-mind normativity and enacted alternative forms of expression, either formally or experimentally. Andy Jackson's *Immune Systems* (2015) and *Music Our Bodies Can't Hold* (2017) exemplify an aesthetics that uses a variety of forms – couplets, haiku, tercets, ghazals, and personae – to stage larger questions about disability, society, and medical systems. Specifically, *Immune Systems* attends to medical tourism in India and the medicalisation of the body. The poems are intimate and personal, although Jackson takes care to tell the reader that they are also "fictional and true" (*Immune* 59). In "Ghazal of the Body" the poet uses formal techniques to play out complex social interactions in India's medical system:

> There's no easy way of knowing if that man's prone body
> will ever move again. An answer stiffens in your body.
> Girlish yearning from a distant, scratch radio. Again,
> as you try to walk past, a man's arm pressing your breast.   (*Immune* 48)

Instead of repeating 'body,' the ghazal however disrupts reader expectations by naming a body part at the end of each couplet – "faces," "limbs," "leg," "teeth," "flesh," and "skin." Coupled with a semi-regular medial caesurae and the second person point of view, the ghazal's speaker enforces a subtle clinical undertone, which jars against the poem's intimacy with the humanity of other subjects: "*Biscuit?*... she pleads again, / wrapping all her limbs around the pillar of your leg" (48; emphasis in original).

Regardless of the condition of truth – or the truthiness – of his poems, *Immune Systems*, like *Music Our Bodies Can't Hold*, demonstrates the ways in which bodies are constructed in medical systems or through interactions with pain and spectacle. In the latter collection, Jackson undertakes a series of portraits or personae of people, who have, or were speculated to have, Marfan syndrome, a disorder of the connective tissues. Arising from interviews and research, the persona poems navigate polyvocality and distance, while producing portraits that reflect variation of experience and affect with the disorder. In the poem "Tal" the speaker draws an analogy between poetic structure and the heart that unravels the embodied normativity of both literary form and the body:

> To reinforce the fraying structure
>   of your own heart sounds like a problem
> of poetry, but it's more about plumbing,
>
> wrapping a garden hose with tape. (*Music* 71)

The variety of voices in Jackson's poetry underscores the resistance to ableist discourses that uphold exemplary disabled figures who have 'triumphed' or 'endured' their respective disabilities or illnesses. Rather he foregrounds the lived body that navigates inclusive representations including its ordinariness: "I'm living a life so normal / all the usual banalities have crowded in" (*Music* 72). Such a tone should remind us that minority identity formations – and by extension communities – are dynamic cultural spaces that cannot be reduced to singular articulations of autonomy or ideas about what constitutes the insular Australian 'body.' In the second decade of the twenty-first century, embodied poetries such as Jackson's are staging complex questions about how cultural systems, including medical care, are inscribed on fluid body-minds. If gay and lesbian poetry in the 1970s cultivated a countercultural discourse centred on sexual autonomy and sexual identity, advances in contemporary LGBTQ+ and disability poetry are instead gesturing to the idea that embodiment and Australian identity are even more decentred and individual than earlier poets may have realised. These embodied poetries have firmly rejected narratives that centre the non-disabled heteronormative body to the exclusion of other experiences.

Works Cited

Altman, Dennis. *Homosexual Oppression and Liberation*. 1971, University of Queensland Press, 2012.

"Foreword." *Edge City on Two Different Plans: A Collection of Lesbian and Gay Writing from Australia*, edited by Margaret Bradstock, Gary Dunne, Davy Sargent, and Louise Wakeling. Sydney Gay Writers Collective, 1983, pp. 12–14.

Atkinson, Graeme. *The Penguin Book of Gay Australian Writing*. Penguin, 2002.

Barnes, Stuart and Quinn Eades. "Introduction." *Cordite: Transqueer* no.88, 2018. http://cordite.org.au/essays/introduction-to-transqueer/.

Bashford, Kerry et al., eds. *Pink Ink: An Anthology of Australian Lesbian and Gay Writers*. Wicked Women Publications, 1991.

Bradstock, Margaret. *Flight of Koalas*. BlackWattle Press, 1993.

Brown, Pam. *Selected Poems 1972–1978*. Wild & Woolley, 1984.

Calder, Bill. *Pink Ink: The Golden Era for Gay and Lesbian Magazines.* Cambridge Scholars, 2016.
Cataldi, Lee. *Invitation to a Marxist Lesbian Party.* Wild & Woolley, 1978.
Clare, Eli. *Exile and Pride: Disability, Queerness, and Liberation.* Duke University Press, 2015.
— *Brilliant Imperfection: Grappling with Cure.* Duke University Press, 2017.
Collinson, Laurence. *Hovering Narcissus.* Overland, 1977.
Copello, Beatrix and Maralyn Rush, eds. *Sappho's Dreams and Delights: The Australian Anthology of Lesbian Poetry.* Bermac Publications, 2001.
Dearborn, Tricia. *Frankenstein's Bathtub.* Interactive Publications, 2001.
— *Autobiochemistry.* UWA Publishing, 2019.
Dessaix, Robert, ed. *Australian Gay and Lesbian Writing: An Anthology.* Oxford University Press, 1993.
Dunsford, Cathie and Susan Hawthorne, eds. *The Exploding Frangipani: Lesbian Writing from Australia and New Zealand.* New Women's Press, 1990.
Eades, Quinn. *all the beginnings: a queer autobiography of the body.* Tantanoola, 2015.
— *Rallying.* UWA Publishing, 2017.
— "Queer Wounds: Writing Autobiography Past the Limits of Language." *Talking Bodies: Interdisciplinary Perspectives on Embodiment, Gender and Identity,* edited by Emma Rees. Palgrave MacMillan, 2017, pp. 183–202.
Eng, David L., Judith Halberstam, and José Esteban Muñoz. "Introduction." *Social Text* vol.23 no. 3-4, 2005, pp. 1–17.
Farrell, Michael and Jill Jones, eds. *Out of the Box: Contemporary Australian Gay and Lesbian Poets.* Puncher & Wattmann, 2009.
Ferris, Jim. "The Enjambed Body: A Step Toward a Crippled Poetics." *The Georgia Review* vol.58 no.2, 2004, pp. 219–33.
— "Crip Poetry: or How I Learned to Love the Limp." *WordGathering* vol.1 no.2, 2007. https://wordgathering.syr.edu/past_issues/issue2/essay/ferris.html/.
Fisher, Jeremy. "Sex, Sleaze and Righteous Anger: The Rise and Fall of Gay Magazines and Newspapers in Australia." *Text* no.25, 2014. www.textjournal.com.au/speciss/issue25/Fisher.pdf.
Gallagher, Alex. *Parenthetical Bodies.* Subbed In, 2019.
Gallagher, Denis. *Love and Death: An Anthology of Poetry and Prose.* Print's Realm, 1987.
— *These Tattoos: A Personal Miscellany, 1975–1990.* BlackWattle Press, 1990.
Hanscombe, Gillian. *Sybil: The Glide of Her Tongue.* Spinifex Press, 1992.
Hawthorne, Susan. *Cow.* Spinifex Press, 2011.
— *Lupa and Lamb.* Spinifex Press, 2014.
Hurley, Michael. "Gay and Lesbian Writing and Publishing in Australia, 1961–2010." *Australian Literary Studies* vol.25 no.1, 2010, pp. 42–70.
Jackson, Andy. *Immune Systems.* Transit Lounge, 2015.
— *Music Our Bodies Can't Hold.* Hunter Publishers, 2017.
Jeffs, Sandy. *Poems from the Madhouse.* Spinifex Press, 1993.
— *Chiaroscuro.* Black Pepper, 2015.

The Mad Poet's Tea Party. Spinifex Press, 2015.
Johnson, David K. *The Lavender Scare: The Cold War Persecution of Gays and Lesbians in the Federal Government*. University of Chicago Press, 2004.
Johnson, Heather Taylor, ed. *Shaping the Fractured Self: Poetry of Chronic Illness and Pain*. UWA Publishing, 2017.
Jones, Chris. *The Time of Zenia Gold: A Verse Novel*. BlackWattle Press, 1992.
Jones, Jill. *A History of What I'll Become*. UWA Publishing, 2020.
Wild Curious Air. Recent Work Press, 2020.
König, Em. *Breathing Plural*. Cordite, 2020.
Lilley, Kate. "Etudes." *Rabbit: A Journal for Nonfiction Poetry* no.24, 2018, pp. 112–24.
MacNeill, Ian. *TV Tricks and Other Poems*. BlackWattle Press, 1989.
Malouf, David. *Bicycle and Other Poems*. University of Queensland Press, 1970.
Neighbours in a Thicket: Poems. University of Queensland Press, 1974.
McRuer, Robert. *Crip Theory: Cultural Signs of Queerness and Disability*. New York University Press, 2006.
Porter, Dorothy. *Little Hoodlum*. Poetry Society of Australia, 1975.
Akhenaten. University of Queensland Press, 1992.
The Monkey's Mask. Hyland House, 1994.
What a Piece of Work. Picador, 1999.
Rees, Emma. "Varieties of Embodiment and 'Corporeal Style.'" *Talking Bodies: Interdisciplinary Perspectives on Embodiment, Gender and Identity*, edited by Emma Rees. Palgrave MacMillan, 2017, pp. 1–15.
Royalle, Candy. *A Trillion Tiny Awakenings*. UWA Publishing, 2018.
Sakr, Omar. *These Wild Houses*. Cordite, 2017.
The Lost Arabs. University of Queensland Press, 2019.
Sedgwick, Eve Kosofsky. *Tendencies*. Duke University Press, 1993.
Siebers, Tobin. *Disability Theory*. University of Michigan Press, 2008.
Simes, Gary. "Gai Saber: Homosexuality and the Poetic Imagination." *Gay Information*, 1984, p. 33.
Sydney Gay Writers Collective. *InVersions*. Sydney Gay Collective, 1980.
Sydney Gay Writers Collective. *InVersions 2*. Sydney Gay Collective, 1981.
Wakeling, Louise Katherine and Margaret Bradstock, eds. *Small Rebellions*. Wentworth Books, 1984.
Weste, Linda. "Don't Let Them Teach You." *The Exploding Frangipani: Lesbian Writing from Australia and New Zealand*. New Women's Press, 1990, pp. 54–55.
White, Rae. *Milk Teeth*. University of Queensland Press, 2018.
Whittaker, Alison. *Lemons in the Chicken Wire*. Magabala Books, 2016.
Blakwork. Magabala Books, 2018.
Whittaker, Alison and Steven Lindsay Ross. "Introduction." *NANGAMAY dream MANA gather DJURALI grow: First Nations LGBTQIA+ Poetry*, edited by Alison Whittaker and Steven Lindsay Ross. Blackbooks, 2023, p. 17.
Willett, Graham. *Living Out Loud: A History of Gay and Lesbian Activism in Australia*. Allen & Unwin, 2000.
Wotherspoon, Garry. *City of the Plain: History of a Gay Sub-culture*. Hale & Iremonger, 1991.

NOTES

1 The Oxford *Australian Gay and Lesbian Writing* anthology attends to the thematic homosexual and homoerotic undercurrents of precolonial and early colonial Australian literature within the context of closed penal microcosms or male friendships associated with bushranging gangs. See particularly Dessaix at 3–8.
2 See Eng, Halberstam, and Muñoz; Siebers; and Clare, *Exile and Pride* and *Brilliant Imperfection*.
3 For a description of body-mind and its relationship to the ideology of cure, see Clare, *Brilliant Imperfection*.
4 See Ferris, "The Enjambed Body."

17

JOHN KINSELLA

Not the Poem Alone

In Medias Res

Rejecting a Category

To 'witness' the country's beauties and corrosions is not enough. To deploy the word 'decolonise' is too often a misdirection, whereby 'eco' poets substitute their own acts of 'artistry' for action. Poetry can be incisive, organic, respectful: it can call out wrongs; but this is simply not enough. To intervene as poets means to make poetry disposable in place of what are not: ecologies. Ecologies require duration beyond the life of the 'poem' but ecologies are also implicated as songs. Each cycle of ecopoetic engagement has its keywords that tick off theoretical justifications and virtues while the poem is still trying to be the poem. The problem with ecopoetry is that it's *about* the poems and their making, not about a poetry of ecological protection in which the poem is one of many interventions.

There has always been ecological poetry; entwining 'song' and ecologically oriented living is a basic premise for many Indigenous cultures who don't have to call what they are doing 'ecopoetry.' What names itself as ecopoetry is typically a response to Western capitalism and an extension of consumer guilt. Poetry is an incredibly effective tool in challenging consumer rapacity, but in celebrating its own capacity, it risks contributing to the very system of destruction it opposes. Poems may advocate protection, respect, and intervention, but if they fetishise the worth of their own aesthetic categories, they are easily absorbed into the market logics of purely aesthetic value. The poem and its purported advocacy is thus compromised, with benefit accruing to the poet rather than the environment. A chapter within a *Cambridge Companion* risks behaving in this way as well, performing a role within the colonialist epistemic and aesthetic hierarchies of the Western academy. Further, and as I have argued elsewhere ("Argonautica"), the 'ecopoem' arising out of a Western guilt-corrective will inevitably lose meaning or even be read against its intention as times change, context shifts, and language alters meaning. If a poem lacks a sense of collective/communal deep connectivity, one that works through layers of time, it often separates off from that it purports to care about and act for. It is, of course, better to act than not act, but a consciousness of the temporal limitations of colonially embellished language seems essential.

The separation of aesthetics from cause and effect seems essential in order to let the poem act as intervention and yet resist fetishisation: when 'I' am gone, the ecology must continue, and 'my' poems are irrelevant beyond their application. But although poetry's meaning changes across shifting contexts, we habitually seek to fix it within a framework that sustains meaning. However, an activist poem is of its moment and ephemeral beyond its application therein. Which is not to say a poem doesn't keep having moments and applications, but rather that they are different. This is why I feel copyright – even 'authorship' – is irrelevant: the poem I wrote to try to protect Walwalinj fifteen years ago is not the poem I must write now, though that earlier poem may be redeployed, made relevant in the now via others' resisting.

To be clear, that doesn't mean I don't think cultural permissions shouldn't be observed – I do. Rather, as a product of the colonial machine, as a poet who enacts a poem as a moment of resistance, I feel I have ceded rights of 'authorship' to the needs of that moment, and future moments. Attention to the complex relationship between respect for, say, Aboriginal 'ownership' of (or relations of co-ownership with) Country, and my disrespect for all notions of property, land ownership, or 'survey,' is necessary to process the contradictions of working to protect bushland that is neither mine to speak over or of, and yet, without my contribution, my poetic and physical (pacifist) intervention might be erased before other resistances can intervene.

While Yamaji poet Charmaine Papertalk Green and I are friends, and that friendship exists in its own terms, we are also poet activists, with a strong shared commitment to resisting the rapacity of mining companies. Our collaborative technique is based on conversation, and 'yarning,' and always works towards trying to find generative ways of rectifying the colonial imposition, of bringing justice for Aboriginal people. We are continuously attentive to or work through the complications of my coming from a particular settler 'history' (mid-nineteenth-century Irish famine escapees with a story of anti-English resistance), and Charmaine being a member of the Wajarri, Badimaya, and Nhanagardi Wilunyu cultural groups of the Yamaji Nation. We found a means of exchange that allowed for intactness of 'poetic voice' and culturality, as well as common purpose. Here are a few exchanges from *False Claims of Colonial Thieves* (2018), that enact an activism of common purpose through difference. I align mining with militarism, and Charmaine aligns colonial privilege with theft and rapacity:

Prologue
The stakeholders want their environmental scientists to deliver
flora and fauna on a platter, and they will do so for a price.
Stygofauna speak up through the land; some listen, more don't.

And so the mining companies reach into our schools,
funding programs that make students in their own image,
filling the holes they make in country with propaganda
sold as learning, gatekeeping into the church of university.
JK   (xi)

*

Prologue Response
Privilege blindness
if environmental scientists say so
water comes from a plastic bottle
what lies on or within country
cannot be seen for the
privileged are privilege blind
CPG   (xi)

Undermining

1

The king brown does not die from its own poison – within
its body, inert.

Uranium within the hold of old ground around Wiluna is
more than history. Leave it there. Intact.

The roo-tails sign the ground with making, and then they move on
and back until stopped in their tracks.

We try to find our way through the world avoiding reactors. Terms
of trade are weapons-grade.

Or see the range folding inwards, burst back out. Scrub, forests,
their contents. All gone. Hole.

Lure of the material – to conjure empathy out of furnaces. Giving
rise to religions honed as bayonets.

Quarry expanding to echo round owl rock its footing shaky and
mice sharp as shrapnel.
JK   (1)

*

> 2
> Balu winja barna real winja
> Real old ones them ones
> Old ground our country
> With ancient ones deep within
> Wrapped tightly away
> For the earth protecting
> Itself from itself knowing
> It can die from its own poison
> Earth's silver grey hair
> Elder belonging to a time
> When the earth was soft
> The little boy went to sleep
> Balu winja barna real winja
> Real old ones them ones
> Man is a greedy monster
> Interfering to satisfy self
> Pulling old ones to surface
> Birthing a dangerous little boy
> Naming after a god and
> Worshipping like a god
> For the warfare toys of
> Other little boys worldwide
> Energy, power, death, destruction and money
> Uranium is safe in the earth
> Like a sleeping Elder
> Balu winja barna real winja
> Real old ones them ones
> CPG (2)

The "Epilogue" from *False Claims of Colonial Thieves* is a specific act of protest participation on my part to save the Beeliar Wetlands on Whadjuk Noongar boodja (Country).[1] It is addressed by Charmaine via her lifelong protest against damage and injustice on her Yamaji barna (Country), contextualising both the colonial impetus of 'development' and the means of its redress by decolonising and restoration of organic systems of exchange with Country:

> **Epilogue**
>
> As the Beeliar bushland is mowed down
> and some of us who aren't traditional owners
> are also torn from the inside out, we look to those
> whose Boodja it is to take it back, to give it health.
> There can be no surrender of spiritual rights

in an agreement made by a government
using bargaining chips they stole
in the first place. Noongar land
yarning with all living things of the world
joined together: land, water, air, spirit.

*

Refuse to hit your head for sadness
Refuse to draw head blood for grief
Refuse to consider death of our land
This barna – our ancestors' land – our land
Exists as long as we exist to protect it
Farmers poison with fertilisers
Salt pans across the wheat belt country
Like seeping green, pink and white wounds
Miners blow up and steal country from country
Property developers bulldoze for urban sprawl
Most Bluff Point shell middens long gone
Consumerism demands highways
Engineers are agents of change – wetlands die
Shall I hit my head to draw blood
To drip into the barna and mix
Letting country know we care
That a sadness exists for settlers don't care
Our ancestors earth memories
Mingled within the grains of country
Are being removed and destroyed
Our old people's spirits are embedded
In a way colonisers can't understand
So I shall hum a lullaby and share a story
To soothe the hurt and pain down generations
A gentle whisper from the past
Visits me in my dreams
Or is it the future that I see
Why are we still invisible?
JK & CPG (144–45)

Charmaine and her community necessarily have an anti-colonial stance in all aspects of their everyday, and for me there's no choice – I have a responsibility to undo what I came out with all its contradictions. This is something I've written about extensively, and it is core to any ecological activism in Australia. Australia is Aboriginal and Torres Strait Island country, and no discussion of its well-being and environmental health can take place without acknowledgement, consultation, and respect for tens of thousands of years of knowledge-accumulation across the botanical, geological, astronomical, agronomical, hydrological, and all other branches of the sciences. And this science finds its organic, ever-expanding memory in the poetry of song, body, and visual expression, in its many forms.

In other words, when Charmaine writes a poetry of social and ecological concern, it is an expression of a knowledge with the deepest roots in place. It doesn't need to be called 'ecopoetry.' I don't see ecological poetry functioning as intervention without taking social rights, justice, and community issues into consideration. Charmaine's poetry of 'place,' which always involves such social-cultural considerations, might seem to epitomise the drives and needs of 'ecopoetry.' It doesn't. The label would be redundant, surely. Which brings us to the point: 'ecopoetry' is a colonial construct that doesn't wish to be colonial and displaces guilt through speaking of the health of natural environment/s. But it's also an act of desperation, as the biosphere collapses under broader human abuse, and reflects a desire to be part of a community of like minds resisting. This paradox allows 'ecopoetry' to exist as category, to reassure itself of its virtue and validate itself as actually 'doing something,' which too often resides in writing rather than doing, in consuming and writing against consuming, in talking the talk and not walking the walk, so to speak.

So, what I propose is an inclusive environmental poetry that doesn't produce waste and is biodegradable, useful as a growing medium, and committed. I acknowledge that while I have long contested the rubric and performative aspects of 'ecopoetry,' my poetry work has frequently been located within its nexus (and gained focus through comparative readings within this discourse). But while my poetry might seem located there, my activism very often (solely) isn't. The space to create a privileged category of poetics is antithetical to the necessity of acting, of being present at a site of protest. The category is a tag and not an act itself. And this is why I now more insistently eschew 'ecopoetics' as a collective act: I feel it is a distraction and lacks immediacy, breadth, and cultural nuance.

I acknowledge that every effort to verbalise a position against rapacity counts and is essential, and that poems written lamenting acts of rapacity, memorialising past acts of damage, and hoping people will listen and restrain their impetus to damage, truly matter. I am speaking in an essentialist way here because the moment demands it, and the stridency is an act of encouragement, almost to the point of compulsion. What I am insisting is that there's a place to doubt our purpose for writing poetry, even 'ecopoetry,' and that this questioning will possibly become part of a resolution to live less impacting lives, to act as we speak, write, poeticise.

Walwalinj/Mount Bakewell – Making the Poem of Protest *Now*!

Targeting natural habitat for their lifestyle entertainment, recreationalists are often as pernicious as miners: claiming to facilitate appreciation of 'nature,' they make arguments similar to those made by 'nature poetry' and 'ecopoetry,' underpinned by a neocolonial entitlement to enrich settler lifestyles through facilitating 'access/connection' to environmental beauty. Further, playing on European pastoral tropes, the 'wild spaces' that abut farmland (usually only uncleared due to 'difficult' topography or other usages such as railway or road reserves) are fetishised as places of 'health' and 'recreation,' of making contact with 'nature' within managed and orderly contexts. In Western Australia, the Western Trails Alliance is a non-profit mountain bike advocacy group which assists and implements the construction of biking trails through forests and bushland. At the time of writing this chapter, its webpage features a picturesque view of Walwalinj, or Mount Bakewell in the colonial renaming. It states that the Western Trails Alliance is working with private 'land owners' and the York Shire to build a series of mountain biking (and walk) trails through the only alpine wheatbelt habitat in existence.

This mountain, sacred to the Ballardong Noongar people, rises to 470 metres above sea level. The highest point in the vast wheatbelt, it holds bushland that should be a World Heritage Area but instead is being targeted for leisure-oriented exploitation in the name of adventure, health, lifestyle, exercise, and the local economy. A campaign against this destruction is gathering pace and as I am part of that, so is poetry. I have been writing poems about the region, and specifically about Walwalinj, all my life. My *Divine Comedy: Journeys through a Regional Geography* (2008) is based on the immediate location.

Over a decade ago, I submitted a long protest against a proposed Equine Precinct that sought to exploit the area, which was part of the success of efforts to limit its impact. This new version of leisure is even more incursive. Hang-gliding and paragliding leisurists have carved a launch area into the south-east crest of the mountain, and at the time they began their incursion I saw a trail bulldozed through the bushland that reached the area they now use. I checked with a government agency at the time, and no approval had been given for this destruction of natural vegetation. Nothing was done about it and the degradation has continued.

The top of the mountain is crowned by communication towers (the legs of Satan, as they are in my version of the *Comedy*), and are already damaging, but this opening is a whole new level. There is a Class 1 orchid up there that exists nowhere else in the world, and at least two Class 2 orchids. It is a refuge, a habitat.

The Ballardong story of its significance (Winmar) is readily promoted by non-Indigenous locals in York, though astonishingly little pragmatic acknowledgement of the impact of exploitation of the mountain is associated with that telling. Contesting the destruction of vegetation on the mountain is a matter of Ballardong rights, and in seeking to control the legal discourse around this, the Shire seeks to prevent challenge before it begins.[2] Though this is an interpolation outside the original timeline of writing this piece, it is worth noting the paucity of the Shire's response to traditional owner Dr Marion Kickett's lodging of a complaint in late 2022 on behalf of traditional owners:

> The Department of Planning, Lands and Heritage (the Department) has investigated the matter and found that breaches of section 17(a) of the Aboriginal Heritage Act 1972 and regulation 13(1)(a) of the Land Administration (Land Management) Regulations 2006 have been substantiated.
>
> In this instance a formal caution has been issued to the involved parties and noted in the Department's records. I can confirm that your complaint has been recorded in the Department's complaint management system   (reference CR-22-000482)

The result of these breaches was a mere caution. It is incumbent on all people who come into contact with the mountain and its environs to act on behalf of its traditional owners. Poems cannot be written, paintings painted, music composed in the vicinity of this place without the ongoing assault on a Ballardong sacred land. We might not be 'creating' about a particular place, but if we are in the ambit of that place then we are implicated in that place.

Without going into the legal 'nitty gritty' of the Western Trails Alliance's interactions with the Shire in order to gain control of the environment, I seek to show how poetry in Australia, even out of a colonial 'heritage,' can seek in real time (it's happening now) to undo the damage and prevent further damage being done without imposing a regime of 'management.' Here is my initial letter to the Shire on coming across the 'proposal'/'plan':

> Dear Shire President
>
> I wish to vigorously protest the plans to exploit the sacred and exceedingly rare and fragile environment of Walwalinj ('Mt Bakewell') as indicated by your declarations to the ABC. The mountain has already been placed under

> stress by clearing for 'recreational' as well as agricultural purposes, and the habitat will not cope with more stress. There are orchids so rare up there they exist nowhere else. The environment should be protected and not exploited, and its sacred essence respected.
>
> I have spent my entire life writing about the region and know the environment of the Dyott Range and surroundings intimately. This is a 'greenwash' act that claims 'nature tourism,' which would simply mean further degradation of a fragile and unique ecosystem.
>
> Cautious walking and care are one thing, but to 'open up' to mountain biking is to consign the bush to destruction. Recently talking on the email with an environmental officer regarding degradation of Perth Hills forests, they noted that the greatest damage came from mountain biking. This opens the door to so many abuses of the habitat. Walwalinj isn't a 'resource' to be 'capitalised' on. In a world suffering under the weight of such exploitation, surely an effort can be made to conserve rather than exploit?
>
> I ask you to reconsider and take this informed protest on board. I will certainly use all my energy, contacts and writing ability to protest this constantly. It is a wrong thing you are aiming to do.
>
> I will speak about this at every public opportunity I get in the wheatbelt, and that will be sooner than later – that is my responsibility, and I take it seriously.

Working my way through the laws and unlaws of Aboriginal heritage acts and attempts to have them altered, seeing the manipulation of definitions of environmental conditions by local, state, and federal government agencies, is to unfold how everyday laws of governance enshrine and enact an ongoing colonialism. Take the case of Class 'A' Reserve 6915 York (on Wongborel/ 'Mount Brown' – the hill across the valley which is part of a complex Ballardong story of young lovers being separated due to breaking taboos[3]) and the Shire's application to the state Department of Planning, Lands and Heritage to adapt the 'purpose' of the 'reserve.' In response, the Department insisted "that a change of purpose is not required as the suggested purpose 'Recreation' is ancillary to the current purpose of 'Parklands.'"[4]

Mountain biking trails require specific infrastructure and are far more impacting than the passive usage the Department has (with the risk of setting precedent) eroded their distinction from. When I objected to this erosion, the Department insisted that concerning itself with this difference "would be an expensive and timely process for the Local Government [which] was deemed to be unnecessary given the reserve is already used for passive recreation."

Not the Poem Alone: *In Medias Res*

As another who I am now working with has pointed out, no 'A Class' reserve can be used in a different way from its original gazetting without the approval of Parliament.[5] Adopting a flexibility of definition that disregards the varying impacts of 'recreational' activity in order to save itself the expense and effort of ongoing environmental consideration, the Department wields a dangerous power to set precedents that further erode and sidestep existing environmental legislation. This definitional flexibility makes the act of trail-making all the easier. Further, and more vitally, because the South West Land and Sea Council is forming an Aboriginal Regional Corporation for the York/wheatbelt region, it is not yet in place to respond collectively to the attempt to convert the sacred mountain to a leisure zone. This is glibly exploited by settler leisurists whose bureaucratic frameworks facilitate their opportunistic incursion onto the mountain, a place of millennial connection for Noongar people.

This is what I just wrote to a fellow activist in this hastily developing 'alliance':

> i will discuss with an elder, b. as that corporation isn't formed yet, we need more immediate points of contact. this is something that should be on hold until all elders and community can discuss it in THEIR way and thoroughly. it's being rushed to avoid this. it's culturally offensive as well as ecologically criminal.

The slippage whereby negotiating red tape leads to distorted forms of permission-getting is a definitive part of greenwash. In virtually the same way, the ecopoem can so easily become this – written as protest, the concern is the act of publication which detaches the poem from its activist impetus, becoming its own route to institutional acknowledgement, an act among peers for peer approval in which definitions of activism are shifted, and in that shifting, 'space' is potentially (and worryingly) opened for continuing exploitation. Poets aware of this slippage will then work within temporal considerations. The path to be read has to be quicker than a resistance can fail, which is difficult, but not if the poems are written *in situ, in medias res*, and read at the sites of invasiveness and destruction, or even printed on recycled paper and handed out in the real time of physical protest. I did this with James Quinton with our *The Other Report: Poems against the Destruction of the Beeliar Wetlands* during the Roe 8 Highway protests in 2016. Quinton wrote:

> **Bandicoot Burial**
>   after Slessor
> On the red North Lake Road foot path
> Convoys of protectors come
> At night they sing and chat by fire light
> But by morning the fight goes on.

> Inside the metal fence trappers catch bandicoots
> And birds, lizards, and snakes,
> When the heat cooks them in their prisons,
> Or a wheel masses their spine
>
> Someone, it seems, has time for this.
> To shoo off the flies, to examine the cadaver
> To show the body to the drivers,
> And turn a spade to open the sepulchre.
>
> This mulch cross, the flame tree drip line
> The fence strung with heart-shaped notes
> Written with such perplexity, with such bewildered pity,
> The words choke as they begin –
>
> *Protect this place* – the rainy texta
> Droops and fades, the purple drips,
> The breath of the bandicoot rises
> As quiet as gravediggers' lips. (JQ 9)

With its evocations of Kenneth Slessor's "Beach Burial," but also "North Country" and "South Country," Quinton's poem compares the damage done to animals as being akin to that done by humans to humans in war. Of course, the difference is that animals have no choice or ability to resist *at all*, en masse or as individuals, no means of countering. But Slessor's poem takes away all hubris in bringing the dead together, in their no longer contesting (if, indeed, as pawns in the greater game, they were in fact ever able to contest). The participants in war become the victims in war, but in being 'enlisted' are also drawn into the human imagining of perpetual conflict, as if there can be no peace. The animal is always conscripted into a conflict in which they can never win. Their agency is only ever a token of a colonial construct of 'nature' to be manipulated in ways that best suit state and capital.

Via Slessor, Quinton creates a broader almost pantheistic merging of human and animal spirits as a collective lifeforce under attack. The plea of the handwritten heart (these were attached to the fence around the woodlands being destroyed to make way for the highway extension, placed by people hurt and in pain at seeing the hurt and pain), is both poignant and also addresses the differing sides of the 'fight': one resists the violence of machinery and development, and the murder of the many animals the 'department' have gone in to 'save' and translocate, while the other commits these acts in systemic ways. The death and burial of a bandicoot, killed by the machinery of development (for the 'general good,' for 'our'? prosperity), shown to those who killed it, and buried, becomes the beyond-analogy, becomes the embodiment of protest.

Elegy is an act of the present regarding the past but we need to change the nature of elegy to also look towards the future. The instigators of death are invited to become witness to their own destructive acts. It's not a matter of we, the protestors, being witness (a useless process if it doesn't intend to disrupt the crime), but of the perpetrator's understanding their crime *in medias res*. James Quinton stayed in camp at the protest, dressed up in a cockatoo costume to highlight the killing of habitat, and enacted a presence under the supervision of Noongar elders. And this made the poem and poems because he was inside the poem of many voices.

My son Tim, a poet himself, struggled for a long time over the violence he saw and found poetry his only means of addressing the trauma. In my sequence of poems in *The Other Report: Poems against the Destruction of the Beeliar Wetlands* I wrote:

> **Accounts – to the Premier of Western Australia**
> I hold you accountable for the trauma our thirteen-year-old
> is going through as habitat for the birds he loves is destroyed.
>
> I hold you accountable for the emphysema of the biosphere,
> that gasp you add to our last gasps, deoxygenated, stranded by the road.
>
> I hold you accountable for the zoo of death, for the ark scuttled
> and going down with all hands on board, for survivors shot on the surface.
>
> I hold you accountable for helping boil the planet in its own oil,
> for encasing it in bitumen dredged from the pits of hell.
>
> I hold you accountable for making science a convenience store
> in which well-fed bullies stuff their baskets without paying.
>
> I hold you accountable for cruelty and torture, for casualties
> you don't acknowledge, for ignoring alternatives to feed your vanity.
>
> I hold you accountable for treating life as a game in which winner
> takes all, a psychology of childhood instilled by abusive adults.   (21)

The main point of the poem in the protests is its immediacy, its non-curatorial ephemerality and, at best, recyclability if it can be reinvented in other contexts and at different times as part of an act of respect and protecting (meaning it would have to become a different poem). So while a number of others are now becoming active and putting a lot of energy into this attempt to save the bushland of Walwalinj, I see my role increasingly in terms of finding the most 'suitable,' useful, and respectful poetic language I can to assist. This is not an issue of clarity, but effectiveness.

For example, parataxis's resistance to meaning, and destabilising or rejection of the unified voice, is often construed as a form of linguistic elitism, narrowing the possibility of reception and response, but this is certainly not my experience. At protest sites, it's the sound and even the movement of the body that has as much effect as the words themselves: the shape of the utterance is the driving force. The mixture of statement, colloquial chat, verbal play/disruption, and expression is what make the protest poem live in its moment. And then there's what one is trying to protect, often among the cacophony of counterprotest, machinery, police and so on – all noises indicative of or literally causing damage to the living bush.

So, I try to write poems of protest for different situations, and no matter what, emulate the organic nature of the place I am trying to protect: the sounds of the poems becoming part of the sounds of the bush. This crosstalking, this antiphonal movement between registering engagement with place and resistance to incursion, is something I have felt *in situ*, especially if I know a place well. From this point, as I feel a need to write a poem now, I am going to work through its making.

Contexts: First, I will distribute the poem among those others who are speaking out and loosely starting to work together. Secondly, later this month I have a shared session at the York Festival and I hope to read the poem then and speak my concerns. I am sharing the session with my photographer collaborator Will Yeoman, and we are doing our second presentation after staging an exhibition of poems and paintings at a York gallery at the beginning of 2020. So I am thinking of the photograph, but no specific photograph. Further, my mother lives at the base of Walwalinj, and I lived there with my family for many years before moving to another wheatbelt bush zone about ninety kilometres away. This familiarity is necessarily borne out of a history of farming colonialism, which ascribes to a version of memory tainted by self-justification. So, I need to disturb this proximity and not take it for granted.

The 'curatorial poem' is one that is primarily concerned with its own longevity, approval, and aesthetic validation, and, to my mind, these priorities are the greatest factor thwarting a poem bringing any real change, making any real challenge to a corrupt status quo. Presenting a poem in a curated situation cannot be allowed to drain it of activist purpose and energy. Indeed, this contradiction can be incredibly generative, but how it is weighted within the expression is pivotal in making those contradictions highlight discomforts and doubts in the listener. The mountain bike rider might be more open to these suggestions than the mountain bike trail advocates, and maybe even more so than anyone employed ('they have to make a living') to carry out construction work (and the same applies to miners, loggers, etc.).

Not the Poem Alone: *In Medias Res*

Figure 17.1 John Kinsella, "Graphology Botanical – Save Wheatbelt Habitat"

The poem has to offer degrees of access or maybe a range of access points even at its most rebarbative. A poem that 'tells' can be effective, but a poem that also suggests or questions (genuinely) its own perceptions is likely to resonate more intensely. Last week, as part of my thinking about how to write this poem (I write on a screen inside my head first off), I decided to do a Graphology drawing poem that would help me arrange concepts into shapes (Figure 17.1).

Now, for the textual, to-be-'spoken' poem, which is not paratactic in its syntax, but its suggestions might be. As further poems come as interventions, they are likely to be more paratactic, as urgency builds. If the rapacious succeed, the poem is irrelevant. If the rapacious are foiled, the poem might be adapted as a gesture encouraging vigilance against future attempts, future incursions.

The Euphemisms of Trails: Save Walwalinj from the Mountain Bike Trails Proposed by the York Shire and the Western Trails Alliance

> It all falls by waysides
> in naming 'prosperity' –
> *whose* is rarely in question
> because it's a state of being
> we can't afford to question?   *Thunderbird reacts!*

Wheatbelt 'alpine' seems
contradictory in the scouring,
but all definitions up for grabs
as vested parties push bikes
hard up the mountain:

parodying watershed,
parodying ley-lines,
parodying ecotones,
parodying lines of naming
parodying duration.   *Thunderbird reacts!*

Adrenaline's fallout
over orchids *so* rare...
last refuge, plethora, haven.
Life out of reach
infuriates
those who claim
what's not theirs to claim,
but they know the ins
and outs of colonial law.
Read the fine detail –

the letter, the clause ... *see
point* ... sub-sectioned.
Behind closed doors
it may seem to some
that Ballardong people

are a 'hurdle to clear' – a jump
on the path to stimulus. Protocols
written by ... see government
guidelines. See trails carved
out of a purple mountain.   *Thunderbird reacts!*[6]

Coda: In Medias Res

The last few days have been a flurry of activity that has first and foremost seen a family of Ballardong elders go physically into the Shire offices and both assert their traditional ownership of Walwalinj and Wongborel, and ensure the listing of Walwalinj on the heritage register. Further, they made clear their objection to the 'trails proposal' for the mountain. As many others become involved in the action, including botanists, members of the wildflower society, local environmentalists, and a former state premier, the movement to stop this wrong 'in its tracks' is gaining momentum.

What becomes clear is that a 'Class A' reserve such as that on Wongborel cannot have its usage changed without an act of Parliament, and that prior wrong usage doesn't validate present and future wrong usage. The Shire has, apparently, decided to place the 'crown land' usage proposal regarding the mountain on 'hold,' which is a major success for activists, but it seems to remain committed to the private land arrangement.

This has a long way to run and persistent commitment is required. As the propaganda of leisurism adjusts to a more 'rights conscious' social media environment, justification for eco-destruction increasingly comes via claims of 'health and well-being' which are going to have a very particular emphasis in a time of pandemic. To challenge their activities is portrayed as challenging health and well-being, the right to a satisfied life. But the argument is circular, if you see well-being as contingent on the health of the biosphere.

The activist poem becomes a site of ambiguities. Some are generative, some political, reflecting anxiety about its own (ambiguous) efficacy: the tension between these (see my *Beyond Ambiguity* (2021)) is the prosodic mechanism that aligns and realigns the disparate parts of syntax, figurative language, and the visual-sound devices of a poem. But they are not a poetics: a poetics is an action around the use of the poems, and this is what interests me as an activist. The poem has to have immediate impact as well as alternative modes of being read, and also reading the conditions it examines.

Chalice Mining and the Threat to Julimar Forest

Over the last decade there have been various attempts by mining companies to get a foothold in the Toodyay shire. There are (and were) already a number of gravel-mining and other 'excavating'-style operations, but the big drive has been for bauxite mining. Many locals were active against the bauxite grab, and though a company set up an office in town, they eventually left (see *Polysituatedness* (2017)). That doesn't mean the grab isn't possible in the future – it is, and sadly likely. Again, it's an ongoing action and there is never any 'winning.' If you think in military terms of 'campaigns' and 'victories' you will discover quickly that the rapacious are committed to strategic, drawn-out engagements.

More recently, and the greatest threat to ecologies here beyond farming/pastoralism (and its attendant philosophies and modes of living), is the discovery and pegging of deposits of nickel, copper, cobalt and platinum group elements by Chalice Mining near Toodyay. Sold as a green project because of the use of the metals in rechargeable battery technologies, this project has gained momentum through a *fait accompli*-style campaign of presence within the community. Working through the acquisition of private landholdings, Chalice Mining has also staked a portion of the great Julimar Conservation Park. This forest has already been stressed by four-wheel drive adventurism and over-prescribed burns. As the deposit reaches a depth of 850 metres, this is a chronic active situation.

Early in 2021 the WA State Government approved non-invasive exploration of the forest covering a massive area (26 km × 7 km), as step by step the process is moved towards destroying a massively diverse habitat of jarrah-marri-wandoo forest. The forest was logged until the mid-1970s, when, its ecological 'value' being so distinct, it was given protections. However, in 2000, the then state government moved to amend this management plan. The (Labor) opposition noted:

> The area has value for its flora and fauna and it has a high ecological rating. Obviously the Opposition supports this motion before the Parliament to amend the forest management plan to change the purpose of this forest zone. We note that the zoning given to this forest will allow the extraction of minerals, but we understand from a commitment given by the minister that as soon as the issue of prospectivity is sorted out, the region will become a conservation zone.[7]

Inbuilt in this was the demise of the forest. The word "prospectivity" is pivotal and its flexibility is grimly poetic. Law and its language is different from the poem, but it's similar. For example, a protest poem that has lacunae for the poet to live a life divergent from the proposed intent of the poem is de rigueur – we expect the poem to do its own work as it is part of language. However, protest poems easily become tools of dilatory evasion through this, and through the fetishisation of their value within literary criticism, which accrues aesthetic capital for the poem that separates it further from making any real concrete change.

Anthologising of 'environmental' poetry frequently deploys the same tactics – a 'wide range' (a good thing) becomes a justification for less 'radical' perspectives to be included via defining ecopoetry as a catch-all regardless of its interventionary intent. I experienced something like this the other day with the attempts to save the Walwalinj bush: a party who admires the bush but defends leisure activities in the zone said to others that they were wary of meeting me because I was a 'radical' who they feared would physically attack them.

I am a pacifist and do not believe in violent direct action. My anger is in my poetry, but I do not 'own' my poetry and it is ultimately not 'angry'; rather, it redirects the language we all use, drawing attention to the contradictions we all live by. Resisting the grabs for forest and bush that goes on in the name of 'clean energy' (a dubious expression that so often distracts from massive environmental damage and exploitation), in December 2020 I wrote the following poem of protest:

> **Villanelle of the Poisoned Chalice**
> Clean energy is sold as the mine over the forest,
> with all those clean miners and their clean equipment
> extracting glorious palladium, nickel copper and cobalt.
>
> These miners who love the biosphere who love the planet
> to its core, who love boldly at a time of pandemic, cement
> their greenish energy when proffering mine over forest.
>
> Who cares about wildlife when the planet can be a tint
> of electrical chemical fiscal green, who cares about a zone of plants
> as opposed to extracting palladium, nickel copper and cobalt?
>
> We've seen the companies come in before, promising to be clear and present
> in the local community – and 5000 bucks for the town's Christmas pageant
> convinces the locals that clean energy is a victory of mine over forest?
>
> And now the local press blooms like a rare orchid, a nest
> of rare birds – the company is worth 1.1 billion in the light
> of glorious palladium, nickel copper and cobalt.
>
> Counting their clean winnings as they bust habitat
> open via the stock market, calling on echidnas and dunnarts
> to help extract glorious palladium, nickel copper and cobalt,
> emitting clean energy as they'd grant us a mine instead of Julimar Forest.[8]

The Julimar region has been subject to a rush of mining exploration as Chalice Gold Mines' shares have skyrocketed in the wake of the company's test drilling for the rare metals demanded by global 'clean' energy markets in the area. The group has inculcated itself into the town, bought an historic homestead (and property) to conduct its operations from *in situ*, and fund local activities including, glibly, a wildlife rescue service. The media campaign back-engineers the mine into the local 'way of life,' casting it as incontestable reality.

Promising prosperity for the locals, and arguing that anyone contesting it is contesting well-being, such intrusion strangely mimics not only propaganda but the didactic protest poem as well. That's why as poet activists we need to disrupt easy reception at times, with a form of disarray that allows people (and nature) space to gather thoughts, even pause, and maybe change direction. Parataxis can shift momentum.

Taken from a long sequence entitled "Fortune" that contests versions of fortune, chance (via Mallarmé), fate, and happiness, such as that sold to us by developers/miners/imperialists, the following poem is part of many I have been working on as I process a connective approach to resisting this company. The "pit viper" refers to the Northern Hemisphere, never far from the rural local 'here':

> 26.
> No pit vipers here but language allows
> there is – descriptor nascent minecreep
> outside territory as pegged to collapse
> without the temporariness of antlions,
> evening blasts and shaky houses where trees
> huddle in own shade before deletion
> as bearers of poisoned chalices expect all-life
> to skulk to their templates. Hollowing out
> a Dante forest is no-forest far more terrifying
> as 'green energy' clean as a whistle over
> scraper diggers crawler haulers crushers
> all salt and battery pilgrimage to sustainable
> eviction of ecotonality and natural occurrences.[9]

These interventions are only 'interventions' and to my mind a poem can only ever be an 'intervention'. A poem has no quiddity, no purpose beyond that we put it to, and if it consents to a fetishisation for aesthetic value, it concedes its impetus as an intervention in the *now*, fails to act effectively against rapacity, greed, and incursions into country. This is not an essay, it is an action. Actions are easily misrepresented, and they expect to be so.

In the ongoing struggle to protect the mountain/Walwalinj, it is the strength and commitment of Noongar Elders such as Dr Marion Kickett that is doing the work. When the mountain is restored to Ballardong Noongar custodianship – that is, returned to its people – it will be safer and happier. And when Julimar Forest is protected by its traditional owners/custodians there will be a much greater chance of protecting its ecology. Poetry resonates or implodes with the health of the environments it is created in.

Works Cited

Hughes-D'Aeth, Tony. "Can Poetry Stop a Highway? Wielding Words in the Battle over Roe 8." *The Conversation*, 11 January 2017. https://theconversation.com/can-poetry-stop-a-highway-wielding-words-in-the-battle-over-roe-8-71005.

Kinsella, John. *Divine Comedy: Journeys through a Regional Geography*. University of Queensland Press, 2008.

Polysituatedness. Manchester University Press, 2017.

Beyond Ambiguity. Manchester University Press, 2021.

Collected Poems Volume Two (2005–2014): Harsh Hakea. UWA Publishing, 2023.

"The Argonautica I Am Re-envisaging and Will Eventually Try to Forget, as I Should?" *Meanjin*, March 2023. https://meanjin.com.au/essays/the-argonautica-i-am-re-envisaging-and-will-eventually-try-to-forget-as-i-should/.

Kinsella, John and J. P. Quinton. *The Other Report: Poems against the Destruction of the Beeliar Wetlands*. Shed Under the Mountain Press, 2017.

Papertalk Green, Charmaine and John Kinsella. *False Claims of Colonial Thieves*. Magabala Books, 2018.

Slessor, Kenneth. "North Country." *Five Bells: XX Poems*. Frank Johnson, 1939, pp. 30–31.

"South Country." *Five Bells: XX Poems*. Frank Johnson, 1939, p. 32.

"Beach Burial." *Southerly* vol.5 no.3, 1944, p. 13.

Winmar, Dorothy. *Walwalinj: The Hill That Cries*. Quik Printing Services, 1996.

NOTES

1 The Western Australian government sought to extend the Roe Highway with the 'Roe 8 section' that would cut through sensitive Beeliar wetlands. When the government announced plans to begin clearing bush, John Kinsella joined poet James Quinton in December 2016 at the front line of the protest. Reading poems was incorporated into the protest. The government announced in early January 2024 that it had cancelled the extension. See Hughes-D'Aeth.

2 See "Confirmed Minutes: Ordinary Council Meeting." Shire of York, Western Australia, 29 September 2020, Greenhills, pp. 105–24.

3 Dr Marion Kickett, Ballardong Noongar traditional owner relates:

> Wongborel means sleeping woman. My sister rented a flat in the main street on the second floor. From the second floor I could see clearly the shape of a woman lying on her side in the hill ... Noongars always saw two groups of people the valley Noongars and the hill/ mountain Noongars. Both being connected through one old man thousands of years ago ... Bilya Googala (Avon River in York) would always run between the two mountains keep the two spirits separate.

> Quoted in John Kinsella's "Magnificence: Wongborel/'Mount Brown.'" *Collected Poems: Volume Two (2005–2014) Harsh Hakea*.

4 Email to author, 8 September 2021. The Department of Planning, Lands and Heritage internal letter was dated 4 September 2020.

5 See section 42 of the Land Administration Act 1997 (WA).

6 See "Mutually Said: Poets Vegan Anarchist Pacifist" (a blog by John Kinsella and Tracy Ryan). https://poetsvegananarchistpacifist.blogspot.com/2021/09/poem-in-support-of-sacred-bushland-of.html.

7 See the Hansard record of the meeting of the Western Australian Legislative Assembly on 17 August 2000, p. 507.

8 See https://poetsvegananarchistpacifist.blogspot.com/2020/12/please-stand-up-and-protect-julimar.html.

9 Forthcoming in *Inlandica Argonautica*, Vagabond Press, 2024, p. 146.

PART V

Expanding Form

18

PAUL HETHERINGTON AND CASSANDRA ATHERTON

Hybrid Forms

The Verse Novel, Prose Poetry, and Poetic Biography

While conventional literary forms continue to offer a great deal to Australian readers, hybrid forms – in sitting outside of canonised generic categories and because they are often fragmentary – acknowledge that there are other ways of speaking and understanding. Poetry is generally considered hybrid when it combines elements of more than one literary mode or genre, and such hybrid works abound in the twenty-first century. They include the prose poem – because it is poetry written in sentences and paragraphs – and novels in verse – because most novels are written in prose. Poetic biographies may also be considered hybrid because the biographical tradition is usually associated with extended works of factual and discursive prose.

In some cases, Australian literary works that fall into these categories are genuinely experimental or explore Australian identity in unique ways; in other cases, the works may be relatively conservative and unadventurous despite their hybridity. Some of them follow American and English examples of hybrid poetry and, especially in the sphere of prose poetry, American models have been fairly influential. However, in general, Australian verse novels, poetic biographies, and prose poetry have their own tonality and many are united in their exploration of the uncanniness of the hybrid. John Kinsella defines the process of literary hybridising as "a conscious undoing of the codes that constitute all possible readings of a text" and as "a theory of unfamiliarity" ("Hybridising" 158–59) and these forms' focus on the fragmentary – and sometimes the subversive – enables the powerful interstitial spaces they create.

Verse Novel

Christopher Pollnitz in a persuasive survey defines the verse novel sensibly as "any extended verse narrative that can be assessed in terms of both its versification and its handling of basic novelistic properties like character, plot and point of view" (229). Linda Weste emphasises "the 'success' of verse narratives [in] combining poetic and narrative elements" ("Verse Novel Research" 113). And, although the verse novel is often discussed in terms of works written for adults, a great deal of energy resides in verse novels for children, juniors, and young adults, which often give priority to multiple narrators or voicings.

The Australian verse novel tradition was inaugurated with conspicuous critical and commercial successes. C. J. Dennis's *The Songs of a Sentimental Bloke* was first published serially in the *Bulletin* between 1909 and 1915, then in book form. A highly influential work, it explores gang life in the Little Lon red-light district of Melbourne, making impressive and comical use of the Australian vernacular. Less well-known, Dennis's *The Moods of Ginger Mick* (1916) uses similar techniques to focus on the Battle of Gallipoli and the ANZAC legend. However, despite such an auspicious and early start, the Australian verse novel did not take off – and, even then, rather stutteringly – until the 1970s, with the publication of Alan Wearne's *Out Here* (1976; published by Bloodaxe as a stand-alone work in 1987), a collection of nine monologues loosely based on Robert Browning's *The Ring and the Book*. Wearne went on to write other verse novels – *The Nightmarkets* (1986), which "voices the whole city [of Melbourne], through multiplicity" (McCooey, "The City" 125), and, in two volumes, the sprawling and somewhat subversive *The Lovemakers* (2001 and 2004).

The renaissance in the Australian verse novel began in earnest in 1979 with Les Murray's *The Boys Who Stole the Funeral*, a book credited with revitalising this tradition (Pierce n.pag.) and which John Barnie claimed "reintroduced the art of story-telling into poetry" (178). However, the work appropriates aspects of Indigenous Australian culture and satirises feminism and sexual politics in ways that have dated. While Murray's second verse novel *Fredy Neptune* (1998) does not develop complex characters apart from Fredy Neptune, it presents its protagonist against a wide historical canvas.

Other notable extended poems from the 1980s and 1990s include the three separate but thematically linked narrative works in John A. Scott's *St Clair* (1986). While barely qualifying as verse novels, they brought an enigmatic European flavour to Australian literature. John Millett's idiosyncratic *Blue Dynamite*, from the same year, focuses on the collision of Australian and Asian commercial practices in the 1980s, ironically contrasting these with Bodhisattva's six virtues. Originally a film script, Ken Bolton's and John Jenkin's verse novel *The Ferrara Poems* (1989) dramatises a visit by young Australian tourists to the re-imagined city of Ferrara; while Chris Jones' *The Times of Zenia Gold* (1992) presents a fairly explicit homoerotic narrative at a time when this was unusual in mainstream Australian literature. The four connected verse narratives of *The Floor of Heaven* (1992), compared by Tranter himself to a movie (Henry and Tranter), represent a self-conscious urbanisation of the verse novel. In contrast, Philip Hodgins' *Dispossessed* (1994) is a blank verse chronicle of rural life. Matt Rubinstein's *Solstice* (1994) focuses on five characters over a twenty-four-hour period in Adelaide and its evocation of a particular city and fast-moving iambic tetrameter owes a debt to Vikram Seth's *The Golden Gate* (1986). A distinctive work in the Australian context is Merlinda Bobis' *Cantata of the Warrior Woman Daragang Magayon* (1993), a poem shaped in both Filipino and English.

Dorothy Porter's accessible verse novels were chiefly responsible for drawing broad attention to the form in Australia. The first of these, *Akhenaten* (1992) is arguably a biographical sequence about the controversial Egyptian pharaoh rather than a verse novel, but it contains enough plot development to be classed as a novel. Porter's next verse novel, *The Monkey's Mask* (1994) was a publishing sensation – a crime thriller subsequently made into an internationally co-produced film directed by Samantha Lang and released in 2000. Its poetry is primarily fast-paced narrative. Porter wrote three more verse novels, including *What a Piece of Work* (1999), before her untimely death in 2008. Her exploration of female agency and sexuality was groundbreaking in the relatively conservative twentieth-century Australian literary culture.

Geoff Page has been another prominent verse novelist. His verse novels include *The Scarring* (1999), which charts the effects of wartime separation on a married couple, and *Drumming on Water* (2003), which follows a group of female dance band musicians on the Sydney Harbour ferries as the drummer, Emma, seeks justice for the lead singer's death. *1953* (2013) and *Cara Carissima* (2015) extend his achievements in the form. Paul Hetherington's *Blood and Old Belief* (2003) depicts the relationships between a married couple and their daughter on a rural property near Cowra, focusing on family dysfunctionality, the urge for connection, and the impact of drought. John Jenkins' *A Break in the Weather* (2003) – written in a free version of *ottava rima* with rhyming end couplets – presents the relationship between an Australian weather scientist and a Japanese woman at Uluru and in the Blue Mountains. In 2004 Justin Clemens published the mock epic, *The Mundiad*, celebrating aspects of modernity, such as new ageism, screen culture, and IVF.

Written over an extended period, Chris Wallace-Crabbe's quest narrative *The Universe Looks Down* (2005) is an eclectic work, narrated from a female point of view. Richard James Allen adapted his extended 'hybrid' poem, *Thursday's Fictions* (1999) for the stage with Karen Pearlman before publishing *The Kamikaze Mind* (2006), capturing via dictionary form the distributed fragments of an astronaut's mind in a black hole. Shé Hawke's fictocritical verse novel, *Depot Girl*, in 2008 and her *Aquamorphia: Falling for Water* (2014) provide often lateral narratives about human understandings of and relationships to water. Judy Johnson's *Jack* (2006) draws on twentieth-century history to portray the travails of a one-eyed captain of a pearling lugger, hiding out in the Torres Strait amid a multicultural world of Japanese, Islanders, Australian Aborigines, and Europeans.

Verse novels in the second decade of the twenty-first century cover diverse thematic areas, both speculative and historical, often relational. Written mainly in relaxed rhyming couplets, Anthony Lawrence's *The Welfare of My Enemy* (2011) addresses the subject of missing persons. Lisa Jacobson's *The Sunlit Zone* (2012) delves into ecological issues, genetic modification and mutation, and issues of guilt, in a futuristic society. In the same year, Ali Cobby Eckermann published *Ruby Moonlight*, a spare, compassionate, and confronting verse novel about nineteenth-century colonisation in South Australia, a massacre of Indigenous people, and the subsequent relationship between Ruby Moonlight and the Irishman, Jack. Stephen Edgar's three interlinked blank verse poems in *Eldershaw* (2013) discontinuously conjure various intimacies amid a house of ghosts. Lesley Lebkowicz's *The Petrov Poems* (2013) examines the famous defection of the Petrovs from the Soviet Union to Australia in 1954, giving prominence to Evdokia Petrov and her uncertainties, and Ivy Alvarez takes on the challenging task of providing various perspectives on family murders and a suicide in *Disturbance* (2013). In a mixture of vernacular poetry and prose, Omar Musa's *Here Come the Dogs* (2014) explores the issues of multiculturalism, drug culture, and personal identity.

Rebecca Jessen's *Gap* (2014), influenced by Porter's *The Monkey's Mask*, uses short, free verse lines to convey the interior life of Ana, who becomes a suspect in a murder investigation. Linda Weste's *Nothing Sacred* (2015) conjures the last period of the Roman Republic in sometimes visceral detail. Jordie Albiston's experimental *Jack & Mollie (& Her)* (2016) charmingly gives voice to two dogs and their "ownee"; while Brian Castro's highly allusive *Blindness and Rage* (2017), set in contemporary Adelaide and various iterations of Paris, meditates on authorship, fame, and human intimacy. Leni Shilton's *Malcolm* (2019) navigates domestic violence, intergenerational trauma, and marginalisation while *Blight Street* (2021), a verse novella by Geoff Goodfellow, brings different perspectives to bear on similar themes, depicting poverty, addiction, and intergenerational relationships among the suburban poor. Joan Fleming's *Song of Less* (2022) employs lineated poetry and prose poetry to explore problematic notions of intimacy, connection, and love in a world destroyed by ecological disaster. Madison Godfrey's *Dress Rehearsals* (2023) presents a series of prose poems about the performance of womanhood and John Kinsella's *Cellnight* (2023) addresses themes of colonisation, military power, and police violence.

Australian verse novels for children and young adults have proliferated since the 1990s and, by 2002, almost 40 per cent of verse novels published in the previous quarter of a century were for young adults (McCooey, "Australian" 200). The prolific Steven Herrick is a prime innovator in this field. His *Love, Ghosts & Nose Hair* (1996) explores first love and enduring grief and has the distinction of being the first Australian young adult verse novel. Other works include *A Place Like This* (1998) and *Pookie Aleera Is Not My Boyfriend* (2012). He often writes in a pared-back style and utilises intertextuality, parataxis, and multiple narrators. Catherine Bateson's verse novels, *A Dangerous Girl* (2000), *The Year It All Happened* (2001), and *His Name in Fire* (2006) are also invested in exploring a "range of voices, which enables the poetry to observe, question and critique the teenage experience" (Hall n.pag.). Bateson incorporates prose sections, haiku, and journal entries into her works.

Other writers of recent verse novels for younger readers include Emma Cameron, Sherryl Clark, Jessica Davidson, Michelle Dennis Evans, Zana Fraillon, Pip Harry, Libby Hathorn, James Laidler, Kathryn Lomer, Sally Murphy, Irini Savvides, Tim Sinclair, Michelle A. Taylor, and Margaret Wild. Sharon Kernot's lyrical *The Art of Taxidermy* (2018) explores postcolonial unsettlement in a series of uncanny moments, and Lorraine Marwood's *Footprints on the Moon* (2021) is set in 1969 during the Vietnam War and associated anti-war protests. And while there are relatively few young adult verse novels by Indigenous authors, Sally Morgan's eloquent *Sister Heart* (2015) about the Stolen Generation and Kirli Saunders' *Bindi* (2020) – which explores bushfires on Gundungurra Country – are powerful texts.

Australian Prose Poetry

Until the last decade, Australian prose poetry was largely neglected by critics and editors. The *Anthology of Australian Prose Poetry* (2020) gathered more than 160 significant prose poems published between the early 1970s and 2020, many of them previously out of print and more than half written by women. While scholarship has sometimes characterised prose poems as contradictory or problematic, this volume demonstrates that they are not only of a comparable quality to lineated poems but also that prose poetry's use of sentences and paragraphs opens up new poetic possibilities, particularly for those who have historically had fewer opportunities to have a voice. This was reinforced by *Prose Poetry: An Introduction* (2020), which discusses selected Australian prose poems within an international context and critically demonstrates prose poetry's role in addressing the quotidian and shaping identity and diversity.

The *Anthology of Australian Prose Poetry* was preceded by the somewhat sketchy anthology *The Indigo Book of Australian Prose Poems* (2011) and more focused anthologies by Recent Work Press from 2015. Additionally, since 2012 Bronwyn Mehan's Spineless Wonders has published microliterature anthologies that include prose poetry. The Prose Poetry Project – created in 2015 by the International Poetry Studies Institute at the University of Canberra – involves international and Australian poets. A number of these writers, including Lucy Alexander, Eugen Bacon, Stephanie Green, Dominique Hecq, and Jen Webb have published books primarily composed of prose poetry.

Bella Li's *Argosy* (2017) – a book combining prose poetry, collage, and photography – won the poetry category in the 2018 Victorian Premier's Literary Awards and the 2018 NSW Premier's Literary Awards, indicating prose poetry's increasingly secure foothold in Australia. The volume explores travel in neo-surreal landscapes, paying homage to the collage novels of Max Ernst and to the early European symbolists and surrealists. Her second full-length collection, *Lost Lake* (2018) comprises eight prose poetry sequences and consolidates her interests in collage and voyage, while *Theory of Colours* (2021) further extends her range and techniques.

Historically, prose poetry derived from the work of various nineteenth-century French practitioners, most notably Charles Baudelaire's posthumously published 1869 collection, usually translated as *Paris Spleen*. Baudelaire's prose poetry, and that of contemporaries such as Arthur Rimbaud, turned "the unaesthetic and 'prosaic' into the object of poetic discourse" (Wanner 8). Prose poetry had no significant place in nineteenth- or early twentieth-century Australia. Although Michael Sawtell published *The Wisdom of a Vagabond: Prose Poems* in 1925 and J. Ward Walters produced a chapbook entitled *The Storehouse and Other Prose Poems* in 1938, neither contain what is now understood to be prose poetry. However, the 1941 book, *Star Dust (Prose Poems)*, by M[aymie Ada] Hamlyn-Harris does contain genuine attempts at prose poetry written in a high Romantic mode. More significantly, many Indigenous writers worked in various forms of poetic prose throughout the twentieth century, including David Unaipon, Oodgeroo Noonuccal, and Paddy Roe – and the original drafts of Noonuccal's "Burr +Nong" and "The Midden" (Jennifer Jones 26, 30) may be conceived of as hybrid works that, among other features, make use of such prose.

The Verse Novel, Prose Poetry, and Poetic Biography

In the 1970s and 1980s an impetus in Australia towards literary renewal included books composed entirely or mainly of prose poetry or prose pieces – and a good deal of Australian poetry has interrogated this relationship between prose poetry and prose pieces ever since. In 1971, Chris Wallace-Crabbe included a suite of five prose poems, "Going to Cythera" in *Where the Wind Came: Poems* and Andrew Taylor's *Parabolas: Prose Poems* (1976), with its focus on momentum and repetition, has been called "the first [Australian] book of prose poems" (Shapcott, "Letters" n.pag.). However, Rudi Krausmann's *From Another Shore* (1975) – published slightly earlier and with drawings by Brett Whiteley – is arguably the first full collection by an Australian writer that "resembles ... something akin to prose poetry" (Petersen 64). Krausmann also wrote further short prose pieces – in his books *Everyman a sentence situation* (1978) and *The Journey and Other Poems* (1999), for example.

An astute critic of prose poetry, Thomas (Tom) Shapcott is also an early skilled practitioner. His most notable prose poems were written in short sequences exploring "certain recurring motifs and a self-conscious preoccupation with 'turning full circle'" (Shapcott, "Letters" n.pag.) – works such as *Turning Full Circle* (1979) and *Stump & Grape & Bopple-Nut: Prose Inventions* (1981). Gary Catalano, a fine and fastidious prose poet until his death in 2002, produced numerous stand-alone, sometimes lyrical prose poems in, for example, *Fresh Linen: Sixty Prose Poems, 1980–1986* (1988) and *Jigsaw: Poems and Prose Poems* (1998). These works examine issues of self-understanding and perception with an occasional neo-surrealist bent.

Women have been at the helm of developing Australian prose poetry, with Moya Costello commenting that "[t]he best exemplary practitioners of the prose poem to be found anywhere at any time are among contemporary Australian women writers" (Costello n.pag.). joanne burns and Ania Walwicz are two of the most prolific and eminent Australian prose poets, whose work interrogates the boundaries between prose and poetry and emphasises its multifarious voicings. Their work is ludic, parodic, and often ironic or satiric. burns has stated "[the] poem is a show off ... but the prose poem ... is more humble" (Mehan n.pag.). In practice, burns often writes prose poetry or works of poetic prose in sequences and demonstrates real ambition. Her work is keenly attuned to language's nuances and her numerous books include *blowing bubbles in the 7th lane* (1988), *on a clear day* (1992), *penelope's knees* (1996), and *apparently* (2019). Walwicz's feminist revision of "Little Red Riding Hood" (7) and her prose poem "Australia" – which begins: "You big ugly. You too empty" (90–91) – are often on school and university curricula. Her work employs associative and disjunctive effects and, while sometimes pithy, often extends over many pages. *Red Roses* (1992), for instance, is a book-length work.

Influenced by the counterculture of the 1960s and 1970s, both Anna Couani and Vicki Viidikas were influential in opening up the expressive possibilities of the prose poem form. Couani has called her writing – in *The Harbour Breathes* (with photographs by Peter Lyssiotis, 1989) and *Italy* (1977), for instance – "experimental prose" (email to Paul Hetherington), although her highly evocative shorter works qualify as prose poetry. Vicki Viidikas' *Condition Red* (1973; mainly lineated poems), *Wrappings* (1974; short stories and prose poems), and *India Ink* (1984; mainly prose poems) memorably form the basis of her reputation as a "confessional surrealist feminist" (Varatharajan n.pag.). Pam Brown's *Keep It Quiet* (1987) is written entirely in prose. Most of these works are too discursive to be called prose poetry, but a few prose poems are included, and *This World, This Place* (1994) also contains some prose poems.

More generally, from the 1970s to the 1990s, prose poems and poetic prose by writers such as Bruce Beaver, Rodney Hall, John Forbes, Susan Hampton, Laurie Duggan, Kevin Hart, Alison Croggon, M. T. C. Cronin, Robert Kenny, and Michael Sarabin have contributed significantly to the development of the prose poem. Since the 1990s, Peter Boyle has innovatively employed prose. A considerable part of his highly inventive *Apocrypha* (2009), for example – which playfully claims to reproduce "texts collected and translated by William O'Shaunessy" – is in prose; some of it prose poetry. Other books, such as *What the Painter Saw in Our Faces* (2001) and *Museum of Space* (2004) have occasional prose poems interspersed among lineated poems.

The prose poetry of Detroit-born Philip Hammial is known for its neo-surrealism with its suggestively wide-ranging, parable-like, and often dream-like qualities. His books of poems and prose poems, such as *With One Skin Less* (1994), *Skin Theory* (2009), *Asylum Nerves: New and Selected Poems* (2014), and *Inveigling Snafus* (2021), span more than four decades and demonstrate an observant, wry, and ironic attitude to experience and language. Paul Hetherington writes both long and short prose poetry sequences as well as individual prose poems. His work is recognised for its celebration of the prose poem's open form. *Burnt Umber* (2016) contains lineated poems and prose poetry, and was followed by eight prose poetry books, including *Gallery of Antique Art* (2016), *Her One Hundred and Seven Words* (2021), and *Ragged Disclosures* (2022). These collections often recast history, exploring negative capability, the movement of time, the hallmarks of memory, ekphrasis, human intimacy, and the luminosity of childhood.

Cassandra Atherton is one of few Australian poets who write prose poetry exclusively. Her prose poetry collections are known for their "nervy style ... post-punk and post-John Forbes" (Farrell, "Fast"). They include *After Lolita* (2010), *Exhumed* (2015), *Trace* (2015), *Pika-Don* (2018; co-authored and illustrated), and *Leftovers* (2020), and are invested in a conscious intertextuality, ekphrasis – particularly connected to the Pre-Raphaelites – black humour, and the expression of a contemporary woman's experience, often through erotic tropes. Atherton and Hetherington have been called "notable practitioners" (Holland-Batt and Jeffrey 342) and co-authored *Fugitive Letters* (2020), as well as undertaking definitive editing and scholarship on the prose poem, most significantly, *Prose Poetry: An Introduction* (2020).

Since 2000, an increasing number of Australian poetry collections contain prose poems. Luke Beesley's and Michael Farrell's collections often exploit the play of poetry and prose. Both poets are influenced by American poet John Ashbery's humour and they revel in word games. This often creates perceptual surprises and, sometimes, a sense of sheer absurdity. Beesley's books, such as *Balance* (2012), *Aqua Spinach* (2018), and *In The Photograph* (2023) are searching and present a rich self-reflexivity and intertextuality. Farrell has produced significant prose poems and more extended works of poetic prose – for example, *a raiders guide* (2008) contains adventurous and experimental prose poems – and *Cocky's Joy* (2015) and *Family Trees* (2020) test the boundaries between prose and poetry, creating sometimes obscure and discontinuous effects.

Prithvi Varatharajan's *Entries* (2020) also experiments with poetic effects in prose. His prose poem "'A clatter of leaves; rain like shiny nails'" (18) is influenced by Vicki Viidikas' example. Many of John Kinsella's numerous collections such as *Lightning Tree* (1996) and *Drowning in Wheat* (2016) contain prose poems, but it is in his three-volume *Graphology Poems 1995–2015* (2016) where he truly experiments with the form as evolving and organic palimpsest. Kevin Brophy's prose poetry is invested in related issues of perception and self-reflexivity. And Anne M. Carson has published a playful illustrated book of prose poetry, *The Detective's Chair: Prose Poems about Fictional Detectives* (2023) that reflects on creativity.

Jordie Albiston, Alyson Miller, and Penelope Layland have also worked with prose poetry, often as creative non-fiction. Albiston's poetic biographies include prose poems and *Element: The Atomic Weight & Radius of Love* (2019) explores her ongoing interest in the relationship between poetry and mathematics. Miller's *Strange Creatures* (2019) contains tightly packed prose poems, many of which are abject re-imaginings of crimes. Layland's

Nigh (2020) features a number of terse prose poems probing the quotidian and aspects of history and ecological concerns.

Prose poetry has also responded to British colonisation, and Bill Ashcroft, Gareth Griffiths, and Helen Tiffin argue that a "major feature of postcolonial literatures is the concern with place and displacement" (8). These are preoccupations suited to the blurring of established boundaries so often apparent in prose poems, and prose poetry by Indigenous poets constitutes powerful contemporary examples of the form. Ali Cobby Eckermann, Brenda Saunders, Ellen van Neerven, Charmaine Papertalk Green, and Alison Whittaker have all published prose poems or poetic prose. Recently, Evelyn Araluen's *Dropbear* (2021), winner of the 2022 Stella Prize, has been described as "something akin to prose poetry" (Fry n.pag.). Judith Nangala Crispin's lyrical prose poem "On Finding Charlotte in the Anthropological Record" won the 2020 Blake Poetry Prize and examines the role of poetry in interrogating diverse discourses about Aboriginal people. Much of Natalie Harkin's *Dirty Words* (2015) and *Archival-Poetics* (2019) – significant works about Indigenous dispossession – are in poetic prose. And Samuel Wagan Watson's *Smoke Encrypted Whispers* (2004) and *Love Poems and Death Threats* (2014) experiment with the prose poem, including via the haibun form. His works are haunting explorations of dark and often satirical ineffability, providing an "urban aboriginal perspective on the world" (Lo n.pag.).

Ali Jane Smith has called the prose poem a "mongrel form," arguing that in the 1960s and 1970s it was "almost perfectly suited to intelligent, purposeful women working to force a place for women's writing and publishing in Australia; [and] to the bi- and multilingual migrants and children of migrants confronted with broad, flat Australian vowel sounds" (9). Migrant experience is addressed in a good deal of Australian prose poetry, including notably in Alex Skovron's *Autographs* (2008) and Tatjana Lukic's *la,la,la* (2009), but also in work by Judith Rodriguez, Merlinda Bobis, Ania Walwicz, Eugen Bacon, and Miriam Wei Wei Lo. Ouyang Yu has an extensive and feisty oeuvre of prose poetry, including in his mixed-mode, bilingual *Flag of Permanent Defeat* (2019).

Because prose poems play with notions of defamilarisation and the uncanny, and are often highly compressed, they will sometimes seem to inflate, balloon-like, as they are read, becoming larger inside than their outward appearance suggests. In such cases, prose poems work a strange magic with the reader's sense of time and space, not unlike a poetic version of the TARDIS. Prose poetry in Australia is now finally achieving recognition for the wide reaches and spaces it explores and, sometimes, destabilises.

Poetic Biography

Despite their similar approaches, Anna Jackson notes, "[internationally] the verse novel is now established as a literary genre, [while] the verse biography has not been similarly acknowledged." In Australia, perhaps this is due to the continuing proliferation of verse novels and the relative dearth of verse biographies. Additionally, nomenclature functions to divide this form of life-writing. For example, two of the earliest examples, Francis Webb's *A Drum for Ben Boyd* (1948) – a work illustrated by Norman Lindsay recounting the life of a Scotsman arriving in New South Wales in 1848 – and James McAuley's *Captain Quiros* (1964), are usually described as long narrative poems.

Yet these books fit within Jackson's definition of the verse biography as "a sequence of poems concerned with the representation of a biographical subject" (iv). Such works are variously called 'verse biographies,' 'verse-portraits,' 'poetic biographies,' 'biographical poetry,' 'biographical long poems,' and, in some instances, 'documentary poetry.' With the proliferation of hybrid works in this field – containing prose poetry and poetic prose as well as lineated poetry – we use the term proposed by one of Australia's leading practitioners, Jessica L. Wilkinson: 'poetic biography.' This embraces a diversity of forms and also draws attention to their poetics. The translation of biography into poetry challenges traditional ideas of biography as a prosaic narrative that fleshes out an individual's life in factual detail. Indeed, poetic biographies are usually highly selective in their inclusion of factual information, often focusing on evocative tropes.

However, some are also based on extensive research in archives and particular places and on the examination of artefacts and ephemera. This allows for the retrieval of largely erased or overlooked lives – something undertaken by Wilkinson in her three poetic biographies. The first, *marionette: a biography of miss marion davies* (2012), is experimental, critiquing patriarchy and employing ludic textual collage and fragments to deconstruct the traditional poetic line and revive a dynamic image of Davies. In *Suite for Percy Grainger: A Biography* (2014) and *Music Made Visible: A Biography of George Balanchine* (2019) Wilkinson conducts and choregraphs poetry so that the reader becomes a collaborator and spectator. The malleability of her poetry enables her to conjure with the individual's subjectivity; she likens this to "a shadow-experience of witnessing and re-presenting traces" (Wilkinson, "Experiments" 20). Wilkinson, along with Atherton, edited *Memory Book: Portraits of Older Australians in Poetry and Watercolours* (2021), a significant set of biographies by Australian poets based on their interviews with Elders and older Australians. The volume is one of the few to foreground older Australians in the community, redressing states of marginality and invisibility.

Jordie Albiston's poetic biographies are grounded in substantial archival research and often have inventive structures. The collective biography, *Botany Bay Document: A Poetic History of the Women of Botany Bay* (1996) focuses on the first white women of colonial settlement. *The Hanging of Jean Lee* (1998) retrieves and characterises the inner life and point of view of a railway worker's daughter who, after an abusive relationship, became the last woman to be executed in Australia. *The Book of Ethel* (2013) is a poetic biography of Albiston's maternal great-grandmother who emigrated to Australia at fifteen, and *Warlines* (2018) creates poetry redactions from letters written by Victorian soldiers in World War I. Toby Fitch's *Jerilderies* (2014) also includes redacted poems created from Ned Kelly's 1879 *Jerilderie Letter*. The extreme redactions of white space are visually reminiscent of Kelly's famous helmet and visor as depicted by Sidney Nolan.

Indeed, many poets have explored historic aspects of settler colonialism. Judy Johnson's *Dark Convicts* (2017) reinvigorates the narrative of two of Johnson's ancestors who were African American convicts on the First Fleet. Ross Gibson's *26 Views of the Starburst World: William Dawes at Sydney Cove 1788–1791* (2012) illuminates the English astronomer's and colonist's career and his relationship with the Indigenous people in the area now named Sydney Harbour. Based on diaries, correspondence, and other archival sources, Benjamin Laird's electronic poetic biography, *The Durham Poems; or Poems on William Denton, Years 1823–1842* (2016) forms an interrupted narrative of Denton's life and experiences, which included a visit to Australia. Viewed online, words and phrases move and float on the screen, demonstrating the tenuousness of connections and the inevitability of biographical fragmentation. The correspondence between Australian poet Bernard O'Dowd and Walt Whitman between 1889 and 1892 informs David Prater's *Leaves of Glass* (2013). Ironic and witty, Prater's poems are intimate experiments in the construction of personae.

Other significant works include Anne M. Carson's *Massaging Himmler: A Poetic Biography of Dr Felix Kersten* (2019), which is narrated from different points of view and focuses on Kersten's success in persuading Himmler to spare the lives of thousands of Jews during the Holocaust. Emily Ballou's *The Darwin Poems* (2009) impressively depicts Charles Darwin's internal struggles and relationships rather than the mythology surrounding his life, and Colleen Keating's *Hildegard of Bingen: A Poetic Journey* (2019) traces the Benedictine abbess' life, with an emphasis on wisdom and ecology. Maureen Gibbons' *The Butter Lady: A Silhouette Biography in Verse* (2016) uses poetic biography to speculate about the missing narrative of a homeless woman who died in Perth in 2001. Julie Chevalier's wonderfully jarring, *Darger: his girls, a sequence of poems about the life of Henry Darger, 1892–1973* (2012) retrieves the life of an outsider artist and writer while also questioning his possibly nefarious activities. Benjamin Dodds' stark and poignant *Airplane Baby Banana Blanket* (2020) advocates for animal rights in the poetic biography of Lucy, a chimpanzee born in 1966 who was raised as a human and then reintroduced into the wild. Magdalena Ball's *Bobish* (2022) is an exploration of twentieth-century history that reanimates the life of her great-grandmother, Rebecca Lieberman, who travels as a teenager from the impoverished Jewish Pale of Settlement in Russia to straitening circumstances in New York.

Geoff Page is especially interested in the creative and elegiac re-imagining of subjects. Written in rousing trimeter and tetrameter, his *Plevna: A Biography in Verse: Sir Charles 'Plevna' Ryan, 1853–1926* (2016) presents his subject set against the horror of war. Page's *Elegy for Emily: A Verse Biography of Emily Remler (1957–1990)* (2019) employs a pared-back rhythm and cadence appropriate to the short life of an American jazz guitarist who died in Sydney. Leni Shilton's *Walking with Camels: The Story of Bertha Strehlow* (2018) gives Bertha Strehlow a voice while rendering the sublimity of the Australian desert and its vast silences.

Demonstrating other biographical approaches, Dominique Hecq's *Hush: A Fugue* (2017) and Albiston's *Vertigo: A Cantata* (2007) have an autobiographical focus, using musical conceits to explore the insufficiencies and redemptive possibilities of language when faced with grief and loss. Extracts from Shari Kocher's *Sonqoqui: A Threnody* (104–13) employ the metaphor of weaving to join the practices of archaeology, history, and poetry in reimagining the lives of three Inca children. Andy Jackson's *Music Our Bodies Can't Hold* (2017) is a series of poetic portraits, some speculative, about historical figures and contemporary people living with Marfan syndrome, including Mary Queen of Scots and Osama bin Laden.

Π.O.'s trilogy *24 Hours* (1996), *Fitzroy: The Biography* (2015), and *Heide* (2019) constitute sprawling poetic biographies of place. In the first two, Π.O explores the history of Fitzroy, intermingling autobiographical moments with the dialects of locals and migrants. In the last, he breaks open much of the mythology surrounding Sunday and John Reed and individuals associated with them, with a broad focus on critiquing social inequality. Carmine Frascarelli's *Sydney Road Poems* (2016) sketches the iconic Melbourne road and its changing identity, while Ross Gibson's *Seven Versions of an Australian Badland* (2002) is a book of poetic prose chronicling a "horror stretch" of road in Queensland from the 1860s to the 1970s. Mark A. Peart's *The Great Eastern* (2016) constitutes a powerful history of 1860s

Collingwood and Fitzroy through the lens of former English convict and sex worker, John Wilson. Patricia Sykes focuses on the lives of girls and women at the Abbotsford Convent, a home for wayward girls in *The Abbotsford Mysteries* (2011).

Wilkinson has argued that "poetic biography tests the boundaries of more conventional modes of life-writing by challenging our relationship to facts" ("Writing Lines" 181) and Australian poets have certainly exercised a generous amount of intervention in their poetic biographies. Often based on extensive archival work and frequently written in free verse, Australian poetic biographies published to date blend the selective use of documentary material with creative insight, focusing on enabling the reader to re-envision their biographical subjects and to journey with them imaginatively. Especially where the lives of culturally marginal people are concerned, when documentary material may be scarce, this is an important strategy in writing about significant contributors to a society whose values and mores are in considerable flux.

Works Cited

Albiston, Jordie. *Botany Bay Document: A Poetic History of the Women of Botany Bay*. Black Pepper, 1996.
    The Hanging of Jean Lee. Black Pepper, 1998.
    Vertigo: A Cantata. John Leonard Press, 2007.
    The Book of Ethel. Puncher & Wattmann, 2013.
    Jack & Mollie (& Her). University of Queensland Press, 2016.
    Warlines. Hybrid Publishers, 2018.
    Element: The Atomic Weight & Radius of Love. Puncher & Wattmann, 2019.
Allen, Richard James. *Thursday's Fictions*. Five Islands Press, 1999.
    The Kamikaze Mind. Brandl & Schlesinger, 2006.
Alvarez, Ivy. *Disturbance*. Seren, 2013.
Araluen, Evelyn. *Dropbear*. University of Queensland Press, 2021.
Ashcroft, Bill, Gareth Griffiths, and Helen Tiffin. *The Empire Writes Back: Theory and Practice in Post-colonial Literatures*, 2nd ed. Routledge, 2002.
Atherton, Cassandra. *After Lolita*. Ahadada Books, 2010.
    Exhumed. Grand Parade Poets, 2015.
    Trace. Finlay Lloyd, 2015.
    Leftovers. Gazebo Books, 2020.
Atherton, Cassandra and Paul Hetherington, eds. *Anthology of Australian Prose Poetry*. Melbourne University Press, 2020.
Atherton, Cassandra and Alyson Miller. *Pika-Don*. Mountains Brown Press, 2018.
Ball, Magdalena. *Bobish*. Puncher & Wattman, 2022.
Ballou, Emily. *The Darwin Poems*. UWA Publishing, 2009.
Barnie, John. "'The Common Dish' and the Uncommon Poet: Les A. Murray's *The Boys Who Stole the Funeral*." *Kunapipi* vol.4 no.1, 1982, pp. 172–78.
Bateson, Catherine. *A Dangerous Girl*. University of Queensland Press, 2000.

The Year It All Happened. University of Queensland Press, 2001.
His Name in Fire. University of Queensland Press, 2006.
Baudelaire, Charles. *Paris Spleen: Little Poems in Prose*. Translated by Keith Waldrop. Wesleyan University Press, 2009.
Beesley, Luke. *Balance*. Whitmore Press, 2012.
Aqua Spinach. Giramondo, 2018.
In the Photograph. Giramondo, 2023.
Bobis, Merlinda. *Cantata of the Warrior Woman Daragang Magayon; An Epic*. Babaylan Women's Publishing Collective, 1993.
Bolton, Ken and John Jenkins. *The Ferrara Poems*. Experimental Art Foundation, 1989.
Boyle, Peter. *What the Painter Saw in Our Faces*. Five Islands Press, 2001.
Museum of Space. University of Queensland Press, 2004.
Apocrypha. Vagabond Press, 2009.
Brown, Pam. *Keep It Quiet*. Sea Cruise Books, 1987.
This World, This Place. University of Queensland Press, 1994.
burns, joanne. *blowing bubbles in the 7th lane*. Fab Press, 1988.
on a clear day. University of Queensland Press, 1992.
penelope's knees. University of Queensland Press, 1996.
apparently. Giramondo, 2019.
Byrne, Michael, ed. *The Indigo Book of Australian Prose Poems*. Ginninderra Press, 2011.
Carson, Anne M. *Massaging Himmler: A Poetic Biography of Dr Felix Kersten*. Hybrid Publishers, 2019.
The Detective's Chair: Prose Poems about Fictional Detectives. Liquid Amber Press, 2023.
Castro, Brian. *Blindness and Rage*. Giramondo, 2017.
Catalano, Gary. *Fresh Linen: Sixty Prose Poems, 1980–1986*. University of Queensland Press, 1988.
Jigsaw: Poems and Prose Poems. Craftsman House, 1998.
Chevalier, Julie. *Darger: his girls, a sequence of poems about the life of Henry Darger, 1892–1973*. Puncher & Wattmann, 2012.
Clemens, Justin. *The Mundiad*. Hunter Publishers, 2013.
Costello, Moya. "Letters to the Editor." *TEXT* vol.6 no.2, 2002. www.textjournal.com.au/oct02/letters.htm.
Couani, Anna. *Italy*. Ragman Productions, 1977.
email to Paul Hetherington, 2 November 2020.
Couani, Anna and Peter Lyssiotis. *The Harbour Breathes*. Sea Cruise Books, 1989.
Crispin, Judith Nangala. "On Finding Charlotte in the Anthropological Record." Casula Powerhouse Arts Centre. www.casulapowerhouse.com/__data/assets/pdf_file/0011/189578/Blake2020_On-finding-Charlotte-in-the-Anthropological-Record_Judith-Crispin.pdf.
Dennis, C. J. *The Songs of a Sentimental Bloke*. Angus & Robertson, 1915.
The Moods of Ginger Mick. Angus & Robertson, 1916.
Dodds, Benjamin. *Airplane Baby Banana Blanket*. Recent Work Press, 2020.
Eckermann, Ali Cobby. *Ruby Moonlight: A Novel of the Impact of Colonisation in Mid-North South Australia around 1880*. Magabala Books, 2012.
Edgar, Stephen. *Eldershaw*. Black Pepper, 2013.

Farrell, Michael. *a raiders guide*. Giramondo, 2008.
   Cocky's Joy. Giramondo, 2015.
   "Fast and Furious." *The Australian*, 7 May 2016. www.theaustralian.com.au/arts/books/australian-poetry-atherton-hose-huppatz-kocher/news-story/1fdf530cdc5d26bc35ea58572e6ffaef.
   Family Trees. Giramondo, 2020.
Fitch, Toby. *Jerilderies*. Vagabond, 2014.
Fleming, Joan. *Song of Less*. Cordite Publishing, 2022.
Frascarelli, Carmine. *Sydney Road Poems*. Rabbit Poetry Journal, 2016.
Fry, Declan. "*Dropbear* by Evelyn Araluen Review – A Stunning Scalpel Wielded through Australian Myths." *The Guardian*, 26 March 2021. www.theguardian.com/books/2021/mar/26/dropbear-by-evelyn-araluen-review-a-stunning-scalpel-wielded-through-australian-myths.
Gibbons, Maureen. *The Butter Lady: A Silhouette Biography in Verse*. Rabbit Poetry Journal, 2016.
Gibson, Ross. *Seven Versions of an Australian Badland*. University of Queensland Press, 2002.
   26 Views of the Starburst World: William Dawes at Sydney Cove 1788–1791. UWA Publishing, 2012.
Godfrey, Madison. *Dress Rehearsals*. Joan, an imprint of Allen & Unwin, 2023.
Goodfellow, Geoff. *Blight Street*. Walleah Press, 2021.
Hall, Rhiannon. "Inside Me, My Voice Struggles to Get Out: Voice in Catherine Bateson's Verse Novel, *His Name in Fire*." *Axon: Creative Explorations* vol.10 no.1, May 2020. www.axonjournal.com.au/issue-vol-10-no-1-may-2020/inside-me-my-voice-struggles-get-out.
Hamlyn-Harris, M[aymie Ada]. *Star Dust (Prose Poems)*. Rallings & Rallings, 1941.
Hammial, Philip. *With One Skin Less*. Hale & Iremonger, 1994.
   Skin Theory. Puncher & Wattmann, 2009.
   Asylum Nerves: New and Selected Poems. Puncher & Wattmann, 2014.
   Inveigling Snafus. Island Press, 2021.
Harkin, Natalie. *Dirty Words*. Cordite Books, 2015.
   Archival-Poetics. Vagabond Press, 2019.
Hawke, Shé. *Depot Girl*. Picaro Press, 2008.
   Aquamorphia: Falling for Water. Interactive Publications, 2014.
Hecq, Dominique. *Hush: A Fugue*. UWA Publishing, 2017.
Henry, Brian and John Tranter. "John Tranter Interview." *The Argotist Online*. www.argotistonline.co.uk/Tranter%20interview.htm.
Hetherington, Paul. *Blood and Old Belief*. Pandanus Books, 2003.
   Burnt Umber. UWA Publishing, 2016.
   Gallery of Antique Art. Recent Work Press, 2016.
   Her One Hundred and Seven Words. Madhat Press, 2021.
   Ragged Disclosures. Recent Work Press, 2022.
Hetherington, Paul and Cassandra Atherton. *Fugitive Letters*. Recent Work Press, 2020.
   Prose Poetry: An Introduction. Princeton University Press, 2020.
Herrick, Steven. *Love, Ghosts & Nose Hair*. University of Queensland Press, 1996.
   A Place Like This. University of Queensland Press, 1998.
   Pookie Aleera Is Not My Boyfriend. University of Queensland Press, 2012.

Hodgins, Philip. *Dispossessed*. Angus & Robertson, 1994.
Holland-Batt, Sarah and Ella Jeffrey. "Twenty-First-Century Australian Poetry." *The Routledge Companion to Australian Literature*, edited by Jessica Gildersleeve. Routledge, 2020, pp. 335–43.
Jackson, Andy. *Music Our Bodies Can't Hold*. Hunter Publishers, 2017.
Jackson, Anna. Abstract for "The Verse Biography: Introduction." *Biography* vol.39 no.1, 2016, p. iii.
Jacobson, Lisa. *The Sunlit Zone*. Five Islands Press, 2012.
Jenkins, John. *A Break in the Weather*. Modern Writing Press, 2003.
Jessen, Rebecca. *Gap*. University of Queensland Press, 2014.
Johnson, Judy. *Jack*. Pandanus Books, 2006.
   Dark Convicts. UWA Publishing, 2017.
Jones, Chris. *The Times of Zenia Gold: A Verse Novel*. Blackwattle Press, 1992.
Jones, Jennifer. *Black Writers, White Editors: Episodes of Collaboration and Compromise in Australian Publishing History*. Australian Scholarly Publishing, 2009.
Keating, Colleen. *Hildegard of Bingen: A Poetic Journey*. Ginninderra Press, 2019.
Kernot, Sharon. *The Art of Taxidermy*. Text, 2018.
Kinsella, John. *Lightning Tree*. Fremantle Arts Centre Press, 1996.
   "The Hybridising of a Poetry: Notes on Modernism & Hybridity – The Colonising Prospect of Modernism and Hybridity as a Means to Closure." *boundary 2* vol.26 no.1, 1999, pp. 156–59.
   Drowning in Wheat: Selected Poems 1980–2015. Picador, 2016.
   Graphology Poems 1995–2015. Five Islands Press, 2016.
   Cellnight: A Verse Novel. Transit Lounge, 2023.
Kocher, Shari. "Excerpts from Part II of the Verse Novel: *Sonqoqui*: 'Unwritten Field Notes: Peru & Argentina, 1998-1999.'" *Rabbit: A Journal for Nonfiction Poetry* no.15, 2015, pp. 104–13.
Krausmann, Rudi. *From Another Shore*. Wild & Woolley, 1975.
   Everyman a sentence situation. Paper Castle, 1978.
   The Journey and Other Poems. Rudi Krausmann and Garry Shead, 1999.
Laird, Benjamin. *The Durham Poems; or Poems on William Denton, Years 1823–1842*. SOd Press, 2016.
Lawrence, Anthony. *The Welfare of My Enemy*. Puncher & Wattmann, 2011.
Layland, Penelope. *Nigh*. Recent Work Press, 2020.
Lebkowicz, Lesley. *The Petrov Poems*. Pitt Street, 2013.
Li, Bella. *Argosy*. Vagabond Press, 2017.
   Lost Lake. Vagabond Press, 2018.
   Theory of Colours. Vagabond Press, 2021.
Lo, Miriam Wei Wei. "Poetry Review by Guest Miriam Wei Wei Lo." *hi spirits*, 28 October 2004. http://hispirits.blogspot.com/2004/10/poetry-review-by-guest-miriam-wei-wei_28.html.
Lukic, Tatjana. *la,la,la*. Five Islands Press, 2009.
Marwood, Lorraine. *Footprints on the Moon*. University of Queensland Press, 2021.
McAuley, James. *Captain Quiros*. Angus & Robertson, 1964.
McCooey, David. "The City and the Contemporary Australian Long Poem." *JASAL: Journal of the Association for the Study of Australian Literature*, Australian Writing and the City, 1999, pp. 122–28.

"Australian Poetry 1970–2005." *A Companion to Australian Literature since 1900*, edited by Nicholas Birns and Rebecca McNeer. Camden House, 2007, pp. 191–205.

Mehan, Bronwyn. "The joanne burns Award." *Spineless Wonders*, 1 June 2013. https://shortaustralianstories.com.au/the-joanne-burns-award/.

Miller, Alyson. *Strange Creatures*. Recent Work Press, 2019.

Millett, John. *Blue Dynamite*. South Head Press, 1986.

Morgan, Sally. *Sister Heart*. Fremantle Press, 2015.

Murray, Les. *The Boys Who Stole the Funeral*. Angus & Robertson, 1979.

   Fredy Neptune. Duffy & Snellgrove, 1998.

Musa, Omar. *Here Come the Dogs*. Penguin, 2014.

Ouyang, Yu. *Flag of Permanent Defeat*. Puncher & Wattmann, 2019.

Page, Geoff. *The Scarring*. Hale & Iremonger, 1999.

   Drumming on Water. Brandl & Schlesinger, 2003.

   1953. University of Queensland Press, 2013.

   Cara Carissima. Picaro Press, 2015.

   Plevna: A Biography in Verse: Sir Charles 'Plevna' Ryan, 1853–1926. UWA Publishing, 2016.

   Elegy for Emily: A Verse Biography of Emily Remler (1957–1990). Puncher & Wattmann, 2019.

Peart, Mark A. *The Great Eastern*. Rabbit, 2016.

Petersen, D. "Rudi Krausmann, *From Another Shore*." *LiNQ* vol.4 no.3–4, 1975, pp. 64–65. https://journals.jcu.edu.au/linq/article/view/517/shore.

Π.O. *24 Hours*. Collective Effort Press, 1996.

   Fitzroy: The Biography. Collective Effort Press, 2015.

   Heide. Giramondo Publishing, 2019.

Pierce, Peter. "The Silver Age of Australian Fiction." *Meanjin*, Summer 2011. https://meanjin.com.au/essays/the-silver-age-of-australian-fiction/.

Pollnitz, Christopher. "Australian Verse Novels." *Heat* no.7, 2004, pp. 229–52.

Porter, Dorothy. *Akhenaten*. University of Queensland Press, 1992.

   The Monkey's Mask. Hyland House, 1994.

   What a Piece of Work. Picador, 1999.

Prater, David. *Leaves of Glass*. Puncher & Wattmann, 2013.

Rubinstein, Matt. *Solstice*. Allen & Unwin, 1994.

Saunders, Kirli. *Bindi*. Magabala Books, 2020.

Sawtell, Michael. *The Wisdom of a Vagabond: Prose Poems*. Cole's Book Arcade, 1925.

Scott, John A. *St Clair: Three Narratives*. University of Queensland Press, 1986.

Seth, Vikram. *The Golden Gate*. Random House, 1986.

Shapcott, Tom. *Turning Full Circle*. New Poetry, 1979.

   Stump & Grape & Bopple-Nut: Prose Inventions. Bullion Publications, 1981.

   "Letters to the Editor." *TEXT* vol.6 no.2, 2002. www.textjournal.com.au/oct02/letters.htm.

Shilton, Leni. *Walking with Camels: The Story of Bertha Strehlow*. UWA Publishing, 2018.

   Malcolm: A Story in Verse. UWA Publishing, 2019.

Skovron, Alex. *Autographs*. Hybrid Publishers, 2008.

Smith, Ali Jane. "The Mongrel: Australian Prose Poetry." *Australian Poetry Journal* vol.4 no.1, 2014, pp. 6–14.
Sykes, Patricia. *The Abbotsford Mysteries*. Spinifex Press, 2011.
Taylor, Andrew. *Parabolas: Prose Poems*. Makar Press, 1976.
Tranter, John. *The Floor of Heaven*. Angus & Robertson, 1992.
Varatharajan, Prithvi. "Confessional Surrealist Feminist: Vicki Viidikas's Poetics and Politics." *JASAL: Journal of the Association for the Study of Australian Literature* vol.18 no.2, 2018. https://openjournals.library.sydney.edu.au/index.php/JASAL/article/view/11723.
—. *Entries*. Cordite Books, 2020.
Viidikas, Vicki. *Condition Red*. University of Queensland Press, 1973.
—. *Wrappings*. Wild & Woolley, 1974.
—. *India Ink: A Collection of Prose Poems Written in India*. Hale & Iremonger, 1984.
Wallace-Crabbe, Chris. *Where the Wind Came: Poems*. Angus & Robertson, 1971.
—. *The Universe Looks Down*. Brandl & Schlesinger, 2005.
Walters, J. Ward. *The Storehouse and Other Prose Poems*. F.W. Preece, 1938.
Walwicz, Ania. "Australia." *Island in the Sun: An Anthology of Recent Australian Prose*, edited by Damien White, Anna Couani, and Tom Thompson. Sea Cruise Books, 1980, pp. 90–91.
—. "Little Red Riding Hood." *Writing*. Rigmarole Books, 1982, p. 7.
—. *Red Roses*. University of Queensland Press, 1992.
Wanner, Adrian. *Russian Minimalism: From the Prose Poem to the Anti-story*. Northwestern University Press, 2003.
Watson, Samuel Wagan. *Smoke Encrypted Whispers*. University of Queensland Press, 2004.
—. *Love Poems and Death Threats*. University of Queensland Press, 2014.
Wearne, Alan. *The Nightmarkets: A Novel*. Penguin, 1986.
—. *Out Here*. Bloodaxe Books, 1987.
—. *The Lovemakers: Book One: Saying All the Great Sexy Things*. Penguin, 2001.
—. *The Lovemakers: Book Two: Money and Nothing*. ABC Books, 2004.
Webb, Francis. *A Drum for Ben Boyd*. Angus & Robertson, 1948.
Weste, Linda. "Verse Novel Research and Reception in the Twenty-First Century." *New Scholar: An International Journal of the Humanities, Creative Arts and Social Sciences* vol.3 no.2, 2014, pp. 113–24.
—. *Nothing Sacred*. Australian Scholarly Publishing, 2015.
Wilkinson, Jessica L. *marionette: a biography of miss marion davies*. Vagabond Press, 2012.
—. *Suite for Percy Grainger: A Biography*. Vagabond Press, 2014.
—. "Experiments in Poetic Biography: Feminist Threads in Contemporary Long Form Poetry." *Biography* vol.39 no.1, 2016, pp. 1–22.
—. *Music Made Visible: A Biography of George Balanchine*. Vagabond Press, 2019.
—. "Writing Lines, Writing Lives: The Art of Poetic Biography." *New and Experimental Approaches to Writing Lives*, edited by Jo Parnell. Red Globe Press, 2019, pp. 170–85.
Wilkinson, Jessica L. and Cassandra Atherton, eds. *Memory Book: Portraits of Older Australians in Poetry and Watercolours*. Hunter Publishers, 2021.

19

A. J. CARRUTHERS

Sound, Visual, Digital, and Conceptual Poetries in Australia

This chapter will firstly introduce the reader to a sense of the scope and achievement of sound poetry, concrete poetry, and visual poetries in Australia from the pre-Invasion era to the present day. It will then move to experimental poetries of the digital age. The 'art' of speaking critically about poetries other than those to which we may feel accustomed in our age – if criticism is to be more than host, parasite, or rival creative artefact – poses a distinct challenge because of the nexus between narration and nation. An additional complexity is that there tends to be a conflation of public and private, such as chapbooks and Mail Art passed from person to person. Such poetries gain value in being shared in communities, and within international and transcultural networks.

Origins

Australian sound begins in sacred song and chant, with what is known as the songlines of First Nations people, or "songspirals," as described by the Gay'wu group of women, a collaboration of five Yolŋu and three non-Aboriginal women. Songspirals encode information simultaneously as song and map: scores for land and Country, and "milkarri," which are songspirals cried and keened by women. The Gay'wu women describe how these songs come into being and their role:

> Women learn by crying milkarri. When we cry our milkarri we are singing the map. We are singing about the dangers, the goodness on the land, what we will find, how we are going to find it, how we are going to survive. The manikay, the ceremonial singing, with the contributions of women and men; the buŋgul, the ceremonial dancing; the ochre body painting, its design; the yidaki; the bilma – they all have to be right. The women's tremulous voices keening the words, the men with their lowerpitched singing, the richness of sound and movement and emotion, the rising dust and sand, the vibrations through the air, the beings of Country coming together as one. This is the land that is never

shown to the rest of Australia. We are sharing a layer of this with you through the milkarri in this book. It is in the milkarri, in the bilma, in the movement of the dancing. It is all a map for Dhuwa and Yirritja. (34)

The harmonising process of the keening tells stories, and pertain to person as well as Country, and it goes without saying that the philosophical underpinnings as well as cultural expression of these songs differ markedly from European paradigms of thinking. The songs were previously disseminated to public readership through T. G. H. Strehlow's *The Songs of Central Australia* (1971), and derived, via notational and prosodic reduction, from ethnographic work on the songlines, including the Arrernte people (26).

Yet these scores, while curiously theorised and framed in Strehlow's record, can only partially explain the type of interworking of external and internal in living song that we can discern in the songspirals, as the Gay'wu women explain:

> The land sang itself into existence and it still sings. At the beginning of time someone had to talk for the land, it was quiet, nothingness. And then it began with the sound from deep within the water, "Hmmm hmmm." That was the starting point. We know that is the water from the land; in all the songspirals, that is where it all began, life and language begin. The first language was the "Hmmm" from the songs, the sound, the sound that we make. Without dhäruk, without language, there is bäyŋu, nothing. (190)

Here a philosophy of origins in which the sheer *interiority* of the emergence of the sound-basis of language is simultaneously exteriorised – emerging from the land against the nothingness outside it, non-language – brings us to the starting point, the hum, of the originary sound. The ground base of the hum as the point of origin of all sound is that of external nature, and hardly just the perception of it at this originary point. Beyond this there is not so much mimesis as an inhabitation of the sound that is the beginning of all life. The chorality in the songs reaches an oratorical breadth or breath, as in these lines:

> Ḏuruku miyamanarawu Dhaŋgala aaaaaaaa ...
> Wana nyerrpu miyaman ŋunha marrtji Baŋupaŋu.
> Miyaman marrtji Balwarri Nepaway, Maywundjiwuy.
>
> *Of that body of water I sing, I sing of the body of water.*
> *The arm of the paddler is knowledgeable, over there is Baŋupaŋu.*
> *I am singing about Balwarri, the whale, Nepaway, the open sea.* (22)

The Whale, Wuymirri, is one of five songspirals in the book; a summary of which remains inferior to an experience of it. Tristan Tzara is known to have attempted to sing Central Australian songs at the 1916 Cabaret Voltaire, a fact chronicled in the history of the early Romanian and European avant-gardes. We can trace historical European interest in the songs, albeit from outsiders in their own context, to the avant-garde, and it is within the distinct legacy of the avant-garde that various kinds of sound poetry would appear after the period of Invasion. Study of this enormously important area has only just begun. Linda Ioanna Kouvaras, in *Loading the Silence: Australian Sound Art in the Post-Digital Age* (2013), looks at Australian sound against the backdrop of other contexts like Futurist noise and Cagean Zen. Manifold types of practices and poetics are presented, from Percy Grainger to Warren Burt, independent label sound artists, feminist sound objects, sound sculptures, and collaborations across the Australian and international avant-gardes.

These types of scholarship are valuable not just because they obliterate certain containments by media but rather because they give us an historical sense of the afterlives of modernism through the greater avant-garde. The post-digital age might have given us an illusion of an experimentalism without the avant-garde. Women writers in Australia, particularly since the 1970s and the anthology *Mother I'm Rooted* (1975), took to visual and intermedia experimentation in a manner that can now be considered part of the longer history of post-avant-garde writing. Australian experimental poetry in general, whether digital, sonic, or visual, could be as resistant to the avant-garde as much as it became the inheritance of it. There is an abiding sense, particularly in experimental poetry from the 1970s, that politics and poetics were colliding in these productions from the margins. Editor Kate Jennings recounts in the introduction how it "metamorphosed into a political statement" about the position of women in Australia, and yet crucially "became, unabashedly, on my part, an attempt to question the standards of what is supposed to be good and bad poetry in the prevailing literary hegemony" (n.pag.).

The full range of sound- and visual-focused Australian poetry from the modernist period and, especially, after the 1970s came to challenge, diverge from, and yet become again part of larger tendencies in world sound and visual poetics, and this happened on and off the page, as was so with the early twentieth-century avant-gardes. Amanda Stewart's *I/T: Selected Poems* (1998) represents a culmination of this transnational, or even more accurately, geopolitical experience of the second- and third-wave avant-garde in Europe and the USA, but with a distinctly Antipodal, anti-Imperial, and geopolitical sense of these inheritances in various experiments with performance and performance scores.

Stewart's performance practices diversified in the twenty-first century, and Stewart's role as co-founder of *Machine for Making Sense, 180°,* and *Allos* is crucial to the history of the Australian performance ensemble. Stewart has travelled to the United States, meeting Jackson Mac Low and many others. There is some antecedent to this in the first moments of Dada in Australia, when, in the early 1970s, Jas H. Duke (whom Stewart knew and performed with) began performing Dada sound poems in Melbourne. After returning from overseas Duke brought his Dada performances to the Melbourne scene. Yet Chris Mann, a key member in Stewart's *Machine for Making Sense*, did the opposite. Mann began performing in the early 1970s in Melbourne yet later lived much of his life in New York, working with compositional linguistics, and engaging both with members of the neo-avant-gardes, and later, conceptual writers. Duke would 'bring' the foreign back, whereas Mann's immersion in the foreign scene became permanent and Mann in turn influenced those scenes. In these instances the exchange with North American avant-gardes cannot be said to only go one way. A little mesostic, gifted by John Cage, captures Mann's performance practice as "body's talk" and "a fast mix of vulgarity and elegance" (quoted by Gallacher 181).

Vulgarity and elegance, refinement and disruption; these are contradictions of Mann's poetics and perhaps the Antipodal avant-garde at large. The Cagean mesostic has been used also by Javant Biarujia, who is responsible for a variety of visualist and sound poetry practices, the creation of a language, Taneraic, and whose experiments confront the inheritance of the twentieth-century avant-garde from an Antipodal standpoint, Through "wo Rds," "config Urations," and "ges Tures," Biarujia proclaims a "neither/ nor/ a ***rad I(c)al*** *Song of Myself*" that has "airs of so Mething competitive"(20). The poem is open to not just variant reading but also plainer recognition of references. The vertical mesostic words are the elements of Ruthenium and Lutetium. On the horizontal lines, besides writers' names like "Kennet H Koch (& Kostelanetz)," there is the "Manifestos" and the plain cipher of "E=N=E=R=G=U=M=E=N=S," a possessed person, presented with equality signs in the way American Language poetry is often written. It is more specific to the Australian context when read alongside "patt Erns & processes," which suggests the work of Ern Malley and Malley's role in making the question of the avant-garde not only an issue of world literature but modernist Australian poetry (20). These are unusual mesostics; how we read from here is a challenge to criticism and to reading. The history of the avant-garde lingers at the edges of Biarujia's experiments, which are carried out with high seriousness and jest, perhaps more than any Antipodal vanguardist this century.

The late Ania Walwicz was a Polish-born poet whose long and often sparsely punctuated works, often directed scriptwards and scored for performance, might be compared with Mann's. Her writing can be put down to the sound of sound, if it isn't put through the channels of amplification and microphonics; which leads it back to poetry, but the difference will be experienced differently by those who would wish to compare them. Ouyang Yu has made some notable forays into the bilingual exploration of sound, visually and in performance. In all the kinds of sound poetry mentioned what occurs is in keeping with its tradition; it makes us focus on the material or *matter of sound itself*; it will always be that exposed and risky process of laying bare the language, and may result in a communicative short circuit, which distinguishes it from Spoken Word, a more popular form. Both kinds of poetry communicate, and may convey messages, sometimes very clear messages, but the laying bare in classical sound poetry comes to the edge of the subliminal or unconscious (or more strictly in psychotheoretical terms, pre-conscious) levels. Person and character narratives of the exploratory Spoken Word artist will require another history, a reception history too. Duke had spoken critically of the 'churches' of the avant-garde and of sound poetry, and much of the time Antipodal engagement with these practices was not blind participation but critique of the form itself, as clearly is the case also with Mann and Stewart (*poems of life & death* 302).

The sound poetry tradition in Australia began, as we noted earlier, with the Indigenous oral and cultural tradition of the songlines and songspirals, and Indigenous poetry in Australia takes with it the oral tradition at its centre, and this continues in uses of Aboriginal English and Indigenous language in performance. Alison Whittaker, who is also a visualist, performs as much as reads poems, and Lionel Fogarty's performances are notable for use of clapsticks and prosodies that have been heard as directed against audience expectation and white bourgeois decorum, even if that was not the sole purpose of the sounding in the first place. The sound of modern Aboriginal poetry is the bedrock of a generalised notion of Australian poetic sound, and is part of the wider study of the intricacies of *reception*. It is on this register of reception because much of our understanding of the poetry of sound, or sound poetry, comes down to problems of reception and attention: Who listens? In poised attention what expectations have we for consonance? Do we relegate its opposite, in the pejorative sense, to dissonance? If, from the wealth of a mass of passing data, an expected smoothness evaporates and a sound strikes us as harsh, is it still poetic language? What might sound smooth for some may sound harsh for others, and so on. Jewish-Viennese psychoanalyst Theodor Reik speaks of "listening with the third ear," and although the critical divination of poetry is a different sphere to the analysis of the self in Reik, it does involve to a great extent the experience and the idea of listening to what has not been said outright. Therefore we should not speak of the material of

Australian sound poetry as object without losing some of the broader questions of attention, conjecture, concealment, and listening. Australian poetry has a *certain sound*, as a way of putting it, and a variety of ways of making sound – tone, accent, diction, lyricism, and sonic effects; sarcasm, staleness, flatness – all part of an Australian poetic sound, but any account of it must curve back outward to the other side, to the analytic and reception. The tools of careful listening here will be of much use to such an analytic.

Australian poets that have worked with sound have drawn attention to sounds that are peculiar to language's constitution or specific to particular languages, and they have interacted with international tendencies of sound poetry in successive generations of avant-gardes not just in the USA but in the Asia-Pacific and Europe. Much the same as other avant-garde and experimental traditions, the visual field in Australian poetry can be said to have evolved in the same sphere as that of the sonic one. The page, especially when it has become *notational*, that is, treated as a *score* in certain kinds of modern poetry, has for itself a new life in the visual field often because of sounded necessity. If we have a tendency to pry apart the active and the passive in the deeper energies of poetry, drawing attention to the visuality of the word gives us something similar to that of its audiality; our attention shifts to the activity of the saturated word in the visual field.

Visualisms

There is no use cordoning off visualism from sound, as above, because sound so often leaves us with its shadow in scored textual space, as is the case in Alex Selenitsch's monotone works, such as *7 More Monotones* (1973) (see Figures 19.1 and 19.2), which might be compared to visual works of the Brazilian Noigandres. The production of visual poetry goes side by side with processes that also have to do with the spatialisation of sound, and often-times it is how sound haunts the edges of the page that causes us to orient ourselves in visual space. The oraliteral interspace is our concern: where calligraphic and pictographic fold into the pictophonetic. Nowadays, the appearance of text in the gallery, whether painted or through remediated bibliographic object, is commonplace, but Indigenous artist Vernon Ah Kee does so in ways that catch the viewer off guard. Ah Kee often eliminates 'tracking,' the space between each word, so that the viewing process takes more than a second glance. In the delay manifold meanings emerge, with both canonical European literature and popular culture implicated in the excess of colonial criminality. In Alison Whittaker's *Blakwork* (2018) there is an emoji poem that also causes the viewer to look again. A quick cryptography that needs to be worked out; "scissors anchor pistol" (162) tells a

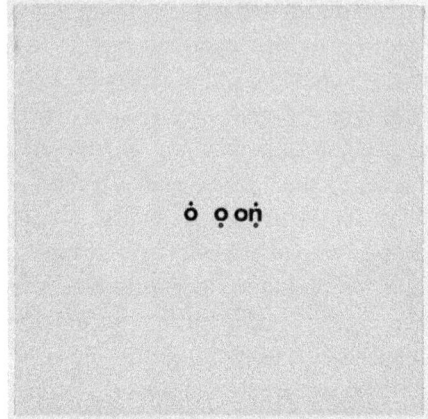

Figure 19.1 Alex Selenitsch, from *7 More Monotones* (1973 n.pag.)

Figure 19.2 Alex Selenitsch, from *7 More Monotones* (1973 n.pag.)

narrative in a similar way to Xu Bing's *Book from the Ground: From Point to Point* (2018), otherwise titled • → ⫫ → •, composed of only symbols and icons. The point here is that the reader must decipher the meaning, which is not meant to be variant but could be. In Whittaker's poem readers will derive their own meaning, which will ultimately be something about the dream of the end of the colonial era, the slump, the fiery end of colonial festivity, the veneration of anchors and explorers, a true new day.

A similar kind of thing happens in some visual work by Michael Farrell, with *Break Me Ouch*, a comic strip narrative poem from 2006, and Chris Edwards' *after Naptime: a poem, profusely illustrated* (2014). Edwards' visualism in multiple works brings together collage, storybook aesthetics, the hieroglyph, and all kinds of experimentation with bookwork and book form. He uses a variety of sources (see Figure 19.3 as example), from Dickens to adventure stories for boys, newspapers, popular books, obscure books, and other curiosities, and the result is a type of narrative scroll that has to be read – or I think is read better – continuously through the pages from 'top' to 'bottom' without pause.

Narrative logic is never far from these and other works of Edwards, like ḥm, a long scroll published in a run of sixteen by binder and printer Nicholas Pounder through Polar Bear Press. Pounder's role in small press and artists' book production is significant. ḥm comes with *A Glyph Glossary*, in standard chapbook form, which is an aid to reading the glyphs and hieroglyphs of the scroll. In operation since 1985, Mike Hudson and Jadwiga Jarvis's Wayzgoose Press has produced works of similar quality such as Jas H. Duke's *Dada kampfen um Leben und Tod: A Prose Poem* (1996) and PiO's *Ockers: A Poem* (1999), a Pop poem. Duke, as mentioned, was as much a concrete or visual poet as sound poet. Duke's *Destiny Wood* (1978) is a part-epic graphic novel that tells a story, in dramatic and visual form, of Jim Arch, "a poet and scientific observer," and Annie, Ann, "a girl from Henry Fuseli" (n.pag.). Figure 19.4 gives a glimpse of its typographical innovation. It is an extraordinary work that has all the trappings of an eighteenth-century novel, and were it further studied one only wonders what could become of it, placed beside, for instance, the dramatic works of Rochelle Owens in a similar period, with its carnival of debauchery, or indeed studied for its visual ingenuity.

It could be said that the generation that began writing and performing in the 1970s and a little earlier is nothing less than the first fruits of an Australian avant-garde. Duke, Selenitsch, PiO, Mann, Thalia, Stewart, Pam Brown, Ian Burn, Pete Spence, Richard Tipping – whose sign works became well-known in the postmodern gallery context – and others pursued a variety of visual practices, each deserving individual attention. From Donnithorne Street, Kyneton, in the state of Victoria, Spence has produced Mail Art, chapbooks, and collaborations with the Dutch-born visual poet Cornelius Vleeskens such as *Alpha-cartography, South by South* (2001). The chapbook includes a note saying that the collaboration developed "back and forth through the mail" (n.pag.). Pat Larter would do 'femail art' on a similar scale and earn international recognition for it.

Post the mail era, some amount of visual poetry has been produced by subsequent generations; those in the zine scene and those who resist the aesthetic and poetic consensus of their time and the conventions and constraints of publishing. Significant visualists of the new century have been

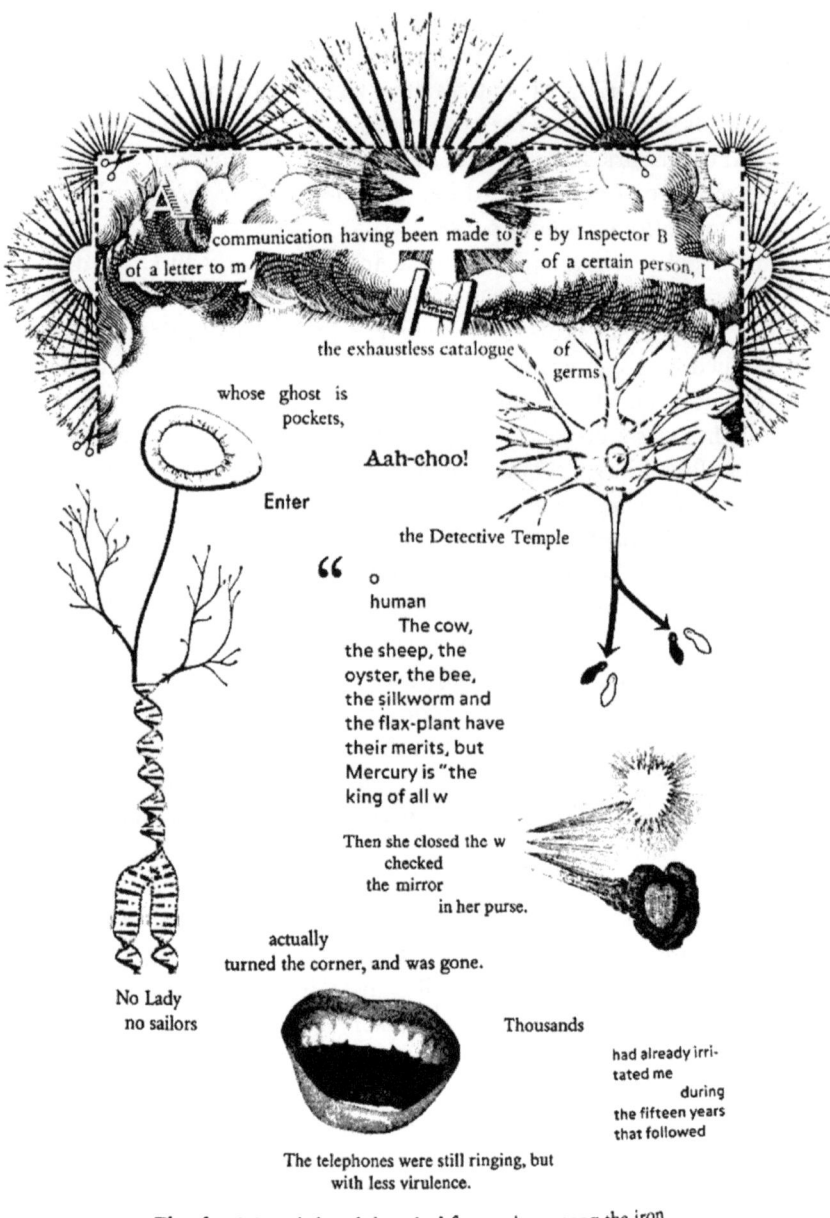

Figure 19.3 Chris Edwards, from *after Naptime* (2014 n.pag.)

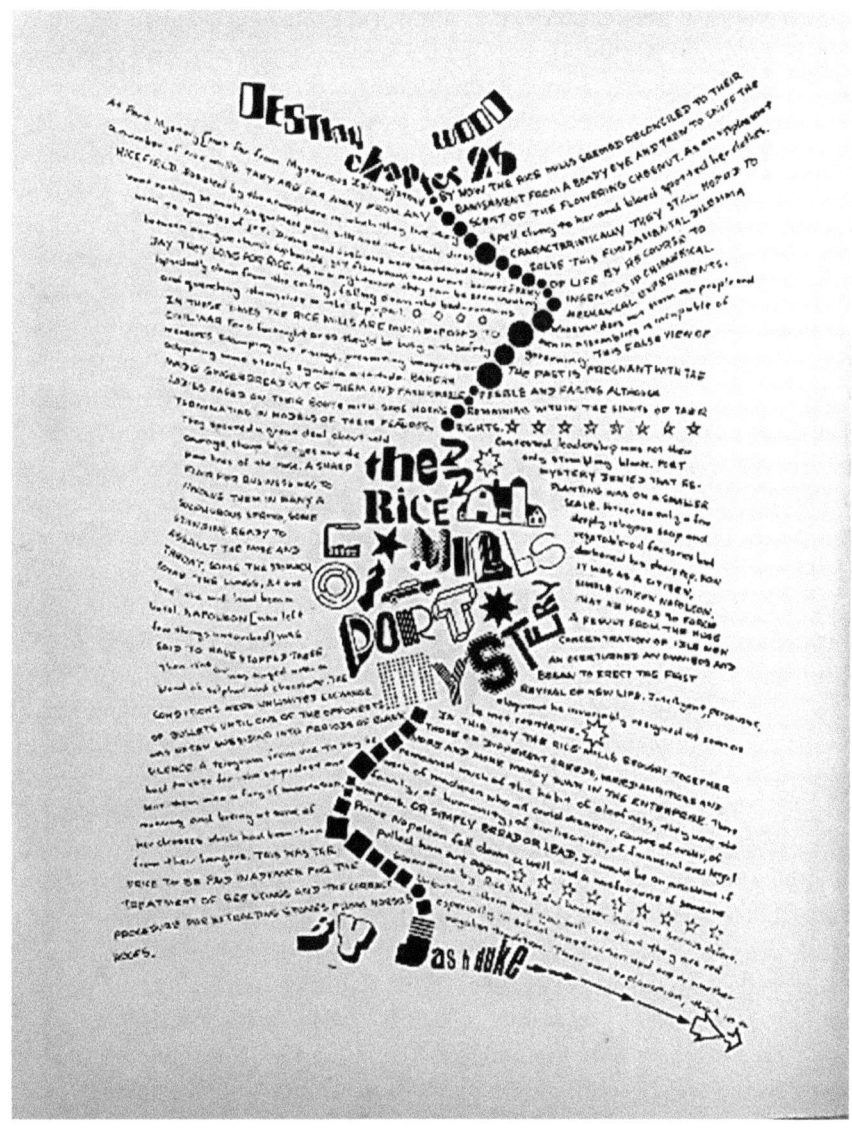

Figure 19.4 Jas H. Duke, from *Destiny Wood* (1978 n.pag.)

Bella Li, Cathy Vidler, Nick Whittock, Whittaker, Natalie Harkin, Jessica L. Wilkinson, and Toby Fitch. Whittock, for instance, has taken the form of the cricket scorebook as a base-level constraint for visual exploration in *hows its* (2014). He extends this to the environment of the game, from its rules, the space of the field and its geometries, schedule, stats, and language, out of the book and into the space of performance.

Two works written decades apart are worth examining side by side rather than by generational chronology. One is a series of *Sonnets* by Alex Selenitsch (1975), and the other, a chapbook titled *Lost Sonnets*, by Cathy Vidler, is part of a series begun in 2015, and indeed part of many sequences by Vidler. Selenitsch's *Sonnets* are not devoid of language. The first page gives structural setting for the Sonnet hypothesis: "antithesis / parenthesis / synthesis" (n.pag.). The second page, however, commits this initial formation to spatial reduction: "above," followed by a clear line of separation, and "below." The third verticalises the second, giving the dimension for a tripartite form in which the first two quatrains, since that is what they would be, are drawn together, and the last quatrain and the couplet are pulled away from each other. Directionality is then squared off, so that the four components are afforded their final relation as a triplicate, with the third a divided square. The final reduction is a number while also revealing the optical level of the sonnet.

The recognition that poetry *has shape* for itself can occur outside the confines of the lexical, and when it does so it is primarily in the "x-ray image of the work," to use Adorno's phrase for musical reproduction (quoted by Cecchi 132). Vidler's *Lost Sonnets* (2018), much more recent, creates another x-ray image of the work of the sonnet. Vidler uses various tools at hand, in MS Word and MS Paint, to image the sonnet's lines and the dynamics thereof. Two senses of form, bulk-shape and word-shape, are exposed in the resulting visual poems. Exposed might not be the right word. Willard Bohn's identification of *eyesight* and *insight* can suffice to explain what a visual poem does not just to perception but conception; what is exposed, uncovered, in the space of a visual poem, is also the communication of insight; what began externally in the shock of raw sight is quickly internalised, made insight. Insight into what? In both Vidler and Selenitsch the insight amounts to *poetic criticism* of the sonnet form, which doesn't mean a lack of enthusiasm with it or its possibilities, one is rather 'exposed' to the x-ray image of the work, which is to say a visual poetics not just of the surface that manifests, but the surface that conceals.

It should be plain to see that modern Australian visual and concrete poetry needs further study, both in the form of genealogy and community, and concerning the general nature of it, whether on the whole it emerges alongside global avant-gardes or neo-avant-gardes, what types and forms have been made – precisionist, processual, loose, Oulipean, collagistic, notational, conceptual – and how various individuals were first published or published themselves; the role of Collective Effort Press, and the work of PiO, here loom large. Some of these names, like Amanda Stewart, Jas H. Duke, Alex Selenitsch, Thalia, Chris Edwards, Vernon Ah Kee, Ian Burn, Cathy Vidler, and Pete Spence, should be examined both in isolation and comparatively, because their practices are sustained and complex. It also needs to be stressed that visual poetry has an ancient history, like sound poetry, and a modern one that intersects with Language Art from the 1960s and in the now. The Indigenous visual tradition has long engaged with language. June Walkutjukurr Richards works often with single words or phrases on canvas, some of which are about art production and exploitation, like "Carpetbagger" (2008), white dealers of Indigenous art, in what Jennifer Loureide Biddle calls "biliterary aesthetics" in *Remote Avant-Garde: Aboriginal Art under Occupation*. In this way Biddle describes Richards' practice:

> In no sense arbitrary vocabulary items or random samples, rather, these painted words, terms, phrases, and idioms are pointed and honed. A precise, chiseled, semantic field of words as art that are *of* art. These expressions bespeak the history of desert art production, market, and demand: greed, possession, profit mongering. Visible and stealth-like witness to otherwise unspeakable, unutterable, silenced histories of Aboriginal experience, Ngaanyatjarra voice. The Western Desert art movement may indeed be the fastest-growing art movement of the twenty-first century and is no small cause for national celebration – but not without cost. Unapologetic, Richards's works are a sharp response but appear as if non sequitur: statements, not questions, flat unadorned facts. Nowhere else and a sense of cauterization – caught, captured, containment – screams. The affect here is thick and instantaneous, poignant and funny. Richards's art hurts, wounding as it hits – an unhealed colonial history not over, not past. (81–82)

National celebration, in an historical period without pillars of sovereignty, in the period of Occupation, that has not reinvented itself or its symbology, would most certainly have to wait, and yet here *nation* can take on the new meaning as First Nations biliterary language art, a history of its own that bears the burden of "unhealed colonial history." This is not to say that colonial writing in itself was monolithic. Michael Farrell, in his 2015 book *Writing Australian Unsettlement: Modes of Poetic Invention 1796–1945* does poetics-based readings of various, and some visualist, works from the colonial and early modernist era, from Jong Ah Sing's unusual handwritten diary *The Case* (from around 1867 to 1872) to Ned Kelly's *Jerilderie Letter* (written in 1878), *Ngarla Songs* (a translation of Ngarla oral texts circa 2019, by Alexander Brown and Brian Geytenbeck), and Christopher Brennan's *Musicopoematographoscope* works (from 1897, inspired by Mallarmé's *En Coup de Dés* and written in the same year). In these and other works Farrell sees an unsettlement of poetics – in making, marking, lettering – and therefore also an unsettlement of the whole concept of a national literature.

The poets whose engagement with visual poetry in the avant-garde tradition is most profound and lasting are those concrete poets of the early 1970s and through to the hypermedia experiments of the 1980s, but outside that cluster attention should be paid to visual poets who are not usually cited in these genealogies like Vietnamese-Australian visualist Lê Văn Tài, Chinese-Australian letter-and-character painter Zhao Baokang, and Indigenous language art like that of Vernon Ah Kee. The manifold forms of visual language, from notation to narrative to glyph, x-ray images of the work, and the processes that lead to such forms – performance, collaboration, unconventional ways of publishing or disseminating such work – may engender a certain historical strangeness, an unsettling sense that poetry by other means does not sit so easily within the constitution of national literature, and by not fitting in stands out. As outstanding, even outsider poetry, poetry that doesn't seek to win prizes, please judges, secure grants, or fit within established expectations, it could retain for itself a certain formal and thematic freedom. Though it lives on the periphery does not mean it should be ignored or is any less worthy than that which occupies the centre.

Digital Poetry

That the potency of sound poetry, which is not succeeded by visual poetry but complementary with it, then leads to a third, digital poetry (also known as electronic poetry), is not just a fact of media convergence and not just a product of media, even if it comes through those things: that makes it acceptable to talk about it then as another kind of poetry. It isn't to say that matters of media are glossed over, but simply to go further and ask what it is that makes digital poetry poetry. The digital poetry *of* Australia is thoroughly international because many of the exhibitions, awards, and fora of such writing take place across continents and hemispheres.

Mez Breeze, one of the longest practising digital-oriented poets, could be said to be writing both in the *idiom* of the digital and writing through the manifold forms – code poetry, net.art, mezangelle (developed in the 1990s), game environments – to get to poetry and to poetics. In a recent work *V[R]ignettes: A Microstory Series*, accessible as of 2021 on mezbreezedesign.com, a reader enters the spatial dimension of the poem, for they are poems with lines as well as storylines, and can navigate them (go 'in' to them) on whichever device they choose to navigate them on. In "Wracking in the Upper Bubble" a daemonic figure stands at the centre of the work against the backdrop of some main text. I swivel round and find the line: "With opinions bred in cloisters ... their odd bra[cken]yish voices / cast from long shear faces." The triple stress of long shear faces lingers; I hear it spondaically before wondering whether it is in fact a sheer, or ferocious molossic. Blake would shiver at the prospect of entering such a space.

Hazel Smith migrated to Australia in the 1980s, and is a foremost electronic poet, using new media, hypertext, music, and, more fundamentally, exploring the interanimation of sound and word. Smith is a member of *austraLYSIS*, an Australian and international ensemble doing intermedia performance. What can be seen here is not just the general historical trend of post-digital media but writing under the influence of such things as exploded font varieties, and different types and means of control over the vectors of the line to that of concrete poetry. Benjamin Laird's *The Durham Poems* are biographical in nature, concerning the life of the psychometrist William Denton (1823–83). The reader enters the JavaScript environment of the poem and notices that the words shuffle into place before settling. Thereafter it is harder to 'move' the poem as it sits in place. Figures 19.5 and 19.6 show two versions 'created' during two 'sittings' of mine with the poem "The Spirit of Reform":

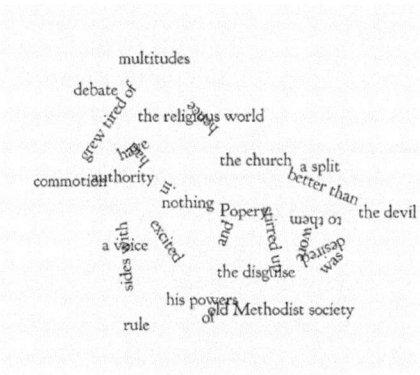

Figure 19.5 Benjamin Laird, from *The Durham Poems* (2016)

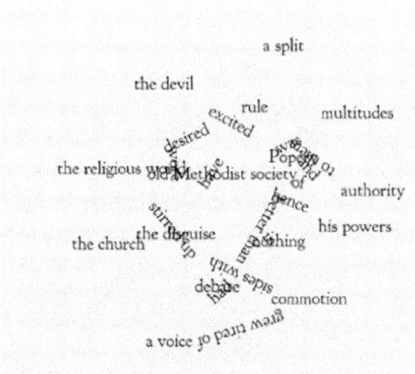

Figure 19.6 Benjamin Laird, from *The Durham Poems* (2016)

Conceptual Poetry

The question of the gallery context and its relation to conceptualism is relevant here, and in the terms of conceptual poetics, we can say that the tradition is not confined to a solely North American context. Like digital writing, conceptual writing is rather a global phenomenon. In the strictest terms available to us then, the kinds of works that can be deemed conceptual are Jonathan Tse's 1998 work *Portrait of an Australian*, in the form and shape of an Australian passport, Natalie Harkin's *Dirty Words*, in the form of a dictionary, Ian Burn's *Xerox Book #1*, iterative photocopies of 'blanks,' and Amelia Dale's *Constitution*, in the form of the Australian Constitution, all of which hang on the edge of the book as object, with its forms and limits. It may be easy to see how this works in tandem with digital writing, but the contexts are different. Digital writing both is and is not bringing into question the context of its appearance; platform is often (but not always) out of the question, whereas the conceptual poem shakes the ground of the work, no matter how essential that ground is to the work's appearance, with the odd fact that this ground is often the printed book. Antipodal digital poetics through Breeze and virtual reality literature, the hypermedia poetics of Hazel Smith, and more recent experiments by Benjamin Laird, extend audiovisualism in the most fundamental sense of *experiment*, testing the new environment and making poetry through the test.

Motives for disruption seem in some ways tied to motives of refinement; it remains to be seen whether this has something to do with the deeper energics of creation and destrudo. An even more penetrating inquiry is that of motives for convention. Motives for convention change. It may be that there is, or will be, such thing as 'convention' in some of these showings: theoretical excursions drawn from this dossier await for those who wish to do so analyses of what may constitute the conventions of experiment. Though not wholly definitive, because nothing is, from here researchers will be able to get to the foundations of experimental sound, visual, and digital poetries from the twentieth-century Antipodal avant-gardes up to contemporary experiment, at least at this time of writing in the vanishing present. I will close without extrapolating any more from this than that lack of access is not the same as the refusal to read. Difficult works demand not just contextual oversight but direct optics, even divination, an optic of the particulars. This and the fact that archives and histories are not for the past: an archive can itself create a future history, an archive, that is, becomes dynamic for works inspired by what it shelves and protects.

In the world of small press, the vanishing present absents itself for the present and materials come briefly into view, but the time-scape is never confined to the present. The present is the greatest risk, of it we know the least. At this point in time, poetry by these means in Australia has an ancient and modern history, is part of those histories, and is unfinished. Nothing has arrived; we aren't *there yet*. "Good times acoming," Kate Jennings jotted in the *Mother I'm Rooted* anthology (n.pag.). The difficulty in bringing this all to light cannot be glossed over: anthologies such as *Mother I'm Rooted* could be digitised for broader access, for example, and the archive expanded, for whatever intellectual property can permit. But for whom? The archive only speaks when it is gestured to in advance for one willing to receive and to listen to it. The good times of sound and visual poetry – notated or spiralling in unsettling mediations across page, screen, book, ground, through the air and in the body – are not yet over, and yet they have happened. In time they will tell their own history, of which this can only be a written fragment.

Works Cited

Biarujia, Javant. *Spelter to Pewter*. Cordite Books, 2016.
Biddle, Jennifer Loureide. *Remote Avant-Garde: Aboriginal Art under Occupation*. Duke University Press, 2016.
Bing, Xu. *Book from the Ground: From Point to Point*. MIT Press, 2018.
Bohn, Willard. *Reading Visual Poetry*. Fairleigh Dickinson University Press, 2011.
Breeze, Mez. *V[R]ignettes: A Microstory Series*. mezbreezedesign.com.
Burn, Ian. *Xerox Book #1*, 1968. Artist book held at National Gallery of Australia.
Cecchi, Alessandro. "To Imitate All That Is Hidden: The Place of Mimesis in Adorno's Musical Performance." *Aisthesis* vol.1 no.1, 2017, pp. 131–38.
Dale, Amelia. *Constitution*. Inken Publisch, 2017.
Duke, Jas H. *Destiny Wood*. Whole Australian Catalogue, 1978, n.pag.
   Dada kampfen um Leben und Tod: A Prose Poem. Wayzgoose, 1996.
   poems of life & death, edited by PiO. Collective Effort Press, 2003.
Edwards, Chris. *after Naptime: a poem, profusely illustrated*. Vagabond Books, 2014.
   hm. Polar Bear Press, 2015.
Farrell, Michael. *Break Me Ouch*. 3 Deep Publishing, 2006.
   Writing Australian Unsettlement: Modes of Poetic Invention, 1796–1945. Palgrave Macmillan, 2015.
Gallacher, Lyn. "Of Course – A Grammatical Tech Check." *Continuum* vol.8 no.1, 1994, pp. 181–91.
Gay'wu Group of Women. *Songspirals: Sharing Women's Wisdom of Country through Songlines*. Allen & Unwin, 2019.
Harkin, Natalie. *Dirty Words*. Cordite Books, 2015.
Jennings, Kate, ed. *Mother I'm Rooted: An Anthology of Australian Women Poets*. Outback Press, 1975.
Kouvaras, Linda Ioanna. *Loading the Silence: Australian Sound Art in the Post-Digital Age*. Routledge, 2013, pp. 3–18.

Laird, Benjamin. *The Durham Poems*. SOd Press, 2016.
PiO. *Ockers: A Poem*. Wayzgoose, 1999.
Reik, Theodor. *Listening with the Third Ear: The Inner Experience of a Psychoanalyst*. Grove Press, 1948.
Selenitsch, Alex. *7 More Monotones*. N.pub, 1973.
— *Sonnets*. bUcKs, 1975.
Spence, Pete and Cornelius Vleeskens. *Alpha-cartography, South by South*. Runaway Spoon Press, 2001.
Stewart, Amanda. *I/T: Selected Poems 1980–1996*. Here and There/Split Records, 1998.
Strehlow, T. G. H. *Songs of Central Australia*. Angus & Robertson, 1971.
Tse, Jonathan. *Portrait of an Australian*, 1998. Artists' book held at State Library of Queensland.
Vidler, Catherine. *Lost Sonnets*. Spacecraft Press, 2018.
Whittaker, Alison. *Blakwork*. Magabala Books, 2018.
Whittock, Nick. *hows its*. Inken Publisch, 2014.

FURTHER READING

The general bibliography below contains a selection of critical studies relating to Australian poetry. Based around the *Companion*'s chapters, it is not intended to be exhaustive. The AustLit database is an indispensable aid in sourcing the works of individual writers, poetry anthologies, and presses, as well as researching further aspects of Australian poetry and its contexts. AustLit is available at www.austlit.edu.au.

Ackland, Michael. *That Shining Band: A Study of Australian Colonial Verse Tradition*. University of Queensland Press, 1994.
   "Poetry from the 1890s to 1970." *The Cambridge Companion to Australian Literature*, edited by Elizabeth Webby. Cambridge University Press, 2000, pp. 74–104.
Adelaide, Debra. *Australian Women Writers: A Bibliographic Guide*. Pandora Press, 1988.
   ed. *A Bright and Fiery Troop: Australian Women Writers of the Nineteenth Century*. Penguin, 1989.
Aitken, Adam. "A Poetics of (Un)Becoming Hybridity." *Southerly* vol.73 no.1, 2013, pp. 123–37.
Alizadeh, Ali. "Sufis of the Antipodes: The Ghazal in Contemporary Australian Poetry." *La Trobe Journal* no.91, 2013, pp. 140–48.
Anderson, Hugh. *Poet Militant: Bernard O'Dowd*. Hill of Content, 1968.
Anderson, Hugh and L. J. Blake. *John Shaw Neilson*. Rigby, 1972.
Araluen, Evelyn. "Resisting the Institution." *Overland* no.227, 2017. https://overland.org.au/previous-issues/issue-227/feature-evelyn-araluen/.
Arnott, Georgina. *The Unknown Judith Wright*. UWA Publishing, 2016.
Atherton, Cassandra. *Flashing Eyes and Floating Hair: A Reading of Gwen Harwood's Pseudonymous Poetry*. Australian Scholarly Publishing, 2006.
   ed. *Travelling without Gods: A Chris Wallace-Crabbe Companion*. Melbourne University Press, 2014.
Attfield, Sarah. "The Invisible Force: Working Class Voices in Contemporary Australian Poetry." *Overland* no.165, 2001, pp. 21–28.
Barnes, Katherine. *The Higher Self in Christopher Brennan's Poems: Esotericism, Romanticism, Symbolism*. Brill, 2006.
Bartlett, Alison. *Jamming the Machinery: Contemporary Australian Women's Writing*. National Library of Australia, 1998.

Bennett, Bruce. *Spirit in Exile: Peter Porter and His Poetry*. Oxford University Press, 1991.
  Dorothy Hewett: Selected Critical Essays. Fremantle Arts Centre Press, 1995.
Bennett, Bruce and Anne Pender, *From a Distant Shore: Australian Writers in Britain 1820–2012*. Monash University Publishing, 2013.
Berryman, Jim and Caitlin Stone. "Australian National Anthologies: A Study of Poems and Poets." *Journal of Australian Studies* vol.41 no.1, 2017, pp. 47–64.
Biddle, Jennifer Loureide. *Remote Avant-Garde Art under Occupation*. Duke University Press, 2016.
Birns, Nicholas. *Contemporary Australian Literature: A World Not Yet Dead*. Sydney University Press, 2015.
Birns, Nicholas and Rebecca McNeer, eds. *A Companion to Australian Literature since 1900*. Camden House, 2007.
Birns, Nicholas, Nicole Moore, and Sarah Schieff, eds. *Teaching Australian and New Zealand Literature*. Modern Language Association, 2017.
Birns, Nicholas and Louis Klee, eds. *The Cambridge Companion to the Australian Novel*. Cambridge University Press, 2023.
Bourke, Lawrence. *A Vivid Steady State: Les Murray and Australian Poetry*. University of New South Wales Press, 1992.
Brewster, Anne. *Giving This Country a Memory: Contemporary Aboriginal Voices of Australia*. Cambria Press, 2015.
Brooks, David. *The Sons of Clovis: Ern Malley, Adoré Floupette and a Secret History of Australian Poetry*. University of Queensland Press, 2011.
Brooks, David and Brenda Walker, eds. *Poetry and Gender: Statements and Essays on Australian Women's Poetry and Poetics*. University of Queensland Press, 1989.
Buckley, Vincent. *Essays In Poetry: Mainly Australian*. Melbourne University Press, 1957.
Cahill, Michelle. "The Poetics of Subalternity." *Mascara Literary Review*, 23 May 2012.
Calder, Bill. *Pink Ink: The Golden Era for Gay and Lesbian Magazines*. Cambridge Scholars, 2016.
Carruthers, A. J. "Who's Afraid of Poetic Invention? Anthologising Australian Poetry in the Twenty-First Century." *JASAL* vol.17 no.2, 2018, pp. 1–23.
Carruthers, A. J., Lia Incognita, Samuel Wagan Watson, and Elena Gomez. "Four Perspectives on Race and Racism in Australian Poetry." *Overland* no.222, 2016, pp. 83–91.
Carter, David. *Always Almost Modern: Australian Print Cultures and Modernity*. Australian Scholarly Publishing, 2013.
Carter, David and Roger Osborne. *Australian Books and Authors in the American Marketplace 1840s–1940s*. Sydney University Press, 2018.
Carter, Paul. *The Road to Botany Bay: An Exploration of Landscape and History*. University of Minneapolis Press, 2010.
Casey, Brendan. "Essential Gossip: Allen Ginsberg, Robert Duncan and U.S.-Australian Poetics." *Cordite Poetry Review*, 15 February 2023. http://cordite.org.au/essays/essential-gossip/.
Cassidy, Bonny. "Reading and Writing to Learn: The Problem of Poetry." *Teaching Australian Literature: From Classroom to National Imaginings*, edited by

Brenton Doecke, Larissa McLean Davies, and Philip Mead. Wakefield Press; Australian Association for the Teaching of English, 2011, pp. 293–306.
Castles, Belinda, ed. *Reading Like an Australian Writer*. NewSouth Publishing, 2021.
Chander, Manu Samriti. *Brown Romantics: Poetry and Nationalism in the Global Nineteenth Century*. Bucknell University Press, 2017.
Clarke, Patricia. *Pen Portraits: Women Writers and Journalists in Nineteenth-Century Australia*. Angus & Robertson, 1988.
Coleman, Deidre and Peter Otto, eds. *Imagining Romanticism: Essays on English and Australian Romanticisms*. Locust Hill, 1992.
Coleman, Peter. *The Heart of James McAuley: Life and Works of the Australian Poet*. Wildcat, 1980.
Cooke, Stuart. *Speaking the Earth's Languages: A Theory for Australian-Chilean Postcolonial Poetics*. Rodopi, 2013.
⸻. "Tracing a Trajectory from Songpoetry to Contemporary Aboriginal Poetry." *A Companion to Australian Aboriginal Literature*, edited by Belinda Wheeler. Camden House, 2013, pp. 89–106.
Corr, Evelyn Araluen. "Silence and Resistance: Aboriginal Women Working within and against the Archive." *Continuum* vol.32 no.4, 2018, pp. 487–502.
Dale, Leigh. *The English Men: Professing Literature in Australian Universities*. Association for the Study of Australian Literature, 1997.
Dalziell, Tanya and Paul Genoni, eds. *Telling Stories: Australian Life and Literature 1935–2012*. Monash University Press, 2013.
Davidson, Toby. *Christian Mysticism and Australian Poetry*. Cambria Press, 2013.
⸻. *Good for the Soul: John Curtin's Life with Poetry*. UWA Publishing, 2021.
Digby, Jenny. *A Woman's Voice: Conversations with Australian Poets*. University of Queensland Press, 1996.
Disney, Dan and Matthew Hall, eds. *New Directions in Contemporary Australian Poetry*. Palgrave Macmillan, 2021.
Dixon, Robert and Veronica Kelly. *The Impact of the Modern: Vernacular Modernities in Australia 1870s–1960s*. University of Sydney Press, 2008.
Dobrez, Livio. *Parnassus Mad Ward: Michael Dransfield and the New Australian Poetry*. University of Queensland Press, 1990.
Dobrez, Patricia. *Michael Dransfield's Lives: A Sixties Biography*. Miegunyah Press, 1999.
Docker, John. *The Nervous Nineties: Australian Cultural Life in the 1890s*. Oxford University Press, 1991.
Dunk, Jonathan. "The Stump: Looking Back on the Republic of Murray." *Overland*, 7 June 2019. https://overland.org.au/2019/06/the-stump-looking-back-on-the-republic-of-murray/.
Duwell, Martin. *A Possible Contemporary Poetry*. Makar Press, 1982.
Eades, Quinn. "Transpoetics: Dialogically Writing the Queer and Trans Body in Fragments." *Axon: Creative Explorations* vol.7 no.2, 2017. www.axonjournal.com.au/issues/7-2/transpoetics.
Edmonds, Phillip. *Tilting at Windmills: The Literary Magazine in Australia, 1968-2012*. University of Adelaide Press, 2015.
Etherington, Ben. "Unsettled Poetics: Contemporary Australian and South African Poetry." *Wasafiri* vol.31 no.2, 2016, pp. 1–4.

Fagan, Kate, ed. "A Matter of Poetry: Why and How Does Poetry Matter?" *Meanjin* vol.60 no.2, 2001, pp. 48–64.

Farrell, Michael. *Writing Australian Unsettlement: Modes of Poetic Invention 1796–1845*. Palgrave Macmillan, 2015.

Ferney, Liam. "Never Be Alone Again: Hip-Hop Sampling as a Technique in Contemporary Australian Poetry." *Cordite Poetry Review*, 2020. http://cordite.org.au/essays/never-be-alone-again/.

Ford, Thomas H. and Justin Clemens. *Barron Field in New South Wales: The Poetics of Terra Nullius*. Melbourne University Press, 2023.

Gay'wu Group of Women. *Songspirals: Sharing Women's Wisdom of Country through Songlines*. Allen & Unwin, 2019.

Giles, Paul. *Antipodean America: Australasia and the Constitution of U.S. Literature*. Oxford University Press, 2013.

Backgazing: Reverse Time in Modernist Culture. Oxford University Press, 2019.

Green, Dorothy. *The Music of Love: Critical Essays on Literature and Life*. Melbourne University Press, 1984.

Green, H. M. *A History of Australian Literature*. 2 vols. Angus & Robertson, 1961.

Griffith, Michael. *God's Fool: The Life and Poetry of Francis Webb*. Angus & Robertson, 1991.

Griffiths, Michael. *The Distribution of Settlement: Appropriation and Refusal in Australian Literature and Culture*. UWA Publishing, 2018.

Hansord, Katie. *Colonial Australian Women Poets: Political Voice and Feminist Traditions*. Anthem Press, 2021.

Harkin, Natalie. "The Poetics of (Re)Mapping Archives: Memory in the Blood." *JASAL* vol.14 no.3, 2014, pp. 1–14.

Harrison, Martin. *Who Wants to Create Australia? Essays on Poetry & Ideas in Contemporary Australia*. Halstead Press, 2004.

Hart, Kevin. "Open, Mixed, and Moving: Recent Australian Poetry." *World Literature Today* vol.67 no.3, 1993, pp. 282–88.

Hawke, John. *Australian Literature and the Symbolist Movement*. University of Woollongong Press, 2009.

Heiss, Anita. *Dhuuluu-Yala = To Talk Straight: Publishing Indigenous Literature*. Aboriginal Studies Press, 2003.

Hergenhan, Laurie and Bruce Clunies Ross, eds. *The Poetry of Les Murray: Critical Essays*. University of Queensland Press, 2002.

Heseltine, Harry, ed. *A Tribute to David Campbell: A Collection of Essays*. University of New South Wales Press, 1987.

Hetherington, Paul and Cassandra Atherton. "Prose Poetry in Australia." *Western Humanities Review* vol.72 no.1, 2018, pp. 67–72.

Prose Poetry: An Introduction. Princeton University Press, 2020.

Heyward, Michael. *The Ern Malley Affair*. University of Queensland Press, 1993.

Hodge, Bob and Vijay Mishra. *Dark Side of the Dream: Australian Literature and the Postcolonial Mind*. Angus & Robertson, 1991.

Holland-Batt, Sarah. *Fishing for Lightning: The Spark of Poetry*. University of Queensland Press, 2021.

Holland-Batt, Sarah and Ella Jeffery. "Twenty-First-Century Australian Poetry," *The Routledge Companion to Australian Literature*, edited by Jessica Gildersleeve. Routledge, 2020, pp. 335–43.

Hope, A. D. *Native Companions: Essays and Comments on Australian Literature, 1936–1966*. Angus & Robertson, 1974.

Hopfer, Sabina. "Reading Lionel Fogarty: An Attempt to Feel into Texts Speaking of Decolonisation." *Southerly* vol.62 no.2, 2002, pp. 45–64.

Hughes-D'Aeth, Tony. *Like Nothing on This Earth: A Literary History of the Wheatbelt*. UWA Publishing, 2018.

Hurley, Michael. "Gay and Lesbian Writing and Publishing in Australia, 1961–2010." *Australian Literary Studies* vol.25, no.1, 2010, pp. 42–70.

Jacklin, Michael. "'Desde Australia para todo elm undo hispano': Australia's Spanish Language Magazines and Latin American/Australian Writing." *Antipodes* vol.24 no.2, 2010, pp. 177–86.

Jackson, Andy. "Caesura and the Deforming Poem: Rupture as a Space for the Other." *Australian Literary Studies* vol.37 no.1, 2022. www.australianliterarystudies.com.au/articles/caesura-and-the-deforming-poem-rupture-as-a-space-for-the-other.

Johnson, Colin. "Guerilla Poetry: Lionel Fogarty's Response to Language Genocide." *Westerly* vol.31 no.3, 1986, pp. 47–55.

Johnson, Judith and Monica Anderson, eds. *Australia Imagined: Views from the British Periodical Press, 1800–1860*. UWA Publishing, 2005.

Johnston, Anna and Elizabeth Webby, eds. *Eliza Hamilton Dunlop*. Sydney University Press, 2021.

Justice, Daniel Heath. *Why Indigenous Literature Matters*. Wilfrid Laurier Press, 2018.

Kane, Paul. *Australian Poetry: Romanticism and Negativity*. Cambridge University Press, 1996.

Keesing, Nancy. *Douglas Stewart*. Oxford University Press, 1965.

Kent, Jacqueline. *A Certain Style: Beatrice Davis, A Literary Life*. Viking, 2001.

Kinsella, John. *Spatial Relations, Vol. 1: Essays, Reviews, Commentaries, and Chorography*. Rodopi, 2013.

Legibility: An Antifascist Poetics. Palgrave Macmillan, 2022.

Kirkby, Joan, ed. *The American Model: Influence and Independence in Australian Poetry*. Hale & Iremonger, 1982.

Kirkpatrick, Peter. *The Sea Coast of Bohemia: Literary Life in the Roaring Twenties*. API Network, 2007.

"Australian Poetry, 1940s–1960s." *Oxford Research Encyclopedia of Literature*, edited by Paula Rabinowitz, Oxford University Press, 2017, pp. 1–46.

Kissane, Andy, David Musgrave, and Carolyn Rickett, eds. *Feeding the Ghost 1: Criticism on Contemporary Australian Poetry*. Puncher & Wattmann, 2018.

Klee, Louis. "Reading Lionel Fogarty." *Textual Practice* vol.36 no.6, 2022, pp. 928–52.

Kohinga, Kyle. "'Soil Is a Toil Needing to Recoil': Lionel Fogarty, Andrew Forrest, and the Settler-Colonial Georgic." *Australian Literary Studies* vol.81 no.1, 2023. www.australianliterarystudies.com.au/articles/soil-is-a-toil-needing-all-to-recoil-lionel-fogarty-andrew-forrest-and-the-settler-colonial-georgic.

Lea, Bronwyn. "Trends in Poetry Publishing, 1995–2008." *Five Bells* vol.15 no.4, 2009, pp. 61–64.

"Australian Poetry Now." *Poetry* vol.208 no.2, 2016, pp. 185–91.

Leane, Jeanine. "Gathering: The Politics of Memory and Contemporary Aboriginal Women's Writing." *Antipodes* vol.31 no.2, 2019, pp. 242–51.

"No Longer Malleable Stuff." *Overland* no.241, 2020, pp. 11–18.

Lee, Christopher. *City Bushman: Henry Lawson and the Australian Imagination*. Curtin University Books, 2004.

Leer, Martin Hugo. "'This Country Is My Mind': Les Murray's Poetics of Place." *Australian Literary Studies* vol.20 no.2, 2001, pp. 15–42.

Lever, Susan. "The Social Tradition in Australian Women's Poetry." *Women's Writing* vol.5 no.2, 1998, pp. 229–39.

Lilley, Kate. "Between Anthologies: Feminism and Genealogies of Australian Women's Poetry." *Australian Feminist Studies* vol.12 no.26, 1997, pp. 265–73.

Lorange, Astrid. "Poetry, Law, and the News: Re-reading the Australian Constitution." *Australian Humanities Review* no.64, 2019, pp. 47–61.

Lucas, Rose and Lyn McCredden, eds. *Bridgings: Readings in Australian Women's Poetry*. Oxford University Press, 1996.

Lucashenko, Melissa. "I Pity the Poor Immigrant." *Journal of the Association for the Study of Australian Literature* vol.17 no.1, 2017, pp. 1–10.

"Writing as a Sovereign Act." *Meanjin Quarterly*, Summer 2018. http://meanjin.com.au/essays/writing-as-a-sovereign-act/.

Lyons, Martin and John Arnold, eds. *A History of the Book in Australia: A National Culture in a Colonial Market*. University of Queensland Press, 2001.

Magner, Brigid. *Locating Australian Literary Memory*. Anthem Press, 2019.

Martin, Sylvia. *Passionate Friends: Mary Fullerton, Mabel Singleton, and Miles Franklin*. Onlywomen, 2001.

McCooey, David. "The City and the Australian Contemporary Long Poem." *Australian Writing and the City*, edited by Frances De Groen and Ken Stewart. Association for the Study of Australian Literature, 2000, pp. 122–28.

"Contemporary Poetry: Across Party Lines." *The Cambridge Companion to Australian Literature*, edited by Elizabeth Webby. Cambridge University Press, 2000, pp. 158–82.

"Surviving Australian Poetry: The New Lyricism." *Agenda* vol.41 no.1, 2005, pp. 22–37.

"Postcolonial Poetry of Australia and Aotearoa/New Zealand." *The Cambridge Companion to Postcolonial Writing*, edited by Jahan Ramazani. Cambridge University Press, 2017, pp. 71–84.

"The Public Life of Contemporary Australian Poetry." *Oxford Research Encyclopedia of Literature*, edited by Paula Rabinowitz, 2018. https://oxfordre.com/literature/view/10.1093/acrefore/9780190201098.001.0001/acrefore-9780190201098-e-296.

McCredden, Lyn. *James McAuley*. Oxford University Press, 1992.

"Contemporary Poetry and the Sacred: Vincent Buckley, Les Murray and Samuel Wagan Watson." *Australian Literary Studies* vol.23 no.2, 2007, pp. 153–68.

"(Un)Belonging in Australia: Poetry and Nation." *Southerly* vol.73 no.1, 2013, pp. 40–56.

McMahon, Elizabeth and Brigitta Olubas, eds. *Antigone Kefala: New Australian Modernities*. UWA Publishing, 2021.
Mead, Philip, ed. *Kenneth Slessor: Critical Readings*. University of Queensland Press, 1997.
  Networked Language: Culture and History in Australian Poetry. Australian Scholarly Publishing, 2008.
Mengham, Rod, ed. *The Salt Companion to John Tranter*. Salt Publishing, 2010.
Mengham, Rod and Glen Phillips, eds. *Fairly Obsessive: Essays on the Works of John Kinsella*. Centre for Studies in Australian Literature, 2000.
Meredith, John and Rex Whalan. *Frank the Poet: The Life and Works of Francis McNamara*. Legacy Books, 1979.
Minter, Peter. "Archipelagos of Sense: Thinking about a Decolonised Australian Poetics." *Southerly* vol.73 no.1, 2013, pp. 155–69.
  "Kath Walker (Oodgeroo Noonuccal), Judith Wright and Decolonised Transcultural Ecopoetics in Frank Heimans' 'Shadow Sister,'" *Sydney Studies in English* no.41, 2015, pp. 61–74.
Moreton-Robinson, Aileen. *Talkin' Up to the White Woman*. University of Queensland Press, 2000.
  ed. *Sovereign Subjects: Indigenous Sovereignty Matters*. Routledge, 2020.
Morris, Meghan. *Ecstasy and Economics: American Essays for John Forbes*. EMPress, 1992.
Morton, Peter. *Lusting for London: Australian Expatriate Writers and the Hub of Empire 1870–1950*. Palgrave Macmillan, 2011.
Munro, Craig and Robyn Sheahan-Bright, eds. *Paper Empires: A History of the Book in Australia, 1946–2005*. University of Queensland Press, 2005.
Murray, Les. "The Boeotian Strain." *Kunapipi* vol.2 no.1, 1980, pp. 4–64.
Musgrave, David. "Genres of Landscape in Australian Poetry." *Five Bells* vol.12 no.4, 2005, pp. 10–12.
Ommundsen, Wenche, ed. *Bastard Moon: Essays on Chinese-Australian Writing*. Otherland Literary Journal, 2001.
  "Transnational Imaginaries: Reading Asian Australian Writing." *JASAL* vol.12 no.2, 2012, pp. 1–8.
Page, Geoff. "Loaded Canons: Australian Poetry Anthologies." *Critical Survey* vol.6 no.1, 1994, pp. 20–27.
  A Reader's Guide to Contemporary Australian Poetry. University of Queensland Press, 1995.
Paisley, Fiona. *The Lone Protester: A.M. Fernando in Australia and Europe*. Aboriginal Studies Press, 2012.
Parsons, Elizabeth. *Poetry and Silence: "A Sequence of Disappearances."* VDM Verlag Dr. Muller, 2008.
Peterson, Irmtraud and Martin Duwell, eds. *And What Books Do You Read: New Studies in Australian Literature*. University of Queensland Press, 1996.
Phillips, Sandra and Clare Archer-Lean. "Decolonising the Reading of Aboriginal and Torres Strait Islander Writing: Reflections as Transformative Practice." *Higher Education Research & Development* vol.38 no.1, 2019, pp. 24–37.
Pierce, Peter, ed. *The Cambridge History of Australian Literature*. Cambridge University Press, 2011.

Pollnitz, Christopher. "Australian Verse Novels." *Heat* no.7, 2004, pp. 229–52.
Pons, Xavier. *Out of Eden: Henry Lawson's Life and Works*. Sirius Books, 1984.
Priest, Ann-Marie. *My Tongue Is My Own: A Life of Gwen Harwood*. Black Inc., 2022.
Reed-Gilbert, Kerry, eds. *The Strength of Us as Women: Black Women Speak*. Ginninderra, 2000.
Rooney, Brigid. *Literary Activists: Writer-Intellectuals and Australian Public Life*. University of Queensland Press, 2009.
Rowe, Noel. *Ethical Investigations: Essays on Australian Literature and Poetics*, edited by Bernadette Brennan. Vagabond Press, 2008.
Ryan, John Charles. "'A Touch of Recognition': Wetlands in Australian Poetry." *ISLE* vol.28 no.3, 2021, pp. 890–916.
Ryan, Judith and Chris Wallace-Crabbe, eds. *Imagining Australia: Literature and Culture in the New World*. Harvard University Committee on Australian Studies, 2004.
Savige, Jaya. "'Creation's Holiday': On Silence and Monsters in Australian Poetry." *Poetry* vol.208 no.2, 2016, pp. 169–84.
Schaffer, Kay. *Women and the Bush: Forces of Desire in the Australian Cultural Tradition*. Cambridge University Press, 1988.
Sefton-Rowston, Adelle. *Politics and Poetics: Race Relations and Reconciliation in Australian Literature*. Peter Lang, 2021.
Semmler, Clement. *Douglas Stewart*. Twayne, 1974.
Sharkey, Michael, ed. *Many Such as She: Victorian Australian Women Poets of World War One*. Walleah Press, 2019.
Sheridan, Susan. *Along the Faultlines: Sex, Race and Nation in Australian Women's Writing, 1880s–1930s*. Allen & Unwin, 1995.
  "Suburban Sonnets: 'Mrs Harwood,' Miriam Stone and Domestic Modernity." *Australian Literary Studies* vol.23 no.2, 2007, pp. 140–52.
  Nine Lives: Postwar Women Writers Making Their Mark. University of Queensland Press, 2011.
Shoemaker, Adam. *Black Words, White Page: Aboriginal Literature*. University of Queensland Press, 1992.
Smith, Ali Jane. "The Mongrel: Australian Prose Poetry." *Australian Poetry Journal* vol.4 no.1, 2014, pp. 6–14.
Smith, Ellen. "Local Moderns: The Jindyworobak Movement and Australian Modernism." *Australian Literary Studies* vol.27 no.1, 2012. www.australianliterarystudies.com.au/articles/local-moderns-the-jindyworobak-movement-and-australian-modernism.
Smith, Linda Tuhiwai. *Decolonizing Methodologies: Research and Indigenous Peoples*. Bloomsbury, 1999.
Smith, Vivian. "Experiment and Renewal: A Missing Link in Modern Australian Poetry." *Southerly* vol.47 no.1, 1987, pp. 3–18.
Standfield, Rachel, ed. *Indigenous Mobilities: Across and Beyond the Antipodes*. ANU Press, 2018.
Stephenson, P. R. *The Foundations of Culture in Australia: An Essay towards National Self-Respect*. W. J. Miles, 1936.

Stewart, Ken, ed. *The 1890s: Australian Literature and Literary Culture*. University of Queensland Press, 1996.
Strauss, Jennifer. *Boundary Conditions: The Poetry of Judith Wright*. Oxford University Press, 1995.
Tate, Audrey. *Ada Cambridge: Her Life and Work, 1844–1926*. Melbourne University Press, 1991.
Taylor, Andrew. *Reading Australian Poetry*. University of Queensland Press, 1987.
Trigg, Stephanie. *Gwen Harwood*. Oxford University Press, 1994.
Van Toorn, Penny. *Writing Never Arrives Naked: Early Aboriginal Cultures of Writing in Australia*. Aboriginal Studies Press, 2006.
Varatharajan, Prithvi. "A Political Radio Poetics: Ouyang Yu's Poetry and Its Adaptation on ABC Radio National's 'poetica.'" *Cultural Studies Review* vol.23 no.2, 2017, pp. 18–34.
Vickery, Ann. *Stressing the Modern: Cultural Politics in Australian Women's Poetry*. Salt Publishing, 2007.
"The Rise of Women's Poetry in the 1970s: An Initial Survey into New Australian Poetry, the Women's Movement, and a Matrix of Revolutions." *Australian Feminist Studies* vol.22 no.53, 2007, pp. 265–85.
Vickery, Ann and Kate Fagan. "'The Whole Reflected World Shuddering': Active Aesthetics and Contemporary Australian Poetry." *Active Aesthetics: Contemporary Australian Poetry*, edited by Daniel Benjamin and Claire Marie Stancek,. Tuumba Press, 2016, pp. 17–-28.
Vickery, Ann and John Hawke, eds. *Poetry and the Trace*. Puncher & Wattmann, 2013.
Vincent, Bridget. "Sorry, Above All, That I Can Make Nothing Right': Public Apology in Judith Wright." *Australian Humanities Review* no.61, May 2017, pp. 160–72.
Yu, Timothy. *Diasporic Poetics: Asian Writing in the United States, Canada and Australia*. Oxford University Press, 2021.
Walker, David. *Dream and Disillusion: A Search for Australian Cultural Identity*. Australian National University Press, 1976.
Walker, Kath [Oodgeroo]. *Kath Walker in China*, translated by Gui Zixin. Jacaranda Press, and the International Culture Publishing Corporation, 1988.
Walker, Shirley. *Flame and Shadow: A Study of Judith Wright's Poetry*. University of Queensland Press, 1991.
Ward, Russel. *The Australian Legend*. Oxford University Press, 1958.
Webby, Elizabeth. *Early Australian Poetry: An Annotated Bibliography of Original Poems Published in Australian Newspapers, Magazines and Almanacks before 1850*. Hale & Iremonger, 1982.
White, Richard. *Inventing Australia: Images and Identity, 1688–1980*. Allen & Unwin, 1981.
Wilkinson, Jessica L. "Experiments in Poetic Biography: Feminist Threads in Contemporary Long Form Poetry." *Biography* vol.39 no.1, 2016, pp. 1–22.
"Writing Lines, Writing Lives: The Art of Poetic Biography." *New and Experimental Approaches to Writing Lives*, edited by Jo Parnell. Red Globe Press, 2019, pp. 170–85.

Williams, Barbara. *In Other Words: Interviews with Australian Poets*. Rodopi, 1998.
Wright, Alexis. "Politics of Writing." *Southerly* vol.62 no.2, 2002, pp. 19–20.
"What Happens When You Tell Someone Else's Story." *Meanjin* vol.75 no.4, 2016. https://meanjin.com.au/essays/what-happens-when-you-tell-somebody-elses-story/.
Wright, Judith. *Preoccupations in Australian Poetry*. Oxford University Press, 1965.
Zwicky, Fay. *The Lyre in the Pawnshop: Essays on Literature and Survival, 1974–1984*. UWA Publishing, 1986.

INDEX

1967 Referendum, 11, 134
925, 67

Aboriginal Tent Embassy, 138, 145
activism, 4, 9, 14, 23, 34, 50, 110, 137–39, 145–47, 158, 164–65, 197–98, 200–1, 204–5, 209, 211, 219–20, 225, 228, 232, 268, 274–76, 280, 282, 292–310
Adamson, Cheryl, 66
Adamson, Robert, 63–66, 68, 141, 144, 236
Ah Kee, Vernon, 16, 339, 344, 346
Ah Sing, Jong, 4, 82–83, 86, 345
AIDS, 286
Aitken, Adam, 66, 237, 249, 259
Albiston, Jordie, 46, 318, 323, 326–27
Alexander, Lucy, 320
Alexander, Peter F., 192
Alizadeh, Ali, 258
Allen, Chadwick, 14
Allen, Richard James, 317
Altman, Dennis, 274–75
Alvarez, Ivy, 15, 318
Andrada, Eunice, 242–44
Angry Penguins, 7, 44, 49, 57–59, 62, 64, 112–14
Angus & Robertson, 8–9, 119, 121–22, 125
Anthropocene, 153, 160, 165
ANZACs, 5, 39–48, 316
Araluen, Evelyn, 21–35, 51, 201, 224, 229–31, 255, 268
  Dropbear, 34, 324
archive, 14–15, 34–35, 83, 86, 158, 219–32, 280, 326, 328
Armand, Louis, 258
Arna, 57
Arnott, Georgina, 154, 156, 158, 165
Ashcroft, Bill, 324
Atherton, Cassandra, 15, 323, 325

Australian Book Review, 8
Australian Poetry, 8, 60, 174
Australian Poetry Journal, 286
Australian Poetry Now (anthology), 64, 134, 168
austraLYSIS, 347
avant-garde, 6–8, 44, 54, 65, 67, 115, 140, 147, 164, 276, 336–49
Azam, Maryam, 247–48

Bacon, Eugen, 320, 324
Bailey, Mary, 89–90, 93–99
Ball, Magdalena, 327
Ballou, Emily, 326
Banning, Lex, 286
Baokang, Zhao, 16, 346
Barjai, 49
Barnes, Stuart, 280, 284, 287
Barnie, John, 316
Barton, Edmund, 26
Bateson, Catherine, 319
Beasley, Jack, 61
Beaver, Bruce, 63–64, 66, 322
Beesley, Luke, 323
Belcourt, Billy-Ray, 51
Bellear, Lisa, 231
Bennelong, 268
Bennett, Bruce, 42
Bennett, Stefanie, 275
Berndt, R.M., 10, 184
Beveridge, Judith, 66, 68
Biarujia, Javant, 68, 258, 276, 337
Biddle, Jennifer Loureide, 345
Biggs, Maurice, 43
Billeter, Walter, 64–65
Bing, Xu, 340
Birch, Tony, 224, 231
Birns, Nicholas, 9, 144

INDEX

Bjelke-Petersen, Joh, 200
Blackman, Wilson, 167
BlackWattle Press, 14, 277
Blight, John, 60
blood memory, 14, 230–31
Bloodaxe, 316
Boake, Barcroft, 80
Bobis, Merlinda, 12, 241–43, 317, 324
Boey, Kim Cheng, 12
Bohn, Willard, 344
Bolton, Alec, 121
Bolton, Ken, 65, 67–68, 135–36, 138, 141, 316
Bonyhady, Tim, 164
Bookfellow, 54, 104
Boyle, Peter, 287, 322
Bradstock, Margaret, 277–79
Brady, Veronica, 157
Breeze, Mez, 16, 346
Brennan, Christopher, 5, 23, 54–56, 60, 62, 82–83, 101, 104, 109, 125, 159, 345
Brereton, Kurt, 141
Brett, Lily, 258–59
Brindabella Press, 121
Brisbane Realist Writers Group, 11
Broom, 261
Brophy, Kevin, 323
Brown, Alexander, 345
Brown, Lachlan, 246–47
Brown, Pam, 14, 137, 141, 144–45, 275, 278, 322, 341
Buchanan, Cheryl, 200–1, 211
Buchanan, Constance, 95
Buckby, Samuel, 43
Buckley, Vincent, 8, 10, 62, 65–66, 119, 123, 126, 128–30, 140, 172–73
Buckmaster, Charles, 63, 137, 141
Buddee, Paul, 43
Bulletin, 5, 8–9, 26, 39, 54–56, 60–61, 104, 119–21, 125, 127, 129, 167, 171, 173, 261, 316
Burgmann, Meredith, 134
Burn, Ian, 341, 344, 348
burns, joanne, 136, 144, 276, 321
Burt, Warren, 336
bush ballad, 5, 54, 127, 256, 262

Caesar, Adrian, 39
Calder, Bill, 276
Callan, Erica, 141
Cambridge, Ada, 4, 89–99
Cameron, Emma, 319
CAMP Ink, 275

Campbell, David, 55, 59–60, 119, 121, 126–28, 130
capitalism, 145, 163, 201, 224, 292
Capp, Fiona, 165
Carey, Peter, 114
cargo, 14, 277
Carmichael, Grace Jennings, 256
Carruthers, A.J., 2, 15
Carson, Anne M., 323, 326
Carter, Paul, 208
Casaliggi, Carmen, 89
Castro, Brian, 318
Catalano, Gary, 321
Cataldi, Lee, 276
Cato, Nancy, 174
censorship, 130, 132, 136, 138–39, 147, 275
Chambers, Iain, 237
Chaos, 136
Chevalier, Julie, 327
Chisholm, A.R., 62
Chong, Eileen, 242, 244–47
Christesen, Clem, 62
Christianity, 73–74, 78, 80, 93, 95, 104, 123–24, 129, 176, 186, 194, 275
Clark, Axel, 83
Clark, Manning, 47, 267
Clark, Sherryl, 319
Clemens, Justin, 3, 317
Clifford, James, 236
Clough, Maurice, 43
Coetzee, J.M., 187
Cold War, 122, 127, 129, 143
Coleman, Aidan, 6
Collective Effort Press, 344
Collett, Anne, 164
Collinson, Laurence, 60, 275
Commonwealth Literary Fund, 8, 119
communism, 61, 123, 129, 136, 138, 274
concrete poetry, 65, 135–36, 334
Confessional, 64, 112, 126, 255, 276, 279, 322
Constitution, 11, 22, 33, 139, 348
  Howard-Murray draft preamble, 10, 23–24, 31–33
convictism, 2, 26, 39, 91, 131
convicts, 3, 48, 75, 78, 91–92, 95, 326, 328
Cook, James, 3, 78, 126, 225
Cooke, Stuart, 162, 164–65, 207, 212
Copello, Beatriz, 279
Cordite Poetry Review, 1, 68, 284
Costello, Moya, 321
Couani, Anna, 67–68, 144, 322

362

INDEX

Country, 22, 34, 50, 207, 220, 222, 232, 293–96, 299, 310, 334
Craig, Alexander, 129
Craven, Peter, 66
crip poetics, 285–88
Crisp, Louise, 165
Crispin, Judith Nangala, 324
Croggon, Alison, 322
Cronin, M.T.C., 322
Cross, Zora, 5–6, 109
Crosscurrents, 137
Cuevas-Morales, Silvia, 258
Curthoys, Ann, 257, 267
Curtin, John, 120

Dale, Amelia, 348
Dale, Leigh, 10
Dark, Eleanor, 159
Davenport, Sarah, 82, 84–85
Davidson, Jessica, 319
Davidson, Toby, 5, 7–8, 10
Davies, Luke, 66
Davis, Beatrice, 8, 59, 121
Davis, Jack, 13, 50, 202, 209–10
Dawe, Bruce, 46, 63, 129
Dawn, 54
Day, Sarah, 164
Deamer, Dulcie, 56
Dearborn, Tricia, 279–80
decolonial, 13, 23, 33, 35, 147, 162, 165, 197, 205, 208, 213, 221, 223–25, 231, 292, 295
Dennis, C.J., 5, 15, 316
Dessaix, Robert, 278
Devanny, James, 11
Devanny, Jean, 61
diaspora, 13, 236–49, 255, 257, 260, 268
Diesendorf, Margaret, 64
digital poetries, 1, 16, 326, 334, 346–48
disability, *see* crip poetics
Disney, Dan, 5, 260
Dixon, Robert, 26, 189, 191
Dobrez, Livio, 141–42
Dobrez, Patricia, 141–42
Dobson, Rosemary, 7, 59–60, 119, 121–22, 130
Dodds, Benjamin, 327
Dodwell, Diane, 167–68
domesticity, 15, 90–94, 97, 112, 159, 169, 171–76, 221–22, 226, 228, 246, 318
Dransfield, Michael, 63–65, 139, 141–45
Druce, Will, 258, 260
Dugan, Michael, 137

Duggan, Laurie, 65–66, 138, 140–41, 144, 254, 322
Duke, Jas H., 15–16, 337–38, 341, 344
Dunk, Jonathan, 184–85
Dunlop, Eliza Hamilton, 3, 89–92, 98
Dunne, Gary, 277
Dunsford, Cathy, 279
Dutton, Geoffrey, 57–58, 106, 142

Eades, Quinn, 283–86
Ear in a Wheatfield, 65, 137
Eckermann, Ali Cobby, 1, 15, 51, 211, 231, 318, 324
ecopoetic, 14, 153, 162, 190, 292, 297–98, 308
Edgar, Stephen, 318
Edge City on Two Different Plans (anthology), 274, 277
Edwards & Shaw, 120, 130
Edwards, Chris, 16, 278, 340, 344
elegy, 6, 44, 107, 179, 187, 239, 256, 303, 327
Elliot, Brian, 60
Elvey, Anne, 165
environmentalism, 9, 146, 153, 158, 162–65, 189, 212, 275, 292–310
epic, 7, 12, 22, 45, 120, 122, 125, 171, 317
ethnopoetics, 245
Etymspheres, 65, 136
Evans, Michelle Dennis, 319
Everett, Jim, 231

Fanoy, Jeltje, 67
Farrell, Michael, 3–4, 16, 68, 278, 280, 323, 340, 345
Federation, 3–5, 23–24, 26–27, 39, 101, 155
Fellowship of Australian Writers, 8
feminism, 6–7, 35, 67, 90, 92–95, 97–99, 110, 134, 138–39, 144, 159, 165, 172, 175, 224, 242, 261, 275–76, 279, 283–84, 316, 321–22, 336
Fermanis, Porscha, 89
Fernando, A.M., 4, 268–69
Ferry, John, 155
Field, Barron, 3, 43, 50, 73–76, 78
Fisher, Andrew, 38
Fitch, Toby, 326, 343
FitzGerald, Robert D., 56, 60, 106, 119, 128, 162
Flannigan, Charlie, 4, 82
Flaunt, 277
Fleming, Joan, 318
Flinders, Matthew, 2, 21

363

INDEX

Fogarty, Lionel, 13, 23, 33, 46, 50–51, 197–213, 231, 338
Forbes, John, 2, 46, 63, 65–67, 141, 143, 147, 256, 322
Fox, Len, 61
Fraillon, Zana, 319
Frank the Poet, *see* McNamara, Francis
Franklin, Miles, 257
Frascarelli, Carmine, 327
Free Poetry, 137
Frost, Lucy, 84
Fullerton, Mary, 111
Furaih, Ameer Chasib, 211

Gallagher, Alex, 283
Gallagher, Denis, 141, 276–78, 286
Gallagher, Katherine, 46
Galligan, Pat, 43
Garrish, Carolyn, 279
Gaskin, Claire, 286
Gay Changes, 276
Gay Community News, 276
Gay'wu group, 334–36
Gellert, Leon, 5, 40–42
Generation of '68, 11, 64, 115, 134–47
georgic, 9–10, 183, 185, 187–94
Geytenbeck, Brian, 345
Gibbons, Maureen, 326
Gibson, Ross, 326–27
Giddens, Anthony, 16
Gilbert, Kevin, 13, 50, 134–47, 202, 209–10
  Inside Black Australia: An Anthology of Aboriginal Poetry, 13
Giles, Paul, 262
Gillam, Kevin, 287
Gilmore, Mary, 4, 11, 23–24, 59–61, 73, 78, 109
Giramondo Press, 68
Glastonbury, Keri, 278
Gleeson, James, 57
Godfrey, Madison, 319
Goodfellow, Geoff, 318
Gordon, Adam Lindsay, 74, 79–80, 84
gothic, 3, 73–86, 158
Gough, Julie, 221, 229
Gould, Alan, 65
Grainger, Percy, 336
Grant, Jamie, 65
Gray, Robert, 63–66, 110, 203
Great Auk, 137
Green, H.M., 8, 60
Green, Stephanie, 320
Grieves, Victoria, 207

Griffith, Michael, 7, 124
Griffiths, Gareth, 324

H/EAR, 67, 137
Hall, Matthew, 146
Hall, Rodney, 61, 63–64, 168, 170, 322
Hamlyn-Harris, M(aymie Ada), 320
Hammial, Philip, 322
Hampton, Susan, 279, 322
Hanscombe, Gillian, 279
Hansord, Katie, 3
Harford, Lesbia, 6, 101, 109–11
Harkin, Natalie, 13, 33, 51, 223, 228, 230, 324, 343, 348
  Archival Poetics, 230
Harpur, Charles, 3, 23–26, 75–76, 78, 101, 157
Harris, Max, 7, 44, 57–59, 61–62, 64, 112–13, 115, 130
Harris, Robert, 68
Harrison, Jennifer, 286
Harrison, Martin, 278
Harrison-Ford, Carl, 63, 65
Harry, J.S., 63–66, 136–37, 144
Harry, Pip, 319
Hart, Kevin, 65, 322
Hart-Smith, William, 59–60
Harwood, Gwen, 9, 64, 109, 119, 123, 126, 167
  "In the Park," 9, 171–74
Hathorn, Libby, 319
Hawke, John, 5
Hawke, Shé, 318
Hawthorne, Susan, 278–79, 287
Haynes, Roslynn D., 126
Healy, J.J., 153
Heat, 68
Hecq, Dominique, 320, 327
Heiss, Anita, 231
Hely, Debra, 279
Hemensley, Kris, 63–65, 67, 137–38
Hermes, 57
Herrick, Steven, 319
Hetherington, Paul, 15, 317, 322
Hewett, Dorothy, 11, 46, 59, 61, 139, 169, 255
Heyward, Michael, 66, 114
Hiatt, Marty, 258, 260
Higgins, Bertram, 56, 59
Hill, Barry, 202
Hodgins, Philip, 317
Holt, Yvette, 228, 231
Homfray, L.E., 40

INDEX

homosexuality, 10, 14, 274–75, 277
Hong, Ee Tiang, 12, 238–39
Honi Soit, 201
Hope, A.D., 8, 10, 27, 30, 46, 49, 59–63, 66,
    119, 121, 123, 128–32, 140–43
    "Australia," 27, 28–30, 50, 62, 130
Hopfer, Sabina, 202, 211
Hore-Ruthven, Patrick, 43
Horne, Donald, 134, 144
Howard, John, 10, 31–32, 34
Howarth, Guy, 61
Hudson, Flexmore, 59
Hudson, Mike, 341
Huggins, Jackie, 228
Hurley, Michael, 276
Hutchinson, C.N., 40

Indyk, Ivor, 67–68, 143, 147
Ingamells, John, 8
Ingamells, Rex, 7, 48–49, 62
InVersions, 276
Island, 63

Jacket, 1, 68
Jacklin, Michael, 13, 258
Jackson, Andy, 15, 286–88, 327
Jackson, Anna, 325
Jacobs, Alan, 12
Jacobson, Lisa, 318
James, Clive, 258, 260
James, Kate, 279
Jarrett, Elizabeth, 51
Jarvis, Jadwiga, 341
Jefferies, Alan, 141
Jeffs, Sandy, 279, 286
Jenkins, John, 63, 65, 136, 138, 316–17
Jenkins, Wendy, 278
Jennings, Kate, 11, 138, 144–45, 336, 349
Jennings, Lynne, 279
Jessen, Rebecca, 318
Jindyworobaks, 8–9, 48–49, 51, 59, 62–63,
    130–31, 146
Johnson, A.A., 40
Johnson, David K., 274
Johnson, Eva, 281
Johnson, Frank, 55
Johnson, Heather Taylor, 287
Johnson, Judy, 318, 326
Johnston, Judith, 97
Johnston, Martin, 63–65, 135–36
Jones, Chris, 277, 316
Jones, Evan, 129
Jones, Gabriele Journey, 281

Jones, Gail, 261
Jones, Jill, 277–80
Jones, Marc, 258
Jones, Rae Desmond, 141
Jose, Nicholas, 267
Justice, Daniel Heath, 220

Kane, Paul, 101
Kantarizis, Sylvia, 64
Keating, Colleen, 326
Kefala, Antigone, 64
Kelly, Ned, 55, 82
    Jerilderie Letter, 326, 345
Kendall, Henry, 77, 101
Kennedy, Victor, 8
Kenny, Robert, 67, 134, 322
Kernot, Sharon, 319
Kershaw, Alister, 61, 257
Kingston, Coralie, 201
Kinsella, John, 1, 14, 68, 165, 197, 315, 319,
    323
Klee, Louis, 10, 13, 16, 197–98, 209
Knobel, Paul, 276, 278
Knowles, Claire, 90
Kocher, Shari, 327
König, Em, 283
Korean War, 38
Koutonin, Mawuna Remarque, 258
Kouvaras, Linda Ioanna, 336
Kramer, Leonie, 64, 131
Krausmann, Rudi, 15, 321

La Crónica, 12
La Mama, 63
Laidler, James, 319
Laird, Benjamin, 16, 326, 347–48
Lambert, Elisabeth, 59
Landon, Leticia E., 91
Lane, William, 4
Langton, Marcia, 198
larrikin, 5, 39–40
Larter, Pat, 341
Lawrence, Anthony, 15, 66, 318
Lawson, Elizabeth, 170, 179
Lawson, Henry, 3–5, 23, 26, 54, 60–61,
    78–80, 256
Lawson, Louisa, 54
Layland, Penelope, 323–24
Lea, Bronwyn, 16
Leakey, Caroline, 89–90, 93
Leakey, Catherine, 98–99
Leane, Jeanine, 13, 51, 205, 231, 267
Lebkowicz, Lesley, 318

365

INDEX

Lee, Alwyn, 56
Leer, Martin, 193
Lehmann, Geoffrey, 64–66, 110, 203
Leves, Kerry, 144, 278
Lew, Emma, 68
Lewis, Cassie, 255
LGBTQ+ poetries, 14, 274–85
  lesbian poetry, 278–80
  trans and genderqueer poetics, 283–85
Li, Bella, 16, 249, 320, 343
Lilley, Kate, 66, 278
Lindsay, Jack, 5, 7, 55–56, 106
Lindsay, Lionel, 58
Lindsay, Norman, 5, 55–56, 60, 106, 120, 125, 141, 325
Ling, Amy, 247
Literature in North Queensland, 63
little magazines, 8, 11, 55, 64–65, 67, 136–37, 140, 275–77
Lomer, Kathryn, 319
London Aphrodite, 7, 56
Loney, Alan, 258
Lowe, Lisa, 243
Lucashenko, Melissa, 204, 224, 229
Lukic, Tatjana, 324
Luna, 67

Mabo decision, 13, 23, 33
MacCarter, Kent, 68
Mackellar, Dorothea, 30, 109
  "My Country," 7, 27–28
Mackenzie, Kenneth, 59–60
MacNeill, Ian, 277
Madsen, Deborah, 245
Magic Sam, 67
Mahadeo, Gemma E., 281
Maiden, Jennifer, 55, 63–64, 68, 135, 138, 144
Malley, Ern, 7, 44, 57, 60, 101, 112–15, 123, 167, 337
Malouf, David, 1, 11, 14, 61, 65, 139, 141, 168, 258, 275
Manifold, J.S., 43–45, 60–61
Mann, Cecil, 119
Mann, Chris, 16, 67, 337–38, 341
Martin, Catherine, 81–82
Martin, David, 129
Martiniello, Jenni Kemarre, 228
Marwood, Lorraine, 319
mateship, 32, 39
McAuley, James, 7–8, 10, 15, 44–45, 49, 57, 59–62, 66, 109, 112–15, 119, 121–24, 128, 130, 162, 171, 325

McCooey, David, 10, 32, 47, 49
McCrae, Hugh, 55, 60, 106
McDonald, Nan, 121
McDonald, Roger, 168
McKenna, Mark, 31–32
McKinney, Jack, 62, 158
McKinnon, Laurin, 277
McNamara, Francis, 3, 73, 78
McRuer, Robert, 285
Mead, Philip, 1–2, 4, 10, 12–13, 86, 115, 199, 203–5
Mead, Rachael, 287
Meanjin, 8, 49, 54–62, 67, 120, 171
Mehan, Bronwyn, 320
Mellor, Anne, 92
Menzies, Robert, 10, 38, 121–22, 135–36, 139, 142
Merri Creek, Or Nero, 137
migrant 7, 67
Miller, Alyson, 323
Millett, John, 65, 316
Minter, Peter, 51, 162, 207, 269
Mitchell, Thomas, 22
Modernism, 6–7, 10, 44, 55–60, 66, 101–15, 120, 134–35, 140, 144–45, 161, 173, 185, 192–94, 255, 257, 261–62, 268, 336–37, 345
  anti, 56, 58, 61, 106, 187, 191–92, 194
modernity, 57–58, 61, 123–24, 127, 140, 158, 161, 175, 186, 317
Modjeska, Drusilla, 6, 109
MOK, 64, 136–37
Montgomery, Alexander, 80
Moore, Dashiell, 13
Morales, Cuevas, 259
Moreton, Romaine, 51, 231
Moreton-Robinson, Aileen, 4, 90
Morgan, Sally, 228, 319
Morrissey, Philip, 200–1, 212
Morton, Peter, 256, 258, 260
Mother I'm Rooted (anthology), 11, 144, 336, 349
Mudie, Ian, 48
Mudrooroo, 13, 202, 205, 207, 255
Munro, Lorna, 33, 165
Mununggurr-Williams, Melanie, 51
Murphy, Fiona, 286
Murphy, Sally, 319
Murray, Les, 1, 9–10, 15, 23–24, 31–32, 34, 47–49, 63–66, 68, 109, 126, 141, 143, 146–47, 183–94, 236, 252–55, 257, 263, 316

366

"The Buladelah-Taree Holiday Cycle," 10, 183–85, 193
Murray-Smith, Stephen, 60–61
Musa, Omar, 15, 318

nationalist myth, 2, 4–5, 7, 21, 23, 27, 29, 34–35, 38–40, 42–51, 156, 188, 224, 227, 257, 267
neo-classicism, 101, 140–41, 143–44
neoliberalism, 139, 143
New Australian Poetry (anthology), 64, 134, 136, 138–39, 141–44, 147
New Impulses in Australian Poetry (anthology), 63–64, 168
New Poetry, 64–66
Ngoc-Tuan, Huang, 12
Nichols, Robert, 40
Nicholson, Barbara, 228
Nixon, Jenni, 278–79
Noyes, George Rapall, 75

O'Brian, Kate, 277
O'Connor, Mark, 65
O'Dowd, Bernard, 26–27, 55, 120, 326
Ommundsen, Wenche, 4–5, 12
Ong, Aihwa, 241
Oodgeroo Noonuccal, 9, 11, 13, 23, 51, 139, 147, 153, 158, 162–63, 165, 202, 209–10, 228, 255, 263–69, 320
  We Are Going, 11, 50, 61
orality, 22, 65, 67, 184, 282, 338–39, 345
others, 261
Otis Rush, 67
Our Glass, 64, 137
Out of the Box (anthology), 15, 278
OutWriters, 279
Ouyang Yu, 12, 239–41, 257, 324, 338
Overland, 8, 60–61, 63

Page, Geoff, 46, 65–66, 179, 317, 327
Paisley, Fiona, 268
Palmer, Nettie, 6, 56, 58
Palmer, Vance, 6
Papertalk Green, Charmaine, 14, 51, 165, 229–31, 293–97, 324
Parkes, Henry, 3, 23
pastoral, 10, 75–76, 127, 145, 179, 183, 185, 187–94, 239, 241, 276, 298
Paterson, A.B. (Banjo), 5, 23, 54, 60, 79–80, 262
  "The Man from Snowy River," 24, 73, 80
  "Waltzing Matilda," 3, 54, 74, 79–80, 267
Pearl, Cyril, 56

Peart, Mark A., 327
Penguin Book of Modern Australian Verse (anthology), 108
performance poetries, 15, 65, 336–38, 346–47
Perry, Grace, 64
Perverse Verse, 277
Phillips, A.A., 55, 60
Phoenix, 59
PiO, 12, 65, 67, 327, 341, 344
poetic biography, 1, 315, 323, 325–28
Poetry (magazine), 59
Poetry Australia, 64–66, 68, 137
Poetry Magazine, 63–64
Poetry Society (Sydney), 63
Polar Bear Press, 341
Pollnitz, Christopher, 185, 315
Pope, Jessie, 40
Porter, Dorothy, 14–15, 65, 275, 279, 317–18
Porter, Hal, 106
Porter, Peter, 10, 23, 65–66, 147, 168–69, 179, 253–55, 257, 260, 263
Post Neo, 67
postmodernism, 67, 144, 193, 236, 341
Pounder, Nicholas, 341
Powell, Nicholas, 259
Prater, David, 255, 326
Prichard, Katharine Susannah, 61
Priest, Ann-Marie, 9
prose poetry, 1, 12, 15, 30–31, 34, 82, 145, 209, 244, 249, 315, 318–25
Prose Poetry Project, 320
Puchner, Martin, 140
Pugliese, Joseph, 224
Punch, 82

Quadrant, 8, 60, 123, 171, 185
Quan, Andy, 281
Quinton, James, 301–3

Rabbit, 278
Ramos, Victor, 13
Rando, Gaetano, 12
Realist, 61
Recent Work Press, 320
Reed, John, 57, 112
Reed, Sunday, 58
Reed-Gilbert, Kerry, 13, 219–20, 228, 231–32
Rees, Emma, 287
regional, 64, 154, 203, 239, 300
Reid, Barrett, 63
republicanism, 4, 25–26, 31–32

INDEX

Richards, June Walkutjukurr, 345
Richards, Kate, 141
Ridge, Lola, 7, 255, 261–63, 269
rights, 3, 89–92, 94, 139, 145, 147, 297, 307
   Aboriginal, 11, 13, 163, 165, 299
   animal, 327
   land, 33, 127, 201
   transgender, 284
   women's, 89–91, 95
Roberts, Nigel, 137, 143, 145
Robinson, Roland, 48, 63, 119–20, 131
Rodriguez, Judith, 324
Roe, Jill, 98
Roe, Paddy, 320
Romanticism, 3, 73, 75, 89–99, 101, 110, 140–41, 143, 145–47, 160, 165, 168
   neo, 58, 141, 144
   new, 66, 141
   post, 194
Rooney, Brigid, 160
Rose, Deborah Bird, 207
Rose, Peter, 66, 278, 280
Rowland, Robyn, 46
Rowlands, Graham, 46, 142
Royal Commission into Aboriginal Deaths in Custody, 211
Royalle, Candy, 282
Rubinstein, Matt, 317
Rush, Maralyn, 279
Ryan, Gig, 11, 66, 68, 137, 144, 185

Sakr, Omar, 248–49, 281–82
Salt, 68
Sarabin, Michael, 322
Saravanamuttu, Dîpti, 281
Sargent, Dave, 276
satire, 3, 34, 58, 61–62, 144, 168, 179, 321, 324
Saunders, Brenda, 324
Saunders, H.D., 43
Saunders, Kirli, 319
Savige, Jaya, 76, 260
Savvides, Irini, 319
Sawtell, Michael, 320
Schur, Owen, 76
Scott, John A., 63–64, 66, 316
Scott, Kim, 231
Scripsi, 66–68
Seita, Sophie, 136
Selenitsch, Alex, 16, 339, 341, 344
Shakti, Uma Kali, 277
Shapcott, Thomas, 63–64, 134–35, 168, 321

Shaw Neilson, John, 5–6, 54, 56, 60, 101–6, 109, 126–27, 162
Sheridan, Susan, 9, 172–73, 175
Shilton, Leni, 318, 327
Shiosaki, Elfie, 14, 230–31
Shoemaker, Adam, 202
Shying, Kerri, 286
Simes, Gary, 277
Simpson, Amelia, 32
Simpson, Leanne Betasamosake, 14, 224–25
Simpson, R.A., 129
Sinclair, Tim, 319
Skovron, Alex, 324
Slessor, Kenneth, 5–7, 44, 55–56, 59–62, 101, 106–9, 111, 120, 125, 127, 302
   "Beach Burial," 5, 44, 46, 59, 302
   "Five Bells," 6, 107–8
small presses, 11, 68, 135–36, 138, 276, 348
Smith, Ali Jane, 324
Smith, Andrew, 80
Smith, Ellen, 8
Smith, Hazel, 16, 346, 348
Smith, Shirley, 228
Social Alternatives, 201
social realism, 60, 62
socialism, 109, 165
song cycles, 2, 10, 22, 184
songlines, 334–36, 338
sonnet, 5–6, 16, 26–27, 40–42, 44–46, 102, 105, 120, 127, 167, 171, 173, 344
sound poetry, 192, 334, 336–39, 345
Southerly, 8, 49, 59–60, 62, 67, 108, 120, 286
sovereignty, 5, 9, 16, 22–24, 31, 33, 39, 86, 134, 139, 153, 206, 223, 231, 345
Spence, Pete, 67, 341, 344
Spineless Wonders, 320
spoken word, 65, 282, 338
Stead, Christina, 159
Steele, Peter, 129
Stephens, A.G., 5, 54, 104, 261
Stephensen, P.R., 39, 48, 51, 62, 257
Stewart, Amanda, 15, 336–38, 341, 344
Stewart, Douglas, 7–8, 22, 44–46, 55–56, 59–60, 63, 119–22, 125, 128–30, 171
Stewart, Harold, 7, 44, 57, 60, 112–15, 123
Stolen Generations, 86, 221, 319
   apology for, 13, 42, 203
Stow, Randolph, 64
Strauss, Jennifer, 40, 42, 169, 175, 179
Stream, 56–57, 59
Strehlow, T.G.H., 335
sublime, 3, 73–86, 159

368

suburbia, 12, 130, 138, 169, 172–76, 239, 318
Sumner, Tyne Daile, 212
surrealism, 7, 56–57, 59, 114, 127, 142, 320–22
Sydney Gay Writers Collective, 276
Sykes, Patricia, 328
Symbolism, 5, 54, 61, 101, 103–4, 114, 122

Tài, Lê Văn, 16, 346
Talbot, Colin, 134
Taylor, Andrew, 65, 109, 321
Taylor, Michelle A., 319
terra nullius, 2–3, 33, 45, 76, 197, 268
Thalia, 341, 344
The Strength of Us as Women (anthology), 219–20
Thiele, Colin, 43
Thompson, John, 61, 108
Thorne, Tim, 63–64, 138
Tierney, Orchid, 10, 14
Tiffin, Helen, 324
Tipping, Richard, 64, 135–36, 138, 341
Torrents, Salvador, 4
Tranter, John, 11, 63–68, 134–35, 139–44, 147, 317
Trigg, Stephanie, 168, 173, 175–78
Tse, Jonathan, 348
Tucker, Margaret, 228
Tulip, James, 64
Turner, Ian, 61
Tyndale, Ray, 277

Uluru Statement from the Heart, 33
Unaipon, David, 74, 320

van Neerven, Ellen, 33, 51, 229, 231, 267, 269, 281, 324
van Toorn, Penny, 203
Varatharajan, Prithvi, 323
vernacular, 5, 12, 143, 146–47, 187–88, 191–92, 281, 284, 316, 318
verse novel, 1, 15, 277, 279, 315–19, 325
Versión, 12
Vickery, Ann, 91–92
Vidler, Cath, 16, 343–44
Vietnam War, 38, 42, 46, 123, 127, 134–36, 138, 142, 275, 319
Viidikas, Vicki, 63–64, 66, 135, 137, 143–45, 322–23
Vincent, Bridget, 164
Vision, 6, 55–56, 106

visual poetry, 4, 16, 67, 82–83, 140, 249, 305, 334, 336–46
Vleeskens, Cornelius, 341

Wagan Watson, Samuel, 51, 231, 324
Wakeling, Corey, 11, 259
Wakeling, Louise Katherine, 277, 279
Walker, Shirley, 159
Wallace-Crabbe, Chris, 15, 61, 64, 129, 168, 317, 321
Walters, J. Ward, 320
Walwicz, Ania, 12, 67, 322, 324, 337
  "Australia," 12, 30, 321
Ward, Glenyse, 228
Waten, Judah, 61
Watson, Irene, 205
Wayzgoose Press, 341
Wearne, Alan, 15, 63–64, 66–67, 138, 316
Webb, Francis, 7, 15, 23, 55–56, 60, 63, 119–21, 124–26, 128–29, 325
Webb, Jen, 320
Wei Wei Lo, Miriam, 324
Wellington, Kaitlen, 51
West, Ida, 228
West, Michael, 277
Westbrook, F.E., 40
Weste, Linda, 279, 315, 318
Westerly, 63
Wharton, Herb, 231
Wheatley, Nadia, 134
White Australia (policy), 4–5, 121, 135, 238
White, Patrick, 7, 61, 130–31, 154, 161, 257
White, Rae, 283–84, 286
whiteness, 14, 45, 223
Whitlam, Gough, 11–12, 139, 142, 238
Whittaker, Alison, 33, 51, 231, 281–82, 324, 338–39, 343
Whittock, Nick, 16, 343
Wickham, Anna, 7, 101, 109, 111–12, 255
Wild, Margaret, 319
Wilkinson, Jessica L., 325, 328, 343
Williams, Ann, 82, 84–86
Williams, George, 32
Williams, Ray, 61
Wilmot, Frank, 55
Wilson, Edmund, 56
Winter, Bronwyn, 277
World War I, 5, 7, 23, 38–40, 42, 326
World War II, 5, 7–8, 12, 24, 38, 42–44, 46, 126–27, 274

INDEX

Wright, Alexis, 197, 223, 228–29, 231
Wright, David Mackie, 55
Wright, Judith, 9, 11, 23, 32, 50, 55, 59–62, 66, 108–9, 119, 122, 130, 139, 141, 147, 153–65
  Preoccupations in Australian Poetry, 8, 130, 162
  "South of My Days," **9**, 154–57, 161

Wright, Tim, 137
Wu, Janet Jiahui, 281

Yocum, Demetrio, 248
Yunupingu, Garralwy, 267
Yuting, Yang, 5

Zhong, Huang, 4–5
Zwicky, Fay, 66, 255

Cambridge Companions To …

AUTHORS

Edward Albee edited by Stephen J. Bottoms

Margaret Atwood edited by Coral Ann Howells (second edition)

W. H. Auden edited by Stan Smith

Jane Austen edited by Edward Copeland and Juliet McMaster (second edition)

James Baldwin edited by Michele Elam

Balzac edited by Owen Heathcote and Andrew Watts

Beckett edited by John Pilling

Bede edited by Scott DeGregorio

Aphra Behn edited by Derek Hughes and Janet Todd

Saul Bellow edited by Victoria Aarons

Walter Benjamin edited by David S. Ferris

William Blake edited by Morris Eaves

Boccaccio edited by Guyda Armstrong, Rhiannon Daniels, and Stephen J. Milner

Jorge Luis Borges edited by Edwin Williamson

Brecht edited by Peter Thomson and Glendyr Sacks (second edition)

The Brontës edited by Heather Glen

Bunyan edited by Anne Dunan-Page

Frances Burney edited by Peter Sabor

Byron edited by Drummond Bone (second edition)

Albert Camus edited by Edward J. Hughes

Willa Cather edited by Marilee Lindemann

Catullus edited by Ian Du Quesnay and Tony Woodman

Cervantes edited by Anthony J. Cascardi

Chaucer edited by Piero Boitani and Jill Mann (second edition)

Chekhov edited by Vera Gottlieb and Paul Allain

Kate Chopin edited by Janet Beer

Caryl Churchill edited by Elaine Aston and Elin Diamond

Cicero edited by Catherine Steel

John Clare edited by Sarah Houghton-Walker

J. M. Coetzee edited by Jarad Zimbler

Coleridge edited by Lucy Newlyn

Coleridge edited by Tim Fulford (new edition)

Wilkie Collins edited by Jenny Bourne Taylor

Joseph Conrad edited by J. H. Stape

H. D. edited by Nephie J. Christodoulides and Polina Mackay

Dante edited by Rachel Jacoff (second edition)

Daniel Defoe edited by John Richetti

Don DeLillo edited by John N. Duvall

Charles Dickens edited by John O. Jordan

Emily Dickinson edited by Wendy Martin

John Donne edited by Achsah Guibbory

Dostoevskii edited by W. J. Leatherbarrow

Theodore Dreiser edited by Leonard Cassuto and Claire Virginia Eby

John Dryden edited by Steven N. Zwicker

W. E. B. Du Bois edited by Shamoon Zamir

George Eliot edited by George Levine and Nancy Henry (second edition)

T. S. Eliot edited by A. David Moody

Ralph Ellison edited by Ross Posnock

Ralph Waldo Emerson edited by Joel Porte and Saundra Morris

William Faulkner edited by Philip M. Weinstein

Henry Fielding edited by Claude Rawson

F. Scott Fitzgerald edited by Ruth Prigozy

F. Scott Fitzgerald edited by Michael Nowlin (second edition)

Flaubert edited by Timothy Unwin

E. M. Forster edited by David Bradshaw

Benjamin Franklin edited by Carla Mulford

Brian Friel edited by Anthony Roche

Robert Frost edited by Robert Faggen

Gabriel García Márquez edited by Philip Swanson

Elizabeth Gaskell edited by Jill L. Matus

Edward Gibbon edited by Karen O'Brien and Brian Young

Goethe edited by Lesley Sharpe

Günter Grass edited by Stuart Taberner

Thomas Hardy edited by Dale Kramer

David Hare edited by Richard Boon

Nathaniel Hawthorne edited by Richard Millington

Seamus Heaney edited by Bernard O'Donoghue

Ernest Hemingway edited by Scott Donaldson

Hildegard of Bingen edited by Jennifer Bain
Homer edited by Robert Fowler
Horace edited by Stephen Harrison
Ted Hughes edited by Terry Gifford
Ibsen edited by James McFarlane
Kazuo Ishiguro edited by Andrew Bennett
Henry James edited by Jonathan Freedman
Samuel Johnson edited by Greg Clingham
Ben Jonson edited by Richard Harp and Stanley Stewart
James Joyce edited by Derek Attridge (second edition)
Kafka edited by Julian Preece
Keats edited by Susan J. Wolfson
Jack Kerouac edited by Steven Belletto
Rudyard Kipling edited by Howard J. Booth
Lacan edited by Jean-Michel Rabaté
D. H. Lawrence edited by Anne Fernihough
Primo Levi edited by Robert Gordon
Lucretius edited by Stuart Gillespie and Philip Hardie
Machiavelli edited by John M. Najemy
David Mamet edited by Christopher Bigsby
Thomas Mann edited by Ritchie Robertson
Christopher Marlowe edited by Patrick Cheney
Andrew Marvell edited by Derek Hirst and Steven N. Zwicker
Ian McEwan edited by Dominic Head
Herman Melville edited by Robert S. Levine
Arthur Miller edited by Christopher Bigsby (second edition)
Milton edited by Dennis Danielson (second edition)
Molière edited by David Bradby and Andrew Calder
William Morris edited by Marcus Waithe
Toni Morrison edited by Justine Tally
Alice Munro edited by David Staines
Nabokov edited by Julian W. Connolly
Eugene O'Neill edited by Michael Manheim
George Orwell edited by John Rodden
Ovid edited by Philip Hardie
Petrarch edited by Albert Russell Ascoli and Unn Falkeid
Harold Pinter edited by Peter Raby (second edition)
Sylvia Plath edited by Jo Gill
Plutarch edited by Frances B. Titchener and Alexei Zadorojnyi
Edgar Allan Poe edited by Kevin J. Hayes
Alexander Pope edited by Pat Rogers
Ezra Pound edited by Ira B. Nadel
Proust edited by Richard Bales
Pushkin edited by Andrew Kahn
Thomas Pynchon edited by Inger H. Dalsgaard, Luc Herman and Brian McHale
Rabelais edited by John O'Brien
Rilke edited by Karen Leeder and Robert Vilain
Philip Roth edited by Timothy Parrish
Salman Rushdie edited by Abdulrazak Gurnah
John Ruskin edited by Francis O'Gorman
Sappho edited by P. J. Finglass and Adrian Kelly
Seneca edited by Shadi Bartsch and Alessandro Schiesaro
Shakespeare edited by Margareta de Grazia and Stanley Wells (second edition)
George Bernard Shaw edited by Christopher Innes
Shelley edited by Timothy Morton
Mary Shelley edited by Esther Schor
Sam Shepard edited by Matthew C. Roudané
Spenser edited by Andrew Hadfield
Laurence Sterne edited by Thomas Keymer
Wallace Stevens edited by John N. Serio
Tom Stoppard edited by Katherine E. Kelly
Harriet Beecher Stowe edited by Cindy Weinstein
August Strindberg edited by Michael Robinson
Jonathan Swift edited by Christopher Fox
J. M. Synge edited by P. J. Mathews
Tacitus edited by A. J. Woodman
Henry David Thoreau edited by Joel Myerson
Thucydides edited by Polly Low
Tolstoy edited by Donna Tussing Orwin
Anthony Trollope edited by Carolyn Dever and Lisa Niles
Mark Twain edited by Forrest G. Robinson
John Updike edited by Stacey Olster
Mario Vargas Llosa edited by Efrain Kristal and John King
Virgil edited by Fiachra Mac Góráin and Charles Martindale (second edition)

Voltaire edited by Nicholas Cronk
David Foster Wallace edited by Ralph Clare
Edith Wharton edited by Millicent Bell
Walt Whitman edited by Ezra Greenspan
Oscar Wilde edited by Peter Raby
Tennessee Williams edited by Matthew C. Roudané
William Carlos Williams edited by Christopher MacGowan
August Wilson edited by

Mary Wollstonecraft edited by Claudia L. Johnson
Virginia Woolf edited by Susan Sellers (second edition)
Wordsworth edited by Stephen Gill
Richard Wright edited by Glenda R. Carpio
W. B. Yeats edited by Marjorie Howes and John Kelly
Xenophon edited by Michael A. Flower
Zola edited by Brian Nelson

TOPICS

The Actress edited by Maggie B. Gale and John Stokes
The African American Novel edited by Maryemma Graham
The African American Slave Narrative edited by Audrey A. Fisch
African American Theatre by Harvey Young
Allegory edited by Rita Copeland and Peter Struck
American Crime Fiction edited by Catherine Ross Nickerson
American Gothic edited by Jeffrey Andrew Weinstock
The American Graphic Novel by Jan Baetens, Hugo Frey and Fabrice Leroy
American Horror edited by Stephen Shapiro and Mark Storey
American Literature of the 1930s edited by William Solomon
American Literature and the Body by Travis M. Foster
American Literature and the Environment edited by Sarah Ensor and Susan Scott Parrish
American Modernism edited by Walter Kalaidjian
American Poetry since 1945 edited by Jennifer Ashton
American Realism and Naturalism edited by Donald Pizer
American Short Story edited by Michael J. Collins and Gavin Jones
American Travel Writing edited by Alfred Bendixen and Judith Hamera
American Utopian Literature and Culture since 1945 edited by Sherryl Vint
American Women Playwrights edited by Brenda Murphy
Ancient Rhetoric edited by Erik Gunderson

Arthurian Legend edited by Elizabeth Archibald and Ad Putter
Australian Literature edited by Elizabeth Webby
Australian Poetry edited by Ann Vickery
The Australian Novel edited by Nicholas Birns and Louis Klee
The Beats edited by Stephen Belletto
The Black Body in American Literature edited by Cherene Sherrard-Johnson
Boxing edited by Gerald Early
British Black and Asian Literature (1945–2010) edited by Deirdre Osborne
British Fiction: 1980–2018 edited by Peter Boxall
British Fiction since 1945 edited by David James
British Literature of the 1930s edited by James Smith
British Literature of the French Revolution edited by Pamela Clemit
British Romantic Poetry edited by James Chandler and Maureen N. McLane
British Romanticism edited by Stuart Curran (second edition)
British Romanticism and Religion edited by Jeffrey Barbeau
British Theatre, 1730–1830, edited by Jane Moody and Daniel O'Quinn
Canadian Literature edited by Eva-Marie Kröller (second edition)
The Canterbury Tales edited by Frank Grady
Children's Literature edited by M. O. Grenby and Andrea Immel
The City in World Literature edited by Ato Quayson and Jini Kim Watson

The Classic Russian Novel edited by Malcolm V. Jones and Robin Feuer Miller

Comics edited by Maaheen Ahmed

Contemporary African American Literature edited by Yogita Goyal

Contemporary Irish Poetry edited by Matthew Campbell

Creative Writing edited by David Morley and Philip Neilsen

Crime Fiction edited by Martin Priestman

Dante's 'Commedia' edited by Zygmunt G. Barański and Simon Gilson

Dracula edited by Roger Luckhurst

Early American Literature edited by Bryce Traister

Early Modern Women's Writing edited by Laura Lunger Knoppers

The Eighteenth-Century Novel edited by John Richetti

Eighteenth-Century Poetry edited by John Sitter

Eighteenth-Century Thought edited by Frans De Bruyn

Emma edited by Peter Sabor

English Dictionaries edited by Sarah Ogilvie

English Literature, 1500–1600 edited by Arthur F. Kinney

English Literature, 1650–1740 edited by Steven N. Zwicker

English Literature, 1740–1830 edited by Thomas Keymer and Jon Mee

English Literature, 1830–1914 edited by Joanne Shattock

English Melodrama edited by Carolyn Williams

English Novelists edited by Adrian Poole

English Poetry, Donne to Marvell edited by Thomas N. Corns

English Poets edited by Claude Rawson

English Renaissance Drama edited by A. R. Braunmuller and Michael Hattaway (second edition)

English Renaissance Tragedy edited by Emma Smith and Garrett A. Sullivan Jr.

English Restoration Theatre edited by Deborah C. Payne Fisk

Environmental Humanities edited by Jeffrey Cohen and Stephanie Foote

The Epic edited by Catherine Bates

Erotic Literature edited by Bradford Mudge

The Essay edited by Kara Wittman and Evan Kindley

European Modernism edited by Pericles Lewis

European Novelists edited by Michael Bell

Fairy Tales edited by Maria Tatar

Fantasy Literature edited by Edward James and Farah Mendlesohn

Feminist Literary Theory edited by Ellen Rooney

Fiction in the Romantic Period edited by Richard Maxwell and Katie Trumpener

The Fin de Siècle edited by Gail Marshall

Frankenstein edited by Andrew Smith

The French Enlightenment edited by Daniel Brewer

French Literature edited by John D. Lyons

The French Novel: from 1800 to the Present edited by Timothy Unwin

Gay and Lesbian Writing edited by Hugh Stevens

German Romanticism edited by Nicholas Saul

Global Literature and Slavery edited by Laura T. Murphy

Gothic Fiction edited by Jerrold E. Hogle

The Graphic Novel edited by Stephen Tabachnick

Greek Comedy edited by Martin Revermann

Greek Lyric edited by Felix Budelmann

Greek Mythology edited by Roger D. Woodard

The Greek and Roman Novel edited by Tim Whitmarsh

Greek and Roman Theatre edited by Marianne McDonald and J. Michael Walton

Greek Tragedy edited by P. E. Easterling

The Harlem Renaissance edited by George Hutchinson

The History of the Book edited by Leslie Howsam

Human Rights and Literature edited by Crystal Parikh

The Irish Novel edited by John Wilson Foster

Irish Poets edited by Gerald Dawe

The Italian Novel edited by Peter Bondanella and Andrea Ciccarelli

The Italian Renaissance edited by Michael Wyatt

Jewish American Literature edited by Hana Wirth-Nesher and Michael P. Kramer

The Latin American Novel edited by Efraín Kristal

Latin American Poetry edited by Stephen Hart

Latina/o American Literature edited by John Morán González

Latin Love Elegy edited by Thea S. Thorsen

The Literature of the American Civil War and Reconstruction edited by Kathleen Diffley and Coleman Hutchison

The Literature of the American Renaissance edited by Christopher N. Phillips

Literature and Animals by Derek Ryan

Literature and the Anthropocene edited by John Parham

The Literature of Berlin edited by Andrew J. Webber

Literature and Climate edited by Adeline Johns-Putra and Kelly Sultzbach

The Literature of the Crusades edited by Anthony Bale

Literature in a Digital Age edited by Adam Hammond

Literature and Disability edited by Clare Barker and Stuart Murray

The Literature of the First World War edited by Vincent Sherry

Literature and Food edited by J. Michelle Coghlan

The Literature of London edited by Lawrence Manley

The Literature of Los Angeles edited by Kevin R. McNamara

The Literature of New York edited by Cyrus Patell and Bryan Waterman

The Literature of Paris edited by Anna-Louise Milne

Literature and the Posthuman edited by Bruce Clarke and Manuela Rossini

Literature and Religion edited by Susan M. Felch

Literature and Science edited by Steven Meyer

Literature on Screen edited by Deborah Cartmell and Imelda Whelehan

The Literature of World War II edited by Marina MacKay

Lyrical Ballads edited by Sally Bushell

Medieval British Manuscripts edited by Orietta Da Rold and Elaine Treharne

Medieval English Culture edited by Andrew Galloway

Medieval English Law and Literature edited by Candace Barrington and Sebastian Sobecki

Medieval English Literature edited by Larry Scanlon

Medieval English Mysticism edited by Samuel Fanous and Vincent Gillespie

Medieval English Theatre edited by Richard Beadle and Alan J. Fletcher (second edition)

Medieval French Literature edited by Simon Gaunt and Sarah Kay

Medieval Romance edited by Roberta L. Krueger

Medieval Romance edited by Roberta L. Krueger (new edition)

Medieval Women's Writing edited by Carolyn Dinshaw and David Wallace

Modern American Culture edited by Christopher Bigsby

Modern British Women Playwrights edited by Elaine Aston and Janelle Reinelt

Modern French Culture edited by Nicholas Hewitt

Modern German Culture edited by Eva Kolinsky and Wilfried van der Will

The Modern German Novel edited by Graham Bartram

The Modern Gothic edited by Jerrold E. Hogle

Modern Irish Culture edited by Joe Cleary and Claire Connolly

Modern Italian Culture edited by Zygmunt G. Baranski and Rebecca J. West

Modern Latin American Culture edited by John King

Modern Russian Culture edited by Nicholas Rzhevsky

Modern Spanish Culture edited by David T. Gies

Modernism edited by Michael Levenson (second edition)

The Modernist Novel edited by Morag Shiach

Modernist Poetry edited by Alex Davis and Lee M. Jenkins

Modernist Women Writers edited by Maren Tova Linett

Narrative edited by David Herman

Narrative Theory edited by Matthew Garrett

Native American Literature edited by Joy Porter and Kenneth M. Roemer

Nineteen Eighty-Four edited by Nathan Waddell

Nineteenth-Century American Literature and Politics edited by John Kerkering

Nineteenth-Century American Poetry edited by Kerry Larson

Nineteenth-Century American Women's Writing edited by Dale M. Bauer and Philip Gould

Nineteenth-Century Thought edited by Gregory Claeys

The Novel edited by Eric Bulson

Old English Literature edited by Malcolm Godden and Michael Lapidge (second edition)

Performance Studies edited by Tracy C. Davis

Piers Plowman by Andrew Cole and Andrew Galloway

The Poetry of the First World War edited by Santanu Das

Popular Fiction edited by David Glover and Scott McCracken

Postcolonial Literary Studies edited by Neil Lazarus

Postcolonial Poetry edited by Jahan Ramazani

Postcolonial Travel Writing edited by Robert Clarke

Postmodern American Fiction edited by Paula Geyh

Postmodernism edited by Steven Connor

Prose edited by Daniel Tyler

The Pre-Raphaelites edited by Elizabeth Prettejohn

Pride and Prejudice edited by Janet Todd

Queer Studies edited by Siobhan B. Somerville

Race and American Literature edited by John Ernest

Renaissance Humanism edited by Jill Kraye

Robinson Crusoe edited by John Richetti

Roman Comedy edited by Martin T. Dinter

The Roman Historians edited by Andrew Feldherr

Roman Satire edited by Kirk Freudenburg

The Romantic Sublime by Cian Duffy

Science Fiction edited by Edward James and Farah Mendlesohn

Scottish Literature edited by Gerald Carruthers and Liam McIlvanney

Sensation Fiction edited by Andrew Mangham

Shakespeare and Contemporary Dramatists edited by Ton Hoenselaars

Shakespeare on Film edited by Russell Jackson (second edition)

Shakespeare and Popular Culture edited by Robert Shaughnessy

Shakespeare and Race edited by Ayanna Thompson

Shakespeare and Religion edited by Hannibal Hamlin

Shakespeare on Screen edited by Russell Jackson

Shakespeare on Stage edited by Stanley Wells and Sarah Stanton

Shakespeare and War edited by David Loewenstein and Paul Stevens

Shakespearean Comedy edited by Alexander Leggatt

Shakespearean Tragedy edited by Claire McEachern (second edition)

Shakespeare's First Folio edited by Emma Smith

Shakespeare's History Plays edited by Michael Hattaway

Shakespeare's Language edited by Lynne Magnusson with David Schalkwyk

Shakespeare's Last Plays edited by Catherine M. S. Alexander

Shakespeare's Poetry edited by Patrick Cheney

Sherlock Holmes edited by Janice M. Allan and Christopher Pittard

The Sonnet edited by A. D. Cousins and Peter Howarth

The Spanish Novel: from 1600 to the Present edited by Harriet Turner and Adelaida López de Martínez

Textual Scholarship edited by Neil Fraistat and Julia Flanders

Theatre History by David Wiles and Christine Dymkowski

Theatre and Science edited by Kristen E. Shepherd-Barr

Transnational American Literature edited by

Travel Writing edited by Peter Hulme and Tim Youngs

The Twentieth-Century American Novel and Politics by Bryan Santin

Twentieth-Century American Poetry and Politics edited by Daniel Morris

Twentieth-Century British and Irish Women's Poetry edited by Jane Dowson

The Twentieth-Century English Novel edited by Robert L. Caserio

Twentieth-Century English Poetry edited by Neil Corcoran

Twentieth-Century Irish Drama edited by Shaun Richards

Twentieth-Century Literature and Politics edited by Christos Hadjiyiannis and Rachel Potter

Twentieth-Century Russian Literature edited by Marina Balina and Evgeny Dobrenko

Utopian Literature edited by Gregory Claeys

Victorian and Edwardian Theatre edited by Kerry Powell

The Victorian Novel edited by Deirdre David (second edition)

Victorian Poetry edited by Joseph Bristow

Victorian Women's Poetry edited by Linda K. Hughes

Victorian Women's Writing edited by Linda H. Peterson

War Writing edited by Kate McLoughlin

Women's Writing in Britain, 1660–1789 edited by Catherine Ingrassia

Women's Writing in the Romantic Period edited by Devoney Looser

World Crime Fiction edited by Jesper Gulddal, Stewart King and Alistair Rolls

World Literature edited by Ben Etherington and Jarad Zimbler

Writing of the English Revolution edited by N. H. Keeble

The Writings of Julius Caesar edited by Christopher Krebs and Luca Grillo

For EU product safety concerns, contact us at Calle de José Abascal, 56–1°,
28003 Madrid, Spain or eugpsr@cambridge.org.

www.ingramcontent.com/pod-product-compliance
Ingram Content Group UK Ltd.
Pitfield, Milton Keynes, MK11 3LW, UK
UKHW040650220625
459949UK00010B/182